NATIONAL GEOGRAPHIC

CONCISE ATLAS *of the* WORLD

GREENLAND
KALAALLIT NUNAAT
CANADA
UNITED STATES
NORTH
NORTH
ATLANTIC
OCEAN
MEXICO
Aleutian Islands
ALASKA
Anchorage
Fairbanks
Whitehorse
Yellowknife
Edmonton
Calgary
Saskatoon
Regina
Winnipeg
Vancouver
Victoria
Seattle
Portland
Eugene
Boise
Salt Lake City
Sacramento
Reno
San Francisco
Las Vegas
Los Angeles
San Diego
Tijuana
Mexicali
Phoenix
Albuquerque
Denver
Kansas City
Oklahoma City
Dallas
Austin
San Antonio
Houston
El Paso
Ciudad Juárez
Chihuahua
Monterrey
Tampico
Mazatlán
Guadalajara
Mexico
Puebla
Veracruz
Acapulco
Mérida
Cancún
Havana
CUBA
Nassau
BAHAMAS
Miami
Tampa
Orlando
Jacksonville
Atlanta
Birmingham
Memphis
Nashville
Charlotte
New Orleans
Chicago
Milwaukee
Minneapolis
Detroit
Toronto
Ottawa
Montreal
Quebec
Buffalo
Boston
New York
Philadelphia
Washington
Halifax
St. John's
ISLAND OF NEWFOUNDLAND
Reykjavík
ICELAND
Dublin
IRELAND
PORTUGAL
Lisbon
Casablanca
MOROCCO
Marrakech
Rabat
WESTERN SAHARA
MAURITANIA
TROPIC OF CANCER

NATIONAL GEOGRAPHIC

CONCISE ATLAS of the WORLD

NATIONAL GEOGRAPHIC, WASHINGTON, D.C.

NATIONAL GEOGRAPHIC

CONCISE ATLAS *of the* WORLD

One of the world's largest nonprofit scientific and educational organizations, the National Geographic Society was founded in 1888 "for the increase and diffusion of geographic knowledge." Fulfilling this mission, the Society educates and inspires millions every day through its magazines, books, television programs, videos, maps and atlases, research grants, the National Geographic Bee, teacher workshops, and innovative classroom materials. The Society is supported through membership dues, charitable gifts, and income from the sale of its educational products. This support is vital to National Geographic's mission to increase global understanding and promote conservation of our planet through exploration, research, and education.

For more information, please call 1-800-NGS LINE (647-5463) or write to the following address:

National Geographic Society
1145 17th Street N.W.
Washington, D.C. 20036-4688 U.S.A.

Visit the Society's Web site at www.nationalgeographic.com.

Library of Congress Cataloging in Publication data is available upon request.

This atlas was made possible by the contributions of numerous experts and organizations around the world, including the following:

Center for International Earth Science Information Network (CIESIN), Columbia University

Central Intelligence Agency (CIA)

Conservation International

Earth Science System Education Program, Michigan State University

Global Land Cover Group, University of Maryland

National Aeronautics and Space Administration (NASA) and the NASA Ames Research Center, NASA Goddard Space Flight Center, NASA Jet Propulsion Laboratory (JPL), NASA Marshall Space Flight Center

National Imagery and Mapping Agency (NIMA)

National Oceanic and Atmospheric Administration (NOAA) and the National Climatic Data Center, National Environmental Satellite, Data, and Information Service; National Geophysical Data Center; National Ocean Service

National Science Foundation

Population Reference Bureau

Smithsonian Institution

United Nations (UN) and the UN Conference on Trade and Development, UN Development Programme, UN Educational, Scientific, and Cultural Organization (UNESCO), UN Environment Programme (UNEP), UN Population Division, Food and Agriculture Organization (FAO), International Telecommunication Union (ITU), World Conservation Monitoring Centre (WCMC)

U.S. Board on Geographic Names

U.S. Department of Agriculture

U.S. Department of Commerce: Bureau of the Census, National Oceanic and Atmospheric Administration

U.S. Department of Energy

U.S. Department of the Interior: Bureau of Land Management, National Park Service, U.S. Geological Survey

U.S. Department of State: Office of the Geographer

World Bank

World Health Organization/Pan American Health Organization (WHO/PAHO)

World Resources Institute (WRI)

World Trade Organization (WTO)

Worldwatch Institute

For a complete listing of contributors, see page 126.

INTRODUCTION

Fifty years ago a quiet New Zealander named Edmund Hillary and a shy Sherpa named Tenzing Norgay attained what no one before them had: the summit of Mount Everest. Their accomplishment inspired worldwide admiration—and curiosity. People turned to maps and atlases to find the nation of Nepal and to pinpoint the location of Earth's highest peak. Through Hillary's exploration, people everywhere learned more about their world. Hillary himself, grateful to the Sherpa people for their help in his conquest of the mountain, returned the favor by building schools, hospitals, and bridges throughout their land.

The National Geographic Society has long been dedicated to helping all people become explorers and discoverers. Under the Geographic banner, the world's finest scientists—anthropologists, archaeologists, botanists, oceanographers—crisscross the Earth, reporting on mysterious blank spots on the maps and the beguiling peoples of faraway places. Governments and research institutions all over the planet open their doors to National Geographic. Such access is a rare privilege, for which we are grateful. In return, we share the information we amass with readers around the world.

The need for accurate and accessible information about our globe has never been greater, and that's what this *Concise Atlas of the World* offers. The most informative and up-to-date concise atlas available today, it presents the findings of leading geographers who use and combine such cutting-edge technologies as enhanced satellite imagery, extensive digital databases, and Geographic Information Systems (GIS).

National Geographic's *Concise Atlas of the World* covers both political and physical geography and the cultures of every continent and country. Thematic maps reveal world economies and populations as well as religions, which continue to exert an extraordinary influence on billions of people. Sections called "Flags and Facts," are organized by continent and offer snapshots of countries and nonsovereign entities such as the Falklands and Svalbard. At a glance you can learn the life expectancy in Mozambique (34 years) or San Marino (81 years), the GDP per capita in Timor-Leste ($500) or Luxembourg ($44,000), or the literacy rate in Iraq (58 percent) or Latvia (100 percent). The world ocean is mapped, and the movement of every tectonic plate is charted. A special component covers the sun-drenched isles of Oceania.

So as you struggle to make sense of the triumphs and tragedies of today's world, keep the *Concise Atlas of the World* at your fingertips. Dig into it, and you'll be delighted with its ease of use and wealth of resources. Most of us will never have the chance, as Hillary did, to chart the unknown, but equipped with this valuable reference book we can all make our own explorations more exciting and meaningful.

President and Chief Executive Officer

TABLE OF CONTENTS

INTRODUCTION 4

HOW TO USE THIS ATLAS 8
Map Policies / Political Maps / Physical Maps / World Thematic Maps / Map Symbols

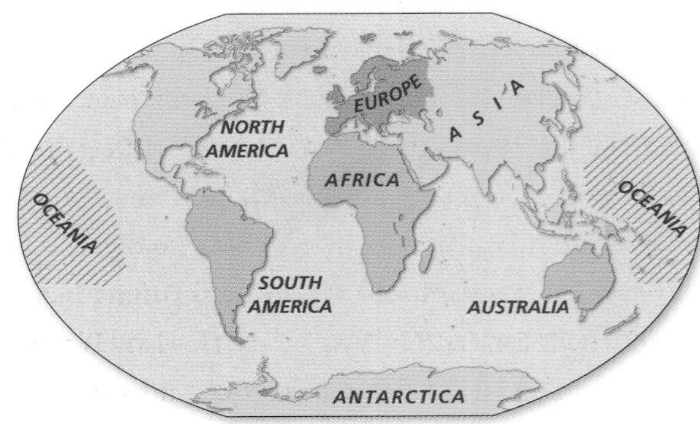

WORLD

WORLD ORBITAL DIAGRAM AND LAND COVER 10

WORLD POLITICAL MAP 12

WORLD PHYSICAL MAP 14

POLITICAL POLES, PHYSICAL HEMISPHERES 16

STRUCTURE OF THE EARTH 18
Continents Adrift in Time / Geologic Time / Geologic Forces Change the Face of the Planet / Plate Tectonics

WORLD OCEANS 20

WORLD POPULATION 22
Lights of the World / Population Pyramids / Population Growth / Population Density / Regional Population Growth Disparities

WORLD POPULATION CONTINUED 24
Fertility / Urban Population Densities / Urban Population Growth / Life Expectancy / Migration / Most Populous Nations / Most Crowded Nations / Demographic Extremes

WORLD RELIGIONS 26
Major Religions / Sacred Places / Adherents Worldwide / Adherents by Continent / Adherents by Country

WORLD ECONOMY 28
Predominant Economy / Labor Migration / Top GDP Growth Rates / The World's Richest and Poorest Countries / World Employment / Gross DomesticProduct / Major Manufacturers

GEOGRAPHICAL COMPARISONS 30
The Earth / The Earth's Extremes / Area of each Continent / Highest Point on each Continent / Lowest Surface Point on each Continent / Largest Islands / Largest Drainage Basin / Longest Rivers / Area of each Ocean / Deepest Point in each Ocean / Largest Lakes by Area / Geopolitical Extremes / Engineering Wonders / Largest Seas By Area

WORLD TIME 32
Time Zones / International Date Line

CONTINENTS

NORTH AMERICA

NORTH AMERICA LAND COVER IMAGE 34

NORTH AMERICA POLITICAL MAP 36

NORTH AMERICA PHYSICAL MAP 38

UNITED STATES POLITICAL MAP 40

UNITED STATES PHYSICAL MAP 42

NORTH AMERICA FLAGS & FACTS, U.S. STATE FLAGS, POPULATION DENSITY, AND DATES OF COUNTRY INDEPENDENCE 44
Antigua and Barbuda, Bahamas, Barbados, Belize, Canada, Costa Rica, Cuba, Dominica, Dominican Republic, El Salvador, Grenada, Guatemala, Haiti, Honduras, Jamaica, Mexico, Nicaragua, Panama, St. Kitts and Nevis, St. Lucia, St. Vincent and the Grenadines, Trinidad and Tobago, United States **DEPENDENCIES:** Anguilla, Aruba, Bermuda, British Virgin Islands, Cayman Islands, Greenland, Guadeloupe, Martinique, Montserrat, Netherlands Antilles, Puerto Rico, St.-Pierre and Miquelon, Turks and Caicos Islands, Virgin Islands

SOUTH AMERICA

SOUTH AMERICA LAND COVER IMAGE 48

SOUTH AMERICA POLITICAL MAP 50

SOUTH AMERICA PHYSICAL MAP 52

SOUTH AMERICA FLAGS & FACTS, POPULATION DENSITY, AND DATES OF COUNTRY INDEPENDENCE 54
Argentina, Bolivia, Brazil, Chile, Colombia, Ecuador, Guyana, Paraguay, Peru, Suriname, Uruguay, Venezuela **DEPENDENCIES:** Falkland Islands, French Guiana

EUROPE

EUROPE LAND COVER IMAGE 56

EUROPE POLITICAL MAP 58

EUROPE PHYSICAL MAP 60

EUROPE FLAGS & FACTS, POPULATION DENSITY, AND DATES OF COUNTRY INDEPENDENCE 62
Albania, Andorra, Austria, Belarus, Belgium, Bosnia and Herzegovina, Bulgaria, Croatia, Czech Republic, Denmark, Estonia, Finland, France, Germany, Greece, Hungary, Iceland, Ireland, Italy, Latvia, Liechtenstein, Lithuania, Luxembourg, Macedonia, Malta, Moldova, Monaco, Netherlands, Norway, Poland, Portugal, Romania, Russia, San Marino, Serbia and Montenegro, Slovakia, Slovenia, Spain, Sweden, Switzerland, Ukraine, United Kingdom, Vatican City **DEPENDENCIES:** Faroe Islands, Gibraltar

ASIA

ASIA LAND COVER IMAGE 66

ASIA POLITICAL MAP 68

ASIA PHYSICAL MAP 70

ASIA FLAGS & FACTS, POPULATION DENSITY, AND DATES OF COUNTRY INDEPENDENCE 72

Afghanistan, Armenia, Azerbaijan, Bahrain, Bangladesh, Bhutan, Brunei, Cambodia, China, Cyprus, Georgia, India, Indonesia, Iran, Iraq, Israel, Japan, Jordan, Kazakhstan, Kuwait, Kyrgyzstan, Laos, Lebanon, Malaysia, Maldives, Mongolia, Myanmar, Nepal, North Korea, Oman, Pakistan, Philippines, Qatar, Saudi Arabia, Singapore, South Korea, Sri Lanka, Syria, Tajikistan, Thailand, Timor-Leste, Turkey, Turkmenistan, United Arab Emirates, Uzbekistan, Vietnam, Yemen **AREA OF SPECIAL STATUS:** Taiwan

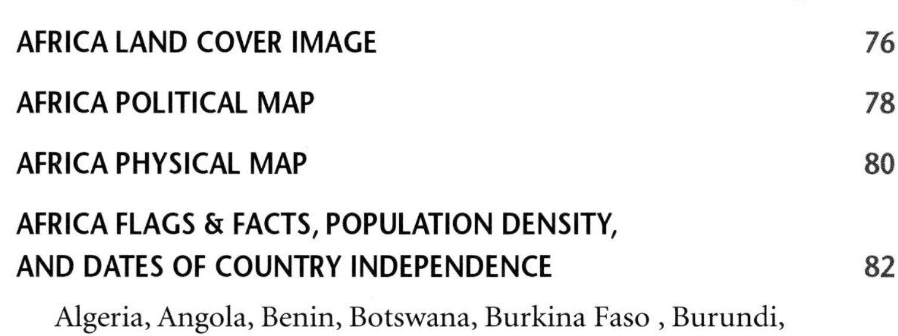

AFRICA

AFRICA LAND COVER IMAGE 76

AFRICA POLITICAL MAP 78

AFRICA PHYSICAL MAP 80

AFRICA FLAGS & FACTS, POPULATION DENSITY, AND DATES OF COUNTRY INDEPENDENCE 82

Algeria, Angola, Benin, Botswana, Burkina Faso , Burundi, Cameroon, Cape Verde, Central African Republic, Chad, Comoros, Congo, Côte d'Ivoire, Democratic Republic of the Congo, Djibouti, Egypt, Equatorial Guinea, Eritrea, Ethiopia, Gabon, Gambia, Ghana, Guinea, Guinea-Bissau, Kenya, Lesotho, Liberia, Libya, Madagascar, Malawi, Mali, Mauritania, Mauritius, Morocco, Mozambique, Namibia, Niger, Nigeria, Rwanda, Sao Tome and Principe, Senegal, Seychelles, Sierra Leone, Somalia, South Africa, Sudan, Swaziland, Tanzania, Togo, Tunisia, Uganda, Zambia, Zimbabwe **DEPENDENCIES:** Mayotte, Réunion, Saint Helena

AUSTRALIA

AUSTRALIA, PAPUA NEW GUINEA, AND NEW ZEALAND LAND COVER IMAGE 86

AUSTRALIA POLITICAL MAP 88

AUSTRALIA PHYSICAL MAP 90

PAPUA NEW GUINEA AND NEW ZEALAND POLITICAL MAPS 92

AUSTRALIA, NEW ZEALAND, AND PAPUA NEW GUINEA FLAGS & FACTS, POPULATION DENSITY, AND DATES OF COUNTRY INDEPENDENCE 93

Australia, New Zealand, Papua New Guinea

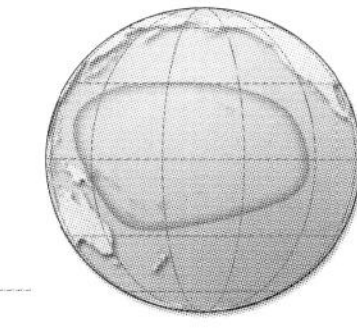

OCEANIA

OCEANIA LAND COVER IMAGE 94

OCEANIA POLITICAL MAP 96

OCEANIA FLAGS & FACTS, POPULATION DENSITY, AND DATES OF COUNTRY INDEPENDENCE 98

Fiji Islands, Kiribati, Marshall Islands, Micronesia, Nauru, Palau, Samoa, Solomon Islands, Tonga, Tuvalu, Vanuatu **DEPENDENCIES:** American Samoa, Cook Islands, French Polynesia, Guam, New Caledonia, Niue, Norfolk Island, Northern Mariana Islands, Pitcairn Islands, Tokelau, Wallis and Futuna Islands, **UNINHABITED DEPENDENCIES:** Baker Island, Howland Island, Jarvis Island, Johnston Atoll, Kingman Reef, Midway Islands, Palmyra Atoll, Wake Island

ANTARCTICA

ANTARCTICA LAND COVER IMAGE 100

ANTARCTICA PHYSICAL MAP AND INSET OF TERRITORIAL CLAIMS 102

APPENDIX

AIRLINE DISTANCES/ABBREVIATIONS 104

METRIC CONVERSIONS 105

FOREIGN TERMS 106

AVERAGE RAINFALL AND TEMPERATURE 108

INDEX

PLACE-NAME INDEX 112

ACKNOWLEDGMENTS 126

Consultants / Art and Illustrations / Satellite Images / Photography / Principal Reference Sources / Principal Online Sources / Key to Flags and Facts

CREDITS 128

Map Policies

Maps are a rich, useful, and—to the extent humanly possible—accurate means of depicting the world. Yet maps inevitably make the world seem a little simpler than it really is. A neatly drawn boundary may in reality be a hotly contested war zone. The government-sanctioned, "official" name of a provincial city in an ethnically diverse region may bear little resemblance to the name its citizens routinely use. These cartographic issues often seem obscure and academic. But maps arouse passions. Despite our carefully reasoned map policies, users of National Geographic maps write us strongly worded letters when our maps are at odds with their worldviews.

How do National Geographic cartographers deal with these realities? With constant scrutiny, considerable discussion, and help from many outside experts.

Examples:

Nations: Issues of national sovereignty and contested borders often boil down to "de facto versus de jure" discussions. Governments and international agencies frequently make official rulings about contested regions. These de jure decisions, no matter how legitimate, are often at odds with the wishes of individuals and groups, and they often stand in stark contrast to real-world situations. The inevitable conclusion: It is simplest and best to show the world as it is—de facto—rather than as we or others wish it to be.

Africa's Western Sahara, for example, was divided by Morocco and Mauritania after the Spanish government withdrew in 1976. Although Morocco now controls the entire territory, the United Nations does not recognize Morocco's sovereignty over this still disputed area. This atlas shows the de facto Moroccan rule but includes an explanatory note.

Place-names: Ride a barge down the Danube, and you'll hear the river called **Donau, Duna, Dunaj, Dunărea, Dunav, Dunay.** These are local names. This atlas uses the conventional name, "Danube," on physical maps. On political maps, local names are used, with the conventional name in parentheses where space permits. Usage conventions for both foreign and domestic place-names are established by the U.S. Board on Geographic Names, a group with representatives from several federal agencies.

Political Maps

Political maps portray features such as international boundaries, the locations of cities, road networks, and other important elements of the world's human geography. Most index entries are keyed to the political maps, listing the page numbers and then the specific locations on the pages. (See page 112 for details on how to use the index.)

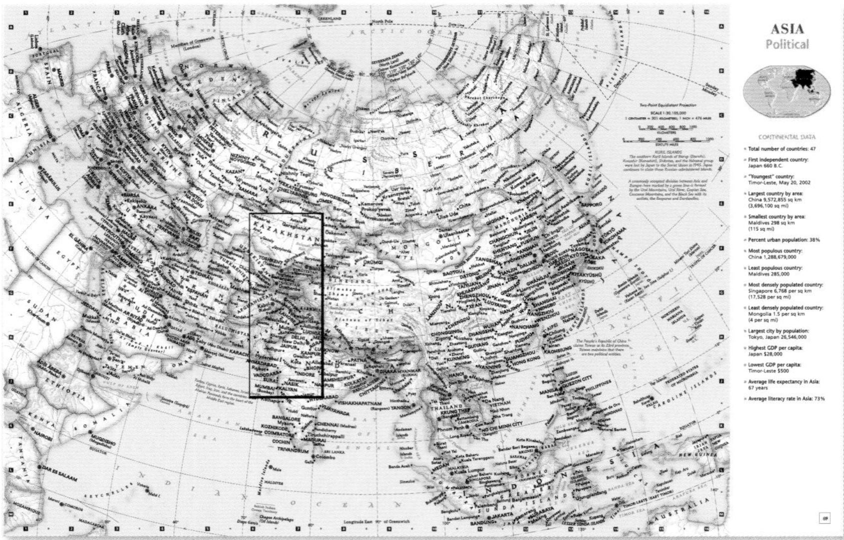

Asia Political, pp. 68-69

Physical features: Gray relief shading depicts surface features such as mountains, hills, and valleys.

Water features are shown in blue. Solid lines and filled-in areas indicate perennial water features; dashed lines and patterns indicate intermittent features.

Boundaries and political divisions are defined with both lines and colored bands; they vary according to whether a boundary is internal or international (for details, see map symbols key at right).

Cities: The regional political maps that form the bulk of this atlas depict four categories of cities or towns. The largest cities are shown in all capital letters (e.g., LONDON).

Physical Maps

Physical maps of the world, the continents, and the ocean floor reveal landforms and vegetation in stunning detail. Painted by relief artists John Bonner and Tibor Tóth, the maps have been edited for accuracy. Although painted maps are human interpretations, these depictions can emphasize subtle features that are sometimes invisible in satellite imagery.

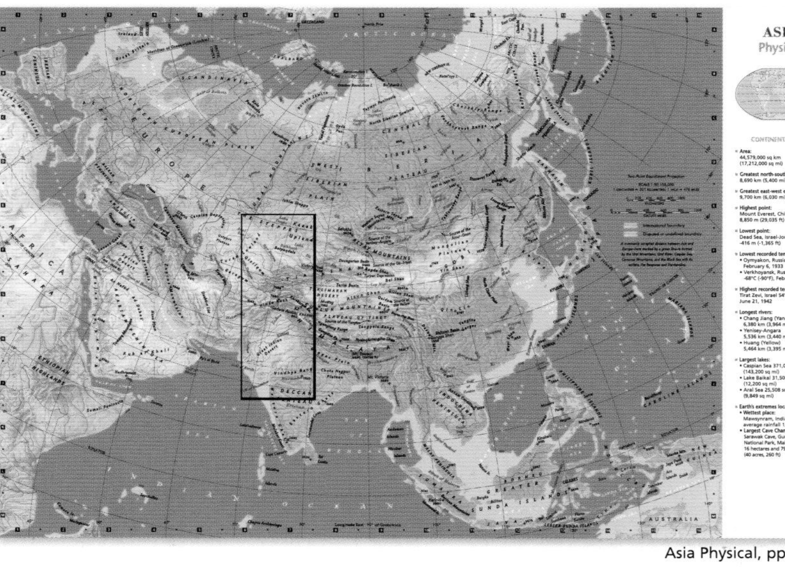

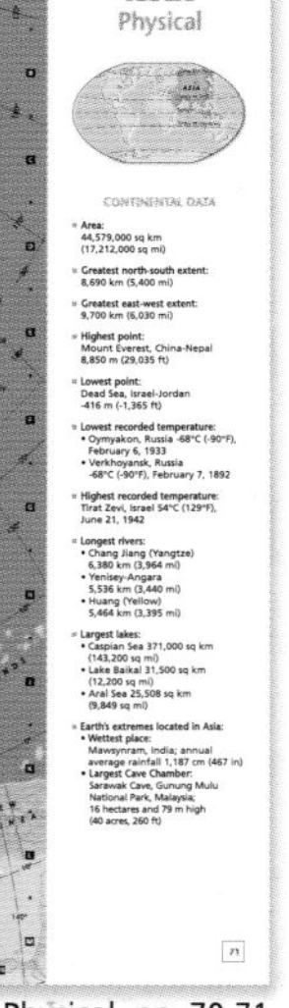

Asia Physical, pp. 70-71

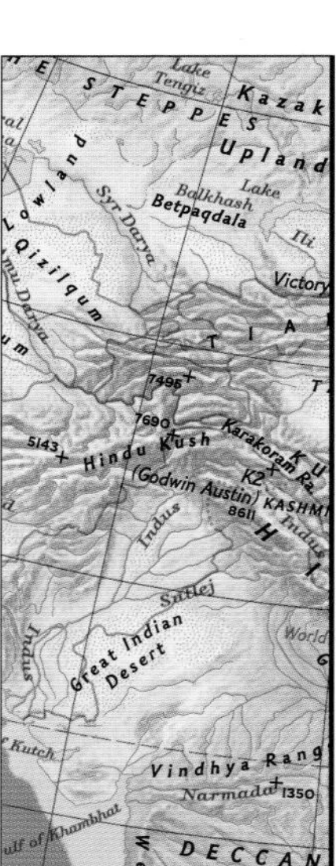

Physical features: Colors and shading illustrate variations in elevation, landforms and vegetation. Patterns indicate specific landscape features, such as sand, glaciers, and swamps.

Water features: Blue lines indicate rivers; other water bodies are shown as areas of blue. Lighter shading reflects the limits of the Continental Shelf.

Boundaries and political divisions are shown in red. Dotted lines indicate disputed or uncertain boundaries.

World Thematic Maps

Thematic maps reveal the rich patchwork and infinite interrelationships of our changing planet. The thematic section at the beginning of the atlas charts human patterns, with information on population, religions, and the world economy. In this section, maps are coupled with charts, diagrams, photographs, and tabular information, which together create a very useful framework for studying geographic patterns.

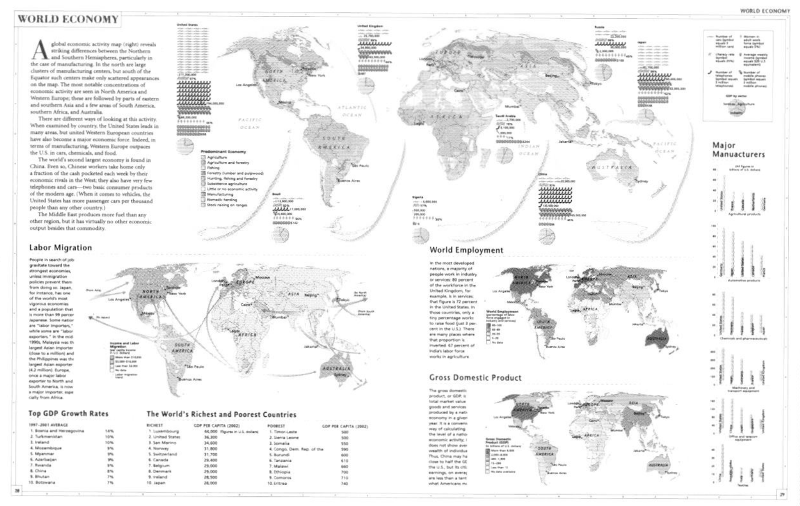

World Economy, pp. 28-29

Flags and Facts

This atlas recognizes 192 independent nations. All of these countries, along with dependencies and U.S. states, are profiled in the continental sections of the atlas. Accompanying each entry are highlights of geographic, demographic, and economic data. These details provide a brief overview of each country, state, or territory; they are not intended to be comprehensive. A detailed description of the sources and policies used in compiling the listings is included in the Key to Flags and Facts on page 127.

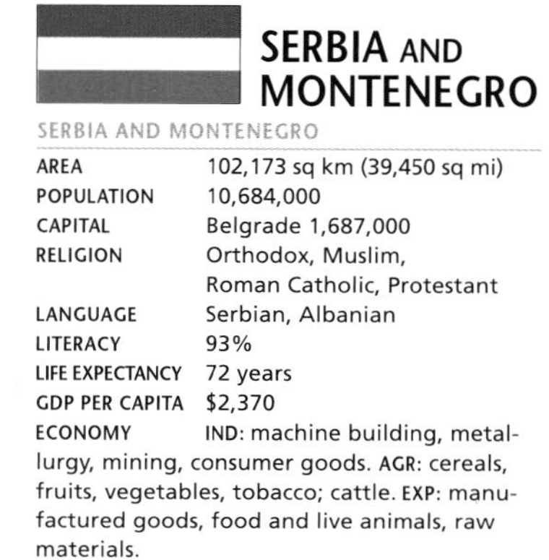

SERBIA AND MONTENEGRO

SERBIA AND MONTENEGRO

AREA	102,173 sq km (39,450 sq mi)
POPULATION	10,684,000
CAPITAL	Belgrade 1,687,000
RELIGION	Orthodox, Muslim, Roman Catholic, Protestant
LANGUAGE	Serbian, Albanian
LITERACY	93%
LIFE EXPECTANCY	72 years
GDP PER CAPITA	$2,370

ECONOMY IND: machine building, metallurgy, mining, consumer goods. AGR: cereals, fruits, vegetables, tobacco; cattle. EXP: manufactured goods, food and live animals, raw materials.

Europe, pp. 62-65

Index and Grid

Beginning on page 112 is a full index of place-names found in this atlas. The edge of each map is marked with letters (in rows) and numbers (in columns), to which the index entries are referenced. As an example, "Cartagena, Col. 50 A2" (see inset below) refers to the grid section on page 50 where row A and column 2 meet. More examples and additional details about the index are included on page 112.

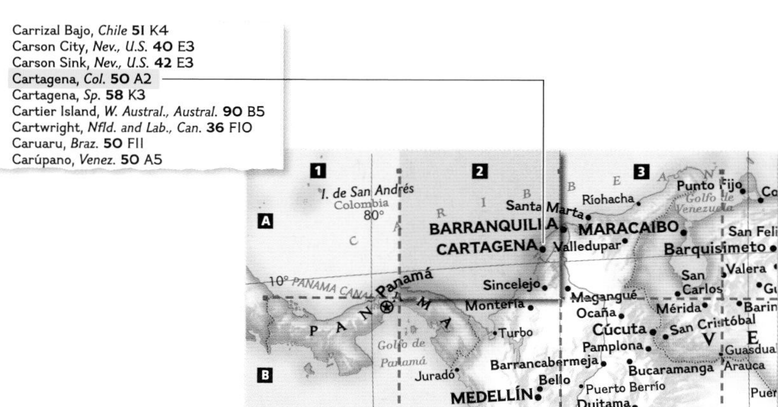

Map Symbols

BOUNDARIES

Defined

Undefined or disputed

Offshore line of separation

International boundary (Physical Plates)

Disputed or undefined boundary (Physical Plates)

CITIES

Capitals

Towns

WATER FEATURES

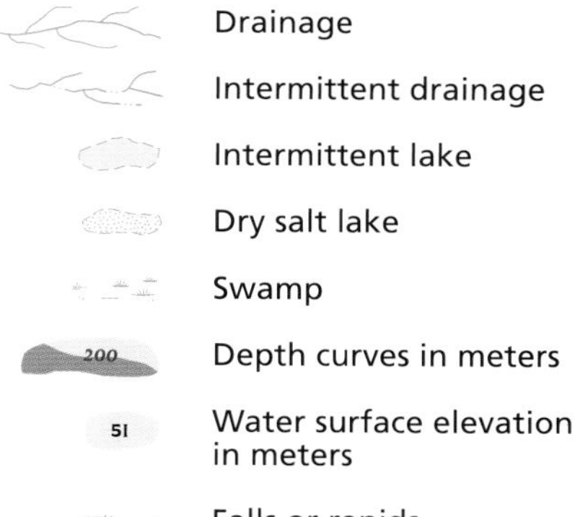

Drainage

Intermittent drainage

Intermittent lake

Dry salt lake

Swamp

200 Depth curves in meters

51 Water surface elevation in meters

Falls or rapids

PHYSICAL FEATURES

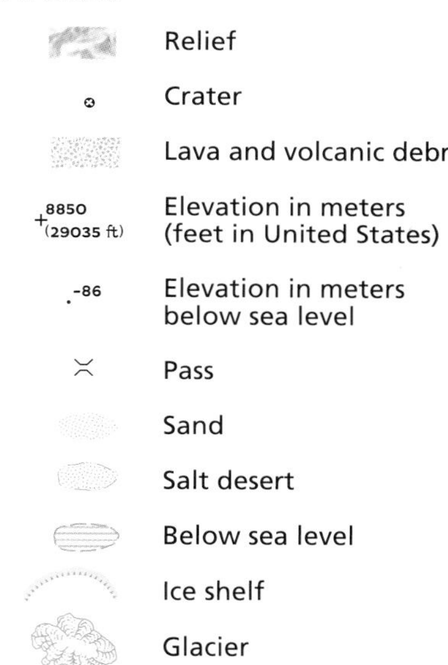

Relief

Crater

Lava and volcanic debris

8850 (29035 ft) Elevation in meters (feet in United States)

-86 Elevation in meters below sea level

Pass

Sand

Salt desert

Below sea level

Ice shelf

Glacier

CULTURAL FEATURES

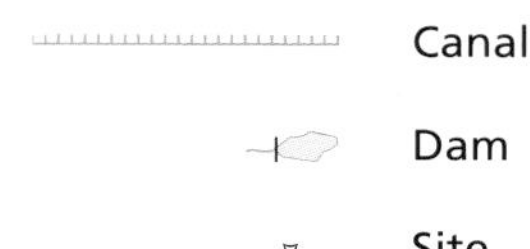

Canal

Dam

Site

MAP SCALE *(Sample)*

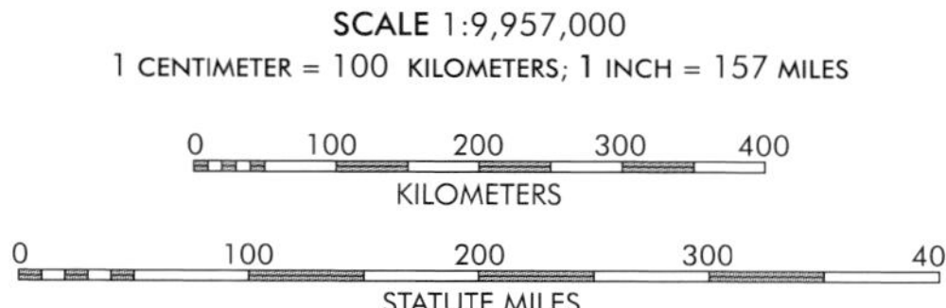

WORLD

VEGETATIVE LAND COVER
Evergreen Needleleaf Forest
Evergreen Broadleaf Forest
Deciduous Needleleaf Forest
Deciduous Broadleaf Forest
Mixed Forest
Woodland
Wooded Grassland
Closed Shrubland
Open Shrubland
Grassland
Cropland
Barren and Desert
Urban and Built-Up
Snow and Ice

WORLD
Political

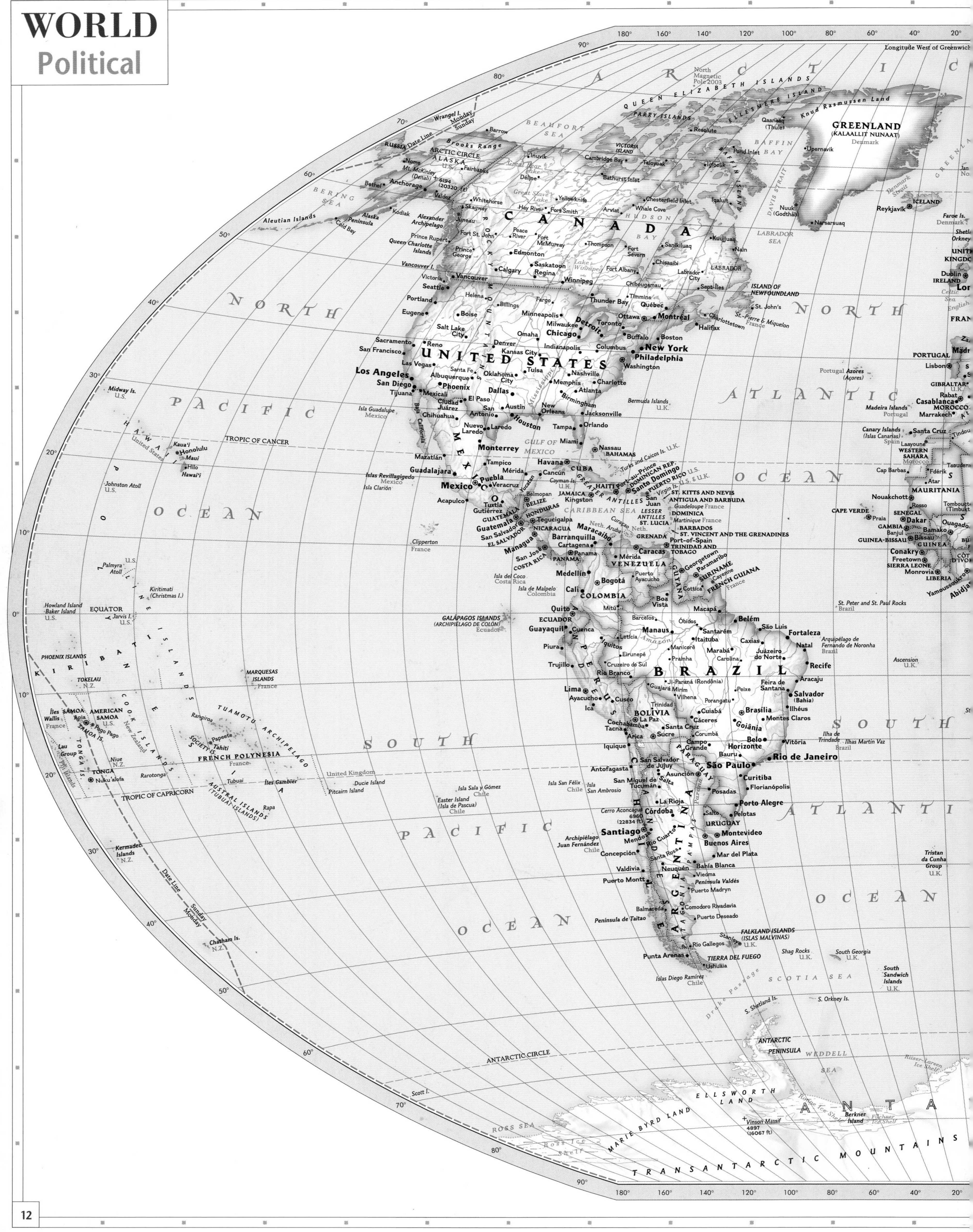

OCEAN
RUSSIA
KAZAKHSTAN
MONGOLIA
CHINA
INDIA
INDONESIA
AUSTRALIA
NORTH PACIFIC OCEAN
INDIAN OCEAN
SOUTH PACIFIC OCEAN
ANTARCTICA
ARCTIC CIRCLE
TROPIC OF CANCER
EQUATOR
TROPIC OF CAPRICORN
ANTARCTIC CIRCLE
Date Line
Winkel Tripel Projection, Central Meridian 0°
SCALE 1:80,471,000
1 CENTIMETER = 805 KILOMETERS; 1 INCH = 1270 MILES AT THE EQUATOR
0 500 1000 1500 2000 2500
KILOMETERS
0 500 1000 1500 2000 2500
STATUTE MILES
International boundaries and disputed territories, where scale permits, reflect de facto status at the time of publication.

WORLD
Physical

NANSEN BASIN
NANSEN RIDGE
POLE PLAIN
MAKAROV BASIN
OCEAN
North East Land
Spitsbergen
Svalbard
Edge Island
Bear Island
NORWEGIAN SEA
BARENTS SEA
CONTINENTAL SHELF
North Cape
George Land
Franz Josef Land
Graham Bell Island
Vize I.
Komsomolets Island
October Revolution Island
Bol'shevik Island
Cape Chelyuskin
North Land
Novaya Zemlya
KARA SEA
Taymyr Peninsula
Lake Taymyr
LAPTEV SEA
New Siberian Islands
CONTINENTAL SLOPE
CONTINENTAL SHELF
EAST SIBERIAN SEA
Wrangel I.
Chukchi Range
ARCTIC CIRCLE
North Siberian Lowland
Gyda Peninsula
Yamal Pen.
Kolguyev I.
Kola Pen.
White Sea
Timan Ridge
Scandinavia
G. of Bothnia
Lake Onega
Lake Ladoga
Gulf of Finland
Baltic Sea
Jutland
Source of the Volga
Volga
Ural Mountains
Ob
West Siberian Plain
Irtysh
Yenisey
Central Siberian Plateau
Lena
Verkhoyansk Range
Cherskiy Range
Kolyma
Kolyma Range
Koryak Range
SIBERIA
ASIA
EUROPE
Northern European Plain
Pinsk Marshes
Central Russian Upland
Carpathian Mts.
Danube
Alps
Apennines
Adriatic Sea
Balkan Peninsula
Black Sea
Bosporus
Crimea
Sea of Azov
Don
Caucasus Mts.
El'brus 5642
Caspian Depression
Caspian Sea
Ural
Kazakh Uplands
The Steppes
Aral Sea
Ustyurt Plateau
Kyzylkum
Turan Lowland
Garagum
Amu Darya
Syr Darya
Lake Balkhash
Dzungarian Basin
Altay Mountains
Belukha 4506
Tian Shan
Turpan Depression
Victory Peak 7439
Taklimakan Desert
Altun Shan
Kunlun Mountains
Muztag 6987
K2 8611
Hindu Kush
Source of the Plateau of Tibet
Plateau of Tibet
HIMALAYA
Mt. Everest 8850 (29035 ft)
Brahmaputra
Ganges
Indus
Great Indian Desert
Mongolian Plateau
GOBI
Eastern Sayan Mts.
Lake Baikal
Yablonovyy Range
Stanovoy Range
Greater Khingan Range
Amur
Manchurian Plain
Sikhote Alin Range
Sakhalin
SEA OF OKHOTSK
Kamchatka Peninsula
ALEUTIAN BASIN
BERING SEA
Attu
Aleutian Is.
ALEUTIAN TRENCH
Detroit Tablemount
EMPEROR SEAMOUNTS
EMPEROR TROUGH
HESS RISE
NORTHWEST PACIFIC BASIN
Kuril Islands
KURIL TRENCH
Hokkaido
JAPAN TRENCH
Honshu
Fuji 3776
Shikoku
Kyushu
SEA OF JAPAN (EAST SEA)
Korea
Yellow Sea
Qinghai Hu
Yellow
Qin Ling
North China Plain
Yangtze
CONTINENTAL SHELF
EAST CHINA SEA
Ryukyu Islands
RYUKYU TRENCH
Taiwan
Taiwan Str.
Luzon Strait
Luzon
Mt. Pinatubo
PHILIPPINE SEA
PHILIPPINE BASIN
Philippine Islands
Philippine Trench
IZU TRENCH
BONIN TRENCH
Nampo Shoto
KYUSHU PALAU RIDGE
WEST MARIANA BASIN
Mariana Islands
MARIANA TROUGH
MARIANA TRENCH
Challenger Deep 10920
Guam
YAP TRENCH
PALAU TRENCH
SHATSKY RISE
Isakov Seamount
Makarov Seamount
Grosvenor Seamount
MAPMAKER SEAMOUNTS
NORTH PACIFIC OCEAN
TROPIC OF CANCER
MID-PACIFIC MOUNTAINS
Wake I.
MAGELLAN SEAMOUNTS
Marshall Islands
Bikini Atoll
Enewetak Atoll
Kwajalein Atoll
Taongi Atoll
EAST MARIANA BASIN
MICRONESIA
Pohnpei (Ponape)
Chuuk
Caroline Islands
EAST CAROLINE BASIN
WEST CAROLINE BASIN
CENTRAL PACIFIC BASIN
Gilbert Islands
EQUATOR
Nauru
Banaba
Beru
Nanumea
Tuvalu
VITIAZ TRENCH
Admiralty Is.
New Ireland
Bismarck Archipelago
New Britain
Bougainville
Solomon Islands
Solomon Sea
Guadalcanal
MELANESIA
New Guinea
Jaya Peak 5029
Arafura Sea
Timor
Timor Sea
CONTINENTAL SHELF
Cape York Pen.
Gulf of Carpentaria
Great Barrier Reef
CORAL SEA BASIN
CORAL SEA
Vanuatu
NORTH FIJI BASIN
Fiji Islands
NEW HEBRIDES TRENCH
New Caledonia
TROPIC OF CAPRICORN
SOUTH FIJI BASIN
SOUTH PACIFIC OCEAN
Lord Howe I.
LORD HOWE RISE
NEW CALEDONIA BASIN
Gascoyne Tablemount
TASMAN BASIN
TASMAN SEA
TASMAN PLAIN
North Island
NEW ZEALAND
Mt. Cook 3754
South Island
Stewart Island
EAST TASMAN PLATEAU
SOUTH TASMAN RISE
CAMPBELL PLATEAU
Auckland
MACQUARIE RIDGE
Macquarie I.
Tasmania
Bass Strait
Mt. Kosciuszko 2228
Murray
Darling
Great Dividing Range
Central Lowlands
Great Artesian Basin
Lake Eyre -16
AUSTRALIA
Western Plateau
Macdonnell Ranges
Great Victoria Desert
Nullarbor Plain
Great Australian Bight
Great Sandy Desert
Kimberley Plateau
NORTH AUSTRALIAN BASIN
Wallaby Plateau
North West Cape
EXMOUTH PLATEAU
Cape Inscription
PERTH BASIN
Cape Naturaliste
CONTINENTAL SLOPE
SOUTH AUSTRALIAN BASIN
DIAMANTINA FRACTURE ZONE
BROKEN RIDGE
EAST INDIAMAN RIDGE
WHARTON BASIN
Christmas I.
Cocos Islands
JAVA TRENCH
JAVA RIDGE
Lesser Sunda Islands
Flores
Java Sea
Greater Sunda Islands
Banda Sea
Buru
Celebes
Moluccas
CELEBES BASIN
Borneo
INDONESIA
Kerinci 3800
Sumatra
Strait of Malacca
Malay Pen.
Kinabalu 4101
Mindanao
SULU BASIN
PALAWAN TROUGH
CONTINENTAL SHELF
SOUTH CHINA SEA
Hainan
G. of Tonkin
Indochina Peninsula
Mekong
Gulf of Thailand
Andaman Sea
Andaman Islands
Nicobar Islands
BAY OF BENGAL
Ganges Fan
Sri Lanka (Ceylon)
INDIA
Deccan Plateau
Western Ghats
Eastern Ghats
Indus Fan
ARABIAN SEA
ARABIAN BASIN
CARLSBERG RIDGE
CHAGOS-LACCADIVE PLATEAU
Maldive Islands
CEYLON PLAIN
COCOS BASIN
NINETYEAST RIDGE
INVESTIGATOR RIDGE
Nikitin Seamount
Chagos Archipelago
Diego Garcia
CHAGOS TRENCH
MID-INDIAN BASIN
MID-INDIAN RIDGE
OSBORN PLATEAU
Seychelles
Coco-de-Mer Seamounts
SOMALI BASIN
OWEN FRACTURE ZONE
Socotra
Gulf of Aden
Somali Peninsula
Ethiopian Highlands
Lake Turkana (L. Rudolf)
ARABIAN PENINSULA
Rub al Khali (Empty Quarter)
An Nafūd
Persian Gulf
G. of Oman
Zagros Mountains
Mesopotamia
Tigris
Euphrates
Syrian Desert
Dead Sea -416 (-1365 ft)
Sinai
Red Sea
Elburz Mts.
Mt. Ararat 5165
ANATOLIA (ASIA MINOR)
Aegean Sea
Ionian Sea
Sicily
Crete
Cyprus
Nile Fan
MEDITERRANEAN SEA
Great Eastern Erg
Qattara Depression -133
Western Desert
Libyan Desert
Nile
Eastern Desert
Nubian Desert
SAHARA
Tibesti 3415
Mt. Tahat 3003
Air (Azbine)
Lake Chad
Marra Mts. 3088
Blue Nile
White Nile
AFRICA
Cameroon Mt. 4100
Bioko
Congo
Congo Basin
Ruwenzori 5109
Lake Albert
Lake Victoria
Sources of the Nile
Kilimanjaro 5895
Lake Tanganyika
Zanzibar I.
Mitumba Mts.
Lower Guinea
Congo Canyon
Katanga Plateau
Lake Malawi
Lake Kariba
Victoria Falls
Zambezi
Amirante Isles
MASCARENE PLATEAU
Aldabra Is.
Comoro Is.
Mozambique Channel
MASCARENE BASIN
Maromokotro
Madagascar
Mascarene Islands
Mauritius
Rodrigues
Réunion
MASCARENE PLAIN
MADAGASCAR BASIN
MADAGASCAR PLATEAU
NATAL BASIN
MOZAMBIQUE PLATEAU
Kalahari Desert
Namib Desert
Thabana Ntlenyana 3482
Drakensberg
Great Karroo
Cape of Good Hope
Cape Agulhas
Vema Seamount
Wyandot Seamount
AGULHAS PLATEAU
AGULHAS RIDGE
AGULHAS BASIN
Meteor Seamount
PRINCE EDWARD FRACTURE ZONE
Prince Edward Islands
SOUTHWEST INDIAN RIDGE
CROZET BASIN
Crozet Islands
Amsterdam
St. Paul
INDIAN OCEAN
SOUTHEAST INDIAN RIDGE
Kerguelen Islands
Heard Island
KERGUELEN PLATEAU
Ob Tablemount
Lena Tablemount
ATLANTIC-INDIAN RIDGE
ENDERBY PLAIN
SOUTH INDIAN BASIN
Cosmonaut Sea
Riiser-Larsen Peninsula
Cape Ann
Enderby Land
Prydz Bay
Cape Poinsett
South Magnetic Pole
ANTARCTIC CIRCLE
Balleny Is.
Queen Maud Land
ANTARCTICA
Ice thickness 4776
Transantarctic Mountains
Victoria Land
Ross Sea
Ross Ice Shelf
Longitude East of Greenwich
Winkel Tripel Projection, Central Meridian 0°
SCALE 1:80,471,000
1 CENTIMETER = 805 KILOMETERS; 1 INCH = 1270 MILES AT THE EQUATOR
0 500 1000 1500 2000 2500
KILOMETERS
0 500 1000 1500 2000 2500
STATUTE MILES
20° 40° 60° 80° 100° 120° 140° 160° 180°
90° 80° 70° 60° 50° 40° 30° 20° 10° 0° 10° 20° 30° 40°

POLITICAL
Poles

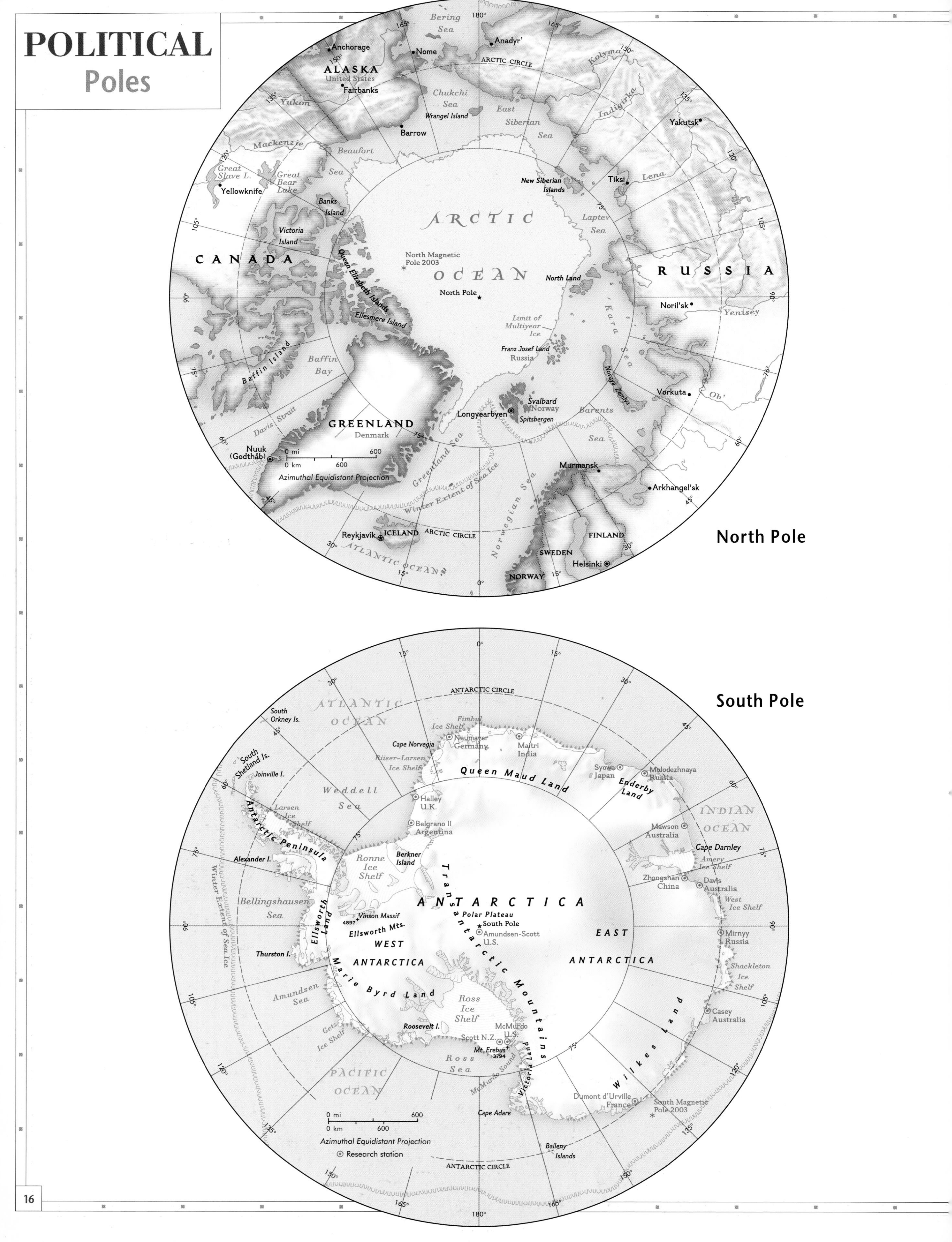

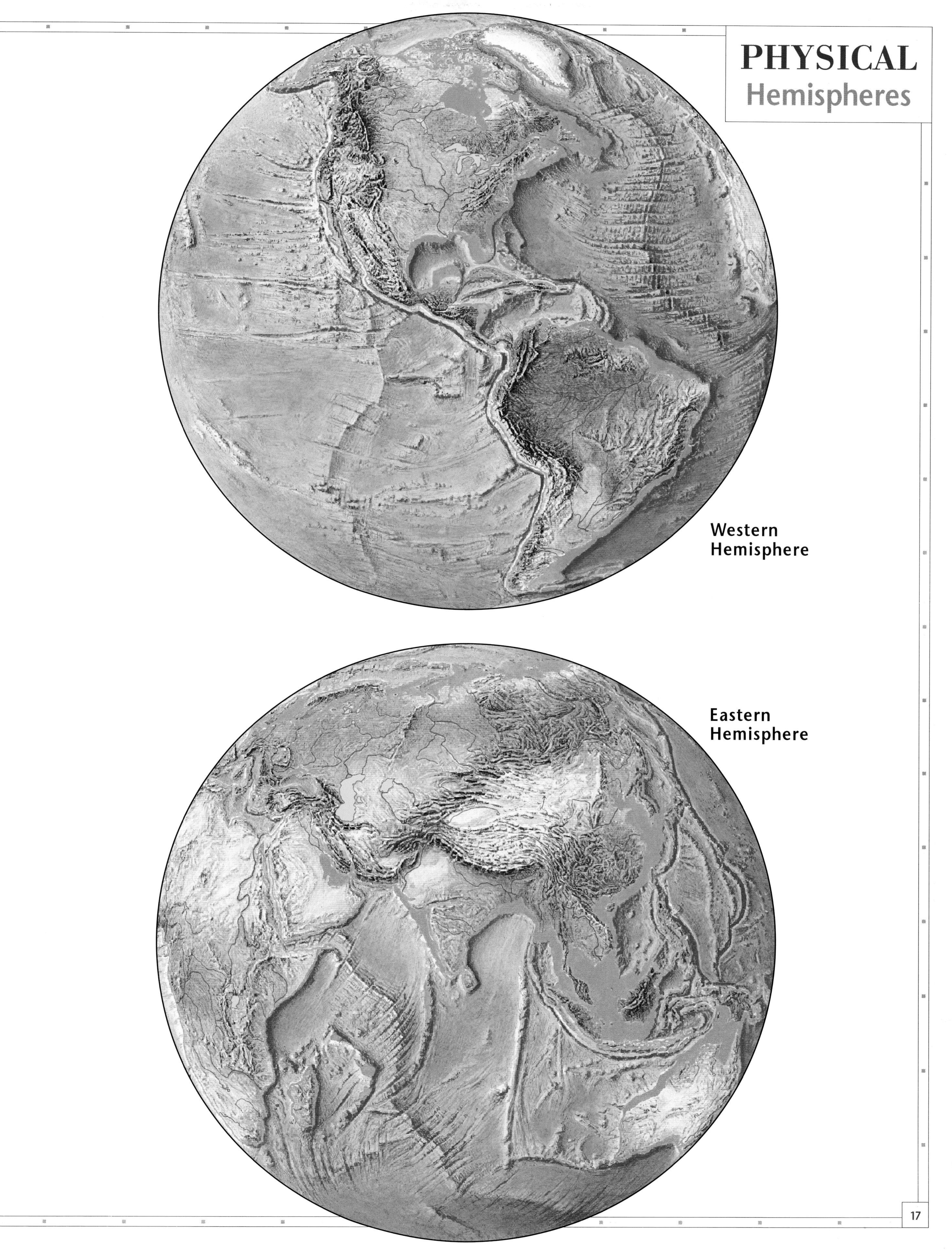
Western
Hemisphere
Eastern
Hemisphere

STRUCTURE OF THE EARTH

Like ice on a great lake, the Earth's crust, or the lithosphere, floats over the planet's molten innards, is cracked in many places, and is in slow but constant movement. Earth's surface is broken into 16 enormous slabs of rock, called plates, averaging thousands of miles wide and having a thickness of several miles. As they move and grind against each other, they push up mountains, spawn volcanoes, and generate earthquakes.

Although these often cataclysmic events capture our attention, the movements that cause them are imperceptible–a slow waltz of rafted rock that continues over eons.

How slow? The Mid-Atlantic Ridge (see "spreading" diagram, opposite) is being built by magma oozing between two plates, separating North America and Africa at the speed of a growing human fingernail.

The dividing lines between plates often mark areas of high volcanic and earthquake activity as plates strain against each other or one dives beneath another. In the Ring of Fire around the Pacific Basin, disastrous earthquakes have occurred in Kobe, Japan, and in Los Angeles and San Francisco, California. Volcanic eruptions have taken place at Pinatubo in the Philippines and Mount St. Helens in Washington State.

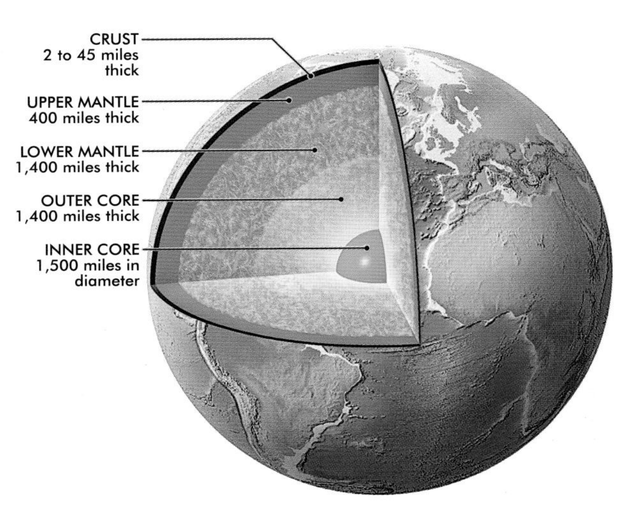

Continents Adrift in Time

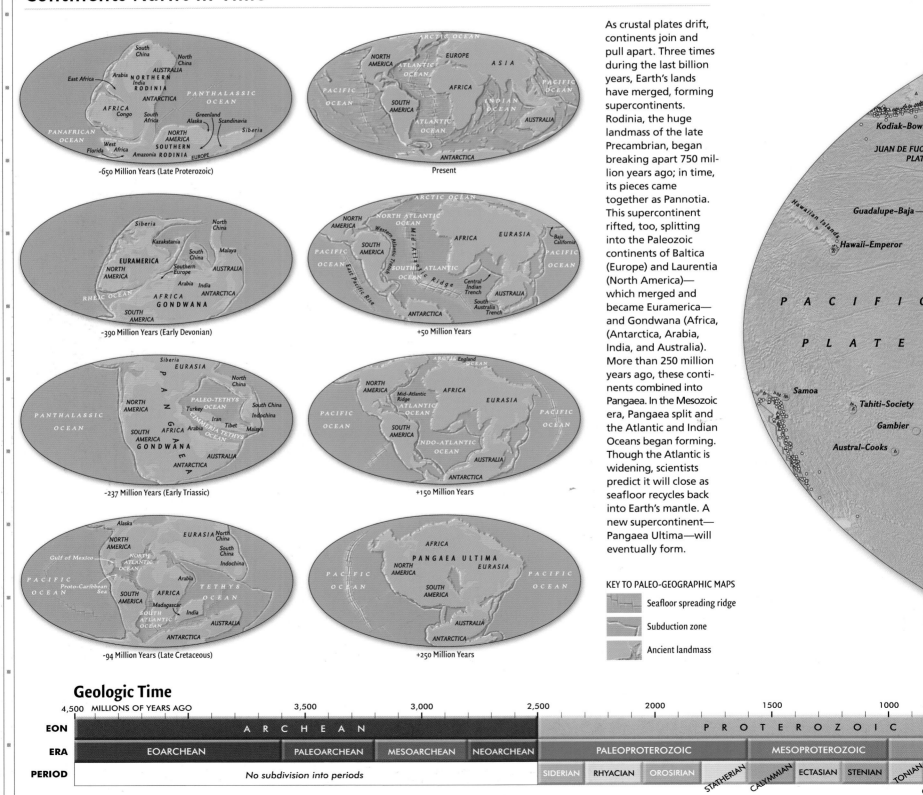

-650 Million Years (Late Proterozoic)

Present

-390 Million Years (Early Devonian)

+50 Million Years

-237 Million Years (Early Triassic)

+150 Million Years

-94 Million Years (Late Cretaceous)

+250 Million Years

As crustal plates drift, continents join and pull apart. Three times during the last billion years, Earth's lands have merged, forming supercontinents. Rodinia, the huge landmass of the late Precambrian, began breaking apart 750 million years ago; in time, its pieces came together as Pannotia. This supercontinent rifted, too, splitting into the Paleozoic continents of Baltica (Europe) and Laurentia (North America)—which merged and became Euramerica—and Gondwana (Africa, (Antarctica, Arabia, India, and Australia). More than 250 million years ago, these continents combined into Pangaea. In the Mesozoic era, Pangaea split and the Atlantic and Indian Oceans began forming. Though the Atlantic is widening, scientists predict it will close as seafloor recycles back into Earth's mantle. A new supercontinent—Pangaea Ultima—will eventually form.

KEY TO PALEO-GEOGRAPHIC MAPS

- Seafloor spreading ridge
- Subduction zone
- Ancient landmass

Kodiak-Bowie
JUAN DE FUCA PLAT
Hawaiian Islands
Guadalupe-Baja
Hawaii-Emperor
PACIFIC PLATE
Samoa
Tahiti-Society
Gambier
Austral-Cooks

Geologic Time

MILLIONS OF YEARS AGO: 4,500 · 3,500 · 3,000 · 2,500 · 2000 · 1500 · 1000

EON	ARCHEAN				PROTEROZOIC							
ERA	EOARCHEAN	PALEOARCHEAN	MESOARCHEAN	NEOARCHEAN	PALEOPROTEROZOIC				MESOPROTEROZOIC			
PERIOD	*No subdivision into periods*				SIDERIAN	RHYACIAN	OROSIRIAN	STATHERIAN	CALYMMIAN	ECTASIAN	STENIAN	TONIAN

Geologic Forces Change the Face of the Planet

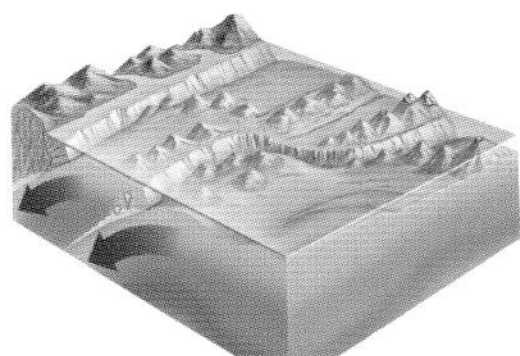
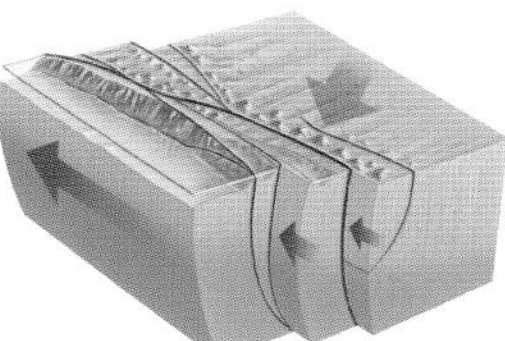
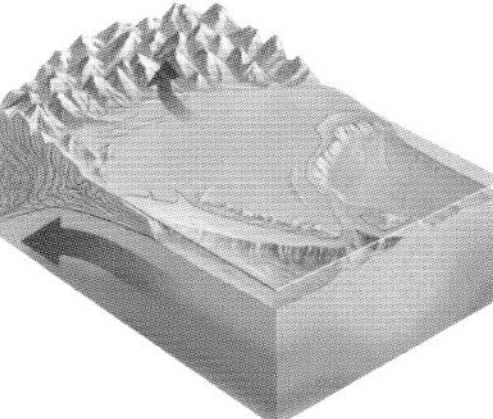
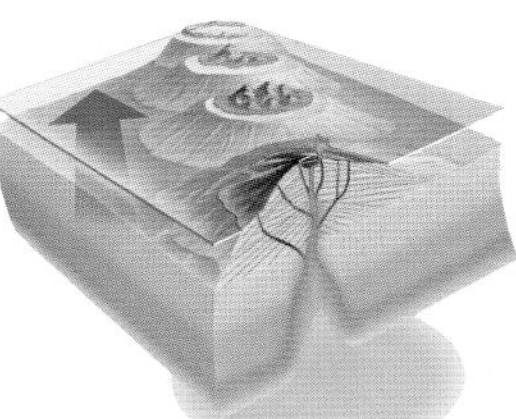
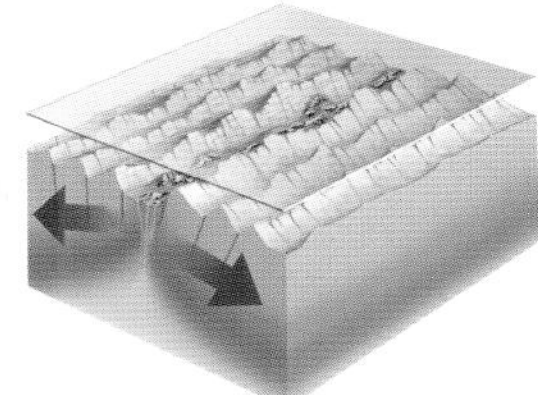
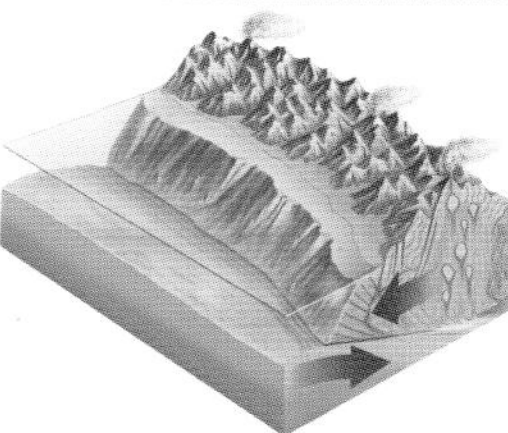

ACCRETION
As ocean plates move toward the edges of continents or island arcs and slide under them, seamounts are skimmed off and piled up in submarine trenches. The buildup can cause continents to grow.

FAULTING
Enormous crustal plates do not slide smoothly. Strain built up along their edges may release in a series of small jumps, felt as minor tremors on land. Extended buildup can cause a sudden jump, producing an earthquake.

COLLISION
When two continental plates converge, the result can be the greatest mountain-building process on Earth. The Himalaya rose when the Indian subcontinent collided with Eurasia, driving the land upward.

HOT SPOTS
In the cauldron of inner Earth, some areas burn hotter than others and periodically blast through their crustal covering as volcanoes. Such a "hot spot" built the Hawaiian Islands, leaving a string of oceanic protuberances.

SPREADING
At the divergent boundary known as the Mid-Atlantic Ridge, oozing magma forces two plates apart by as much as eight inches a year. If that rate had been constant, the ocean could have reached its current width in 30 million years.

SUBDUCTION
When an oceanic plate and a continental plate converge, the older and heavier sea plate takes a dive. Plunging back into the interior of the Earth, it is transformed into molten material, only to rise again as magma.

Plate Tectonics

Tectonic boundaries mark areas of geologic change in ocean floors, on the margins of continents, and even within continents, as seen in the Great Rift Valley of East Africa. Clusters of volcanoes and frequent earthquakes indicate unstable areas.

EURASIAN PLATE
NORTH AMERICAN PLATE
ROCKY MOUNTAINS
Yellowstone
Raton
Iceland
Mid-Atlantic Ridge
Azores
New England
ALPS
HIMALAYA
Plateau of Tibet
ARABIAN PLATE
Tibesti Uplift
Cape Verde
CARIBBEAN PLATE
COCOS PLATE
Galápagos
Afar
AFRICAN PLATE
Great Rift Valley
SOMALI PLATE
East Africa
INDIAN PLATE
PHILIPPINE PLATE
PACIFIC PLATE
Caroline
CAROLINE PLATE
SOUTH AMERICAN PLATE
ANDES
NAZCA PLATE
Easter
Juan Fernández
Trindade
St. Helena
Comoros
Réunion
Walvis Ridge
AUSTRALIAN PLATE
East Australia
Tasmantid
Crozet
Kerguélen
Bouvet
SCOTIA PLATE
ANTARCTIC PLATE

Kilometers: 0 1000 2000 3000
Statute Miles: 0 1000 2000 3000
Nautical Miles: 0 1000 2000 3000

Winkel Tripel Projection

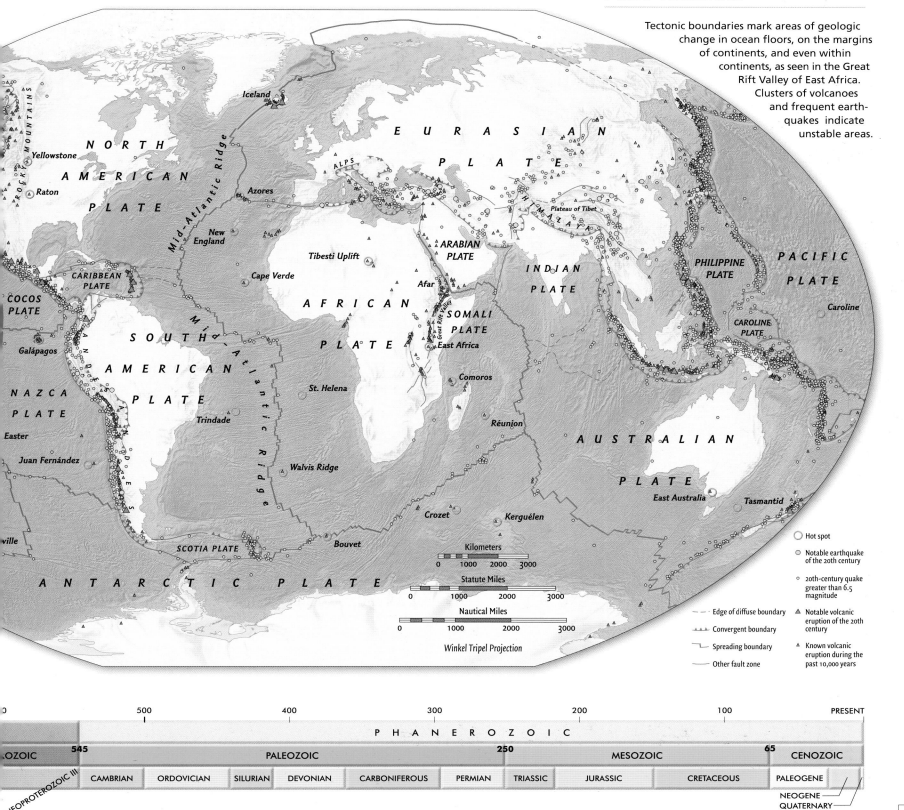

Edge of diffuse boundary
Convergent boundary
Spreading boundary
Other fault zone
Hot spot
Notable earthquake of the 20th century
20th-century quake greater than 6.5 magnitude
Notable volcanic eruption of the 20th century
Known volcanic eruption during the past 10,000 years

0 | 500 | 400 | 300 | 200 | 100 | PRESENT

PHANEROZOIC

OZOIC | 545 PALEOZOIC | 250 MESOZOIC | 65 CENOZOIC

NEOPROTEROZOIC III | CAMBRIAN | ORDOVICIAN | SILURIAN | DEVONIAN | CARBONIFEROUS | PERMIAN | TRIASSIC | JURASSIC | CRETACEOUS | PALEOGENE | NEOGENE | QUATERNARY

WORLD
Oceans

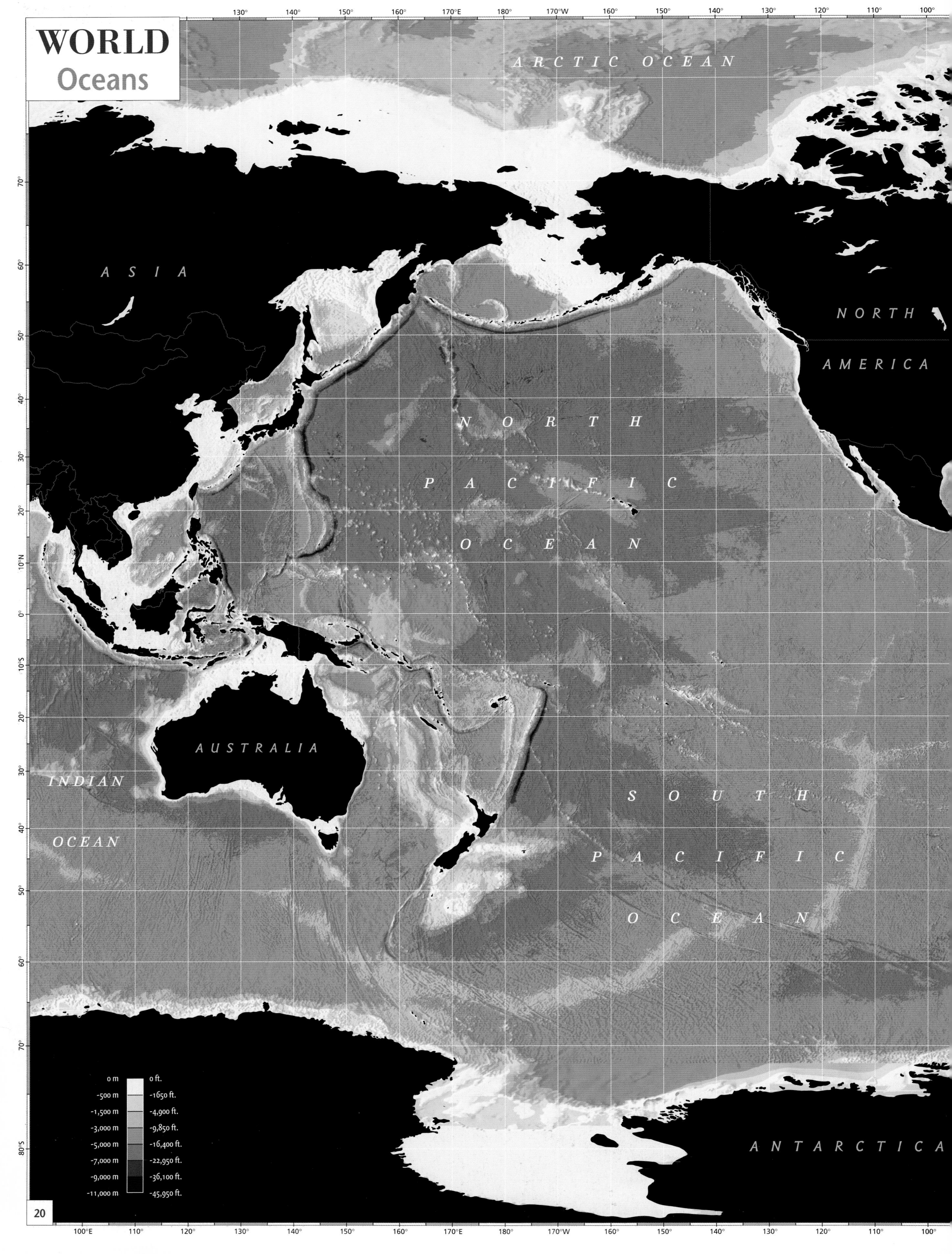

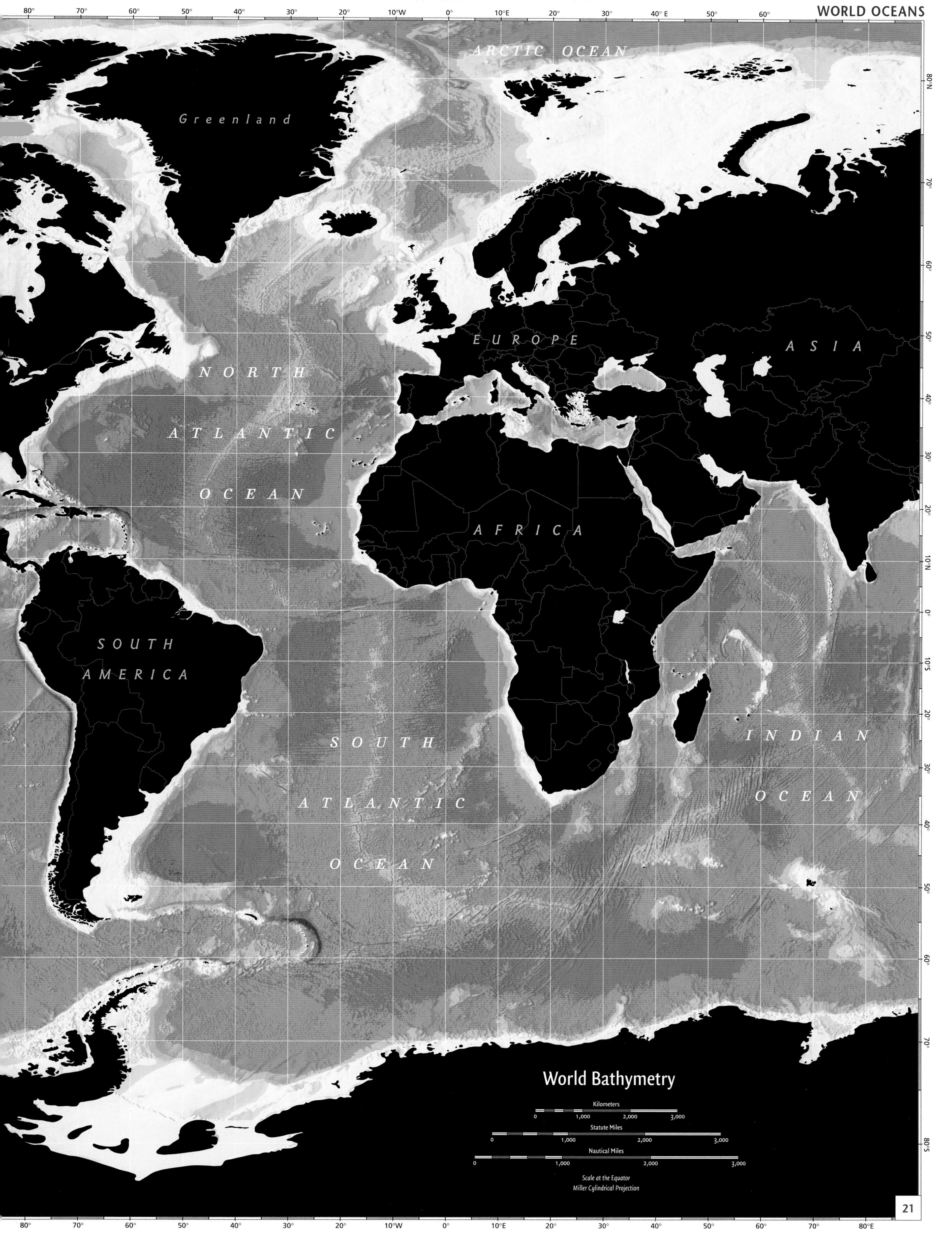

ARCTIC OCEAN
Greenland
EUROPE
ASIA
NORTH ATLANTIC OCEAN
AFRICA
SOUTH AMERICA
SOUTH ATLANTIC OCEAN
INDIAN OCEAN
World Bathymetry
Kilometers
0 1,000 2,000 3,000
Statute Miles
0 1,000 2,000 3,000
Nautical Miles
0 1,000 2,000 3,000
Scale at the Equator
Miller Cylindrical Projection

While populations in many parts of the world are expanding, those of Europe, Australia, New Zealand, Japan, and other rich industrial areas show little to no growth, or may actually be shrinking. Many such countries must bring in immigrant workers to keep their economies thriving.

A clear correlation exists between wealth and low fertility: the higher the incomes and educational levels, the lower the rates of reproduction.

Many governments keep vital statistics, recording births and deaths, and count their populations regularly to try to plan ahead. The United States has taken a census every ten years since 1790, recording the ages, the occupations, and other important facts about its people. The United Nations helps less developed countries carry out censuses and improve their demographic information.

Governments of poor countries, with an average per capita income of $380 a year, may find that half their populations are under the age of 20. They are faced with the overwhelming tasks of providing adequate education and jobs while encouraging better family planning programs. Governments of nations with low birthrates find themselves with growing numbers of elderly people but fewer workers able to provide tax money for health care and pensions.

In a mere 150 years, world population has grown fivefold, at an ever increasing pace. The industrial revolution helped bring about improvements in food supplies and advances in both medicine and public health, which allowed people to live longer and to have healthier babies. Today, 15,000 people are born into the world every hour, and nearly all of them are in poor African, Asian, and South American nations. This situation concerns planners, who look to demographers (professionals who study all aspects of population) for important data.

Lights of the World

Satellite imagery offers a surprising view of the world at night. Bright lights in Europe, Asia, and the United States give a clear picture of densely populated areas with ample electricity. Reading this map requires great care, however. Some totally dark areas, like most of Australia, do in fact have very small populations, but other light-free areas—in China and Africa, for example—may simply hide dense populations with not enough electricity to be seen by a satellite. Wealthy areas with fewer people, such as Florida, may be using their energy wastefully. Ever since the 1970s, demographers have supplemented census data with information from satellite imagery.

Population Pyramids

A population pyramid shows the number of males and females in every age group of a population. A pyramid for Ethiopia reveals that people younger than 20 far outnumber older people; one for Spain shows that most people are between 25 and 40.

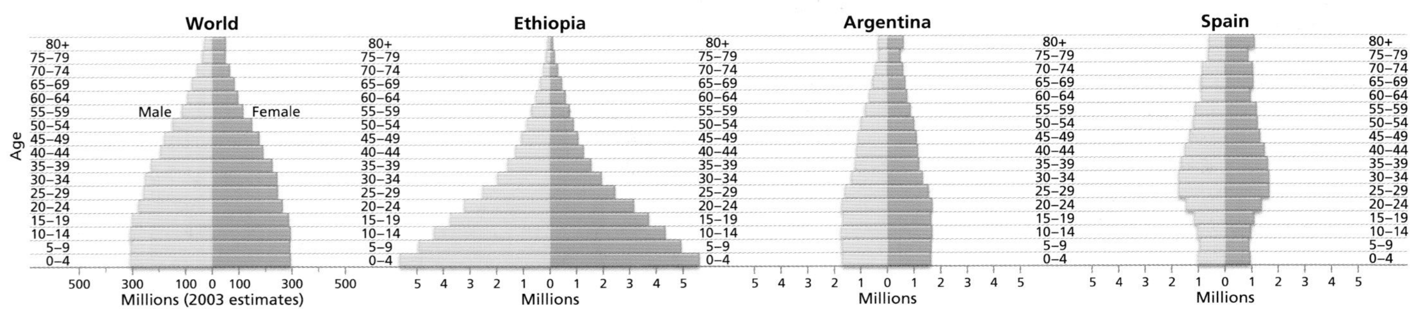

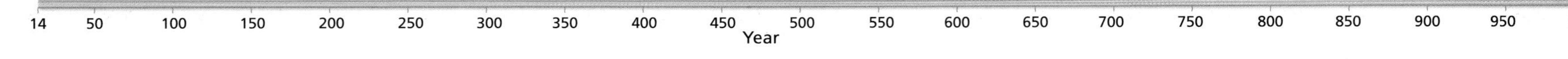

Population Growth

The population of the world is not distributed evenly. In this cartogram Canada is almost invisible, while China looks enormous because its population is 41 times greater than Canada's. In reality, both countries are similar in size. The shape of almost every country looks distorted when populations are compared in this way. Population sizes are constantly changing, however. In countries that are experiencing many more births than deaths, population totals are ballooning. In others, too few babies are born to replace the number of people who die, and populations are shrinking. A cartogram devoted solely to growth rates around the world would look quite different from this one.

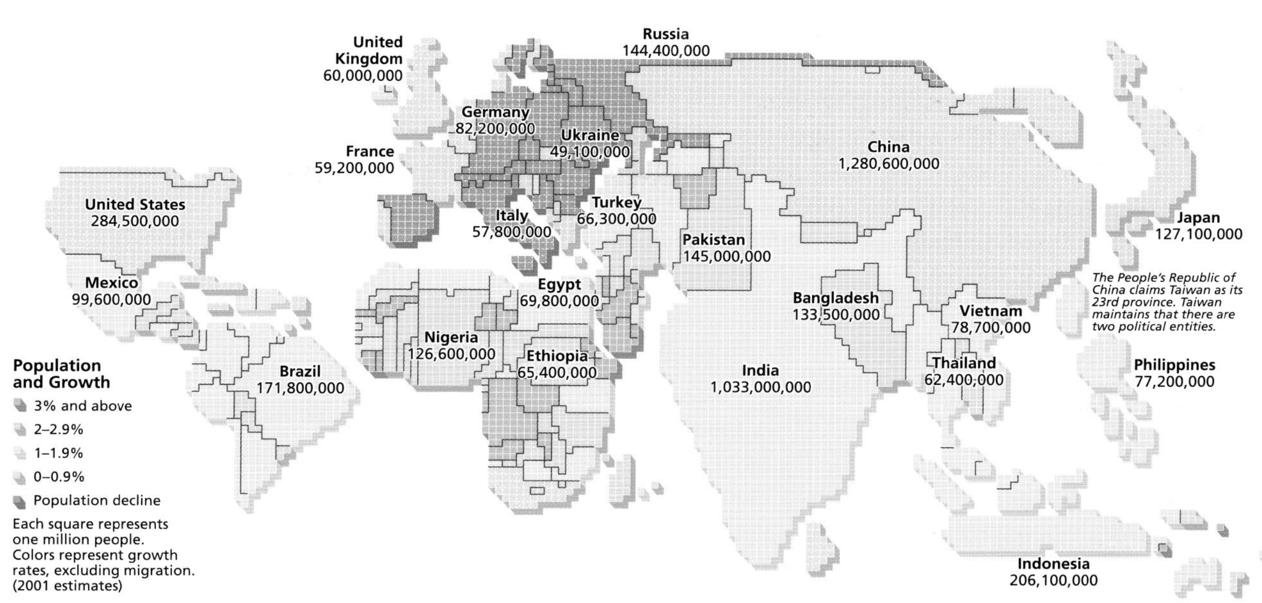

Population Density

A country's population density is estimated by figuring out how many people would occupy one square mile if they were all spread out evenly. In reality, people live together most closely in cities, on seacoasts, and in river valleys. Singapore, a tiny country largely composed of a single city, has a high population density—more than 17,000 people per square mile. Greenland, by comparison, has less than one person per square mile because it is mostly covered by ice. Its people mainly fish for a living and dwell in small groups near the shore.

Regional Population Growth Disparities

Two centuries ago, the population of the world began a phenomenal expansion. Even so, North America and Australia still have a long way to go before their population numbers equal those of Asia and Africa. China and India now have more than a billion people each, making Asia the most populous continent. Africa, which has the second greatest growth, does not yet approach Asia in numbers.

According to some experts, the world's population, now totaling more than six billion, will not start to level off until about the year 2200, when it could reach eleven billion. Nearly all the new growth will take place in Asia, Africa, and Latin America; however, Africa's share will be almost double that of its present level and China's share will decline.

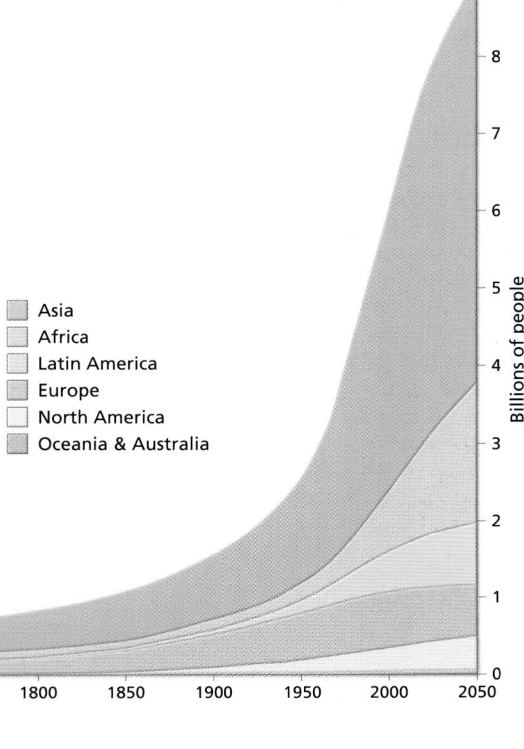

Fertility

Fertility, or birthrate, measures the average number of children born to women in a given population. It can also be expressed as the number of live births per thousand people in a population per year. In low-income countries, with limited educational opportunities for girls and women, birthrates reach their highest levels.

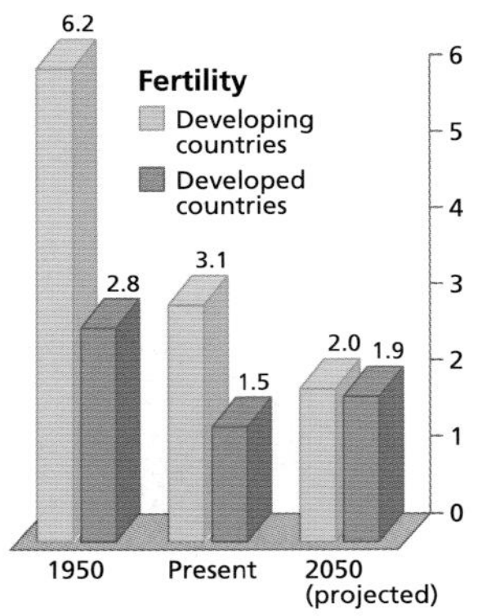

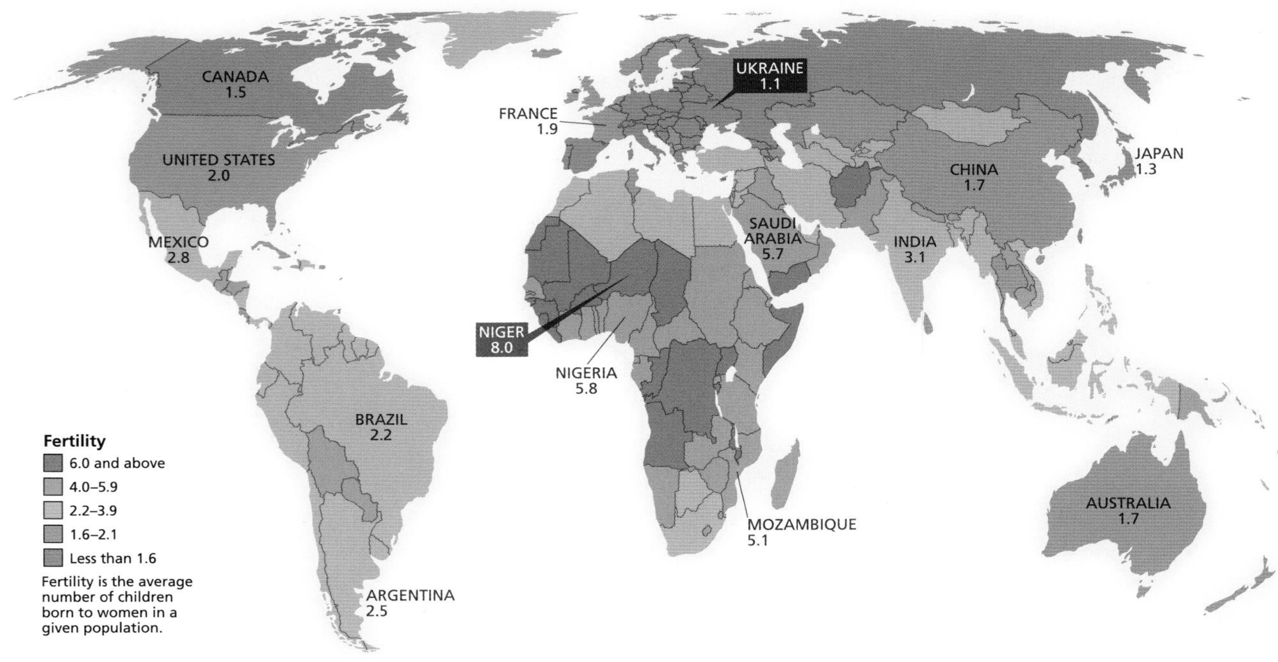

Urban Population Densities

People around the world are leaving farms and moving to cities, where jobs and opportunities are better. In the year 2000 almost half the world's people lived in cities. The shift of population from the countryside to urban centers will probably continue in less developed countries for many years to come.

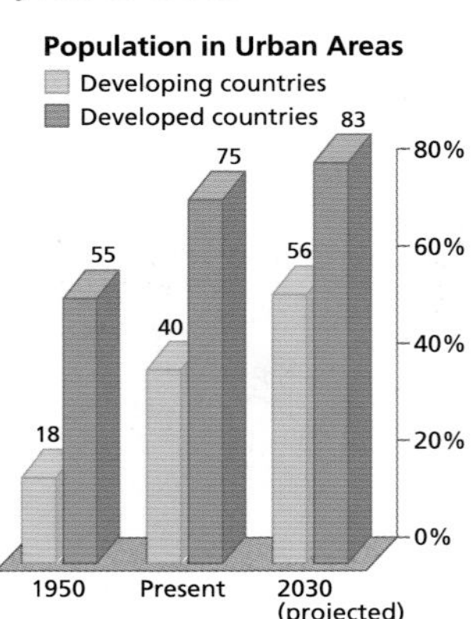

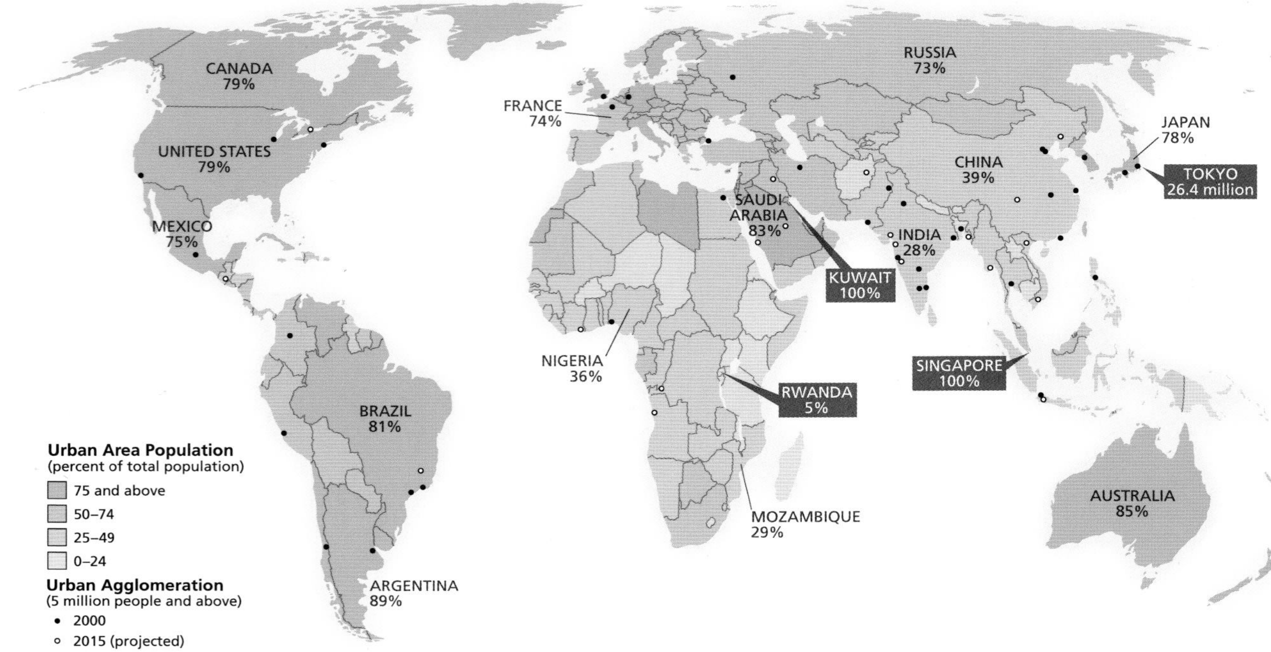

Urban Population Growth

Urban populations are growing more than twice as fast as populations as a whole. Soon, the world's city dwellers will outnumber its rural inhabitants as towns become cities and cities merge into megacities with more than ten million people. Globalization speeds the process. Although cities generate wealth and provide better health care along with electricity, clean water, sewage treatment, and other benefits, they can also cause great ecological damage. Squatter settlements and slums may develop if cities cannot keep up with millions of new arrivals. Smog, congestion, pollution, and crime are other dangers. Good city management is a key to future prosperity.

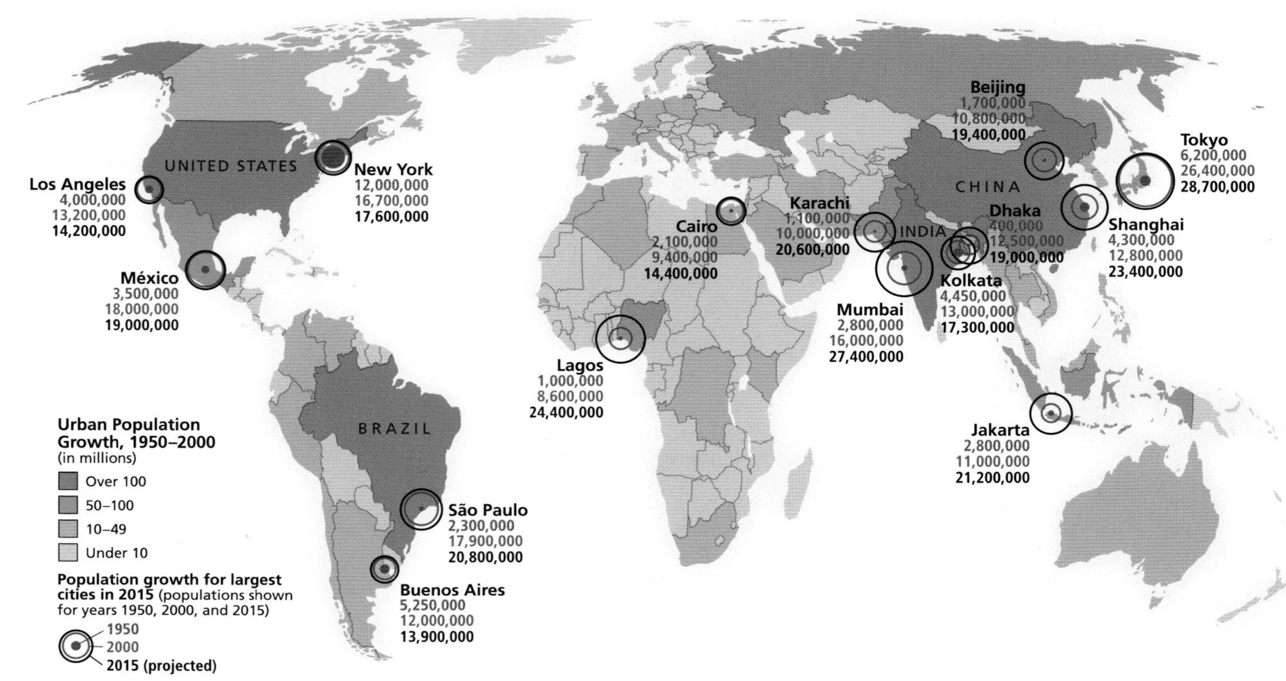

Life Expectancy

Life expectancy for population groups does not mean that all people die by a certain age. It is an average of death statistics. High infant mortality equals low life expectancy: People who live to adulthood will probably reach old age; there are just fewer of them.

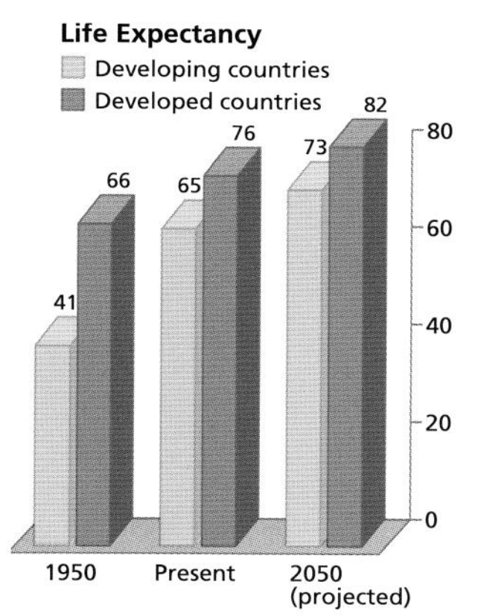

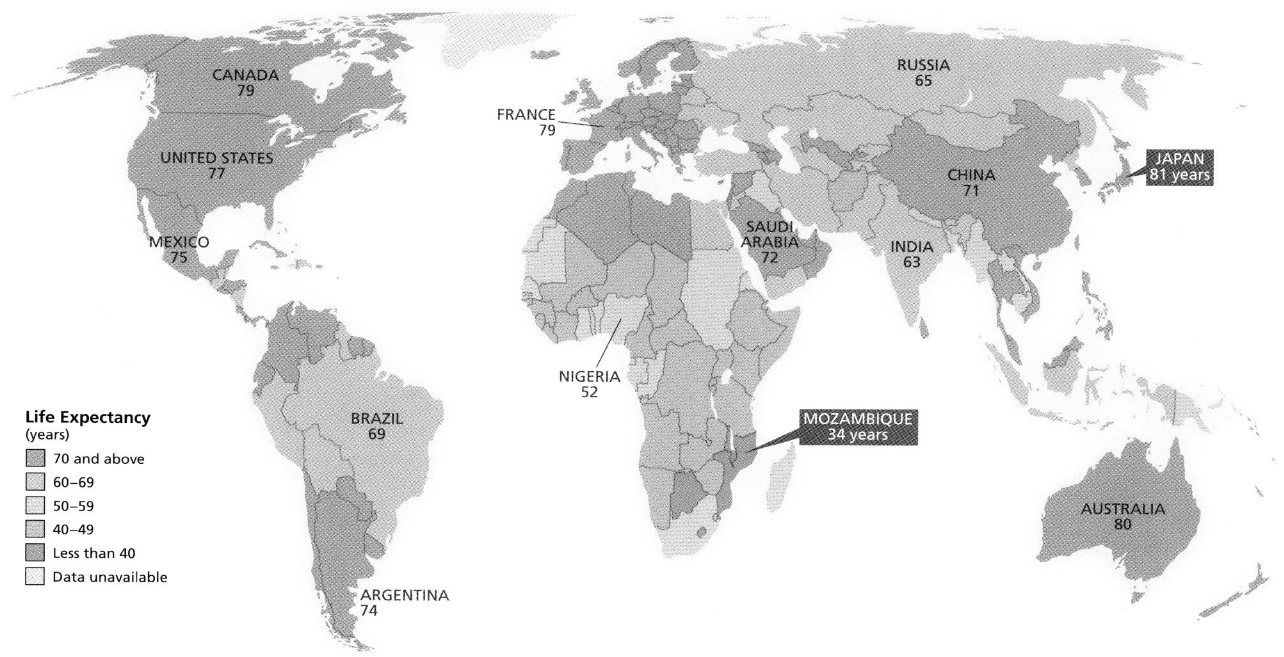

Migration

International migration has reached its highest level, with foreign workers now providing the labor in several Middle Eastern nations and immigrant workers proving essential to rich countries with low birthrates. Refugees continue to escape grim political and environmental conditions, while businesspeople and tourists keep many economies spinning.

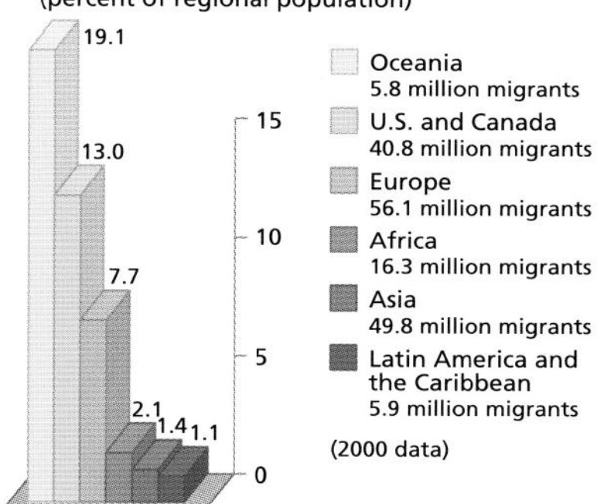

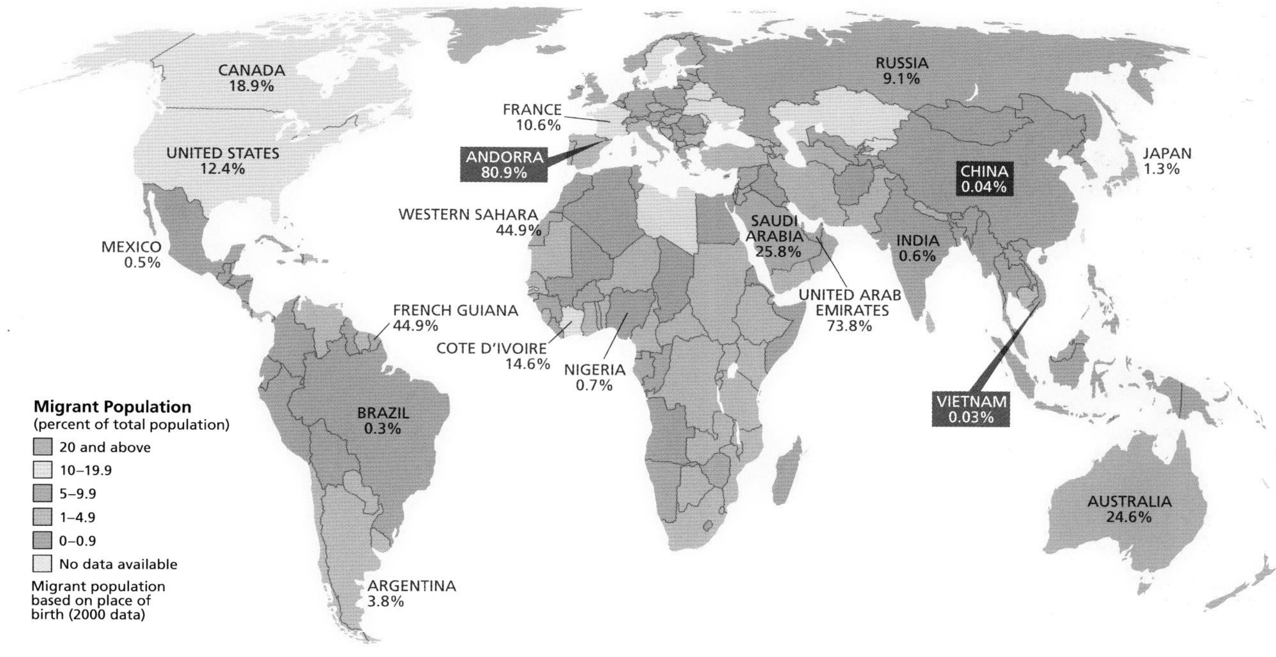

Most Populous Nations

(mid-2003 data)

1. China 1,288,679,000
2. India 1,068,572,000
3. United States 291,512,000
4. Indonesia 220,483,000
5. Brazil 176,464,000
6. Pakistan 149,147,000
7. Bangladesh 146,733,000
8. Russia 145,546,000
9. Nigeria 133,882,000
10. Japan 127,508,000
11. Mexico 104,878,000
12. Germany 82,621,000
13. Philippines 81,578,000
14. Vietnam 80,786,000
15. Egypt 72,062,000
16. Turkey 71,224,000
17. Ethiopia 70,677,000
18. Iran 66,582,000
19. Thailand 63,063,000
20. France 59,771,000

Most Crowded Nations

Population Density (pop/sq. mi.)

1. Monaco 45,333
2. Singapore 17,528
3. Malta 3,205
4. Bangladesh 2,639
5. Bahrain 2,545
6. Maldives 2,461
7. Mauritius 1,550
8. Barbados 1,524
9. Nauru 1,412
10. San Marino 1,295
11. South Korea 1,251
12. Lebanon 1,045
13. Netherlands 1,030
14. Vatican City 1,000
15. Tuvalu 1,000
16. Belgium 881
17. Japan 874
18. India 842
19. Israel 825
20. Rwanda 817

Demographic Extremes

Life Expectancy at Birth

Lowest (female):
34 Mozambique
38 Botswana, Lesotho
40 Malawi, Zambia, Zimbabwe
41 Angola, Rwanda

Lowest (male):
33 Mozambique
36 Botswana
37 Lesotho
39 Angola, Malawi, Rwanda

Highest (female):
85 Japan
84 San Marino
83 France, Italy, Spain, Switzerland
82 Australia, Austria, Canada, Finland, Iceland, Norway, Sweden

Highest (male):
78 Iceland, Japan, Sweden
77 Australia, Canada, Israel, Italy, Kuwait, San Marino, Singapore, Switzerland
76 Austria, Costa Rica, France, Greece, Netherlands, New Zealand, Norway, Spain
75 Belgium, Cyprus, Denmark, Finland, Germany, Georgia, Ireland, Luxembourg, United Kingdom

Population Age Structure

Highest % Population under Age 15
51% Uganda
50% Niger
49% Burkina Faso
48% Burundi, Chad, Sao Tome and Principe, Yemen

Highest % Population over Age 65
19% Greece, Italy, Japan
17% Belgium, Bulgaria, Germany, Spain, Sweden
16% Austria, Croatia, Estonia, France, Portugal, San Marino, Switzerland, United Kingdom
15% Denmark, Finland, Hungary, Latvia, Norway

WORLD RELIGIONS

The great power of religion comes from its ability to speak to the heart of individuals and societies. Since earliest human times, the urge to honor nature spirits or the belief in a supreme being has brought comfort and security in the face of fundamental questions of life and death.

Billions of people are now adherents of Hinduism, Buddhism, Judaism, Christianity, and Islam, all of which began in Asia. Universal elements of these faiths include ritual and prayer, sacred sites and pilgrimage, saints and martyrs, ritual clothing and implements, dietary laws and fasting, festivals and holy days, and special ceremonies for life's major moments. Sometimes otherworldly, most religions have moral and ethical guidelines that attempt to make life better on Earth as well. Their tenets and goals are taught not only at the church, synagogue, mosque, or temple but also through schools, storytelling, parables, painting, sculpture, and even dance and drama.

The world's major religions blossomed from the teachings and revelations of individuals who heeded and transmitted the voice of God or discovered a way to salvation that could be understood by others. Abraham and Moses for Jews, the Buddha for Buddhists, Jesus Christ for Christians, and Muhammad for Muslims fulfilled the roles of divine teachers who experienced essential truths of existence.

Throughout history priests, rabbis, clergymen, and imams have recited, interpreted, and preached the holy words of sacred texts and writings to the faithful. Today the world's religions, with their guidance here on Earth and hopes and promises for the afterlife, continue to exert an extraordinary force on billions of people.

NORTH AMERICA
Toronto
New York
Los Angeles
México
PACIFIC OCEAN
ATLANTIC OCEAN
SOUTH AMERICA
São Paulo
Buenos Aires

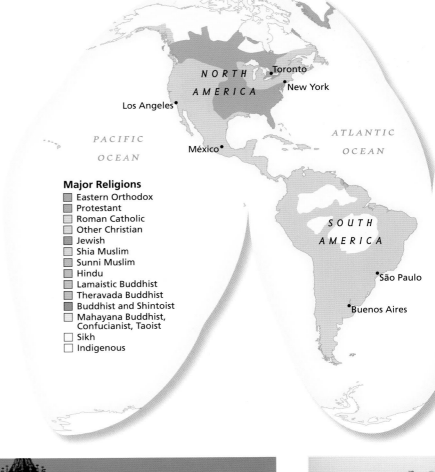

Major Religions
- Eastern Orthodox
- Protestant
- Roman Catholic
- Other Christian
- Jewish
- Shia Muslim
- Sunni Muslim
- Hindu
- Lamaistic Buddhist
- Theravada Buddhist
- Buddhist and Shintoist
- Mahayana Buddhist, Confucianist, Taoist
- Sikh
- Indigenous

BUDDHISM
Founded about 2,500 years ago by Siddhartha Gautama—an Indian prince who became the Buddha, or Enlightened One—Buddhism accepts "four noble truths": Life is suffering; suffering has a cause (desire); the cause can be overcome; the way to overcome the cause is through ethical conduct, meditation, and wisdom.

CHRISTIANITY
Christian belief in eternal life is based on the example of Jesus Christ, a Jew born 2,000 years ago. The New Testament tells of his teaching, persecution, crucifixion, and resurrection. Today Christianity is found around the world in three main forms: Roman Catholicism, Eastern Orthodox, and Protestantism.

HINDUISM
Hinduism began in India more than 4,000 years ago and is still flourishing. Sacred texts known as the *Vedas* form the basis of Hindu faith

Adherents Worldwide

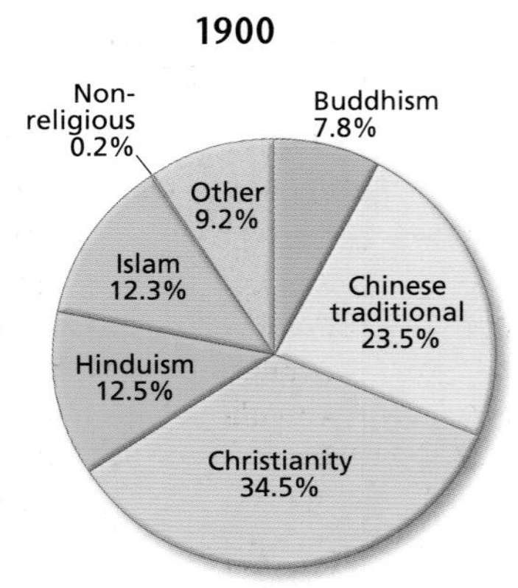

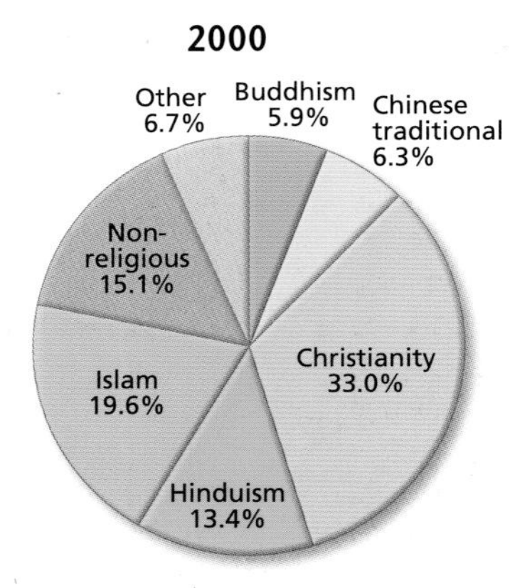

The growth of Islam and the decline of Chinese traditional religion stand out as significant changes over the past one hundred years. Christianity, largest of the world's main faiths, has remained largely stable in number of adherents. Today more than one out of six people claim to be atheistic or nonreligious.

Adherents by Continent

In terms of religious adherents, Asia ranks first. This is not only because half the world's people live on that continent but also because three of the five major faiths are practiced there: Hinduism in South Asia; Buddhism in East and Southeast Asia; and Islam from Indonesia to the Central Asian republics to Turkey. Australia, Europe, North America, and South America are overwhelmingly Christian. Africa, with many millions of Muslims and Christians, retains large numbers of animists.

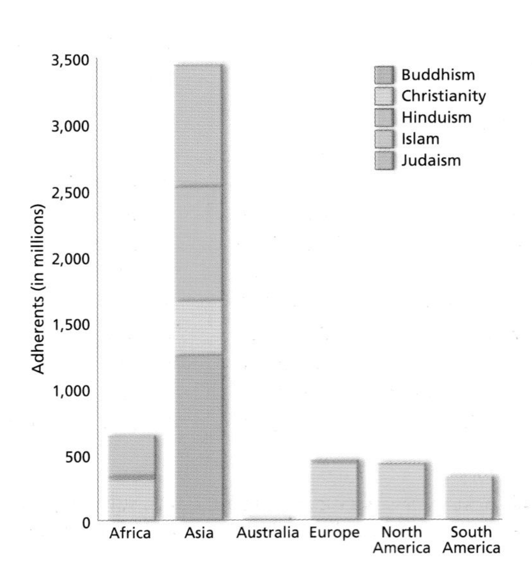

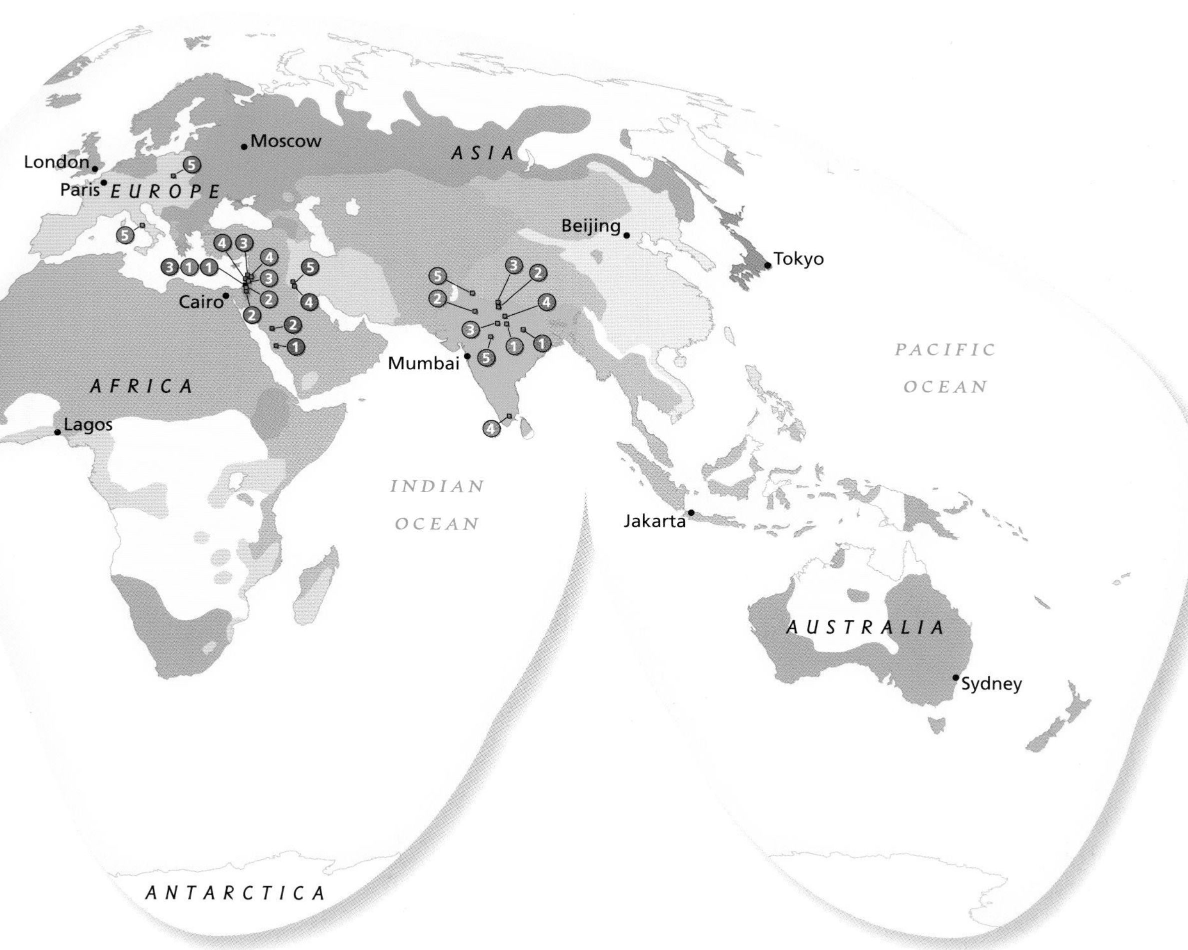

Sacred Places

BUDDHISM

1. Bodhgaya: Where Buddha reached enlightenment
2. Kusinagara: Place of Buddha's death
3. Lumbini: Buddha's birthplace
4. Sarnath: Place where Buddha delivered his first sermon
5. Sanchi: Location of stupa that contains relics of Buddha

CHRISTIANITY

1. Jerusalem: Church of the Holy Sepulchre, Jesus's crucifixion
2. Bethlehem: Jesus's birthplace
3. Nazareth: Where Jesus grew up
4. Shore of the Sea of Galilee: Where Jesus gave the Sermon on the Mount
5. Rome and the Vatican: Tombs of St. Peter and St. Paul

HINDUISM

1. Varanasi (Benares): Most holy Hindu site, home of Shiva
2. Vrindavan: Krishna's birthplace
3. Allahabad: At confluence of Ganges and Yamuna rivers, purest place to bathe
4. Madurai: Temple of Minakshi, great goddess of the south
5. Badrinath: Vishnu's shrine

ISLAM

1. Mecca: Muhammad's birthplace; destination of the pilgrimage, or *hajj*
2. Medina: City of Muhammad's flight, or *hegira*
3. Jerusalem: Dome of the Rock, Muhammad's stepping-stone to heaven
4. Najaf (Shi'ite): Tomb of Imam Ali
5. Kerbala (Shi'ite): Tomb of Imam Hoseyn

JUDAISM

1. Jerusalem: Location of the Western Wall and first and second temples; the ancient and modern capital of Israel
2. Hebron: Burial spot of patriarchs and matriarchs
3. Safed: Where Kabbalah (Jewish mysticism) flourished
4. Tiberias: Where Talmud (source of Jewish law) first composed
5. Auschwitz: Symbol of six million Jews who perished in the Holocaust

nd ritual. The main trinity of ods comprises Brahma the reator, Vishnu the preserver, nd Shiva the destroyer. Hinus believe in reincarnation.

ISLAM
Muslims believe that the Koran, Islam's sacred book, accurately records the spoken word of God (Allah) as revealed to the Prophet Muhammad, born in Mecca around 570 C.E. Strict adherents pray five times a day, fast during the holy month of Ramadan, and make at least one pilgrimage to Mecca, Islam's holiest city.

JUDAISM
The 4,000-year-old religion of the Jews stands as the oldest of the major faiths that believe in a single god. Judaism's traditions, customs, laws, and beliefs date back to Abraham, the founder, and to the Torah—the first five books of the Old Testament, believed to have been handed down to Moses on Mount Sinai.

Adherents by Country

COUNTRIES WITH THE MOST BUDDHISTS

Country	Buddhists
1. China	105,829,000
2. Japan	69,931,000
3. Thailand	52,383,000
4. Vietnam	39,534,000
5. Myanmar	33,145,000
6. Sri Lanka	12,879,000
7. Cambodia	9,462,000
8. India	7,249,000
9. South Korea	7,174,000
10. Taiwan	4,686,000

COUNTRIES WITH THE MOST CHRISTIANS

Country	Christians
1. United States	235,742,000
2. Brazil	155,545,000
3. Mexico	95,169,000
4. China	89,056,000
5. Russia	84,308,000
6. Philippines	68,151,000
7. India	62,341,000
8. Germany	62,326,000
9. Nigeria	51,123,000
10. Congo, Dem. Rep.	49,256,000

COUNTRIES WITH THE MOST HINDUS

Country	Hindus
1. India	755,135,000
2. Nepal	18,354,000
3. Bangladesh	15,995,000
4. Indonesia	7,259,000
5. Sri Lanka	2,124,000
6. Pakistan	1,868,000
7. Malaysia	1,630,000
8. United States	1,032,000
9. South Africa	959,000
10. Myanmar	893,000

COUNTRIES WITH THE MOST MUSLIMS

Country	Muslims
1. Indonesia	181,368,000
2. Pakistan	141,650,000
3. India	123,960,000
4. Bangladesh	110,805,000
5. Turkey	65,637,000
6. Egypt	65,612,000
7. Iran	65,439,000
8. Nigeria	63,300,000
9. China	38,208,000
10. Algeria	30,690,000

COUNTRIES WITH THE MOST JEWS

Country	Jews
1. United States	5,621,000
2. Israel	3,951,000
3. Russia	951,000
4. France	591,000
5. Argentina	490,000
6. Canada	403,000
7. Brazil	357,000
8. Britain	302,000
9. Palestine*	273,000
10. Ukraine	220,000

**Nonsovereign nation*

All figures are estimates based on data for the year 2000.
Countries with the highest reported nonreligious populations include China, Russia, United States, Germany, North Korea, Japan, India, Vietnam, France, and Italy.

WORLD ECONOMY

A global economic activity map (right) reveals striking differences between the Northern and Southern Hemispheres, particularly in the case of manufacturing. In the north are large clusters of manufacturing centers, but south of the Equator such centers make only scattered appearances on the map. The most notable concentrations of economic activity are seen in North America and Western Europe; these are followed by parts of eastern and southern Asia and a few areas of South America, southern Africa, and Australia.

There are different ways of looking at this activity. When examined by country, the United States leads in many areas, but united Western European countries have also become a major economic force. Indeed, in terms of manufacturing, Western Europe outpaces the U.S. in cars, chemicals, and food.

The world's second largest economy is found in China. Even so, Chinese workers take home only a fraction of the cash pocketed each week by their economic rivals in the West; they also have very few telephones and cars—two basic consumer products of the modern age. (When it comes to vehicles, the United States has more passenger cars per thousand people than any other country.)

The Middle East produces more fuel than any other region, but it has virtually no other economic output besides that commodity.

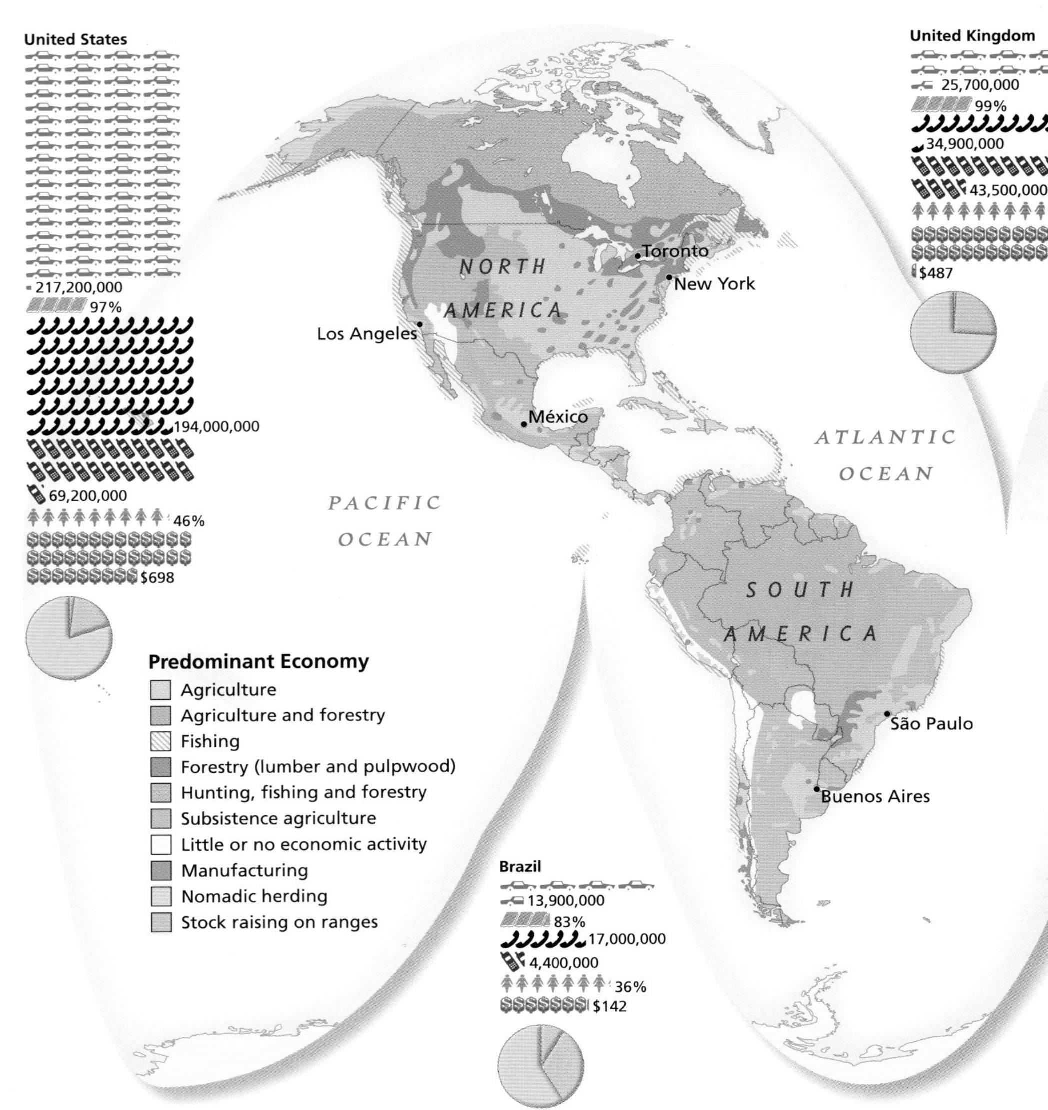

Labor Migration

People in search of jobs gravitate toward the strongest economies, unless immigration policies prevent them from doing so. Japan, for instance, has one of the world's most vigorous economies and a population that is more than 99 percent Japanese. Some nations are "labor importers," while some are "labor exporters." In the mid-1990s, Malaysia was the largest Asian importer (close to a million) and the Philippines was the largest Asian exporter (4.2 million). Europe, once a major labor exporter to North and South America, is now a major importer, especially from Africa.

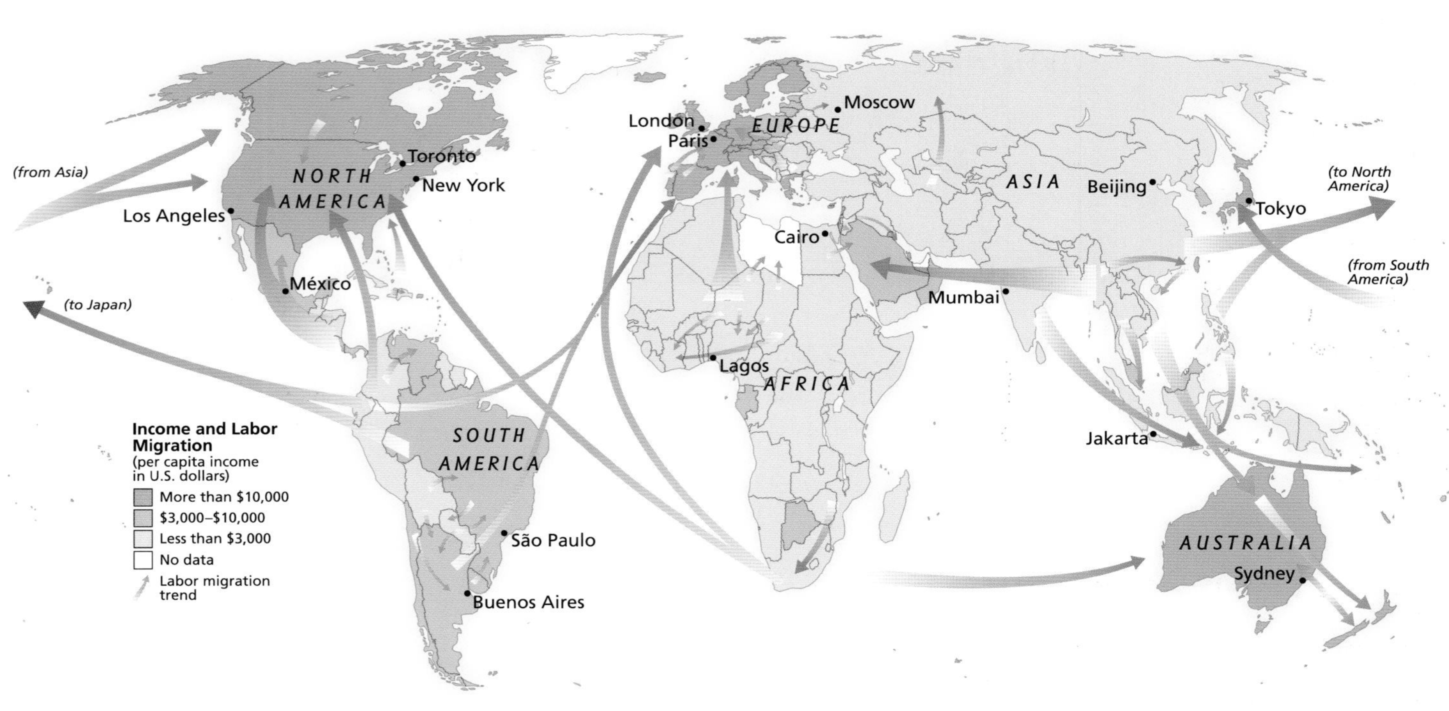

Top GDP Growth Rates

1997–2001 AVERAGE	
1. Bosnia and Herzegovina	14%
2. Turkmenistan	10%
3. Ireland	10%
4. Mozambique	9%
5. Myanmar	9%
6. Azerbaijan	9%
7. Rwanda	9%
8. China	8%
9. Bhutan	7%
10. Botswana	7%

The World's Richest and Poorest Countries

RICHEST	GDP PER CAPITA (2002)	POOREST	GDP PER CAPITA (2002)
1. Luxembourg	44,000 (figures in U.S. dollars)	1. Timor-Leste	500
2. United States	36,300	2. Sierra Leone	500
3. San Marino	34,600	3. Somalia	550
4. Norway	31,800	4. Congo, Dem. Rep. of the	590
5. Switzerland	31,700	5. Burundi	600
6. Canada	29,400	6. Tanzania	610
7. Belgium	29,000	7. Malawi	660
8. Denmark	29,000	8. Ethiopia	700
9. Ireland	28,500	9. Comoros	710
10. Japan	28,000	10. Eritrea	740

EUROPE
London
Paris
Moscow
ASIA
Beijing
Tokyo
Cairo
Mumbai
AFRICA
Lagos
INDIAN OCEAN
Jakarta
PACIFIC OCEAN
AUSTRALIA
Sydney

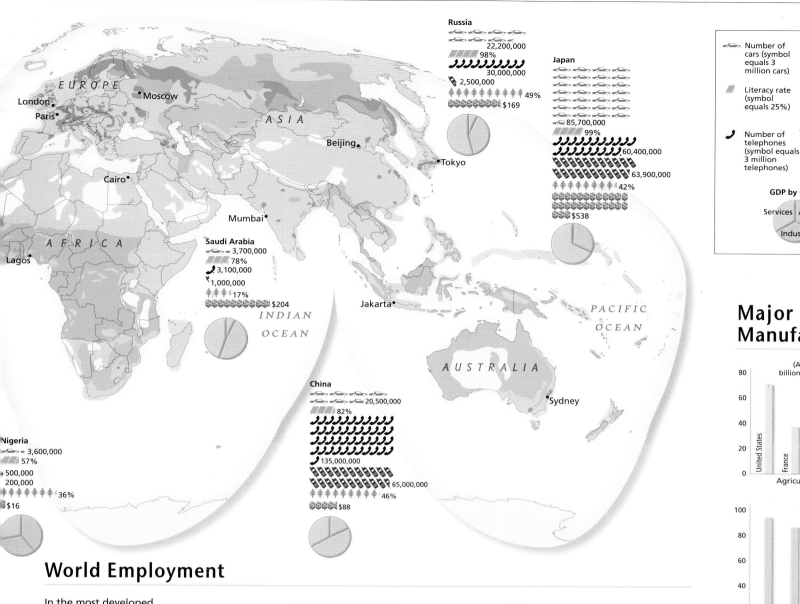

Russia
22,200,000
98%
30,000,000
2,500,000
49%
$169

Japan
85,700,000
99%
60,400,000
63,900,000
42%
$538

Saudi Arabia
3,700,000
78%
3,100,000
1,000,000
17%
$204

China
20,500,000
82%
135,000,000
65,000,000
46%
$88

Nigeria
3,600,000
57%
500,000
200,000
36%
$16

Number of cars (symbol equals 3 million cars)
Women in adult workforce (symbol equals 5%)
Literacy rate (symbol equals 25%)
Average weekly income (symbol equals $20 U.S. equivalent)
Number of telephones (symbol equals 3 million telephones)
Number of mobile phones (symbol equals 3 million mobile phones)

GDP by sector
Services
Agriculture
Industry

World Employment

In the most developed nations, a majority of people work in industry or services: 80 percent of the workforce in the United Kingdom, for example, is in services; that figure is 72 percent in the United States. In those countries, only a tiny percentage works to raise food (just 3 percent in the U.S.). There are many places where that proportion is inverted: 67 percent of India's labor force works in agriculture.

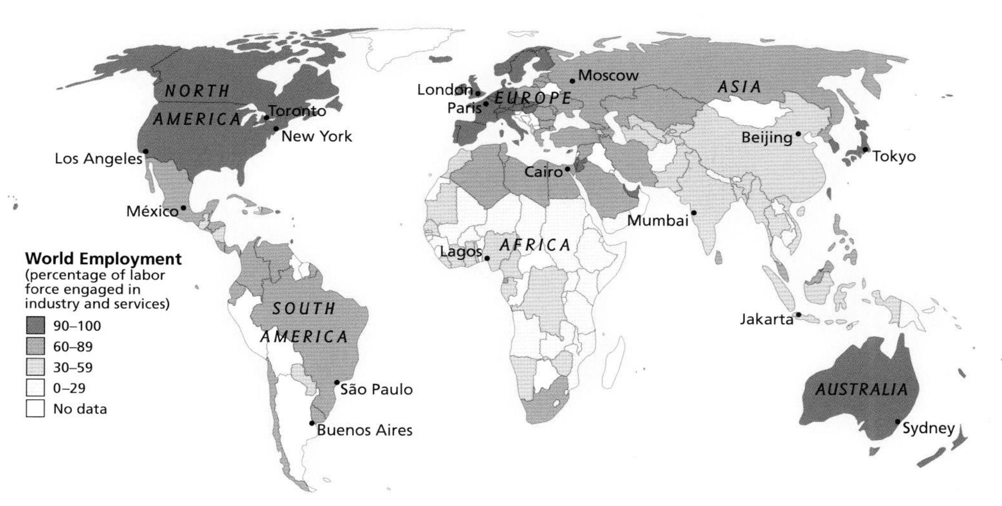

Gross Domestic Product

The gross domestic product, or GDP, is the total market value of goods and services produced by a nation's economy in a given year. It is a convenient way of calculating the level of a nation's economic activity; it does not show average wealth of individuals. Thus, China may have close to half the GDP of the U.S., but its citizens' earnings, on average, are less than a tenth of what Americans make.

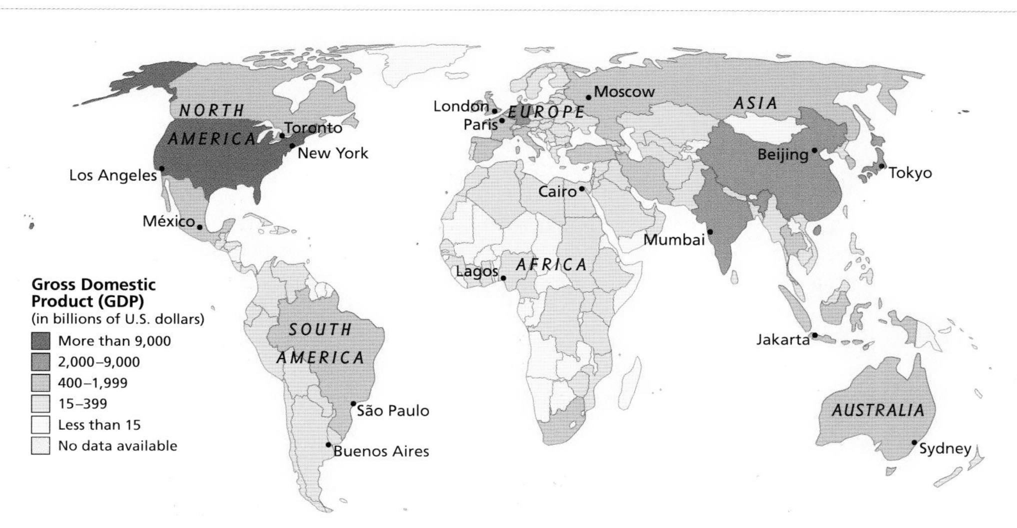

Major Manufacturers

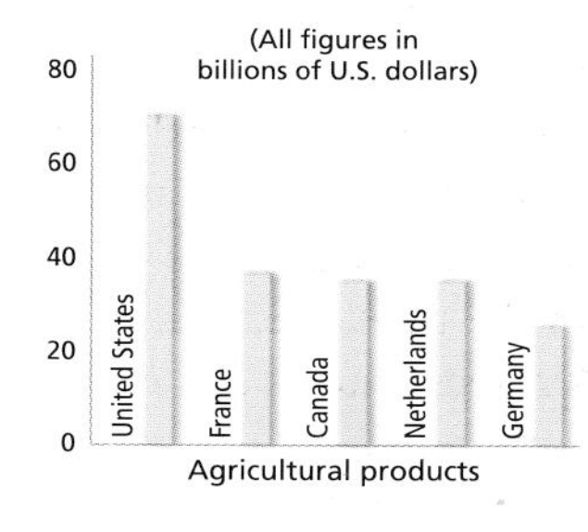

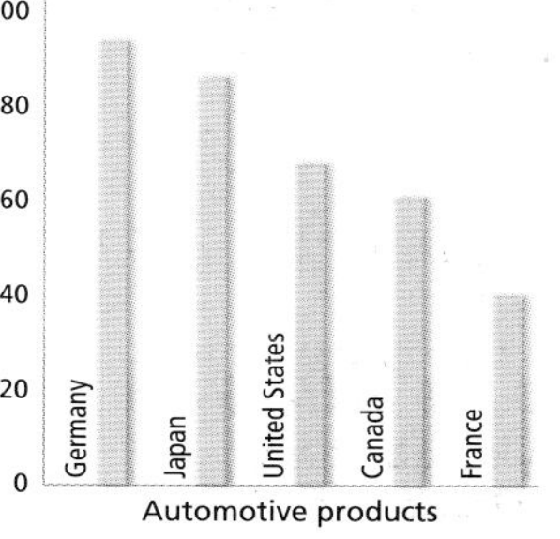

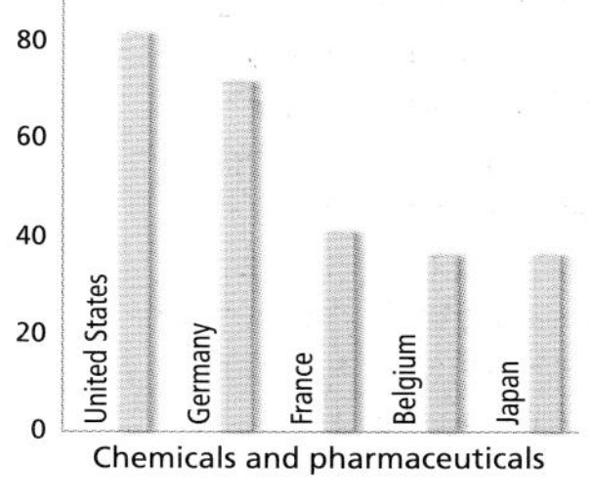

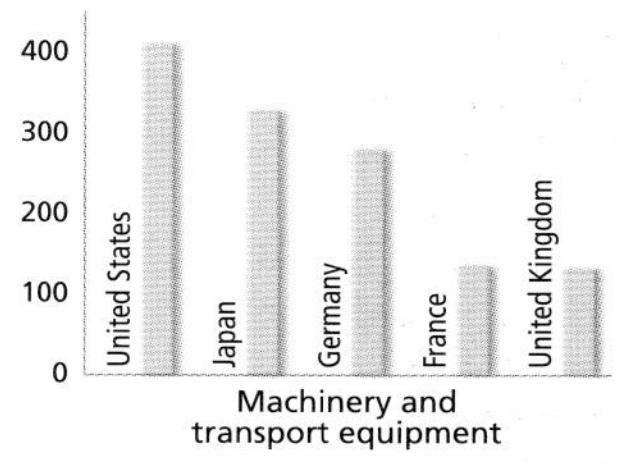

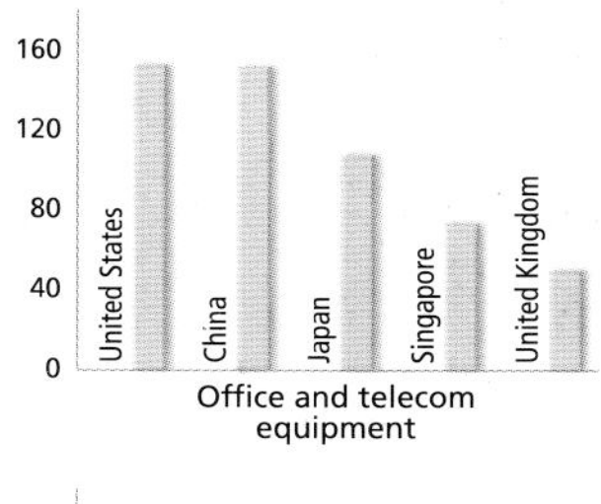

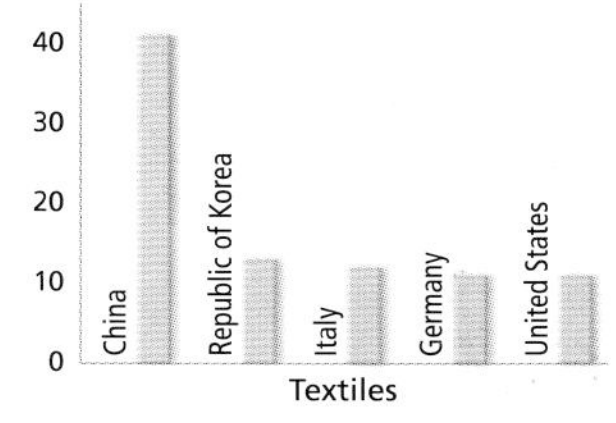

GEOGRAPHICAL COMPARISONS

THE EARTH

Mass: 5,974,000,000,000,000,000,000 (5.974 sextillion) metric tons

Total Area: 510,066,000 sq km (196,938,000 sq mi)

Land Area: 148,647,000 sq km (57,393,000 sq mi), 29.1% of total

Water Area: 361,419,000 sq km (139,545,000 sq mi), 70.9% of total

Population: 6,313,558,000

THE EARTH'S EXTREMES

Hottest Place: Dalol, Denakil Depression, Ethiopia, annual average temperature 34°C (93°F)

Coldest Place: Plateau Station, Antarctica, annual average temperature -56.7°C (-70°F)

Hottest Recorded Temperature: Al Aziziyah, Libya 58°C (136.4°F), September 3, 1922

Coldest Recorded Temperature: Vostok, Antarctica -89.2°C (-128.6°F), July 21, 1983

Wettest Place: Mawsynram, Assam, India, annual average rainfall 1,187 cm (467 in)

Driest Place: Arica, Atacama Desert, Chile, rainfall barely measurable

Highest Waterfall: Angel Falls, Venezuela 979 m (3,212 ft)

Largest Desert: Sahara, Africa 9,000,000 sq km (3,475,000 sq mi)

Largest Canyon: Grand Canyon, Colorado River, Arizona 446 km (277 mi) long along river, 549 m (1,801 ft) to 29 km (18 mi) wide, about 1.6 km (1 mi) deep

Largest Cave Chamber: Sarawak Cave, Gunung Mulu National Park, Malaysia 16 hectares and 79 meters high (40.2 acres and 260 feet)

Largest Cave System: Mammoth Cave, Kentucky, over 530 km (330 mi) of passageways mapped

Most Predictable Geyser: Old Faithful, Wyoming, annual average interval 75 to 79 minutes

Longest Reef: Great Barrier Reef, Australia 2,012 km (1,250 mi)

Greatest Tides: Bay of Fundy, Nova Scotia 16 m (52 ft)

AREA OF EACH CONTINENT

	SQ KM	SQ MI	PERCENT OF EARTH'S LAND
Asia	44,579,000	17,212,000	30.0
Africa	30,065,000	11,608,000	20.2
North America	24,474,000	9,449,000	16.5
South America	17,819,000	6,880,000	12.0
Antarctica	13,209,000	5,100,000	8.9
Europe	9,938,000	3,837,000	6.7
Australia	7,687,000	2,968,000	5.2

HIGHEST POINT ON EACH CONTINENT

	METERS	FEET
Mount Everest, Asia	8,850	29,035
Cerro Aconcagua, South America	6,960	22,834
Mount McKinley (Denali), N. America	6,194	20,320
Kilimanjaro, Africa	5,895	19,340
El'brus, Europe	5,642	18,510
Vinson Massif, Antarctica	4,897	16,067
Mount Kosciuszko, Australia	2,228	7,310

LOWEST SURFACE POINT ON EACH CONTINENT

	METERS	FEET
Dead Sea, Asia	-416	-1,365
Lake Assal, Africa	-156	-512
Death Valley, North America	-86	-282
Valdés Peninsula, South America	-40	-131
Caspian Sea, Europe	-28	-92
Lake Eyre, Australia	-16	-52
Bentley Subglacial Trench, Antarctica	-2,550	-8,366

LARGEST ISLANDS

	AREA SQ KM	AREA SQ MI
1 Greenland	2,175,600	840,000
2 New Guinea	792,500	306,000
3 Borneo	725,100	280,100
4 Madagascar	587,000	226,600
5 Baffin Island	507,500	196,000
6 Sumatra	427,300	165,000
7 Honshu	227,400	87,800
8 Great Britain	218,100	84,200
9 Victoria Island	217,300	83,900
10 Ellesmere Island	196,200	75,800
11 Celebes	178,700	69,000
12 South Island (New Zealand)	151,000	58,300
13 Java	126,700	48,900
14 North Island (New Zealand)	114,000	44,000
15 Island of Newfoundland	108,900	42,000

LARGEST DRAINAGE BASINS

	AREA SQ KM	AREA SQ MI
1 Amazon, South America	7,050,000	2,721,000
2 Congo, Africa	3,700,000	1,428,000
3 Mississippi-Missouri, North America	3,250,000	1,255,000
4 Paraná, South America	3,100,000	1,197,000
5 Yenisey-Angara, Asia	2,700,000	1,042,000
6 Ob-Irtysh, Asia	2,430,000	938,000
7 Lena, Asia	2,420,000	934,000
8 Nile, Africa	1,900,000	733,400
9 Amur, Asia	1,840,000	710,000
10 Mackenzie-Peace, North America	1,765,000	681,000
11 Ganges-Brahmaputra, Asia	1,730,000	668,000
12 Volga, Europe	1,380,000	533,000
13 Zambezi, Africa	1,330,000	513,000
14 Niger, Africa	1,200,000	463,000
15 Chang Jiang (Yangtze), Asia	1,175,000	454,000

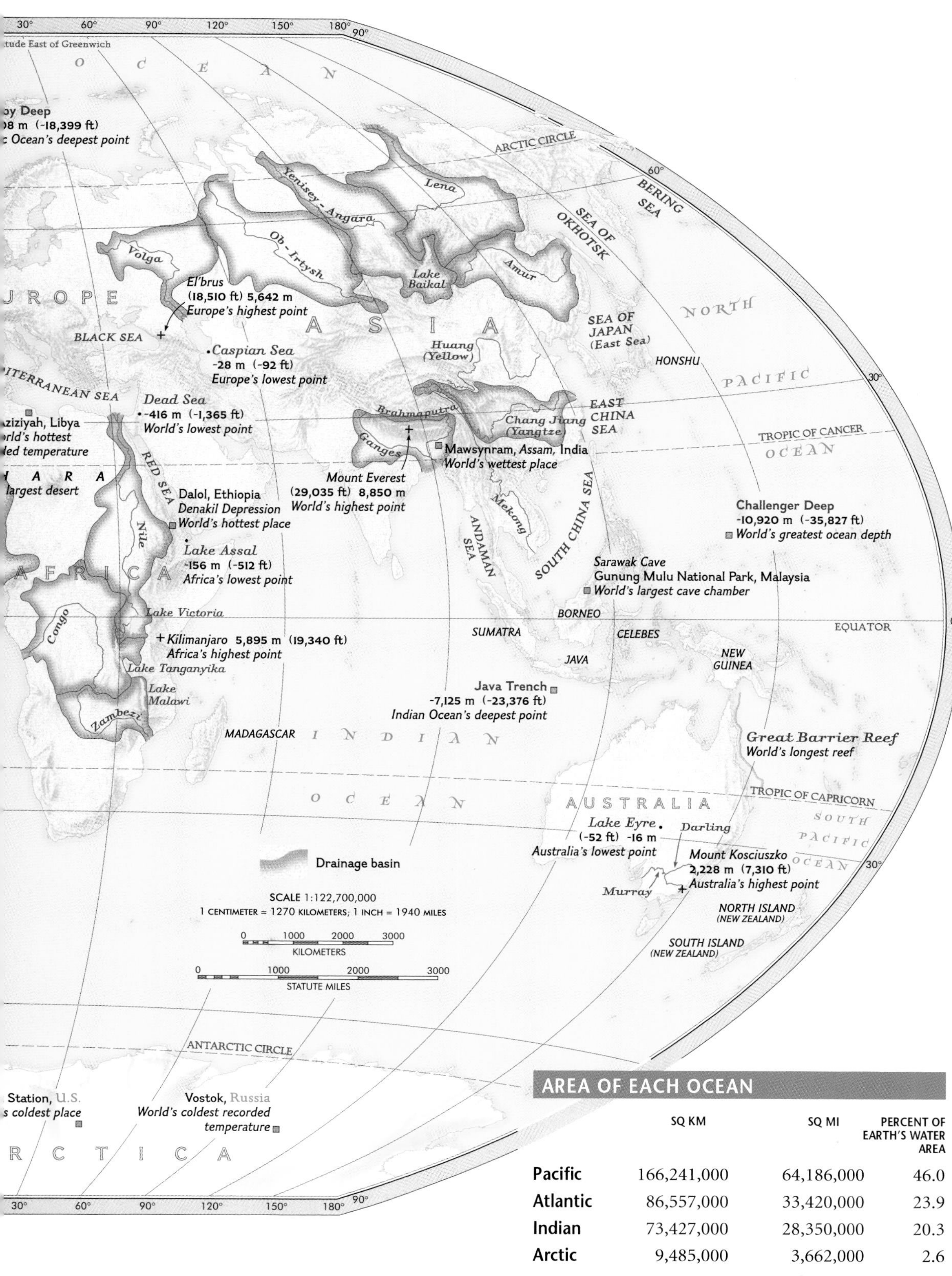

GEOPOLITICAL EXTREMES

Largest Country: Russia 17,074,993 sq km (6,592,692 sq mi)

Smallest Country: Vatican City 0.4 sq km (0.2 sq mi)

Most Populous Country: China 1,288,679,000 people

Least Populous Country: Vatican City 1,000 people

Most Crowded Country: Monaco 17,503 per sq km (45,333 per sq mi)

Least Crowded Country: Mongolia 1.5 per sq km (4 per sq mi)

Largest Metropolitan Area: Tokyo 26,546,000 people

Country with the Greatest Number of Bordering Countries: China 14, Russia 14

ENGINEERING WONDERS

Tallest Office Building: Petronas Towers, Kuala Lumpur, Malaysia 452 meters, 1483 feet

Tallest Tower (Freestanding): CN Tower, Toronto, Canada 553 meters, 1,815 feet

Tallest Manmade Structure: KVLY TV tower, near Fargo, North Dakota 629 meters, 2,063 feet

Longest Wall: Great Wall of China, approx. 3,460 km (2,150 miles)

Longest Road: Pan-American highway (not including gap in Panama and Colombia), more than 24,140 km (15,000 miles)

Longest Railroad: Trans-Siberian Railroad, Russia 9,286 km (5,770 miles)

Longest Road Tunnel: Laerdal Tunnel, Norway 24.5 km, 15.2 miles

Longest Rail Tunnel: Seikan rail tunnel, Japan 53.9 km (33.5 miles)

Highest Bridge (over water): Royal Gorge Bridge, Colorado 321 meters, 1,053 feet above water

Longest Highway Bridge: Lake Pontchartrain Causeway, Louisiana 38.4 km (23.9 miles)

Longest Suspension Bridge: Akashi-Kaikyo Bridge, Japan 3,911 meters (12,831 feet)

Longest Boat Canal: Grand Canal, China, over 1,770 km (1,100 miles)

Longest Irrigation Canal: Garagum Canal, Turkmenistan, nearly 1,100 km (700 miles)

Largest Artificial Lake: Lake Volta, Volta River, Ghana 9,065 sq km (3,500 sq mi)

Tallest Dam: Nurek Dam, Vakhsh River, Tajikistan 300 meters (984 feet)

Tallest Pyramid: Great Pyramid of Khufu, Egypt 137 meters, 450 feet

Deepest Mine: Western Deep Levels Mine, South Africa, approx. 4 km (2.5 miles) deep

Longest Submarine Cable: Sea-Me-We 3 cable, connects 34 countries on four continents, 39,000 km (24,200 miles) long

AREA OF EACH OCEAN

	SQ KM	SQ MI	PERCENT OF EARTH'S WATER AREA
Pacific	166,241,000	64,186,000	46.0
Atlantic	86,557,000	33,420,000	23.9
Indian	73,427,000	28,350,000	20.3
Arctic	9,485,000	3,662,000	2.6

LONGEST RIVERS

		KM	MI
1	Nile, Africa	6,825	4,241
2	Amazon, South America	6,437	4,000
3	Chang Jiang (Yangtze), Asia	6,380	3,964
4	Mississippi-Missouri, North America	5,971	3,710
5	Yenisey-Angara, Asia	5,536	3,440
6	Huang (Yellow), Asia	5,464	3,395
7	Ob-Irtysh, Asia	5,410	3,362
8	Amur, Asia	4,416	2,744
9	Lena, Asia	4,400	2,734
10	Congo, Africa	4,370	2,715
11	Mackenzie-Peace, North America	4,241	2,635
12	Mekong, Asia	4,184	2,600
13	Niger, Africa	4,170	2,591
14	Paraná-Río de la Plata, S. America	4,000	2,485
15	Murray-Darling, Australia	3,718	2,310
16	Volga, Europe	3,685	2,290
17	Purus, South America	3,380	2,100

DEEPEST POINT IN EACH OCEAN

	METERS	FEET
Challenger Deep, Pacific Ocean	-10,920	-35,827
Puerto Rico Trench, Atlantic Ocean	-8,605	-28,232
Java Trench, Indian Ocean	-7,125	-23,376
Molloy Deep, Arctic Ocean	-5,608	-18,399

LARGEST LAKES BY AREA

		AREA		MAXIMUM DEPTH	
		SQ KM	SQ MI	METERS	FEET
1	Caspian Sea	371,000	143,200	1,025	3,363
2	Lake Superior	82,100	31,700	406	1,332
3	Lake Victoria	69,500	26,800	82	269
4	Lake Huron	59,600	23,000	229	751
5	Lake Michigan	57,800	22,300	281	922
6	Lake Tanganyika	32,600	12,600	1,470	4,823
7	Lake Baikal	31,500	12,200	1,637	5,371
8	Great Bear Lake	31,300	12,100	446	1,463
9	Lake Malawi	28,900	11,200	695	2,280
10	Great Slave L.	28,600	11,000	614	2,014

LARGEST SEAS BY AREA

		AREA		AVGERAGE DEPTH	
		SQ KM	SQ MI	METERS	FEET
1	South China Sea	2,974,600	1,148,500	1,464	4,803
2	Caribbean Sea	2,515,900	971,400	2,575	8,448
3	Mediterranean Sea	2,510,000	969,100	1,501	4,925
4	Bering Sea	2,261,100	873,000	1,491	4,892
5	Gulf of Mexico	1,507,600	582,100	1,615	5,299
6	Sea of Okhotsk	1,392,100	537,500	973	3,192
7	Sea of Japan	1,012,900	391,100	1,667	5,469
8	Hudson Bay	730,100	281,900	93	305
9	East China Sea	664,600	256,600	189	620
10	Andaman Sea	564,900	218,100	1,118	3,668
11	Black Sea	507,900	196,100	1,191	3,907
12	Red Sea	453,000	174,900	538	1,765

WORLD TIME

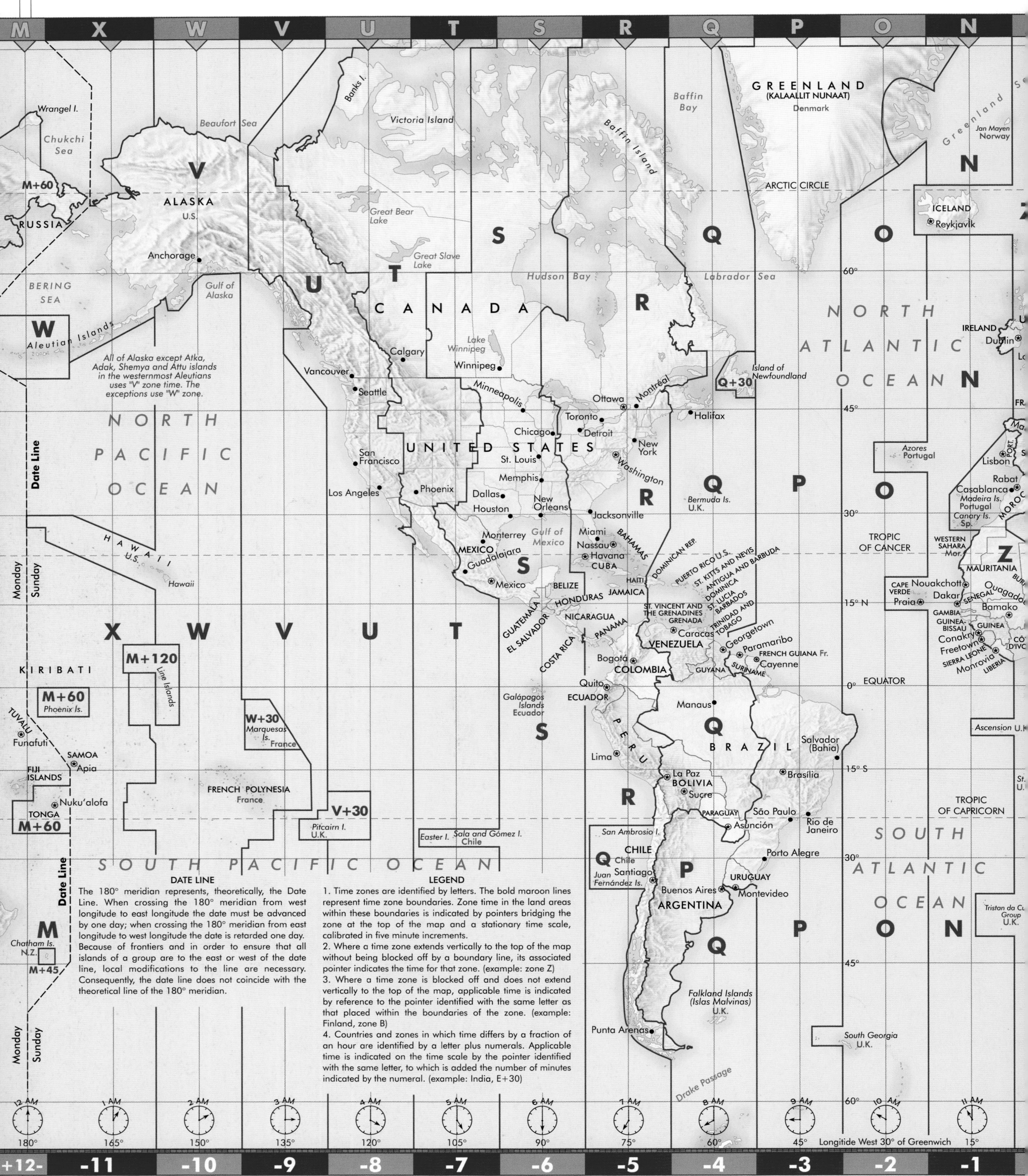

The numeral in each tab directly above shows the number of hours to be added to, or subtracted from, Greenwich time (Z).

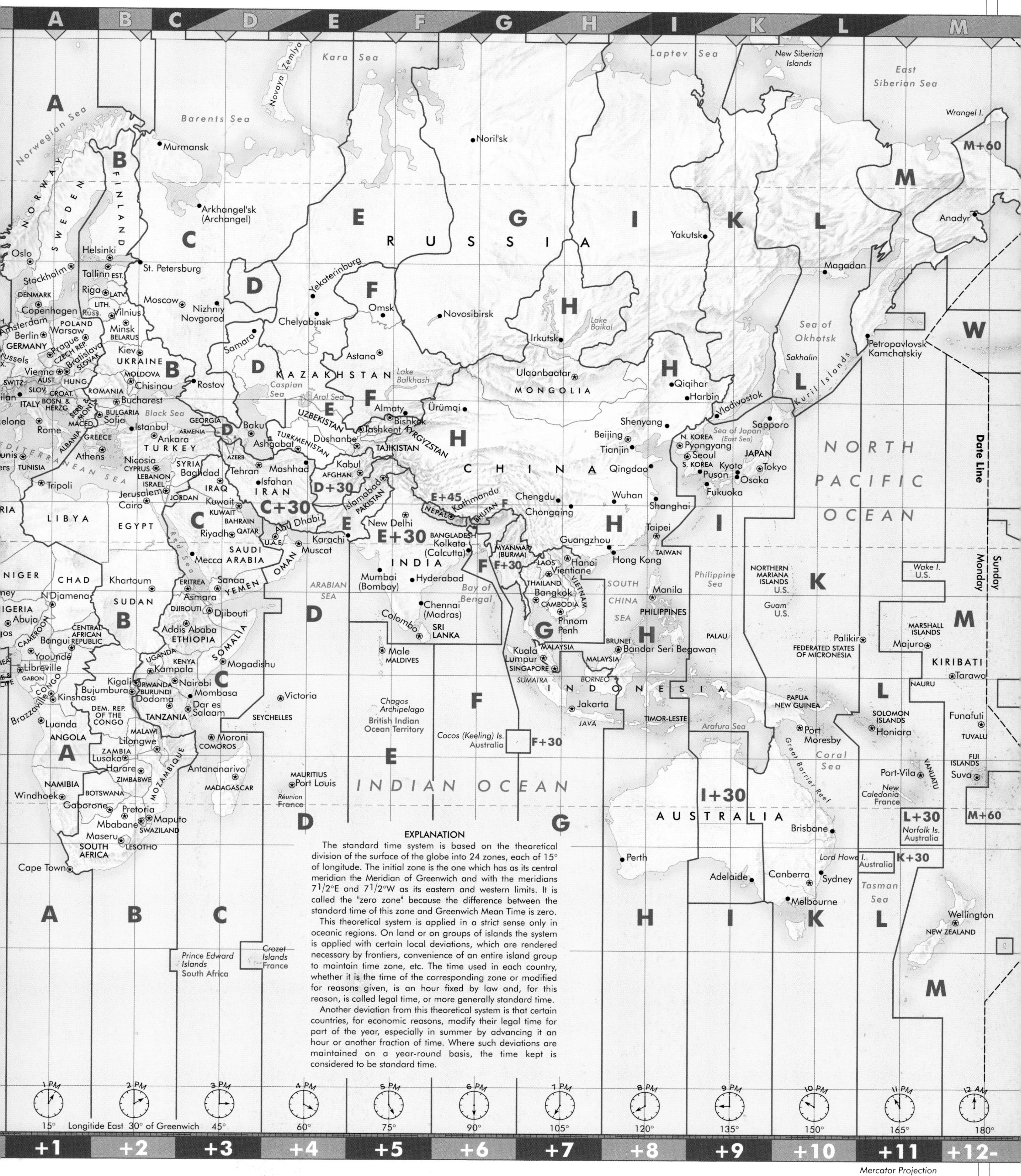

EXPLANATION

The standard time system is based on the theoretical division of the surface of the globe into 24 zones, each of 15° of longitude. The initial zone is the one which has as its central meridian the Meridian of Greenwich and with the meridians $7^1/2$°E and $7^1/2$°W as its eastern and western limits. It is called the "zero zone" because the difference between the standard time of this zone and Greenwich Mean Time is zero.

This theoretical system is applied in a strict sense only in oceanic regions. On land or on groups of islands the system is applied with certain local deviations, which are rendered necessary by frontiers, convenience of an entire island group to maintain time zone, etc. The time used in each country, whether it is the time of the corresponding zone or modified for reasons given, is an hour fixed by law and, for this reason, is called legal time, or more generally standard time.

Another deviation from this theoretical system is that certain countries, for economic reasons, modify their legal time for part of the year, especially in summer by advancing it an hour or another fraction of time. Where such deviations are maintained on a year-round basis, the time kept is considered to be standard time.

NORTH AMERICA

Located between the Atlantic, Pacific, and Arctic Oceans, North America is almost an island unto itself, connected to the rest of the world only by the tenuous thread running through the Isthmus of Panama. Geologically old in some places, young in others, and diverse throughout, the continent sweeps from Arctic tundra in the north through the plains, prairies, and deserts of the interior to the tropical rain forests of Central America. Its eastern coastal plain is furrowed by broad rivers that drain worn and ancient mountain ranges, while in the West younger and more robust ranges thrust their still growing high peaks skyward. Though humans have peopled the continent for perhaps as long as 40,000 years, political boundaries were unknown there until some 400 years ago when European settlers imprinted the land with their ideas of ownership. Despite, or perhaps because of, its relative youth—and its geographic location—most of North America has remained remarkably stable. In the past century, when country borders throughout much of the rest of the world have altered dramatically, they have changed little in North America, while the system of government by democratic rule, first rooted in this continent's soil in the 18th century, has spread to many corners of the globe.

Third largest of the Earth's continents, North America seems made for human habitation. Its waterways—the inland seas of Hudson Bay and the Great Lakes, the enormous Mississippi system draining its midsection, and the countless navigable rivers of the East—have long provided natural corridors for human commerce. In its vast interior, the nurturing soils of plains and prairies have offered up bountiful harvests, while rich deposits of oil and gas have fueled industrial growth, making this continent's mainland one of the world's economic powerhouses.

Just in the past couple of centuries, North America has experienced dramatic changes in its population, landscapes, and environment, an incredible transformation brought about by waves of immigration, booming economies, and relentless development. During the 20th century, the United States and Canada managed to propel themselves into the ranks of the world's richest nations. But success has brought a host of concerns, not the least of which involves the continued exploitation of natural resources. North America is home to roughly eight percent of the planet's people, yet its per capita consumption of energy is almost six times as great as the average for all other continents.

The United States ended the 20th century as the only true superpower, with a military presence and political, economic, and cultural influences that extend around the globe. But the rest of the continent south of the U.S. failed to keep pace, plagued by poverty, despotic governments, and social unrest. Poverty has spurred millions of Mexicans, Central Americans, and Caribbean islanders to migrate northward (legally and illegally) in search of better lives. Finding ways to integrate these disenfranchised masses into the continent's economic miracle is one of the greatest challenges facing North America in the 21st century.

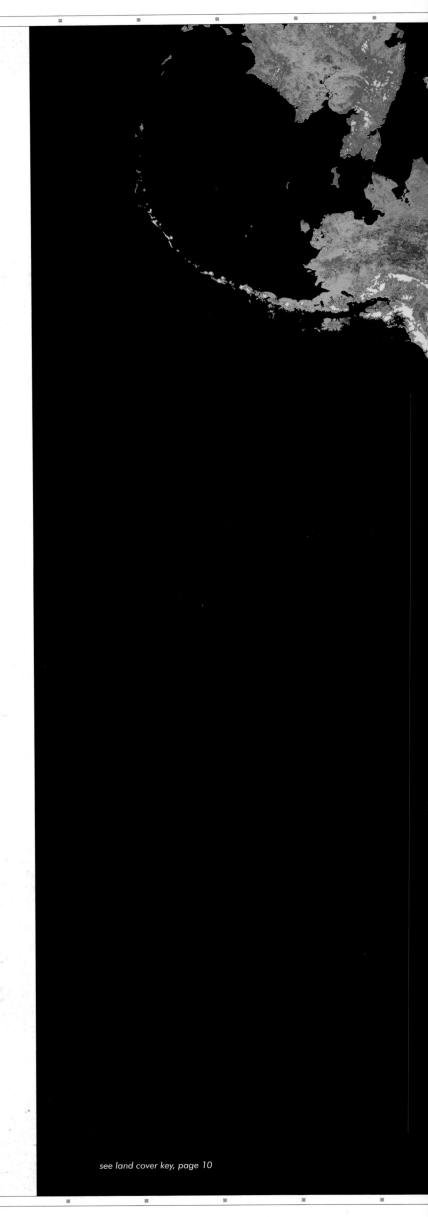

see land cover key, page 10

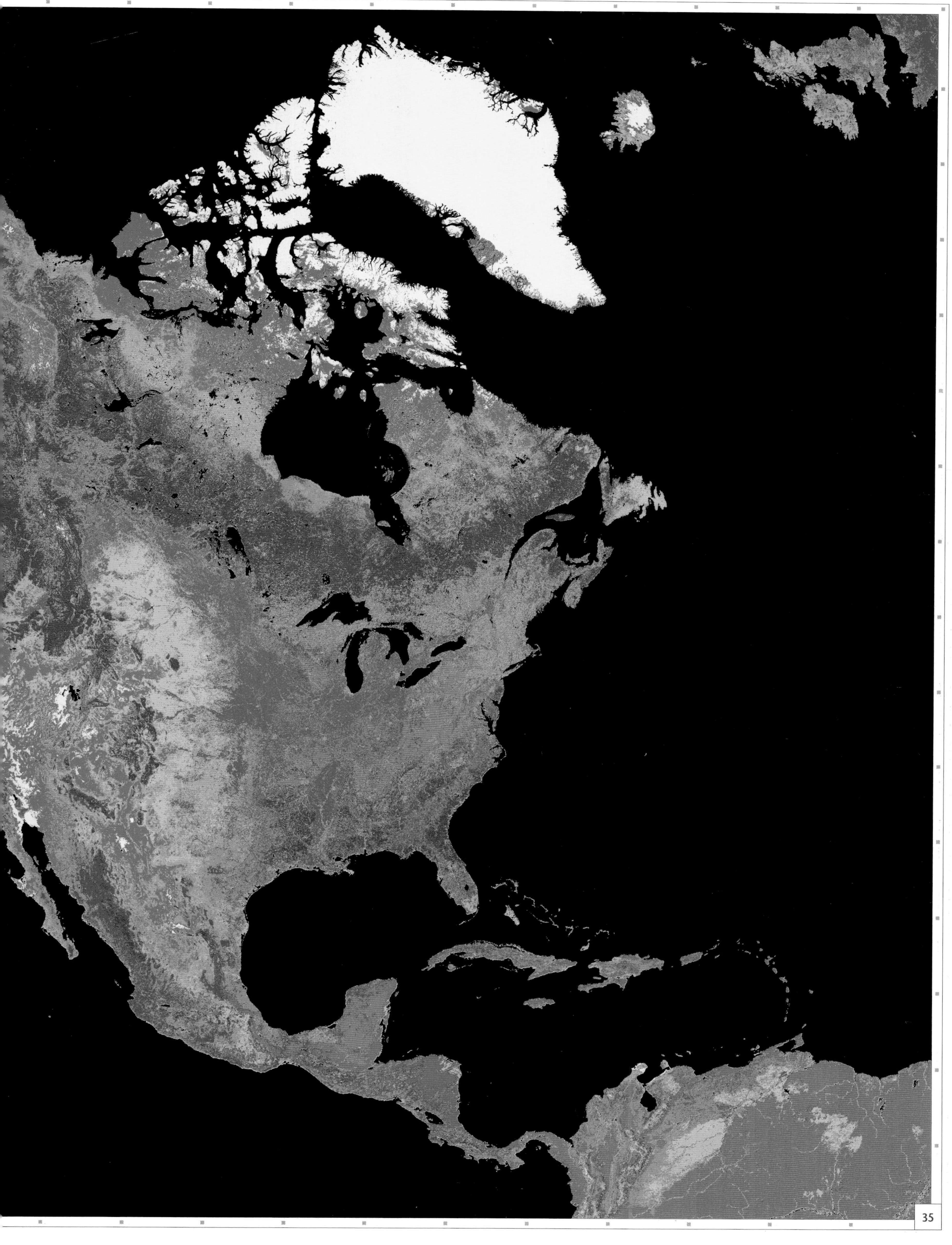

ASIA
RUSSIA
ARCTIC OCEAN
North Magnetic Pole 2003
QUEEN ELIZABETH ISLANDS
PARRY ISLANDS
Ellesmere Island
Devon Island
Banks Island
Victoria Island
Prince of Wales Island
Somerset Island
Boothia Peninsula
Southampton Island
Baffin Island
Bylot Island
CHUKCHI SEA
BERING SEA
BEAUFORT SEA
Lincoln Sea
BAFFIN BAY
Davis Strait
Denmark Strait
Hudson Strait
Foxe Basin
Ungava Bay
HUDSON BAY
James Bay
LABRADOR SEA
GREENLAND SEA
NORWEGIAN SEA
ARCTIC CIRCLE
GULF OF ALASKA
PACIFIC OCEAN
ATLANTIC OCEAN
GREENLAND (KALAALLIT NUNAAT)
Denmark
KNUD RASMUSSEN LAND
ICELAND
Reykjavík
UNITED KINGDOM
ALASKA
Brooks Range
North Slope
Barrow
Prudhoe Bay
Kaktovik
Fairbanks
Anchorage
Juneau
Nome
Kodiak Island
YUKON TERRITORY
Whitehorse
Dawson
NORTHWEST TERRITORIES
Yellowknife
Great Bear Lake
Great Slave Lake
NUNAVUT
Iqaluit
Rankin Inlet
CANADA
BRITISH COLUMBIA
Vancouver
Victoria
ALBERTA
Edmonton
Calgary
SASKATCHEWAN
Regina
Saskatoon
MANITOBA
Winnipeg
Churchill
ONTARIO
Thunder Bay
TORONTO
Ottawa
QUEBEC
MONTREAL
Québec
NEWFOUNDLAND AND LABRADOR
LABRADOR
Island of Newfoundland
St. John's
N.B.
Fredericton
NOVA SCOTIA
Halifax
P.E.I.
Charlottetown
St.-Pierre & Miquelon
France
U.S.
WASH.
Seattle
OREGON
Portland
IDAHO
Boise
MONTANA
Helena
WYOMING
Cheyenne
NORTH DAKOTA
Bismarck
SOUTH DAKOTA
Pierre
NEBRASKA
MINN.
Minneapolis
St. Paul
WIS.
MILWAUKEE
MICHIGAN
DETROIT
CHICAGO
CLEVELAND
PITTSBURGH
NEW YORK
BOSTON
PHILADELPHIA
SAN FRANCISCO
Sacramento
NEVADA
Salt Lake City
Lake Superior
Lake Michigan
Lake Huron
Lake Erie
Lake Ontario
St. Lawrence

NORTH AMERICA
Political

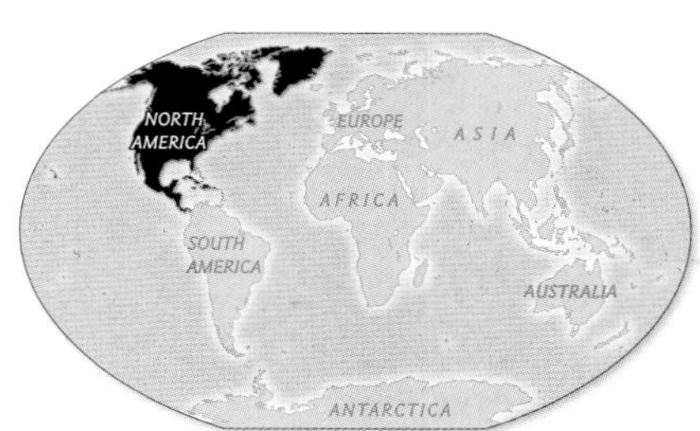

CONTINENTAL DATA

- **Total number of countries:** 23
- **First independent country:** United States, July 4, 1776
- **"Youngest" country:** St. Kitts and Nevis, Sept. 19, 1983
- **Largest country by area:** Canada 9,984,670 sq km (3,855,101 sq mi)
- **Smallest country by area:** St. Kitts and Nevis 269 sq km (104 sq mi)
- **Percent urban population:** 75%
- **Most populous country:** United States 291,512,000
- **Least populous country:** St. Kitts and Nevis 46,000
- **Most densely populated country:** Barbados 588 per sq km (1,524 per sq mi)
- **Least densely populated country:** Canada 3.1 per sq km (8 per sq mi)
- **Largest city by population:** Mexico City, Mexico 18,268,000
- **Highest GDP per capita:** United States $36,300
- **Lowest GDP per capita:** Haiti $1,700
- **Average life expectancy in North America:** 76 years
- **Average literacy rate in North America:** 92%

ARCTIC OCEAN
GREENLAND
GREENLAND SEA
NORWEGIAN SEA
Meridian of Greenwich (London)
ARCTIC CIRCLE
BRITISH ISLES
Faroe Islands
ICELAND
Jan Mayen
Denmark Strait
Kangerdlugssuaq
Cape Morris Jesup
Peary Land
Crown Prince Christian Land
King Frederik VIII Land
King Wilhelm Land
King Christian X Land
King Christian IX Land
King Frederik VI Coast
Gunnbjørn 3700
Mont Forel 3360
Ice thickness 3410
3270
KNUD RASMUSSEN LAND
J.A.D. Jensen Nunatakker 1680
Cape Farewell
Lincoln Sea
North Magnetic Pole 2003
QUEEN ELIZABETH ISLANDS
Axel Heiberg Island
Ellesmere Island
Hayes Pen.
Smith Bay
Cape York
Melville Bay
Jones Sd.
Devon I.
PARRY ISLANDS
Melville I.
Bathurst I.
Cornwallis I.
Prince Patrick Island
M'Clure Str.
Viscount Melville Sound
Banks Island
Cape Prince Alfred
Victoria Island
Prince of Wales I.
Somerset Island
Lancaster Sd.
Bylot Island
BAFFIN BAY
Qeqertarsuaq
Davis Strait
Brodeur Pen.
Borden Pen.
Baffin Island
M'Clintock Chan.
G. of Boothia
Boothia Peninsula
Wollaston Peninsula
Collinson Peninsula
Amundsen Gulf
Franklin Bay
Queen Maud Gulf
Melville Hills
Melville Pen.
Foxe Basin
Prince Charles I.
Cumberland Peninsula
Cumberland Sd.
Foxe Pen.
Meta Incognita Peninsula
Hudson Strait
Killiniq Island
LABRADOR SEA
Southampton Island
Cape Dobbs
Chesterfield Inlet
Coats I.
Mansel I.
HUDSON BAY
Ungava Peninsula
Ungava Bay
Torngat Mts.
Labrador
Cape Harrison
Leaf
Caniapiscau
Réservoir Caniapiscau
Smallwood Reservoir
Mts. Otish 1135
Eastmain
Rés. Manicouagan
Laurentide Scarp
Str. of Belle Isle
Bonavista Bay
Long Range Mts.
ISLAND OF NEWFOUNDLAND
Avalon Peninsula
Anticosti I.
Gulf of St. Lawrence
Cabot Str.
Cape Breton Island
St. Lawrence
Gaspé Pen.
Prince Edward I.
Sable I.
Rés. Gouin
NOVA SCOTIA
Cape Sable
Bay of Fundy
Mt. Katahdin 1606
Mt. Washington 1917
White Mts.
Gulf of Maine
Cape Cod
Long Island
Mt. Tremblant 968
Laurentian Scarp
Ottawa
L. Champlain
Adirondack Mts.
L. Ontario
Niagara Falls
L. Erie
Hudson
Delaware
MOUNTAINS
Georgian Bay
L. Huron
Lower Peninsula
L. Michigan
Upper Pen.
L. Superior
Lake Abitibi
Abitibi
Lake Nipigon
Lake of the Woods
James Bay
Akimiski I.
Attawapiskat
Belcher Islands
Cape Churchill
Cape Tatnam
Severn
Nelson
Churchill
Wollaston Lake
Reindeer Lake
Lake Athabasca
Lac la Ronge
Lake Winnipeg
Lake Winnipegosis
Lake St. Joseph
Trout Lake
Lake Manitoba
Saskatchewan
N. Saskatchewan
S. Saskatchewan
CANADIAN SHIELD
Dubawnt Lake
Thelon
Back
Great Bear Lake
Great Slave Lake
Hay
Laird
Virginia Falls
Caribou Mts.
Birch Mts.
Athabasca
Peace
Source of the Mackenzie-Peace
Williston Lake
Franklin Mts.
Mackenzie
Mackenzie Mts.
Selwyn Mts.
Richardson Mts.
Mackenzie Bay
BEAUFORT SEA
Point Barrow
North Slope
Brooks Range
Davidson Mts.
Porcupine
Ogilvie Mountains
YUKON PLATEAU
Source of the Yukon
Cassiar Mts.
Mt. Logan 5959
COAST MOUNTAINS
ROCKY MOUNTAINS
GREAT PLAINS
Fraser
Columbia Mts.
Selkirk Mts.
Bitterroot Ra.
Source of the Missouri-Red Rock
Missouri
Yellowstone
Big Horn Mts.
Grand Teton 4197
Snake River Plain
Snake
Columbia Plateau
Columbia
Great Sandy Desert
Badlands
Black Hills 2207
Lake Sakakawea
Source of the Mississippi (Lake Itasca)
Lake Oahe
St. Croix
Mississippi
Des Moines
Geographical Center of the
CENTRAL
Front Ra.
Wasatch Ra.
Great Salt Lake
Great Basin
Sierra Nevada
Sacramento Valley
Mt. Shasta 4317
CASCADE RANGE
Mt. Rainier 4392
Mt. St. Helens 2550
Cape Flattery
Vancouver I.
Str. of Georgia
Hecate Str.
Queen Charlotte Is.
Alexander Archipelago
Cape Blanco
Cape Mendocino
Farallon Islands
Monterey
PACIFIC OCEAN
GULF OF ALASKA
Prince William Sd.
Chugach Mts.
Kenai Peninsula
Kodiak Island
Cook Inlet
Alaska Range
Mt. McKinley (Denali) 6194 (20320 ft)
Highest point in North America
Kuskokwim Mts.
Kuskokwim
White Mts.
Yukon
ARCTIC CIRCLE
Kobuk
Noatak
Baird Mts.
Seward Peninsula
Norton Sound
Bering Str.
BERING SEA
St. Lawrence Island
Nunivak I.
SIBERIA
ASIA

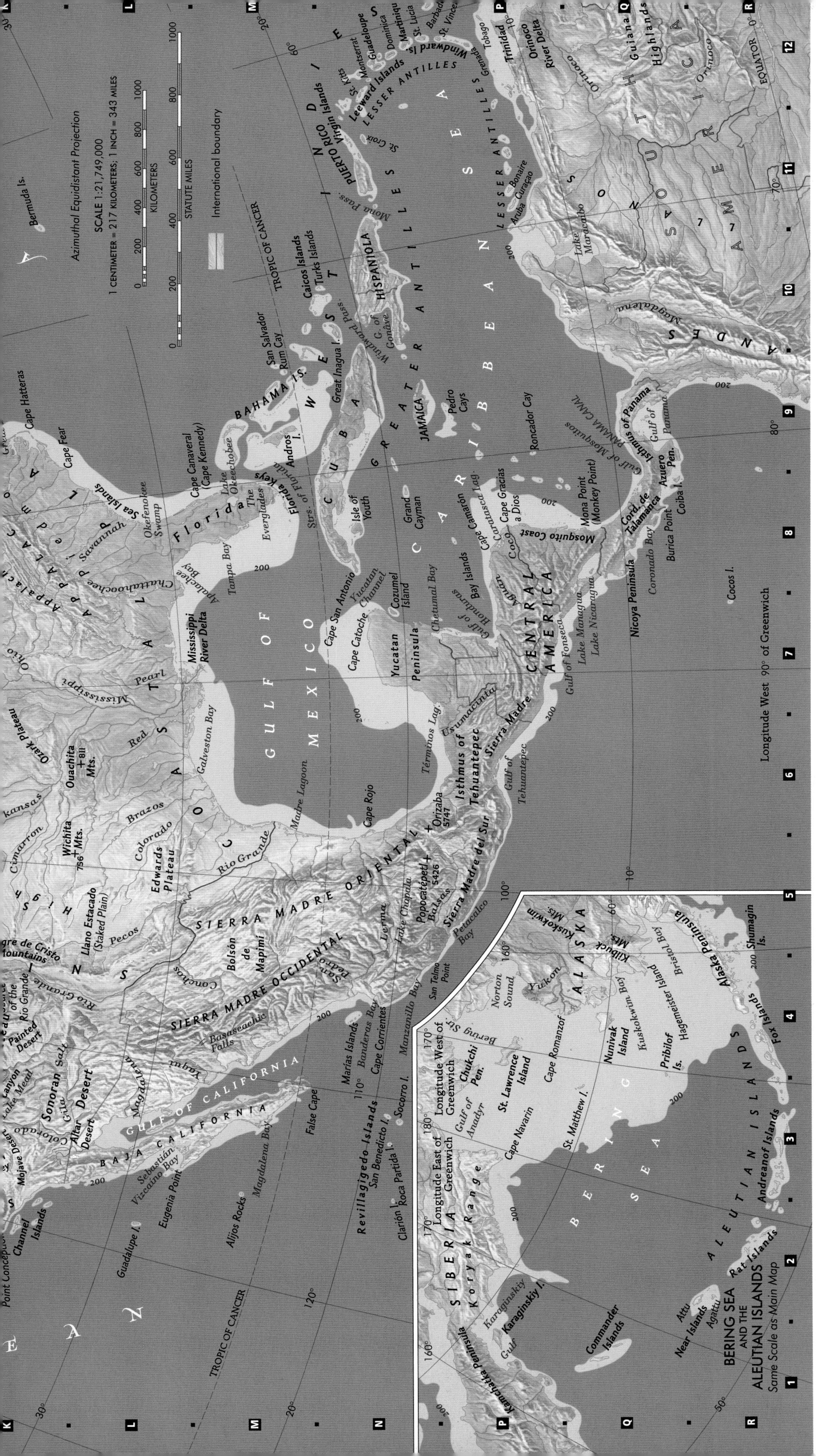

NORTH AMERICA
Physical

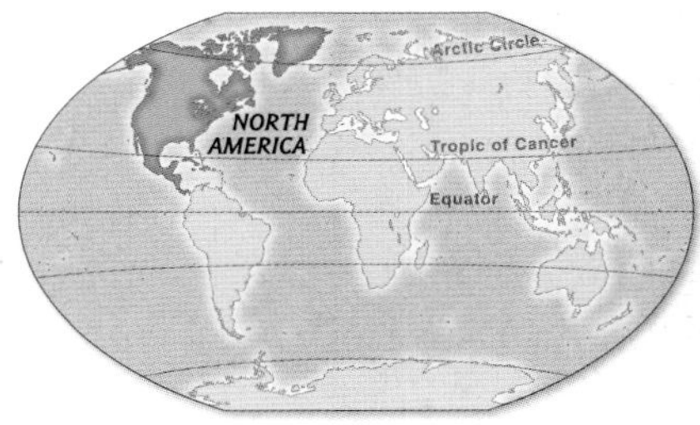

CONTINENTAL DATA

- **Area:**
  24,474,000 sq km
  (9,449,000 sq mi)
- **Greatest north-south extent:**
  7,200 km (4,470 mi)
- **Greatest east-west extent:**
  6,400 km (3,980 mi)
- **Highest point:**
  Mount McKinley (Denali), Alaska, United States 6,194 m (20,320 ft)
- **Lowest point:**
  Death Valley, California, United States -86 m (-282 ft)
- **Lowest recorded temperature:**
  Snag, Yukon Territory, Canada -63°C (-81.4°F), February 3 1947
- **Highest recorded temperature:**
  Death Valley, California, United States 56.6°C (134°F), July 10, 1913
- **Longest rivers:**
  - Mississippi-Missouri 5,971 km (3,710 mi)
  - Mackenzie-Peace 4,241 km (2,635 mi)
  - Yukon 3,220 km (2,000 mi)
- **Largest lakes:**
  - Lake Superior 82,100 sq km (31,700 sq mi)
  - Lake Huron 59,600 sq km (23,000 sq mi)
  - Lake Michigan 57,800 sq km (22,300 sq mi)
- **Earth's extremes located in North America:**
  - **Largest Canyon:** Grand Canyon, Arizona, United States; Length: 446 km (277 mi), Width: 549 m to 29 km (1,801 ft to 18 mi), Depth: about 1.6 km (1 mi)
  - **Largest Cave System:** Mammoth Cave, Kentucky, United States; over 530 km (330 mi) of mapped passageways
  - **Most Predictable Geyser:** Old Faithful, Wyoming, United States; annual average interval 75 to 79 minutes

BRITISH COLUMBIA
ALBERTA
SASKATCHEWAN
MANITOBA
CANADA
ROCKY MOUNTAINS
PACIFIC OCEAN
Str. of Juan de Fuca
Str. of Georgia
Bellingham
Everett
Seattle
Bremerton
Mt. Olympus 7965
Aberdeen
Centralia
Olympia
Tacoma
Mt. Rainier 14411
Mt. St. Helens 8366
Longview
Kelso
Astoria
Vancouver
WASHINGTON
Colville
Sandpoint
Wenatchee
Coeur d'Alene
Spokane
Yakima
Richland
Pullman
Walla Walla
Wallace
Columbia
Lewiston
Portland
Newport
Salem
Albany
Corvallis
Mt. Hood 11239
The Dalles
Pendleton
La Grande
Baker City
Snake
Eugene
Springfield
North Bend
Coos Bay
OREGON
John Day
Roseburg
Grants Pass
Medford
Ashland
Klamath Falls
Burns
Crane
Ontario
Payette
Caldwell
Boise
Nampa
Mountain Home
Sun Valley
IDAHO
Borah Pk. 12662
Idaho Falls
Salmon
Bonners Ferry
Kalispell
Polson
Missoula
Deer Lodge
Helena
Butte
Dillon
Bozeman
Livingston
Cut Bank
Shelby
Havre
Great Falls
Fort Benton
Lewistown
Turner
Malta
Glasgow
Fort Peck Lake
Wolf Point
Missouri
Williston
Sidney
MONTANA
Roundup
Glendive
Miles City
Billings
Laurel
Forsyth
Hardin
Baker
Crescent City
Yreka
Goose L.
Eureka
Mt. Shasta 14162
Redding
Red Bluff
Susanville
Fort Bragg
Ukiah
Yuba City
Tahoe
Sacramento
Santa Rosa
Vallejo
SAN FRANCISCO
Oakland
Stockton
San Mateo
Palo Alto
SAN JOSE
Modesto
Santa Cruz
Monterey
Salinas
Fresno
Visalia
Coalinga
Paso Robles
San Luis Obispo
Santa Maria
Lompoc
Santa Barbara
Bakersfield
Delano
Bishop
Mt. Whitney 14494
Death Valley
-282
Beatty
Ridgecrest
Mojave
Glendale
Pasadena
LOS ANGELES
Long Beach
Santa Ana
San Bernardino
Palm Springs
Riverside
Salton Sea
SAN DIEGO
National City
El Centro
Yuma
CALIFORNIA
SIERRA NEVADA
Denio
McDermitt
Winnemucca
Lovelock
Carlin
Elko
Wells
Reno
Carson City
NEVADA
GREAT BASIN
McGill
Ely
Hawthorne
Mt. Jefferson 11949
Tonopah
Goldfield
Pioche
Caliente
Las Vegas
Boulder City
Lake Mead
Needles
Jerome
Twin Falls
Burley
Pocatello
Rupert
Blackfoot
Montpelier
Preston
Logan
Ogden
Great Salt Lake
Salt Lake City
Tooele
Provo
Utah L.
Nephi
Manti
Price
Sevier Lake
Fillmore
Richfield
UTAH
Vernal
Kings Pk. 13528
Grand Junction
Moab
Parowan
Cedar City
Panguitch
St. George
Kanab
Monticello
Lake Powell
Powell
Cody
Sheridan
Buffalo
Worland
Thermopolis
Grand Teton 13766
Gannett Pk. 13804
WYOMING
Riverton
Lander
Casper
Douglas
Lusk
Gillette
Newcastle
Kemmerer
Green River
Rock Springs
Rawlins
Evanston
Laramie
Cheyenne
Scottsbluff
Craig
Fort Collins
Greeley
Longmont
Boulder
Glenwood Springs
DENVER
Aurora
Fort Morgan
COLORADO
Delta
Gunnison
Montrose
Pikes Pk. 14110
Colorado Springs
Pueblo
Salida
Canon City
Lamar
La Junta
Silverton
Cortez
Durango
Alamosa
Walsenburg
Trinidad
Farmington
Raton
COLORADO PLATEAU
Grand Canyon
Kingman
Williams
Flagstaff
Prescott
Winslow
Holbrook
ARIZONA
Wickenburg
PHOENIX
Scottsdale
Mesa
Baldy Peak 11403
Globe
Gila Bend
Casa Grande
Eloy
Ajo
Morenci
Safford
Tucson
Willcox
Benson
Tombstone
Nogales
Bisbee
Douglas
Wheeler Peak 13161
Los Alamos
Santa Fe
Springer
Clayton
Gallup
Grants
Las Vegas
Albuquerque
Belen
NEW MEXICO
Tucumcari
Vaughn
Magdalena
Socorro
Fort Sumner
Clovis
Truth or Consequences
Roswell
Alamogordo
Silver City
Artesia
Lordsburg
Deming
Las Cruces
Hobbs
Carlsbad
El Paso
Portal
Stanley
Minot
Rugby
St. John
Devils Lake
Grafton
Lake Sakakawea
Harvey
Grand Forks
NORTH DAKOTA
Dickinson
Mandan
Bismarck
Jamestown
Valley City
Fargo
Moorhead
Mott
Fort Yates
Ashley
Oakes
Lemmon
Mobridge
Aberdeen
Lake Oahe
Faith
Belle Fourche
SOUTH DAKOTA
Watertown
Lead
Rapid City
Pierre
Huron
Brookings
Hot Springs
Martin
Mitchell
Lake Francis Case
Sioux Falls
Yankton
Chadron
Valentine
Ainsworth
Alliance
Norfolk
NEBRASKA
Sidney
North Platte
Grand Island
Columbus
Kearney
Platte
Hastings
Lincoln
McCook
Beatrice
Norton
Colby
Goodland
Russell
Hays
Salina
Manhattan
KANSAS
Great Bend
Hutchinson
Garden City
Arkansas
Dodge City
Wichita
Liberal
Arkansas City
Guymon
Woodward
Ponca City
Enid
Stillwater
Dalhart
Dumas
Borger
Pampa
Amarillo
Oklahoma City
Shawnee
OKLAHOMA
Chickasha
Hereford
Childress
Lawton
Red
Plainview
Vernon
Ardmore
Wichita Falls
Lubbock
Brownfield
Lamesa
Snyder
Sweetwater
Abilene
Big Spring
Fort Worth
DALLAS
Midland
Odessa
Brownwood
Pecos
TEXAS
San Angelo
Waco
Temple
Van Horn
Fort Stockton
Marfa
Alpine
Sanderson
Ozona
Sonora
Amistad Reservoir
Rio Grande
Austin
New Braunfels
SAN ANTONIO
Del Rio
Uvalde
Eagle Pass
Cuero
Victoria
Beeville
Aransas Pass
Laredo
Alice
Kingsville
Falfurrias
Raymondville
Edinburg
McAllen
Harlingen
Brownsville
MEXICO
ALASKA
ARCTIC OCEAN
BEAUFORT SEA
CHUKCHI SEA
ARCTIC CIRCLE
RUSSIA
Bering Str.
BERING SEA
Barrow
Wainwright
Atqasuk
Point Lay
Prudhoe Bay
Kaktovik
Point Hope
Umiat
North Slope
BROOKS RANGE
Kivalina
Noatak
Shungnak
Kotzebue
Kiana
Kobuk
Wiseman
Shishmaref
Selawik
Wales
Deering
Allakaket
Beaver
Fort Yukon
Teller
Hughes
Circle
Yukon
Nome
Koyuk
Galena
Nulato
Tanana
Rampart
Gambell
Golovin
Kaltag
Ruby
Fairbanks
Eagle
Savoonga
St. Lawrence Island
Unalakleet
Lake Minchumina
Nenana
Big Delta
Alakanuk
St. Michael
Kotlik
ALASKA RANGE
Cantwell
Tanacross
Mountain Village
Anvik
McGrath
Mt. McKinley (Denali) 20320
Northway
Hooper Bay
Holy Cross
Flat
Farewell
Gulkana
Tununak
Aniak
Red Devil
Skwentna
Palmer
Mekoryuk
Bethel
Nyac
Anchorage
Valdez
Nunivak Island
Kashegelok
Whittier
Cordova
Quinhagak
Kenai
Goodnews Bay
Newhalen
Seward
Cape Yakataga
Yakutat
Iliamna Lake
Homer
Seldovia
Togiak
Dillingham
Naknek
King Salmon
Egegik
Pilot Point
Kodiak
Karluk
Kodiak Island
Chignik
Sand Point
Cold Bay
GULF OF ALASKA
PACIFIC OCEAN
YUKON TERRITORY
NORTHWEST TERRITORIES
BRITISH COLUMBIA
CANADA
U.S.
Skagway
Haines
Juneau
Gustavus
Hoonah
Sitka
Petersburg
Wrangell
Ketchikan
Hydaburg
0 100 200 300 km
0 50 100 150 statute mi

UNITED STATES
Political
Albers Conic Equal-Area Projection
SCALE 1:10,824,000
1 CENTIMETER = 108 KILOMETERS; 1 INCH = 171 MILES
KILOMETERS
STATUTE MILES
ATLANTIC OCEAN
GULF OF MEXICO
GULF OF MAINE
TROPIC OF CANCER
ONTARIO
QUEBEC
NEW BRUNSWICK
PRINCE EDWARD ISLAND
NOVA SCOTIA
BAHAMAS
CUBA
HAITI
MINNESOTA
WISCONSIN
MICHIGAN
IOWA
ILLINOIS
INDIANA
OHIO
PENNSYLVANIA
NEW YORK
VERMONT
NEW HAMPSHIRE
MAINE
MASSACHUSETTS
CONN.
RHODE ISLAND
NEW JERSEY
DELAWARE
MARYLAND
WEST VIRGINIA
VIRGINIA
MISSOURI
KENTUCKY
TENNESSEE
NORTH CAROLINA
SOUTH CAROLINA
ARKANSAS
MISSISSIPPI
ALABAMA
GEORGIA
LOUISIANA
FLORIDA
APPALACHIAN MOUNTAINS
Lake Superior
Lake Michigan
Lake Huron
Lake Erie
Lake Ontario
Georgian Bay
L. Champlain
St. Lawrence
Bay of Fundy
Long Island
Delaware Bay
Chesapeake Bay
Albemarle Sound
Pamlico Sound
Port Royal Sound
Mobile Bay
Tampa Bay
L. Okeechobee
Florida Keys
Straits of Florida
Mississippi
Ohio
WASHINGTON, D.C.
NEW YORK
PHILADELPHIA
BALTIMORE
BOSTON
PITTSBURGH
CLEVELAND
DETROIT
CHICAGO
MILWAUKEE
INDIANAPOLIS
COLUMBUS
ST. LOUIS
MEMPHIS
ATLANTA
JACKSONVILLE
NEW ORLEANS
PRINCIPAL HAWAIIAN ISLANDS
Longitude West 159° of Greenwich
Longitude West 90° of Greenwich
PACIFIC OCEAN
KAUA'I
Ni'ihau
O'AHU
Honolulu
MOLOKA'I
LĀNA'I
MAUI
Kaho'olawe
HAWAI'I
Mauna Loa 13679
Kilauea 4077
Kalae (South Point)
100 km
100 statute mi

PACIFIC OCEAN
CAN
ROCKY MOUNTAINS
GREAT PLAINS
CASCADE RANGE
SIERRA NEVADA
COAST RANGES
GREAT BASIN
COLORADO PLATEAU
Columbia Plateau
Str. of Georgia
Str. of Juan de Fuca
Cape Flattery
Mt. Olympus 7965
Puget Sd.
Mt. Baker 10778
Okanogan
Columbia
Pend Oreille L.
Bitterroot Range
Flathead Lake
Cape Disappointment
Mt. Rainier 14411
Mt. St. Helens 8366
Mt. Adams 12307
Columbia
Snake
Illinois Pk. 7690
Clearwater Mts.
Continental Divide
Missouri
Milk
Bear Paw Mts.
Fort Peck Lake
Lake Sakakawea
Souris
Sheyenne
L. Ashtabula
Mt. Hood 11239
Willamette
John Day
Blue Mountains
Wallowa Mts.
Buffalo Hump 8924
Salmon
Musselshell
Yellowstone
Little Missouri
Badlands
Heart
White Butte 3506
Cape Blanco
Salmon River Mountains
10340 Twin Peaks
Borah Pk. 12662
Granite Pk. 12799
Absaroka Range
Bighorn
Bighorn Mts.
Tongue
Powder
Grand
Lake Oahe
Moreau
Geographical Center of the 50 United States
Harney Basin
Great Sandy Desert
Yellowstone L.
Jackson L.
Grand Teton 13770
Cloud Pk. 13166
Belle Fourche
Cheyenne
Black Hills
Harney Pk. 7242
L. Sharpe
James
Snake
Steens Mt. 9733
Snake River Plain
Wind River Ra.
Gannett Pk. 13804
Goose L.
Warner Mts.
Shoshone Falls
American Falls Res.
Cape Mendocino
Mt. Shasta 14162
Klamath Mountains
Eagle Pk. 9892
Granite Pk. 9732
Black Rock Desert
Sherman Pk. 9682
Bear River Ra.
Lake Francis Case
White
Niobrara
Lassen Peak 10457
Sacramento
Sacramento Valley
Great Salt Lake
Great Divide Basin
Laramie Pk. 10272
Laramie Mts.
Sand Hills
Elkhorn
Pyramid L.
Humboldt
Ruby Dome 11387
Ruby Mts.
Great Salt Lake Desert
Wasatch Ra.
Flaming Gorge Reservoir
Medicine Bow Mts.
N. Platte
Front Range
N. Platte
Point Arena
Carson Sink
Donner Pass 7088
L. Tahoe
Kings Pk. 13528
Uinta Mts.
Utah Lake
5424
S. Platte
Loup
Platte
Point Reyes
Farallon Is.
San Francisco Bay
Shoshone Mts.
Toiyabe Ra.
Monitor Ra.
Schell Cr. Ra.
Mt. Moriah 12050
Wheeler Pk. 13063
Sevier Lake
Roan Cliffs
Green
Colorado
Longs Peak 14255
Republican
Mono L.
Diablo Range
San Joaquin
Monterey Bay
Point Sur
Boundary Peak 13140
Troy Pk. 11298
Mt. Elbert 14433
Geographical Center of the 48 Contiguous United States
Solomon
Smoky Hills 1654
Santa Lucia Ra.
San Joaquin Valley
Mt. Whitney 14494 (4418 m)
Bald Mt. 9380
Uncompahgre Plateau
Uncompahgre Pk. 14309
Pikes Peak 14110
Mt. Sunflower 4039
Smokey Hill
Arkansas
Death Valley −282 (−86 m)
Mojave Desert
Spring Mts.
Lake Mead
Lake Powell
Rio Grande
Blanca Pk. 14345
San Juan Mts.
Sangre de Cristo Mts.
Point Buchon
Mount Trumbull 8029
Kaibab Plateau
Matthews Pk. 9512
Chuska Mts.
2265 Red Hills
Point Conception
Santa Barbara Chan.
San Miguel
Santa Rosa
Santa Cruz
Channel Islands
San Nicolas
Santa Catalina
San Clemente
Gulf of Santa Catalina
Black Mts.
Grand Canyon
San Francisco Mt. 12633
Painted Desert
Wheeler Pk. 13161
Black Mesa 4973
Cimarron
Canadian
N. Canadian
Mt. San Antonio 10064
L. Meredith
Washita
Continental Divide
Palomar Mt. 6140
−232
Salton Sea
Imperial Valley
Colorado
Mogollon Rim
Baldy Peak 11403
2479 Wichita Mts.
Sonoran Desert
Salt
Gila
Black Range
Elephant Butte Res.
Sierra Blanca Pk. 12003
Sacramento Mts.
Llano Estacado
Cap Rock Escarpment
Red
Gila
Caballo Res.
San Andres Mts.
Guadalupe Mts.
Guadalupe Pk. 8749
Brazos
Red Bluff Lake
Colorado
Rio Grande
Pecos
Edwards Plateau 2487
Amistad Reservoir
Guadalupe
Rio Grande
Nueces
Corpus Christi Bay
Baffin Bay
Falcon Lake
MEXICO
ALASKA
BEAUFORT SEA
CHUKCHI SEA
Point Barrow
Dease Inlet
Smith Bay
Harrison Bay
Prudhoe Bay
Camden Bay
Demarcation Point
Icy Cape
Teshekpuk Lake
North Slope
Mt. Isto 9060
British Mts.
Cape Lisburne
Point Hope
Tingmerkpuk Mt. 3787
Colville
BROOKS RANGE
De Long Mountains
Philip Smith Mts.
Davidson Mts.
ARCTIC CIRCLE
RUSSIA
Noatak
Baird Mountains
Endicott Mts.
Kotzebue Sd.
Kobuk
Porcupine
Bering Str.
Diomede Is.
C. Prince of Wales
Selawik Lake
SEWARD PENINSULA
Koyukuk
Yukon Flats
White Mts.
Ray Mts.
CANADA
U.S.
Norton Bay
Yukon
2207 St. Lawrence Island
Norton Sound
Stuart I.
Kaiyuh Mts.
ALASKA
Tanana
Yukon Delta
Cape Romanzof
Kuskokwim Mountains
ALASKA RANGE
Mt. McKinley (Denali) 20320 (6194 m)
Susitna
Talkeetna Mts.
Copper
Wrangell Mts.
Mt. Blackburn 16390
Yukon
Yukon
Kuskokwim
Mt. Gerdine 11258
Nunivak I.
Roberts Mt. 1675
Kilbuck Mts.
Chugach Mountains
St. Elias Mountains
Mt. St. Elias 18008
KENAI PENINSULA
Cook Inlet
Prince William Sd.
Montague I.
BERING SEA
Kuskokwim Bay
Iliamna Lake
Cape Newenham
Yakutat Bay
Mt. Fairweather 15300
COAST MOUNTAINS
Kennedy Entrance
GULF OF ALASKA
Cross Sound
Admiralty Island
Bristol Bay
ALASKA PENINSULA
ALEUTIAN RANGE
Mt. Katmai 6715
Afognak I.
Chichagof Island
Kruzof I.
Baranof I.
Kupreanof I.
Shelikof Str.
4470
Kodiak Island
ALEXANDER ARCHIPELAGO
Kuiu I.
Revillagigedo Island
Mt. Veniaminof 8225
Trinity Is.
Prince of Wales I.
Dall I.
ALASKA
0 100 200 300 km
0 50 100 150 statute mi

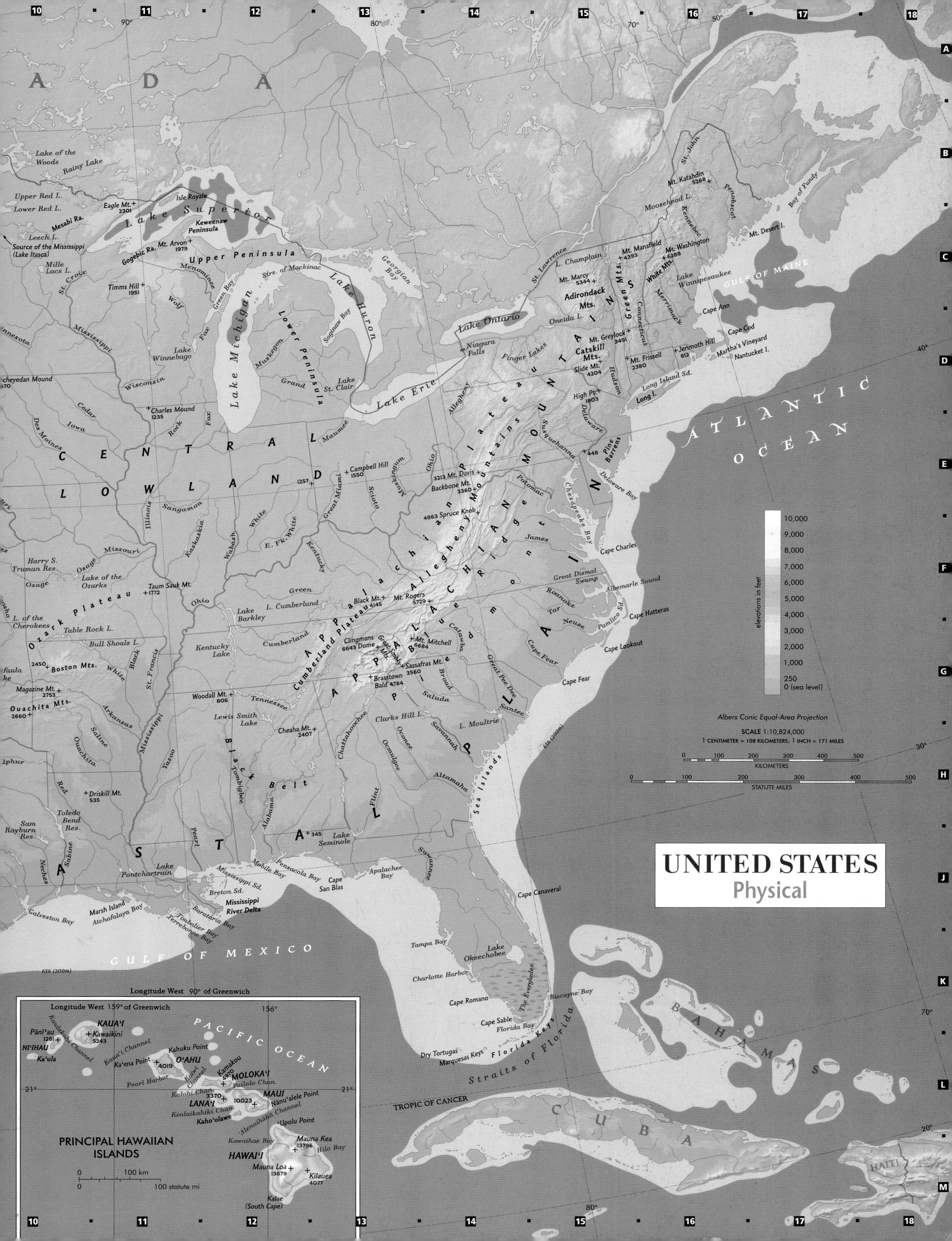

UNITED STATES
Physical
Albers Conic Equal-Area Projection
SCALE 1:10,824,000
1 CENTIMETER = 108 KILOMETERS; 1 INCH = 171 MILES
0 100 200 300 400 500
KILOMETERS
0 100 200 300 400 500
STATUTE MILES
elevations in feet
10,000
9,000
8,000
7,000
6,000
5,000
4,000
3,000
2,000
1,000
250
0 (sea level)
656 (200m)
A D A
Lake of the Woods
Rainy Lake
Upper Red L.
Lower Red L.
Mesabi Ra.
Leech L.
Source of the Mississippi (Lake Itasca)
Mille Lacs L.
St. Croix
Eagle Mt. 2301
Isle Royale
Lake Superior
Keweenaw Peninsula
Gogebic Ra.
Mt. Arvon 1979
Upper Peninsula
Timms Hill 1951
Menominee
Wolf
Green Bay
Strs. of Mackinac
Lake Michigan
Lower Peninsula
Saginaw Bay
Lake Huron
Georgian Bay
Lake Winnebago
Fox
Mississippi
Wisconsin
Muskegon
Grand
Lake St. Clair
Lake Erie
Niagara Falls
Lake Ontario
St. Lawrence
L. Champlain
Mt. Marcy 5344
Adirondack Mts.
Oneida L.
Finger Lakes
Catskill Mts.
Slide Mt. 4204
Mt. Greylock 3491
Mt. Frissell 2380
Jerimoth Hill 812
Green Mts.
White Mts.
Mt. Mansfield 4393
Mt. Washington 6288
Lake Winnipesaukee
Connecticut
Merrimack
Hudson
Moosehead L.
Kennebec
Penobscot
St. John
Mt. Katahdin 5268
Bay of Fundy
Mt. Desert I.
GULF OF MAINE
Cape Ann
Cape Cod
Martha's Vineyard
Nantucket I.
Long Island Sd.
Long I.
High Pt. 1803
Delaware
Susquehanna
Pine Barrens
448
Allegheny
Delaware Bay
Chesapeake Bay
Potomac
Cape Charles
ATLANTIC OCEAN
Minnesota
Cheyedan Mound 1670
Charles Mound 1235
Cedar
Iowa
Des Moines
Rock
Fox
CENTRAL LOWLAND
Maumee
1257
Campbell Hill 1550
Great Miami
Scioto
Muskingum
Ohio
3213 Mt. Davis
Backbone Mt. 3360
4863 Spruce Knob
Appalachian Plateau
Allegheny Mountains
APPALACHIAN MOUNTAINS
Blue Ridge
Piedmont
James
Great Dismal Swamp
Albemarle Sound
Roanoke
Tar
Neuse
Pamlico Sd.
Cape Hatteras
Cape Lookout
Cape Fear
Illinois
Sangamon
Kaskaskia
Wabash
White
E. Fk. White
Kentucky
Missouri
Harry S. Truman Res.
Osage
Lake of the Ozarks
Taum Sauk Mt. 1772
Ozark Plateau
Ohio
Green
L. Cumberland
Lake Barkley
Black Mt. 4145
Mt. Rogers 5729
Cumberland Plateau
L. of the Cherokees
Table Rock L.
Bull Shoals L.
Kentucky Lake
Cumberland
Clingmans Dome 6643
Great Smoky Mts.
Mt. Mitchell 6684
Catawba
Sassafras Mt. 3560
Brasstown Bald 4784
Broad
Saluda
Great Pee Dee
Santee
2450 Boston Mts.
White
Black
St. Francis
Magazine Mt. 2753
Ouachita Mts. 2660
Arkansas
Woodall Mt. 806
Tennessee
Lewis Smith Lake
Cheaha Mt. 2407
Clarks Hill L.
L. Moultrie
Savannah
Chattahoochee
Oconee
Ocmulgee
Altamaha
Saline
Ouachita
Yazoo
Black Belt
Tombigbee
Red
Driskill Mt. 535
Toledo Bend Res.
Sam Rayburn Res.
Sabine
Neches
Pearl
Alabama
Flint
345
Lake Seminole
Suwannee
Sea Islands
COASTAL PLAIN
Lake Pontchartrain
Mississippi Sd.
Mobile Bay
Pensacola Bay
Cape San Blas
Apalachee Bay
Breton Sd.
Mississippi River Delta
Barataria Bay
Timbalier Bay
Terrebonne Bay
Marsh Island
Atchafalaya Bay
Galveston Bay
GULF OF MEXICO
Cape Canaveral
Tampa Bay
Lake Okeechobee
Charlotte Harbor
The Everglades
Cape Romano
Biscayne Bay
Cape Sable
Florida Bay
Dry Tortugas
Marquesas Keys
Florida Keys
Straits of Florida
TROPIC OF CANCER
BAHAMAS
CUBA
HAITI
Longitude West 90° of Greenwich
Longitude West 159° of Greenwich
PRINCIPAL HAWAIIAN ISLANDS
PACIFIC OCEAN
KAUA'I
Kawaikini 5243
Pānī'au 1281
NI'IHAU
Ka'ula
Kaulakahi Channel
Kaua'i Channel
Kahuku Point
O'AHU
Ka'ena Point
4019
Pearl Harbor
Kaiwi Channel
Kamakou 4970
MOLOKA'I
Pailolo Chan.
Kalohi Chan.
3370
LANA'I
MAUI
10023
Nānu'alele Point
Kealaikahiki Chan.
Kaho'olawe
'Alenuihāhā Channel
'Upolu Point
Kawaihae Bay
Mauna Kea 13796
Hilo Bay
HAWAI'I
Mauna Loa 13679
Kilauea 4077
Kalae (South Cape)
0 100 km
0 100 statute mi

NORTH AMERICA
FLAGS & FACTS

ANTIGUA AND BARBUDA

ANTIGUA AND BARBUDA

AREA 442 sq km (171 sq mi)
POPULATION 74,000
CAPITAL St. John's 24,000
RELIGION Anglican, other Protestant denominations, Roman Catholic
LANGUAGE English, local dialects
LITERACY 89%
LIFE EXPECTANCY 71 years
GDP PER CAPITA $10,000
ECONOMY **IND:** tourism, construction, light manufacturing. **AGR:** cotton, fruits, vegetables, bananas; livestock. **EXP:** petroleum products, manufactures, machinery and transport equipment, food and live animals.

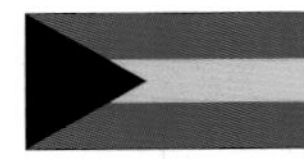

BAHAMAS

COMMONWEALTH OF THE BAHAMAS

AREA 13,939 sq km (5,382 sq mi)
POPULATION 311,000
CAPITAL Nassau 220,000
RELIGION Baptist, Anglican, Roman Catholic
LANGUAGE English, Creole
LITERACY 98%
LIFE EXPECTANCY 72 years
GDP PER CAPITA $16,800
ECONOMY **IND:** tourism, banking, cement, oil refining and transshipment. **AGR:** citrus, vegetables; poultry. **EXP:** pharmaceuticals, cement, rum, crawfish.

BARBADOS

BARBADOS

AREA 430 sq km (166 sq mi)
POPULATION 253,000
CAPITAL Bridgetown 136,000
RELIGION Protestant, Roman Catholic
LANGUAGE English
LITERACY 97%
LIFE EXPECTANCY 73 years
GDP PER CAPITA $14,500
ECONOMY **IND:** tourism, sugar, light manufacturing, component assembly. **AGR:** sugarcane, vegetables, cotton. **EXP:** sugar and molasses, rum, other foods and beverages, chemicals.

BELIZE

BELIZE

AREA 22,965 sq km (8,867 sq mi)
POPULATION 271,000
CAPITAL Belmopan 9,000
RELIGION Roman Catholic, Protestant
LANGUAGE English, Spanish, Mayan, Garifuna, Creole
LITERACY 70%
LIFE EXPECTANCY 67 years
GDP PER CAPITA $3,250
ECONOMY **IND:** garment production, food processing, tourism, construction. **AGR:** bananas, coca, citrus, sugarcane; lumber. **EXP:** sugar, bananas, citrus, clothing.

CANADA

CANADA

AREA 9,984,670 sq km (3,855,101 sq mi)
POPULATION 31,630,000
CAPITAL Ottawa 1,094,000
RELIGION Roman Catholic, Protestant
LANGUAGE English, French
LITERACY 97%
LIFE EXPECTANCY 79 years
GDP PER CAPITA $29,400
ECONOMY **IND:** processed and unprocessed minerals, food products, wood and paper products, transportation equipment. **AGR:** wheat, barley, oilseed, tobacco; dairy products; forest products; fish. **EXP:** motor vehicles and parts, newsprint, wood pulp, timber.

COSTA RICA

REPUBLIC OF COSTA RICA

AREA 51,100 sq km (19,730 sq mi)
POPULATION 4,171,000
CAPITAL San José 983,000
RELIGION Roman Catholic, Evangelical Christian
LANGUAGE Spanish, English
LITERACY 96%
LIFE EXPECTANCY 79 years
GDP PER CAPITA $8,500
ECONOMY **IND:** microprocessors, food processing, textiles and clothing, construction materials. **AGR:** coffee, pineapples, bananas, sugar; beef; timber. **EXP:** coffee, bananas, sugar, pineapples.

CUBA

REPUBLIC OF CUBA

AREA 110,860 sq km (42,803 sq mi)
POPULATION 11,279,000
CAPITAL Havana 2,268,000
RELIGION Roman Catholic, Protestant, Jehovah's Witnesses, Jewish, Santeria
LANGUAGE Spanish
LITERACY 96%
LIFE EXPECTANCY 76 years
GDP PER CAPITA $2,300
ECONOMY **IND:** sugar, mining, tobacco, chemicals. **AGR:** sugar, tobacco, citrus, coffee; livestock. **EXP:** sugar, nickel, tobacco, fish.

DOMINICA

COMMONWEALTH OF DOMINICA

AREA 751 sq km (290 sq mi)
POPULATION 70,000
CAPITAL Roseau 26,000
RELIGION Roman Catholic, Protestant
LANGUAGE English, French patois
LITERACY 94%
LIFE EXPECTANCY 73 years
GDP PER CAPITA $3,700
ECONOMY **IND:** soap, coconut oil, tourism, copra. **AGR:** bananas, citrus, mangoes, root crops. **EXP:** bananas, soap, bay oil, vegetables.

DOMINICAN REPUBLIC

DOMINICAN REPUBLIC

AREA 48,671 sq km (18,792 sq mi)
POPULATION 8,716,000
CAPITAL Santo Domingo 2,629,000
RELIGION Roman Catholic
LANGUAGE Spanish
LITERACY 82%
LIFE EXPECTANCY 69 years
GDP PER CAPITA $3,700
ECONOMY **IND:** tourism, sugar processing, ferronickel and gold mining, textiles. **AGR:** sugarcane, coffee, cotton, cocoa. **EXP:** ferronickel, sugar, gold, silver.

EL SALVADOR

REPUBLIC OF EL SALVADOR

AREA 21,041 sq km (8,124 sq mi)
POPULATION 6,640,000
CAPITAL San Salvador 1,381,000
RELIGION Roman Catholic, Evangelical Christian
LANGUAGE Spanish, Nahua
LITERACY 72%
LIFE EXPECTANCY 70 years
GDP PER CAPITA $4,600
ECONOMY **IND:** food processing, beverages, textiles, chemicals. **AGR:** coffee, sugar, corn, rice; shrimp, beef. **EXP:** raw materials, consumer goods, capital goods, fuels.

GRENADA

GRENADA

AREA 344 sq km (133 sq mi)
POPULATION 105,000
CAPITAL St. George's 36,000
RELIGION Roman Catholic, Anglican, other Protestant denominations
LANGUAGE English, French patois
LITERACY 98%
LIFE EXPECTANCY 71 years
GDP PER CAPITA $4,750
ECONOMY **IND:** food and beverages, textiles, light assembly operations, tourism. **AGR:** bananas, cocoa, nutmeg, mace. **EXP:** bananas, cocoa, nutmeg, fruits and vegetables.

GUATEMALA

REPUBLIC OF GUATEMALA

AREA 108,889 sq km (42,042 sq mi)
POPULATION 12,360,000
CAPITAL Guatemala City 3,366,000
RELIGION Roman Catholic, Protestant, indigenous Mayan beliefs
LANGUAGE Spanish, Amerindian languages
LITERACY 64%
LIFE EXPECTANCY 66 years
GDP PER CAPITA $3,700
ECONOMY **IND:** sugar, textiles and clothing, furniture, chemicals. **AGR:** sugarcane, corn, bananas, coffee; cattle. **EXP:** coffee, sugar, bananas, fruits and vegetables.

HAITI

REPUBLIC OF HAITI

AREA 27,750 sq km (10,714 sq mi)
POPULATION 7,528,000
CAPITAL Port-au-Prince 1,838,000
RELIGION Roman Catholic, Protestant, Voodoo
LANGUAGE French, Creole
LITERACY 45%
LIFE EXPECTANCY 51 years
GDP PER CAPITA $1,700
ECONOMY **IND:** sugar refining, flour milling, textiles, cement. **AGR:** coffee, mangoes, sugarcane, rice; wood. **EXP:** manufactures, coffee, oils, mangoes.

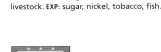

HONDURAS

REPUBLIC OF HONDURAS

AREA 112,492 sq km (43,433 sq mi)
POPULATION 6,876,000
CAPITAL Tegucigalpa 980,000
RELIGION Roman Catholic, Protestant
LANGUAGE Spanish, Amerindian dialects
LITERACY 74%
LIFE EXPECTANCY 71 years
GDP PER CAPITA $2,600
ECONOMY **IND:** sugar, coffee, textiles, clothing. **AGR:** sugarcane, corn, bananas, coffee; cattle. **EXP:** coffee, bananas, shrimp, lobster.

JAMAICA

JAMAICA

AREA 10,991 sq km (4,244 sq mi)
POPULATION 2,646,000
CAPITAL Kingston 672,000
RELIGION Protestant, Roman Catholic, African beliefs
LANGUAGE English, Creole
LITERACY 85%
LIFE EXPECTANCY 75 years
GDP PER CAPITA $3,700
ECONOMY **IND:** tourism, bauxite, textiles, food processing. **AGR:** sugarcane, bananas, coffee, citrus; poultry. **EXP:** alumina, bauxite, sugar, bananas.

MEXICO

UNITED MEXICAN STATES

AREA 1,964,375 sq km (758,449 sq mi)
POPULATION 104,878,000
CAPITAL Mexico City 18,268,000
RELIGION Roman Catholic, Protestant
LANGUAGE Spanish, various Mayan, Nahuatl, and other indigenous languages
LITERACY 90%
LIFE EXPECTANCY 75 years
GDP PER CAPITA $9,000
ECONOMY **IND:** food and beverages, tobacco, chemicals, iron and steel. **AGR:** corn, wheat, soybeans, rice; beef; wood products. **EXP:** manufactured goods, oil and oil products, silver, fruits.

NICARAGUA

REPUBLIC OF NICARAGUA

AREA 130,000 sq km (50,193 sq mi)
POPULATION 5,482,000
CAPITAL Managua 1,039,000
RELIGION Roman Catholic, Protestant
LANGUAGE Spanish, English, indigenous languages
LITERACY 68%
LIFE EXPECTANCY 69 years
GDP PER CAPITA $2,500
ECONOMY **IND:** food processing, chemicals, machinery and metal products. **AGR:** coffee, bananas, sugarcane, cotton; beef. **EXP:** coffee, shrimp and lobster, cotton, tobacco.

PANAMA

REPUBLIC OF PANAMA

AREA 75,517 sq km (29,157 sq mi)
POPULATION 2,981,000
CAPITAL Panama City 1,202,000
RELIGION Roman Catholic, Protestant
LANGUAGE Spanish, English
LITERACY 91%
LIFE EXPECTANCY 74 years
GDP PER CAPITA $5,900
ECONOMY **IND:** construction, petroleum refining, brewing, cement and other construction materials. **AGR:** bananas, rice, corn, coffee; livestock; shrimp. **EXP:** bananas, shrimp, sugar, coffee.

ST. KITTS AND NEVIS

FEDERATION OF ST. KITTS AND NEVIS

AREA 269 sq km (104 sq mi)
POPULATION 46,000
CAPITAL Basseterre 12,000
RELIGION Anglican, other Protestant denominations, Roman Catholic
LANGUAGE English
LITERACY 97%
LIFE EXPECTANCY 71 years
GDP PER CAPITA $8,700
ECONOMY **IND:** sugar processing, tourism, cotton, salt. **AGR:** sugarcane, rice, yams, vegetables; fish. **EXP:** machinery, food, electronics, beverages.

ST. LUCIA

SAINT LUCIA

AREA	616 sq km (238 sq mi)
POPULATION	162,000
CAPITAL	Castries 57,000
RELIGION	Roman Catholic, Protestant
LANGUAGE	English, French patois
LITERACY	67%
LIFE EXPECTANCY	72 years
GDP PER CAPITA	$4,400
ECONOMY	**IND:** clothing, assembly of electronic components, beverages, corrugated cardboard boxes. **AGR:** bananas, coconuts, vegetables, citrus. **EXP:** bananas, clothing, cocoa, vegetables.

ST. VINCENT AND THE GRENADINES

SAINT VINCENT AND THE GRENADINES

AREA	389 sq km (150 sq mi)
POPULATION	110,000
CAPITAL	Kingstown 28,000
RELIGION	Anglican, Methodist, Roman Catholic, other Protestant
LANGUAGE	English, French patois
LITERACY	96%
LIFE EXPECTANCY	72 years
GDP PER CAPITA	$2,900
ECONOMY	**IND:** food processing, cement, furniture, clothing. **AGR:** bananas, coconuts, sweet potatoes, spices; cattle; fish. **EXP:** bananas, eddoes and dasheen (taro), arrowroot starch, tennis racquets.

TRINIDAD AND TOBAGO

REPUBLIC OF TRINIDAD AND TOBAGO

AREA	5,128 sq km (1,980 sq mi)
POPULATION	1,309,000
CAPITAL	Port-of-Spain 54,000
RELIGION	Roman Catholic, Hindu, Anglican, Muslim, Presbyterian
LANGUAGE	English, Hindi, French, Spanish, Chinese
LITERACY	94%
LIFE EXPECTANCY	71 years
GDP PER CAPITA	$9,000
ECONOMY	**IND:** petroleum, chemicals, tourism, food processing. **AGR:** cocoa, sugarcane, rice, citrus; poultry. **EXP:** petroleum and petroleum products, chemicals, steel products, fertilizer.

UNITED STATES

UNITED STATES OF AMERICA

AREA	9,629,091 sq km (3,717,811 sq mi)
POPULATION	291,512,000
CAPITAL	Washington, D.C. 3,997,000
RELIGION	Protestant, Roman Catholic, Jewish
LANGUAGE	English, Spanish
LITERACY	97%
LIFE EXPECTANCY	77 years
GDP PER CAPITA	$36,300
ECONOMY	**IND:** petroleum, steel, motor vehicles, aerospace. **AGR:** wheat, other grains, corn, fruits; beef; forest products; fish. **EXP:** capital goods, automobiles, industrial supplies and raw materials, consumer goods.

DEPENDENCIES

SOVEREIGN LOCAL

ANGUILLA (UNITED KINGDOM)

ANGUILLA

AREA	96 sq km (37 sq mi)
POPULATION	12,000
CAPITAL	The Valley 1,000
RELIGION	Anglican, Methodist, Seventh-Day Adventist, Baptist, Roman Catholic
LANGUAGE	English
LITERACY	95%
LIFE EXPECTANCY	76 years
GDP PER CAPITA	$8,600
ECONOMY	**IND:** tourism, boat building, offshore financial services. **AGR:** small quantities of tobacco, vegetables; cattle. **EXP:** lobster, fish, livestock, salt.

SOVEREIGN LOCAL

CAYMAN ISLANDS (U K.)

CAYMAN ISLANDS

AREA	262 sq km (101 sq mi)
POPULATION	42,000
CAPITAL	George Town 21,000
RELIGION	Protestant, Roman Catholic
LANGUAGE	English
LITERACY	98%
LIFE EXPECTANCY	79 years
GDP PER CAPITA	$30,000
ECONOMY	**IND:** tourism, banking, insurance and finance, construction. **AGR:** vegetables, fruits; livestock. **EXP:** turtle products, manufactured consumer goods.

SOVEREIGN LOCAL

MONTSERRAT (U. K.)

MONTSERRAT

AREA	102 sq km (39 sq mi)
POPULATION	5,000
CAPITAL	Plymouth (abandoned)
RELIGION	Anglican, Methodist, Roman Catholic, other Protestant
LANGUAGE	English
LITERACY	97%
LIFE EXPECTANCY	78 years
GDP PER CAPITA	$2,400
ECONOMY	**IND:** tourism, textiles, electronic appliances. **AGR:** cabbages, carrots, cucumbers, tomatoes; livestock products. **EXP:** electronic components, plastic bags, apparel, hot peppers.

SOVEREIGN LOCAL

TURKS AND CAICOS IS. (U.K.)

TURKS AND CAICOS ISLANDS

AREA	430 sq km (166 sq mi)
POPULATION	19,000
CAPITAL	Grand Turk 5,000
RELIGION	Baptist, Methodist, Anglican
LANGUAGE	English
LITERACY	98%
LIFE EXPECTANCY	74 years
GDP PER CAPITA	$7,300
ECONOMY	**IND:** tourism, offshore financial services. **AGR:** corn, beans, cassava (tapioca), citrus; fish. **EXP:** lobster, dried and fresh conch, conch shells.

SOVEREIGN LOCAL

ARUBA (NETHERLANDS)

ARUBA

AREA	193 sq km (75 sq mi)
POPULATION	95,000
CAPITAL	Oranjestad 23,000
RELIGION	Roman Catholic, Protestant
LANGUAGE	Dutch, Papiamento, English, Spanish
LITERACY	97%
LIFE EXPECTANCY	79 years
GDP PER CAPITA	$28,000
ECONOMY	**IND:** tourism, transshipment facilities, oil refining. **AGR:** aloes; livestock; fish. **EXP:** live animals and animal products, art and collectibles, machinery and electrical equipment, transport equipment.

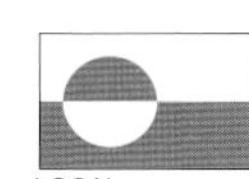

SOVEREIGN LOCAL

GREENLAND (DENMARK)

GREENLAND

AREA	2,166,086 sq km (836,086 sq mi)
POPULATION	58,000
CAPITAL	Nuuk (Godthåb) 14,000
RELIGION	Evangelical Lutheran
LANGUAGE	Greenlandic (East Inuit), Danish, English
LITERACY	NA
LIFE EXPECTANCY	68 years
GDP PER CAPITA	$20,000
ECONOMY	**IND:** fish processing (shrimp and halibut), handicrafts, furs. **AGR:** forage crops, garden and greenhouse vegetables; sheep; fish. **EXP:** fish and fish products.

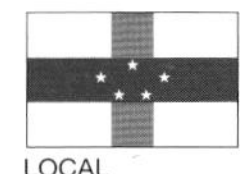

SOVEREIGN LOCAL

NETH. ANTILLES (NETH.)

NETHERLANDS ANTILLES

AREA	800 sq km (309 sq mi)
POPULATION	179,000
CAPITAL	Willemstad 125,000
RELIGION	Roman Catholic, Protestant, Jewish, Seventh-Day Adventist
LANGUAGE	Dutch, Papiamento, English, Spanish
LITERACY	98%
LIFE EXPECTANCY	76 years
GDP PER CAPITA	$11,400
ECONOMY	**IND:** tourism, petroleum refining, petroleum transshipment facilities, light manufacturing. **AGR:** aloes, sorghum, peanuts, vegetables. **EXP:** petroleum products.

SOVEREIGN LOCAL

VIRGIN ISLANDS (U. S.)

UNITED STATES VIRGIN ISLANDS

AREA	352 sq km (136 sq mi)
POPULATION	110,000
CAPITAL	Charlotte Amalie 11,000
RELIGION	Baptist, Roman Catholic, Episcopalian
LANGUAGE	English, Spanish, Creole
LITERACY	NA
LIFE EXPECTANCY	78 years
GDP PER CAPITA	$15,000
ECONOMY	**IND:** tourism, petroleum refining, watch assembly, rum distilling. **AGR:** fruits, vegetables, sorghum; cattle. **EXP:** refined petroleum products.

SOVEREIGN LOCAL

BERMUDA (UNITED KINGDOM)

BERMUDA

AREA	53 sq km (21 sq mi)
POPULATION	64,000
CAPITAL	Hamilton 1,000
RELIGION	Protestant, Anglican, Roman Catholic
LANGUAGE	English, Portuguese
LITERACY	98%
LIFE EXPECTANCY	77 years
GDP PER CAPITA	$34,800
ECONOMY	**IND:** tourism, finance, structural concrete products, paints, perfumes. **AGR:** bananas, vegetables, flowers, dairy products. **EXP:** pharmaceuticals.

GUADELOUPE (FRANCE)

DEPARTMENT OF GUADELOUPE

AREA	1,705 sq km (658 sq mi)
POPULATION	441,000
CAPITAL	Basse-Terre 12,000
RELIGION	Roman Catholic, Hindu, Pagan African
LANGUAGE	French
LITERACY	90%
LIFE EXPECTANCY	78 years
GDP PER CAPITA	$9,000
ECONOMY	**IND:** construction, cement, rum, sugar. **AGR:** bananas, sugarcane, tropical fruits and vegetables; cattle. **EXP:** bananas, sugar, rum.

SOVEREIGN LOCAL

PUERTO RICO (UNITED STATES)

COMMONWEALTH OF PUERTO RICO

AREA	9,104 sq km (3,515 sq mi)
POPULATION	3,879,000
CAPITAL	San Juan 1,404,000
RELIGION	Roman Catholic, Protestant
LANGUAGE	Spanish, English
LITERACY	89%
LIFE EXPECTANCY	77 years
GDP PER CAPITA	$11,200
ECONOMY	**IND:** pharmaceuticals, electronics, apparel, food products. **AGR:** sugarcane, coffee, pineapples, plantains; livestock. **EXP:** pharmaceuticals, electronics, apparel, canned tuna.

SOVEREIGN LOCAL

BRITISH VIRGIN IS. (U.K.)

BRITISH VIRGIN ISLANDS

AREA	153 sq km (59 sq mi)
POPULATION	21,000
CAPITAL	Road Town 11,000
RELIGION	Methodist, Anglican, other Protestant denominations, Roman Catholic
LANGUAGE	English
LITERACY	98%
LIFE EXPECTANCY	76 years
GDP PER CAPITA	$16,000
ECONOMY	**IND:** tourism, light industry, construction, rum. **AGR:** fruits, vegetables; livestock; fish. **EXP:** rum, fresh fish, fruits, animals.

MARTINIQUE (FRANCE)

DEPARTMENT OF MARTINIQUE

AREA	1,100 sq km (425 sq mi)
POPULATION	392,000
CAPITAL	Fort-de-France 93,000
RELIGION	Roman Catholic, Hindu, Pagan African
LANGUAGE	French, Creole patois
LITERACY	93%
LIFE EXPECTANCY	79 years
GDP PER CAPITA	$11,000
ECONOMY	**IND:** construction, cement, rum, sugar. **AGR:** pineapples, avocados, bananas, flowers. **EXP:** refined petroleum products, bananas, rum, pineapples.

SOVEREIGN LOCAL

ST.-PIERRE AND MIQUELON (Fr.)

TERRITORIAL COLLECTIVITY OF ST.-PIERRE AND MIQUELON

AREA	242 sq km (93 sq mi)
POPULATION	7,000
CAPITAL	St.-Pierre 6,000
RELIGION	Roman Catholic
LANGUAGE	French
LITERACY	99%
LIFE EXPECTANCY	78 years
GDP PER CAPITA	$11,000
ECONOMY	**IND:** fish processing and supply base for fishing fleets, tourism. **AGR:** vegetables; poultry; fish. **EXP:** fish and fish products, soybeans, animal feed, mollusks and crustaceans.

NORTH AMERICA
FLAGS & FACTS

UNITED STATES' STATE FLAGS

ALABAMA
POPULATION 4,464,000
CAPITAL Montgomery

ALASKA
POPULATION 635,000
CAPITAL Juneau

ARIZONA
POPULATION 5,307,000
CAPITAL Phoenix

ARKANSAS
POPULATION 2,692,000
CAPITAL Little Rock

CALIFORNIA
POPULATION 34,501,000
CAPITAL Sacramento

COLORADO
POPULATION 4,418,000
CAPITAL Denver

CONNECTICUT
POPULATION 3,425,000
CAPITAL Hartford

DELAWARE
POPULATION 796,000
CAPITAL Dover

FLORIDA
POPULATION 16,397,000
CAPITAL Tallahassee

GEORGIA
POPULATION 8,384,000
CAPITAL Atlanta

HAWAII
POPULATION 1,224,000
CAPITAL Honolulu

IDAHO
POPULATION 1,321,000
CAPITAL Boise

ILLINOIS
POPULATION 12,482,000
CAPITAL Springfield

INDIANA
POPULATION 6,115,000
CAPITAL Indianapolis

IOWA
POPULATION 2,923,000
CAPITAL Des Moines

KANSAS
POPULATION 2,695,000
CAPITAL Topeka

KENTUCKY
POPULATION 4,066,000
CAPITAL Frankfort

LOUISIANA
POPULATION 4,465,000
CAPITAL Baton Rouge

MAINE
POPULATION 1,287,000
CAPITAL Augusta

MARYLAND
POPULATION 5,375,000
CAPITAL Annapolis

MASSACHUSETTS
POPULATION 6,379,000
CAPITAL Boston

MICHIGAN
POPULATION 9,991,000
CAPITAL Lansing

MINNESOTA
POPULATION 4,972,000
CAPITAL St. Paul

MISSISSIPPI
POPULATION 2,858,000
CAPITAL Jackson

MISSOURI
POPULATION 5,630,000
CAPITAL Jefferson City

MONTANA
POPULATION 904,000
CAPITAL Helena

NEBRASKA
POPULATION 1,713,000
CAPITAL Lincoln

NEVADA
POPULATION 2,106,000
CAPITAL Carson City

NEW HAMPSHIRE
POPULATION 1,259,000
CAPITAL Concord

NEW JERSEY
POPULATION 8,484,000
CAPITAL Trenton

NEW MEXICO
POPULATION 1,829,000
CAPITAL Santa Fe

NEW YORK
POPULATION 19,011,000
CAPITAL Albany

NORTH CAROLINA
POPULATION 8,186,000
CAPITAL Raleigh

NORTH DAKOTA
POPULATION 634,000
CAPITAL Bismarck

OHIO
POPULATION 11,374,000
CAPITAL Columbus

OKLAHOMA
POPULATION 3,460,000
CAPITAL Oklahoma City

OREGON
POPULATION 3,473,000
CAPITAL Salem

PENNSYLVANIA
POPULATION 12,287,000
CAPITAL Harrisburg

RHODE ISLAND
POPULATION 1,059,000
CAPITAL Providence

SOUTH CAROLINA
POPULATION 4,063,000
CAPITAL Columbia

SOUTH DAKOTA
POPULATION 757,000
CAPITAL Pierre

TENNESSEE
POPULATION 5,740,000
CAPITAL Nashville

TEXAS
POPULATION 21,325,000
CAPITAL Austin

UTAH
POPULATION 2,270,000
CAPITAL Salt Lake City

VERMONT
POPULATION 613,000
CAPITAL Montpelier

VIRGINIA
POPULATION 7,188,000
CAPITAL Richmond

WASHINGTON
POPULATION 5,988,000
CAPITAL Olympia

WEST VIRGINIA
POPULATION 1,802,000
CAPITAL Charleston

WISCONSIN
POPULATION 5,402,000
CAPITAL Madison

WYOMING
POPULATION 494,000
CAPITAL Cheyenne

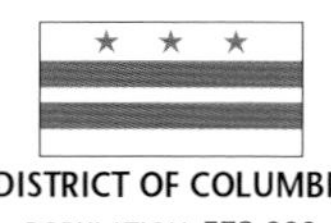

DISTRICT OF COLUMBIA
POPULATION 572,000
United States' Capital

POPULATION DENSITY

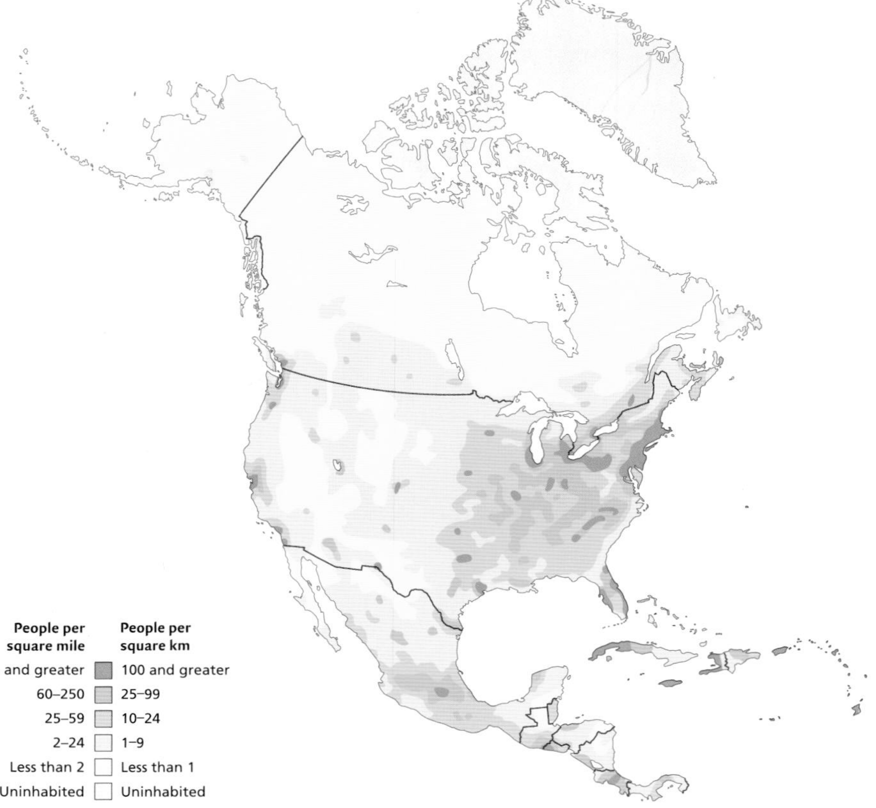

DATES OF COUNTRY INDEPENDENCE

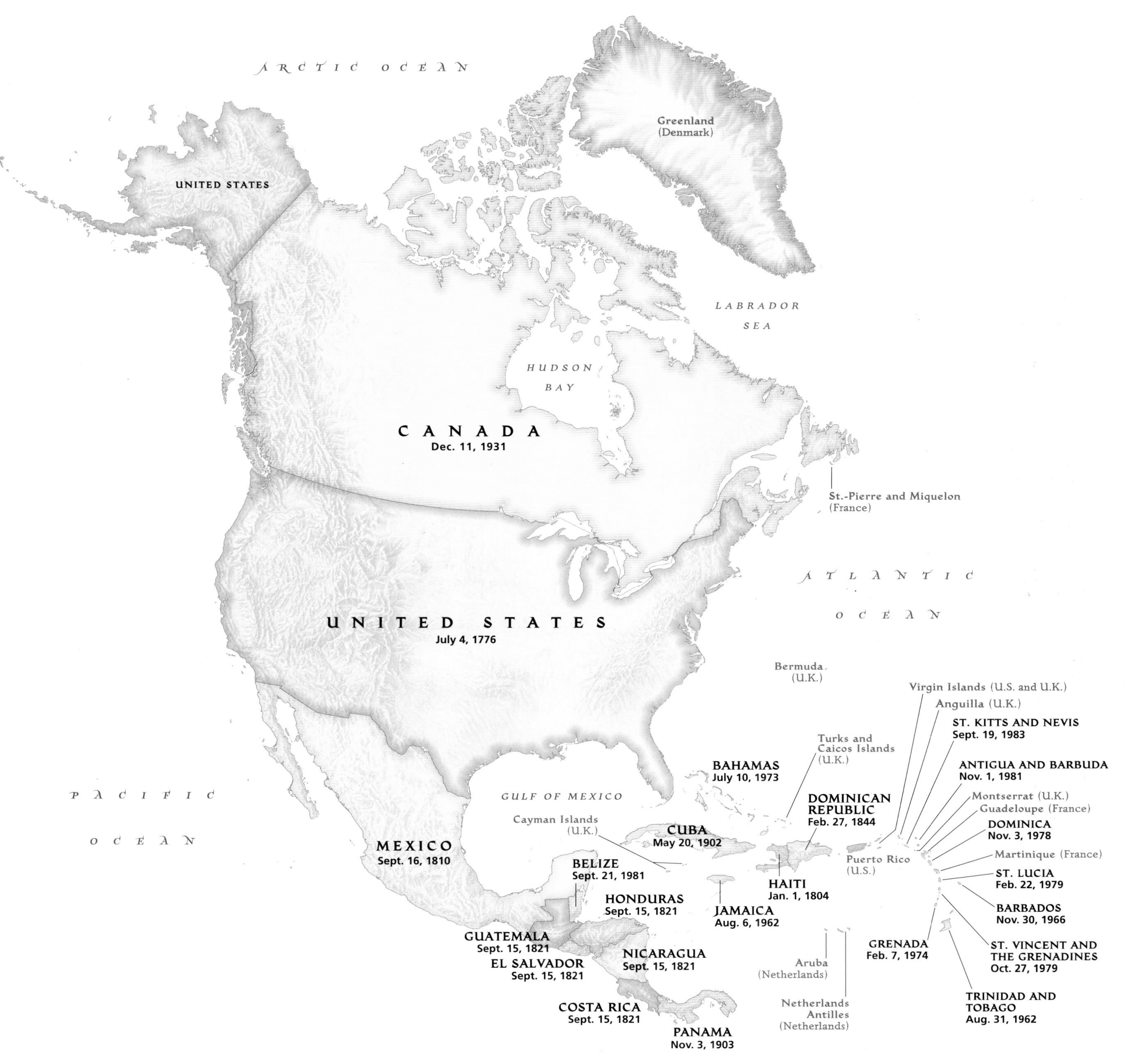
ARCTIC OCEAN
Greenland (Denmark)
UNITED STATES
LABRADOR SEA
HUDSON BAY
CANADA
Dec. 11, 1931
St.-Pierre and Miquelon (France)
ATLANTIC OCEAN
UNITED STATES
July 4, 1776
Bermuda (U.K.)
Virgin Islands (U.S. and U.K.)
Anguilla (U.K.)
ST. KITTS AND NEVIS
Sept. 19, 1983
Turks and Caicos Islands (U.K.)
BAHAMAS
July 10, 1973
ANTIGUA AND BARBUDA
Nov. 1, 1981
PACIFIC OCEAN
GULF OF MEXICO
DOMINICAN REPUBLIC
Feb. 27, 1844
Montserrat (U.K.)
Guadeloupe (France)
Cayman Islands (U.K.)
CUBA
May 20, 1902
DOMINICA
Nov. 3, 1978
MEXICO
Sept. 16, 1810
Martinique (France)
Puerto Rico (U.S.)
BELIZE
Sept. 21, 1981
HAITI
Jan. 1, 1804
ST. LUCIA
Feb. 22, 1979
HONDURAS
Sept. 15, 1821
JAMAICA
Aug. 6, 1962
BARBADOS
Nov. 30, 1966
GUATEMALA
Sept. 15, 1821
NICARAGUA
Sept. 15, 1821
GRENADA
Feb. 7, 1974
ST. VINCENT AND THE GRENADINES
Oct. 27, 1979
EL SALVADOR
Sept. 15, 1821
Aruba (Netherlands)
COSTA RICA
Sept. 15, 1821
Netherlands Antilles (Netherlands)
TRINIDAD AND TOBAGO
Aug. 31, 1962
PANAMA
Nov. 3, 1903

SOUTH AMERICA

Continent of extremes, South America extends from the Isthmus of Panama, in the Northern Hemisphere, to a ragged tail less than 700 miles from Antarctica. There the Andes, a continuous continental rampart that forms the world's second highest range, finally dives undersea to continue as a submarine ridge. Occupying nearly half the continent, the world's largest and biologically richest rain forest spans the Equator, drained by the Amazon River, second longest river but largest by volume anywhere.

These formidable natural barriers shaped lopsided patterns of settlement in South America, the fourth largest continent. As early as 1531, when Spaniard Francisco Pizarro began his conquest of the Inca Empire, Iberians were pouring into coastal settlements that now hold most of the continent's burgeoning population. Meanwhile, Portuguese planters imported millions of African slaves to work vast sugar estates on Brazil's littoral. There and elsewhere, wealth and power coalesced in family oligarchies and in the Roman Catholic Church, building a system that 19th-century liberal revolutions failed to dismantle.

But eventual independence did not necessarily bring regional unity: Boundary wars dragged on into the 20th century before yielding the present-day borders of 12 nations. French Guiana remains an overseas department ruled from Paris; the Falkland Islands are a dependent territory of the United Kingdom. Natural riches still dominate economies, in the form of processed agricultural goods and minerals, as manufacturing matures. Privatization of nationalized industries in the 1990s followed free-market policies instituted by military regimes in the '70s and '80s, sometimes adding tumult to nations troubled by debt and inflation. By the end of the century however, democracy had flowered across the continent, spurring an era of relative prosperity.

A rich blend of Iberian, African, and Amerindian traditions, South America has one of the world's most lively and distinctive cultures. Although the majority of people can still trace their ancestors back to Spain or Portugal, waves of immigration have transformed South America into an ethnic smorgasbord. This blend has produced a vibrant modern culture with influence far beyond the bounds of its South American cradle.

The vast majority of South Americans live in cities rather than the rain forest or mountains. A massive rural exodus since the 1950s has transformed South America into the second most urbanized continent (after Australia), a region that now boasts three of the world's 15 largest cities—Sao Paulo, Buenos Aires, and Rio de Janeiro. Ninety percent of the people live within 200 miles (320 km) of the coast, leaving huge expanses of the interior virtually unpopulated. Despite protests from indigenous tribes and environmental groups, South American governments have tried to spur growth by opening up the Amazon region to economic exploitation, thereby wreaking ecological havoc. The Amazon could very well be the key to the region's economic future—not by the decimation of the world's richest forest, but by the sustainable management and commercial development of its largely untapped biodiversity into medical, chemical, and nutritional products.

see land cover key, page 10

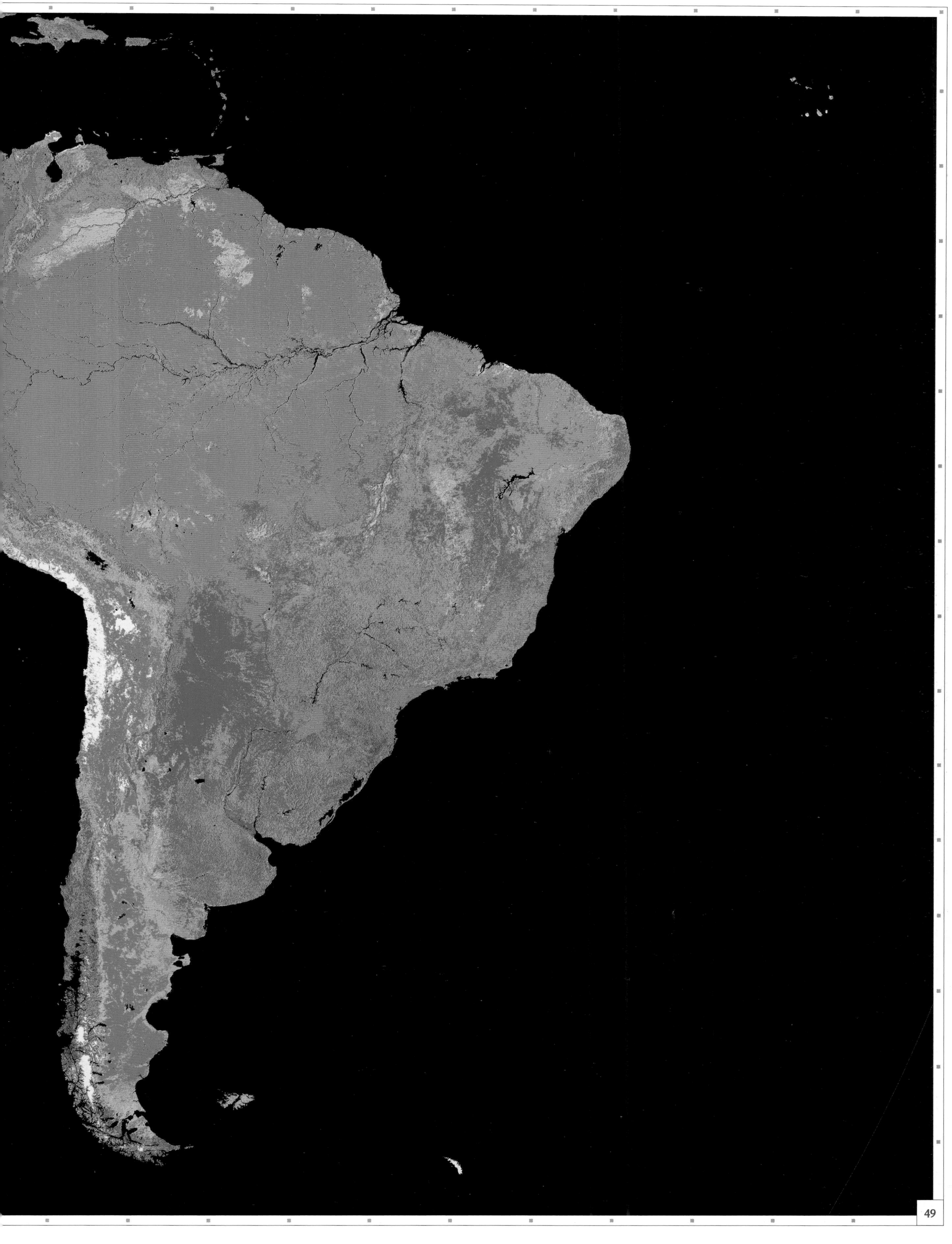

Longitude West 55° of Greenwich
EQUATOR
TROPIC OF CAPRICORN
PANAMA
COLOMBIA
VENEZUELA
GUYANA
SURINAME
FRENCH GUIANA
France
Boundary claimed by Suriname
ECUADOR
PERU
BRAZIL
BOLIVIA
PARAGUAY
ANDES
TRINIDAD AND TOBAGO
Tobago
Trinidad
I. de San Andrés
Colombia
Isla de Malpelo
Colombia
Golfo de Panamá
Golfo de Venezuela
Golfo de Guayaquil
Lago Titicaca
Arquipélago de Fernando de Noronha
Brazil
Atol das Rocas
Brazil
Ilha de Marajó
Represa da Balbina
Represa de Sobradinho
PANAMA CANAL
Panamá
BARRANQUILLA
CARTAGENA
Santa Marta
Ríohacha
MARACAIBO
Valledupar
Punto Fijo
Coro
Barquisimeto
San Felipe
Los Teques
Maracay
CARACAS
VALENCIA
Barcelona
Cumaná
Porlamar
Carúpano
Port-of-Spain
Maturín
Tucupita
Ciudad Guayana
Ciudad Bolívar
El Tigre
San Fernando de Apure
Calabozo
Acarigua
Guanare
Barinas
Valera
San Carlos
Mérida
San Cristóbal
Cúcuta
Guasdualito
Arauca
Sincelejo
Montería
Magangué
Ocaña
Turbo
Pamplona
Bucaramanga
Barrancabermeja
Jurado
MEDELLÍN
Bello
Puerto Berrío
Quibdó
La Dorada
Duitama
Sogamoso
Tunja
Manizales
Pereira
BOGOTÁ
Villavicencio
Armenia
Tuluá
Buenaventura
CALI
Palmira
Neiva
Guapí
Popayán
Florencia
Tumaco
Pasto
Mocoa
Ipiales
Esmeraldas
QUITO
Manta
Portoviejo
Babahoyo
GUAYAQUIL
Milagro
Riobamba
Cuenca
Machala
Tumbes
Loja
Talara
Sullana
Paita
Piura
Chiclayo
TRUJILLO
Chimbote
Huaraz
Cajamarca
Chachapoyas
Moyobamba
Tarapoto
Yurimaguas
Iquitos
Nauta
Pucallpa
Huánuco
Cerro de Pasco
Huacho
Huaral
Callao
LIMA
Chorrillos
La Oroya
Huancayo
Huancavelica
Ayacucho
Cusco
Chincha Alta
Pisco
Ica
Nasca
Arequipa
Puno
Mollendo
Moquegua
Tacna
Arica
Iquique
Tocopilla
Calama
Antofagasta
Taltal
LA PAZ
COCHABAMBA
Oruro
Sucre
Potosí
Santa Cruz
Trinidad
Tarija
Riberalta
Cobija
Puerto Maldonado
Georgetown
Lethem
Paramaribo
Nieuw Nickerie
Cayenne
Oiapoque
Macapá
Amapá
Boa Vista
Caracaraí
MANAUS
Santarém
Altamira
Tefé
Coari
Leticia
Porto Velho
Rio Branco
Ji-Paraná (Rondônia)
BELÉM
São Luís
FORTALEZA
Teresina
Natal
João Pessoa
RECIFE
Maceió
Aracaju
SALVADOR (Bahia)
Feira de Santana
Marabá
Imperatriz
Palmas
BRASÍLIA
Goiânia
Anápolis
Cuiabá
Campo Grande
Corumbá
BELO HORIZONTE
Uberlândia
Uberaba
Vitória
RIO DE JANEIRO
Niterói
Duque de Caxias
NOVA IGUAÇU
SÃO PAULO
Santos
Campinas
Santo André
Sorocaba
Londrina
Maringá
CURITIBA
Paranaguá
Foz do Iguaçu
Ciudad del Este
Asunción
Pedro Juan Caballero
Concepción
Amazonas (Amazon)
Solimões (Amazonas)
Negro
Branco
Madeira
Purus
Tapajós
Xingu
Tocantins
Araguaia
São Francisco
Paraná
Paraguay
Orinoco
Marañón

SOUTH AMERICA

Political

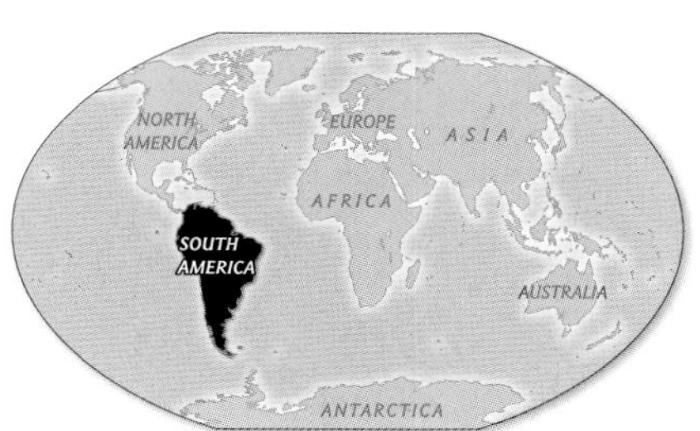

CONTINENTAL DATA

- **Total number of countries:** 12
- **First independent country:** Colombia, July 20, 1810
- **"Youngest" country:** Suriname, Nov. 25, 1975
- **Largest country by area:** Brazil 8,547,403 sq km (3,300,169 sq mi)
- **Smallest country by area:** Suriname 163,265 sq km (63,037 sq mi)
- **Percent urban population:** 79%
- **Most populous country:** Brazil 176,464,000
- **Least populous country:** Suriname 444,000
- **Most densely populated country:** Ecuador 44 per sq km (115 per sq mi)
- **Least densely populated country:** Suriname 2.7 per sq km (7 per sq mi)
- **Largest city by population:** São Paulo, Brazil 17,962,000
- **Highest GDP per capita:** Argentina $10,200
- **Lowest GDP per capita:** Bolivia $2,600
- **Average life expectancy in South America:** 70 years
- **Average literacy rate in South America:** 91%

Longitude West 55° of Greenwich
EQUATOR
TROPIC OF CAPRICORN
CARIBBEAN SEA
LESSER ANTILLES
Guajira Peninsula
Gulf of Venezuela
Paraguaná Pen.
Tortuga I.
Margarita I.
Paria Pen.
Tobago
Trinidad
Serra Nevada de Santa Marta 5775
Lake Maracaibo
L. Valencia
Coast Range 2660
Orinoco River Delta
PANAMA CANAL
Gulf of Morrosquillo
Gulf of Urabá
Isthmus of Panama
Gulf of Panama
Magdalena
Maracaibo Basin
5007
Cordillera de Mérida
Apure
LLANOS
Orinoco
Shell Beach
Angel Falls
Total drop 979 meters
World's highest waterfall
Cauca
Serranía de Baudó
4080
Cordillera Central
Cordillera Oriental
5493
Tomo
Pakaraima Mts.
Mt. Roraima 2772
GUIANA HIGHLANDS
Essequibo
Devil's Island
Maroni
Cape Orange
Wilhelmina Mts.
Sierra Pacaraima
Kanuku Mts.
854
Serra de Tumucumaque
Malpelo Island
Buenaventura Bay
Guaviare
Source of the Orinoco
Tacutu
Maracá Island
Mouths of the Amazon
Paru
Pico da Neblina 3014
Galera Point
Ajajú
Negro
Branco
Balbina Reservoir
Gurupá I.
Marajó Island
Marajó Bay
Cape Gurupi
AMAZON
Chimborazo 6310
Napo
Amazon
Amazon (Solimões)
Xingu
São Marcos Bay
Pt. Jericoacoara
Tocantins
Serra do Tiracambu
Santa Elena Peninsula
Gulf of Guayaquil
Pongo de Manseriche
Juruá
Purus
Madeira
Tapajós
Selvas
Caatinga
Parnaíba
Sa. da Ibiapaba 725
Fernando de Noronha
Atol das Rocas
Cape São Roque
Marañón
Aguja Point
Sechura Desert
Lobos Islands
Cordillera Oriental
Cordillera Central
Ucayali
LA MONTAÑA
BASIN
Araguaia
Teles Pires
Sa. do Uruçuí
Sobradinho Reservoir
Borborema Plateau 1123
São Francisco
Sertão
Nevado Huascarán 6768
ANDES
OCCIDENTAL
Beni
Jiparaná
Juruena
Serra do Tombador
Serra Formosa
Serra dos Parecis
640
670
Sa. do Roncador
BRAZILIAN HIGHLANDS
Espigão Mestre
Manguinho Point
Mamoré
Guaporé
MATO GROSSO PLATEAU
Serra Dourada
1349
Campos
Todos os Santos Bay
Chincha Is.
Apurímac
Source of the Amazon
Lake Titicaca
3810
Illampu 6362
Yungas
Illimani 6462
Securé
Cord. Oriental
Cordillera Central
Altiplano
5453
Grande
Bañados del Izozog
Paraguay
Pantanal
Serra de Maracaju 558
Paranaíba
Serra do Espinhaço
2040
Baleia Point
Madrid Point
Salar de Uyuni
Atacama Desert
Chaco Boreal
Pilcomayo
Paraná
Pico de la Bandeira 2890
Source of the Paraná
Serra da Mantiqueira
Cape São Tomé
Cape Frio
Angamos Point
Sete Quedas Falls
Iguaçu Falls
Cerro Galan 6600
PACIFIC OCEAN
200

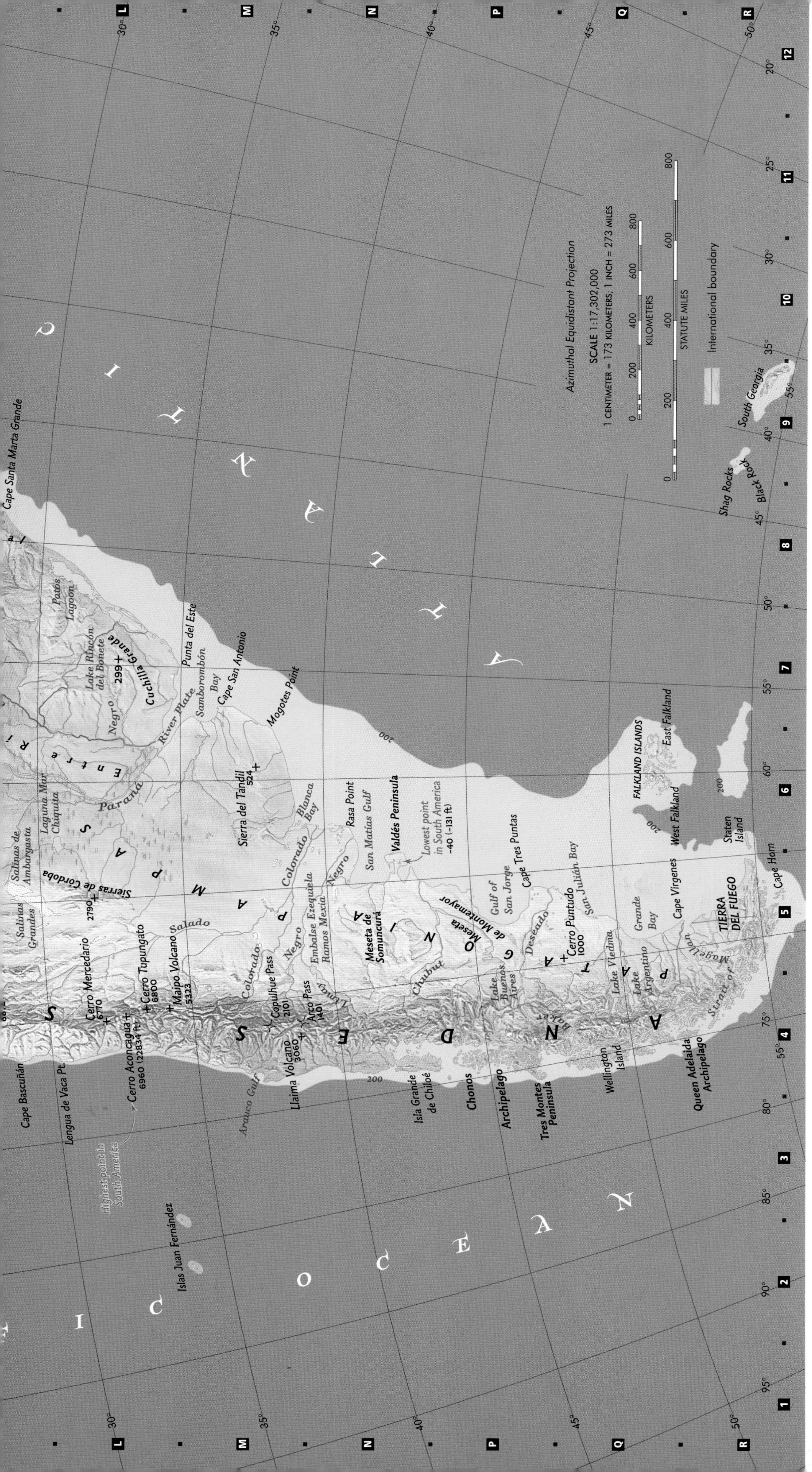

SOUTH AMERICA
Physical

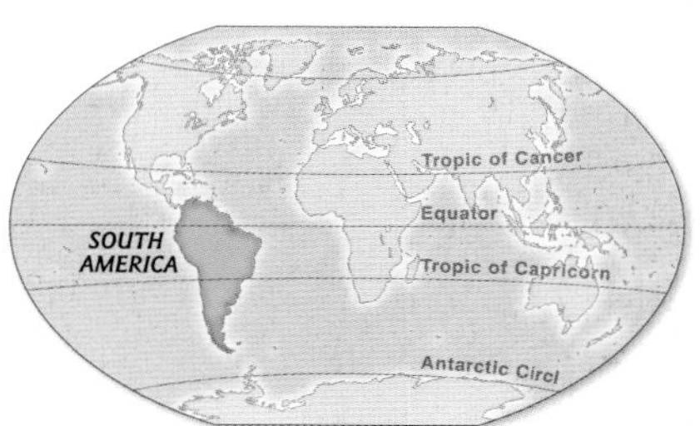

CONTINENTAL DATA

- **Area:**
  17,819,000 sq km
  (6,880,000 sq mi)
- **Greatest north-south extent:**
  7,645 km (4,750 mi)
- **Greatest east-west extent:**
  5,150 km (3,200 mi)
- **Highest point:**
  Cerro Aconcagua, Argentina
  6,960 m (22,834 ft)
- **Lowest point:**
  Valdés Peninsula, Argentina
  -40 m (-131 ft)
- **Lowest recorded temperature:**
  Sarmiento, Argentina -33°C
  (-27°F), June 1, 1907
- **Highest recorded temperature:**
  Rivadavia, Argentina 49°C (120°F),
  December 11, 1905
- **Longest rivers:**
  - Amazon 6,437 km (4,000 mi)
  - Paraná-Río de la Plata 4,000 km (2,485 mi)
  - Purus 3,380 km (2,100 mi)
- **Largest lakes:**
  - Lake Titicaca 8,290 sq km (3,200 sq mi)
  - Lake Poopó, 2,499 sq km (965 sq mi)
  - Lake Buenos Aires, 2,240 sq km (865 sq mi)
- **Earth's extremes located in South America:**
  - **Driest place:** Arica, Atacama Desert, Chile; rainfall barely measurable
  - **Highest Waterfall:** Angel Falls, Venezuela 979 m (3,212 ft)

SOUTH AMERICA
FLAGS & FACTS

ARGENTINA
ARGENTINE REPUBLIC

AREA 2,780,400 sq km (1,073,518 sq mi)
POPULATION 36,925,000
CAPITAL Buenos Aires 12,106,000
RELIGION Roman Catholic
LANGUAGE Spanish, English, Italian, German, French
LITERACY 96%
LIFE EXPECTANCY 74 years
GDP PER CAPITA $10,200
ECONOMY **IND:** food processing, motor vehicles, consumer durables, textiles. **AGR:** sunflower seeds, lemons, soybeans, grapes; livestock. **EXP:** edible oils, fuels and energy, cereals, feed.

BOLIVIA
REPUBLIC OF BOLIVIA

AREA 1,098,581 sq km (424,164 sq mi)
POPULATION 8,595,000
CAPITAL La Paz (administrative) 1,499,000; Sucre (legal) 183,000
RELIGION Roman Catholic
LANGUAGE Spanish, Quechua, Aymara
LITERACY 83%
LIFE EXPECTANCY 63 years
GDP PER CAPITA $2,600
ECONOMY **IND:** mining, smelting, petroleum, food and beverages. **AGR:** soybeans, coffee, coca, cotton; timber. **EXP:** soybeans, natural gas, zinc, gold.

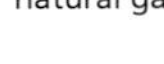

BRAZIL
FEDERATIVE REPUBLIC OF BRAZIL

AREA 8,547,403 sq km (3,300,169 sq mi)
POPULATION 176,464,000
CAPITAL Brasília 2,073,000
RELIGION Roman Catholic
LANGUAGE Portuguese, Spanish, English, French
LITERACY 83%
LIFE EXPECTANCY 69 years
GDP PER CAPITA $7,400
ECONOMY **IND:** textiles, shoes, chemicals, cement. **AGR:** coffee, soybeans, wheat, rice; beef. **EXP:** manufactures, iron ore, soybeans, footwear.

CHILE
REPUBLIC OF CHILE

AREA 756,096 sq km (291,930 sq mi)
POPULATION 15,774,000
CAPITAL Santiago 5,551,000
RELIGION Roman Catholic, Protestant
LANGUAGE Spanish
LITERACY 95%
LIFE EXPECTANCY 76 years
GDP PER CAPITA $10,000
ECONOMY **IND:** copper, other minerals, foodstuffs, fish processing. **AGR:** wheat, corn, grapes, beans; beef; timber; fish. **EXP:** copper, fish, fruits, paper and pulp.

COLOMBIA
REPUBLIC OF COLOMBIA

AREA 1,138,910 sq km (439,735 sq mi)
POPULATION 44,172,000
CAPITAL Bogotá 6,957,000
RELIGION Roman Catholic
LANGUAGE Spanish
LITERACY 91%
LIFE EXPECTANCY 71 years
GDP PER CAPITA $6,300
ECONOMY **IND:** textiles, food processing, oil, clothing and footwear. **AGR:** coffee, cut flowers, bananas, rice; forest products; shrimp. **EXP:** petroleum, coffee, coal, apparel.

ECUADOR
REPUBLIC OF ECUADOR

AREA 283,560 sq km (109,483 sq mi)
POPULATION 12,558,000
CAPITAL Quito 1,660,000
RELIGION Roman Catholic
LANGUAGE Spanish, Quechua
LITERACY 90%
LIFE EXPECTANCY 71 years
GDP PER CAPITA $3,000
ECONOMY **IND:** petroleum, food processing, textiles, metal work. **AGR:** bananas, coffee, cocoa, rice; cattle; balsa wood; fish. **EXP:** petroleum, bananas, shrimp, coffee.

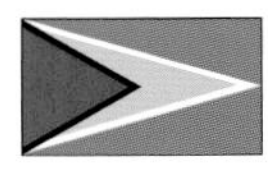

GUYANA
CO-OPERATIVE REPUBLIC OF GUYANA

AREA 214,969 sq km (83,000 sq mi)
POPULATION 765,000
CAPITAL Georgetown 280,000
RELIGION Christian, Hindu, Muslim
LANGUAGE English, Amerindian dialects, Creole, Hindi, Urdu
LITERACY 98%
LIFE EXPECTANCY 63 years
GDP PER CAPITA $3,600
ECONOMY **IND:** bauxite, sugar, rice milling, timber. **AGR:** sugar, rice, wheat, vegetable oils; beef. **EXP:** sugar, gold, bauxite/alumina, rice.

PARAGUAY
REPUBLIC OF PARAGUAY

AREA 406,752 sq km (157,048 sq mi)
POPULATION 6,188,000
CAPITAL Asunción 1,302,000
RELIGION Roman Catholic
LANGUAGE Spanish, Guaraní
LITERACY 92%
LIFE EXPECTANCY 71 years
GDP PER CAPITA $4,600
ECONOMY **IND:** sugar, cement, textiles, beverages. **AGR:** cotton, sugarcane, soybeans, corn; beef; timber. **EXP:** electricity, soybeans, feed, cotton.

PERU
REPUBLIC OF PERU

AREA 1,285,216 sq km (496,224 sq mi)
POPULATION 27,126,000
CAPITAL Lima 7,594,000
RELIGION Roman Catholic
LANGUAGE Spanish, Quechua, Aymara
LITERACY 88%
LIFE EXPECTANCY 69 years
GDP PER CAPITA $4,800
ECONOMY **IND:** mining of metals, petroleum, fishing, textiles. **AGR:** coffee, cotton, sugarcane, rice; poultry; fish. **EXP:** fish and fish products, copper, zinc, gold.

SURINAME
REPUBLIC OF SURINAME

AREA 163,265 sq km (63,037 sq mi)
POPULATION 444,000
CAPITAL Paramaribo 240,000
RELIGION Hindu, Protestant, Roman Catholic, Muslim
LANGUAGE Dutch, English, Sranang Tongo, Hindustani, Javanese
LITERACY 93%
LIFE EXPECTANCY 70 years
GDP PER CAPITA $3,500
ECONOMY **IND:** bauxite and gold mining, alumina production, lumbering. **AGR:** paddy rice, bananas; beef; forest products. **EXP:** alumina, crude oil, lumber, shrimp and fish.

URUGUAY
ORIENTAL REPUBLIC OF URUGUAY

AREA 176,215 sq km (68,037 sq mi)
POPULATION 3,380,000
CAPITAL Montevideo 1,329,000
RELIGION Roman Catholic
LANGUAGE Spanish, Portunol, or Brazilero
LITERACY 97%
LIFE EXPECTANCY 75 years
GDP PER CAPITA $9,200
ECONOMY **IND:** food processing, electrical machinery, transportation equipment, petroleum products. **AGR:** wheat, rice, barley, corn; livestock; fish. **EXP:** meat, rice, leather products, vehicles.

VENEZUELA
BOLIVARIAN REPUBLIC OF VENEZUELA

AREA 912,050 sq km (352,144 sq mi)
POPULATION 25,698,000
CAPITAL Caracas 3,177,000
RELIGION Roman Catholic
LANGUAGE Spanish
LITERACY 91%
LIFE EXPECTANCY 73 years
GDP PER CAPITA $6,100
ECONOMY **IND:** petroleum, iron ore mining, construction materials, food processing. **AGR:** corn, sorghum, sugarcane, rice; beef; fish. **EXP:** petroleum, bauxite and aluminum, steel, chemicals.

DEPENDENCIES

SOVEREIGN

LOCAL

FALKLAND ISLANDS (U.K.)
FALKLAND ISLANDS

AREA 12,173 sq km (4,700 sq mi)
POPULATION 3,000
CAPITAL Stanley 2,000
RELIGION Anglican, Roman Catholic, other Protestant
LANGUAGE English
LITERACY NA
LIFE EXPECTANCY NA
GDP PER CAPITA $19,000
ECONOMY **IND:** wool and fish processing, sale of stamps and coins. **AGR:** fodder and vegetable crops; sheep. **EXP:** wool, hides, meat.

FRENCH GUIANA (FRANCE)
DEPARTMENT OF FRENCH GUIANA

AREA 90,000 sq km (34,749 sq mi)
POPULATION 182,000
CAPITAL Cayenne 53,000
RELIGION Roman Catholic
LANGUAGE French
LITERACY 83%
LIFE EXPECTANCY 76 years
GDP PER CAPITA $6,000
ECONOMY **IND:** construction, shrimp processing, forestry products, rum. **AGR:** rice, manioc (tapioca), sugar, cocoa; cattle. **EXP:** shrimp, timber, gold, rum.

POPULATION DENSITY

People per square mile	People per square km
250 and greater	100 and greater
60–250	25–99
25–59	10–24
2–24	1–9
Less than 2	Less than 1
Uninhabited	Uninhabited

DATES OF COUNTRY INDEPENDENCE

CARIBBEAN SEA
VENEZUELA
July 5, 1811
SURINAME
November 25, 1975
French Guiana (France)
COLOMBIA
July 20, 1810
GUYANA
May 26, 1966
ECUADOR
May 24, 1822
BRAZIL
September 7, 1822
PERU
July 28, 1821
BOLIVIA
August 6, 1825
PARAGUAY
May 14, 1811
PACIFIC
OCEAN
ARGENTINA
July 9, 1816
CHILE
September 18, 1810
URUGUAY
August 25, 1825
ATLANTIC
OCEAN
Falkland Islands
(United Kingdom)

EUROPE

Europe appears from space as a cluster of peninsulas and islands thrusting westward from Asia into the Atlantic Ocean. The smallest continent except Australia, Europe nonetheless has a population density second only to Asia's. Colliding tectonic plates and retreating Ice Age glaciers continue to shape Europe's fertile plains and rugged mountains, and the North Atlantic's Gulf Stream tempers the continent's climate. Europe's highly irregular coastline measures more than one and a half times the length of the Equator, leaving only 13 out of 43 counties landlocked.

Europe has been inhabited for some 40,000 years. During the last millennium Europeans explored the planet and established far-flung empires, leaving their imprint on every corner of the Earth. Europe led the world in science and invention, and launched the industrial revolution. Great periods of creativity in the arts have occurred at various times all over the continent and shape its collective culture. By the end of the 19th century Europe dominated world commerce, spreading European ideas, languages, legal systems, and political patterns around the globe. But the Europeans who explored, colonized, and knitted the world's regions together knew themselves only as Portuguese, Spanish, Dutch, British, French, German, Russian. After centuries of rivalry and war, the two devastating world wars launched from its soil in the 20th century ended Europe's world dominance. By the 1960s nearly all its colonies had gained independence.

European countries divided into two blocs, playing out the new superpowers' Cold War—the west allied to North America and the east bound to the Soviet Union, with Germany split between them. From small beginnings in the 1950s, Western Europe began to unify. Germany's unification and the Soviet Union's unexpected breakup in the early 1990s sped the movement. Led by former enemies France and Germany, 15 countries of Western Europe now form the European Union (EU), with common European citizenship. Several Eastern European countries clamor to join. In 1999, 12 of the EU members adopted a common currency, the euro, creating a single economic market, one of the largest in the world. Political union will come harder. A countercurrent of nationalism and ethnic identity has splintered the Balkan Peninsula, and the future of Russia is impossible to predict.

Next to Asia, Europe has the world's densest population. Scores of distinct ethnic groups, speaking some 40 languages, inhabit more than 40 countries, which vary in size from European Russia to tiny Luxembourg, each with its own history and traditions. Yet Europe has a more uniform culture than any other continent. Its population is overwhelmingly of one race, Caucasian, despite the recent arrival of immigrants from Africa and Asia. Most of its languages fall into three groups with Indo-European roots: Germanic, Romance, or Slavic. One religion, Christianity, predominates in various forms, and social structures nearly everywhere are based on economic classes. However, immigrant groups established as legitimate and illegal workers, refugees, and asylum seekers cling to their own habits, religions, and languages. Every European society is becoming more multicultural, with political as well as cultural consequences.

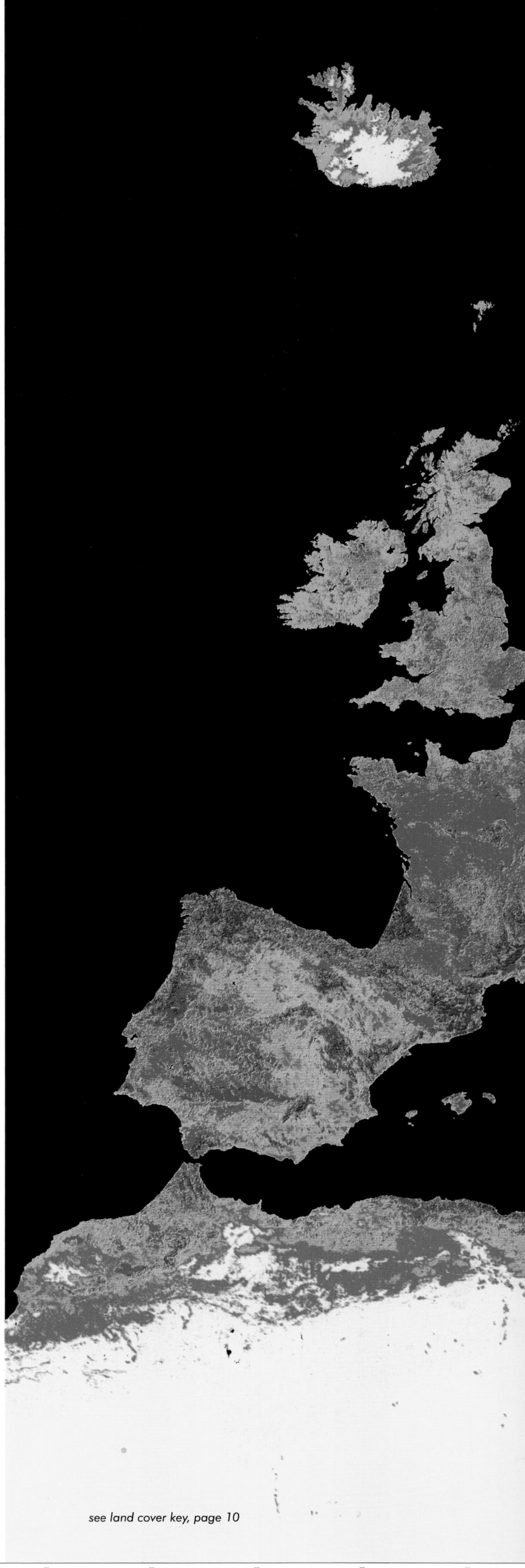

see land cover key, page 10

Azimuthal Equidistant Projection
SCALE 1:13,664,000
1 CENTIMETER = 137 KILOMETERS; 1 INCH = 215 MILES
0 100 200 300 400 500
KILOMETERS
0 100 200 300 400 500
STATUTE MILES
Small country
ICELAND
Ísafjörður
Akureyri
Keflavík
Reykjavík
Surtsey
Vestmannaeyjar
Höfn
Neskaupstadur
NORWEGIAN SEA
ARCTIC CIRCLE
FAROE ISLANDS (FØROYAR) Denmark
Tórshavn
Meridian of Greenwich (London)
SHETLAND ISLANDS
Mainland
Lerwick
ORKNEY ISLANDS
Kirkwall
Thurso
Stornoway
Isle of Lewis
Outer Hebrides
Island of Skye
Rockall U.K.
ATLANTIC OCEAN
Inverness
Aberdeen
SCOTLAND
Perth
Dundee
Greenock
Glasgow
Edinburgh
Londonderry
NORTHERN IRELAND
Sligo
Dundalk
Belfast
Baile Átha Cliath (Dublin)
Galway
Limerick
IRELAND
Tralee
Waterford
Cork
IRISH SEA
Newcastle
Sunderland
UNITED KINGDOM
Leeds
Liverpool
Manchester
Sheffield
WALES
ENGLAND
Swansea
Cardiff
BIRMINGHAM
Bristol
LONDON
Plymouth
Southampton
CELTIC SEA
Isles of Scilly
ENGLISH CHANNEL
Channel Islands U.K.
NORTH SEA
Hammerfest
Sørøya
Berlevåg
Vadsø
Lakselv
Alta
Tromsø
Kirkenes
Nikel
Polyarny
Murmansk
Ivalo
Inari
Harstad
Lofoten
Vesterålen
Svolvær
Narvik
Kiruna
Monchegorsk
Apatity
Kandalaksha
Kemijärvi
Gällivare
Bodø
Mo i Rana
Mosjøen
Rovaniemi
Boden
Kemi
Luleå
Arvidsjaur
Piteå
Oulu
Storuman
Namsos
Gäddede
Skellefteå
Raahe
Steinkjer
Kajaani
Kokkola
Jakobstad
Umeå
Trondheim
Kristiansund
Molde
Ålesund
Örnsköldsvik
Östersund
Kramfors
Vaasa
Seinäjoki
Nurmes
Kuopio
Joensuu
Røros
Sundsvall
Jyväskylä
Savonlinna
Florø
Bergen
Sognefjorden
Lillehammer
Gjøvik
Hamar
Hønefoss
Bollnäs
Pori
Rauma
Tampere
Mikkeli
Lappeenranta
Imatra
Lahti
Hämeenlinna
Turku
Kotka
Helsinki
GULF OF BOTHNIA
Haugesund
Oslo
Drammen
Falun
Borlänge
Gävle
ÅLAND
Stavanger
Skien
Karlstad
Västerås
Uppsala
Egersund
Kristiansand
Mandal
Fredrikstad
Arendal
Örebro
Stockholm
GULF OF FINLAND
Tallinn
Narva
Slantsy
Luga
NORWAY
SWEDEN
FINLAND
ESTONIA
Pärnu
Tartu
Lake Peipus
Pskov
Novgor
Göteborg
Trollhättan
Norrköping
Linköping
Jönköping
GOTLAND
Visby
Ventspils
Gulf of Riga
Riga
Valmiera
Frederikshavn
Ålborg
Randers
Århus
JUTLAND
Esbjerg
DENMARK
Borås
Växjö
Kalmar
Halmstad
ÖLAND
Karlskrona
Liepāja
LATVIA
Jelgava
Rēzekne
Daugavpils
Šiauliai
Panevėžys
Vitsyebsk
Polatsk
København (Copenhagen)
Odense
Malmö
Helsingborg
Klaipėda
LITHUANIA
Kaunas
Vilnius
Navapolatsk
Mahilyo
BALTIC SEA
Kiel
Lübeck
Rostock
Słupsk
Koszalin
Kaliningrad
Russia
Gdańsk
Lida
MINSK
Hrodna
BELARUS
Bremerhaven
Groningen
Oldenburg
NETHERLANDS
Amsterdam
Bremen
HAMBURG
Szczecin
Bydgoszcz
Toruń
Olsztyn
Białystok
Baranavichy
Babruysk
Salihorsk
Rotterdam
Hannover
Braunschweig
BERLIN
Poznań
Wisła
WARSZAWA (Warsaw)
Brest
Pinsk
Mazyr
Antwerpen
Bielefeld
Magdeburg
Łódź
Essen
Dortmund
Bruxelles (Brussels)
BELGIUM
Lille
Charleroi
Köln
Bonn
GERMANY
Leipzig
POLAND
Lublin
Kovel'
Zhytomyr
Cherbourg
Le Havre
Amiens
Caen
Brest
Rennes
Rouen
LUXEMBOURG
Luxembourg
Wiesbaden
Frankfurt
Erfurt
Zwickau
Dresden
Chemnitz
Wrocław
Radom
Częstochowa
Kielce
Wałbrzych
Lutsk
Rivne
Berdychiv
Khmel'nyts'kyy
Lorient
Alençon
Le Mans
PARIS
Reims
Darmstadt
Würzburg
Plzeň
PRAHA (Prague)
Katowice
Kraków
Rzeszów
Przemyśl
L'viv
Ternopil'
Vinny
Angers
Nantes
Tours
Orléans
Troyes
Nancy
Karlsruhe
Mannheim
Nürnberg
CZECH REP.
Olomouc
Ostrava
České Budějovice
Brno
Ivano-Frankivs'k
Strasbourg
Stuttgart
Augsburg
MÜNCHEN (Munich)
WIEN (Vienna)
Bratislava
SLOVAKIA
Košice
CARPATHIAN MOUNTAINS
Chernivtsi
La Rochelle
Poitiers
FRANCE
Dijon
Besançon
Mulhouse
Freiburg
Basel
Bern
Zürich
Innsbruck
Salzburg
Linz
Miskolc
Nyíregyháza
Baia Mare
Bălți
Chișinău
BAY OF BISCAY
Limoges
Clermont-Ferrand
Lausanne
Genève
SWITZERLAND
LIECH.
AUSTRIA
Graz
Győr
BUDAPEST
Debrecen
Oradea
Bacău
Bordeaux
Lyon
MASSIF CENTRAL
Saint-Étienne
Grenoble
Bergamo
MILANO (Milan)
Trento
Bolzano
Maribor
SLOVENIA
Ljubljana
Zagreb
HUNGARY
Cluj-Napoca
Târgu Mureș
Arad
ROMANIA
Brașov
Galați
Sibiu
Szeged
Subotica
Timișoara
A Coruña
Santiago de Compostela
Gijón
Oviedo
Santander
Donostia-San Sebastián
Bayonne
Bilbao
Lugo
Vigo
Ourense
León
Vitoria-Gasteiz
Burgos
Agen
Montauban
Toulouse
Pau
Valence
Torino
Verona
Brescia
Padova
Venezia (Venice)
Trieste
Rijeka
CROATIA
Osijek
Novi Sad
Buzău
Porto
Braga
PORTUGAL
Coimbra
Valladolid
Duero
Ebro
Pamplona
PYRENEES
ANDORRA
Andorra
Montpellier
Nîmes
Aix-en-Provence
Marseille
Toulon
MONACO
Nice
Genova (Genoa)
Riviera
La Spezia
Modena
Ferrara
Bologna
Rimini
Banja Luka
BOSNIA & HERZEGOVINA
Tuzla
BEOGRAD (Belgrade)
SERBIA
Craiova
Ploiești
Slatina
BUCUR
Constan
Zadar
Sarajevo
Zaječar
Ruse
Varna
Danube
Pleven
Salamanca
Segovia
Zaragoza
Perpignan
Pisa
Firenze
SAN MARINO
Ancona
Split
MONTENEGRO
Mostar
Niš
Novi Pazar
Priština
Vratsa
Gabrovo
Santarém
Lisboa (Lisbon)
Setúbal
MADRID
SPAIN
Tagus
Tarragona
Lleida
BARCELONA
Bastia
Elba
Perugia
Terni
Teramo
Dubrovnik
Podgorica
Prizren
SOFIYA (Sofia)
BULGARIA
Stara
Zagora
Cáceres
Mérida
Badajoz
Toledo
CORSE (CORSICA) France
Ajaccio
Civitavecchia
Pescara
Shkodër
Skopje
Plovdiv
Khaskovo
Castelló de la Plana
Valencia
VATICAN CITY
ROMA (Rome)
ITALY
Foggia
Bari
Tiranë (Tirana)
Elbasan
MACEDONIA
Xánthi
Guadiana
Ciudad Real
Linares
Albacete
BALEARIC SEA
Menorca
Sassari
Olbia
Benevento
NAPOLI (NAPLES)
Brindisi
ALBANIA
Bitola
Kavála
Faro
Huelva
Córdoba
Lucena
Jaén
Murcia
Palma de Mallorca
Mallorca
BALEARIC ISLANDS Spain
Ibiza
SARDEGNA (SARDINIA) Italy
Nuoro
Salerno
Potenza
Taranto
Vlorë
Lecce
Korçë
Thessaloníki
Sevilla
Granada
Alicante
TYRRHENIAN SEA
Oristano
Iglesias
Carbonia
Cagliari
Castrovillari
Ioánina
Lárissa
Balkan
Cádiz
Jerez
Strait of Gibraltar
Algeciras
GIBRALTAR U.K.
Málaga
Almería
Cartagena
Ceuta Sp.
Alborán Spain
ALBORAN SEA
Melilla Sp.
Cosenza
Catanzaro
Kérkira (Corfu)
Vólos
GREECE
Lésvos
Híos
Lefkáda
Évia
Kefallinía
Zákinthos
IONIAN SEA
Pátra
Pireás
Athína (Athens)
PELOPONNISOS
Kikládes
DODEKA
AEGEAN SEA
MEDITERRANEAN SEA
ALGER (Algiers)
Palermo
Messina
Marsala
Reggio di Calabria
SICILY
Catania
Ragusa
Siracusa
Kalamáta
RABAT
TUNIS
Pantelleria Italy
Isole Pelagie Italy
MALTA
Valletta
Thíra
SEA OF CRETE
Kárpathos
Haniá (Canea)
Iráklio
KRÍTI (CRETE)
MOROCCO
ALGERIA
TUNISIA
AFRICA
LIBYA
TARĀBULUS (Tripoli)
Longitude West 5° of Greenwich
Longitude East 5° of Greenwich

EUROPE
Political

A commonly accepted division between Asia and Europe–here marked by a green line–is formed by the Ural Mountains, Ural River, Caspian Sea, Caucasus Mountains, and the Black Sea with its outlets, the Bosporus and Dardanelles.

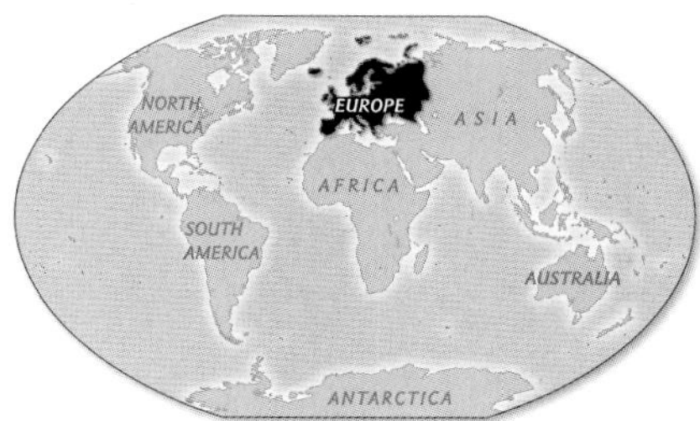

CONTINENTAL DATA

- **Total number of countries:** 43
- **First independent country:** San Marino, September 3, 301
- **"Youngest" countries:** Czech Republic, January 1, 1993; Slovakia, January 1, 1993
- **Largest country by area:** Russia 17,074,993 sq km (6,592,692 sq mi)
- **Smallest country by area:** Vatican City 0.4 sq km (0.2 sq mi)
- **Percent urban population:** 73%
- **Most populous country:** Russia 145,546,000
- **Least populous country:** Vatican City 1,000
- **Most densely populated country** Monaco 17,503 per sq km (45,333 per sq mi)
- **Least densely populated country:** Iceland 2.7 per sq km (7 per sq mi)
- **Largest city by population:** Paris, France 9,658,000
- **Highest GDP per capita:** Luxembourg $44,000
- **Lowest GDP per capita:** Bosnia and Herzegovina $1,800
- **Average life expectancy in Europe:** 74 years
- **Average literacy rate in Europe:** 97%

A commonly accepted division between Asia and Europe–here marked by a green line–is formed by the Ural Mountains, Ural River, Caspian Sea, Caucasus Mountains, and the Black Sea with its outlets, the Bosporus and Dardanelles.
Azimuthal Equidistant Projection
SCALE 1:13,664,000
1 CENTIMETER = 137 KILOMETERS; 1 INCH = 215 MILES
0 100 200 300 400 500
KILOMETERS
0 100 200 300 400 500
STATUTE MILES
International boundary
Breidafjördur
Húnaflói
Faxaflói
Rifstangi
Reykjanes
1446
ICELAND
Hekla
1491
Vatnajökull
Surtsey
Vestmannaeyjar
Hvannadalshnúkur
2119
NORWEGIAN SEA
ARCTIC CIRCLE
ATLANTIC OCEAN
Faroe Islands
Shetland Islands
Orkney Islands
Outer Hebrides
Inner Hebrides
Moray Firth
Ben Nevis
1343
Highlands
Grampian Mts.
BRITISH ISLES
GREAT BRITAIN
Donegal B.
L. Neagh
Firth of Forth
Southern Uplands
IRELAND
IRISH SEA
Isle of Man
The Pennines
Shannon
Snowdon
1085
Carrantuohill
1041
Cambrian Mts.
Thames
CELTIC SEA
Land's End
English Channel
Channel Islands
Point St.-Mathieu
Armorican Massif
417
NORTH SEA
Trondheimsfjorden
Sognefjorden
Hardangerfjorden
Galdhøpiggen
2469
1796
Mjøsa
Glåma
Klarälven
Mälaren
Vänern
Vättern
Skagerrak
Kattegat
JUTLAND
FYN
ZEALAND
SCANDINAVIA
North Cape
Varangerfjorden
Finnmark Plateau
Inari
Lofoten
Vesterålen
Vestfjorden
Kebnekaise
2111
Torneälven
Luleälven
Storavan
Umeälven
Ångermanälven
Indalsälven
Kemi
Oulu
Oulujärvi
Pielinen
Suomen Ridge
Lake Region
231
Päijänne
Saimaa
Salpaus Ridge
Maan Ridge
651
Lake Imandra
L. Pya
GULF OF BOTHNIA
Åland Is.
GULF OF FINLAND
Hiiumaa
Saaremaa
Gulf of Riga
L. Peipus
L. Pskov
Velikaya
Western Dvina
Gotland
Öland
BALTIC SEA
BALTIC PLAINS
Neman
Gulf of Gdańsk
Vistula
Frisian Islands
IJsselmeer
Weser
Elbe
Oder
Rhine
NORTHERN EUROPEAN
MITTELLAND CANAL
Harz
1141
Meuse
Ardennes
Moselle
Main
Ore Mts.
1244
Sudeten
1602
Bohemian Forest
Pinsk Marshes
Bug
Prypyats'
Volyn-Podolian
Seine
PARIS BASIN
Loire
Vosges
1424
Black Forest
1493
Source of the Danube
Danube
Lake Constance
Sources of the Rhine
Jura Mts.
L. of Geneva
Grossglockner
3798
Neusiedler Lake
CARPATHIAN MOUNTAINS
Gerlach
2655
Dniester
301
Saône
Puy de Sancy
1886
MASSIF CENTRAL
Mont Blanc
4807
4476
Matterhorn
ALPS
L. Como
L. Garda
Bakony
Balaton
Great Hungarian Plain
Tisza
2303
Transylvania
Mures
Olt
2543
Transylvanian Alps
BAY OF BISCAY
Cape Finisterre
Cantabrian Mountains
2648
AQUITAINE BASIN
Garonne
Cévennes
1702
Rhône
Piedmont
Po
Gulf of Venice
Drava
Sava
DINARIC ALPS
Iron Gate
PYRENEES
Pico de Aneto
3404
Ebro
IBERIAN PENINSULA
Douro
Iberian Mountains
2316
MESETA
Tagus
Gulf of Lions
3297
Riviera
LIGURIAN SEA
APENNINES
ADRIATIC SEA
Corno Grande
2912
Dalmatia
Durmitor
2522
Morava
BALKAN PENINSULA
Balkan Mountains
2376
Ludogorie
Maritsa
2925
Rhodope Mts.
CORSICA
2710
Tiber
Guadiana
Sierra Morena
1300
Cape St. Vincent
Guadalquivir
Baetic Mountains
Mulhacén
3478
Strait of Gibraltar
ALBORAN SEA
BALEARIC SEA
1445
Minorca
Majorca
Iviza
BALEARIC ISLANDS
SARDINIA
1834
TYRRHENIAN SEA
Vesuvius
1281
Strait of Otranto
L. Ohrid
2637
Pindus Mts.
Olympus
2917
Thessaly
Northern Sporades
Euboea
Dardanelles
Calabria
IONIAN SEA
IONIAN ISLANDS
Parnassus
2457
PELOPONNESUS
Cyclades
SICILY
Etna
3322
Malta
MALTESE ISLANDS
SEA OF CRETE
CRETE
MEDITERRANEAN
Er Rif
ATLAS MOUNTAINS
SAHARA
AFRICA
Gulf of Sidra
Longitude West 5° of Greenwich
Longitude East 5° of Greenwich

EUROPE
Physical

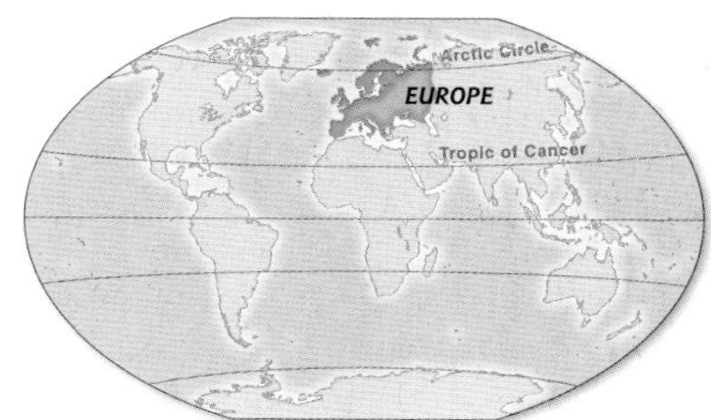

CONTINENTAL DATA

- **Area:**
  9,938,000 sq km
  (3,837,000 sq mi)
- **Greatest north-south extent:**
  4,800 km (2,980 mi)
- **Greatest east-west extent:**
  6,400 km (3,980 mi)
- **Highest point:**
  El'brus, Republic of Georgia-Russia
  5,642 m (18,510 ft)
- **Lowest point:**
  Caspian Sea -28 m (-92 ft)
- **Lowest recorded temperature:**
  Ust'Shchugor, Russia -55°C (-67°F),
  Date unknown
- **Highest recorded temperature:**
  Seville, Spain 50°C (122°F),
  August 4, 1881
- **Longest rivers:**
  - Volga 3,685 km (2,290 mi)
  - Danube 2,848 km (1,770 mi)
  - Dnieper 2,285 km (1,420 mi)
- **Largest lakes:**
  - Caspian Sea 371,000 sq km (143,200 sq mi)
  - Lake Ladoga 17,872 sq km (6,900 sq mi)
  - Lake Onega 9,842 sq km (3,800 sq mi)

ALBANIA

REPUBLIC OF ALBANIA

AREA	28,748 sq km (11,100 sq mi)
POPULATION	3,135,000
CAPITAL	Tirana 299,000
RELIGION	Muslim, Albanian Orthodox, Roman Catholic
LANGUAGE	Albanian, Greek
LITERACY	93%
LIFE EXPECTANCY	74 years
GDP PER CAPITA	$4,500

ECONOMY IND: food processing, textiles and clothing, lumber, oil. AGR: wheat, corn, potatoes, vegetables; meat. EXP: textiles and footwear, asphalt, metals and metallic ores, crude oil.

ANDORRA

PRINCIPALITY OF ANDORRA

AREA	468 sq km (181 sq mi)
POPULATION	67,000
CAPITAL	Andorra 21,000
RELIGION	Roman Catholic
LANGUAGE	Catalan, French, Castilian Spanish
LITERACY	100%
LIFE EXPECTANCY	83 years
GDP PER CAPITA	$19,000

ECONOMY IND: tourism, cattle raising, timber. AGR: tobacco, rye, wheat, barley; sheep. EXP: tobacco products, furniture.

AUSTRIA

REPUBLIC OF AUSTRIA

AREA	83,858 sq km (32,378 sq mi)
POPULATION	8,157,000
CAPITAL	Vienna 2,066,000
RELIGION	Roman Catholic, Protestant
LANGUAGE	German
LITERACY	98%
LIFE EXPECTANCY	79 years
GDP PER CAPITA	$27,700

ECONOMY IND: construction, machinery, vehicles and parts, food. AGR: grains, potatoes, sugar beets, wine; dairy products; lumber. EXP: machinery and equipment, paper and paperboard, metal goods, chemicals.

BELARUS

REPUBLIC OF BELARUS

AREA	207,595 sq km (80,153 sq mi)
POPULATION	9,873,000
CAPITAL	Minsk 1,664,000
RELIGION	Eastern Orthodox, Roman Catholic, Protestant, Jewish, Muslim
LANGUAGE	Belarusian, Russian
LITERACY	98%
LIFE EXPECTANCY	69 years
GDP PER CAPITA	$8,200

ECONOMY IND: metal-cutting machine tools, tractors, trucks, earth movers. AGR: grain, potatoes, vegetables, sugar beets; beef. EXP: machinery and equipment, chemicals, metals, textiles.

BELGIUM

KINGDOM OF BELGIUM

AREA	30,528 sq km (11,787 sq mi)
POPULATION	10,380,000
CAPITAL	Brussels 1,134,000
RELIGION	Roman Catholic, Protestant
LANGUAGE	Dutch, French, German
LITERACY	98%
LIFE EXPECTANCY	78 years
GDP PER CAPITA	$29,000

ECONOMY IND: engineering and metal products, motor vehicle assembly, processed food and beverages, chemicals. AGR: sugar beets, fresh vegetables, fruits, grain; beef. EXP: machinery and equipment, chemicals, diamonds, metals and metal products.

BOSNIA AND HERZEGOVINA

BOSNIA AND HERZEGOVINA

AREA	51,129 sq km (19,741 sq mi)
POPULATION	3,892,000
CAPITAL	Sarajevo 552,000
RELIGION	Muslim, Orthodox, Roman Catholic, Protestant
LANGUAGE	Croatian, Serbian, Bosnian
LITERACY	NA
LIFE EXPECTANCY	72 years
GDP PER CAPITA	$1,800

ECONOMY IND: vehicle assembly, textiles, tobacco products, wooden furniture. AGR: wheat, corn, fruits, vegetables; livestock. EXP: NA.

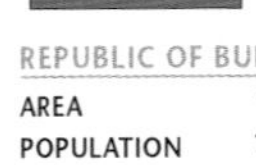

BULGARIA

REPUBLIC OF BULGARIA

AREA	110,994 sq km (42,855 sq mi)
POPULATION	7,519,000
CAPITAL	Sofia 1,187,000
RELIGION	Bulgarian Orthodox, Muslim
LANGUAGE	Bulgarian
LITERACY	98%
LIFE EXPECTANCY	72 years
GDP PER CAPITA	6,600

ECONOMY IND: electricity, gas and water, food, beverages and tobacco. AGR: vegetables, fruits, tobacco; livestock. EXP: clothing, footwear, iron and steel, machinery and equipment.

CROATIA

REPUBLIC OF CROATIA

AREA	56,542 sq km (21,831 sq mi)
POPULATION	4,287,000
CAPITAL	Zagreb 1,081,000
RELIGION	Roman Catholic, Orthodox
LANGUAGE	Croatian
LITERACY	97%
LIFE EXPECTANCY	74 years
GDP PER CAPITA	$8,800

ECONOMY IND: chemicals and plastics, machine tools, fabricated metal, electronics. AGR: wheat, corn, sugar beets, sunflower seed; livestock. EXP: transport equipment, textiles, chemicals, foodstuffs.

CZECH REPUBLIC

CZECH REPUBLIC

AREA	78,866 sq km (30,450 sq mi)
POPULATION	10,177,000
CAPITAL	Prague 1,202,000
RELIGION	Atheist, Roman Catholic, Protestant, Orthodox
LANGUAGE	Czech
LITERACY	100%
LIFE EXPECTANCY	75 years
GDP PER CAPITA	$15,300

ECONOMY IND: metallurgy, machinery and equipment, motor vehicles, glass. AGR: wheat, potatoes, sugar beets, hops; pigs. EXP: machinery and transport equipment, other manufactured goods, chemicals, raw materials and fuel.

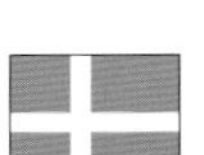

DENMARK

KINGDOM OF DENMARK

AREA	43,098 sq km (16,640 sq mi)
POPULATION	5,395,000
CAPITAL	Copenhagen 1,332,000
RELIGION	Evangelical Lutheran
LANGUAGE	Danish, Faroese, Greenlandic
LITERACY	100%
LIFE EXPECTANCY	77 years
GDP PER CAPITA	$29,000

ECONOMY IND: food processing, machinery and equipment, textiles and clothing, chemical products. AGR: grain, potatoes, rape, sugar beets; pork and beef; fish. EXP: machinery and instruments, meat and meat products, dairy products, fish.

ESTONIA

REPUBLIC OF ESTONIA

AREA	45,227 sq km (17,462 sq mi)
POPULATION	1,353,000
CAPITAL	Tallinn 401,000
RELIGION	Evangelical Lutheran, Russian Orthodox, Eastern Orthodox
LANGUAGE	Estonian, Russian, Ukrainian
LITERACY	100%
LIFE EXPECTANCY	71 years
GDP PER CAPITA	$10,900

ECONOMY IND: oil shale, shipbuilding, electric motors, cement. AGR: potatoes, fruits, vegetables; livestock and dairy products; fish. EXP: machinery and equipment, wood products, textiles, food products.

FINLAND

REPUBLIC OF FINLAND

AREA	338,145 sq km (130,558 sq mi)
POPULATION	5,212,000
CAPITAL	Helsinki 936,000
RELIGION	Evangelical Lutheran
LANGUAGE	Finnish, Swedish
LITERACY	100%
LIFE EXPECTANCY	78 years
GDP PER CAPITA	$26,200

ECONOMY IND: metal products, shipbuilding, pulp and paper, copper refining. AGR: cereals, sugar beets, potatoes; dairy; fish. EXP: machinery and equipment, chemicals, metals, timber.

FRANCE

FRENCH REPUBLIC

AREA	543,965 sq km (210,026 sq mi)
POPULATION	59,771,000
CAPITAL	Paris 9,658,000
RELIGION	Roman Catholic
LANGUAGE	French
LITERACY	99%
LIFE EXPECTANCY	79 years
GDP PER CAPITA	$25,700

ECONOMY IND: machinery, chemicals, automobiles, metallurgy. AGR: wheat, cereals, sugar beets, potatoes; beef; fish. EXP: machinery and transportation equipment, aircraft, plastics, chemicals.

GERMANY

FEDERAL REPUBLIC OF GERMANY

AREA	357,022 sq km (137,847 sq mi)
POPULATION	82,621,000
CAPITAL	Berlin 3,319,000
RELIGION	Protestant, Roman Catholic
LANGUAGE	German
LITERACY	99%
LIFE EXPECTANCY	78 years
GDP PER CAPITA	$26,600

ECONOMY IND: iron, steel, coal, cement. AGR: potatoes, wheat, sugar beets, fruits; cattle. EXP: machinery, vehicles, chemicals, metals and manufactures.

GREECE

HELLENIC REPUBLIC

AREA	131,957 sq km (50,949 sq mi)
POPULATION	10,988,000
CAPITAL	Athens 3,120,000
RELIGION	Greek Orthodox
LANGUAGE	Greek
LITERACY	97%
LIFE EXPECTANCY	78 years
GDP PER CAPITA	$19,000

ECONOMY IND: tourism, food and tobacco processing, textiles, chemicals. AGR: wheat, corn, barley, sugar beets; beef. EXP: manufactured goods, food and beverages, petroleum products.

HUNGARY

REPUBLIC OF HUNGARY

AREA	93,030 sq km (35,919 sq mi)
POPULATION	10,141,000
CAPITAL	Budapest 1,812,000
RELIGION	Roman Catholic, Calvinist, Lutheran
LANGUAGE	Hungarian
LITERACY	99%
LIFE EXPECTANCY	72 years
GDP PER CAPITA	$13,300

ECONOMY IND: mining, metallurgy, construction materials, processed foods. AGR: wheat, corn, sunflower seed, potatoes; pigs. EXP: machinery and equipment, other manufactures, food products, raw materials.

ICELAND

REPUBLIC OF ICELAND

AREA	103,000 sq km (39,769 sq mi)
POPULATION	289,000
CAPITAL	Reykjavík 175,000
RELIGION	Evangelical Lutheran
LANGUAGE	Icelandic
LITERACY	100%
LIFE EXPECTANCY	80 years
GDP PER CAPITA	$27,100

ECONOMY IND: fish processing, aluminum smelting, ferrosilicon production, geothermal power. AGR: potatoes, turnips; cattle; fish. EXP: fish and fish products, animal products, aluminum, diatomite.

IRELAND

REPUBLIC OF IRELAND

AREA	70,273 sq km (27,133 sq mi)
POPULATION	3,990,000
CAPITAL	Dublin 993,000
RELIGION	Roman Catholic
LANGUAGE	English , Irish (Gaelic)
LITERACY	98%
LIFE EXPECTANCY	77 years
GDP PER CAPITA	$28,500

ECONOMY IND: food products, brewing, textiles, clothing. AGR: turnips, barley, potatoes, sugar beets; beef. EXP: machinery and equipment, computers, chemicals, pharmaceuticals.

ITALY

ITALIAN REPUBLIC

AREA	301,338 sq km (116,347 sq mi)
POPULATION	57,166,000
CAPITAL	Rome 2,651,000
RELIGION	Roman Catholic
LANGUAGE	Italian, German, French, Slovene
LITERACY	98%
LIFE EXPECTANCY	80 years
GDP PER CAPITA	$25,000

ECONOMY IND: tourism, machinery, iron and steel, chemicals. AGR: fruits, vegetables, grapes, potatoes; beef; fish. EXP: engineering products, textiles and clothing, production machinery, motor vehicles.

LATVIA

REPUBLIC OF LATVIA

AREA 64,589 sq km (24,938 sq mi)
POPULATION 2,320,000
CAPITAL Riga 756,000
RELIGION Lutheran, Roman Catholic, Russian Orthodox
LANGUAGE Latvian, Lithuanian, Russian
LITERACY 100%
LIFE EXPECTANCY 71 years
GDP PER CAPITA $8,300
ECONOMY **IND:** buses, vans, street and railroad cars, synthetic fibers. **AGR:** grain, sugar beets, potatoes, vegetables; beef; fish. **EXP:** wood and wood products, machinery and equipment, metals, textiles.

LIECHTENSTEIN

PRINCIPALITY OF LIECHTENSTEIN

AREA 160 sq km (62 sq mi)
POPULATION 35,000
CAPITAL Vaduz 5,000
RELIGION Roman Catholic, Protestant
LANGUAGE German, Alemannic dialect
LITERACY 100%
LIFE EXPECTANCY 79 years
GDP PER CAPITA $23,000
ECONOMY **IND:** electronics, metal manufacturing, textiles, ceramics. **AGR:** wheat, barley, corn, potatoes; livestock. **EXP:** small specialty machinery, dental products, stamps, hardware

LITHUANIA

REPUBLIC OF LITHUANIA

AREA 65,301 sq km (25,213 sq mi)
POPULATION 3,458,000
CAPITAL Vilnius 579,000
RELIGION Roman Catholic, Lutheran, Russian Orthodox, Protestant
LANGUAGE Lithuanian, Polish, Russian
LITERACY 98%
LIFE EXPECTANCY 72 years
GDP PER CAPITA $8,400
ECONOMY **IND:** metal-cutting machine tools, electric motors, television sets, refrigerators and freezers. **AGR:** grain, potatoes, sugar beets, flax; beef; fish. **EXP:** machinery and equipment, mineral products, chemicals, textiles and clothing.

LUXEMBOURG

GRAND DUCHY OF LUXEMBOURG

AREA 2,586 sq km (998 sq mi)
POPULATION 452,000
CAPITAL Luxembourg 82,000
RELIGION Roman Catholic
LANGUAGE Luxembourgish, German, French
LITERACY 100%
LIFE EXPECTANCY 78 years
GDP PER CAPITA $44,000
ECONOMY **IND:** banking, iron and steel, food processing, chemicals. **AGR:** barley, oats, potatoes, wheat; livestock. **EXP:** machinery and equipment, steel products, chemicals, rubber products.

MACEDONIA

FORMER YUGOSLAV REPUBLIC OF MACEDONIA

AREA 25,713 sq km (9,928 sq mi)
POPULATION 2,059,000
CAPITAL Skopje 437,000
RELIGION Macedonian Orthodox, Muslim
LANGUAGE Macedonian, Albanian
LITERACY NA
LIFE EXPECTANCY 73 years
GDP PER CAPITA $5,000
ECONOMY **IND:** textiles, mining, metal fabrication and electrical equipment, chemicals. **AGR:** rice, tobacco, wheat, corn; beef. **EXP:** food, beverages, tobacco, miscellaneous manufactures.

MALTA

REPUBLIC OF MALTA

AREA 316 sq km (122 sq mi)
POPULATION 396,000
CAPITAL Valletta 82,000
RELIGION Roman Catholic
LANGUAGE Maltese, English
LITERACY 89%
LIFE EXPECTANCY 77 years
GDP PER CAPITA $17,000
ECONOMY **IND:** tourism, electronics, ship building and repair, construction. **AGR:** potatoes, cauliflower, grapes, wheat; pork. **EXP:** machinery and transport equipment, manufactures.

MOLDOVA

REPUBLIC OF MOLDOVA

AREA 33,800 sq km (13,050 sq mi)
POPULATION 4,253,000
CAPITAL Chisinau 662,000
RELIGION Eastern Orthodox
LANGUAGE Moldovan, Russian, Gagauz
LITERACY 96%
LIFE EXPECTANCY 68 years
GDP PER CAPITA $3,000
ECONOMY **IND:** food processing, agricultural machinery, foundry equipment, refrigerators and freezers. **AGR:** vegetables, fruits, wine, grain; beef. **EXP:** foodstuffs, wine, tobacco, textiles and footwear.

MONACO

PRINCIPALITY OF MONACO

AREA 2 sq km (1 sq mi)
POPULATION 34,000
CAPITAL Monaco 34,000
RELIGION Roman Catholic
LANGUAGE French, English, Italian, Monégasque
LITERACY 99%
LIFE EXPECTANCY 79 years
GDP PER CAPITA $27,000
ECONOMY **IND:** tourism, construction, small-scale industrial and consumer products. **AGR:** NA. **EXP:** full customs integration with France.

NETHERLANDS

KINGDOM OF THE NETHERLANDS

AREA 41,528 sq km (16,034 sq mi)
POPULATION 16,237,000
CAPITAL Amsterdam 1,105,000
RELIGION Roman Catholic, Protestant, Muslim
LANGUAGE Dutch
LITERACY 99%
LIFE EXPECTANCY 78 years
GDP PER CAPITA $26,900
ECONOMY **IND:** agroindustries, metal and engineering products, electrical machinery and equipment, chemicals. **AGR:** grains, potatoes, sugar beets, fruits; livestock. **EXP:** machinery and equipment, chemicals, fuels, foodstuffs.

NORWAY

KINGDOM OF NORWAY

AREA 323,759 sq km (125,004 sq mi)
POPULATION 4,568,000
CAPITAL Oslo 787,000
RELIGION Evangelical Lutheran
LANGUAGE Norwegian
LITERACY 100%
LIFE EXPECTANCY 79 years
GDP PER CAPITA $31,800
ECONOMY **IND:** petroleum and gas, food processing, ship building, pulp and paper products. **AGR:** barley, other grains, potatoes; beef; fish. **EXP:** petroleum and petroleum products, machinery and equipment, metals, chemicals.

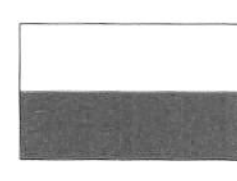

POLAND

REPUBLIC OF POLAND

AREA 312,685 sq km (120,728 sq mi)
POPULATION 38,599,000
CAPITAL Warsaw 2,282,000
RELIGION Roman Catholic
LANGUAGE Polish
LITERACY 99%
LIFE EXPECTANCY 74 years
GDP PER CAPITA $9,500
ECONOMY **IND:** machine building, iron and steel, coal mining, chemicals. **AGR:** grains, fruits, vegetables; meat. **EXP:** machinery and transport equipment, intermediate manufactured goods, miscellaneous manufactured goods, food and live animals.

PORTUGAL

PORTUGUESE REPUBLIC

AREA 92,345 sq km (35,655 sq mi)
POPULATION 10,446,000
CAPITAL Lisbon 3,942,000
RELIGION Roman Catholic
LANGUAGE Portuguese
LITERACY 87%
LIFE EXPECTANCY 77 years
GDP PER CAPITA $18,000
ECONOMY **IND:** textiles and footwear, wood pulp, paper and cork, metalworking. **AGR:** grain, potatoes, olives, grapes; sheep. **EXP:** clothing and footwear, machinery, chemicals, cork and paper products.

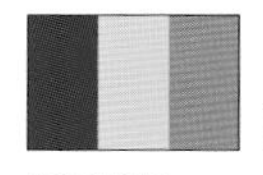

ROMANIA

ROMANIA

AREA 238,391 sq km (92,043 sq mi)
POPULATION 21,622,000
CAPITAL Bucharest 1,998,000
RELIGION Romanian Orthodox, Protestant Roman Catholic, Uniate Catholic
LANGUAGE Romanian, Hungarian, German
LITERACY 97%
LIFE EXPECTANCY 71 years
GDP PER CAPITA $6,800
ECONOMY **IND:** textiles and footwear, light machinery and auto assembly, mining, timber. **AGR:** wheat, corn, sugar beets, sunflower seed; eggs. **EXP:** textiles and footwear, metals and metal products, machinery and equipment, minerals and fuels.

RUSSIA

RUSSIAN FEDERATION

AREA 17,074,993 sq km (6,592,692 sq mi)
POPULATION 145,546,000
CAPITAL Moscow 8,316,000
RELIGION Russian Orthodox, Muslim
LANGUAGE Russian
LITERACY 98%
LIFE EXPECTANCY 65 years
GDP PER CAPITA $8,800
ECONOMY **IND:** mining, machine building, road and rail transportation equipment, communications equipment. **AGR:** grain, sugar beets, sunflower seed, vegetables; beef. **EXP:** petroleum and petroleum products, natural gas, wood and wood products, metals.

SAN MARINO

REPUBLIC OF SAN MARINO

AREA 61 sq km (24 sq mi)
POPULATION 30,000
CAPITAL San Marino 5,000
RELIGION Roman Catholic
LANGUAGE Italian
LITERACY 96%
LIFE EXPECTANCY 81 years
GDP PER CAPITA $34,600
ECONOMY **IND:** tourism, banking, textiles, electronics. **AGR:** wheat, grapes, corn, olives; cattle. **EXP:** NA.

SERBIA AND MONTENEGRO

SERBIA AND MONTENEGRO

AREA 102,173 sq km (39,450 sq mi)
POPULATION 10,684,000
CAPITAL Belgrade 1,687,000
RELIGION Orthodox, Muslim, Roman Catholic, Protestant
LANGUAGE Serbian, Albanian
LITERACY 93%
LIFE EXPECTANCY 73 years
GDP PER CAPITA $2,370
ECONOMY **IND:** machine building, metallurgy, mining, consumer goods. **AGR:** cereals, fruits, vegetables, tobacco; cattle. **EXP:** manufactured goods, food and live animals, raw materials.

SLOVAKIA

SLOVAK REPUBLIC

AREA 49,034 sq km (18,932 sq mi)
POPULATION 5,355,000
CAPITAL Bratislava 464,000
RELIGION Roman Catholic, Atheist, Protestant
LANGUAGE Slovak, Hungarian
LITERACY NA
LIFE EXPECTANCY 74 years
GDP PER CAPITA $12,200
ECONOMY **IND:** metal and metal products, food and beverages, electricity, gas. **AGR:** grains, potatoes, sugar beets, hips; pigs; forest products. **EXP:** machinery and transport equipment, intermediate manufactured goods, miscellaneous manufactured goods, chemicals.

SLOVENIA

REPUBLIC OF SLOVENIA

AREA 20,273 sq km (7,827 sq mi)
POPULATION 1,999,000
CAPITAL Ljubljana 250,000
RELIGION Roman Catholic
LANGUAGE Slovenian, Serbo-Croatian
LITERACY 99%
LIFE EXPECTANCY 76 years
GDP PER CAPITA $18,000
ECONOMY **IND:** ferrous metallurgy and rolling mill products, aluminum reduction and rolled products, lead and zinc smelting, trucks. **AGR:** potatoes, hops, wheat, sugar beets; cattle. **EXP:** manufactured goods, machinery and transport equipment, chemicals, food.

SPAIN

KINGDOM OF SPAIN

AREA 505,988 sq km (195,363 sq mi)
POPULATION 41,334,000
CAPITAL Madrid 3,969,000
RELIGION Roman Catholic
LANGUAGE Castilian Spanish, Catalan, Galician, Basque
LITERACY 97%
LIFE EXPECTANCY 79 years
GDP PER CAPITA $20,700
ECONOMY **IND:** textiles and apparel, food and beverages, metals and metal manufactures, chemicals. **AGR:** grain, vegetables, olives, wine grapes; beef; fish. **EXP:** machinery, motor vehicles, foodstuffs, other consumer goods.

SWEDEN

KINGDOM OF SWEDEN

AREA 449,964 sq km (173,732 sq mi)
POPULATION 8,960,000
CAPITAL Stockholm 1,626,000
RELIGION Lutheran
LANGUAGE Swedish
LITERACY 99%
LIFE EXPECTANCY 80 years
GDP PER CAPITA $25,400
ECONOMY **IND:** iron and steel, precision equipment, wood pulp and paper products, processed foods. **AGR:** grains, sugar beets, potatoes; meat. **EXP:** machinery, motor vehicles, paper products, pulp and wood.

SWITZERLAND

SWISS CONFEDERATION

AREA	41,284 sq km (15,940 sq mi)
POPULATION	7,341,000
CAPITAL	Bern 316,000
RELIGION	Roman Catholic, Protestant
LANGUAGE	German, French, Italian
LITERACY	99%
LIFE EXPECTANCY	80 years
GDP PER CAPITA	$31,700

ECONOMY **IND:** machinery, chemicals, watches, textiles. **AGR:** grains, fruits, vegetables; meat. **EXP:** machinery, chemicals, metals, watches.

UKRAINE

UKRAINE

AREA	603,700 sq km (233,090 sq mi)
POPULATION	47,793,000
CAPITAL	Kiev 2,488,000
RELIGION	Ukrainian Orthodox, Ukrainian Catholic, Protestant, Jewish
LANGUAGE	Ukrainian, Russian, Romanian Polish, Hungarian
LITERACY	98%
LIFE EXPECTANCY	68 years
GDP PER CAPITA	$4,200

ECONOMY **IND:** coal, electric power, ferrous and nonferrous metals, machinery and transport equipment. **AGR:** grain, sugar beets, sunflower seeds, vegetables; beef. **EXP:** ferrous and nonferrous metals, fuel and petroleum products, machinery and transport equipment, food products.

UNITED KINGDOM

UNITED KINGDOM OF GREAT BRITAIN AND N. IRELAND

AREA	242,910 sq km (93,788 sq mi)
POPULATION	59,200,000
CAPITAL	London 7,640,000
RELIGION	Anglican, Roman Catholic
LANGUAGE	English, Welsh, Scottish form of Gaelic
LITERACY	99%
LIFE EXPECTANCY	78 years
GDP PER CAPITA	$25,300

ECONOMY **IND:** machinery tools, electric power equipment, automation equipment, railroad equipment. **AGR:** cereals, oilseed, potatoes, vegetables; cattle; fish. **EXP:** manufactured goods, fuels, chemicals, food.

VATICAN CITY

STATE OF THE VATICAN CITY (THE HOLY SEE)

AREA	0.4 sq km (0.2 sq mi)
POPULATION	1,000
CAPITAL	Vatican City 1,000
RELIGION	Roman Catholic
LANGUAGE	Italian, Latin, French
LITERACY	100%
LIFE EXPECTANCY	NA
GDP PER CAPITA	NA

ECONOMY **IND:** printing and production of a small amount of mosaics and staff uniforms, worldwide banking and financial activities. **AGR:** NA. **EXP:** NA.

DEPENDENCIES

SOVEREIGN

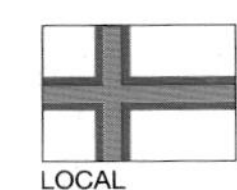

LOCAL

FAROE ISLANDS (DENMARK)

FAROE ISLANDS

AREA	1,399 sq km (540 sq mi)
POPULATION	48,000
CAPITAL	Tórshavn 17,000
RELIGION	Evangelical Lutheran
LANGUAGE	Faroese (derived from old Norse), Danish
LITERACY	NA
LIFE EXPECTANCY	79 years
GDP PER CAPITA	$20,000

ECONOMY **IND:** fishing, fish processing, shipbuilding, construction. **AGR:** milk, potatoes, vegetables; sheep; salmon. **EXP:** fish and fish products, stamps, ships.

SOVEREIGN

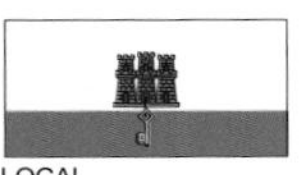

LOCAL

GIBRALTAR (UNITED KINGDOM)

GIBRALTAR

AREA	6 sq km (2 sq mi)
POPULATION	27,000
CAPITAL	Gibraltar 27,000
RELIGION	Roman Catholic, Anglican, Muslim, Jewish
LANGUAGE	English, Spanish, Italian, Portuguese, Russian
LITERACY	80%
LIFE EXPECTANCY	79 years
GDP PER CAPITA	$17,500

ECONOMY **IND:** tourism, banking and finance, shipbuilding and repairing, support to large UK naval and air bases. **AGR:** NA. **EXP:** petroleum, manufactured goods.

People per square mile	People per square km
250 and greater	100 and greater
60–250	25–99
25–59	10–24
2–24	1–9
Less than 2	Less than 1

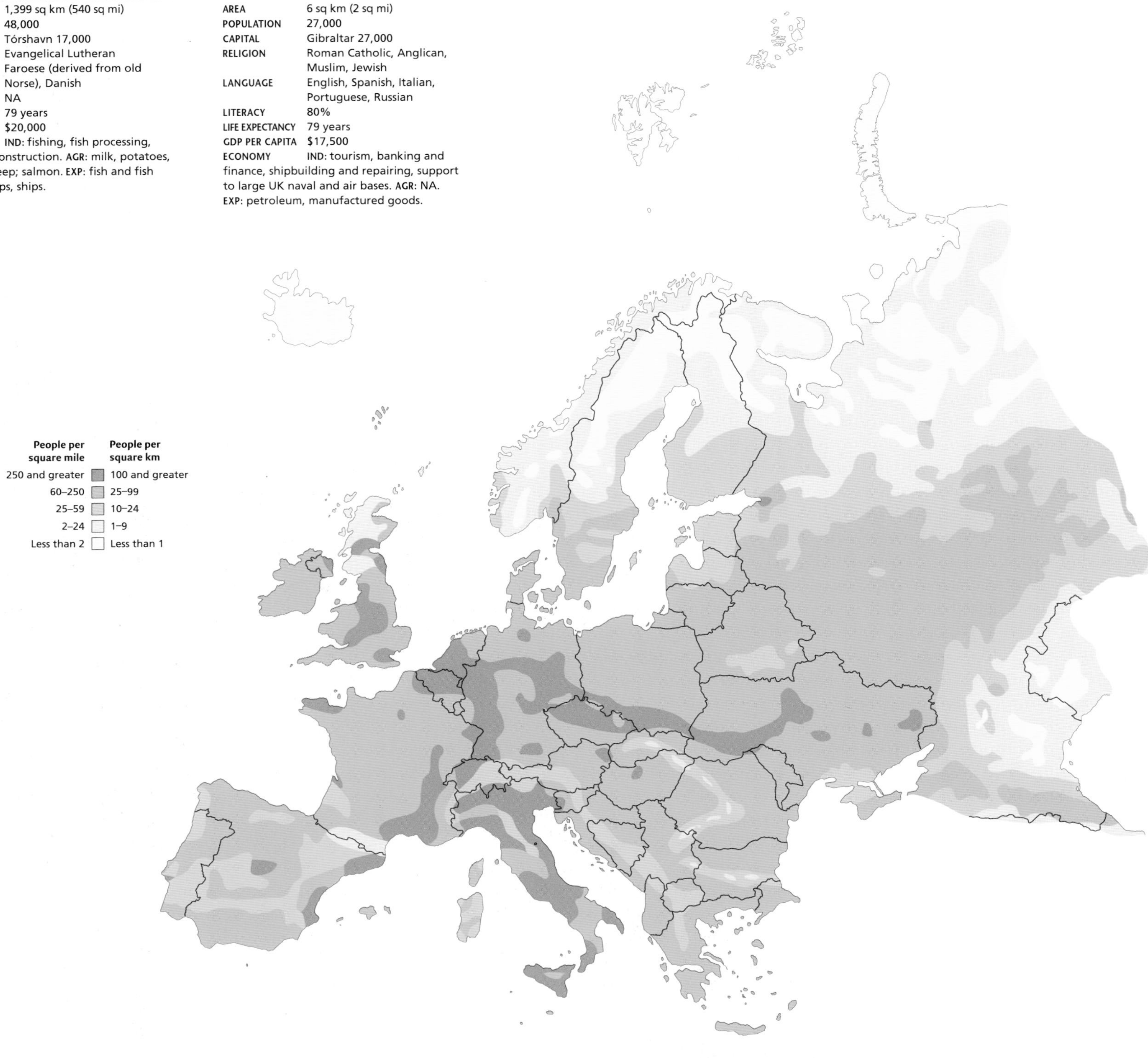

DATES OF COUNTRY INDEPENDENCE

Svalbard (Norway)
KARA SEA
ARCTIC OCEAN
BARENTS SEA
ICELAND June 17, 1944
NORWEGIAN SEA
NORWAY June 7, 1905
Faroe Islands (Denmark)
FINLAND Dec. 6, 1917
ATLANTIC OCEAN
SWEDEN June 6, 1523
RUSSIA Aug. 24, 1991
ASIA
EUROPE
ESTONIA May 1919
NORTH SEA
IRELAND Dec. 6, 1921
LATVIA Dec. 1919
BALTIC SEA
UNITED KINGDOM 10th century
DENMARK 10th century
Kaliningrad (Russia)
LITHUANIA April 1919
BELARUS Aug. 25, 1991
NETHERLANDS 1579 A.D.
POLAND Nov. 11, 1918
BELGIUM July 21, 1831
GERMANY Jan. 18, 1871
KAZAKHSTAN see page 75
UKRAINE Aug. 24, 1991
LUXEMBOURG 1839 A.D.
CZECH REP. Jan. 1, 1993
FRANCE 486 A.D.
SLOVAKIA Jan. 1, 1993
CASPIAN SEA
SWITZERLAND Aug. 1, 1291
AUSTRIA 1156 A.D.
MOLDOVA Aug 27, 1991
HUNGARY 1001 A.D.
LIECHTENSTEIN Jan. 23, 1719
SLOVENIA June 25, 1991
ROMANIA Mar. 26, 1881
CROATIA June 25, 1991
PORTUGAL 1140 A.D.
SAN MARINO Sept. 3, 301
MONACO 1419 A.D.
ANDORRA 1278 A.D.
BOSN. & HERZG. March 1, 1992
SERB. & MONT. April 27, 1992
GEORGIA see page 75
AZERBAIJAN see page 75
BLACK SEA
ITALY March 17, 1861
BULGARIA March 3, 1878
SPAIN 1492 A.D.
VATICAN CITY Feb. 11, 1929
MACEDONIA Sept. 17, 1991
ALBANIA Nov. 28, 1912
TURKEY see page 75
GREECE 1829 A.D.
Gibraltar (U.K.)
MALTA Sept. 21, 1964
MEDITERRANEAN SEA

ASIA

The continent of Asia, occupying four-fifths of the giant Eurasian landmass, stretches across ten time zones from the Pacific Ocean in the east to the Ural Mountains and Black Sea in the west. It is the largest of the continents, with dazzling geographic diversity and 30 percent of the Earth's land surface. Asia includes numerous island nations, such as Japan, the Philippines, Indonesia, and Sri Lanka, as well as many of the world's major islands: Borneo, Sumatra, Honshu, Celebes, Java, and half of New Guinea. Siberia, the huge Asian section of Russia, reaches deep inside the Arctic Circle and fills the continent's northern quarter. To its south lie the large countries of Kazakhstan, Mongolia, and China. Within its 47 countries, Asia holds 60 percent of humanity, yet deserts, mountains, jungles, and inhospitable zones render much of the continent empty or underpopulated.

Great river systems allowed the growth of the world's first civilizations in the Middle East, the Indian subcontinent, and North China. Numerous cultural forces, each linked to these broad geographical areas, have formed and influenced Asia's rich civilizations and hundreds of ethnic groups. The two oldest are the cultural milieus of India and China. India's culture still reverberates throughout countries as varied as Sri Lanka, Pakistan, Nepal, Burma, Cambodia, and Indonesia. The world religions of Hinduism and Buddhism originated in India and spread as traders, scholars, and priests sought distant footholds. China's ancient civilization has profoundly influenced the development of all of East Asia, much of Southeast Asia, and parts of Central Asia. Most influential of all Chinese institutions were the Chinese written language, a complex script with thousands of characters, and Confucianism, an ethical worldview that affected philosophy, politics, and relations within society. Islam, a third great influence in Asia, proved formidable in its energy and creative genius. Arabs from the 7th century onwards, spurred on by faith, moved rapidly into Southwest Asia. Their religion and culture, particularly Arabic writing, spread through Iran and Afghanistan to the Indian subcontinent.

Today nearly all of Asia's people continue to live beside rivers or along coastal zones. Dense concentrations of population fill Japan, China's eastern half, Java, parts of Southeast Asia, and much of the Indian subcontinent. China and India, acting as demographic, political, and cultural counterweights, hold nearly half of Asia's population. India, with a billion people, expects to surpass China as the world's most populous nation by 2050. As China seeks to take center stage, flexing economic muscle and pushing steadily into the oil-rich South China Sea, many Asian neighbors grow concerned. The development of nuclear weapons by India and Pakistan complicate international relations. Economic recovery after the financial turmoil of the late 1990s preoccupies many countries, while others yearn to escape dire poverty. Religious, ethnic, and territorial conflicts continue to beset the continent, from the Middle East to Korea, from Cambodia to Uzbekistan. Asians also face the threats of overpopulation, resource depletion, pollution, and the growth of megacities. Yet if vibrant Asia meets the challenges of rebuilding and reconciliation, overcoming age-old habits of rivalry, corruption, and cronyism, it may yet fulfill the promise to claim the first hundred years of the new millennium as Asia's century.

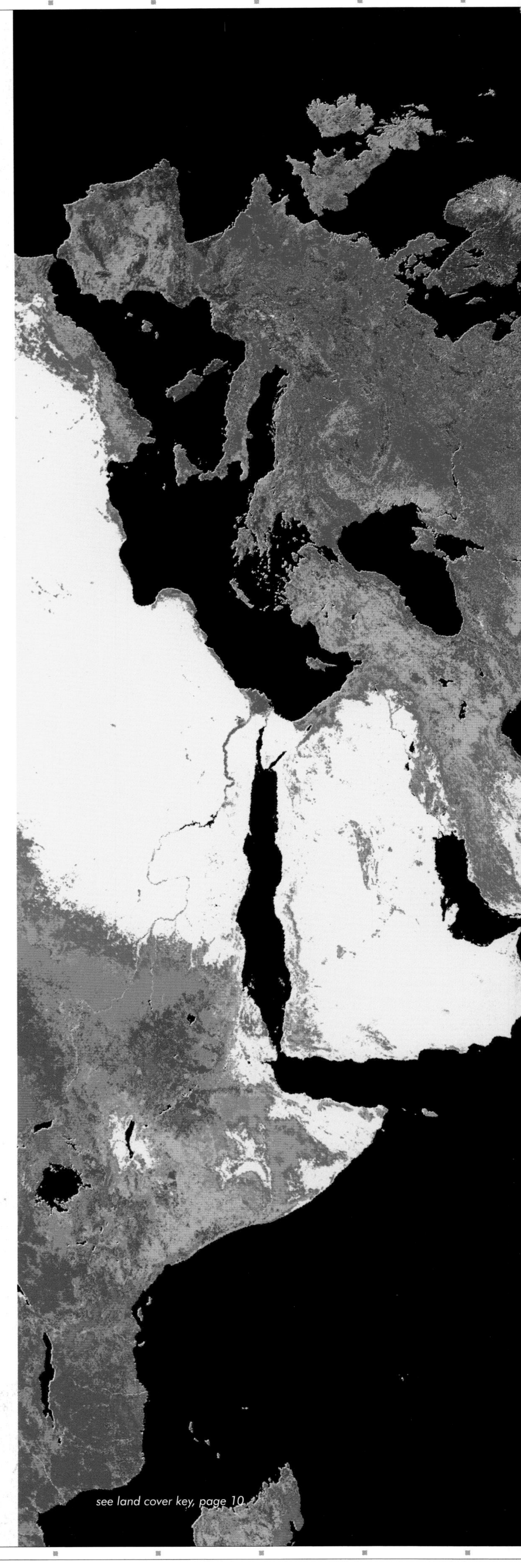

see land cover key, page 10

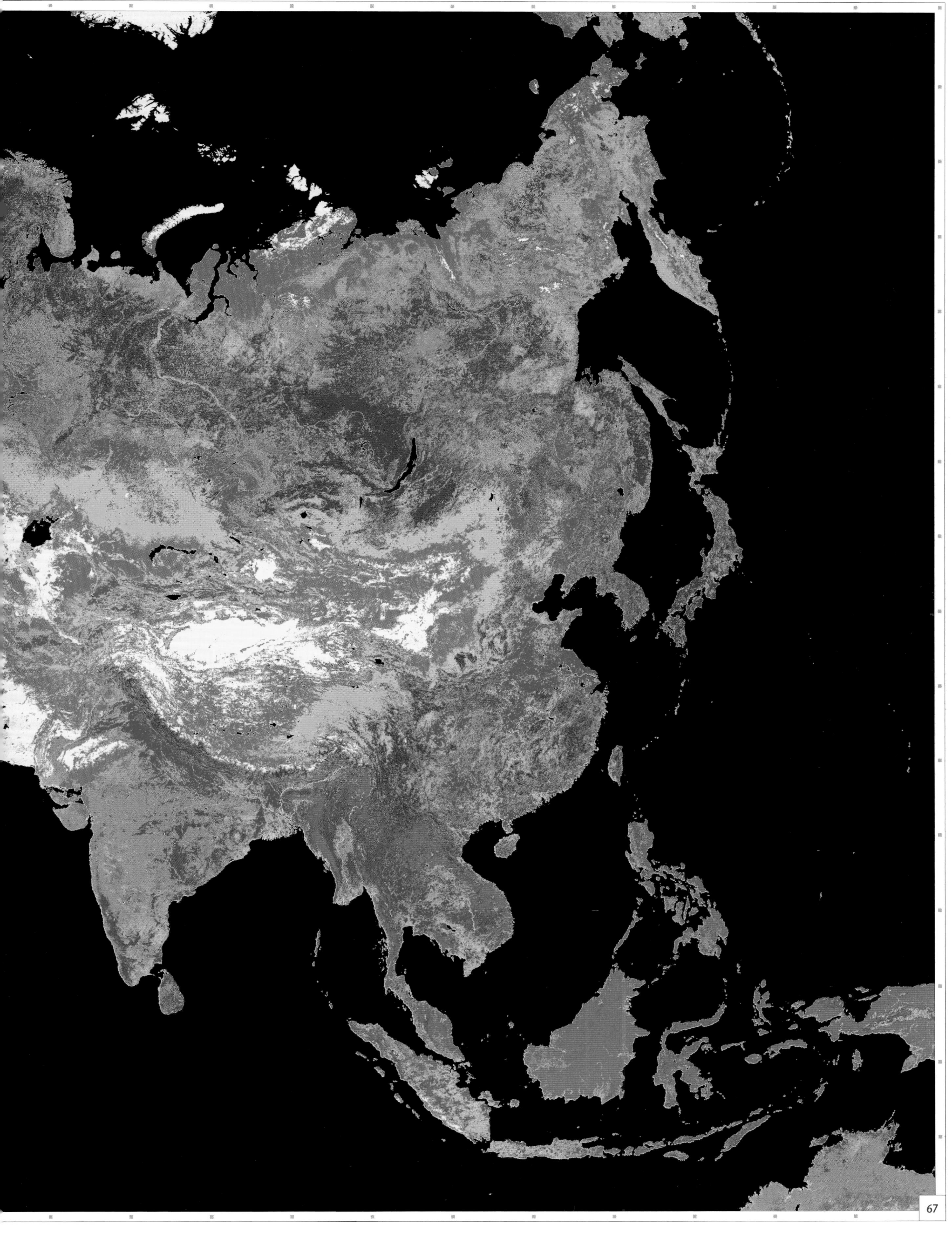

ATLANTIC OCEAN
IRELAND
Baile Átha Cliath (Dublin)
UNITED KINGDOM
LONDON
Lisboa (Lisbon)
PORTUGAL
SPAIN
MADRID
MOROCCO
ALGER (Algiers)
ALGERIA
TUNIS
TUNISIA
MALTA
FRANCE
PARIS
Bern
SWITZERLAND
NETHERLANDS
Amsterdam
Bruxelles (Brussels)
BELGIUM
LUX.
GERMANY
BERLIN
DENMARK
København (Copenhagen)
NORTH SEA
NORWEGIAN SEA
GREENLAND SEA
GREENLAND
Denmark
North Pole
ARCTIC
ICELAND
Meridian of Greenwich (London)
ARCTIC CIRCLE
NORWAY
Oslo
SWEDEN
Stockholm
Gulf of Bothnia
FINLAND
Helsinki
LAPLAND
SVALBARD
Norway
Spitsbergen
Edgeøya
Nordaustlandet
BARENTS SEA
FRANZ JOSEF LAND (Zemlya Frantsa Iosifa)
Russia
SEVERNAYA ZEMLYA (North Land)
Ostrov Komsomolets
O. Oktyabr'skoy Revolyutsii
Ostrov Bol'shevik
Novaya Zemlya
KARA SEA
Gulf of Ob
BALTIC SEA
Kaliningrad
Russia
POLAND
WARSZAWA (Warsaw)
PRAHA (Prague)
CZECH REP.
AUSTRIA
WIEN (Vienna)
Bratislava
SLOVAKIA
HUNGARY
BUDAPEST
SLOVENIA
Ljubljana
CROATIA
Zagreb
BOSNIA & HERZEGOVINA
Sarajevo
SERBIA & MONTENEGRO
BEOGRAD (Belgrade)
ROMANIA
BUCUREŞTI (Bucharest)
MOLDOVA
Chişinău
ALBANIA
Tiranë
MACEDONIA
Skopje
BULGARIA
SOFIYA (Sofia)
GREECE
Athína (Athens)
ITALY
ROMA (Rome)
MEDITERRANEAN SEA
AEGEAN SEA
LITHUANIA
Vilnius
LATVIA
Rīga
ESTONIA
Tallinn
BELARUS
MINSK
UKRAINE
KYYIV (Kiev)
CRIMEA
BLACK SEA
Bosporus
Dardanelles
ISTANBUL
BURSA
Eskişehir
ANKARA
İZMİR
Konya
Samsun
Kayseri
TURKEY
Adana
İskenderun
Diyarbakır
Trabzon
CYPRUS
Lefkosia (Nicosia)
LEBANON
BEYROUTH (Beirut)
SYRIA
HALAB (Aleppo)
DIMASHQ (Damascus)
ISRAEL
Jerusalem
GAZA STRIP
WEST BANK
JORDAN
'AMMĀN
SUEZ CANAL
EL QĀHIRA (Cairo)
EGYPT
Nile
LIBYA
ṬARĀBULUS (Tripoli)
TROPIC OF CANCER
SUDAN
Khartoum
ERITREA
Asmara
ĀDĪS ĀBEBA (Addis Ababa)
ETHIOPIA
DJIBOUTI
Djibouti
GULF OF ADEN
SOMALIA
MUQDISHO (Mogadishu)
UGANDA
KENYA
NAIROBI
Lake Victoria
EQUATOR
TANZANIA
DAR ES SALAAM
MOZAMBIQUE
COMOROS
Moroni
MADAGASCAR
SEYCHELLES
Victoria
Mahé I.
RED SEA
AL ḤIJĀZ
Tabūk
Yanbu' al Baḩr
JEDDAH
Makkah (Mecca)
Al Madīnah (Medina)
Aṭ Ṭā'if
Khamīs Mushayṭ
'ASĪR
Jīzān
SAUDI ARABIA
AR RIYĀḌ (Riyadh)
Buraydah
Ḥā'il
Dawmat al Jandal
Ad Dammām
Hufūf
Al Manāmah (Manama)
BAHRAIN
QATAR
Ad Dawḥah (Doha)
UNITED ARAB EMIRATES
Abū Ẓaby (Abu Dhabi)
Dubayy
Ar Rub' al Khālī (Empty Quarter)
Qal'at Bīshah
YEMEN
Ṣan'ā'
Ṣa'dah
Al Ḥudaydah
Ta'izz
'Adan
Saywūn
Ash Shiḩr
Al Mukallā
OMAN
Nizwá
Masqaṭ (Muscat)
Ṣūr
Jazīrat Maşīrah
Şalālah
Socotra (Suquṭrá) Yemen
IRAQ
MESOPOTAMIA
BAGHDĀD
Karbalā'
An Najaf
An Nāṣirīyah
Al Başrah
Kirkūk
Al Mawşil
KUWAIT
Al Kuwayt
PERSIAN GULF
GULF OF OMAN
IRAN
TEHRĀN
Tabrīz
Ardabīl
Qazvīn
Rasht
Hamadān
Sanandaj
Kermānshāh
Qom
Arāk
Ahvāz
Ābādān
EŞFAHĀN
Yazd
Shīrāz
Kermān
Bandar-e Būshehr
Jahrom
Bandar-e 'Abbās
Zāhedān
Zābol
Bīrjand
Mashhad
Sabzevār
Bojnūrd
Bābol
KHORĀSĀN
ARMENIA
YEREVAN
GEORGIA
T'BILISI
AZERBAIJAN
BAKI (Baku)
CASPIAN SEA
Euphrates
Tigris
RUSSIA
ST. PETERSBURG
Petrozavodsk
Segezha
Kandalaksha
Murmansk
Severodvinsk
Arkhangel'sk
Mezen'
BELOYE MORE (WHITE SEA)
Ladozhskoye Ozero
Onezhskoye Ozero
Vologda
Yaroslavl'
Tver'
MOSKVA (Moscow)
Smolensk
Bryansk
Kursk
Tula
Orel
Ryazan'
Tambov
Voronezh
Penza
Saratov
Volgograd
ROSTOV NA DONU
Krasnodar
Sochi
Stavropol'
Vladikavkaz
Groznyy
Astrakhan'
NIZHNIY NOVGOROD
KAZAN'
Kirov
Perm'
Izhevsk
Ul'yanovsk
SAMARA
Ufa
Volga
Kama
Syktyvkar
Ukhta
Nar'yan Mar
Vorkuta
Pechora
Dvina
URAL MOUNTAINS
Nizhniy Tagil
Serov
YEKATERINBURG
CHELYABINSK
Magnitogorsk
Orenburg
Orsk
Oral
Ural
Aqtöbe
Atyraū
Fort Shevchenko
Aqtaū
Salekhard
Nadym
Novyy Urengoy
Khanty Mansiysk
Nizhnevartovsk
Surgut
Tavda
Tyumen'
Tobol'sk
Irtysh
Ob
Petropavl
Qostanay
Kökshetaū
Ekibastuz
Astana
Pavlodar
OMSK
NOVOSIBIRSK
Tomsk
Kolpashevo
Barnaul
Semey
Rubtsovsk
Öskemen
KAZAKHSTAN
Oktyabr'sk
Qaraghandy
Aral Sea
Aral
Qazaly
Syr Darya
Qyzylorda
Zaysan Köli
Balqash Köli
Balqash
Ayaköz
Shymkent
Taraz
Saryözek
Taldyqorghan
ALMATY
UZBEKISTAN
Nukus
Dashhowuz
TURKMENISTAN
Türkmenbashy
Ashgabat
Mary
Chärjew
Amu Darya
Buxoro (Bukhara)
Samarqand
TOSHKENT (Tashkent)
Farg'ona
Namangan
KYRGYZSTAN
Bishkek
TAJIKISTAN
Dushanbe
Termiz
Mazar-e Sharif
Konduz
AFGHANISTAN
Herat
Farah
Kabol (Kabul)
Kandahar
Gilgit
KASHMIR
Islamabad
Peshawar
Rawalpindi
LAHORE
Faisalabad
Srinagar
Quetta
BALUCHISTAN
PAKISTAN
Multan
Bahawalpur
Khanpur
Sukkur
Indus
Turbat
KARACHI
Hyderabad
Amritsar
Jullundur
LUDHIANA
DELHI
New Delhi
MEERUT
AGRA
JAIPUR
Jodhpur
Udaipur
LUCKNOW
KANPUR
Gwalior
Kota
Allahabad
Varanasi
PATNA
BHOPAL
INDORE
Jabalpur
INDIA
AHMADABAD
Rajkot
VADODARA
SURAT
Amravati
NASIK
NAGPUR
MUMBAI (Bombay)
KALYAN
PUNE
Sholapur
Kolhapur
HYDERABAD
Guntur
VIJAYAWADA
VISHAKHAPATNAM
Hubli
Nellore
BANGALORE
Mysore
Salem
CHENNAI (Madras)
Pondicherry
KOZHIKODE
COIMBATORE
Tiruchchirappalli
MADURAI
COCHIN
TRIVANDRUM
Jaffna
SRI LANKA
Colombo
Galle
Lakshadweep India
Maldive Islands
Male
MALDIVES
British Indian Ocean Territory
Chagos Archipelago (Oil Islands)
Diego Garcia
ARABIAN SEA
INDIAN OCEAN
BAY OF BENGAL
Andaman Islands India
Nicobar Islands India
Banda Aceh
Ranchi
JAMSHEDPUR
KOLKATA (Calcutta)
Khulna
DHAKA
BANGLADESH
CHITTAGONG
Rajshahi
Shiliguri
Guwahati
Imphal
Brahmaputra
Ganga (Ganges)
Kathmandu
NEPAL
Thimphu
BHUTAN
Lhasa
Xigazê
Gyangzê
HIMALAYA
TIBET
Plateau of Tibet
Boundary claimed by India
Sittwe
Mandalay
Hinthada
YANGON (Rangoon)
Monywa
SIBERIA
Dickson
Poluostrov Taymyr
Novorybnoye
Khatanga
Yeniseyskiy Zaliv
Dudinka
Noril'sk
Igarka
Chirinda
Nizhnyaya Tunguska
Tura
Yenisey
Severo Yeniseyskiy
Yeniseysk
Angara
Achinsk
Krasnoyarsk
Kansk
Bratsk
Kemerovo
Prokop'yevsk
Novokuznetsk
Abakan
Biysk
Kyzyl
Ulaangom
Dund-Us
Altay
ALTAY MOUNTAINS
Tacheng
Yining
Shihezi
ÜRÜMQI
Turpan
Hami
SINKIANG
Aksu
Kuqa
Korla
Kashi
Tarim
Taklimakan Shamo
Shache
Hotan
Qiemo
ALTUN SHAN
KUNLUN SHAN
Lenghu
Da Qaidam
Golmud
CHINA
Longitude East 90° of Greenwich
Turkey, Cyprus, Syria, Lebanon, Israel, Jordan, Egypt, Iraq, Iran, and the countries of the Arabian Peninsula form the heart of the Middle East region.

ASIA
Political

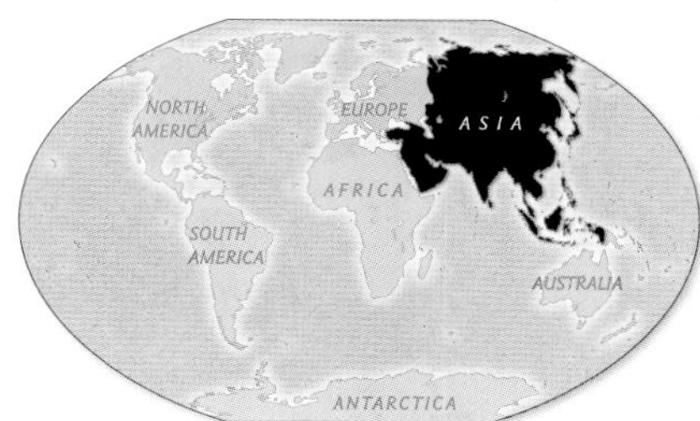

Two-Point Equidistant Projection

SCALE 1:30,105,000
1 CENTIMETER = 301 KILOMETERS; 1 INCH = 476 MILES

0 200 400 600 800 1000 KILOMETERS

0 200 400 600 800 1000 STATUTE MILES

KURIL ISLANDS
The southern Kuril Islands of Iturup (Etorofu), Kunashir (Kunashiri), Shikotan, and the Habomai group were lost by Japan to the Soviet Union in 1945. Japan continues to claim these Russian-administered islands.

A commonly accepted division between Asia and Europe–here marked by a green line–is formed by the Ural Mountains, Ural River, Caspian Sea, Caucasus Mountains, and the Black Sea with its outlets, the Bosporus and Dardanelles.

The People's Republic of China claims Taiwan as its 23rd province. Taiwan maintains that there are two political entities.

CONTINENTAL DATA

- **Total number of countries:** 47
- **First independent country:** Japan 660 B.C.
- **"Youngest" country:** Timor-Leste, May 20, 2002
- **Largest country by area:** China 9,572,855 sq km (3,696,100 sq mi)
- **Smallest country by area:** Maldives 298 sq km (115 sq mi)
- **Percent urban population:** 38%
- **Most populous country:** China 1,288,679,000
- **Least populous country:** Maldives 285,000
- **Most densely populated country:** Singapore 6,768 per sq km (17,528 per sq mi)
- **Least densely populated country:** Mongolia 1.5 per sq km (4 per sq mi)
- **Largest city by population:** Tokyo, Japan 26,546,000
- **Highest GDP per capita:** Japan $28,000
- **Lowest GDP per capita:** Timor-Leste $500
- **Average life expectancy in Asia:** 67 years
- **Average literacy rate in Asia:** 73%

ATLANTIC OCEAN
ARCTIC
GREENLAND
GREENLAND SEA
North Pole
Ireland
BRITISH ISLES
Great Britain
NORWEGIAN SEA
Meridian of Greenwich (London)
ARCTIC CIRCLE
NORTH SEA
SVALBARD
FRANZ JOSEF LAND
Komsomolets I.
NORTH LAND
October Revolution I.
Bol'shevik I.
BARENTS SEA
IBERIAN PENINSULA
SCANDINAVIA
Gulf of Bothnia
ATLAS MOUNTAINS
ALPS
NORTHERN EUROPEAN PLAIN
BALTIC SEA
Kola Peninsula
White Sea
NOVAYA ZEMLYA
KARA SEA
Taymyr Peninsula
Lake Taymyr
Yenisey Gulf
North Siberian L
Gyda Pen.
Yamal Peninsula
Gulf of Ob
Lake Ladoga
Lake Onega
MEDITERRANEAN SEA
EUROPE
Volga
Narodnaya 1895
URAL MOUNTAINS
Ob
Taz
Yenisey
WEST SIBERIAN PLAIN
BALKAN PENINSULA
Kama
Irtysh
Vasyugan'ye
Angara
Crimea
BLACK SEA
AEGEAN SEA
Dardanelles
Bosporus
Don
Volga
Ural
Tobol
Ishim Steppe
ANATOLIA (ASIA MINOR)
Taurus Mts.
3916
Caucasus Mountains
El'brus 5642
Caspian Depression
THE STEPPES
Lake Tengiz
Kazakh Uplands
Eastern Sayan Mts.
Western Sayan Mountains
Belukha 4506
ALTAY MOUNTAINS
Source of the Yenisey-Angara
AFRICA
TROPIC OF CANCER
Cyprus
Mt. Ararat 5165
L. Van
Aral Sea
Ustyurt Plateau
Syr Darya
Lake Balkhash
Betpaqdala
Ili
Black Irtysh
Dzungarian Basin
5445
Source of the Ob
Bogda Sha
154
Turpan Depression
Levant Coast
3088
Euphrates
Mesopotamia
Tigris
Lake Urmia
Kura
CASPIAN SEA
Turan Lowland
Qizilqum
Amu Darya
Garabogaz Bay
Garagum
Kopet Mts.
Victory Peak 7439
TIAN SHAN
Tarim
Tarim Basin
Lop Nur
SUEZ CANAL
SINAI
Nile
Dead Sea -416 (-1356 ft) World's lowest point
Gulf of Aqaba
Syrian Desert
Hawr al Hammar
-28
Elburz Mts.
5671
Zagros Mountains
4548
Dasht-e Lut
Hejaz
An Nafūd
SAHARA
RED SEA
ARABIAN PENINSULA
Ad Dahnā
PERSIAN GULF
Hasa Plain
TAKLIMAKAN DESERT
Altun Shan
Qaidam Basin
7495
7690
5143
Hindu Kush
Karakoram Ra.
Muztag 7282
K2 (Godwin Austen) 8611
KASHMIR
KUNLUN MOUNTAINS
6300
PLATEAU OF TIBET
Source of the Yangtze
Tanggula Range
Nganglong Range
Gangdise Ra.
7059
Nyainqêntanglha Shan
Salween
Helmand
Indus
Sutlej
2386
Tihamah
Tuwayq Mountains
GULF OF OMAN
2980
Great Indian Desert
HIMALAYA
World's highest point
Mt. Everest 8850 (29035 ft)
Brahmaputra
Rub al Khali
Ra's al Hadd
Gulf of Kutch
Ganges Plain
Ganges
3760
ETHIOPIAN HIGHLANDS
Hadhramaut
1730
Gulf of Masira
Vindhya Range
Narmada
1350
Chota Nagpur Plateau
Mt. Victoria 3053
GULF OF ADEN
Gulf of Khambhat
DECCAN PLATEAU
Eastern Ghats
1589
Krishna
Western Ghats
Irrawaddy
Socotra
ARABIAN SEA
Somali Peninsula
Coromandel Coast
BAY OF BENGAL
Lakshadweep
LACCADIVE SEA
Malabar Coast
2695
Andaman Islands
Nicobar Islan
EQUATOR
Cape Comorin
2524
Sri Lanka
Maldive Islands
INDIAN OCEAN
Seychelles
Comoro Is.
Madagascar
Chagos Archipelago
Longitude East 90° of Greenwich

ASIA
Physical

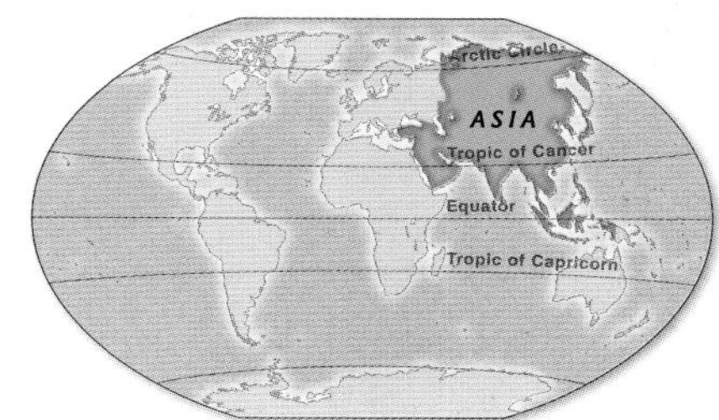

Two-Point Equidistant Projection

SCALE 1:30,105,000
1 CENTIMETER = 301 KILOMETERS; 1 INCH = 476 MILES

0 200 400 600 800 1000
KILOMETERS

0 200 400 600 800 1000
STATUTE MILES

International boundary

Disputed or undefined boundary

A commonly accepted division between Asia and Europe–here marked by a green line–is formed by the Ural Mountains, Ural River, Caspian Sea, Caucasus Mountains, and the Black Sea with its outlets, the Bosporus and Dardanelles.

CONTINENTAL DATA

- **Area:**
  44,579,000 sq km
  (17,212,000 sq mi)
- **Greatest north-south extent:**
  8,690 km (5,400 mi)
- **Greatest east-west extent:**
  9,700 km (6,030 mi)
- **Highest point:**
  Mount Everest, China-Nepal
  8,850 m (29,035 ft)
- **Lowest point:**
  Dead Sea, Israel-Jordan
  -416 m (-1,365 ft)
- **Lowest recorded temperature:**
  - Oymyakon, Russia -68°C (-90°F), February 6, 1933
  - Verkhoyansk, Russia -68°C (-90°F), February 7, 1892
- **Highest recorded temperature:**
  Tirat Zevi, Israel 54°C (129°F), June 21, 1942
- **Longest rivers:**
  - Chang Jiang (Yangtze) 6,380 km (3,964 mi)
  - Yenisey-Angara 5,536 km (3,440 mi)
  - Huang (Yellow) 5,464 km (3,395 mi)
- **Largest lakes:**
  - Caspian Sea 371,000 sq km (143,200 sq mi)
  - Lake Baikal 31,500 sq km (12,200 sq mi)
  - Aral Sea 25,508 sq km (9,849 sq mi)
- **Earth's extremes located in Asia:**
  - **Wettest place:**
    Mawsynram, India; annual average rainfall 1,187 cm (467 in)
  - **Largest Cave Chamber:**
    Sarawak Cave, Gunung Mulu National Park, Malaysia; 16 hectares and 79 m high (40 acres, 260 ft)

ASIA
FLAGS & FACTS

AFGHANISTAN

TRANSITIONAL ISLAMIC STATE OF AFGHANISTAN

AREA 652,090 sq km (251,773 sq mi)
POPULATION 28,717,000
CAPITAL Kabul 2,734,000
RELIGION Sunni and Shiite Muslim
LANGUAGE Pashtu, Afghan Persian (Dari), Uzbek, Turkmen, Balochi, Pashai
LITERACY 36%
LIFE EXPECTANCY 46 years
GDP PER CAPITA $800
ECONOMY **IND**: small-scale production of textiles, soap, furniture, shoes. **AGR**: opium poppies, wheat, fruits, nuts; wool. **EXP**: opium, fruits and nuts, handwoven carpets, wool.

ARMENIA

REPUBLIC OF ARMENIA

AREA 29,743 sq km (11,484 sq mi)
POPULATION 3,220,000
CAPITAL Yerevan 1,420,000
RELIGION Armenian Apostolic
LANGUAGE Armenian, Russian
LITERACY 99%
LIFE EXPECTANCY 72 years
GDP PER CAPITA $3,350
ECONOMY **IND**: metal-cutting machine tools, forging-pressing machines, electric motors, tires. **AGR**: fruits (grapes), vegetables; livestock. **EXP**: diamonds, scrap metal, machinery and equipment, brandy.

AZERBAIJAN

REPUBLIC OF AZERBAIJAN

AREA 86,600 sq km (33,436 sq mi)
POPULATION 8,233,000
CAPITAL Baku 1,964,000
RELIGION Muslim, Russian Orthodox, Armenian Orthodox
LANGUAGE Azerbaijani, Russian, Armenian
LITERACY 97%
LIFE EXPECTANCY 72 years
GDP PER CAPITA $3,300
ECONOMY **IND**: petroleum, natural gas, chemicals and petrochemicals, textiles. **AGR**: cotton, grain, rice, grapes; cattle. **EXP**: oil and gas, machinery, cotton, foodstuffs.

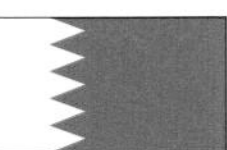

BAHRAIN

KINGDOM OF BAHRAIN

AREA 712 sq km (275 sq mi)
POPULATION 678,000
CAPITAL Manama 150,000
RELIGION Shiite and Sunni Muslim
LANGUAGE Arabic, English, Farsi, Urdu
LITERACY 89%
LIFE EXPECTANCY 74 years
GDP PER CAPITA $13,000
ECONOMY **IND**: petroleum processing and refining, aluminum smelting, offshore banking, tourism. **AGR**: fruit, vegetables; poultry; shrimp. **EXP**: petroleum and petroleum products, aluminum.

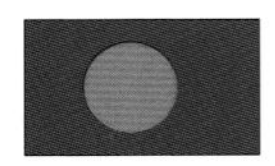

BANGLADESH

PEOPLE'S REPUBLIC OF BANGLADESH

AREA 147,570 sq km (56,977 sq mi)
POPULATION 146,733,000
CAPITAL Dhaka 13,181,000
RELIGION Muslim, Hindu
LANGUAGE Bangla, English
LITERACY 56%
LIFE EXPECTANCY 59 years
GDP PER CAPITA $1,750
ECONOMY **IND**: cotton textiles, jute, garments, tea processing. **AGR**: rice, jute, tea, wheat; beef. **EXP**: garments, jute and jute goods, leather, frozen fish and seafood.

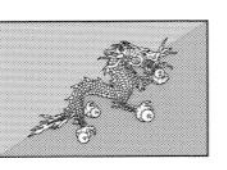

BHUTAN

KINGDOM OF BHUTAN

AREA 46,500 sq km (17,954 sq mi)
POPULATION 945,000
CAPITAL Thimphu 32,000
RELIGION Lamaistic Buddhist, Hindu
LANGUAGE Dzonkha, Tibetan and Nepali dialects
LITERACY 42%
LIFE EXPECTANCY 66 years
GDP PER CAPITA $1,200
ECONOMY **IND**: cement, wood products, processed fruits, alcoholic beverages. **AGR**: rice, corn, root crops, citrus; dairy products. **EXP**: cardamom, gypsum, timber, handicrafts.

BRUNEI

NEGARA BRUNEI DARUSSALAM

AREA 5,765 sq km (2,226 sq mi)
POPULATION 360,000
CAPITAL Bandar Seri Begawan 46,000
RELIGION Muslim, Buddhist, Christian, indigenous beliefs
LANGUAGE Malay, English, Chinese
LITERACY 88%
LIFE EXPECTANCY 76 years
GDP PER CAPITA $18,000
ECONOMY **IND**: petroleum, petroleum refining, liquefied natural gas, construction. **AGR**: rice, vegetables, fruits; chickens. **EXP**: crude oil, natural gas, refined products.

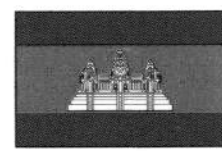

CAMBODIA

KINGDOM OF CAMBODIA

AREA 181,035 sq km (69,898 sq mi)
POPULATION 12,558,000
CAPITAL Phnom Penh 1,109,000
RELIGION Theravada Buddhist
LANGUAGE Khmer, French, English
LITERACY 35%
LIFE EXPECTANCY 56 years
GDP PER CAPITA $1,500
ECONOMY **IND**: garments, tourism, rice, milling, fishing. **AGR**: rice, rubber, corn, vegetables. **EXP**: timber, garments, rubber, rice.

CHINA

PEOPLE'S REPUBLIC OF CHINA

AREA 9,572,855 sq km (3,696,100 sq mi)
POPULATION 1,288,679,000
CAPITAL Beijing 10,836,000
RELIGION Daoist, Buddhist, Muslim
LANGUAGE Chinese (Mandarin), Cantonese, other dialects and minority languages
LITERACY 82%
LIFE EXPECTANCY 71 years
GDP PER CAPITA $4,600
ECONOMY **IND**: iron and steel, coal, machine building, armaments. **AGR**: rice, wheat, potatoes, sorghum; pork; fish. **EXP**: machinery and equipment, textiles and clothing, footwear, toys and sporting goods.

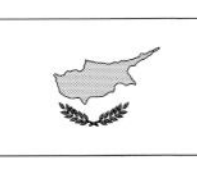

CYPRUS

REPUBLIC OF CYPRUS

AREA 5,897 sq km (2,277 sq mi)
POPULATION 934,000
CAPITAL Nicosia 199,000
RELIGION Greek Orthodox, Muslim
LANGUAGE Greek, Turkish, English
LITERACY 97%
LIFE EXPECTANCY 77 years
GDP PER CAPITA $15,000
ECONOMY **IND**: food, beverages, textiles, chemicals. **AGR**: potatoes, citrus, vegetables, barley. **EXP**: citrus, potatoes, grapes, textiles.

GEORGIA

REPUBLIC OF GEORGIA

AREA 69,700 sq km (26,911 sq mi)
POPULATION 4,660,000
CAPITAL T'bilisi 1,406,000
RELIGION Georgian Orthodox, Muslim, Russian Orthodox, Armenian Apostolic
LANGUAGE Georgian, Russian, Armenian, Azeri
LITERACY 99%
LIFE EXPECTANCY 77 years
GDP PER CAPITA $3,100
ECONOMY **IND**: aircraft, food processing, machine tools, electric locomotives. **AGR**: citrus, grapes, tea, vegetables; livestock. **EXP**: citrus fruits, diverse types of machinery and metals, chemicals, fuel exports.

INDIA

REPUBLIC OF INDIA

AREA 3,287,263 sq km (1,269,219 sq mi)
POPULATION 1,068,572,000
CAPITAL New Delhi 301,000
RELIGION Hindu, Muslim, Christian, Sikh
LANGUAGE Hindi, English, 14 other official languages
LITERACY 52%
LIFE EXPECTANCY 63 years
GDP PER CAPITA $2,540
ECONOMY **IND**: textiles, chemicals, food processing, steel. **AGR**: rice, wheat, oilseed, cotton; cattle; fish. **EXP**: textile goods, gems and jewelry, engineering goods, chemicals.

INDONESIA

REPUBLIC OF INDONESIA

AREA 1,904,570 sq km (735,358 sq mi)
POPULATION 220,483,000
CAPITAL Jakarta 11,429,000
RELIGION Muslim, Protestant, Roman Catholic, Hindu, Buddhist
LANGUAGE Bahasa Indonesia, English, Dutch,Javanese,and other local dialects
LITERACY 84%
LIFE EXPECTANCY 68 years
GDP PER CAPITA $3,000
ECONOMY **IND**: petroleum and natural gas, textiles, mining, rubber. **AGR**: rice, cassava (tapioca), peanuts, rubber; poultry. **EXP**: oil and gas, plywood, textiles, rubber.

IRAN

ISLAMIC REPUBLIC OF IRAN

AREA 1,648,000 sq km (636,296 sq mi)
POPULATION 66,582,000
CAPITAL Tehran 7,038,000
RELIGION Shiite and Sunni Muslim
LANGUAGE Persian, Turkic, Kurdish, various local dialects
LITERACY 72%
LIFE EXPECTANCY 69 years
GDP PER CAPITA $7,000
ECONOMY **IND**: petroleum, petrochemicals, textiles, cement and other construction materials. **AGR**: wheat, rice, other grains, sugar beets; dairy products; caviar. **EXP**: petroleum, carpets, fruits and nuts, iron and steel.

IRAQ

REPUBLIC OF IRAQ

AREA 438,317 sq km (169,235 sq mi)
POPULATION 24,205,000
CAPITAL Baghdad 4,958,000
RELIGION Shiite and Sunni Muslim
LANGUAGE Arabic, Kurdish, Assyrian, Armenian
LITERACY 58%
LIFE EXPECTANCY 58 years
GDP PER CAPITA $2,500
ECONOMY **IND**: petroleum, chemicals, textiles, construction materials. **AGR**: wheat, barley, rice, vegetables; cattle. **EXP**: crude oil.

ISRAEL

STATE OF ISRAEL

AREA 22,145 sq km (8,550 sq mi)
POPULATION 6,707,000
CAPITAL Jerusalem 661,000
RELIGION Jewish, Muslim, Christian
LANGUAGE Hebrew, Arabic, English
LITERACY 95%
LIFE EXPECTANCY 79 years
GDP PER CAPITA $19,000
ECONOMY **IND**: high-technology projects (aviation, communications), wood and paper products, potash and phosphates, food. **AGR**: citrus, vegetables cotton; beef. **EXP**: machinery and equipment, software, cut diamonds, agricultural products.

JAPAN

JAPAN

AREA 377,880 sq km (145,900 sq mi)
POPULATION 127,508,000
CAPITAL Tokyo 26,546,000
RELIGION Shinto, Buddhist
LANGUAGE Japanese
LITERACY 99%
LIFE EXPECTANCY 81 years
GDP PER CAPITA $28,000
ECONOMY **IND**: motor vehicles, electronic equipment, machine tools, steel and nonferrous metals. **AGR**: rice, sugar beets, vegetables, fruits; pork; fish. **EXP**: motor vehicles, semiconductors, office machinery, chemicals.

JORDAN

HASHEMITE KINGDOM OF JORDAN

AREA 89,342 sq km (34,495 sq mi)
POPULATION 5,480,000
CAPITAL Amman 1,181,000
RELIGION Sunni Muslim, Christian
LANGUAGE Arabic, English
LITERACY 87%
LIFE EXPECTANCY 69 years
GDP PER CAPITA $4,300
ECONOMY **IND**: phosphate mining, petroleum refining, cement, potash. **AGR**: wheat, barley, citrus, tomatoes; sheep. **EXP**: phosphates, fertilizers, potash, agricultural products.

KAZAKHSTAN

REPUBLIC OF KAZAKHSTAN

AREA 2,717,300 sq km (1,049,155 sq mi)
POPULATION 14,787,000
CAPITAL Astana 328,000
RELIGION Muslim, Russian Orthodox
LANGUAGE Kazakh, Russian
LITERACY 98%
LIFE EXPECTANCY 66 years
GDP PER CAPITA $5,900
ECONOMY **IND**: oil, coal, copper, chromite. **AGR**: grain (mostly spring wheat), cotton; wool. **EXP**: oil, ferrous and nonferrous metals, machinery, chemicals.

KUWAIT

STATE OF KUWAIT

AREA 17,818 sq km (6,880 sq mi)
POPULATION 2,384,000
CAPITAL Kuwait City 888,000
RELIGION Sunni and Shiite Muslim, Christian, Hindu, Parsi
LANGUAGE Arabic, English
LITERACY 79%
LIFE EXPECTANCY 78 years
GDP PER CAPITA $15,100
ECONOMY **IND:** petroleum, petrochemicals, desalination, food processing. **AGR:** practically no crops; fish. **EXP:** oil and refined products, fertilizers.

KYRGYZSTAN

KYRGYZ REPUBLIC

AREA 198,500 sq km (76,641 sq mi)
POPULATION 5,033,000
CAPITAL Bishkek 736,000
RELIGION Muslim, Russian Orthodox
LANGUAGE Kyrgyz, Russian
LITERACY 97%
LIFE EXPECTANCY 69 years
GDP PER CAPITA $2,800
ECONOMY **IND:** small machinery, textiles, food processing, cement. **AGR:** tobacco, cotton, potatoes, vegetables; sheep. **EXP:** cotton, gold, machinery, shoes.

LAOS

LAO PEOPLE'S DEMOCRATIC REPUBLIC

AREA 236,800 sq km (91,429 sq mi)
POPULATION 5,593,000
CAPITAL Vientiane 663,000
RELIGION Buddhist, animist
LANGUAGE Lao, French, English, various indigenous languages
LITERACY 57%
LIFE EXPECTANCY 54 years
GDP PER CAPITA $1,630
ECONOMY **IND:** small-scale tin and gypsum mining, timber, electric power, agricultural processing. **AGR:** sweet potatoes, vegetables, corn, coffee; water buffalo. **EXP:** wood products, garments, electricity, coffee.

LEBANON

LEBANESE REPUBLIC

AREA 10,452 sq km (4,036 sq mi)
POPULATION 4,198,000
CAPITAL Beirut 2,115,000
RELIGION Muslim, Christian
LANGUAGE Arabic, French, English, Armenian
LITERACY 86%
LIFE EXPECTANCY 73 years
GDP PER CAPITA $5,200
ECONOMY **IND:** banking, jewelry, mineral and chemical products, oil refining. **AGR:** citrus, grapes, tomatoes, apples; sheep. **EXP:** foodstuffs and tobacco, textiles, chemicals, precious stones.

MALAYSIA

MALAYSIA

AREA 329,847 sq km (127,355 sq mi)
POPULATION 25,061,000
CAPITAL Kuala Lumpur 1,410,000
RELIGION Muslim, Buddhist, Daoist, Hindu, Christian, Sikh, Shamanist
LANGUAGE Bahasa Melayu, English, Chinese
LITERACY 84%
LIFE EXPECTANCY 73 years
GDP PER CAPITA $9,000
ECONOMY **IND:** rubber and palm oil processing, light manufacturing, logging, agriculture processing. **AGR:** rubber, palm oil, timber. **EXP:** electronic equipment, petroleum and liquefied natural gas, chemicals, palm oil.

MALDIVES

REPUBLIC OF MALDIVES

AREA 298 sq km (115 sq mi)
POPULATION 285,000
CAPITAL Male 84,000
RELIGION Sunni Muslim
LANGUAGE Maldivian Dhivehi (dialect of Sinhala), English
LITERACY 93%
LIFE EXPECTANCY 67 years
GDP PER CAPITA $3,870
ECONOMY **IND:** fish processing, tourism shipping, boat building. **AGR:** coconuts, corn, sweet potatoes; fish. **EXP:** consumer goods, intermediate and capital goods, petroleum products.

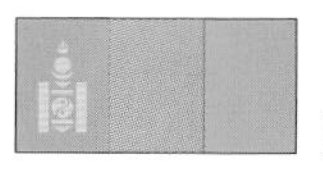

MONGOLIA

MONGOLIA

AREA 1,565,000 sq km (604,250 sq mi)
POPULATION 2,500,000
CAPITAL Ulaanbaatar 781,000
RELIGION Tibetan Buddhist, Lamaism
LANGUAGE Khalkha Mongol, Turkic, Russian
LITERACY 98%
LIFE EXPECTANCY 65 years
GDP PER CAPITA $1,770
ECONOMY **IND:** construction materials, mining, food and beverages, processing of animal products. **AGR:** wheat, barley, potatoes, forage crops; sheep. **EXP:** copper, livestock, animal products, cashmere.

MYANMAR

UNION OF MYANMAR

AREA 676,552 sq km (261,218 sq mi)
POPULATION 49,481,000
CAPITAL Yangon (Rangoon) 4,504,000
RELIGION Buddhist, Christian, Muslim
LANGUAGE Burmese, minor languages
LITERACY 83%
LIFE EXPECTANCY 57 years
GDP PER CAPITA $1,500
ECONOMY **IND:** agricultural processing, textiles and footwear, wood and wood products, construction materials. **AGR:** rice, corn, oilseed, sugarcane; hardwood. **EXP:** apparel, foodstuffs, wood products, precious stones.

NEPAL

KINGDOM OF NEPAL

AREA 147,181 sq km (56,827 sq mi)
POPULATION 25,164,000
CAPITAL Kathmandu 755,000
RELIGION Hindu, Buddhist, Muslim
LANGUAGE Nepali, English, many other languages and dialects
LITERACY 28%
LIFE EXPECTANCY 59 years
GDP PER CAPITA $1,400
ECONOMY **IND:** tourism, rice, cigarettes, cement and brick production. **AGR:** rice, corn, wheat, sugarcane; milk. **EXP:** carpets, clothing, leather goods, jute goods.

NORTH KOREA

DEMOCRATIC PEOPLE'S REPUBLIC OF KOREA

AREA 120,538 sq km (46,540 sq mi)
POPULATION 22,661,000
CAPITAL Pyongyang 3,164,000
RELIGION Buddhist, Confucianist
LANGUAGE Korean
LITERACY 99%
LIFE EXPECTANCY 63 years
GDP PER CAPITA $1,000
ECONOMY **IND:** military products, machine building, mining, textiles. **AGR:** rice, corn, potatoes, soybeans; cattle. **EXP:** minerals, metallurgical products, manufactures, agricultural and fishery products.

OMAN

SULTANATE OF OMAN

AREA 212,460 sq km (82,031 sq mi)
POPULATION 2,637,000
CAPITAL Muscat 540,000
RELIGION Ibadhi Muslim, Sunni Muslim, Shiite Muslim, Hindu
LANGUAGE Arabic, English, Baluchi, Urdu, Indian dialects
LITERACY 80%
LIFE EXPECTANCY 73 years
GDP PER CAPITA $8,200
ECONOMY **IND:** crude oil production and refining, natural gas production, construction, cement. **AGR:** dates, limes, bananas, alfalfa; camels; fish. **EXP:** petroleum, reexports, fish, metals.

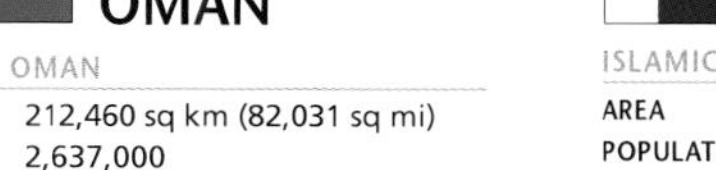

PAKISTAN

ISLAMIC REPUBLIC OF PAKISTAN

AREA 796,095 sq km (307,374 sq mi)
POPULATION 149,147,000
CAPITAL Islamabad 636,000
RELIGION Sunni and Shiite Muslim, Christian, Hindu
LANGUAGE Punjabi, Sindhi, Siraiki, Pashtu, Urdu, English, Balochi
LITERACY 43%
LIFE EXPECTANCY 60 years
GDP PER CAPITA $2,100
ECONOMY **IND:** textiles, food processing, beverages, construction materials. **AGR:** cotton, wheat, rice, sugarcane; milk. **EXP:** textiles (garments, cotton cloth), rice, other agricultural products.

PHILIPPINES

REPUBLIC OF THE PHILIPPINES

AREA 300,000 sq km (115,831 sq mi)
POPULATION 81,578,000
CAPITAL Manila 10,069,000
RELIGION Roman Catholic, Protestant, Muslim, Buddhist
LANGUAGE Filipino (based on Tagalog), English, and 8 major dialects
LITERACY 95%
LIFE EXPECTANCY 70 years
GDP PER CAPITA $4,000
ECONOMY **IND:** textiles, pharmaceuticals, chemicals, wood products. **AGR:** rice, coconuts, corn, sugarcane; pork; fish. **EXP:** electronic equipment, machinery and transport equipment, garments, coconut products.

QATAR

STATE OF QATAR

AREA 11,521 sq km (4,448 sq mi)
POPULATION 629,000
CAPITAL Doha 285,000
RELIGION Muslim
LANGUAGE Arabic, English
LITERACY 79%
LIFE EXPECTANCY 72 years
GDP PER CAPITA $21,200
ECONOMY **IND:** crude oil production and refining, fertilizers, petrochemicals, steel reinforcing bars. **AGR:** fruits, vegetables; poultry; fish. **EXP:** petroleum products, fertilizers, steel.

SAUDI ARABIA

KINGDOM OF SAUDI ARABIA

AREA 1,960,582 sq km (756,985 sq mi)
POPULATION 24,070,000
CAPITAL Riyadh 4,761,000
RELIGION Muslim
LANGUAGE Arabic
LITERACY 78%
LIFE EXPECTANCY 72 years
GDP PER CAPITA $10,600
ECONOMY **IND:** crude oil production, petroleum refining, basic petrochemicals, cement. **AGR:** wheat, barley, tomatoes, melons; mutton. **EXP:** petroleum and petroleum products.

SINGAPORE

REPUBLIC OF SINGAPORE

AREA 660 sq km (255 sq mi)
POPULATION 4,196,000
CAPITAL Singapore 4,108,000
RELIGION Buddhist, Muslim, Christian, Hindu, Sikh, Taoist, Confucianist
LANGUAGE Chinese, Malay, Tamil, English
LITERACY 94%
LIFE EXPECTANCY 79 years
GDP PER CAPITA $24,700
ECONOMY **IND:** electronics, chemicals, financial services, oil drilling equipment. **AGR:** rubber, copra, fruit, orchids; poultry. **EXP:** machinery and equipment (including electronics), chemicals, mineral fuels.

SOUTH KOREA

REPUBLIC OF KOREA

AREA 99,250 sq km (38,321 sq mi)
POPULATION 47,939,000
CAPITAL Seoul 9,862,000
RELIGION Christian, Buddhist
LANGUAGE Korean, English
LITERACY 98%
LIFE EXPECTANCY 76 years
GDP PER CAPITA $19,400
ECONOMY **IND:** military products,machine building, mining, textiles. **AGR:** rice, corn, potatoes, soybeans; cattle. **EXP:** minerals, metallurgical products, manufactures, agricultural and fishery products.

SRI LANKA

DEMOCRATIC SOCIALIST REPUBLIC OF SRI LANKA

AREA 65,525 sq km (25,299 sq mi)
POPULATION 19,273,000
CAPITAL Colombo 681,000
RELIGION Buddhist, Hindu, Christian, Muslim
LANGUAGE Sinhala, Tamil, English
LITERACY 90%
LIFE EXPECTANCY 72 years
GDP PER CAPITA $3,250
ECONOMY **IND:** processing of rubber, tea and other agricultural products, clothing, cement. **AGR:** rice, sugarcane, grains, pulses; milk. **EXP:** textiles and apparel, tea, diamonds, coconut products.

SYRIA

SYRIAN ARAB REPUBLIC

AREA 185,180 sq km (71,498 sq mi)
POPULATION 17,537,000
CAPITAL Damascus 2,195,000
RELIGION Sunni, Alawite, Druze and other Muslim sects, Circassian
LANGUAGE Arabic, Kurdish, Armenian, Aramaic, Circassian
LITERACY 71%
LIFE EXPECTANCY 70 years
GDP PER CAPITA $3,200
ECONOMY **IND:** petroleum, textiles, food processing, beverages. **AGR:** wheat, barley, cotton, lentils; beef. **EXP:** petroleum, textiles, manufactured goods, fruits and vegetables.

TAJIKISTAN

REPUBLIC OF TAJIKISTAN

AREA 143,100 sq km (55,251 sq mi)
POPULATION 6,574,000
CAPITAL Dushanbe 522,000
RELIGION Sunni and Shiite Muslim
LANGUAGE Tajik, Russian
LITERACY 98%
LIFE EXPECTANCY 68 years
GDP PER CAPITA $1,140
ECONOMY **IND:** aluminum processing, mining, textiles, chemicals and fertilizers. **AGR:** cotton, grain, fruits, grapes; cattle. **EXP:** aluminum, electricity, cotton, fruits.

THAILAND

KINGDOM OF THAILAND

AREA 513,115 sq km (198,115 sq mi)
POPULATION 63,063,000
CAPITAL Bangkok 7,527,000
RELIGION Buddhist, Muslim
LANGUAGE Thai, English, ethnic and regional dialects
LITERACY 94%
LIFE EXPECTANCY 71 years
GDP PER CAPITA $6,600
ECONOMY **IND:** tourism, textiles and garments, electric appliances and components, tungsten. **AGR:** rice, cassava (tapioca), rubber, corn. **EXP:** computers and parts, textiles, integrated circuits, rice.

TIMOR-LESTE

DEMOCRATIC REPUBLIC OF TIMOR-LESTE

AREA 14,874 sq km (5,743 sq mi)
POPULATION 778,000
CAPITAL Dili 56,000
RELIGION Christian (mostly Catholic)
LANGUAGE Tetum, Portuguese, Bahasa Indonesian
LITERACY 48%
LIFE EXPECTANCY 49 years
GDP PER CAPITA $500
ECONOMY **IND:** logging. **AGR:** coffee, coconuts, cacao; fish. **EXP:** potential for oil.

TURKEY

REPUBLIC OF TURKEY

AREA 779,452 sq km (300,948 sq mi)
POPULATION 71,224,000
CAPITAL Ankara 3,208,000
RELIGION Muslim (mostly Sunni)
LANGUAGE Turkish, Kurdish, Arabic, Armenian, Greek
LITERACY 85%
LIFE EXPECTANCY 69 years
GDP PER CAPITA $7,000
ECONOMY **IND:** textiles, food processing, autos, mining. **AGR:** tobacco, cotton, grain, olives; livestock. **EXP:** apparel, foodstuffs, textiles, metal manufactures.

TURKMENISTAN

TURKMENISTAN

AREA 488,100 sq km (188,456 sq mi)
POPULATION 5,703,000
CAPITAL Ashgabat 558,000
RELIGION Muslim, Eastern Orthodox
LANGUAGE Turkmen, Russian, Uzbek
LITERACY 98%
LIFE EXPECTANCY 67 years
GDP PER CAPITA $4,700
ECONOMY **IND:** natural gas, oil, petroleum products, textiles. **AGR:** cotton, grain; livestock. **EXP:** gas, oil, cotton fiber, textiles.

UNITED ARAB EMIRATES

UNITED ARAB EMIRATES

AREA 82,880 sq km (32,000 sq mi)
POPULATION 3,888,000
CAPITAL Abu Dhabi 471,000
RELIGION Sunni and Shiite Muslim, Christian, Hindu
LANGUAGE Arabic, Persian, English, Hindi, Urdu
LITERACY 79%
LIFE EXPECTANCY 74 years
GDP PER CAPITA $21,100
ECONOMY **IND:** petroleum, fishing, petrochemicals, construction materials. **AGR:** dates, vegetables, watermelons; poultry; fish. **EXP:** crude oil, natural gas, reexports, dried fish.

UZBEKISTAN

REPUBLIC OF UZBEKISTAN

AREA 447,400 sq km (172,742 sq mi)
POPULATION 25,672,000
CAPITAL Tashkent 2,157,000
RELIGION Muslim, Eastern Orthodox
LANGUAGE Uzbek, Russian, Tajik
LITERACY 99%
LIFE EXPECTANCY 70 years
GDP PER CAPITA $2,500
ECONOMY **IND:** textiles, food processing, machine building, metallurgy. **AGR:** cotton, vegetables, fruits, grain; livestock. **EXP:** cotton, gold, natural gas, mineral fertilizers.

VIETNAM

SOCIALIST REPUBLIC OF VIETNAM

AREA 329,560 sq km (127,244 sq mi)
POPULATION 80,786,000
CAPITAL Hanoi 3,822,000
RELIGION Buddhist, Hoa Hao, Cao Dai, Christian, indigenous beliefs, Muslim
LANGUAGE Vietnamese, English, French, Chinese, Khmer, tribal languages
LITERACY 94%
LIFE EXPECTANCY 72 years
GDP PER CAPITA $2,100
ECONOMY **IND:** petroleum, natural gas, light industries, mining. **AGR:** wheat, barley, oats, grapes; sheep. **EXP:** crude oil, marine products, rice, coffee.

YEMEN

REPUBLIC OF YEMEN

AREA 536,869 sq km (207,286 sq mi)
POPULATION 19,350,000
CAPITAL Sanaa 1,410,000
RELIGION Sunni and Shiite Muslim
LANGUAGE Arabic
LITERACY 38%
LIFE EXPECTANCY 60 years
GDP PER CAPITA $820
ECONOMY **IND:** crude oil production and petroleum refining, small-scale production of cotton textiles and leather goods, food processing, handicrafts. **AGR:** grain, fruits and vegetables, pulses, qat; dairy products; fish. **EXP:** crude oil, coffee, dried and salted fish.

AREA OF SPECIAL STATUS

TAIWAN

TAIWAN

AREA 35,980 sq km (13,891 sq mi)
POPULATION 22,568,000
CAPITAL Taipei 2,550,000
RELIGION mixture of Buddhist, Confucian, and Taoist; Christian
LANGUAGE Mandarin Chinese, Taiwanese
LITERACY 86%
LIFE EXPECTANCY 76 years
GDP PER CAPITA $17,200
ECONOMY **IND:** electronics, petroleum refining, chemicals, textiles, iron and steel, machinery, cement, food processing. **AGR:** rice corn, vegetables, fruits,tea; pigs, poultry, beef, milk; fish. **EXP:** machinery and electrical equipment, minerals, precision instruments.

The People's Republic of China claims Taiwan as its 23rd province. Taiwan maintains that there are two political entities.

POPULATION DENSITY

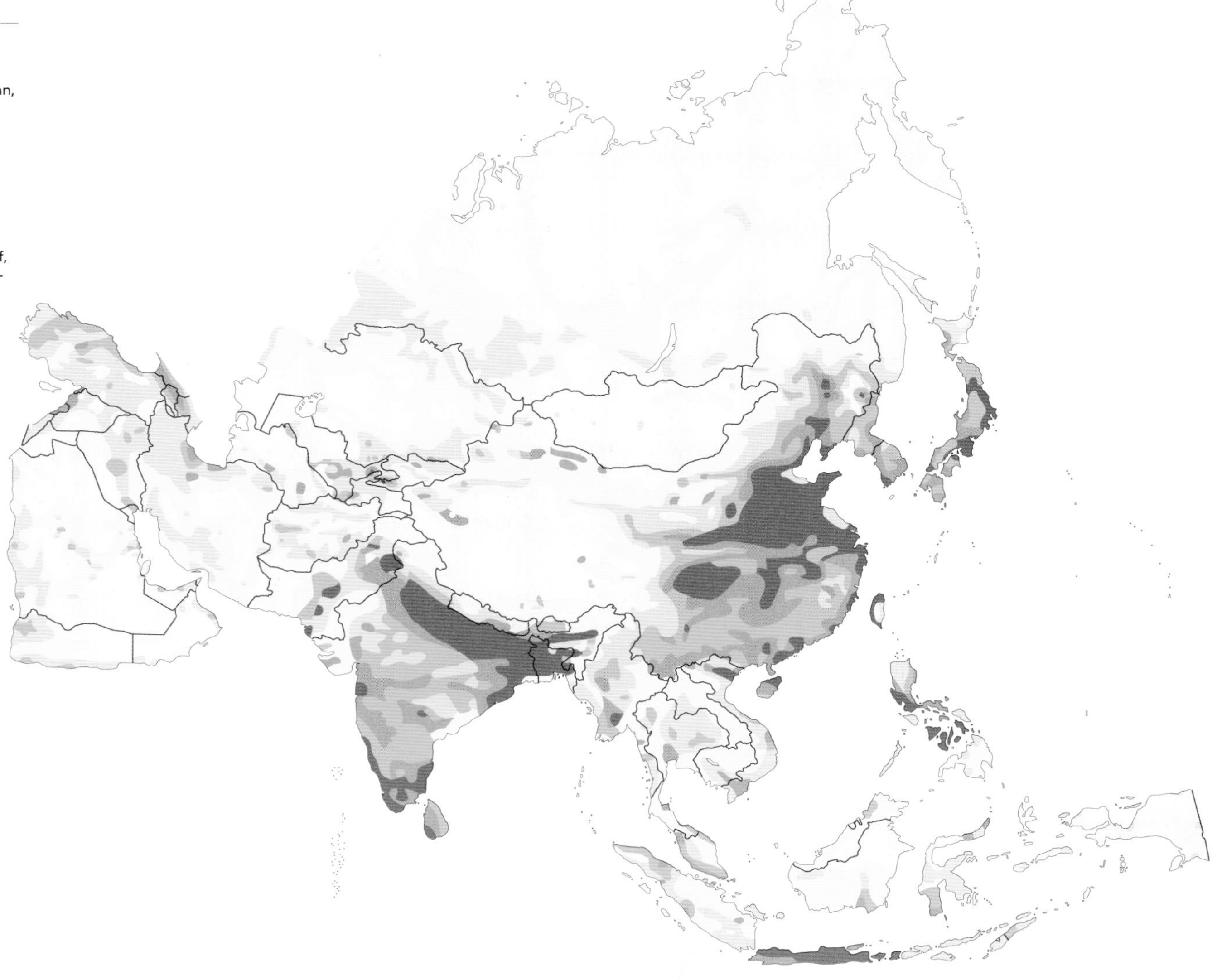

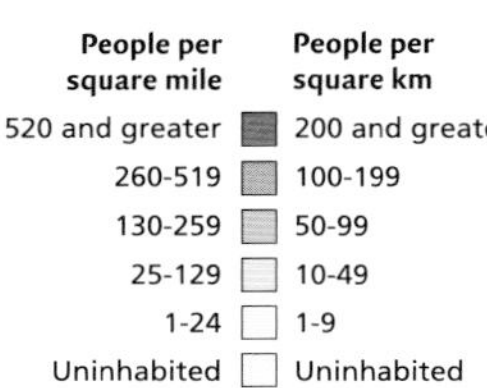

DATES OF COUNTRY INDEPENDENCE

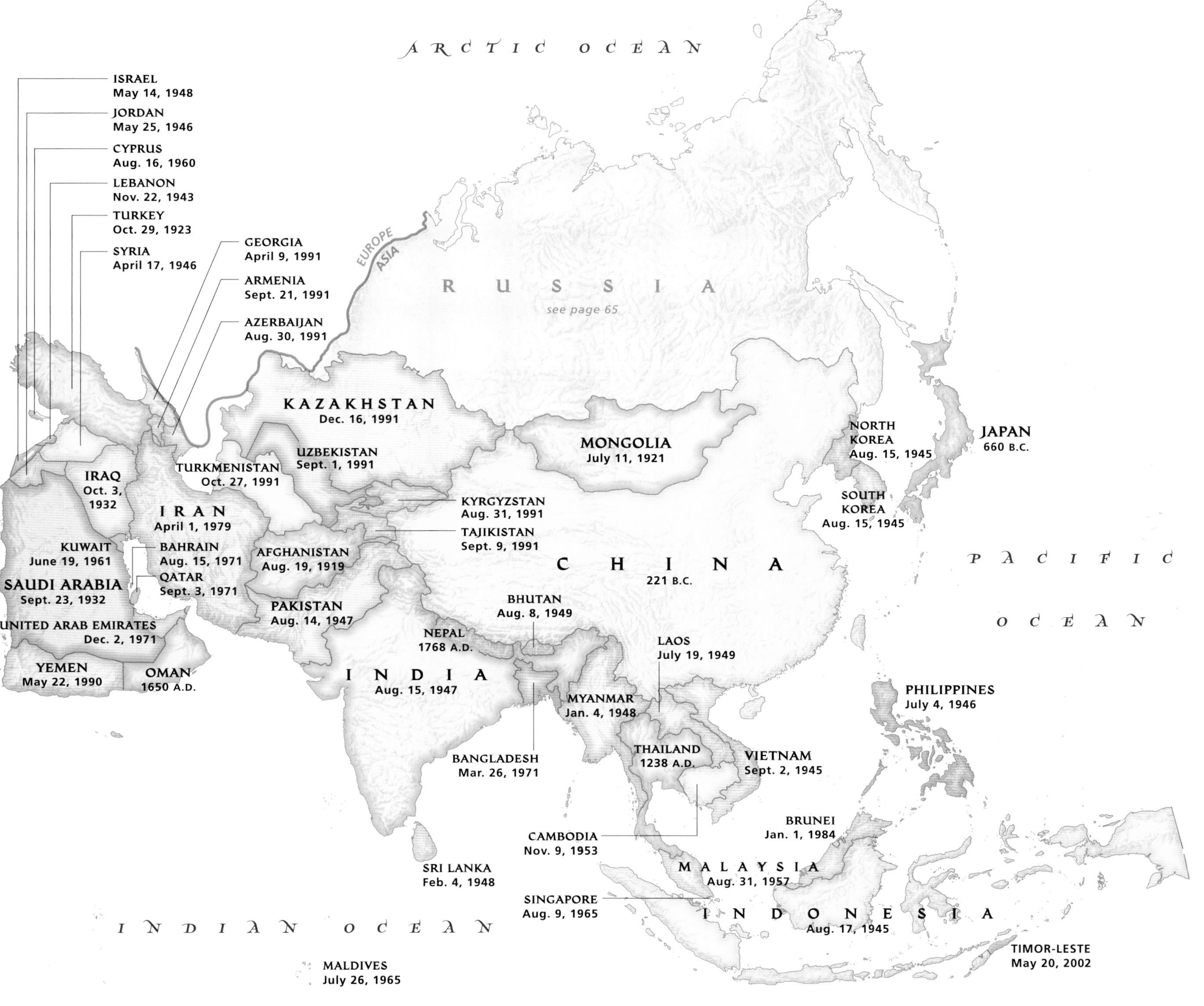
ARCTIC OCEAN
ISRAEL May 14, 1948
JORDAN May 25, 1946
CYPRUS Aug. 16, 1960
LEBANON Nov. 22, 1943
TURKEY Oct. 29, 1923
SYRIA April 17, 1946
GEORGIA April 9, 1991
ARMENIA Sept. 21, 1991
AZERBAIJAN Aug. 30, 1991
EUROPE
ASIA
RUSSIA
see page 65
KAZAKHSTAN Dec. 16, 1991
MONGOLIA July 11, 1921
UZBEKISTAN Sept. 1, 1991
TURKMENISTAN Oct. 27, 1991
IRAQ Oct. 3, 1932
IRAN April 1, 1979
KYRGYZSTAN Aug. 31, 1991
TAJIKISTAN Sept. 9, 1991
NORTH KOREA Aug. 15, 1945
SOUTH KOREA Aug. 15, 1945
JAPAN 660 B.C.
KUWAIT June 19, 1961
BAHRAIN Aug. 15, 1971
AFGHANISTAN Aug. 19, 1919
QATAR Sept. 3, 1971
SAUDI ARABIA Sept. 23, 1932
CHINA 221 B.C.
PACIFIC OCEAN
PAKISTAN Aug. 14, 1947
BHUTAN Aug. 8, 1949
UNITED ARAB EMIRATES Dec. 2, 1971
NEPAL 1768 A.D.
LAOS July 19, 1949
YEMEN May 22, 1990
OMAN 1650 A.D.
INDIA Aug. 15, 1947
MYANMAR Jan. 4, 1948
PHILIPPINES July 4, 1946
BANGLADESH Mar. 26, 1971
THAILAND 1238 A.D.
VIETNAM Sept. 2, 1945
BRUNEI Jan. 1, 1984
CAMBODIA Nov. 9, 1953
SRI LANKA Feb. 4, 1948
MALAYSIA Aug. 31, 1957
SINGAPORE Aug. 9, 1965
INDONESIA Aug. 17, 1945
INDIAN OCEAN
TIMOR-LESTE May 20, 2002
MALDIVES July 26, 1965

AFRICA

Elemental and unconquerable, Africa remains something of a paradox among continents. Birthplace of humankind and of the great early civilizations of Egypt and Kush, also called Nubia, the continent has since thwarted human efforts to exploit many of its resources. The forbidding sweep of the Sahara, largest desert in the world, holds the northern third of Africa in thrall, while the bordering Sahel sands alternately advance and recede in unpredictable, drought-invoking rhythms. In contrast to the long, life-giving thread of the Nile, the lake district in the east, and the Congo drainage in central Africa, few major waterways provide irrigation and commercial navigation to large, arid segments of the continent.

Africa's unforgettable form, bulging to the west, lies surrounded by oceans and seas. The East African Rift System is the continent's most dramatic geologic feature. This great rent actually begins in the Red Sea, then cuts southward to form the stunning landscape of lakes, volcanoes, and deep valleys that finally ends near the mouth of the Zambezi River. Caused by the Earth's crust pulling apart, the rift may one day separate East Africa from the rest of the continent.

Most of Africa is made up of savannah—high, rolling, grassy plains. These savannahs have been home since earliest times to people often called Bantu, a reference to both social groupings and their languages. Other distinct physical types exist around the continent as well: BaMbuti (Pygmies), San (Bushmen), Nilo-Saharans, and Hamito-Semitics (Berbers and Cushites). Africa's astonishing 1,600 spoken languages—more than any other continent— reflect the great diversity of ethnic and social groups.

Africa ranks among the richest regions in the world in natural resources; it contains vast reserves of fossil fuels, precious metals, ores, and gems, including almost all of the world's chromium, much uranium, copper, enormous underground gold reserves, and diamonds. Yet Africa accounts for a mere one percent of world economic output. South Africa's economy alone nearly equals that of all other sub-Saharan countries. Many obstacles complicate the way forward. African countries experience great gaps in wealth between city and country, and many face growing slums around megacities such as Lagos and Cairo. Nearly 40 other African cities have populations over a million. Lack of clean water and the spread of diseases—malaria, tuberculosis, cholera, and AIDS—undermine people's health. More than 29million Africans are now infected with HIV/AIDS, which killed 2.4 millionAfricans in 2002. AIDS has shortened life expectancy to 47 years in partsof Africa, destroyed families, and erased decades of social progress andeconomic activity by killing people in their prime working years. In addition, war and huge concentrations of refugees displaced by fighting, persecution, and famine deter any chance of growth and stability.

Africa's undeveloped natural beauty—along with its wealth of animal life, despite a vast dimunition in their numbers due to poaching and habitat loss—has engendered a booming tourist industry. Names such as "Serengeti Plain," "Kalahari Desert," "Okavanga Delta," and "Victoria Falls" still evoke images of an Africa unspoiled, unconquerable, and, throughout the Earth, unsurpassed.

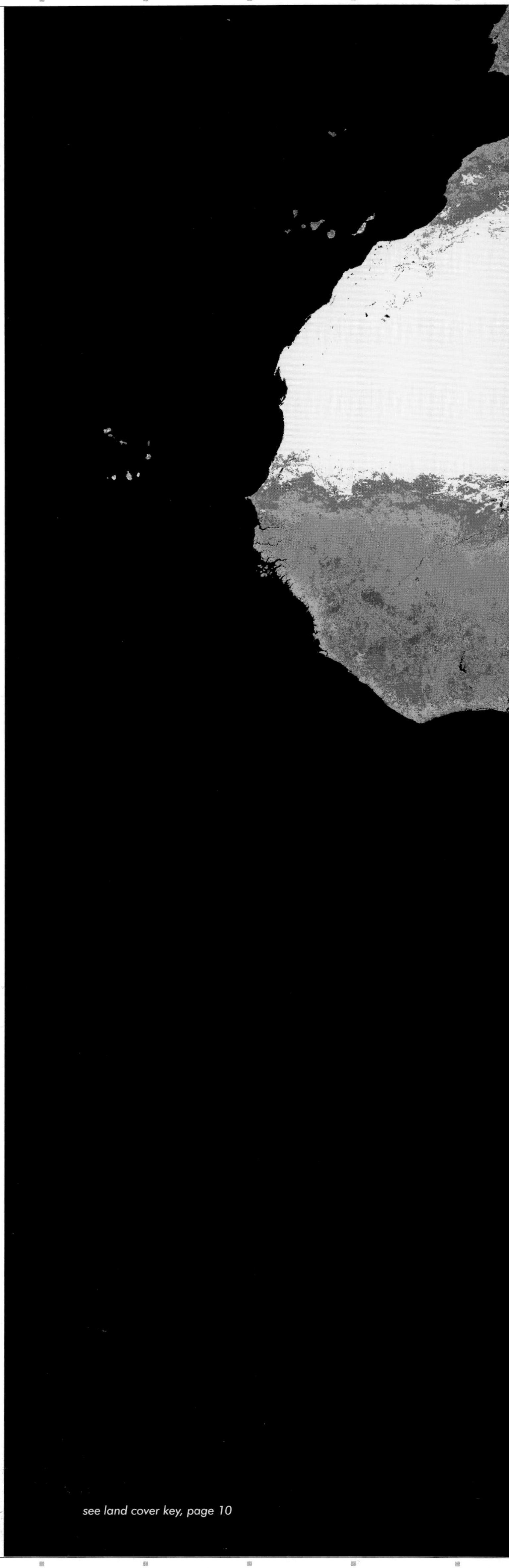

see land cover key, page 10

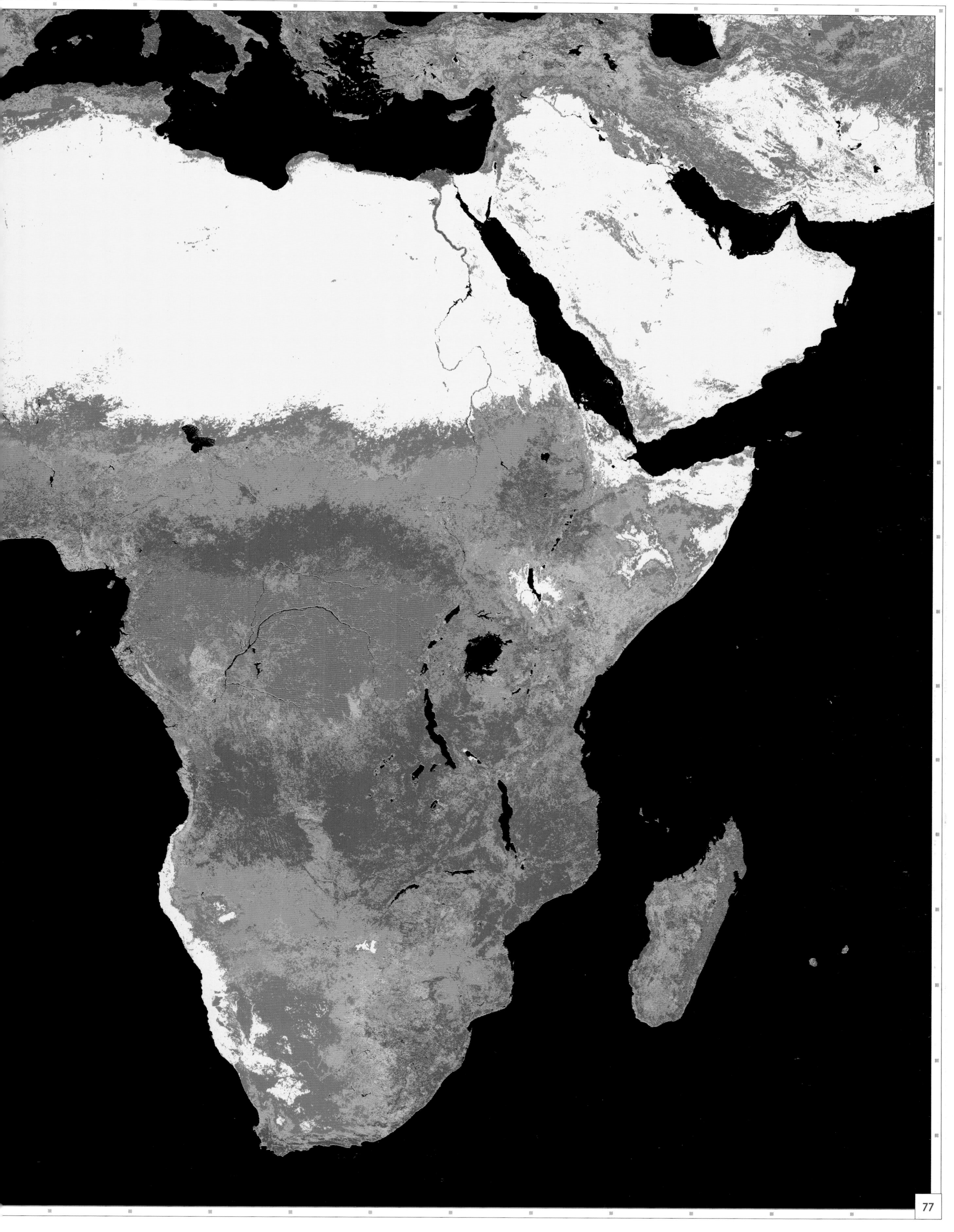

Longitude West 20° of Greenwich
U.K.
LONDON
Bruxelles (Brussels)
BELGIUM
LUX.
PARIS
FRANCE
SWITZERLAND
Bern
GERMANY
POLAND
PRAHA (Prague)
CZECH REP.
WIEN (Vienna)
AUSTRIA
SLOVAKIA
Bratislava
BUDAPEST
HUNGARY
Ljubljana
SLOVENIA
Zagreb
CROATIA
BOSNIA & HERZEGOVINA
Sarajevo
SERBIA
MONTENEGRO
BEOGRAD (Belgrade)
ROMANIA
BUCUREŞTI (Bucharest)
SOFIYA (Sofia)
BULGARIA
Skopje
MACEDONIA
(Tirana) Tiranë
ALBANIA
GREECE
Athína (Athens)
ITALY
ROMA (Rome)
MALTA
UKRAINE
KYIV (Kiev)
MOLDOVA
Chişinău
RUSSIA
KAZAKHSTAN
UZBEKISTAN
TURKMENISTAN
Ashgabat
CASPIAN SEA
BLACK SEA
GEORGIA
T'BILISI
ARMENIA
AZERBAIJAN
BAKI (Baku)
YEREVAN
ANKARA
TURKEY
TEHRĀN
IRAN
BAGHDĀD
IRAQ
SYRIA
Lefkosia (Nicosia)
CYPRUS
LEBANON
(Beirut) BEYROUTH
DIMASHQ (Damascus)
ISRAEL
Jerusalem
ʻAMMĀN
JORDAN
KUWAIT
Al Kuwayt (Kuwait)
PERSIAN GULF
BAHRAIN
Al Manāmah (Manama)
QATAR
Ad Dawhah (Doha)
U.A.E.
SAUDI ARABIA
AR RIYĀD (Riyadh)
TROPIC OF CANCER
AZORES (AÇORES) Portugal
PORTUGAL
Lisboa (Lisbon)
SPAIN
MADRID
ANDORRA
GIBRALTAR U.K.
Strait of Gibraltar
MEDITERRANEAN SEA
MADEIRA ISLANDS Portugal
CANARY ISLANDS (ISLAS CANARIAS) Spain
Santa Cruz
Las Palmas
MOROCCO
RABAT
CASABLANCA
Tangier
Tétouan
Fès (Fez)
Meknès
Marrakech
Agadir
Laayoune
WESTERN SAHARA
ALGERIA
ALGER (Algiers)
Oran
Constantine
Annaba
TUNISIA
TUNIS
LIBYA
ṬARĀBULUS (Tripoli)
Banghāzī (Benghazi)
TRIPOLITANIA
CYRENAICA
FEZZAN
EGYPT
EL QÂHIRA (Cairo)
EL ISKANDARÎYA (Alexandria)
EL GÎZA
Bûr Saʻîd (Port Said)
El Suweis (Suez)
Nile
Boundary claimed by Sudan
Treaty boundary
SAHARA
AOZOU STRIP
MAURITANIA
Nouakchott
Nouadhibou
MALI
BAMAKO
Tombouctou (Timbuktu)
Niger
NIGER
Niamey
CHAD
N'Djamena
Lake Chad
SUDAN
KHARTOUM
OMDURMAN (Umm Durmān)
Khartoum North
Bûr Sūdān (Port Sudan)
White Nile
Blue Nile
ERITREA
Asmara
DJIBOUTI
Djibouti
YEMEN
Şan'ā' (Sanaa)
GULF OF ADEN
ETHIOPIA
ĀDĪS ĀBEBA (Addis Ababa)
SOMALILAND
Hargeysa
PUNTLAND
SOMALIA
MUQDISHO (Mogadishu)
Historic capital
No central government
Boundary undemarcated and in dispute
KENYA
UGANDA
KAMPALA
DAKAR
SENEGAL
GAMBIA
Banjul
GUINEA-BISSAU
Bissau
GUINEA
CONAKRY
SIERRA LEONE
Freetown
LIBERIA
Monrovia
CÔTE D'IVOIRE
ABIDJAN
Administrative capital
Yamoussoukro
Legislative capital
BURKINA FASO
OUAGADOUGOU
GHANA
ACCRA
TOGO
Lomé
BENIN
Porto-Novo
Cotonou
NIGERIA
Abuja
LAGOS
KANO
CAMEROON
YAOUNDÉ
DOUALA
CENTRAL AFRICAN REPUBLIC
Bangui
EQUATORIAL GUINEA
Malabo
Bioko
RIO MUNI
SAO TOME &
GULF OF GUINEA
EQUATOR

AFRICA
Political

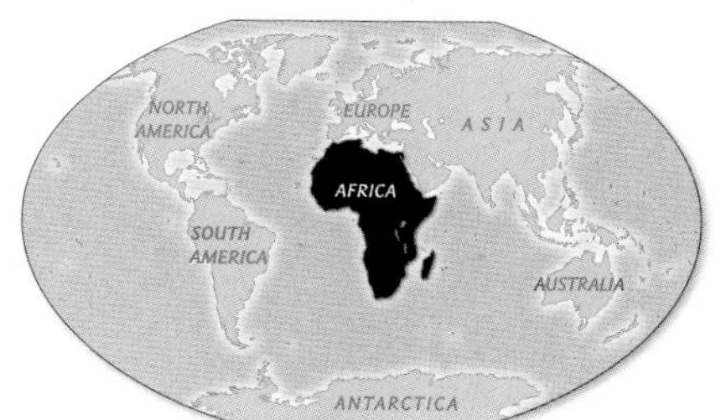

CONTINENTAL DATA

- **Total number of countries:** 53
- **First independent country:** Ethiopia, over 2,000 years old
- **"Youngest" country:** Eritrea, May 24, 1993
- **Largest country in area:** Sudan 2,505,810 sq km (967,498 sq mi)
- **Smallest country in area:** Seychelles 455 sq km (176 sq mi)
- **Percent urban population:** 33%
- **Most populous country:** Nigeria 133,882,000
- **Least populous country:** Seychelles 87,000
- **Most densely populated country:** Mauritius 598 per sq km (1,550 per sq mi)
- **Least densely populated country:** Namibia 2.3 per sq km (6 per sq mi)
- **Largest city by population:** Cairo, Egypt 9,586,000
- **Highest GDP per capita:** Mauritius $10,800
- **Lowest GDP per capita:** Sierra Leone $500
- **Average life expectancy in Africa:** 52 years
- **Average literacy rate in Africa:** 57%

Longitude West 20° of Greenwich
Longitude East 20° of Greenwich
TROPIC OF CANCER
EQUATOR
E U R O P E
A S I A
IBERIAN PENINSULA
BALKAN PENINSULA
ANATOLIA (ASIA MINOR)
ARABIAN PENINSULA
BLACK SEA
CASPIAN SEA
MEDITERRANEAN SEA
RED SEA
PERSIAN GULF
GULF OF ADEN
GULF OF GUINEA
AZORES
Madeira
MADEIRA ISLANDS
Salvage Islands
CANARY ISLANDS
La Palma
Tenerife
Gomera
Ferro
Gran Canaria
Lanzarote
Fuerteventura
C. Beddouza
Cape Rhir
C. Boujdour
C. Blanc
C. Timiris
C. Verde
Bissagos Is.
Strait of Gibraltar
Corsica
Sardinia
Balearic Is.
Sicily
Peloponnesus
Crete
Rhodes
Cyprus
Cape Blanc
G. of Tunis
G. of Hamamet
G. of Gabes
Jerba I.
Gulf of Sidra
Cape Misurata
Ras al Hilāl
G. of Bomba
G. of Salûm
Arabs Gulf
Nile River Delta
SUEZ CANAL
SINAI
Mt. Sinai 2285
G. of Suez
Gulf of Aqaba
Râs Muhammad
Râs Banas
Cape Elba (Ras Hadarba)
Suakin Archipelago
Ras Kasar
Dahlak Archipelago
Lowest point in Africa
Bab al Mandab
G. of Tadjoura
Cape Gwardafuy
ATLAS MOUNTAINS
Tell Atlas
Er Rif 2456
2308
2326
High Atlas
Saharan Atlas
Jebel Toubkal 4165
Chott Melrhir
Shott el Jerid
Oued Drâa
Hamada du Drâa
Great Western Erg
Great Eastern Erg
Gefara
Jabal Nafūsah
Jabal al Akhḑar
Libyan Plateau 264
Qattara Depression
-133
Tademaït Plateau
Hamada de Tinrhert
Jabal as Sawdā'
Al Harūj al Aswad
1200
Ṣaḩrā' Awbārī
Sand Sea of Calanscio
Sarīr Calanscio
Western Desert
Libyan Desert
Eastern Desert
Nile
Erg Iguidi
Erg Chech
Sebkha Mekerrhane
Sebkha Azzel Matti
Tassili-n-Ajjer
Zednes 460
Tanezrouft
Mount Tahat 3003
Ahaggar Mts.
Ṣaḩrā' Marzūq
Rebiana Sand Sea
Kufra Oasis
Abu Ballâs 467
Gilf Kebîr Plateau
Lake Nasser
Jabal Sīrī 420
Lake Nubia
Nubian Desert
SAHARA
Akchâr
El Djouf
Trarza
Tagant
El Mreyyé
1000
Adrar des Iforas
Tassili Oua-n-Ahaggar
Tarazit Massif
Aïr (Azbine)
Mt. Bagzane 2022
Ténéré
Mangueni Plateau
Pic Touside 3315
Tibesti
Emi Koussi 3415
Jebel 'Uweinat 1893
Jabel Abyad Plateau
Jebel Sabidana 1907
Bodele Depression
Ennedi
1310
Lake Faguibine
Lake Débo
Niger
Sénégal
Gambia
Falémé
Bafing
Bani
Fouta Djallon
1116
Loma Mts. 1948
Source of the Niger
765
Nimba Mts.
SUDAN
White Volta
Black Volta
Komoé
Lake Volta
UPPER GUINEA
Cavalla
Grain Coast
Cape Palmas
Ivory Coast
Gold Coast
Slave Coast
Bight of Benin
Niger River Delta
Bioko
Príncipe
Kainji Res.
Bauchi Plateau 1781
Benue
Hadejia
Gana
Yobe
Manga
Lake Chad
Guéra Massif 1613
Chari
Logone
Dar Rounga
1400
Chaîne des Mongos
Tondou Massif
Mbang Mts.
1213
Karre Mts.
Cameroon Mt. 4100
Sanaga
Ntem
Ngoko
Lobaya
Ubangi
Kotto
Bomu
Uele
Itimbiri
Aruwimi
Congo
CONGO
Jebel Teljo 1954
3088
Marra Mts.
Jebel ed Dair 1412
Nuba Mts. 1325
Bahr el 'Arab
Sudd
White Nile
Mountain Nile
Blue Nile
El Gezira
Atbara
Albert Nile
Lake Albert
Ruwenzori
Mt. Elgon 4321
KENYA
Swamp
Lake Turkana (L. Rudolf)
Chalbi Desert
Lorian
L. Chew Bahir
Dawa
Jubba
Shebele
Ras Dashen Terara 4620
Guna Terara 4231
Lake Tana
Lake Assal -156 (-512 ft)
ETHIOPIAN HIGHLANDS
Gurage 3719
Lake Abaya
Mendebo Mts.
Batu 4307
RIFT VALLEY
Ogadēn
Haud
SOMALI PENINSULA
2408
200
10°
20°
30°
40°
50°
60°
0°
1 2 3 4 5 6 7 8 9 10 11 12
A B C D E F G H J

AFRICA
Physical

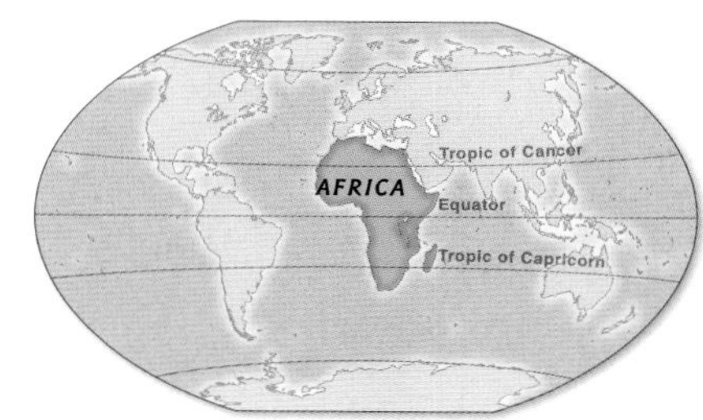

CONTINENTAL DATA

- **Area:**
  30,065,000 sq km
  (11,608,000 sq mi)
- **Greatest north-south extent:**
  8,047 km (5,000 mi)
- **Greatest east-west extent:**
  7,564 km (4,700 mi)
- **Highest point:**
  Kilimanjaro, Tanzania
  5,895 m (19,340 ft)
- **Lowest point:**
  Lake Assal, Djibouti
  -156 m (-512 ft)
- **Lowest recorded temperature:**
  Ifrane, Morocco -24°C (-11°F),
  February 11, 1935
- **Highest recorded temperature:**
  Al Aziziyah, Libya 58°C (136.4°F)
  September 13, 1922
- **Longest rivers:**
  - Nile 6,825 km (4,241 mi)
  - Congo 4,370 km (2,715 mi)
  - Niger 4,170 km (2,591 mi)
- **Largest lakes:**
  - Lake Victoria 69,500 sq km (26,800 sq mi)
  - Lake Tanganyika 32,600 sq km (12,600 sq mi)
  - Lake Malawi 28,900 sq km (11,200 sq mi)
- **Earth's extremes located in Africa:**
  - **Largest desert on Earth:** Sahara 9,000,000 sq km (3,475,000 sq mi)
  - **Hottest place on Earth:** Dalol, Denakil Depression, Ethiopia; annual average temperature 34°C (93°F)

AFRICA
FLAGS & FACTS

ALGERIA
PEOPLE'S DEMOCRATIC REPUBLIC OF ALGERIA

AREA 2,381,741 sq km (919,595 sq mi)
POPULATION 31,746,000
CAPITAL Algiers 2,861,000
RELIGION Sunni Muslim
LANGUAGE Arabic, French, Berber dialects
LITERACY 62%
LIFE EXPECTANCY 70 years
GDP PER CAPITA $5,600
ECONOMY **IND:** petroleum, natural gas, light industries, mining. **AGR:** wheat, barley, oats, grapes; sheep. **EXP:** petroleum, natural gas, petroleum products.

ANGOLA
REPUBLIC OF ANGOLA

AREA 1,246,700 sq km (481,354 sq mi)
POPULATION 13,087,000
CAPITAL Luanda 2,819,000
RELIGION indigenous beliefs, Roman Catholic, Protestant
LANGUAGE Portuguese, Bantu
LITERACY 42%
LIFE EXPECTANCY 40 years
GDP PER CAPITA $1,330
ECONOMY **IND:** petroleum, diamonds, cement, food. **AGR:** bananas, sugarcane, coffee, sisal; livestock; forest products; fish. **EXP:** crude oil, diamonds, refined petroleum products, gas.

BENIN
REPUBLIC OF BENIN

AREA 112,622 sq km (43,484 sq mi)
POPULATION 7,041,000
CAPITAL Porto-Novo 225,000
RELIGION indigenous beliefs, Christian, Muslim
LANGUAGE French, Fon, Yoruba, tribal languages
LITERACY 38%
LIFE EXPECTANCY 51 years
GDP PER CAPITA $1,040
ECONOMY **IND:** textiles, cigarettes, beverages, food. **AGR:** corn, sorghum, cassava (tapioca), yams; poultry. **EXP:** cotton, crude oil, palm products, cocoa.

BOTSWANA
REPUBLIC OF BOTSWANA

AREA 581,730 sq km (224,607 sq mi)
POPULATION 1,573,000
CAPITAL Gaborone 225,000
RELIGION indigenous beliefs, Christian
LANGUAGE English, Setswana
LITERACY 70%
LIFE EXPECTANCY 37 years
GDP PER CAPITA $7,800
ECONOMY **IND:** diamonds, copper, nickel, coal. **AGR:** sorghum, corn, millet, pulses; livestock. **EXP:** diamonds, vehicles, copper, nickel.

BURKINA FASO
BURKINA FASO

AREA 274,200 sq km (105,869 sq mi)
POPULATION 13,228,000
CAPITAL Ouagadougou 862,000
RELIGION Muslim, indigenous beliefs, Roman Catholic
LANGUAGE French, African languages
LITERACY 36%
LIFE EXPECTANCY 45 years
GDP PER CAPITA $1,040
ECONOMY **IND:** cotton lint, beverages, agricultural processing, soap. **AGR:** peanuts, shea nuts, sesame, cotton; livestock. **EXP:** cotton, animal products, gold.

BURUNDI
REPUBLIC OF BURUNDI

AREA 27,834 sq km (10,747 sq mi)
POPULATION 6,096,000
CAPITAL Bujumbura 346,000
RELIGION Roman Catholic, indigenous beliefs, Protestant, Muslim
LANGUAGE Kirundi, French, Swahili
LITERACY 35%
LIFE EXPECTANCY 43 years
GDP PER CAPITA $600
ECONOMY **IND:** light consumer goods (blankets, shoes, soap), assembly of imported components. **AGR:** coffee, cotton, tea, corn; beef. **EXP:** coffee, tea, sugar, cotton.

CAMEROON
REPUBLIC OF CAMEROON

AREA 475,442 sq km (183,569 sq mi)
POPULATION 15,746,000
CAPITAL Yaoundé 1,481,000
RELIGION indigenous beliefs, Christian, Muslim
LANGUAGE French, English, 24 major African language groups
LITERACY 63%
LIFE EXPECTANCY 48 years
GDP PER CAPITA $1,700
ECONOMY **IND:** petroleum production and refining, food processing, light consumer goods. **AGR:** coffee, cocoa, cotton, rubber; livestock. **EXP:** crude oil and petroleum products, lumber, cocoa beans, aluminum.

CAPE VERDE
REPUBLIC OF CAPE VERDE

AREA 4,056 sq km (1,566 sq mi)
POPULATION 474,000
CAPITAL Praia 82,000
RELIGION Roman Catholic, Protestant
LANGUAGE Portuguese, Crioulo
LITERACY 72%
LIFE EXPECTANCY 69 years
GDP PER CAPITA $1,500
ECONOMY **IND:** food and beverages, fish processing, shoes and garments, salt mining. **AGR:** bananas, corn, beans, sweet potatoes; fish. **EXP:** fuel, shoes, garments, fish.

CENTRAL AFRICAN REPUBLIC
CENTRAL AFRICAN REPUBLIC

AREA 622,984 sq km (240,535 sq mi)
POPULATION 3,684,000
CAPITAL Bangui 666,000
RELIGION Protestant, Roman Catholic, Indigenous beliefs, Muslim
LANGUAGE French, Sangho, Arabic, Hunsa, Swahili
LITERACY 60%
LIFE EXPECTANCY 43 years
GDP PER CAPITA $1,300
ECONOMY **IND:** diamond mining, sawmills, breweries, textiles. **AGR:** cotton, coffee, tobacco, manioc (tapioca); timber. **EXP:** food, textiles, petroleum products, machinery.

CHAD
REPUBLIC OF CHAD

AREA 1,284,000 sq km (495,755 sq mi)
POPULATION 9,253,000
CAPITAL N'Djamena 735,000
RELIGION Muslim, Christian, indigenous beliefs
LANGUAGE French, Arabic, Sara, Sango, 100 other local languages
LITERACY 40%
LIFE EXPECTANCY 49 years
GDP PER CAPITA $1,030
ECONOMY **IND:** cotton textiles, meat packing, beer brewing, natron (sodium carbonate). **AGR:** cotton, sorghum, millet, peanuts; cattle. **EXP:** cotton, cattle, textiles.

COMOROS
UNION OF THE COMOROS

AREA 1,862 sq km (719 sq mi)
POPULATION 633,000
CAPITAL Moroni 49,000
RELIGION Sunni Muslim, Roman Catholic
LANGUAGE Arabic, French, Shikomoro
LITERACY 57%
LIFE EXPECTANCY 56 years
GDP PER CAPITA $710
ECONOMY **IND:** tourism, perfume distillation, textiles, furniture. **AGR:** vanilla, cloves, perfume essences, copra. **EXP:** vanilla, ylang-ylang, cloves, perfume oil.

CONGO
REPUBLIC OF THE CONGO

AREA 342,000 sq km (132,047 sq mi)
POPULATION 3,723,000
CAPITAL Brazzaville 1,360,000
RELIGION Christian, animist, Muslim
LANGUAGE French, Lingala, Monokutuba
LITERACY 75%
LIFE EXPECTANCY 50 years
GDP PER CAPITA $900
ECONOMY **IND:** petroleum extraction, cement kilning, lumbering, brewing. **AGR:** cassava (tapioca), sugar, rice, corn; forest products. **EXP:** crude oil and petroleum products, lumber, cocoa beans, aluminum.

CÔTE D'IVOIRE
REPUBLIC OF CÔTE D'IVOIRE

AREA 322,462 sq km (124,503 sq mi)
POPULATION 16,962,000
CAPITAL Abidjan (administrative capital) 3,956,000; Yamoussourkro (legislative capital) 110,000
RELIGION Christian, Muslim, indigenous beliefs
LANGUAGE French, Dioula, 60 native languages
LITERACY 49%
LIFE EXPECTANCY 43 years
GDP PER CAPITA $1,550
ECONOMY **IND:** mining, mineral processing, consumer products, cement. **AGR:** coffee, sugar, palm oil, rubber; wood products. **EXP:** diamonds, copper, coffee, cobalt.

DEMOCRATIC REPUBLIC OF THE CONGO
DEMOCRATIC REPUBLIC OF THE CONGO

AREA 2,344,885 sq km (905,365 sq mi)
POPULATION 56,625,000
CAPITAL Kinshasa 5,253,000
RELIGION Roman Catholic, Protestant, Kimbanguist, Muslim, traditional
LANGUAGE French, Lingala, Kingwana, Kikongo, Tshiluba
LITERACY 77%
LIFE EXPECTANCY 48 years
GDP PER CAPITA $590
ECONOMY **IND:** mining (diamonds, copper), mineral processing, consumer products. **AGR:** coffee, sugar, palm oil, rubber; wood products. **EXP:** diamonds, copper, coffee, cobalt.

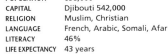

DJIBOUTI
REPUBLIC OF DJIBOUTI

AREA 23,200 sq km (8,958 sq mi)
POPULATION 658,000
CAPITAL Djibouti 542,000
RELIGION Muslim, Christian
LANGUAGE French, Arabic, Somali, Afar
LITERACY 46%
LIFE EXPECTANCY 43 years
GDP PER CAPITA $1,400
ECONOMY **IND:** small-scale enterprises (dairy products, mineral-water bottling). **AGR:** fruits, vegetables; goats. **EXP:** reexports, hides and skins, coffee.

EGYPT
ARAB REPUBLIC OF EGYPT

AREA 1,002,000 sq km (386,874 sq mi)
POPULATION 72,062,000
CAPITAL Cairo 9,586,000
RELIGION Sunni Muslim, Coptic Christian
LANGUAGE Arabic, English, French
LITERACY 51%
LIFE EXPECTANCY 68 years
GDP PER CAPITA $3,700
ECONOMY **IND:** textiles, food processing, tourism, chemicals. **AGR:** cotton, rice, corn, wheat; cattle. **EXP:** crude oil and petroleum, cotton, textiles, metal products.

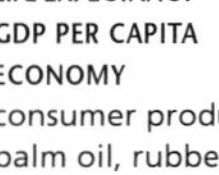

EQUATORIAL GUINEA
REPUBLIC OF EQUATORIAL GUINEA

AREA 28,051 sq km (10,831 sq mi)
POPULATION 510,000
CAPITAL Malabo 33,000
RELIGION Roman Catholic, indigenous beliefs
LANGUAGE Spanish, French, pidgin English, Fang, Bubi, Ibo
LITERACY 79%
LIFE EXPECTANCY 54 years
GDP PER CAPITA $2,100
ECONOMY **IND:** petroleum, fishing, sawmilling, natural gas. **AGR:** coffee, cocoa, rice, yams; livestock; timber. **EXP:** petroleum, timber, cocoa.

ERITREA
STATE OF ERITREA

AREA 121,144 sq km (46,774 sq mi)
POPULATION 4,362,000
CAPITAL Asmara 503,000
RELIGION Muslim, Coptic Christian, Roman Catholic, Protestant
LANGUAGE Afar, Amharic, Arabic, Tigre, Kunama, Tigrinya
LITERACY 25%
LIFE EXPECTANCY 54 years
GDP PER CAPITA $740
ECONOMY **IND:** food processing, beverages, clothing and textiles. **AGR:** sorghum, lentils, vegetables, corn; livestock; fish. **EXP:** coffee, gold, leather products, oilseeds.

ETHIOPIA
FEDERAL DEMOCRATIC REPUBLIC OF ETHIOPIA

AREA 1,133,380 sq km (437,600 sq mi)
POPULATION 70,677,000
CAPITAL Addis Ababa 2,753,000
RELIGION Muslim, Ethiopian Orthodox, animist
LANGUAGE Amharic, Tigrinya, Orominga, Guaraginga, Somali, Arabic, local languages
LITERACY 36%
LIFE EXPECTANCY 42 years
GDP PER CAPITA $700
ECONOMY **IND:** food processing, beverages, textiles, chemicals. **AGR:** cereals, pulses, coffee, oilseeds; hides. **EXP:** coffee, gold, leather products, oilseeds.

GABON

GABONESE REPUBLIC

AREA 267,667 sq km (103,347 sq mi)
POPULATION 1,327,000
CAPITAL Libreville 573,000
RELIGION Christian, indigenous beliefs
LANGUAGE French, Fang, Myene, Nzebi, Bapounou/Eschira, Bandjabi
LITERACY 63%
LIFE EXPECTANCY 59 years
GDP PER CAPITA $5,500
ECONOMY **IND:** food and beverage, textiles, lumbering and plywood, cement. **AGR:** cocoa, coffee, sugar, palm oil; cattle; okoume; fish. **EXP:** crude oil, timber, manganese, uranium.

GAMBIA

REPUBLIC OF THE GAMBIA

AREA 11,295 sq km (4,361 sq mi)
POPULATION 1,501,000
CAPITAL Banjul 418,000
RELIGION Muslim, Christian
LANGUAGE English, Mandinka, Wolof, Fula
LITERACY 48%
LIFE EXPECTANCY 53 years
GDP PER CAPITA $1,770
ECONOMY **IND:** processing peanuts, fish and hides, tourism, beverages. **AGR:** peanuts, millet, sorghum, rice; cattle. **EXP:** peanuts and peanut products, fish, cotton lint, palm kernels.

GHANA

REPUBLIC OF GHANA

AREA 238,537 sq km (92,100 sq mi)
POPULATION 20,468,000
CAPITAL Accra 1,925,000
RELIGION Muslim, Christian, indigenous beliefs.
LANGUAGE English, Akan, Moshi, Dagomba, Ewe, Ga
LITERACY 65%
LIFE EXPECTANCY 57 years
GDP PER CAPITA $1,980
ECONOMY **IND:** mining, lumbering, light manufacturing, aluminum smelting. **AGR:** cocoa, rice, coffee, cassava (tapioca); timber. **EXP:** gold, cocoa, timber, tuna.

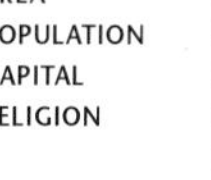

GUINEA

REPUBLIC OF GUINEA

AREA 245,857 sq km (94,926 sq mi)
POPULATION 9,030,000
CAPITAL Conakry 1,272,000
RELIGION Muslim, Christian, indigenous beliefs
LANGUAGE French, tribal languages
LITERACY 36%
LIFE EXPECTANCY 49 years
GDP PER CAPITA $1,970
ECONOMY **IND:** bauxite, gold, diamonds, light manufacturing. **AGR:** rice, coffee, pineapples, palm kernels; cattle; timber. **EXP:** bauxite, alumina, gold diamonds.

GUINEA-BISSAU

REPUBLIC OF GUINEA-BISSAU

AREA 36,125 sq km (13,948 sq mi)
POPULATION 1,288,000
CAPITAL Bissau 292,000
RELIGION indigenous beliefs, Muslim, Christian
LANGUAGE Portuguese, Crioulo, African languages
LITERACY 34%
LIFE EXPECTANCY 45 years
GDP PER CAPITA $900
ECONOMY **IND:** agricultural products processing, beer, soft drinks. **AGR:** rice, corn, beans, cassava (tapioca); timber; fish. **EXP:** cashew nuts, shrimp, peanuts, palm kernels.

KENYA

REPUBLIC OF KENYA

AREA 580,367 sq km (224,081 sq mi)
POPULATION 31,639,000
CAPITAL Nairobi 2,343,000
RELIGION Protestant , Roman Catholic, indigenous beliefs, Muslim
LANGUAGE English, Kiswahili, indigenous languages
LITERACY 78%
LIFE EXPECTANCY 46 years
GDP PER CAPITA $1,000
ECONOMY **IND:** small scale consumer goods (plastic, furniture), agricultural products processing, oil refining. **AGR:** coffee, tea, corn, wheat; dairy products. **EXP:** tea, coffee, horticultural products, petroleum products.

LESOTHO

KINGDOM OF LESOTHO

AREA 30,355 sq km (11,720 sq mi)
POPULATION 1,800,000
CAPITAL Maseru 271,000
RELIGION Christian, indigenous beliefs
LANGUAGE English, Sesotho, Zulu, Xhosa
LITERACY 83%
LIFE EXPECTANCY 37 years
GDP PER CAPITA $2,450
ECONOMY **IND:** food, beverages, textiles, handicrafts. **AGR:** corn, wheat, pulses, sorghum; livestock. **EXP:**manufactures (clothing, footwear), wool and mohair, food and live animals.

LIBERIA

REPUBLIC OF LIBERIA

AREA 111,370 sq km (43,000 sq mi)
POPULATION 3,317,000
CAPITAL Monrovia 491,000
RELIGION indigenous beliefs, Christian, Muslim
LANGUAGE English, tribal languages
LITERACY 38%
LIFE EXPECTANCY 49 years
GDP PER CAPITA $1,100
ECONOMY **IND:** rubber processing, palm oil processing, diamonds. **AGR:** rubber, coffee, cocoa, rice; sheep; timber. **EXP:** diamonds, iron ore, rubber, timber.

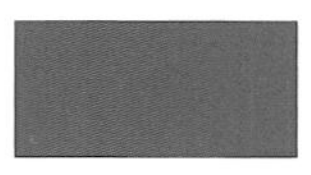

LIBYA

GREAT SOCIALIST PEOPLE'S LIBYAN ARAB JAMAHIRIYA

AREA 1,759,540 sq km (679,362 sq mi)
POPULATION 5,499,000
CAPITAL Tripoli 1,776,000
RELIGION Sunni Muslim
LANGUAGE Arabic, Italian, English
LITERACY 76%
LIFE EXPECTANCY 76 years
GDP PER CAPITA $7,600
ECONOMY **IND:** petroleum, food processing, textiles, handicrafts. **AGR:** wheat, barley, olives, dates; sheep. **EXP:** crude oil, refined petroleum products.

MADAGASCAR

REPUBLIC OF MADAGASCAR

AREA 587,041 sq km (226,658 sq mi)
POPULATION 16,980,000
CAPITAL Antananarivo 1,689,000
RELIGION indigenous beliefs, Christian, Muslim
LANGUAGE French, Malagasy
LITERACY 80%
LIFE EXPECTANCY 55 years
GDP PER CAPITA $870
ECONOMY **IND:** meat processing, soap, breweries, tanneries. **AGR:** coffee, vanilla, sugarcane, cloves; livestock products. **EXP:** coffee, vanilla, shellfish, sugar.

MALAWI

REPUBLIC OF MALAWI

AREA 118,484 sq km (45,747 sq mi)
POPULATION 11,651,000
CAPITAL Lilongwe 523,000
RELIGION Protestant, Roman Catholic, indigenous beliefs
LANGUAGE English, Chichewa
LITERACY 58%
LIFE EXPECTANCY 39 years
GDP PER CAPITA $660
ECONOMY **IND:** tobacco, tea, sugar, sawmill products. **AGR:** tobacco, sugarcane, cotton, tea; cattle. **EXP:** tobacco, tea, sugar, cotton.

MALI

REPUBLIC OF MALI

AREA 1,240,192 sq km (478,841 sq mi)
POPULATION 11,626,000
CAPITAL Bamako 1,161,000
RELIGION Muslim, indigenous beliefs
LANGUAGE French, Bambara, numerous African languages
LITERACY 38%
LIFE EXPECTANCY 45 years
GDP PER CAPITA $840
ECONOMY **IND:** minor local consumer good production and food processing, construction, textiles, gold mining. **AGR:** cotton, millet, rice, corn; cattle. **EXP:** cotton, gold, livestock.

MAURITANIA

ISLAMIC REPUBLIC OF MAURITANIA

AREA 1,030,700 sq km (397,955 sq mi)
POPULATION 2,914,000
CAPITAL Nouakchott 626,000
RELIGION Muslim
LANGUAGE Hassaniya Arabic, Wolof, Pulaar, Soninke, French
LITERACY 41%
LIFE EXPECTANCY 53 years
GDP PER CAPITA $1,800
ECONOMY **IND:** fish processing, mining of iron ore and gypsum. **AGR:** dates, millet, sorghum, rice; cattle. **EXP:** iron ore, fish and fish products, gold.

MAURITIUS

REPUBLIC OF MAURITIUS

AREA 2,040 sq km (788 sq mi)
POPULATION 1,221,000
CAPITAL Port Louis 176,000
RELIGION Hindu, Roman Catholic, Muslim, Protestant
LANGUAGE English, Creole, French, Hindi, Urdu, Hakka, Bojpoori
LITERACY 83%
LIFE EXPECTANCY 72 years
GDP PER CAPITA $10,800
ECONOMY **IND:** food processing (largely sugar milling), textiles, chemicals, tourism. **AGR:** sugarcane, tea, corn, tomatoes; cattle; fish. **EXP:** clothing and textiles, sugar, cut flowers, molasses.

MOROCCO

KINGDOM OF MOROCCO

AREA 710,850 sq km (274,461 sq mi)
POPULATION 30,366,000
CAPITAL Rabat 1,668,000
RELIGION Muslim
LANGUAGE Arabic, Berber dialects, French
LITERACY 44%
LIFE EXPECTANCY 70 years
GDP PER CAPITA $3,700
ECONOMY **IND:** phosphate rock mining and processing, food processing, leather goods, textiles. **AGR:** barley, wheat, citrus, wine; livestock. **EXP:** phosphates and fertilizers, food and beverages, minerals.

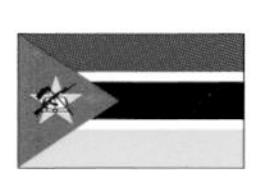

MOZAMBIQUE

REPUBLIC OF MOZAMBIQUE

AREA 799,380 sq km (308,642 sq mi)
POPULATION 17,479,000
CAPITAL Maputo 1,134,000
RELIGION indigenous beliefs, Christian,Muslim
LANGUAGE Portuguese, indigenous dialects
LITERACY 42%
LIFE EXPECTANCY 34 years
GDP PER CAPITA $900
ECONOMY **IND:** food, beverages, chemicals (fertilizer, soap), petroleum products. **AGR:** cotton, cashew nuts, sugarcane, tea; beef. **EXP:** prawns, cashews, cotton, sugar.

NAMIBIA

REPUBLIC OF NAMIBIA

AREA 824,292 sq km (318,261 sq mi)
POPULATION 1,927,000
CAPITAL Windhoek 216,000
RELIGION Christian, indigenous beliefs
LANGUAGE English, Afrikaans, German, indigenous languages
LITERACY 38%
LIFE EXPECTANCY 49 years
GDP PER CAPITA $4,500
ECONOMY **IND:** meatpacking, fish processing, dairy products, mining (diamonds, uranium). **AGR:** millet, sorghum, peanuts; livestock; fish. **EXP:** fish, diamonds, copper, gold.

NIGER

REPUBLIC OF NIGER

AREA 1,267,000 sq km (489,191 sq mi)
POPULATION 12,073,000
CAPITAL Niamey 821,000
RELIGION Muslim, indigenous beliefs, Christian
LANGUAGE French, Hausa, Djerma
LITERACY 15%
LIFE EXPECTANCY 45 years
GDP PER CAPITA $820
ECONOMY **IND:** uranium mining, cement, brick, textiles. **AGR:** cowpeas, cotton, peanuts, millet; cattle. **EXP:** uranium ore, livestock products, cowpeas, onions.

NIGERIA

FEDERAL REPUBLIC OF NIGERIA

AREA 923,768 sq km (356,669 sq mi)
POPULATION 133,882,000
CAPITAL Abuja 420,000
RELIGION Muslim, Christian, indigenous beliefs
LANGUAGE English, Hausa, Yoruba, Ibo, Fulani
LITERACY 57%
LIFE EXPECTANCY 52 years
GDP PER CAPITA $840
ECONOMY **IND:** crude oil, mining, palm oil, cement. **AGR:** cocoa, peanuts, palm oil, corn; cattle; timber; fish. **EXP:** petroleum and petroleum products, cocoa, rubber.

RWANDA

RWANDESE REPUBLIC

AREA 26,338 sq km (10,169 sq mi)
POPULATION 8,306,000
CAPITAL Kigali 412,000
RELIGION Roman Catholic, Protestant, Seventh-Day Adventist, indigenous beliefs
LANGUAGE Kinyarwanda, English, Kiswahili
LITERACY 48%
LIFE EXPECTANCY 40 years
GDP PER CAPITA $1,000
ECONOMY **IND:** cement, agricultural products, small-scale beverages, soap. **AGR:** coffee, tea, pyrethrum, bananas; livestock. **EXP:** coffee, tea, hides, tin ore.

AFRICA
FLAGS & FACTS

SAO TOME AND PRINCIPE

DEM. REP. OF SAO TOME AND PRINCIPE

AREA 1,001 sq km (386 sq mi)
POPULATION 176,000
CAPITAL São Tomé 67,000
RELIGION Roman Catholic, Evangelical Christian, Protestant, Seventh-Day Adventist
LANGUAGE Portuguese
LITERACY 79%
LIFE EXPECTANCY 65 years
GDP PER CAPITA $1,200
ECONOMY **IND:** light construction, textiles, soap, beer; fish processing; timber. **AGR:** cocoa, coconuts, palm kernels, copra; poultry; fish. **EXP:** cocoa, copra, coffee, palm oil.

SENEGAL

REPUBLIC OF SENEGAL

AREA 196,722 sq km (75,955 sq mi)
POPULATION 10,580,000
CAPITAL Dakar 2,160,000
RELIGION Muslim, indigenous beliefs
LANGUAGE French, Wolof, Pulaar, Diola, Jola, Mandinka
LITERACY 39%
LIFE EXPECTANCY 53 years
GDP PER CAPITA $1,580
ECONOMY **IND:** agricultural and fish processing, phosphate mining, fertilizer production, petroleum refining. **AGR:** peanuts, millet, corn, sorghum; cattle; fish. **EXP:** fish, ground nuts, petroleum products, phosphates.

SEYCHELLES

REPUBLIC OF SEYCHELLES

AREA 455 sq km (176 sq mi)
POPULATION 87,000
CAPITAL Victoria 30,000
RELIGION Roman Catholic, Anglican
LANGUAGE English, French, Creole
LITERACY 58%
LIFE EXPECTANCY 70 years
GDP PER CAPITA $7,600
ECONOMY **IND:** fishing, tourism, processing of coconuts and vanilla, beverages. **AGR:** coconuts, chickens; tuna fish. **EXP:** fish, cinnamon bark, copra, petroleum products.

SIERRA LEONE

REPUBLIC OF SIERRA LEONE

AREA 71,740 sq km (27,699 sq mi)
POPULATION 5,733,000
CAPITAL Freetown 837,000
RELIGION Muslim, indigenous beliefs, Christian
LANGUAGE English, Mende, Temne, Krio
LITERACY 31%
LIFE EXPECTANCY 43 years
GDP PER CAPITA $500
ECONOMY **IND:** diamond mining, small-scale manufacturing (beverages, textiles). **AGR:** rice, coffee, cocoa, palm kernels; poultry; fish. **EXP:** diamonds, rutile, cocoa, coffee.

SOMALIA

SOMALIA

AREA 637,657 sq km (246,201 sq mi)
POPULATION 8,025,000
CAPITAL Mogadishu 1,212,000
RELIGION Sunni Muslim
LANGUAGE Somali, Arabic, Italian, English
LITERACY 38%
LIFE EXPECTANCY 46 years
GDP PER CAPITA $550
ECONOMY **IND:** sugar refining, textiles, petroleum refining, wireless communications. **AGR:** bananas, sorghum, corn, sugarcane; cattle; fish. **EXP:** livestock, bananas, hides, fish.

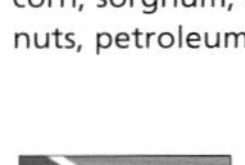

SOUTH AFRICA

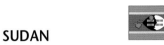

REPUBLIC OF SOUTH AFRICA

AREA 1,219,090 sq km (470,693 sq mi)
POPULATION 44,024,000
CAPITAL Pretoria (adm.) 1,651,000; Cape Town (leg.) 2,993,000; Bloemfontein (jud.) 364,000
RELIGION Christian, indigenous beliefs
LANGUAGE Afrikaans, English, Ndebele
LITERACY 85%
LIFE EXPECTANCY 53 years
GDP PER CAPITA $9,400
ECONOMY **IND:** mining (platinum, gold), automobile assembly, metalworking, machinery. **AGR:** corn, wheat, sugarcane, fruits; beef. **EXP:** gold, diamonds, other metals and minerals, machinery and equipment.

SUDAN

REPUBLIC OF THE SUDAN

AREA 2,505,810 sq km (967,498 sq mi)
POPULATION 38,114,000
CAPITAL Khartoum 2,853,000
RELIGION Sunni Muslim, indigenous beliefs, Christian
LANGUAGE Arabic, Nubian, Ta Bedawie, many local dialects
LITERACY 46%
LIFE EXPECTANCY 57 years
GDP PER CAPITA $1,360
ECONOMY **IND:** agricultural processing (sugar, beer), gold mining, oil refining, shoes. **AGR:** coffee, sisal, tea, cotton; cattle. **EXP:** coffee, manufactured goods, cotton, cashew nuts.

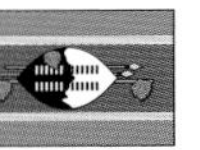

SWAZILAND

KINGDOM OF SWAZILAND

AREA 17,363 sq km (6,704 sq mi)
POPULATION 1,161,000
CAPITAL Mbabane 80,000
RELIGION Protestatnt, indigenous beliefs, Muslim, Roman Catholic
LANGUAGE English, Swazi
LITERACY 78%
LIFE EXPECTANCY 45 years
GDP PER CAPITA $4,200
ECONOMY **IND:** mining (coal and asbestos), wood pulp, sugar, soft drink concentrates. **AGR:** sugarcane, cotton, corn, tobacco; cattle. **EXP:** soft drink concentrates, sugar, wood pulp, cotton yarn.

TANZANIA

UNITED REPUBLIC OF TANZANIA

AREA 945,087 sq km (364,900 sq mi)
POPULATION 35,363,000
CAPITAL Dar es Salaam (adm.)2,115,000; Dodoma (leg.) 180,000
RELIGION Christian, Muslim, indigenous beliefs
LANGUAGE Swahili, English, Arabic, many local languages
LITERACY 68%
LIFE EXPECTANCY 45 years
GDP PER CAPITA $610
ECONOMY **IND:** agricultural processing, diamond and gold mining, oil refining. **AGR:** coffee, sisal, tea, cotton; cattle. **EXP:** coffee, manufactured goods, cotton, cashew nuts.

TOGO

TOGOLESE REPUBLIC

AREA 56,785 sq km (21,925 sq mi)
POPULATION 5,429,000
CAPITAL Lomé 732,000
RELIGION indigenous beliefs, Christian, Muslim
LANGUAGE French, Ewe, Mina, Kabye, Dagomba
LITERACY 52%
LIFE EXPECTANCY 54 years
GDP PER CAPITA $1,500
ECONOMY **IND:** phosphate mining, agricultural processing, cement, handicrafts. **AGR:** coffee, cocoa, cotton, yams; livestock; fish. **EXP:** cotton, phosphates, coffee, cocoa.

TUNISIA

TUNISIAN REPUBLIC

AREA 163,610 sq km (63,170 sq mi)
POPULATION 9,898,000
CAPITAL Tunis 1,927,000
RELIGION Muslim
LANGUAGE Arabic, French
LITERACY 67%
LIFE EXPECTANCY 73 years
GDP PER CAPITA $6,600
ECONOMY **IND:** petroleum, mining, tourism, textiles, footwear. **AGR:** olives, olive oil, grain, dairy products. **EXP:** textiles, mechanical goods, phosphates and chemicals, agricultural products.

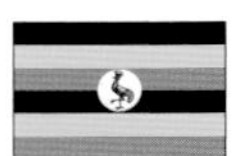

UGANDA

REPUBLIC OF UGANDA

AREA 241,139 sq km (93,104 sq mi)
POPULATION 25,262,000
CAPITAL Kampala 1,274,000
RELIGION Roman Catholic, Protestant, indigenous beliefs, Muslim
LANGUAGE English, Ganda or Luganda, many local languages
LITERACY 63%
LIFE EXPECTANCY 44 years
GDP PER CAPITA $1,200
ECONOMY **IND:** sugar, brewing, tobacco, cotton textiles. **AGR:** coffee, tea, tobacco, cassava (tapioca); beef. **EXP:** coffee, fish and fish products, tea, electrical products.

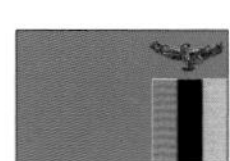

ZAMBIA

REPUBLIC OF ZAMBIA

AREA 752,614 sq km (290,586 sq mi)
POPULATION 10,896,000
CAPITAL Lusaka 1,718,000
RELIGION Christian, Muslim, Hindu
LANGUAGE English, indigenous languages
LITERACY 79%
LIFE EXPECTANCY 41 years
GDP PER CAPITA $870
ECONOMY **IND:** copper mining and processing, construction, foodstuffs, beverages. **AGR:** corn, sorghum, rice, peanuts; cattle; coffee. **EXP:** copper, cobalt, electricity, tobacco.

ZIMBABWE

REPUBLIC OF ZIMBABWE

AREA 390,757 sq km (150,872 sq mi)
POPULATION 12,577,000
CAPITAL Harare 1,868,000
RELIGION Syncretic (part Christian, part indigenous beliefs), Christian, indigenous beliefs
LANGUAGE English, Shona, Sindebele
LITERACY 85%
LIFE EXPECTANCY 41 years
GDP PER CAPITA $2,450
ECONOMY **IND:** mining (coal, gold), wood products, cement, textiles. **AGR:** corn, cotton, tobacco, wheat; cattle. **EXP:** tobacco, gold, ferroalloys, cotton.

POPULATION DENSITY

DEPENDENCIES

MAYOTTE (FRANCE)

TERRITORIAL COLLECTIVITY OF MAYOTTE

AREA 374 sq km (144 sq mi)
POPULATION 167,000
CAPITAL Mamoudzou 43,000
RELIGION Muslim, Christian
LANGUAGE Mahorian, French
LITERACY NA
LIFE EXPECTANCY 60 years
GDP PER CAPITA $600
ECONOMY **IND:** lobster and shrimp industry, construction. **AGR:** wheat, barley, oats, grapes; sheep. **EXP:** ylang-ylang (perfume essence), coffee, copra.

RÉUNION (FRANCE)

DEPARTMENT OF RÉUNION

AREA 2,507 sq km (968 sq mi)
POPULATION 754,000
CAPITAL St.-Denis 169,000
RELIGION Roman Catholic, Hindu, Muslim, Buddhist
LANGUAGE French, Creole
LITERACY 79%
LIFE EXPECTANCY 75 years
GDP PER CAPITA $4,800
ECONOMY **IND:** sugar, rum, cigarettes, handicraft items. **AGR:** sugarcane, vanilla, tobacco, tropical fruits. **EXP:** sugar, rum and molasses, perfume essences, lobster.

SOVEREIGN LOCAL

SAINT HELENA (U.K.)

SAINT HELENA

AREA 411 sq km (159 sq mi).
POPULATION 7,000
CAPITAL Jamestown 2,000
RELIGION Anglican, Baptist, Seventh-Day Adventist
LANGUAGE English
LITERACY 97%
LIFE EXPECTANCY 77 years
GDP PER CAPITA $2,500
ECONOMY **IND:** construction, crafts, fishing. **AGR:** corn, potatoes, vegetables, timber, fish. **EXP:** fish, coffee, handicrafts.

DATES OF COUNTRY INDEPENDENCE

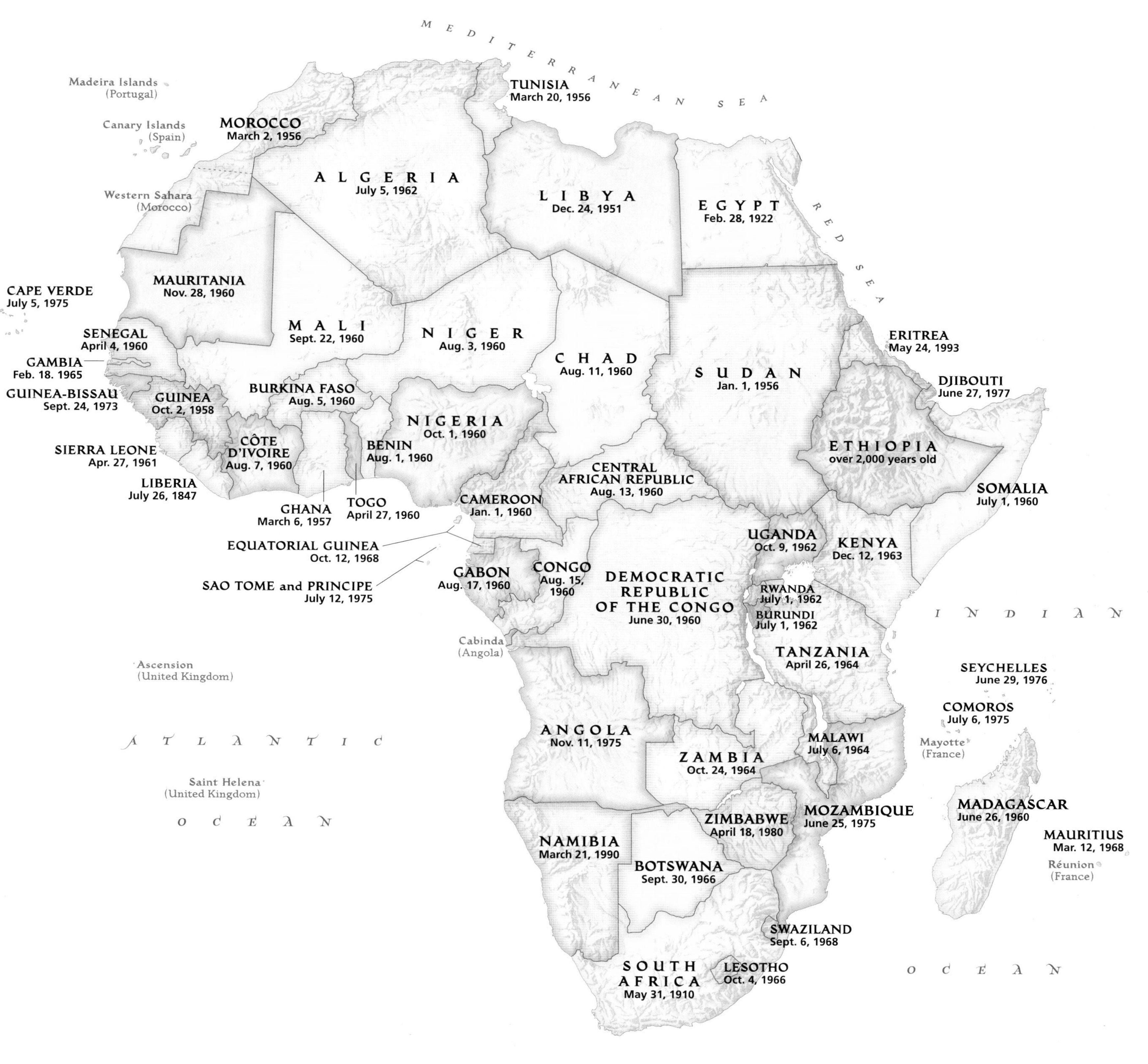

People per square mile		People per square km
520 and greater	■	200 and greater
260–519	■	100–199
130–259	■	50–99
25–129	□	10–49
1-24	□	1-9
Uninhabited	□	Uninhabited

AUSTRALIA

PAPUA NEW GUINEA AND NEW ZEALAND

Uniquely both a continent and a nation, Australia ranks as the smallest continent but sixth largest nation. Its landmass is relatively arid, but varied climatic zones give it surprising diversity and a rich ecology. Australia's land is many millions of years old; it retains an ancient feeling and distinctive geography and endures extremes of droughts, floods, tropical cyclones, and bushfires. North of Australia, off the tip of Cape York and across the Torres Strait, is the island of New Guinea. Papua New Guinea, which became an independent nation in 1975, comprises the eastern side of the island and many small islands, including Bougainville and the Bismark Archipelago. The island of Tasmania lies off Australia's southeast coast. East from there, across the Tasman Sea, is the island nation of New Zealand, composed of North Island and South Island, respectively the 12th and 14th largest islands on Earth. Eons of isolation have allowed outstanding and bizarre life forms to evolve, such as the duck-billed platypus—a monotreme, or egg-laying mammal native to Australia and Tasmania—and New Zealand's kiwi, a timid, nocturnal, wingless bird.

Off the coast of the northeastern Australian state of Queensland lies the Great Barrier Reef, the world's largest coral reef, which extends about 1,250 miles (2,012 km). The Great Barrier Reef was formed and expanded over millions of years as tiny marine animals deposited their skeletons. Coral reefs, and the Great Barrier Reef especially, are considered the rain forests of the ocean for their complex life-forms and multilayered diversity.

Australia's landmass nearly equals that of the United States' lower 48. Despite its size, however, Australia holds fewer people than any other inhabited continent. The most densely populated one percent of the continent—the southeast and south coast— is home to 84 percent of the population. The daunting, sunbaked landscapes and extreme aridity of the vast interior outback offered a small measure of protection to Aboriginal hunter-gatherers who lived there; their brethren in coastal areas were virtually extinguished by disease and brutality following Sydney's settlement as a British penal colony in 1788. Later, the prospect of greater personal freedom and of owning land drew large numbers of immigrants.

Australia's aborigines were hunters and gatherers moving with the seasons. Their society was based on a complex network of intricate kinship relationships. Social control was maintained by a system of beliefs called the Dreaming. A rich oral tradition existed in which stories of the Dreamtime, the time of creation, or recent history were passed down. Aboriginal rock carvings and paintings date back at least 30,000 years. The Maori—indigenous Polynesian people of New Zealand—arrived in different migrations starting around 1150, and a "great fleet" arrived in the 14th century, probably from Tahiti. Maori art boasts of beautiful wood carvings that adorn houses and fish hooks carved out of whalebone. In the 1840 Treaty of Waitingi, the Maori gave formal control of their land to the British, though they kept all other rights of livelihood.

Australia dominates the region economically. Its economic ties with Asia and the Pacific Rim have become increasingly important. Jet-age transportation and instant communication, along with trade, forge worldwide links, while the continent's unique fauna and flora point to its past isolation.

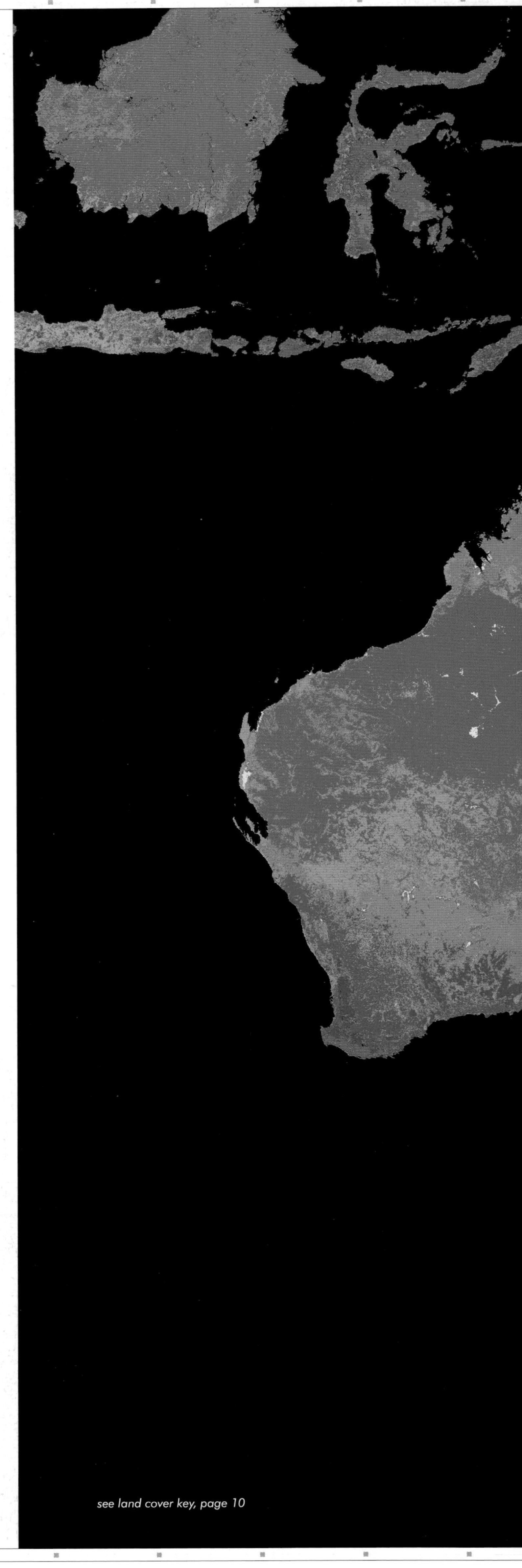

see land cover key, page 10

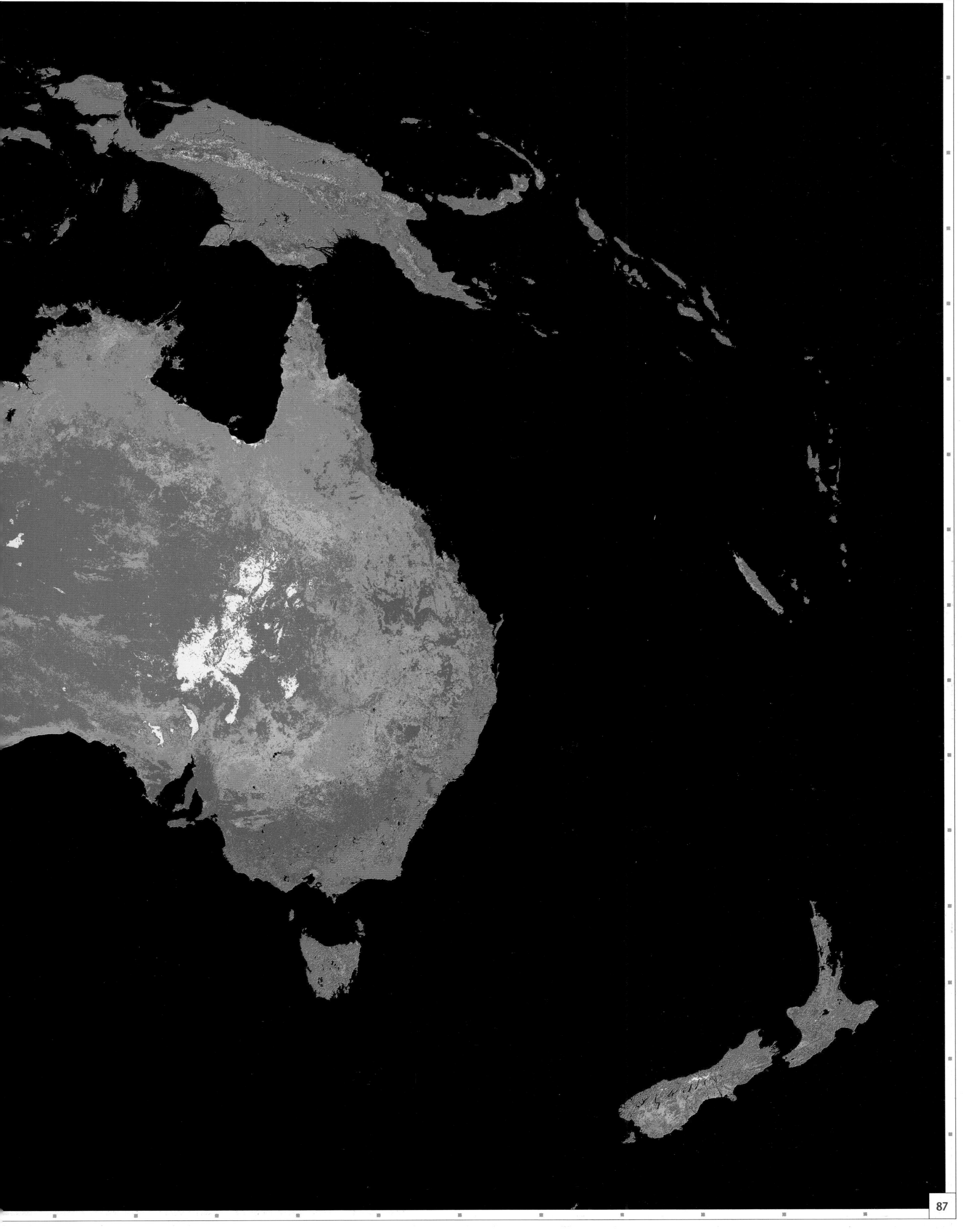

INDONESIA
TIMOR SEA
ARAFURA
Azimuthal Equidistant Projection
SCALE 1:9,957,000
1 CENTIMETER = 100 KILOMETERS; 1 INCH = 157 MILES
0 100 200 300 400
KILOMETERS
0 100 200 300 400
STATUTE MILES
Aboriginal Lands
Homesteads
Ashmore Islands
Australia
Cartier Island
Australia
Browse Island
Melville Island
Bathurst Island
Garden Point
Milikapiti
Nguiu
Minjilang
Van Diemen Gulf
Darwin
Delissaville
Humpty Doo
Adelaide River
Burrundie
Tipperary
Wadeye
Maningrida
Oenpelli
Jabiru
Milingimbi
Galiwink
ARNHEM LAND
Goodparla
El Sharana
Pine Creek
Mainoru
Katherine
Bamyili-Beswick
Maranboy
Ngukurr
Mataranka
Willeroo
Roper Valley
Larrimah
Nutwood Downs
Delamere
Joseph Bonaparte Gulf
Kalumburu
Port Warrender
Forrest River
Wyndham
Legune
Bullo River
Timber Creek
Ivanhoe
Kununurra
Kuri Bay
Collier Bay
Karunjie
Gibb River
Mt. Barnett
Mt. House
L. Argyle
Spring Creek
Turkey Creek
KIMBERLEY
Glenroy
Lansdowne
Ord River
Alice Downs
Newry
Victoria River Downs
Waterloo
Mt. Sanford
Wave Hill
Inverway
Nicholson
Birrindudu
Lajamanu
Daly Waters
Top Springs
Tanumbirini
O.T. Downs
McArthur River
Newcastle Waters
Beetaloo
Elliott
NORTHERN TERRITORY
Eva Downs
Anthony Lagoon
Helen Springs
Brunette Downs
Muckety
Banka Banka
Rockhampton Downs
Lombadina
King Sd.
Beagle Bay
Derby
Yeeda
Roebuck Plains
Camballin
Fitzroy Crossing
Halls Creek
Broome
Dampier Downs
Nerrima
Margaret River
Gordon Downs
Cherrabun
Christmas Creek
Lagrange
Anna Plains
GREAT SANDY DESERT
Billiluna
Tanami Desert
Tanami
Tennant Creek
Frewena
Balgo
Wallal Downs
Pardoo
DeGrey
Goldsworthy
Shay Gap
Port Hedland
Warrawagine
Wauchope
Warrabri
Hatches Creek
Point Samson
Mundabullangana
Karratha
Roebourne
Whim Creek
Bamboo
Willowra
Barrow Creek
Elkedra
Barrow Island
Marble Bar
Lake Mackay
Anningie
Ammaroo
Argadargada
Tea Tree
Fortescue
Hillside
Nullagine
Yuendumu
Pine Hill
Utopia
Exmouth Gulf
Onslow
Pannawonica
Bonney Downs
WESTERN
Mt. Wedge
Aileron
Alcoota
Lucy Creek
Exmouth
Peedamulla
Wittenoom
Roy Hill
Papunya
Bushy Park
Mt. Riddock
Learmonth
Nanutarra
Mt. Stuart
Marillana
Balfour Downs
Haast Bluff
Alice Springs
Ross River
Ringwood
Wyloo
Tom Price
Rocklea
Jiggalong
Bullara
Uaroo
Parraburdoo
Newman
Hermannsburg
Ewaninga
Santa Teresa
Cardabia
Ashburton Downs
WESTERN
Gibson Desert
Lake Amadeus
Wallara
Henbury
Deep Well
Rodinga
TROPIC OF CAPRICORN
Lyndon
Ashburton
Mundiwindi
Docker River
Mount Ebenezer
Bundooma
Gnaraloo
Minilya
Mount Vernon
Bulloo Downs
Yulara
Curtin Springs
Finke
Erldunda
Rumbalara
Finke
Simpson Desert
Quobba
Gascoyne Junction
Milgun
Glenelya
PLATEAU
Mt. Cavenagh
Kulgera
Duffield
Landor
Gascoyne
Carnarvon
Peak Hill
New Springs
Lake Carnegie
Carnegie
Warburton
Amata
Ernabella
Tieyon
Dairy Creek
Cunyu
Wongawal
Agnes Creek
Ilbunga
Shark Bay
Wooramel
Carey Downs
Mooloogool
Everard Park
Mount Sarah
Denham
Milly Milly
Belele
Paroo
Lake Violet
Wiluna
Todmorden
Murchison
Mileura
Meekatharra
AUSTRALIA
Welbourn Hill
Oodnadatta
Hamelin
Curbur
Carrarang
Meadow
Mount Keith
Mount Willoughby
Big Bell
Cosmo Newberry
Warrina
SOUTH
Murgoo
Daydawn
Sandstone
Melrose
Eurardy
Pinegrove
Agnew
William Creek
Kalbarri
Galina Mine
Yalgoo
Edah
Mt. Magnet
Laverton
Coober Pedy
Strangways
Great Victoria Desert
Lake Maurice
Lynton
Northampton
Geraldton
Mullewa
Wurarga
Fields Find
Narndee
Leonora
Murrin Murrin
Mt. Ida
Malcolm
Ingomar
McDouall Peak
The Twins
Tardun
Lake Barlee
Kookynie
Yerilla
Walkaway
Nangulu
Pintharuka
Paynes Find
Diemal Find
Menzies
Maralinga
AUSTRAL
Dongara
Mingenew
Perenjori
Lake Moore
Mouroubra
Riverina
Wynbring
Tarcoola
Bon Bon
Carnamah
Coorow
Davyhurst
Bardoc
Yindi
Fisher
Watson
Cook
Immarna
Barton Siding
Andamooka
Jurien
Wubin
Kalannie
Wialki
Bonnie Rock
Kalgoorlie
Golden Ridge
Coonana
Kitchener
Rawlinna
Nurina
Reid
Forrest
Deakin
Hughes
Kingoonya
Coondambo
Woomera
Pimba
Moora
Pithara
Burakin
Mukinbudin
Bullfinch
Coolgardie
Karonie
Zanthus
Naretha
Haig
Loongana
Koonalda
Koonibba
Wongan Hills
Trayning
Southern Cross
Chinta
Lake Gairdner
Konnongorring
Goomalling
Merredin
Marvel Loch
Cocklebiddy Motel
Mundrabilla
Eucla Motel
Bookabie
Fowlers Bay
Mudamuckla
Toodyay
Lake Cowan
Madura
Muchea
Wundowie
Bruce Rock
Fraser Range
John Eyre Motel
Smoky Bay
Wirrulla
Norseman
Balladonia
Poochera
Iron Knob
PERTH
Quairading
Narembeen
FREMANTLE
Kwinana
Corrigin
Hyden
Streaky Bay
Rockingham
Pingelly
Kondinin
Salmon Gums
Wudinna
GREAT AUSTRALIAN BIGHT
Mandurah
Wickepin
Kulin
Lake King
Red Lake
Grass Patch
Talia
Pinjarra
Narrogin
Newdegate
Gibson
Elliston
Cowell
Waroona
Williams
Wagin
Lake Grace
Ravensthorpe
Esperance
Arno Bay
Bunbury
Collie
Katanning
Hopetoun
Tumby Bay
Capel
Busselton
Jerramungup
Wangary
Dunsborough
Cowaramup
Bridgetown
Borden
Port Lincoln
Witchcliffe
Nannup
Karridale
Pemberton
Porongurup
Flinders Bay
Mt. Barker
Northcliffe
Albany
Nornalup
Denmark
Torbay
Kingscote
Kangaroo Island
INDIAN OCEAN
Longitude East 124° of Greenwich
112° 116° 120° 124° 128° 132° 136°
12° 16° 20° 24° 28° 32° 36°
1 2 3 4 5 6 7 8 9
A B C D E F G H J K L M

AUSTRALIA
Political

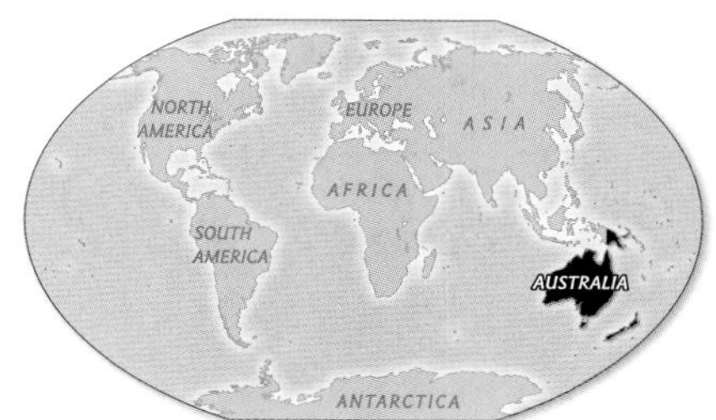

CONTINENTAL DATA

- **Total number of countries:** 1
- **Date of independence:** January 1, 1901
- **Area of Australia:** 7,687,000 sq km (2,968,000 sq mi)
- **Percent urban population:** 85%
- **Population of Australia:** 19,917,000
- **Population density:** 2.7 per sq km (7 per sq mi)
- **Largest city by population:** Sydney, Australia 3,907,000
- **GDP per capita:** Australia $27,000
- **Average life expectancy in Australia:** 80 years
- **Average literacy rate in Australia:** 100%

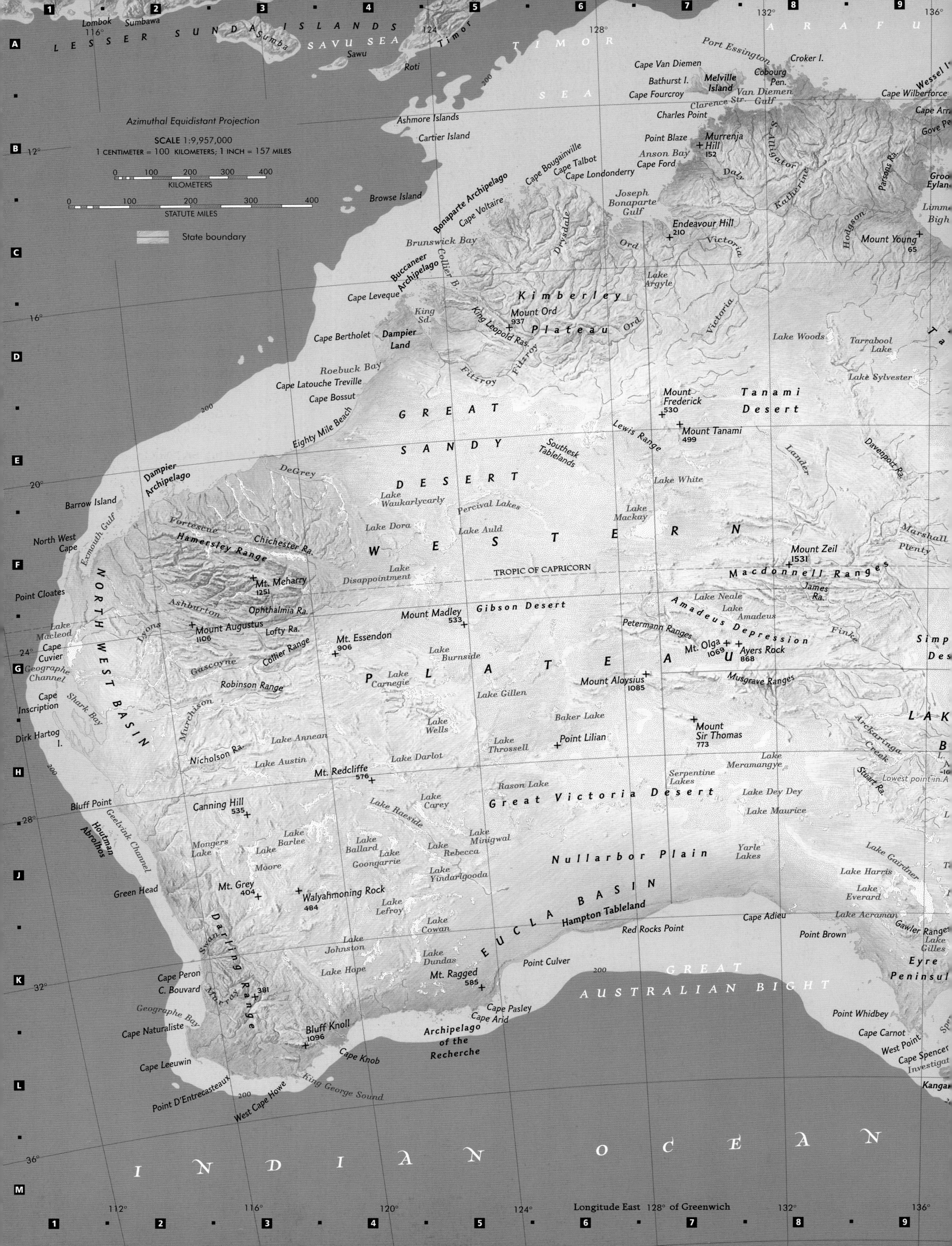

Lombok
Sumbawa
LESSER SUNDA ISLANDS
Sumba
SAVU SEA
Sawu
Roti
Timor
TIMOR SEA
ARAFURA
Port Essington
Croker I.
Cape Van Diemen
Bathurst I.
Melville Island
Cobourg Pen.
Cape Fourcroy
Van Diemen Gulf
Clarence Str.
Charles Point
Wessel Is.
Cape Wilberforce
Cape Arnhem
Gove Pen.
Azimuthal Equidistant Projection
SCALE 1:9,957,000
1 CENTIMETER = 100 KILOMETERS; 1 INCH = 157 MILES
0 100 200 300 400
KILOMETERS
0 100 200 300 400
STATUTE MILES
State boundary
Ashmore Islands
Cartier Island
Point Blaze
Murrenja Hill 152
Anson Bay
Cape Ford
S. Alligator
Daly
Parsons Ra.
Groote Eylandt
Cape Bougainville
Cape Talbot
Cape Londonderry
Joseph Bonaparte Gulf
Browse Island
Bonaparte Archipelago
Cape Voltaire
Drysdale
Katherine
Hodgson
Limmen Bight
Endeavour Hill 210
Mount Young 65
Brunswick Bay
Ord
Victoria
Buccaneer Archipelago
Collier B.
Lake Argyle
Cape Leveque
Kimberley Plateau
King Sd.
Mount Ord 937
King Leopold Ras.
Cape Bertholet
Dampier Land
Lake Woods
Tarrabool Lake
Roebuck Bay
Fitzroy
Cape Latouche Treville
Cape Bossut
Lake Sylvester
Mount Frederick 530
Tanami Desert
GREAT SANDY DESERT
Mount Tanami 499
Eighty Mile Beach
Lewis Range
Southesk Tablelands
Lander
Davenport Ra.
DeGrey
Dampier Archipelago
Lake White
Lake Waukarlycarly
Percival Lakes
Barrow Island
Lake Mackay
Exmouth Gulf
Fortescue
Lake Dora
Lake Auld
Marshall
North West Cape
Hamersley Range
Chichester Ra.
WESTERN
Plenty
Mount Zeil 1531
Lake Disappointment
TROPIC OF CAPRICORN
Macdonnell Ranges
Mt. Meharry 1251
NORTH WEST BASIN
James Ra.
Point Cloates
Lake Neale
Ashburton
Ophthalmia Ra.
Amadeus Depression
Lake Amadeus
Mount Madley 533
Gibson Desert
Lake Macleod
Mount Augustus 1106
Lofty Ra.
Petermann Ranges
Finke
Lyons
Mt. Essendon 906
Mt. Olga 1069
Ayers Rock 868
Cape Cuvier
Collier Range
Lake Burnside
Simpson Desert
Geographe Channel
Gascoyne
PLATEAU
Lake Carnegie
Mount Aloysius 1085
Musgrave Ranges
Robinson Range
Lake Gillen
Cape Inscription
Shark Bay
Murchison
Baker Lake
Mount Sir Thomas 773
LAKE
Lake Wells
Arckaringa Creek
Dirk Hartog I.
Lake Annean
Lake Throssell
Point Lilian
Nicholson Ra.
Lake Austin
Lake Darlot
Lake Meramangye
Mt. Redcliffe 576
Serpentine Lakes
Stuart Ra.
Lowest point in A.
Rason Lake
Lake Dey Dey
Bluff Point
Lake Raeside
Lake Carey
Great Victoria Desert
Lake Maurice
Canning Hill 535
Houtman Abrolhos
Geelvink Channel
Mongers Lake
Lake Barlee
Lake Minigwal
Lake Ballard
Lake Rebecca
Lake Goongarrie
Nullarbor Plain
Yarle Lakes
Lake Gairdner
Lake Moore
Lake Yindarlgooda
Lake Harris
Green Head
Mt. Grey 404
Walyahmoning Rock 484
EUCLA BASIN
Lake Everard
Lake Lefroy
Hampton Tableland
Cape Adieu
Lake Acraman
Darling Range
Swan
Lake Cowan
Red Rocks Point
Point Brown
Gawler Ranges
Lake Gilles
Lake Johnston
Lake Dundas
Point Culver
Eyre Peninsula
Cape Peron
Lake Hope
Mt. Ragged 585
GREAT AUSTRALIAN BIGHT
C. Bouvard
Murray
381
Geographe Bay
Cape Pasley
Cape Arid
Point Whidbey
Cape Naturaliste
Bluff Knoll 1096
Archipelago of the Recherche
Cape Carnot
Cape Knob
West Point
Cape Spencer
Investigator
Cape Leeuwin
King George Sound
Kangaroo
Point D'Entrecasteaux
West Cape Howe
INDIAN OCEAN
200
12°
16°
20°
24°
28°
32°
36°
112°
116°
120°
124°
128°
132°
136°
Longitude East 128° of Greenwich
1 2 3 4 5 6 7 8 9
A B C D E F G H J K L M

AUSTRALIA
Physical

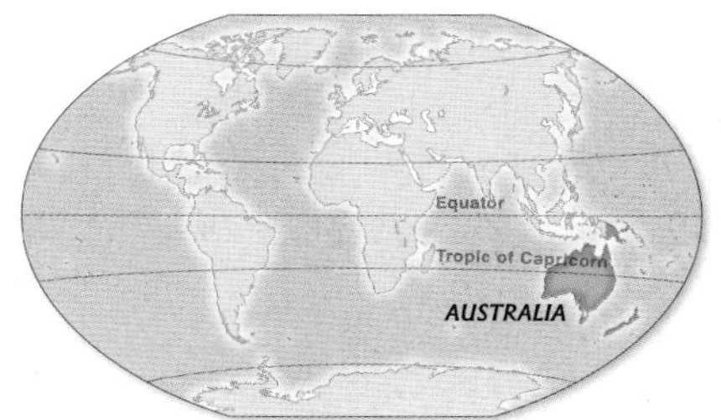

CONTINENTAL DATA

- **Area :**
  7,687,000 sq km (2,968,000 sq mi)
- **Greatest north-south extent :**
  3,138 km (1,950 mi)
- **Greatest east-west extent :**
  3,983 km (2,475 mi)
- **Highest point :**
  Mount Kosciuszko, New South Wales 2,228 m (7,310 ft)
- **Lowest point :**
  Lake Eyre -16 m (-52 ft)
- **Lowest recorded temperature :**
  Charlotte Pass, New South Wales -23°C (-9.4°F), June 29, 1994
- **Highest recorded temperature:**
  Cloncurry, Queensland 53.3°C (128 °F), January 16, 1889
- **Longest rivers :**
  - Murray-Darling 3,718 km (2,310 mi)
  - Murrumbidgee 1575 km (979 mi)
  - Lachlan 1370 km (851 mi)
- **Largest lakes (Aus.):**
  - Lake Eyre 9,500 sq km (3,668 sq mi)
  - Lake Mackay 3,494 sq km (1349 sq mi)
  - Lake Amadeus 1,032 sq km (398 sq mi)
- **Earth's extremes located in Australia:**
  - **Longest Reef:**
    Great Barrier Reef 2,012 km (1,250 mi)

PAPUA NEW GUINEA AND NEW ZEALAND

Political

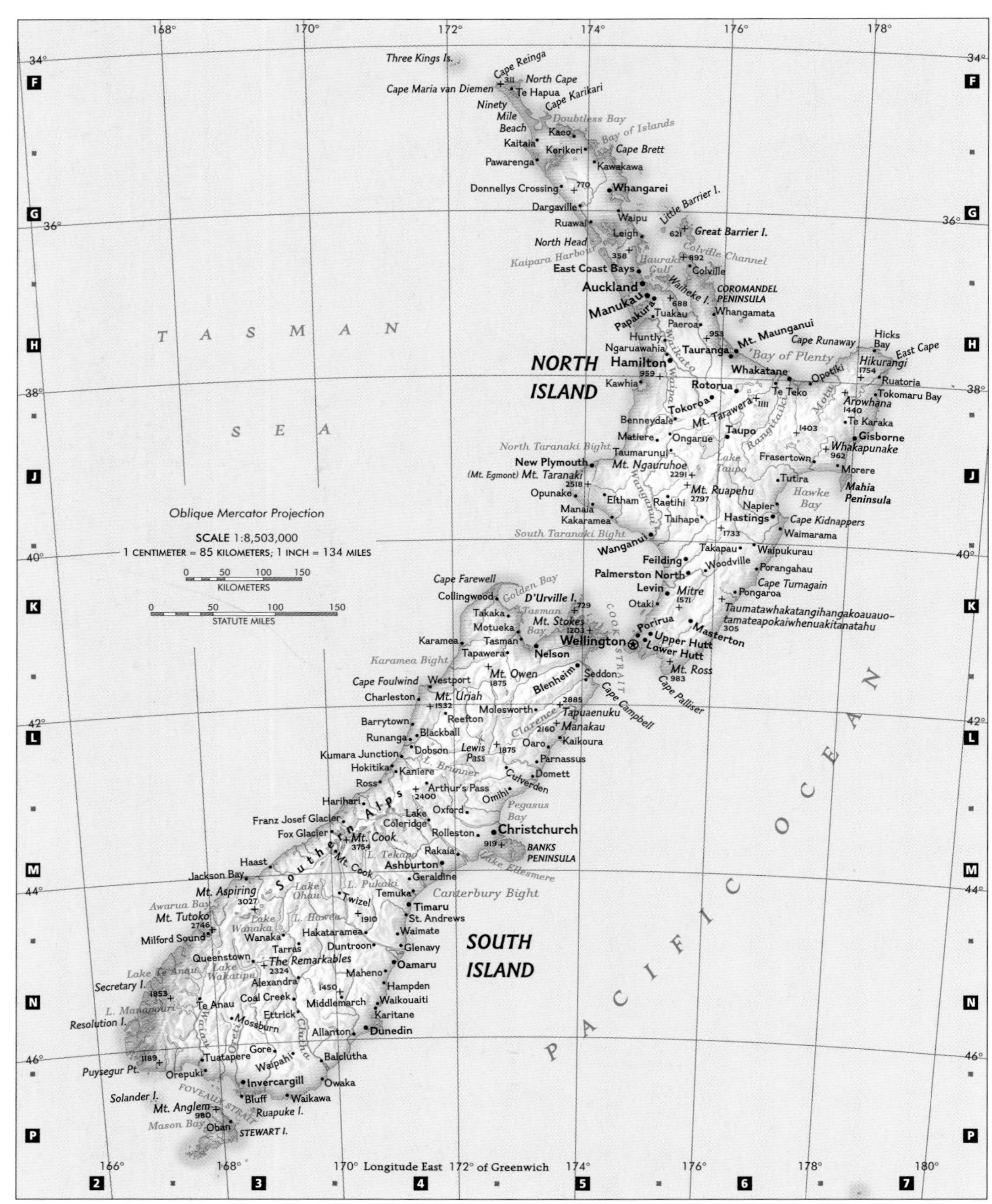

AUSTRALIA

COMMONWEALTH OF AUSTRALIA

AREA	7,687,000 sq km (2,968,000 sq mi)
POPULATION	19,917,000
CAPITAL	Canberra 387,000
RELIGION	Protestant, Roman Catholic
LANGUAGE	English, indigenous languages
LITERACY	100%
LIFE EXPECTANCY	80 years
GDP PER CAPITA	$27,000

ECONOMY IND: mining, industrial and transportation equipment, food processing, chemicals. AGR: wheat, barley, sugarcane, fruits; cattle. EXP: coal, gold, meat, wool.

NEW ZEALAND

NEW ZEALAND

AREA	270,534 sq km (104,454 sq mi)
POPULATION	4,008,000
CAPITAL	Wellington 345,000
RELIGION	Protestant, Roman Catholic
LANGUAGE	English, Maori
LITERACY	99%
LIFE EXPECTANCY	78 years
GDP PER CAPITA	$19,500

ECONOMY IND: food processing, wood and paper products, textiles, machinery. AGR: wheat, barley, potatoes, pulses; wool; fish. EXP: dairy products, meat, fish, wool.

PAPUA NEW GUINEA

INDEPENDENT STATE OF PAPUA NEW GUINEA

AREA	462,840 sq km (178,703 sq mi)
POPULATION	5,525,000
CAPITAL	Port Moresby 259,000
RELIGION	Protestant, indigenous beliefs, Roman Catholic
LANGUAGE	715 indigenous languages
LITERACY	65%
LIFE EXPECTANCY	57 years
GDP PER CAPITA	$2,400

ECONOMY IND: copra crushing, mining (gold, silver), crude oil production, construction. AGR: coffee, cocoa, coconuts, palm kernels; poultry. EXP: oil, gold, copper ore, logs, gas, petroleum products.

DATES OF COUNTRY INDEPENDENCE

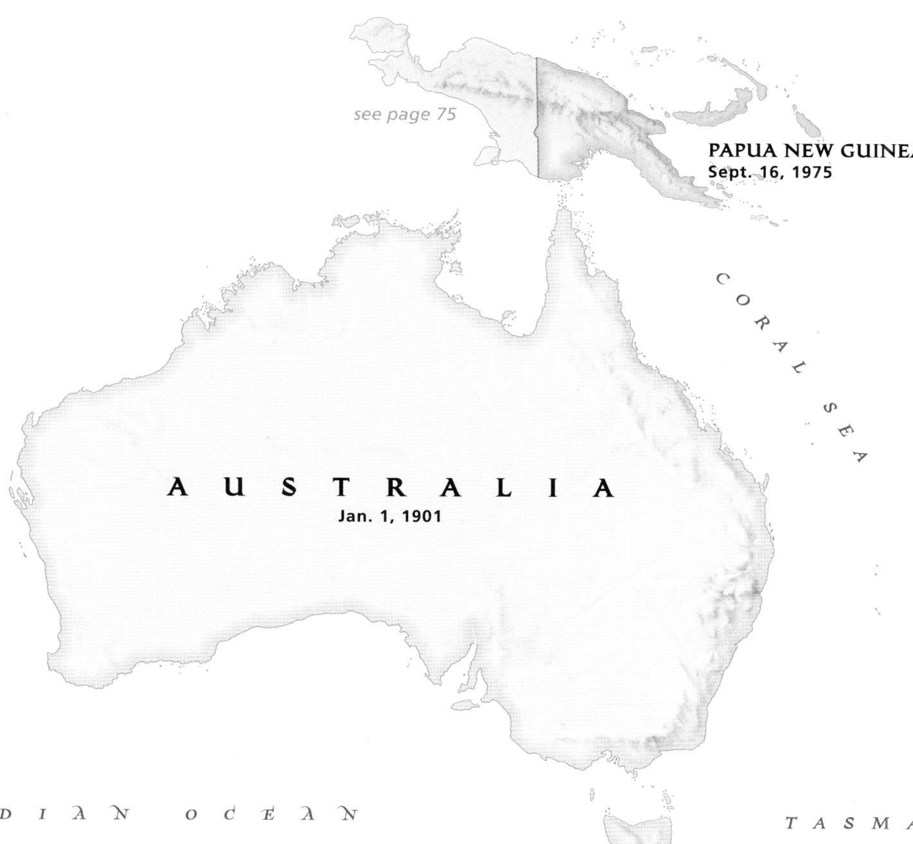

POPULATION DENSITY

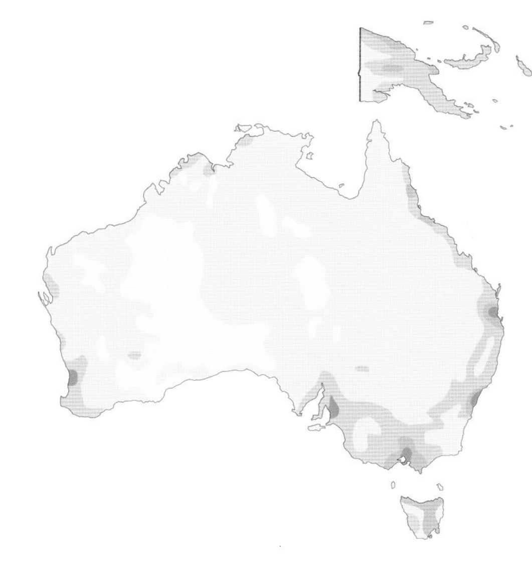

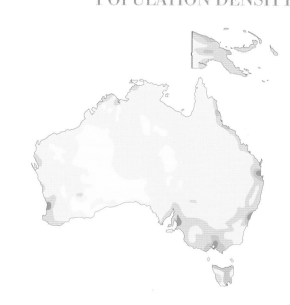

People per square mile	People per square km
60 and greater	25 and greater
25–59	10-24
2–24	1-9
Less than 2	Less than 1
Uninhabited	Uninhabited

OCEANIA

The Pacific Ocean's vastness covers nearly a third of the world's surface, and at the Equator embraces nearly half the Earth's circumference (11,000 miles, 17,600 km.). At the heart of this watery realm lies the region of Oceania, with more than 10,000 islands in the central and South Pacific. Geographers divide Oceania into three major ethnogeographic regions, known as Polynesia ("many islands"), Melanesia ("black islands"), and Micronesia ("tiny islands").

Largest is Polynesia, an immense oceanic triangle, with apexes at Hawaii in the north, Easter Island in the east and New Zealand in the southwest. The best known island groups are Hawaii, French Polynesia—including Tahiti—Samoa, the Cook Islands, Tonga, Tuvalu, and Wallis and Futuna. Enigmatic Easter Island, incredibly isolated with a population of just 2,000 people today, is famous for its gigantic stone statues in human form.

The islands of Melanesia cluster in the southwest, south of the equator and northeast of Australia. The name originally referred to either the dark island landscapes or the dark colored skin of most inhabitants. Major island groups here are the Bismarck Archipelago, the Solomon Islands, Vanuatu, New Caledonia, and Fiji.

Micronesia, mostly north of the Equator and in the west-central part of Oceania, comprises a vast number of small islands and atolls, including the Caroline Islands, Marshall Islands, Palau, Gilbert Islands, Nauru, and the Mariana Islands, including Guam, a territory of the United States. South of Guam lies the world's deepest ocean point, known as Challenger Deep of the Mariana Trench (35,827 feet, 10,920 m.).

Oceania's myriad islands fall generally into two categories, the "high islands," which are larger and of volcanic origin, and the "low islands," formed by coral and which often combine with reefs or other small islands to form atolls surrounding lagoons. Climate throughout the huge region tends towards high humidity and high temperatures all year round.

The discovery and settlement of the whole Pacific took place gradually over thousands of years. Some 30,000 years ago there were no people at all in Oceania, but settlers slowly came, first to Melanesia, then fanning outward to the north, south, and east. Double-hulled canoes of great seaworthiness carried these amazing navigators, who knew the sea, stars, wind, clouds, and currents intimately. They came to Fiji by about 1000 B.C., Tonga by 500 B.C., and the Marquesas by around A.D. 500. Hawaii and Easter Island were the last of the Polynesian settlements.

European contact began with Ferdinand Magellan's round-the-world voyage (1519-22). Throughout the 16th to 18th centuries successive Spanish, Dutch, British, and French mariners probed the extent of Oceania in the name of treasure hunting, commerce, national expansion, adventure, and science. Capt. James Cook, a British seaman, made three heroic voyages of discovery to the Pacific between 1768 and 1779. The 19th century saw the arrival of permanent missionaries, later followed by foreign governments. Ever since, modernization, communications, air travel, and tourism have altered forever the indigenous cultures. Today about 12 million islanders live in Oceania, and it is fair to say that, despite massive changes, a broad cultural unity still exists throughout this far-flung region.

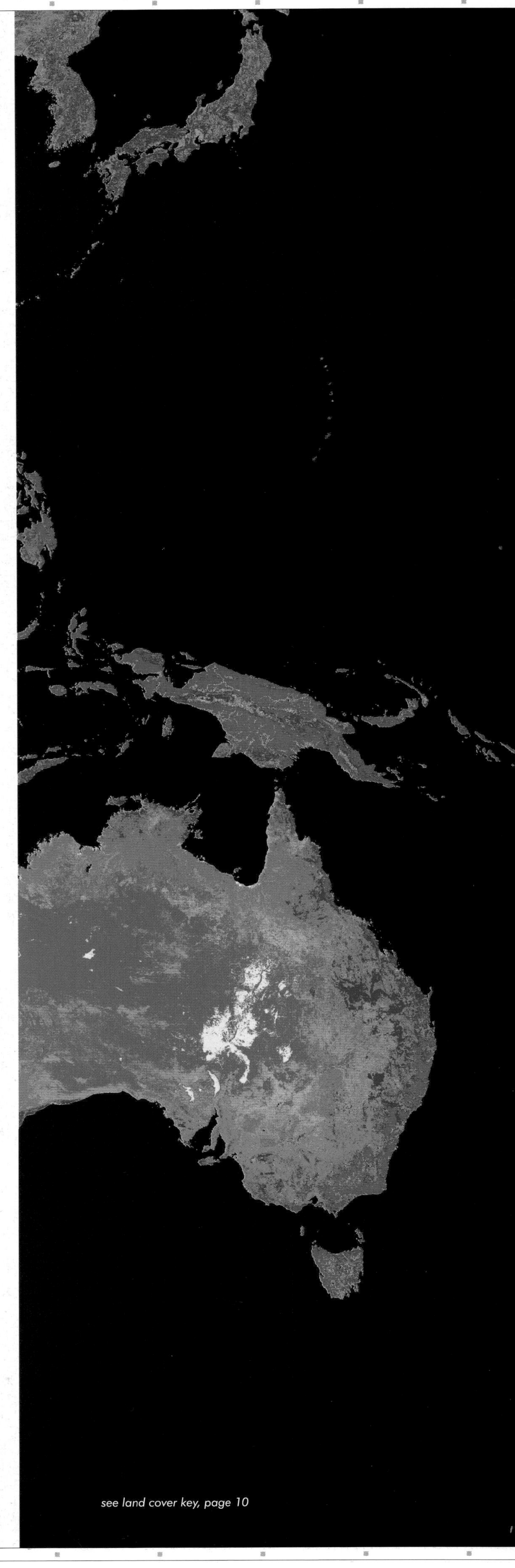

see land cover key, page 10

CHINA
NORTH KOREA
P'YŎNGYANG
SEOUL
SOUTH KOREA
YELLOW SEA
Cheju Do
SEA OF JAPAN (EAST SEA)
JAPAN
HONSHŪ
TŌKYŌ
YOKOHAMA
NAGOYA
KŌBE
ŌSAKA
HIROSHIMA
SHIKOKU
KYŪSHŪ
Hachijō Jima
Nampō Shotō
Japan
Sumisu (Smith)
Sōfu Gan (Lot's Wife)
Yaku Shima
Tanega Shima
EAST CHINA SEA
Amami Ō Shima
Okinawa
Sakishima Shotō
RYUKYU ISLANDS
Japan
Kita Daitō Jima
Daitō Islands
Japan
Okino Daitō Jima
Bonin Islands
(Ogasawara Guntō)
Muko Jima Rettō
Chichi Jima Rettō
Haha Jima Rettō
Volcano Islands
(Kazan Rettō)
Japan
Kita Iwo Jima
Iwo Jima
Minami Iwo Jima
Minami Tori Shima
(Marcus)
Japan
TROPIC OF CANCER
NORTH PACIFIC
Monday
Sunday
Kure Atoll
Midway Islands
HAWAII
Pearl and Hermes Atoll
Lisianski I.
Laysan I.
United States
Gardner Pinnacles
La Perouse Pinnacle
Necker I.
Nihoa
Ni'ihau
Ka'ula
Kaua'i
O'ahu
Honolulu
Moloka'i
Lāna'i
Maui
Kaho'olawe
Hawai'i
Batan Is.
Babuyan Is.
Parece Vela
Japan
Farallon de Pajaros
Asuncion
Agrihan
Pagan
Alamagan
Sarigan
Anatahan
Saipan
Tinian
Rota
Guam
U.S.
NORTHERN MARIANA ISLANDS
U.S.
PHILIPPINE SEA
PHILIPPINES
LUZON
Samar
Leyte
MINDANAO
Davao
Wake Island
U.S.
Johnston Atoll
U.S.
Taongi Atoll
Bikini Atoll
Rongelap Atoll
Enewetak Atoll
Utirik Atoll
Ailuk Atoll
Wotje Atoll
Maloelap Atoll
Majuro
Arno Atoll
Mili Atoll
Jaluit Atoll
Kili I.
MARSHALL ISLANDS
Ralik Chain
Ratak Chain
Date Line
Ujelang Atoll
Kwajalein Atoll
Ailinglapalap Atoll
Namorik Atoll
Ebon Atoll
MICRONESIA
Ulithi Atoll
Fais
Yap Islands
Gaferut
Woleai Atoll
Ifalik Atoll
Satawal
Namonuito Atoll
Hall Is.
Chuuk
(Truk Is.)
Oroluk Atoll
Senyavin Is.
Pohnpei (Ponape)
Palikir
Pulap Atoll
Pulusuk
Puluwat Atoll
Mortlock Is.
Ngatik Atoll
Kosrae
(Kusaie)
Nukuoro Atoll
Kapingamarangi Atoll
PALAU
Koror
Ngulu Atoll
Eauripik Atoll
CAROLINE ISLANDS
FEDERATED STATES OF MICRONESIA
Sonsorol Is.
Pulo Anna
Merir
Helen I.
Tobi
Miangas
Kepulauan Talaud
Celebes Sea
Morotai
Molucca Sea
Halmahera
SULAWESI
(Celebes)
Kep. Asia
Waigeo
Kep. Mapia
EQUATOR
Biak
Teluk Cenderawasih
Peleng
Kep. Sula
Buru
Ceram
MOLUCCAS
INDONESIA
Banda Sea
Buton
Kep. Kai
Kep. Aru
Wetar
Alor
Lomblen
Timor
Dili
Moa
Babar
Kep. Tanimbar
TIMOR-LESTE
(EAST TIMOR)
Roti
Timor Sea
Arafura Sea
Torres Str.
NEW GUINEA
PAPUA NEW GUINEA
Port Moresby
Admiralty Islands
Manus
Mussau Is.
New Hanover
BISMARCK ARCHIPELAGO
Bismarck Sea
New Ireland
Rabaul
New Britain
Green Islands
Bougainville
Huon G.
Trobriand Is.
Woodlark
Solomon Sea
D'Entrecasteaux Islands
Louisiade Archipelago
MELANESIA
Nukumanu Islands
Choiseul
SOLOMON ISLANDS
New Georgia
Santa Isabel
Malaita
Honiara
Guadalcanal
Rennell
San Cristobal
Duff Islands
NAURU
GILBERT ISLANDS
Butaritari
Abaiang
Marakei
Tarawa (Bairiki)
Abemama
Nonouti
Banaba
(Ocean I.)
Tabiteuea
Beru
Tamana
Arorae
KIRIBATI
Howland Island
Baker Island
U.S.
Kanton
Enderbury I.
McKean Island
Birnie I.
Rawaki
Nikumaroro
Orona
Manra
PHOENIX ISLANDS
Nanumea
Niutao
Nanumanga
Nui
Vaitupu
Nukufetau
Funafuti
Nukulaelae
Niulakita
TUVALU
POLYNESIA
Palmyra Atoll
U.S.
Teraina (Washington I.)
Tabuaeran (Fanning I.)
Kiribati
Kiritimati
(Christmas I.)
Kiribati
Jarvis Island
U.S.
LINE ISLANDS
Malden Island
Starbuck Island
Atafu
Nukunono
TOKELAU
Fakaofu
(Tongareva) Penrhyn Atoll
Rakahanga Atoll
Pukapuka Atoll
(Danger Is.)
Manihiki Atoll
Nassau
Vostok Isl.
Flint
Swains I.
AMERICAN SAMOA
U.S.
SAMOA
Apia
Savai'i
Upolu
Pago Pago
Tutuila
Manua Is.
Rose Atoll
SAMOA ISLANDS
Suwarrow Atoll
New Zealand
COOK ISLANDS
Îles Wallis
Uvea
France
Îles de Horne
Rotuma
Fiji
Niuafo'ou
Tafahi
Niuatoputapu
Nupani
Nendo
(Ndeni)
Santa Cruz Islands
Utupua
Vanikolo Is.
Anuta (Cherry I.)
Fataka (Mitre I.)
Tikopia
Torres Islands
Banks Islands
Espiritu Santo
Maéwo
Malakula
Port-Vila
Éfaté
Erromango
Futuna
Tanna
Anatom
VANUATU
Vanua Levu
FIJI ISLANDS
Taveuni
Viti Levu
Suva
Lau Group
Kadavu
Vatoa
Ono-i-Lau
TONGA ISLANDS
Vava'u Group
Ha'apai Group
TONGA
Nuku'alofa
Tongatapu Group
'Eua
Ata
Niue
Palmerston Atoll
Aitutaki Atoll
Hervey Is.
Manuae
Maupihaa
Motu One
Mitiaro
Atiu
Mauke
Rarotonga
Mangaia
Îles Maria
AUSTRAL
(TUBUAI)
Willis Islets
CORAL SEA ISLANDS TERRITORY
Australia
Îles Chesterfield
Île Huon
Îles Bélep
Ouvéa
Lifou
Loyalty Is.
Maré
NEW CALEDONIA
Nouméa
France
Île des Pins
(Kunié)
Matthew
Hunter
TROPIC OF CAPRICORN
CORAL SEA
Cape York
Gulf of Carpentaria
Great Dividing Range
AUSTRALIA
Fraser Island
BRISBANE
Norfolk Island
Australia
Phillip Island
Raoul I.
(Sunday)
Macauley I.
Curtis I.
Kermadec Islands
N.Z.
L'Esperance Rock
Lord Howe I.
Ball's Pyramid
Australia
GREAT AUSTRALIAN BIGHT
ADELAIDE
Kangaroo I.
SYDNEY
Canberra
MELBOURNE
Wilsons Promontory
Bass Strait
King I.
Furneaux Group
TASMANIA
Hobart
South East Cape
TASMAN SEA
SOUTH
Three Kings Islands
Cape Maria van Diemen
North Cape
Great Barrier Island
Bay of Plenty
East Cape
NORTH ISLAND
Cook Str.
Cape Farewell
Wellington
NEW ZEALAND
SOUTH ISLAND
Chatham Islands
Chatham Is.
N.Z.
Pitt Island
Puysegur Point
Foveaux Strait
Stewart Island
The Snares
Bounty Islands
N.Z.
Antipodes Islands
N.Z.
Auckland Islands
N.Z.
Campbell I.
N.Z.
Macquarie I.
Australia
Longitude East 140° of Greenwich

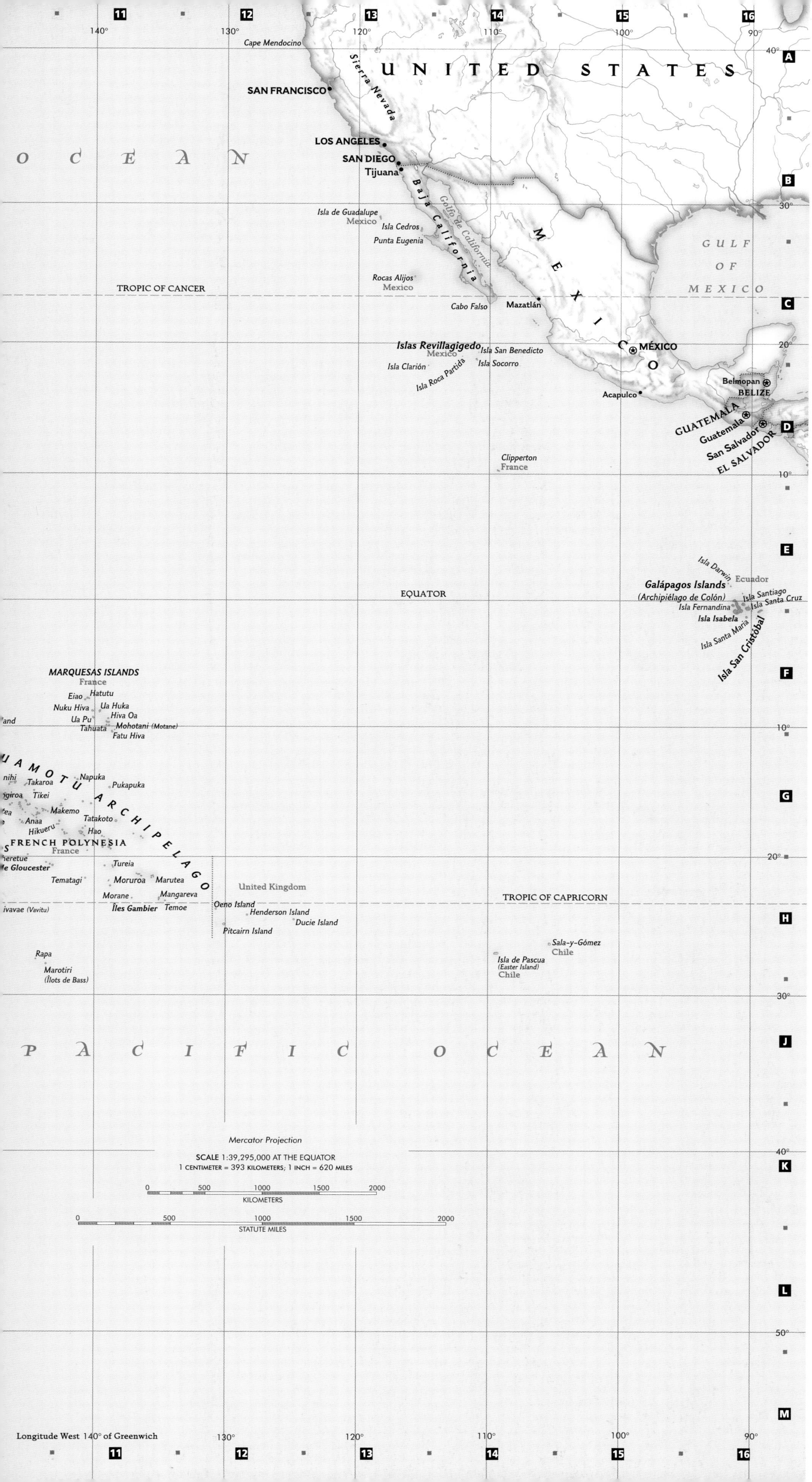

OCEANIA
Political

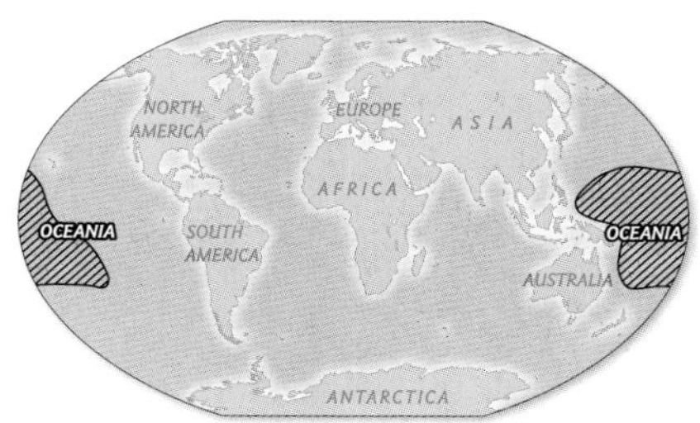

REGIONAL DATA

- **Total number of countries:** 11
- **First independent country:** Samoa, January 1, 1962
- **"Youngest" country:** Palau, October 1, 1994
- **Largest country by area:** Solomon Islands 28,450 sq km (10,985 sq mi)
- **Smallest country by area:** Nauru 21 sq km (8 sq mi)
- **Percent urban population:** 39%
- **Most populous country:** Fiji Islands 865,000
- **Least populous country:** Tuvalu 10,000
- **Most densely populated country:** Nauru 545 per sq km (1,412 per sq mi)
- **Least densely populated country:** Solomon Islands 17 per sq km (44 per sq mi)
- **Largest city by population:** Suva, Fiji Islands 203,000
- **Highest GDP per capita:** Palau $9,000
- **Lowest GDP per capita:** Kiribati $840
- **Average life expectancy in Oceania:** 67 years
- **Average literacy rate in Oceania:** 89%

Mercator Projection

SCALE 1:39,295,000 AT THE EQUATOR

1 CENTIMETER = 393 KILOMETERS; 1 INCH = 620 MILES

Longitude West 140° of Greenwich

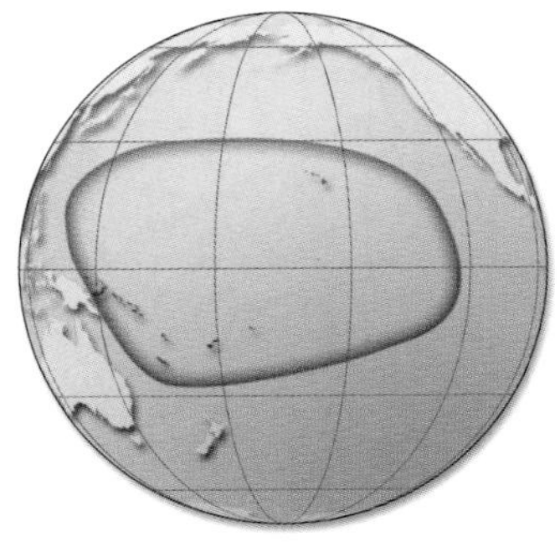

FIJI ISLANDS

REPUBLIC OF THE FIJI ISLANDS

AREA 18,376 sq km (7,095 sq mi)
POPULATION 865,000
CAPITAL Suva 203,000
RELIGION Christian, Hindu, Muslim
LANGUAGE English, Fijian, Hindustani
LITERACY 93%
LIFE EXPECTANCY 67 years
GDP PER CAPITA $5,200
ECONOMY IND: tourism, sugar, clothing, copra. AGR: sugarcane, coconuts, cassava (tapioca), rice; cattle; fish. EXP: sugar, garments, gold, timber.

KIRIBATI

REPUBLIC OF KIRIBATI

AREA 811 sq km (313 sq mi)
POPULATION 98,000
CAPITAL Tarawa 32,000
RELIGION Roman Catholic, Protestant
LANGUAGE English, I-Kiribati
LITERACY NA
LIFE EXPECTANCY 62 years
GDP PER CAPITA $840
ECONOMY IND: fishing, handicrafts. AGR: copra, taro, breadfruit, sweet potatoes; fish. EXP: copra, coconuts, seaweed, fish.

MARSHALL ISLANDS

REPUBLIC OF THE MARSHALL ISLANDS

AREA 181 sq km (70 sq mi)
POPULATION 55,000
CAPITAL Majuro 25,000
RELIGION Christian (mostly Protestant)
LANGUAGE English, local dialects, Japanese
LITERACY 94%
LIFE EXPECTANCY 68 years
GDP PER CAPITA $1,600
ECONOMY IND: copra, fish, tourism, craft items from shell, wood, and pearls. AGR: coconuts, tomatoes, melons, cacao; pigs. EXP: fish, coconut oil, trochus shells.

MICRONESIA

FEDERATED STATES OF MICRONESIA

AREA 702 sq km (271 sq mi)
POPULATION 115,000
CAPITAL Palikir 11,000
RELIGION Roman Catholic, Protestant
LANGUAGE English, Trukese, Pohnpeian, Yapese, Kosraean
LITERACY 89%
LIFE EXPECTANCY 68 years
GDP PER CAPITA $2,000
ECONOMY IND: tourism, construction, fish processing, craft items from shell, wood, and pearls. AGR: black pepper, tropical fruits and vegetables, coconuts, cassava (tapioca); pigs. EXP: fish, garments, bananas, black pepper.

NAURU

REPUBLIC OF NAURU

AREA 21 sq km (8 sq mi)
POPULATION 12,000
CAPITAL Yaren 13,000
RELIGION Protestant, Roman Catholic
LANGUAGE Nauruan, English
LITERACY NA
LIFE EXPECTANCY 61 years
GDP PER CAPITA $5,000
ECONOMY IND: phosphate mining, financial services, coconut products. AGR: coconuts. EXP: phosphates.

PALAU

REPUBLIC OF PALAU

AREA 487 sq km (188 sq mi)
POPULATION 20,000
CAPITAL Koror 14,000
RELIGION Roman Catholic, Protestant, Modekngei (indigenous)
LANGUAGE English, Palauan, Sonsorolese, Tobi, Angaur, Japanese
LITERACY 92%
LIFE EXPECTANCY 69 years
GDP PER CAPITA $9,000
ECONOMY IND: tourism, craft items, construction, garment making. AGR: coconuts, copra cassava (tapioca), sweet potatoes. EXP: trochus (type of shellfish), tuna, copra, handicrafts.

SAMOA

INDEPENDENT STATE OF SAMOA

AREA 2,831 sq km (1,093 sq mi)
POPULATION 172,000
CAPITAL Apia 35,000
RELIGION Protestant, Roman Catholic
LANGUAGE Samoan, English
LITERACY 80%
LIFE EXPECTANCY 69 years
GDP PER CAPITA $3,500
ECONOMY IND: food processing, building materials, auto parts. AGR: coconuts, bananas, taro, yams. EXP: coconut oil and cream, copra, fish, beer.

SOLOMON ISLANDS

SOLOMON ISLANDS

AREA 27,556 sq km (10,639 sq mi)
POPULATION 491,000
CAPITAL Honiara 78,000
RELIGION Protestant, Roman Catholic, indigenous beliefs
LANGUAGE Melanesian pidgin, English, 120 indigenous languages
LITERACY NA
LIFE EXPECTANCY 71 years
GDP PER CAPITA $1,700
ECONOMY IND: fish (tuna), mining, timber. AGR: cocoa, beans, coconuts, palm kernels; cattle; timber; fish. EXP: timber, fish, palm oil, cocoa.

TONGA

KINGDOM OF TONGA

AREA 748 sq km (289 sq mi)
POPULATION 107,000
CAPITAL Nuku'alofa 33,000
RELIGION Christian
LANGUAGE Tongan, English
LITERACY 99%
LIFE EXPECTANCY 68 years
GDP PER CAPITA $2,200
ECONOMY IND: tourism, fishing. AGR: squash, coconuts, copra, bananas. EXP: squash, fish, vanilla beans.

TUVALU

TUVALU

AREA 26 sq km (10 sq mi)
POPULATION 10,000
CAPITAL Funafuti 5,000
RELIGION Church of Tuvalu (Congregationalist), Seventh-Day Adventist, Baha'I
LANGUAGE Tuvaluan, English, Samoan, Kiribati
LITERACY 55%
LIFE EXPECTANCY 66 years
GDP PER CAPITA $1,100
ECONOMY IND: fishing, tourism, copra. AGR: coconuts; fish. EXP: copra.

VANUATU

REPUBLIC OF VANUATU

AREA 12,190 sq km (4,707 sq mi)
POPULATION 214,000
CAPITAL Port-Vila 31,000
RELIGION Protestant, Catholic, indigenous beliefs
LANGUAGE English, French, pidgin (Bislama)
LITERACY 53%
LIFE EXPECTANCY 67 years
GDP PER CAPITA $1,300
ECONOMY IND: petroleum, natural gas, light industries, mining. AGR: copra, coconuts, cocoa, coffee; fish. EXP: copra, kava, beef, cocoa.

DEPENDENCIES

SOVEREIGN

LOCAL

AMERICAN SAMOA (U.S.)

AMERICAN SAMOA

AREA 199 sq km (77 sq mi)
POPULATION 62,000
CAPITAL Pago Pago 15,000
RELIGION Christian Congregationalist, Roman Catholic, Protestant
LANGUAGE Samoan, English
LITERACY 97%
LIFE EXPECTANCY 75 years
GDP PER CAPITA $8,000
ECONOMY IND: tuna canneries, handicrafts. AGR: bananas, coconuts, vegetables, taro; dairy products. EXP: canned tuna.

SOVEREIGN

LOCAL

COOK ISLANDS (NEW ZEALAND)

COOK ISLANDS

AREA 240 sq km (93 sq mi)
POPULATION 18,000
CAPITAL Avarua 12,000
RELIGION Christian
LANGUAGE English, Maori
LITERACY 95%
LIFE EXPECTANCY NA
GDP PER CAPITA $5,000
ECONOMY IND: fruit processing, tourism, fishing. AGR: copra, citrus, pineapples, tomatoes; pigs. EXP: copra, papayas, fresh and canned citrus fruit, coffee.

SOVEREIGN

LOCAL

FRENCH POLYNESIA (FRANCE)

TERRITORY OF FRENCH POLYNESIA

AREA 4,167 sq km (1,608 sq mi)
POPULATION 245,000
CAPITAL Papeete 125,000
RELIGION Protestant, Roman Catholic
LANGUAGE French, Tahitian
LITERACY 98%
LIFE EXPECTANCY 72 years
GDP PER CAPITA $5,000
ECONOMY IND: tourism, pearls, agricultural processing, handicrafts. AGR: coconuts, vanilla, vegetables, fruits; poultry. EXP: cultured pearls, coconut products, mother-of-pearl, vanilla.

SOVEREIGN

LOCAL

GUAM (U.S.)

GUAM

AREA 549 sq km (212 sq mi)
POPULATION 164,000
CAPITAL Hagåtña (Agana) 2,000
RELIGION Roman Catholic
LANGUAGE English, Chamorro, Japanese
LITERACY 99%
LIFE EXPECTANCY 78 years
GDP PER CAPITA $21,000
ECONOMY IND: US military, tourism, construction, transshipment services. AGR: fruits, copra, vegetables; eggs. EXP: mostly transshipments of refined petroleum products, construction materials, fish, food and beverage products.

NEW CALEDONIA (FRANCE)

TERRITORY OF NEW CALEDONIA AND DEPENDENCIES

AREA 18,575 sq km (7,172 sq mi)
POPULATION 222,000
CAPITAL Nouméa 138,000
RELIGION Roman Catholic, Protestant
LANGUAGE French, 33 Melanesian-Polynesian dialects
LITERACY 91%
LIFE EXPECTANCY 73 years
GDP PER CAPITA $15,000
ECONOMY IND: nickel mining and smelting. AGR: vegetables, beef. EXP: ferronickels, nickel ore, fish.

SOVEREIGN

LOCAL

NIUE (NEW ZEALAND)

NIUE

AREA 263 sq km (102 sq mi)
POPULATION 1,600
CAPITAL Alofi 1,000
RELIGION Ekalesia Niue (a Protestant Church), Latter-Day Saints, other Christian
LANGUAGE Polynesian, English
LITERACY 95%
LIFE EXPECTANCY NA
GDP PER CAPITA $3,600
ECONOMY IND: tourism, handicrafts, food processing. AGR: coconuts, passion fruit, honey, limes; pigs. EXP: canned coconut cream, copra, honey, passion fruit products.

SOVEREIGN

LOCAL

NORFOLK ISLAND (AUSTRALIA)

TERRITORY OF NORFOLK ISLAND

AREA 35 sq km (14 sq mi)
POPULATION 2,482
CAPITAL Kingston 1,000
RELIGION Protestant, Roman Catholic
LANGUAGE English, Norfolk
LITERACY NA
LIFE EXPECTANCY NA
GDP PER CAPITA $4,420
ECONOMY IND: tourism. AGR: pine seed, palm seed, cereals, vegetables; cattle. EXP: postage stamps, pine and palm seed, avocados.

SOVEREIGN

LOCAL

NORTHERN MARIANA ISLANDS (U.S.)

COMMONWEALTH OF THE NORTHERN MARIANA ISLANDS

AREA 477 sq km (184 sq mi)
POPULATION 78,000
CAPITAL Saipan 7,000
RELIGION Christian, traditional beliefs
LANGUAGE English, Chamorro, Carolinian
LITERACY 97%
LIFE EXPECTANCY 76 years
GDP PER CAPITA $12,500
ECONOMY IND: tourism, construction, garments, handicrafts. AGR: coconuts, fruits, vegetables; cattle. EXP: garments.

SOVEREIGN

LOCAL

PITCAIRN ISLANDS (U.K.)

PITCAIRN, HENDERSON, DUCIE, AND OENO ISLANDS

AREA	47 sq km (18 sq mi)
POPULATION	50
CAPITAL	Adamstown 50
RELIGION	Seventh-Day Adventist
LANGUAGE	English, Pitcairnese
LITERACY	NA
LIFE EXPECTANCY	NA
GDP PER CAPITA	NA
ECONOMY	IND: postage stamps, handicrafts. AGR: fruits and vegetables; goats, chickens. EXP: fruits, vegetables, curios, stamps.

SOVEREIGN

LOCAL

TOKELAU (NEW ZEALAND)

TOKELAU

AREA	12 sq km (5 sq mi)
POPULATION	1,500
CAPITAL	administered from Wellington
RELIGION	Congregational Christian Church, Roman Catholic
LANGUAGE	Tokelauan, English
LITERACY	NA
LIFE EXPECTANCY	NA
GDP PER CAPITA	$1,000
ECONOMY	IND: small-scale enterprises for copra production and wood working, stamps, coins, fishing. AGR: coconuts, copra, breadfruit, papayas; pigs. EXP: stamps, copra, handicrafts.

SOVEREIGN

LOCAL

WALLIS AND FUTUNA ISLANDS (FRANCE)

TERRITORY OF THE WALLIS AND FUTUNA ISLANDS

AREA	161 sq km (62 sq mi)
POPULATION	15,000
CAPITAL	Matâ'utu 1,000
RELIGION	Roman Catholic
LANGUAGE	French, Wallisian (indigenous Polynesian language)
LITERACY	50%
LIFE EXPECTANCY	NA
GDP PER CAPITA	$2,000
ECONOMY	IND: copra, handicrafts, fishing, lumber. AGR: breadfruit, yams, taro, bananas; pigs. EXP: copra, chemicals, construction materials.

UNINHABITED DEPENDENCIES

BAKER ISLAND (U.S.)

BAKER ISLAND

AREA	1.4 sq km (0.5 sq mi)
POPULATION	None

HOWLAND ISLAND (U.S.)

HOWLAND ISLAND

AREA	1.6 sq km (0.6 sq mi)
POPULATION	None

JARVIS ISLAND (U.S.)

JARVIS ISLAND

AREA	4.5 sq km (1.7 sq mi)
POPULATION	None

JOHNSTON ATOLL (U.S.)

JOHNSTON ATOLL

AREA	2.8 sq km (1.1 sq mi)
POPULATION	None

KINGMAN REEF (U.S.)

KINGMAN REEF

AREA	1 sq km (0.4 sq mi)
POPULATION	None

MIDWAY ISLAND (U.S.)

MIDWAY ISLAND

AREA	6.2 sq km (2.4 sq mi)
POPULATION	None

PALMYRA ATOLL (U.S.)

PALMYRA ATOLL

AREA	11.9 sq km (4.6 sq mi)
POPULATION	None

WAKE ISLAND (U.S.)

WAKE ISLAND

AREA	6.5 sq km (2.5 sq mi)
POPULATION	None

DATES OF COUNTRY INDEPENDENCE

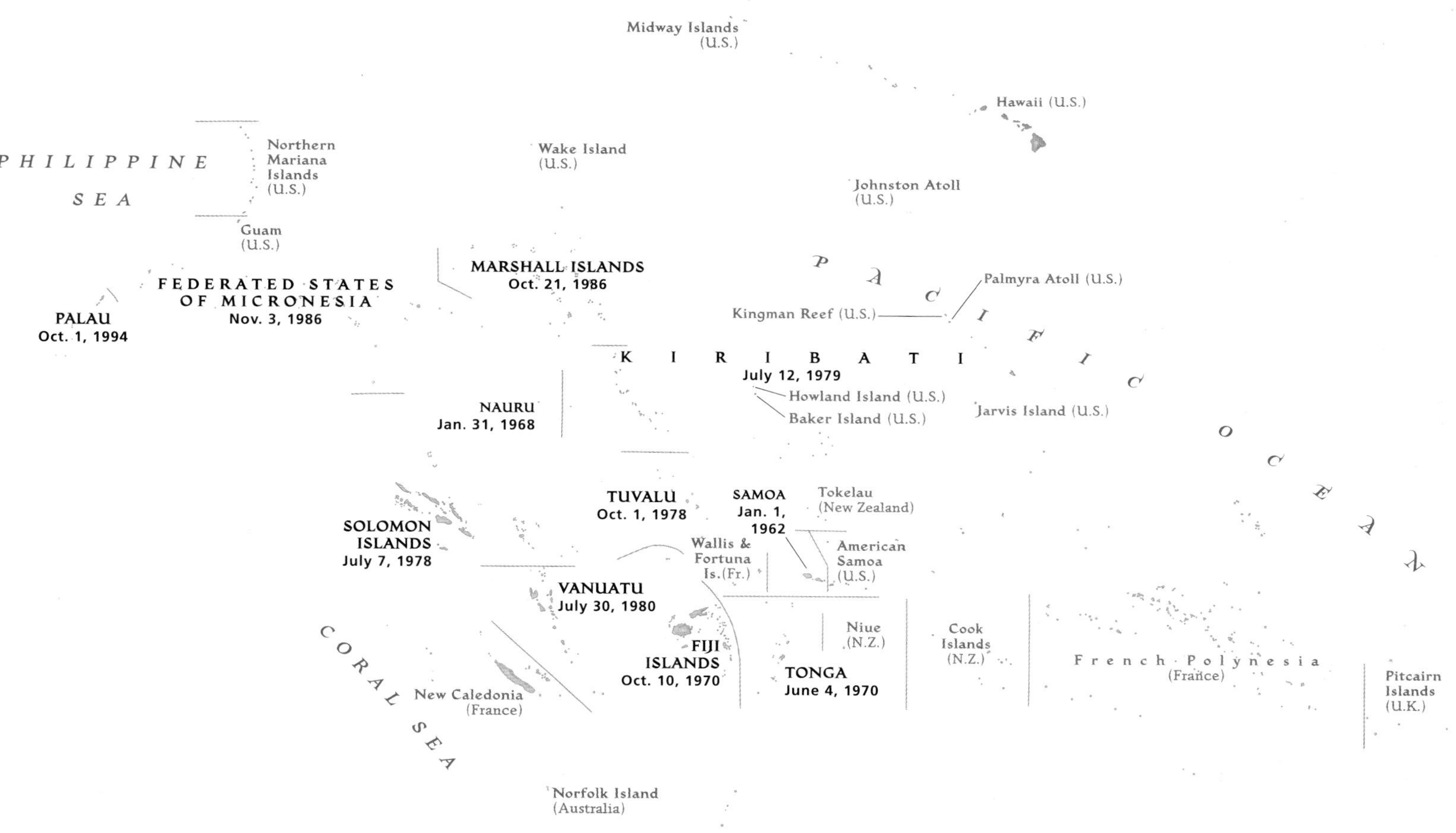

ANTARCTICA

Antarctica, at the southern extreme of the world, ranks as the coldest, highest, driest, and windiest of Earth's continents. At the South Pole the continent experiences the extremes of day and night, banished from sunlight half the year, bathed in continuous light the other half. As best we know, no indigenous peoples ever lived on this continent. Unlike the Arctic, an ocean surrounded by continents, Antarctica is a continent surrounded by ocean. The only people who live there today, mostly scientists and support staff at research stations, ruefully call Antarctica "the Ice," and with good reason. All but two percent of the continent is covered year-round in ice up to 15,000 feet (4,550 meters) thick.

Not until the early 20th century did men explore the heart of the Antarctic to find an austere beauty and an unmatched hardship. "The crystal showers carpeted the pack ice and the ship," wrote Frank Hurley, "until she looked like a tinseled beauty on a field of diamonds." Wrote Apsley Cherry-Garrard in his book, *The Worst Journey in the World*, "Polar exploration is... the cleanest and most isolated way of having a bad time... [ever] devised." Despite its remoteness, Antarctica has been called the frontier of today's ecological crisis. Temperatures are rising, and a hole in the ozone (caused by atmospheric pollutants) allows harmful ultraviolet radiation to bombard land and sea.

The long tendril of the Antarctic Peninsula reaches to within 700 miles of South America, separated by the tempestuous Drake Passage where furious winds build mountainous waves. This "banana belt" of the Antarctic is not nearly so cold as the polar interior, where a great plateau of ice reaches 10,000 feet (3,050 meters) above sea level and winter temperatures can drop lower than –80°C. In the Antarctic summer (Dec. to March), light fills the region, yet heat is absent. Glaciers flow from the icy plateau, coalescing into massive ice shelves; the largest of these, the Ross Ice Shelf, is the size of France.

Antarctica's ice cap holds some 70 percent of the Earth's fresh water. Yet despite all this ice and water, the Antarctic interior averages only two inches of precipitation a year, making it the largest desert in the world. The little snow that does fall, however, almost never melts. The immensely heavy ice sheet, averaging over a mile (1.6 km) thick compresses the land surface over most of the continent to below sea level. The weight actually deforms the South Pole, creating a slightly pear-shaped Earth.

Beneath the ice exists a continent of valleys, lakes, islands, and mountains, little dreamed of until the compilation of more than 2.5 million ice-thickness measurements revealed startling topography below. Ice and sediment cores provide insight into the world's ancient climate and allow for comparison with conditions today. Studies of the Antarctic ice sheet help predict future sea levels, important news for the three billion people who live in coastal areas. If the ice sheet were to melt, global seas would rise by an estimated 200 feet (61 meters), inundating many oceanic islands and gravely altering the world's coastlines.

Antarctica's animal life has adapted extremely well to the harsh climate. Seasonal feeding and energy storage in fats exemplify this specialization. Well-known animals of the far south include seals, whales, and distinctive birds such as flightless penguins, albatrosses, terns, and petrels.

see land cover key, page 10

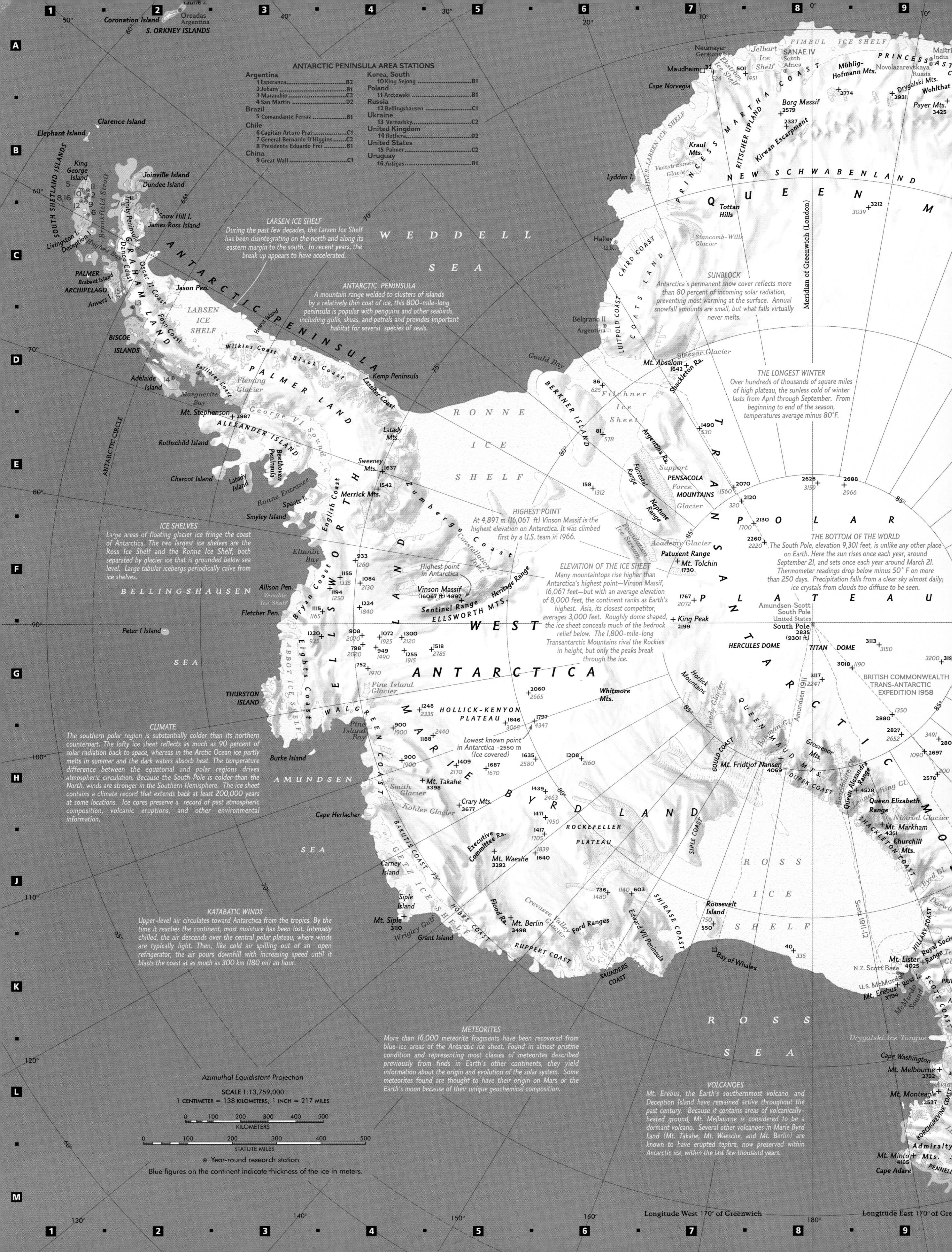

ANTARCTIC PENINSULA AREA STATIONS
Argentina
1 Esperanza B2
2 Jubany B1
3 Marambio C2
4 San Martín D2
Brazil
5 Comandante Ferraz B1
Chile
6 Capitán Arturo Prat C1
7 General Bernardo O'Higgins C2
8 Presidente Eduardo Frei B1
China
9 Great Wall C1
Korea, South
10 King Sejong B1
Poland
11 Arctowski B1
Russia
12 Bellingshausen C1
Ukraine
13 Vernadsky C2
United Kingdom
14 Rothera D2
United States
15 Palmer C2
Uruguay
16 Artigas B1
LARSEN ICE SHELF
During the past few decades, the Larsen Ice Shelf has been disintegrating on the north and along its eastern margin to the south. In recent years, the break up appears to have accelerated.
ANTARCTIC PENINSULA
A mountain range welded to clusters of islands by a relatively thin coat of ice, this 800-mile-long peninsula is popular with penguins and other seabirds, including gulls, skuas, and petrels and provides important habitat for several species of seals.
SUNBLOCK
Antarctica's permanent snow cover reflects more than 80 percent of incoming solar radiation, preventing most warming at the surface. Annual snowfall amounts are small, but what falls virtually never melts.
THE LONGEST WINTER
Over hundreds of thousands of square miles of high plateau, the sunless cold of winter lasts from April through September. From beginning to end of the season, temperatures average minus 80°F.
HIGHEST POINT
At 4,897 m (16,067 ft) Vinson Massif is the highest elevation on Antarctica. It was climbed first by a U.S. team in 1966.
THE BOTTOM OF THE WORLD
The South Pole, elevation 9,301 feet, is unlike any other place on Earth. Here the sun rises once each year, around September 21, and sets once each year around March 21. Thermometer readings drop below minus 50° F on more than 250 days. Precipitation falls from a clear sky almost daily; ice crystals from clouds too diffuse to be seen.
ICE SHELVES
Large areas of floating glacier ice fringe the coast of Antarctica. The two largest ice shelves are the Ross Ice Shelf and the Ronne Ice Shelf, both separated by glacier ice that is grounded below sea level. Large tabular icebergs periodically calve from ice shelves.
ELEVATION OF THE ICE SHEET
Many mountaintops rise higher than Antarctica's highest point—Vinson Massif, 16,067 feet—but with an average elevation of 8,000 feet, the continent ranks as Earth's highest. Asia, its closest competitor, averages 3,000 feet. Roughly dome shaped, the ice sheet conceals much of the bedrock relief below. The 1,800-mile-long Transantarctic Mountains rival the Rockies in height, but only the peaks break through the ice.
CLIMATE
The southern polar region is substantially colder than its northern counterpart. The lofty ice sheet reflects as much as 90 percent of solar radiation back to space, whereas in the Arctic Ocean ice partly melts in summer and the dark waters absorb heat. The temperature difference between the equatorial and polar regions drives atmospheric circulation. Because the South Pole is colder than the North, winds are stronger in the Southern Hemisphere. The ice sheet contains a climate record that extends back at least 200,000 years at some locations. Ice cores preserve a record of past atmospheric composition, volcanic eruptions, and other environmental information.
KATABATIC WINDS
Upper-level air circulates toward Antarctica from the tropics. By the time it reaches the continent, most moisture has been lost. Intensely chilled, the air descends over the central polar plateau, where winds are typically light. Then, like cold air spilling out of an open refrigerator, the air pours downhill with increasing speed until it blasts the coast at as much as 300 km (180 mi) an hour.
METEORITES
More than 16,000 meteorite fragments have been recovered from blue-ice areas of the Antarctic ice sheet. Found in almost pristine condition and representing most classes of meteorites described previously from finds in Earth's other continents, they yield information about the origin and evolution of the solar system. Some meteorites found are thought to have their origin on Mars or the Earth's moon because of their unique geochemical composition.
VOLCANOES
Mt. Erebus, the Earth's southernmost volcano, and Deception Island have remained active throughout the past century. Because it contains areas of volcanically-heated ground, Mt. Melbourne is considered to be a dormant volcano. Several other volcanoes in Marie Byrd Land (Mt. Takahe, Mt. Waesche, and Mt. Berlin) are known to have erupted tephra, now preserved within Antarctic ice, within the last few thousand years.
Azimuthal Equidistant Projection
SCALE 1:13,759,000
1 CENTIMETER = 138 KILOMETERS; 1 INCH = 217 MILES
KILOMETERS
STATUTE MILES
Year-round research station
Blue figures on the continent indicate thickness of the ice in meters.
Coronation Island
S. ORKNEY ISLANDS
Elephant Island
Clarence Island
SOUTH SHETLAND ISLANDS
King George Island
Joinville Island
Dundee Island
Snow Hill I.
James Ross Island
Livingston I.
Deception I.
PALMER ARCHIPELAGO
Anvers I.
BISCOE ISLANDS
Adelaide Island
Mt. Stephenson 2987
ALEXANDER ISLAND
Rothschild Island
Charcot Island
Smyley Island
ANTARCTIC CIRCLE
GRAHAM LAND
ANTARCTIC PENINSULA
PALMER LAND
LARSEN ICE SHELF
WEDDELL SEA
Jason Pen.
Kemp Peninsula
RONNE ICE SHELF
BELLINGSHAUSEN SEA
Allison Pen.
Fletcher Pen.
Peter I Island
THURSTON ISLAND
Burke Island
AMUNDSEN SEA
Cape Herlacher
Carney Island
Siple Island
Mt. Siple 3110
Grant Island
ELLSWORTH LAND
ELLSWORTH MTS.
Sentinel Range
Heritage Range
Vinson Massif (16067 ft) 4897
Highest point in Antarctica
WEST ANTARCTICA
MARIE BYRD LAND
HOLLICK-KENYON PLATEAU
Lowest known point in Antarctica -2550 m (Ice covered)
Whitmore Mts.
Mt. Takahe 3398
Crary Mts. 3677
Executive Committee Ra.
Mt. Waesche 3292
Flood Ra.
Mt. Berlin 3498
Ford Ranges
ROCKEFELLER PLATEAU
Edward VII Peninsula
Roosevelt Island
Bay of Whales
ROSS ICE SHELF
ROSS SEA
QUEEN MAUD LAND
NEW SCHWABENLAND
PRINCESS MARTHA COAST
FIMBUL ICE SHELF
Neumayer Germany
SANAE IV South Africa
Maudheim
Cape Norvegia
Lyddan I.
Halley U.K.
Belgrano II Argentina
COATS LAND
CAIRD COAST
LUITPOLD COAST
BERKNER ISLAND
Filchner Ice Shelf
Gould Bay
Mt. Absalom 1642
Shackleton Ra.
PENSACOLA MOUNTAINS
Patuxent Range
Mt. Tolchin 1730
King Peak 2199
TRANSANTARCTIC MOUNTAINS
POLAR PLATEAU
Amundsen-Scott South Pole United States
South Pole 2835 (9301 ft)
HERCULES DOME
TITAN DOME
BRITISH COMMONWEALTH TRANS-ANTARCTIC EXPEDITION 1958
Meridian of Greenwich (London)
Amundsen 1911
Scott 1911-12
Mt. Fridtjof Nansen 4069
Queen Alexandra Range
Mt. Kirkpatrick 4528
Queen Elizabeth Range
Mt. Markham 4351
Churchill Mts.
Mt. Lister 4025
Mt. Erebus 3794
Cape Washington
Mt. Melbourne 2732
Mt. Monteagle 2537
Mt. Minto 4165
Admiralty Mts.
Cape Adare
Longitude West 170° of Greenwich
Longitude East 170° of Greenwich

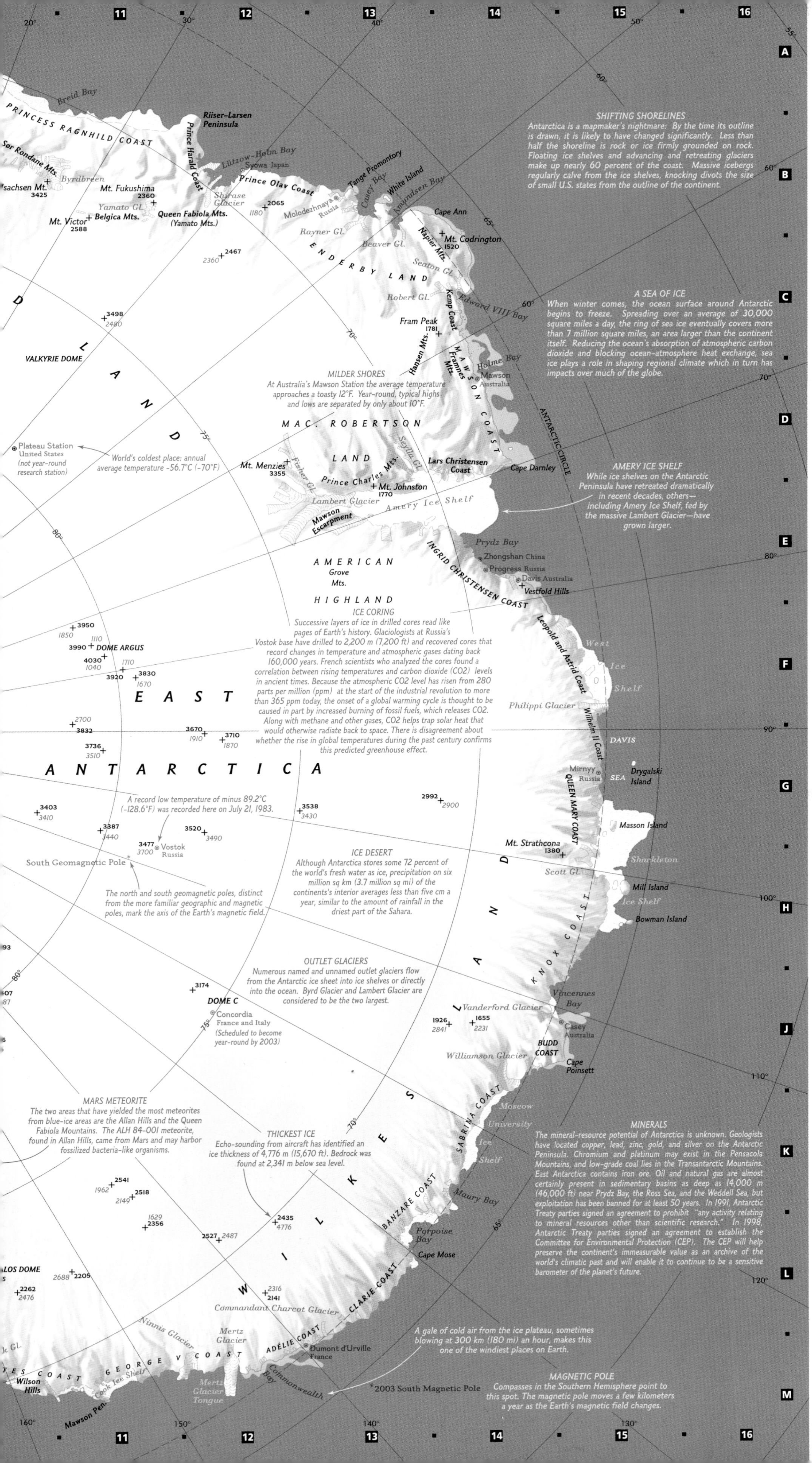

ANTARCTICA

Physical

SHIFTING SHORELINES
Antarctica is a mapmaker's nightmare: By the time its outline is drawn, it is likely to have changed significantly. Less than half the shoreline is rock or ice firmly grounded on rock. Floating ice shelves and advancing and retreating glaciers make up nearly 60 percent of the coast. Massive icebergs regularly calve from the ice shelves, knocking divots the size of small U.S. states from the outline of the continent.

A SEA OF ICE
When winter comes, the ocean surface around Antarctic begins to freeze. Spreading over an average of 30,000 square miles a day, the ring of sea ice eventually covers more than 7 million square miles, an area larger than the continent itself. Reducing the ocean's absorption of atmospheric carbon dioxide and blocking ocean-atmosphere heat exchange, sea ice plays a role in shaping regional climate which in turn has impacts over much of the globe.

MILDER SHORES
At Australia's Mawson Station the average temperature approaches a toasty 12°F. Year-round, typical highs and lows are separated by only about 10°F.

World's coldest place: annual average temperature -56.7°C (-70°F)

AMERY ICE SHELF
While ice shelves on the Antarctic Peninsula have retreated dramatically in recent decades, others—including Amery Ice Shelf, fed by the massive Lambert Glacier—have grown larger.

ICE CORING
Successive layers of ice in drilled cores read like pages of Earth's history. Glaciologists at Russia's Vostok base have drilled to 2,200 m (7,200 ft) and recovered cores that record changes in temperature and atmospheric gases dating back 160,000 years. French scientists who analyzed the cores found a correlation between rising temperatures and carbon dioxide (CO2) levels in ancient times. Because the atmospheric CO2 level has risen from 280 parts per million (ppm) at the start of the industrial revolution to more than 365 ppm today, the onset of a global warming cycle is thought to be caused in part by increased burning of fossil fuels, which releases CO2. Along with methane and other gases, CO2 helps trap solar heat that would otherwise radiate back to space. There is disagreement about whether the rise in global temperatures during the past century confirms this predicted greenhouse effect.

A record low temperature of minus 89.2°C (-128.6°F) was recorded here on July 21, 1983.

The north and south geomagnetic poles, distinct from the more familiar geographic and magnetic poles, mark the axis of the Earth's magnetic field.

ICE DESERT
Although Antarctica stores some 72 percent of the world's fresh water as ice, precipitation on six million sq km (3.7 million sq mi) of the continent's interior averages less than five cm a year, similar to the amount of rainfall in the driest part of the Sahara.

OUTLET GLACIERS
Numerous named and unnamed outlet glaciers flow from the Antarctic ice sheet into ice shelves or directly into the ocean. Byrd Glacier and Lambert Glacier are considered to be the two largest.

MARS METEORITE
The two areas that have yielded the most meteorites from blue-ice areas are the Allan Hills and the Queen Fabiola Mountains. The ALH 84-001 meteorite, found in Allan Hills, came from Mars and may harbor fossilized bacteria-like organisms.

THICKEST ICE
Echo-sounding from aircraft has identified an ice thickness of 4,776 m (15,670 ft). Bedrock was found at 2,341 m below sea level.

MINERALS
The mineral-resource potential of Antarctica is unknown. Geologists have located copper, lead, zinc, gold, and silver on the Antarctic Peninsula. Chromium and platinum may exist in the Pensacola Mountains, and low-grade coal lies in the Transantarctic Mountains. East Antarctica contains iron ore. Oil and natural gas are almost certainly present in sedimentary basins as deep as 14,000 m (46,000 ft) near Prydz Bay, the Ross Sea, and the Weddell Sea, but exploitation has been banned for at least 50 years. In 1991, Antarctic Treaty parties signed an agreement to prohibit "any activity relating to mineral resources other than scientific research." In 1998, Antarctic Treaty parties signed an agreement to establish the Committee for Environmental Protection (CEP). The CEP will help preserve the continent's immeasurable value as an archive of the world's climatic past and will continue to be a sensitive barometer of the planet's future.

A gale of cold air from the ice plateau, sometimes blowing at 300 km (180 mi) an hour, makes this one of the windiest places on Earth.

MAGNETIC POLE
Compasses in the Southern Hemisphere point to this spot. The magnetic pole moves a few kilometers a year as the Earth's magnetic field changes.

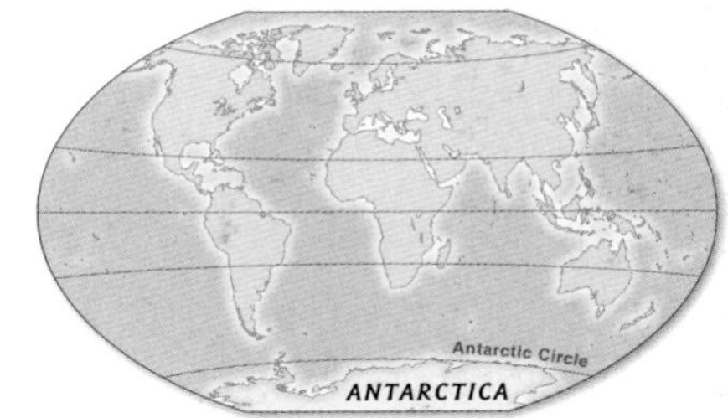

CONTINENTAL DATA

- **Area:**
  13,209,000 sq km
  (5,100,000 sq mi)
- **Greatest extent:**
  5,500 km (3,400 mi), from Trinity Peninsula to Cape Poinsett
- **Highest point:**
  Vinson Massif 4,897 m (16,067 ft)
- **Lowest point:**
  Bentley Subglacial Trench -2,550m (-8,366 ft), ice covered
- **Lowest recorded temperature:**
  Vostok -89.2°C (-128.6°F), July 21, 1983
- **Highest recorded temperature:**
  Vanda Station, Scott Coast
  15°C (59°F), January 5, 1974
- **Earth's extremes located in Antarctica:**
  - **Coldest place on Earth:**
    Plateau Station, annual average temperature -56.7°C (-70°F)
  - **Coldest recorded temperature on Earth:**
    Vostok -89.2°C (-128.6°F), July 21, 1983

TERRITORIAL CLAIMS

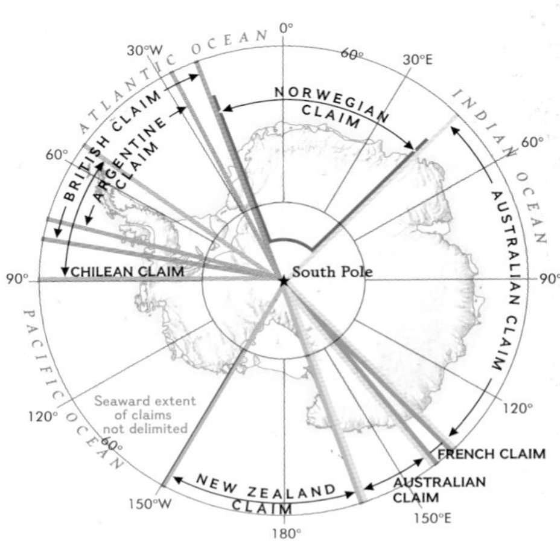

The Antarctic Treaty of 1959 preserves Antarctica for scientific research by all nations. The treaty made static all claims and prohibits any new claims.

APPENDIX

Airline Distances in Kilometers

	BEIJING	CAIRO	CAPE TOWN	CARACAS	HONG KONG	HONOLULU	LONDON	MELBOURNE	MEXICO	MONTRÉAL	MOSCOW	NEW DELHI	NEW YORK	PARIS	RIO DE JANEIRO	ROME	SAN FRANCISCO	SINGAPORE	STOCKHOLM	TOKYO
BEIJING		7557	12947	14411	1972	8171	8160	9093	12478	10490	5809	3788	11012	8236	17325	8144	9524	4465	6725	2104
CAIRO	7557		7208	10209	8158	14239	3513	13966	12392	8733	2899	4436	9042	3215	9882	2135	12015	8270	3404	9587
CAPE TOWN	12947	7208		10232	11867	18562	9635	10338	13703	12744	10101	9284	12551	9307	6075	8417	16487	9671	10334	14737
CARACAS	14411	10209	10232		16380	9694	7500	15624	3598	3932	9940	14221	3419	7621	4508	8363	6286	18361	8724	14179
HONG KONG	1972	8158	11867	16380		8945	9646	7392	14155	12462	7158	3770	12984	9650	17710	9300	11121	2575	8243	2893
HONOLULU	8171	14239	18562	9694	8945		11653	8862	6098	7915	11342	11930	7996	11988	13343	12936	3857	10824	11059	6208
LONDON	8160	3513	9635	7500	9646	11653		16902	8947	5240	2506	6724	5586	341	9254	1434	8640	10860	1436	9585
MELBOURNE	9093	13966	10338	15624	7392	8862	16902		13557	16730	14418	10192	16671	16793	13227	15987	12644	6050	15593	8159
MEXICO	12478	12392	13703	3598	14155	6098	8947	13557		3728	10740	14679	3362	9213	7669	10260	3038	16623	9603	11319
MONTRÉAL	10490	8733	12744	3932	12462	7915	5240	16730	3728		7077	11286	533	5522	8175	6601	4092	14816	5900	10409
MOSCOW	5809	2899	10101	9940	7158	11342	2506	14418	10740	7077		4349	7530	2492	11529	2378	9469	8426	1231	7502
NEW DELHI	3788	4436	9284	14221	3770	11930	6724	10192	14679	11286	4349		11779	6601	14080	5929	12380	4142	5579	5857
NEW YORK	11012	9042	12551	3419	12984	7996	5586	16671	3362	533	7530	11779		5851	7729	6907	4140	15349	6336	10870
PARIS	8236	3215	9307	7621	9650	11988	341	16793	9213	5522	2492	6601	5851		9146	1108	8975	10743	1546	9738
RIO DE JANEIRO	17325	9882	6075	4508	17710	13343	9254	13227	7669	8175	11529	14080	7729	9146		9181	10647	15740	10682	18557
ROME	8144	2135	8417	8363	9300	12936	1434	15987	10260	6601	2378	5929	6907	1108	9181		10071	10030	1977	9881
SAN FRANCISCO	9524	12015	16487	6286	11121	3857	8640	12644	3038	4092	9469	12380	4140	8975	10647	10071		13598	8644	8284
SINGAPORE	4465	8270	9671	18361	2575	10824	10860	6050	16623	14816	8426	4142	15349	10743	15740	10030	13598		9646	5317
STOCKHOLM	6725	3404	10334	8724	8243	11059	1436	15593	9603	5900	1231	5579	6336	1546	10682	1977	8644	9646		8193
TOKYO	2104	9587	14737	14179	2893	6208	9585	8159	11319	10409	7502	5857	10870	9738	18557	9881	8284	5317	8193	

Abbreviations

Adm. *Administrative*
Af. *Africa*
Afghan. *Afghanistan*
Agr. *Agriculture*
Ala. *Alabama*
Alas. *Alaska*
Alban. *Albania*
Alg. *Algeria*
Alta. *Alberta*
Arch. *Archipelago, Archipiélago*
Arg. *Argentina*
Ariz. *Arizona*
Ark. *Arkansas*
Arm. *Armenia*
Atl. Oc. *Atlantic Ocean*
Aust. *Austria*
Austral. *Australia*
Azerb. *Azerbaijan*
B. *Baai, Baía, Baie, Bahía, Bay, Buḩayrat*
B.C. *British Columbia*
Belg. *Belgium*
Bol. *Bolivia*
Bosn. & Herzg. *Bosnia and Herzegovina*
Braz. *Brazil*
Bulg. *Bulgaria*
C. *Cabo, Cap, Cape, Capo*
Calif. *California*
Can. *Canada*
Cen. Af. Rep. *Central African Republic*
C.H. *Court House*
Chan. *Channel*
Chap. *Chapada*
Cmte. *Comandante*
Cnel. *Coronel*
Co.-s. *Cerro-s*
Col. *Colombia*
Colo. *Colorado*
Conn. *Connecticut*
Cord. *Cordillera*
C.R. *Costa Rica*
Cr. *Creek, Crique*
C.S.I. Terr. *Coral Sea Islands Territory*
D.C. *District of Columbia*
Del. *Delaware*
Den. *Denmark*
Dom. Rep. *Dominican Republic*
D.R.C. *Democratic Republic of the Congo*
E. *East-ern*
Ecua. *Ecuador*
El Salv. *El Salvador*
Eng. *England*
Ens. *Ensenada*
Eq. *Equatorial*
Est. *Estonia*
Eth. *Ethiopia*
Exp. *Exports*
Falk. Is. *Falkland Islands*
Fd. *Fiord, Fiordo, Fjord*
Fin. *Finland*
Fk. *Fork*
Fla. *Florida*
Fn. *Fortín*
Fr. *France, French*
F.S.M. *Federated States of Micronesia*
ft *feet*
Ft. *Fort*
G. *Golfe, Golfo, Gulf*
Ga. *Georgia*
Ger. *Germany*
Gl. *Glacier*
Gr. *Greece*
Gral. *General*
Hbr. *Harbor, Harbour*
Hist. *Historic, -al*
Hond. *Honduras*
Hts. *Heights*
Hung. *Hungary*
Hwy. *Highway*
I.-s. *Île-s, Ilha-s, Isla-s, Island-s, Isle, Isol-a, -e*
Ice. *Iceland*
I.H.S. *International Historic Site*
Ill. *Illinois*
Ind. *Indiana*
Ind. *Industry*
Ind. Oc. *Indian Ocean*
Intl. *International*
Ire. *Ireland*
It. *Italy*
Jap. *Japan*
Jct. *Jonction, Junction*
Kans. *Kansas*
Kaz. *Kazakhstan*
Kep. *Kepulauan*
Ky. *Kentucky*
Kyrg. *Kyrgyzstan*
L. *Lac, Lago, Lake, Límni Loch, Lough*
La. *Louisiana*
Lab. *Labrador*
Lag. *Laguna*
Latv. *Latvia*
Leb. *Lebanon*
Lib. *Libya*
Liech. *Liechtenstein*
Lith. *Lithuania*
Lux. *Luxembourg*
m *meters*
Maced. *Macedonia*
Madag. *Madagascar*
Maurit. *Mauritius*
Mass. *Massachusetts*
Md. *Maryland*
Me. *Maine*
Medit. Sea *Mediterranean Sea*
Mex. *Mexico*
Mich. *Michigan*
Minn. *Minnesota*
Miss. *Mississippi*
Mo. *Missouri*
Mon. *Monument*
Mont. *Montana*
Mor. *Morocco*
Mt.-s. *Mont-s, Mount-ain-s*
N. *North-ern*
Nat. *National*
Nat. Mem. *National Memorial*
Nat. Mon. *National Monument*
N.B. *National Battlefield*
N.B. *New Brunswick*
N.C. *North Carolina*
N. Dak. *North Dakota*
N.E. *Northeast*
Nebr. *Nebraska*
Neth. *Netherlands*
Nev. *Nevada*
Nfld. *Newfoundland*
N.H. *New Hampshire*
Nicar. *Nicaragua*
Nig. *Nigeria*
N. Ire. *Northern Ireland*
N.J. *New Jersey*
N. Mex. *New Mexico*
N.M.P. *National Military Park*
N.M.S. *National Marine Sanctuary*
Nor. *Norway*
N.P. *National Park*
N.S. *Nova Scotia*
N.S.W. *New South Wales*
N.V.M. *National Volcanic Monument*
N.W.T. *Northwest Territories*
N.Y. *New York*
N.Z. *New Zealand*
O. *Ostrov, Oued*
Oc. *Ocean*
Okla. *Oklahoma*
Ont. *Ontario*
Oreg. *Oregon*
Oz. *Ozero*
Pa. *Pennsylvania*
Pac. Oc. *Pacific Ocean*
Pak. *Pakistan*
Pan. *Panama*
Para. *Paraguay*
Pass. *Passage*
Peg. *Pegunungan*
P.E.I. *Prince Edward Island*
Pen. *Peninsula, Péninsule*
Pk. *Peak*
P.N.G. *Papua New Guinea*
Pol. *Poland*
Pol. *Poluostrov*
Port. *Portugal, Portuguese*
P.R. *Puerto Rico*
Prov. *Province, Provincial*
Pt.-e. *Point-e*
Pta. *Ponta, Punta*
Qnsld. *Queensland*
Que. *Quebec*
R. *Río, River, Rivière*
Ra.-s. *Range-s*
Rec. *Recreation*
Rep. *Republic*
Res. *Reservoir, Reserve, Reservatório*
R.I. *Rhode Island*
Rom. *Romania*
Russ. *Russia*
S. *South-ern*
Sa.-s. *Serra, Sierra-s*
S. Af. *South Africa*
Sask. *Saskatchewan*
S.C. *South Carolina*
Scot. *Scotland*
Sd. *Sound*
S. Dak. *South Dakota*
Serb. & Mont. *Serbia and Montenegro*
Sev. *Severn-yy, -aya, -oye*
Sk. *Shankou*
Slov. *Slovenia*
Sp. *Spain, Spanish*
Spr.-s. *Spring-s*
St.-e. *Saint-e, Sankt, Sint*
Str.-s. *Straat, Strait-s*
Switz. *Switzerland*
Syr. *Syria*
Taj. *Tajikistan*
Tas. *Tasmania*
Tenn. *Tennessee*
Terr. *Territory*
Tex. *Texas*
Tg. *Tanjung*
Thai. *Thailand*
Trin. *Trinidad*
Tun. *Tunisia*
Turk. *Turkey*
Turkm. *Turkmenistan*
U.A.E. *United Arab Emirates*
U.K. *United Kingdom*
Ukr. *Ukraine*
U.N. *United Nations*
Uru. *Uruguay*
U.S. *United States*
Uzb. *Uzbekistan*
Va. *Virginia*
Vdkhr. *Vodokhranilishche*
Vdskh. *Vodoskhovyshche*
Venez. *Venezuela*
V.I. *Virgin Islands*
Vic. *Victoria*
Viet. *Vietnam*
Vol. *Volcán, Volcano*
Vt. *Vermont*
W. *Wadi, Wādī, Webi*
W. *West-ern*
Wash. *Washington*
Wis. *Wisconsin*
W. Va. *West Virginia*
Wyo. *Wyoming*
Yug. *Yugoslavia*
Zakh. *Zakhod-ni, -nyaya, -nye*
Zimb. *Zimbabwe*

Metric Conversions

QUICK REFERENCE CHART FOR METRIC TO ENGLISH CONVERSION

1 METER	1 METER = 100 CENTIMETERS
1 FOOT	1 FOOT = 12 INCHES
1 KILOMETER	1 KILOMETER = 1,000 METERS
1 MILE	1 MILE = 5,280 FEET

METERS	1	10	20	50	100	200	500	1,000	2,000	5,000	10,000
FEET	3.281	32.81	65.62	164.04	328.1	656.2	1,640.4	3,280.8	6,567.7	16,404.2	32,808.4

KILOMETERS	1	10	20	50	100	200	500	1,000	2,000	5,000	10,000
MILES	0.621	6.21	12.43	31.05	62.1	124.3	310.7	621.4	1,242.7	3,105.7	6,213.7

CONVERSION FROM METRIC MEASURES

SYMBOL	WHEN YOU KNOW	MULTIPLY BY	TO FIND	SYMBOL
		LENGTH		
cm	centimeters	0.393701	inches	in
m	meters	3.280840	feet	ft
m	meters	1.093613	yards	yd
km	kilometers	0.621371	miles	mi
		AREA		
cm^2	square centimeters	0.155000	square inches	in^2
m^2	square meters	10.76391	square feet	ft^2
m^2	square meters	1.195990	square yards	yd^2
km^2	square kilometers	0.386102	square miles	mi^2
ha	hectares	2.471054	acres	—
		MASS		
g	grams	0.035274	ounces	oz
kg	kilograms	2.204623	pounds	lb
t	metric tons	1.102311	short tons	—
		VOLUME		
mL	milliliters	0.061024	cubic inches	in^3
mL	milliliters	0.033814	liquid ounces	liq oz
L	liters	2.113376	pints	pt
L	liters	1.056688	quarts	qt
L	liters	0.264172	gallons	gal
m^3	cubic meters	35.31467	cubic feet	ft^3
m^3	cubic meters	1.307951	cubic yards	yd^3
		TEMPERATURE		
°C	degrees Celsius (centigrade)	9/5 then add 32	degrees Fahrenheit	°F

CONVERSION TO METRIC MEASURES

SYMBOL	WHEN YOU KNOW	MULTIPLY BY	TO FIND	SYMBOL
		LENGTH		
in	inches	2.54	centimeters	cm
ft	feet	0.3048	meters	m
yd	yards	0.9144	meters	m
mi	miles	1.609344	kilometers	km
		AREA		
in^2	square inches	6.4516	square centimeters	cm^2
ft^2	square feet	0.092903	square meters	m^2
yd^2	square yards	0.836127	square meters	m^2
mi^2	square miles	2.589988	square kilometers	km^2
—	acres	0.404686	hectares	ha
		MASS		
oz	ounces	28.349523	grams	g
lb	pounds	0.453592	kilograms	kg
—	short tons	0.907185	metric tons	t
		VOLUME		
in^3	cubic inches	16.387064	milliliters	mL
liq oz	liquid ounces	29.57353	milliliters	mL
pt	pints	0.473176	liters	L
qt	quarts	0.946353	liters	L
gal	gallons	3.785412	liters	L
ft^3	cubic feet	0.028317	cubic meters	m^3
yd^3	cubic yards	0.764555	cubic meters	m^3
		TEMPERATURE		
°F	degrees Fahrenheit	5/9 after subtracting 32	degrees Celsius (centigrade)	°C

FOREIGN TERMS

Aaglet: *well*
Aain: *spring*
Aauinat: *spring*
Āb: *river, water*
Ache: *stream*
Açude: *reservoir*
Ada,-si: *island*
Adrar: *mountain-s, plateau*
Aguada: *dry lake bed*
Aguelt: *water hole, well*
'Ain, Aïn: *spring, well*
Aïoun-et: *spring-s, well*
Aivi: *mountain*
Ákra, Akrotírion: *cape, promontory*
Alb: *mountain, ridge*
Alföld: *plain*
Alin': *mountain range*
Alpe-n: *mountain-s*
Altiplanicie: *high-plain, plateau*
Alto: *hill-s, mountain-s, ridge*
Älv-en: *river*
Āmba: *hill, mountain*
Anou: *well*
Anse: *bay, inlet*
Ao: *bay, cove, estuary*
Ap: *cape, point*
Archipel, Archipiélago: *archipelago*
Arcipelago, Arkhipelag: *archipelago*
Arquipélago: *archipelago*
Arrecife-s: *reef-s*
Arroio, Arroyo: *brook, gully, rivulet, stream*
Ås: *ridge*
Ava: *channel*
Aylagy: *gulf*
'Ayn: *spring, well*

Ba: *intermittent stream, river*
Baai: *bay, cove, lagoon*
Bāb: *gate, strait*
Badia: *bay*
Bælt: *strait*
Bagh: *bay*
Bahar: *drainage basin*
Bahía: *bay*
Bahr, Baḥr: *bay, lake, river, sea, wadi*
Baía, Baie: *bay*
Bajo-s: *shoal-s*
Ban: *village*
Bañado-s: *flooded area, swamp-s*
Banc, Banco-s: *bank-s, sandbank-s, shoal-s*
Band: *lake*
Bandao: *peninsula*
Baño-s: *hot spring-s, spa*
Baraj-ı: *dam, reservoir*
Barra: *bar, sandbank*
Barrage, Barragem: *dam, lake, reservoir*
Barranca: *gorge, ravine*
Bazar: *marketplace*
Ben, Benin: *mountain*
Belt: *strait*
Bereg: *bank, coast, shore*
Berg-e: *mountain-s*
Bil: *lake*
Biq'at: *plain, valley*
Bir, Bîr, Bi'r: *spring, well*
Birket: *lake, pool, swamp*
Bjerg-e: *mountain-s, range*
Boca, Bocca: *channel, river, mouth*
Bocht: *bay*
Bodden: *bay*
Boğaz, -i: *strait*
Bögeni: *reservoir*
Boka: *gulf, mouth*
Bol'sh-oy, -aya, -oye: *big*
Bolsón: *inland basin*
Boubairet: *lagoon, lake*
Bras: *arm, branch of a stream*
Braţ, -ul: *arm, branch of a stream*
Bre, -en: *glacier, ice cap*
Bredning: *bay, broad water*
Bruch: *marsh*
Bucht: *bay*
Bugt-en: *bay*
Buḥayrat, Buheirat: *lagoon, lake, marsh*
Bukhta, Bukta, Bukt-en: *bay*
Bulak, Bulaq: *spring*
Bum: *hill, mountain*
Burnu, Burun: *cape, point*
Busen: *gulf*
Buuraha: *hill-s, mountain-s*
Buyuk: *big, large*

Cabeza-s: *head-s, summit-s*
Cabo: *cape*
Cachoeira: *rapids, waterfall*
Cal: *hill, peak*
Caleta: *cove, inlet*
Campo-s: *field-s, flat country*
Canal: *canal, channel, strait*
Caño: *channel, stream*
Cao Nguyen: *mountain, plateau*
Cap, Capo: *cape*
Capitán: *captain*
Càrn: *mountain*
Castillo: *castle, fort*
Catarata-s: *cataract-s, waterfall-s*
Causse: *upland*
Çay: *brook, stream*
Cay-s, Cayo-s: *island-s, key-s, shoal-s*
Cerro-s: *hill-s, peak-s*
Chaîne, Chaînons: *mountain chain, range*
Chapada-s: *plateau, upland-s*
Chedo: *archipelago*
Chenal: *river channel*
Chersónisos: *peninsula*
Chhung: *bay*
Chi: *lake*
Chiang: *bay*
Chiao: *cape, point, rock*
Ch'ih: *lake*
Chink: *escarpment*
Chott: *intermittent salt lake, salt marsh*
Chou: *island*
Ch'ü: *canal*
Ch'üntao: *archipelago, islands*
Chute-s: *cataract-s, waterfall-s*
Chyrvony: *red*
Cima: *mountain, peak, summit*
Ciudad: *city*
Co: *lake*
Col: *pass*
Collina, Colline: *hill, mountains*
Con: *island*
Cordillera: *mountain chain*
Corno: *mountain, peak*
Coronel: *colonel*
Corredeira: *cascade, rapids*
Costa: *coast*
Côte: *coast, slope*
Coxilha, Cuchilla: *range of low hills*
Crique: *creek, stream*
Csatorna: *canal, channel*
Cul de Sac: *bay, inlet*

Da: *great, greater*
Daban: *pass*
Dağ, -ı, Dagh: *mountain*
Dağlar, -ı: *mountains*
Dahr: *cliff, mesa*
Dake: *mountain, peak*
Dal-en: *valley*
Dala: *steppe*
Dan: *cape, point*
Danau: *lake*
Dao: *island*
Dar'ya: *lake, river*
Daryācheh: *lake, marshy lake*
Dasht: *desert, plain*
Dawan: *pass*
Dawḥat: *bay, cove, inlet*
Deniz, -i: *sea*
Dent-s: *peak-s*
Deo: *pass*
Desēt: *hummock, island, land-tied island*
Desierto: *desert*
Détroit: *channel, strait*
Dhar: *hills, ridge, tableland*
Ding: *mountain*
Distrito: *district*
Djebel: *mountain, range*
Do: *island-s, rock-s*
Doi: *hill, mountain*
Dome: *ice dome*
Dong: *village*
Dooxo: *floodplain*
Dzong: *castle, fortress*

Eiland-en: *island-s*
Eilean: *island*
Ejland: *island*
Elv: *river*
Embalse: *lake, reservoir*
Emi: *mountain, rock*
Enseada, Ensenada: *bay, cove*
Ér: *rivulet, stream*
Erg: *sand dune region*
Est: *east*
Estación: *railroad station*
Estany: *lagoon, lake*
Estero: *estuary, inlet, lagoon, marsh*
Estrecho: *strait*
Étang: *lake, pond*
Eylandt: *island*
Ežeras: *lake*
Ezers: *lake*

Falaise: *cliff, escarpment*
Farvand-et: *channel, sound*
Fell: *mountain*
Feng: *mount, peak*
Fiord-o: *inlet, sound*
Fiume: *river*
Fjäll-et: *mountain*
Fjällen: *mountains*
Fjärd-en: *fjord*
Fjardar, Fjörður: *fjord*
Fjeld: *mountain*
Fjell-ene: *mountain-s*
Fjöll: *mountain-s*
Fjord-en: *inlet, fjord*
Fleuve: *river*
Fljót: *large river*
Flói: *bay, marshland*
Foci: *river mouths*
Főcsatorna: *principal canal*
Förde: *fjord, gulf, inlet*
Forsen: *rapids, waterfall*
Fortaleza: *fort, fortress*
Fortín: *fortified post*
Foss-en: *waterfall*
Foum: *pass, passage*
Foz: *mouth of a river*
Fuerte: *fort, fortress*
Fwafwate: *waterfalls*

Gacan-ka: *hill, peak*
Gal: *pond, spring, waterhole, well*
Gang: *harbor*
Gangri: *peak, range*
Gaoyuan: *plateau*
Garaet, Gara'et: *lake, lake bed, salt lake*
Gardaneh: *pass*
Garet: *hill, mountain*
Gat: *channel*
Gata: *bay, inlet, lake*
Gattet: *channel, strait*
Gaud: *depression, saline tract*
Gave: *mountain stream*
Gebel: *mountain-s, range*
Gebergte: *mountain range*
Gebirge: *mountains, range*
Geçidi: *mountain pass, passage*
Geçit: *mountain pass, passage*
Gezâir: *islands*
Gezîra-t, Gezîret: *island, peninsula*
Ghats: *mountain range*
Ghubb-at, -et: *bay, gulf*
Giri: *mountain*
Gletscher: *glacier*
Gobernador: *governor*
Gobi: *desert*
Gol: *river, stream*
Göl, -ü: *lake*
Golets: *mountain, peak*
Golf, -e, -o: *gulf*
Gor-a, -y, Gór-a, -y: *mountain,-s*
Got: *point*
Gowd: *depression*
Goz: *sand ridge*
Gran, -de: *great, large*
Gryada: *mountains, ridge*
Guan: *pass*
Guba: *bay, gulf*
Guelta: *well*
Guntō: *archipelago*
Gunung: *mountain*
Gura: *mouth, passage*
Guyot: *table mount*

Haḍabat: *plateau*
Haehyŏp: *strait*
Haff: *lagoon*
Hai: *lake, sea*
Haihsia: *strait*
Haixia: *channel, strait*
Hakau: *reef, rock*
Hakuchi: *anchorage*
Halvø, Halvøy-a: *peninsula*
Hama: *beach*
Hamada, Ḩammādah: *rocky desert*
Hamn: *harbor, port*
Hāmūn, Hamun: *depression, lake*
Hana: *cape, point*
Hantō: *peninsula*
Har: *hill, mound, mountain*
Ḩarrat: *lava field*
Hasi, Hassi: *spring, well*
Hauteur: *elevation, height*
Hav-et: *sea*
Havn, Havre: *harbor, port*
Hawr: *lake, marsh*
Häyk': *lake, reservoir*
Hegy, -ség: *mountain, -s, range*
Heiau: *temple*
Ho: *canal, lake, river*
Hoek: *hook, point*
Hög-en: *high, hill*
Höhe, -n: *height, high*
Høj: *height, hill*
Holm, -e, Holmene: *island-s, islet -s*
Ḩolot: *dunes*
Hon: *island-s*
Hor-a, -y: *mountain, -s*
Horn: *horn, peak*
Houma: *point*
Hoved: *headland, peninsula, point*
Hraun: *lava field*
Hsü: *island*
Hu: *lake, reservoir*
Huk: *cape, point*
Hüyük: *hill, mound*

Idehan: *sand dunes*
Île-s, Ilha-s, Illa-s, Îlot-s: *island-s, islet-s*
Îlet, Ilhéu-s: *islet, -s*
Irhil: *mountain-s*
'Irq: *sand dune-s*
Isblink: *glacier, ice field*
Is-en: *glacier*
Isla-s, Islote: *island-s, islet*
Isol-a, -e: *island, -s*
Istmo: *isthmus*
Iwa: *island, islet, rock*

Jabal, Jebel: *mountain-s, range*
Järv, -i, Jaure, Javrre: *lake*
Jazā'ir, Jazīrat, Jazīreh: *island-s*
Jehīl: *lake*
Jezero, Jezioro: *lake*
Jiang: *river, stream*
Jiao: *cape*
Jibāl: *hill, mountain, ridge*
Jima: *island-s, rock-s*
Jøkel, Jökull: *glacier, ice cap*
Joki, Jokka: *river*
Jökulsá: *river from a glacier*
Jūn: *bay*

Kaap: *cape*
Kafr: *village*
Kaikyō: *channel, strait*
Kaise: *mountain*
Kaiwan: *bay, gulf, sea*
Kanal: *canal, channel*
Kangri: *mountain, peak*
Kap, Kapp: *cape*
Kavīr: *salt desert*
Kefar: *village*
Kënet': *lagoon, lake*
Kep: *cape, point*
Kepulauan: *archipelago, islands*
Khalīg, Khalīj: *bay, gulf*
Khirb-at, -et: *ancient site, ruins*
Khrebet: *mountain range*
Kinh: *canal*
Klint: *bluff, cliff*
Kō: *bay, cove, harbor*
Ko: *island, lake*
Koh: *island, mountain, range*
Köl-i: *lake*
Kólpos : *gulf*
Kong: *mountain*
Körfez, -i: *bay, gulf*
Kosa: *spit of land*
Kou: *estuary, river mouth*
Kowtal-e: *pass*
Krasn-yy, -aya, -oye: *red*
Kryazh: *mountain range, ridge*
Kuala: *estuary, river mouth*
Kuan: *mountain pass*
Kūh, Kūhhā: *mountain-s, range*
Kul', Kuli: *lake*
Kum: *sandy desert*
Kundo: *archipelago*
Kuppe: *hill-s, mountain-s*
Kust: *coast, shore*
Kyst: *coast*
Kyun: *island*

La: *pass*
Lac, Lac-ul, -us: *lake*
Lae: *cape, point*
Lago, -a: *lagoon, lake*
Lagoen, Lagune: *lagoon*
Laguna-s: *lagoon-s, lake-s*
Laht: *bay, gulf, harbor*
Laje: *reef, rock ledge*
Laut: *sea*
Lednik: *glacier*
Leida: *channel*
Lhari: *mountain*
Li: *village*
Liedao: *archipelago, islands*
Liehtao: *archipelago, islands*
Liman-ı: *bay, estuary*

Límni: *lake*
Ling: *mountain-s, range*
Linn: *pool, waterfall*
Lintasan: *passage*
Liqen: *lake*
Llano-s: *plain-s*
Loch, Lough: *lake, arm of the sea*
Loma-s: *hill-s, knoll-s*

Mal: *mountain, range*
Mal-yy, -aya, -oye: *little, small*
Mamarr: *pass, path*
Man: *bay*
Mar, Mare: *large lake, sea*
Marsa, Marsá: *bay, inlet*
Masabb: *mouth of river*
Massif: *massif, mountain-s*
Mauna: *mountain*
Mēda: *plain*
Meer: *lake, sea*
Melkosopochnik: *undulating plain*
Mesa, Meseta: *plateau, tableland*
Mierzeja: *sandspit*
Minami: *south*
Mios: *island*
Misaki: *cape, peninsula, point*
Mochun: *passage*
Mong: *town, village*
Mont-e, -i, -s: *mount, -ain, -s*
Montagne, -s: *mount, -ain, -s*
Montaña, -s: *mountain, -s*
More: *sea*
Morne: *hill, peak*
Morro: *bluff, headland, hill*
Motu, -s: *islands*
Mouïet: *well*
Mouillage: *anchorage*
Muang: *town, village*
Mui: *cape, point*
Mull: *headland, promontory*
Munkhafad: *depression*
Munte: *mountain*
Munţi-i: *mountains*
Muong: *town, village*
Mynydd: *mountain*
Mys: *cape*

Nacional: *national*
Nada: *gulf, sea*
Næs, Näs: *cape, point*
Nafūd: *area of dunes, desert*
Nagor'ye: *mountain range, plateau*
Nahar, Nahr: *river, stream*
Nakhon: *town*
Namakzār: *salt waste*
Ne: *island, reef, rock-s*
Neem: *cape, point, promontory*
Nes, Ness: *peninsula, point*
Nevado-s: *snow-capped mountain-s*
Nez: *cape, promontory*
Ni: *village*
Nísi, Nísia, Nisís, Nísoi: *island-s, islet-s*
Nisídhes: *islets*
Nizhn-iy, -yaya, -eye: *lower*
Nizmennost': *low country*
Noord: *north*
Nord-re: *north-ern*
Nørre: *north-ern*
Nos: *cape, nose, point*
Nosy: *island, reef, rock*
Nov-yy, -aya, -oye: *new*
Nudo: *mountain*
Numa: *lake*
Nunatak, -s, -ker: *peak-s: surrounded by ice cap*
Nur: *lake, salt lake*
Nuruu: *mountain range, ridge*
Nut-en: *peak*
Nuur: *lake*

Ö-n, Ø-er: *island-s*
Oblast': *administrative division, province, region*
Oceanus: *ocean*
Odde-n: *cape, point*
Øer-ne: *islands*
Oglat: *group of wells*
Oguilet: *well*
Ór-os, -i: *mountain, -s*
Órmos: *bay, port*
Ort: *place, point*
Øst-er: *east*
Ostrov, -a, Ostrv-o, -a: *island, -s*
Otoci, Otok: *islands, island*
Ouadi, Oued: *river, watercourse*
Øy-a: *island*
Øyane: *islands*
Ozer-o, -a: *lake, -s*

Pää: *mountain, point*
Palus: *marsh*
Pampa-s: *grassy plain-s*
Pantà: *lake, reservoir*
Pantanal: *marsh, swamp*
Pao, P'ao: *lake*
Parbat: *mountain*
Parque: *park*
Pas, -ul: *pass*
Paso, Passo: *pass*
Passe: *channel, pass*
Pasul: *pass*
Pedra: *rock*
Pegunungan: *mountain range*
Pellg: *bay, bight*
Peña: *cliff, rock*
Pendi: *basin*
Penedo-s: *rock-s*
Péninsule: *peninsula*
Peñón: *point, rock*
Pereval: *mountain pass*
Pertuis: *strait*
Peski: *sands, sandy region*
Phnom: *hill, mountain, range*
Phou: *mountain range*
Phu: *mountain*
Piana-o: *plain*
Pic, Pik, Piz: *peak*
Picacho: *mountain, peak*
Pico-s: *peak-s*
Pistyll: *waterfall*
Piton-s: *peak-s*
Pivdennyy: *southern*
Plaja, Playa: *beach, inlet, shore*
Planalto, Plato: *plateau*
Planina: *mountain, plateau*
Plassen: *lake*
Ploskogor'ye: *plateau, upland*
Pointe: *point*
Polder: *reclaimed land*
Poluostrov: *peninsula*
Pongo: *water gap*
Ponta, -l: *cape, point*
Ponte: *bridge*
Poolsaar: *peninsula*
Portezuelo: *pass*
Porto: *port*
Poulo: *island*
Praia: *beach, seashore*
Presa: *reservoir*
Presidente: *president*
Presqu'île: *peninsula*
Prokhod: *pass*
Proliv: *strait*
Promontorio: *promontory*
Průsmyk: *mountain pass*
Przylądek: *cape*
Puerto: *bay, pass, port*
Pulao: *island-s*
Pulau, Pulo: *island*
Puncak: *peak, summit, top*
Punt, Punta, -n: *point, -s*
Pun: *peak*
Puu: *hill, mountain*
Puy: *peak*

Q, Qal'eh: *castle, fort*
Qā': *depression, marsh, mud flat*
Qal'at: *fort*
Qanâ: *canal*
Qārat: *hill-s, mountain-s*
Qaşr: *castle, fort, hill*
Qila: *fort*
Qiryat: *settlement, suburb*
Qolleh: *peak*
Qooriga: *anchorage, bay*
Qoz: *dunes, sand ridge*
Qu: *canal*
Quebrada: *ravine, stream*
Qullai: *peak, summit*
Qum: *desert, sand*
Qundao: *archipelago, islands*
Qurayyāt: *hills*

Raas: *cape, point*
Rabt: *hill*
Rada: *roadstead*
Rade: *anchorage, roadstead*
Rags: *point*
Ramat: *hill, mountain*
Rand: *ridge of hills*
Rann: *swamp*
Raqaba: *wadi, watercourse*
Ras, Râs, Ra's: *cape*
Ravnina: *plain*
Récif-s: *reef-s*
Regreg: *marsh*
Represa: *reservoir*
Reservatório: *reservoir*
Restinga: *barrier, sand area*
Rettō: *chain of islands*
Ri: *mountain range, village*
Ría: *estuary*
Ribeirão: *stream*
Río, Rio: *river*
Roca-s: *cliff, rock-s*
Roche-r, -s: *rock-s*
Rosh: *mountain, point*
Rt: *cape, point*
Rubha: *headland*
Rupes: *scarp*

Saar: *island*
Saari, Sari: *island*
Sabkha-t, Sabkhet: *lagoon, marsh, salt lake*
Sagar: *lake, sea*
Sahara, Şaḩrā': *desert*
Sahl: *plain*
Saki: *cape, point*
Salar: *salt flat*
Salina: *salt pan*
Salin-as, -es: *salt flat-s, salt marsh-es*
Salto: *waterfall*
Sammyaku: *mountain range*
San: *hill, mountain*
San, -ta, -to: *saint*
Sandur: *sandy area*
Sankt: *saint*
Sanmaek: *mountain range*
São: *saint*
Sarīr: *gravel desert*
Sasso: *mountain, stone*
Savane: *savanna*
Scoglio: *reef, rock*
Se: *reef, rock-s, shoal-s*
Sebjet: *salt lake, salt marsh*
Sebkha: *salt lake, salt marsh*
Sebkhet: *lagoon, salt lake*
See: *lake, sea*
Selat: *strait*
Selkä: *lake, ridge*
Semenanjung: *peninsula*
Sen: *mountain*
Seno: *bay, gulf*
Serra, Serranía: *range of hills or mountains*
Severn-yy, -aya, -oye: *northern*
Sgùrr: *peak*
Sha: *island, shoal*
Sha'ib: *ravine, watercourse*
Shamo: *desert*
Shan: *island-s, mountain-s, range*
Shankou: *mountain pass*
Shanmo: *mountain range*
Sharm: *cove, creek, harbor*
Shaţţ: *large river*
Shi: *administrative division, municipality*
Shima: *island-s, rock-s*
Shō: *island, reef, rock*
Shotō: *archipelago*
Shott: *intermittent salt lake*
Shuiku: *reservoir*
Shuitao: *channel*
Shyghanaghy: *bay, gulf*
Sierra: *mountain range*
Silsilesi: *mountain chain, ridge*
Sint: *saint*
Sinus: *bay, sea*
Sjö-n: *lake*
Skarv-et: *barren mountain*
Skerry: *rock*
Slieve: *mountain*
Sø: *lake*
Sønder, Søndre: *south-ern*
Sopka: *conical mountain, volcano*
Sor: *lake, salt lake*
Sør, Sör: *south-ern*
Sory: *salt lake, salt marsh*
Spitz-e: *peak, point, top*
Sredn-iy, -yaya, -eye: *central, middle*
Stagno: *lake, pond*
Stantsiya: *station*
Stausee: *reservoir*
Stenón: *channel, strait*
Step'-i: *steppe-s*
Štít: *summit, top*
Stor-e: *big, great*
Straat: *strait*
Straum-en: *current-s*
Strelka: *spit of land*
Stretet, Stretto: *strait*
Su: *reef, river, rock, stream*
Sud: *south*
Sudo: *channel, strait*
Suidō: *channel, strait*
Şummān: *rocky desert*
Sund: *sound, strait*
Sunden: *channel, inlet, sound*
Svyat-oy, -aya, -oye: *holy, saint*
Sziget: *island*

Tagh: *mountain-s*
Tall: *hill, mound*
T'an: *lake*
Tanezrouft: *desert*
Tang: *plain, steppe*
Tangi: *peninsula, point*
Tanjong, Tanjung: *cape, point*
Tao: *island-s*
Tarso: *hill-s, mountain-s*
Tassili: *plateau, upland*
Tau: *mountain-s, range*
Taūy: *hills, mountains*
Tchabal: *mountain-s*
Te Ava: *tidal flat*
Tel-l: *hill, mound*
Telok, Teluk: *bay*
Tepe, -si: *hill, peak*
Tepuí: *mesa, mountain*
Terara: *hill, mountain, peak*
Testa: *bluff, head*
Thale: *lake*
Thang: *plain, steppe*
Tien: *lake*
Tierra: *land, region*
Ting: *hill, mountain*
Tir'at: *canal*
Tó: *lake, pool*
To, Tō: *island-s, rock-s*
Tonle: *lake*
Tope: *hill, mountain, peak*
Top-pen: *peak-s*
Träsk: *bog, lake*
Tso: *lake*
Tsui: *cape, point*
Tübegi: *peninsula*
Tulu: *hill, mountain*
Tunturi-t: *hill-s, mountain-s*

Uad: *wadi, watercourse*
Udde-m: *point*
Ujong, Ujung: *cape, point*
Umi: *bay, lagoon, lake*
Ura: *bay, inlet, lake*
'Urūq: *dune area*
Uul, Uula: *mountain, range*
'Uyûn: *springs*

Vaara: *mountain*
Vaart: *canal*
Vær: *fishing station*
Vaïn: *channel, strait*
Valle, Vallée: *valley, wadi*
Vallen: *waterfall*
Valli: *lagoon, lake*
Vallis: *valley*
Vanua: *land*
Varre: *mountain*
Vatn, Vatten, Vatnet: *lake, water*
Veld: *grassland, plain*
Verkhn-iy, -yaya, -eye: *higher, upper*
Vesi: *lake, water*
Vest-er: *west*
Via: *road*
Vidda: *plateau*
Vig, Vík, Vik, -en: *bay, cove*
Vinh: *bay, gulf*
Vodokhranilishche: *reservoir*
Vodoskhovyshche: *reservoir*
Volcan, Volcán: *volcano*
Vostochn-yy, -aya, -oye: *eastern*
Vötn: *stream*
Vozvyshennost': *plateau, upland*
Vozyera: *lake-s*
Vrchovina: *mountains*
Vrch-y: *mountain-s*
Vrh: *hill, mountain*
Vrŭkh: *mountain*
Vyaliki: *big, large*
Vysočina: *highland*

Wabē: *stream*
Wadi, Wâdi, Wādī: *valley, watercourse*
Wâhât, Wāḩat: *oasis*
Wald: *forest, wood*
Wan: *bay, gulf*
Water: *harbor*
Webi: *stream*
Wiek: *cove, inlet*

Xia: *gorge, strait*
Xiao: *lesser, little*

Yanchi: *salt lake*
Yang: *ocean*
Yarymadasy: *peninsula*
Yazovir: *reservoir*
Yōlto: *island group*
Yoma: *mountain range*
Yü: *island*
Yumco: *lake*
Yunhe: *canal*
Yuzhn-yy, -aya, -oye: *southern*

Zaki: *cape, point*
Zaliv: *bay, gulf*
Zan: *mountain, ridge*
Zangbo: *river, stream*
Zapadn-yy, -aya, -oye: *western*
Zatoka: *bay, gulf*
Zee: *bay, sea*
Zemlya: *land*

AVERAGE RAINFALL AND TEMPERATURE

Average daily high and low temperatures and monthly rainfall for selected world locations:

	JAN.			FEB.			MARCH			APRIL			MAY			JUNE			JULY			AUG.			SEPT.			OCT.			NOV.			DEC.		
CANADA																																				
CALGARY, *Alberta*	-4	-16	14	-2	-14	15	3	-9	20	11	-3	27	17	3	54	20	7	82	24	9	65	23	8	57	18	3	40	12	-1	18	3	-9	16	-2	-13	14
CHARLOTTETOWN, *P.E.I.*	-3	-11	100	-3	-12	83	1	-7	83	7	-1	77	14	4	79	20	10	75	24	14	78	23	14	86	18	10	91	13	5	106	6	0	106	0	-7	111
CHURCHILL, *Manitoba*	-23	-31	15	-22	-30	12	-15	-25	18	-6	-15	23	2	-5	27	11	1	43	17	7	55	16	7	62	9	2	53	2	-4	44	-9	-16	31	-18	-26	18
EDMONTON, *Alberta*	-9	-18	23	-5	-15	18	0	-9	19	10	-1	24	17	5	45	21	9	79	23	12	87	22	10	64	17	5	36	11	0	20	0	-8	18	-6	-15	22
FORT NELSON, *B.C.*	-18	-27	23	-11	-23	21	-2	-15	21	8	-4	20	16	3	44	21	8	65	23	10	76	21	8	58	15	3	39	6	-4	28	-9	-17	26	-16	-24	23
GOOSE BAY, *Nfld.*	-12	-22	1	-10	-21	4	-4	-15	4	3	-7	15	10	0	46	17	5	97	21	10	119	19	9	98	14	4	87	6	-2	58	0	-8	21	-9	-18	7
HALIFAX, *Nova Scotia*	0	-8	139	0	-9	121	3	-5	123	8	0	109	14	5	110	18	9	96	22	13	93	22	14	103	19	10	93	13	5	127	8	1	142	2	-5	141
MONTRÉAL, *Quebec*	-6	-15	71	-4	-13	66	2	-7	71	11	1	74	18	8	69	24	13	84	26	16	87	25	14	91	20	10	84	13	4	76	5	-2	90	-3	-11	85
MOOSONEE, *Ontario*	-14	-27	39	-12	-25	32	-5	-19	37	3	-8	36	11	0	55	18	5	72	22	9	79	20	8	78	15	5	77	8	0	66	-1	-9	53	-11	-21	41
OTTAWA, *Ontario*	-6	-16	67	-5	-15	59	1	-8	67	11	0	60	19	7	72	24	12	82	27	15	86	25	13	80	20	9	77	13	3	69	4	-3	70	-4	-12	74
PRINCE RUPERT, *B.C.*	4	-3	237	6	-1	198	7	0	202	9	2	179	12	5	133	14	8	110	16	10	115	16	10	149	15	8	218	11	5	345	7	1	297	5	-1	275
QUÉBEC, *Quebec*	-7	-17	85	-6	-16	75	0	-9	79	8	-1	76	17	5	93	22	10	108	25	13	112	23	12	109	18	7	113	11	2	89	3	-4	100	-5	-13	104
REGINA, *Saskatchewan*	-12	-23	17	-9	-21	13	-2	-13	18	10	-3	20	18	3	45	23	9	77	26	11	59	25	10	44	19	4	35	11	-2	20	0	-11	16	-8	-19	14
SAINT JOHN, *N.B.*	-3	-14	141	-2	-14	115	3	-7	111	10	-1	111	17	4	116	22	9	103	25	12	100	24	11	100	19	7	108	14	2	118	6	-3	149	-1	-10	157
ST. JOHN'S, *Nfld.*	-1	-8	69	-1	-9	69	1	-6	74	5	-2	80	10	1	91	16	6	95	20	11	78	20	11	122	16	8	125	11	3	147	6	0	122	2	-5	91
TORONTO, *Ontario*	-1	-8	68	-1	-9	60	3	-4	66	11	2	65	17	7	71	23	13	68	26	16	77	25	15	70	21	11	73	14	5	62	7	0	70	1	-6	67
VANCOUVER, *B.C.*	5	0	146	8	1	121	10	2	102	13	5	69	17	8	56	19	11	47	22	13	31	22	13	37	19	10	60	14	6	116	9	3	155	6	1	172
WHITEHORSE, *Yukon Terr.*	-14	-23	17	-9	-18	13	-2	-13	13	5	-5	9	13	1	14	18	5	30	20	8	37	18	6	39	12	3	31	4	-3	21	-6	-13	20	-12	-20	19
WINNIPEG, *Manitoba*	-13	-23	21	-10	-21	19	-2	-13	26	9	-2	34	18	5	55	23	10	81	26	14	74	25	12	66	19	6	55	12	1	35	-1	-9	26	-9	-18	22
YELLOWKNIFE, *N.W.T.*	-24	-32	14	-20	-30	12	-12	-24	11	-1	-13	10	10	0	16	18	8	20	21	12	35	18	10	39	10	4	29	1	-4	32	-10	-18	23	-20	-28	17
UNITED STATES																																				
ALBANY, *New York*	-1	-12	61	1	-10	59	7	-4	76	14	2	77	21	7	86	26	13	83	29	15	80	27	14	87	23	10	78	17	4	77	9	-1	80	2	-8	74
AMARILLO, *Texas*	9	-6	13	12	-4	14	16	0	23	22	6	28	26	11	71	31	16	88	33	19	70	32	18	74	28	14	50	23	7	35	15	0	15	10	-5	15
ANCHORAGE, *Alaska*	-6	-13	20	-3	-11	21	1	-8	17	6	-2	15	12	4	17	16	8	26	18	11	47	17	10	62	13	5	66	5	-2	47	-3	-9	29	-5	-12	28
ASPEN, *Colorado*	0	-18	32	2	-16	26	5	-11	35	10	-6	28	16	-2	39	22	1	34	26	5	44	25	4	45	21	0	34	15	-5	36	6	-10	31	1	-15	32
ATLANTA, *Georgia*	10	0	117	13	1	117	18	6	139	23	10	103	26	15	100	30	19	92	31	21	134	31	21	93	28	18	91	23	11	77	17	6	95	12	2	105
ATLANTIC CITY, *N.J.*	5	-6	83	6	-5	78	11	0	98	16	4	86	22	10	82	27	15	63	29	18	103	29	18	103	25	13	78	19	7	72	13	2	84	7	-3	81
AUGUSTA, *Maine*	-2	-11	76	0	-10	71	4	-5	84	11	1	92	19	7	95	23	12	85	26	16	85	25	15	84	20	10	80	14	4	92	7	-1	114	0	-8	93
BIRMINGHAM, *Alabama*	11	0	128	14	1	114	19	6	150	24	10	114	27	14	112	31	18	97	32	21	132	32	20	95	29	17	105	24	10	75	18	5	103	13	2	120
BISMARCK, *N. Dak.*	-7	-19	12	-3	-15	11	4	-8	20	13	-1	37	20	6	56	25	11	74	29	14	59	28	12	44	22	6	38	15	0	21	4	-8	14	-4	-16	12
BOISE, *Idaho*	2	-6	38	7	-3	28	12	0	32	16	3	31	22	7	31	27	11	22	32	14	8	31	14	9	25	9	16	18	4	18	9	-1	35	3	-5	35
BOSTON, *Massachusetts*	2	-6	95	3	-5	91	8	0	100	13	5	93	19	10	84	25	15	79	28	18	73	27	18	92	23	14	82	17	8	87	11	4	110	5	-3	105
BROWNSVILLE, *Texas*	21	10	37	22	11	36	26	15	16	29	19	41	31	22	64	33	24	74	34	24	39	34	24	69	32	23	134	30	19	89	26	15	41	22	11	30
BURLINGTON, *Vermont*	-4	-14	46	-3	-13	44	4	-6	55	12	1	71	20	7	78	24	13	85	27	15	90	26	14	101	21	9	85	14	4	77	7	-1	76	-1	-9	59
CHARLESTON, *S.C.*	14	3	88	16	4	80	20	9	114	24	12	71	28	17	97	31	21	155	32	23	180	32	22	176	29	20	135	25	14	77	21	8	63	16	5	82
CHARLESTON, *W. Va.*	5	-5	87	7	-4	82	14	2	100	19	6	85	24	11	99	28	15	92	30	18	126	29	17	102	26	14	81	20	7	67	14	2	85	8	-2	85
CHEYENNE, *Wyoming*	3	-9	10	5	-8	11	7	-6	26	13	-1	35	18	4	64	24	9	56	28	13	51	27	12	42	22	7	31	16	1	19	8	-5	15	4	-9	10
CHICAGO, *Illinois*	-1	-10	48	1	-7	42	8	-1	72	15	5	97	22	10	83	27	16	103	29	19	103	28	18	89	24	14	79	18	7	70	9	1	73	2	-6	65
CINCINNATI, *Ohio*	3	-6	89	5	-4	67	12	1	97	18	7	94	24	12	101	28	17	99	30	19	102	30	18	86	26	14	75	19	8	62	12	3	81	5	-3	75
CLEVELAND, *Ohio*	1	-7	62	2	-6	58	8	-2	78	15	4	85	21	9	90	26	14	89	28	17	88	27	16	86	23	12	80	17	7	65	10	2	80	3	-4	70
DALLAS, *Texas*	13	1	47	15	4	58	20	8	74	25	13	105	29	18	125	33	22	86	35	24	56	35	24	60	31	20	82	26	14	100	19	8	64	14	3	60
DENVER, *Colorado*	6	-9	14	8	-7	16	11	-3	34	17	1	45	22	6	63	27	11	43	31	15	47	30	14	38	25	9	28	19	2	26	11	-4	23	7	-8	15
DES MOINES, *Iowa*	-2	-12	26	1	-9	30	8	-2	57	17	4	85	23	11	103	28	16	108	30	19	97	29	18	105	24	13	80	18	6	58	9	-1	46	0	-9	31
DETROIT, *Michigan*	-1	-7	42	1	-7	43	7	-2	62	14	4	75	21	10	69	26	15	85	29	18	86	27	18	87	23	14	78	16	7	55	9	2	67	2	-4	67
DULUTH, *Minnesota*	-9	-19	31	-6	-16	21	1	-9	44	9	-2	59	17	4	84	22	9	105	25	13	102	23	12	101	18	7	95	11	2	62	2	-6	48	-6	-15	32
EL PASO, *Texas*	13	-1	11	17	1	11	21	5	8	26	9	7	31	14	9	36	18	17	36	20	38	34	19	39	31	16	34	26	10	20	19	4	11	14	-1	14
FAIRBANKS, *Alaska*	-19	-28	14	-14	-26	11	-5	-19	9	5	-6	7	15	3	15	21	10	35	22	11	45	19	8	46	13	2	28	0	-8	21	-12	-21	18	-17	-26	19
HARTFORD, *Connecticut*	1	-9	83	2	-7	79	8	-2	97	16	3	97	22	9	95	27	14	85	29	17	86	28	16	104	24	11	101	18	5	96	11	0	105	3	-6	99
HELENA, *Montana*	-1	-12	15	3	-9	12	7	-5	18	13	-1	24	19	4	45	24	9	53	29	12	28	28	11	27	21	5	28	15	0	19	6	-6	14	0	-12	16
HONOLULU, *Hawaii*	27	19	80	27	19	68	28	20	72	28	20	32	29	21	25	30	22	10	31	23	15	32	23	14	31	23	18	31	22	53	29	21	67	27	19	89
HOUSTON, *Texas*	16	4	98	19	6	75	22	10	88	26	15	91	29	18	142	32	21	133	34	22	85	34	22	95	31	20	106	28	14	120	22	10	97	18	6	91
INDIANAPOLIS, *Indiana*	1	-8	69	4	-6	61	11	0	92	17	5	94	23	11	98	28	16	98	30	18	111	29	17	88	25	13	74	19	6	69	11	1	89	4	-5	77
JACKSONVILLE, *Florida*	18	5	83	19	6	89	23	10	100	26	13	77	29	17	92	32	21	140	33	22	164	33	22	186	31	21	199	27	15	99	23	10	52	19	6	65
JUNEAU, *Alaska*	-1	-7	139	1	-5	116	4	-3	113	8	0	105	13	4	109	16	7	88	18	9	120	17	8	160	13	6	217	8	3	255	3	-2	186	0	-5	153
KANSAS CITY, *Missouri*	2	-9	30	5	-6	32	12	0	62	18	7	88	24	12	138	29	17	102	32	20	115	30	19	99	26	14	120	20	8	83	11	1	56	4	-6	43
LAS VEGAS, *Nevada*	14	0	14	17	4	12	20	7	13	25	10	5	31	16	5	38	21	3	41	25	9	40	23	13	35	19	7	28	12	6	20	6	11	14	1	10
LITTLE ROCK, *Arkansas*	9	-1	85	12	1	88	17	6	120	23	11	134	26	15	141	31	20	84	33	22	83	32	21	80	28	18	85	23	11	102	16	6	153	10	1	123
LOS ANGELES, *California*	19	9	70	19	10	61	19	10	51	20	12	20	21	14	3	22	15	1	24	17	1	25	18	2	25	17	5	24	15	7	21	12	38	19	9	43
LOUISVILLE, *Kentucky*	5	-5	85	7	-3	88	14	2	113	20	7	101	24	13	114	29	17	90	31	20	106	30	19	84	27	15	76	21	8	68	14	3	92	7	-2	89
MEMPHIS, *Tennessee*	9	-1	118	12	2	114	17	6	136	23	11	142	27	16	126	32	21	98	34	23	101	33	22	87	29	18	83	24	11	74	17	6	124	11	2	135
MIAMI, *Florida*	24	15	52	25	16	53	26	18	63	28	20	82	30	22	150	31	24	227	32	25	152	32	25	198	31	24	215	29	22	178	27	19	80	25	16	47
MILWAUKEE, *Wisconsin*	-3	-11	32	-1	-8	31	5	-3	54	12	2	87	18	7	73	24	13	87	27	17	85	26	16	94	22	12	95	15	6	66	7	-1	65	0	-7	53
MINNEAPOLIS, *Minnesota*	-6	-16	21	-3	-13	22	4	-5	45	14	2	58	21	9	80	26	14	103	29	17	97	27	16	95	22	10	70	15	4	49	5	-4	37	-4	-12	24
NASHVILLE, *Tennessee*	8	-3	108	10	-1	100	16	4	127	22	9	104	26	14	118	30	18	99	32	21	99	31	20	85	28	16	89	23	9	67	16	4	101	10	-1	112
NEW ORLEANS, *Louisiana*	16	5	136	18	7	147	22	11	124	26	15	119	29	18	135	32	22	147	33	23	167	32	23	157	30	21	138	26	15	76	22	11	101	18	7	132
NEW YORK, *New York*	3	-4	80	4	-3	76	9	1	99	15	7	94	21	12	93	26	17	80	29	21	101	28	20	107	24	16	85	18	10	81	12	5	96	6	-1	90
OKLAHOMA CITY, *Okla.*	8	-4	28	11	-1	36	17	4	61	22	9	76	26	14	145	31	19	107	34	21	74	34	21	65	29	17	97	23	10	80	16	4	43	10	-2	37
OMAHA, *Nebraska*	-1	-12	18	2	-9	21	9	-2	61	17	5	73	23	11	118	28	16	105	30	19	96	29	18	95	24	13	90	18	6	60	9	-1	35	1	-9	23
PENSACOLA, *Florida*	15	5	109	17	7	126	21	11	150	25	15	112	28	19	105	32	22	168	32	23	187	32	23	176	30	21	166	26	15	102	21	11	91	17	7	105
PHILADELPHIA, *Pa.*	3	-5	82	5	-4	70	11	1	95	17	6	88	23	12	94	28	17	87	30	20	108	29	19	97	25	15	86	19	8	67	13	3	85	6	-2	86
PHOENIX, *Arizona*	19	3	21	22	5	21	25	7	30	29	9	7	33	13	5	38	18	3	39	23	21	38	22	30	36	18	23	30	12	14	23	7	18	19	3	28
PITTSBURGH, *Pa.*	1	-8	66	3	-7	60	9	-1	85	16	4	80	21	9	92	26	14	91	28	16	98	27	16	83	24	12	74	17	6	61	10	1	69	4	-4	71
PORTLAND, *Oregon*	7	1	133	11	2	105	13	4	92	16	5	61	20	8	53	23	12	38	27	14	15	27	14	23	24	11	41	18	7	76	11	4	135	8	2	149
PROVIDENCE, *R.I.*	3	-7	101	4	-6	91	8	-2	111	14	3	102	20	9	89	25	14	77	28	17	77	27	17	102	24	12	88	18	6	93	12	2	117	5	-4	110
RALEIGH, *N.C.*	9	-2	89	11	0	88	17	4	94	22	8	70	26	13	96	29	18	91	31	20	111	30	20	110	27	16	79	22	9	77	17	4	76	12	0	79
RAPID CITY, *S. Dak.*	2	-12	10	4	-10	12	8	-6	26	14	0	52	20	6	84	25	12	89	30	15	63	29	13	43	23	7	32	17	1	26	8	-5	12	3	-11	10
RENO, *Nevada*	7	-6	28	11	-4	24	14	-2	20	18	1	11	23	5	17	28	8	11	33	11	7	32	10	6	26	5	9	20	1	10	12	-3	19	8	-7	27
ST. LOUIS, *Missouri*	3	-6	50	6	-4	54	13	2	84	19	8	97	25	13	100	30	19	103	32	21	92	31	20	76	27	16	73	20	9	70	13	3	78	5	-3	64
SALT LAKE CITY, *Utah*	2	-7	32	6	-4	30	11	0	45	16	3	52	22	8	46	28	13	23	33	18	18	32	17	21	26	11	27	19	5	34	10	-1	34	3	-6	34
SAN DIEGO, *California*	19	9	56	19	10	41	19	12	50	20	13	20	21	15	5	22	17	2	25	19	1	25	20	2	25	19	5	24	16	9	21	12	30	19	9	35
SAN FRANCISCO, *Calif.*	14	8	112	16	9	77	16	9	78	17	10	34	17	10	10	18	11	4	18	12	1	19	13	2	20	13	7	20	13	28	17	11	73	14	8	91

RED FIGURES: Average daily high temperature (°C) **BLUE FIGURES:** Average daily low temperature (°C) **BLACK FIGURES:** Average monthly rainfall (mm)

UNITED STATES	JAN.			FEB.			MARCH			APRIL			MAY			JUNE			JULY			AUG.			SEPT.			OCT.			NOV.			DEC.		
SANTA FE, *New Mexico*	6	-10	11	9	-7	9	13	-5	12	18	-1	13	24	4	23	29	9	31	31	12	52	29	11	64	25	7	38	20	1	32	13	-5	14	7	-9	12
SEATTLE, *Washington*	7	2	141	10	3	107	12	4	94	14	5	64	18	8	42	21	11	38	24	13	20	24	13	27	21	11	47	15	8	89	10	5	149	7	2	149
SPOKANE, *Washington*	1	-6	52	5	-3	39	9	-1	37	14	2	28	19	6	35	24	10	33	28	12	15	28	12	16	22	8	20	15	2	31	5	-2	51	1	-6	57
TAMPA, *Florida*	21	10	54	22	11	73	25	14	90	28	16	44	31	20	76	32	23	143	32	24	189	32	24	196	32	23	160	29	18	60	25	14	46	22	11	54
VICKSBURG, *Mississippi*	14	2	155	16	3	131	21	8	160	25	12	147	29	16	130	32	20	88	33	22	106	33	21	80	30	18	85	26	12	106	20	8	126	16	4	168
WASHINGTON, *D.C.*	6	-3	71	8	-2	66	14	3	90	19	8	72	25	14	94	29	19	80	31	22	97	31	21	104	27	17	84	21	10	78	15	5	76	8	0	79
WICHITA, *Kansas*	4	-7	19	8	-5	23	14	1	57	20	7	57	25	12	99	30	18	105	34	21	82	33	20	78	27	15	85	21	8	62	13	1	37	6	-5	29
MIDDLE AMERICA																																				
ACAPULCO, *Mexico*	29	21	8	31	21	1	31	21	0	31	22	1	32	23	36	32	24	325	32	24	231	32	24	236	31	24	353	31	23	170	31	22	30	31	21	10
BALBOA, *Panama*	31	22	34	32	22	16	32	22	14	32	23	73	31	23	198	30	23	203	31	23	176	31	23	200	30	23	197	29	23	271	29	23	260	31	23	133
CHARLOTTE AMALIE, *V.I.*	28	23	50	27	22	41	28	23	49	28	23	63	29	24	105	30	25	67	31	26	71	31	26	112	31	26	132	31	25	139	29	24	131	28	23	69
GUATEMALA, *Guatemala*	23	12	4	25	12	5	27	14	10	28	14	32	29	16	110	27	16	257	26	16	197	26	16	193	26	16	235	24	16	98	23	14	33	22	13	13
GUAYMAS, *Mexico*	23	13	17	24	14	6	26	16	5	29	18	1	31	21	2	34	24	1	34	27	46	35	27	71	35	26	28	32	22	17	28	18	8	23	13	18
HAVANA, *Cuba*	26	18	71	26	18	46	27	19	46	29	21	58	30	22	119	31	23	165	32	24	124	32	24	135	31	24	150	29	23	173	27	21	79	26	19	58
KINGSTON, *Jamaica*	30	19	29	30	19	24	30	20	23	31	21	39	31	22	104	32	23	96	32	23	46	32	23	107	32	23	127	31	23	181	31	22	95	31	21	41
MANAGUA, *Nicaragua*	33	21	2	33	21	3	35	22	4	36	23	3	35	24	136	32	23	237	32	23	132	32	23	121	33	23	213	32	23	315	32	22	42	32	22	10
MÉRIDA, *Mexico*	28	17	30	29	17	23	32	19	18	33	21	20	34	22	81	33	23	142	33	23	132	33	23	142	32	23	173	31	22	97	29	19	33	28	18	33
MEXICO, *Mexico*	19	6	8	21	6	5	24	8	11	25	11	19	26	12	49	24	13	106	23	12	129	23	12	121	23	12	110	21	10	44	20	8	15	19	6	7
MONTERREY, *Mexico*	20	9	18	22	11	23	24	14	16	29	17	29	31	20	40	33	22	68	32	22	62	33	22	76	30	21	151	27	18	78	22	13	26	18	10	20
NASSAU, *Bahamas*	25	18	48	25	18	43	26	19	41	27	21	65	29	22	132	31	23	178	31	24	153	32	24	170	31	24	180	29	23	171	27	21	71	26	19	43
PORT-AU-PRINCE, *Haiti*	31	20	32	31	20	50	32	21	79	32	22	156	32	22	218	33	23	96	34	23	73	34	23	139	33	23	166	32	22	164	31	22	84	31	21	35
PORT OF SPAIN, *Trinidad*	29	19	69	30	19	41	31	19	46	31	21	53	32	21	94	31	22	193	31	21	218	31	22	246	31	22	193	31	22	170	31	21	183	30	21	124
SAN JOSÉ, *Costa Rica*	24	14	11	24	14	5	26	15	14	26	17	46	27	17	224	26	17	276	25	17	215	26	16	243	26	16	326	25	16	323	25	16	148	24	14	42
SAN JUAN, *Puerto Rico*	27	21	75	27	21	56	27	21	59	28	22	95	29	23	156	29	24	112	29	24	115	29	24	133	30	24	136	29	24	140	29	23	148	27	22	118
SAN SALVADOR, *El Salv.*	32	16	7	33	16	7	34	17	13	34	18	53	33	19	179	31	19	315	32	18	312	32	19	307	31	19	317	31	18	230	31	17	40	32	16	12
SANTO DOMINGO, *Dom. R.*	29	19	57	29	19	43	29	19	49	29	21	77	30	22	179	31	22	154	31	22	155	31	23	162	31	22	173	31	22	164	30	21	111	29	19	63
TEGUCIGALPA, *Honduras*	25	13	9	27	14	4	29	14	8	30	17	32	29	18	151	28	18	159	28	17	82	28	17	87	28	17	185	27	17	135	26	16	38	25	15	12
SOUTH AMERICA																																				
ANTOFAGASTA, *Chile*	24	17	0	24	17	0	23	16	0	21	14	0	19	13	0	18	11	1	17	11	1	17	11	1	18	12	0	19	13	0	21	14	0	22	16	0
ASUNCIÓN, *Paraguay*	35	22	150	34	22	133	33	21	142	29	18	145	25	14	120	22	12	73	23	12	51	26	14	48	28	16	83	30	17	136	32	18	144	34	21	142
BELÉM, *Brazil*	31	22	351	30	22	412	31	23	441	31	23	370	31	23	282	31	22	164	31	22	154	31	22	122	32	22	129	32	22	105	32	22	101	32	22	202
BOGOTÁ, *Colombia*	19	9	48	20	9	52	19	10	81	19	11	119	19	11	103	18	11	61	18	10	47	18	10	48	19	9	58	19	10	142	19	10	115	19	9	67
BRASÍLIA, *Brazil*	27	18	262	27	18	213	28	18	202	28	17	103	26	13	20	25	11	4	26	11	4	28	13	6	31	16	35	28	18	140	28	19	238	26	18	329
BUENOS AIRES, *Arg.*	29	17	93	28	17	81	26	16	117	22	12	90	18	8	77	14	5	64	14	6	59	16	6	65	18	8	78	21	10	97	24	13	89	28	16	96
CARACAS, *Venezuela*	24	13	41	25	13	27	26	14	22	27	16	20	27	17	36	26	17	52	26	16	53	26	16	53	27	16	48	26	16	47	25	16	50	26	14	58
COM. RIVADAVIA, *Arg.*	26	13	16	25	13	11	22	11	21	18	8	21	13	6	34	11	3	21	11	3	25	12	3	22	14	5	13	19	9	13	22	10	13	24	12	15
CÓRDOBA, *Argentina*	31	16	110	30	16	102	28	14	96	24	11	45	21	7	25	18	3	10	18	3	10	21	4	13	23	7	27	25	11	69	28	13	97	30	16	118
GUAYAQUIL, *Ecuador*	31	21	224	31	22	278	31	22	287	32	22	180	31	20	53	31	20	17	29	19	2	30	18	0	31	19	2	30	20	3	31	20	3	31	21	30
LA PAZ, *Bolivia*	17	6	130	17	6	105	18	6	72	18	4	47	18	3	13	17	1	6	17	1	9	17	2	14	18	3	29	19	4	40	19	6	50	18	6	93
LIMA, *Peru*	28	19	1	28	19	1	28	19	1	27	17	0	23	16	1	20	14	2	19	14	4	19	13	3	20	14	3	22	14	2	23	16	1	26	17	1
MANAUS, *Brazil*	31	24	264	31	24	262	31	24	298	31	24	283	31	24	204	31	24	103	32	24	67	33	24	46	33	24	63	33	24	111	33	24	161	32	24	220
MARACAIBO, *Venezuela*	32	23	5	32	23	5	33	23	6	33	24	39	33	25	65	34	25	55	34	24	53	34	25	53	34	25	76	33	24	119	33	24	55	33	24	22
MONTEVIDEO, *Uruguay*	28	17	95	28	16	100	26	15	111	22	12	83	18	9	76	15	6	74	14	6	86	15	6	84	17	8	90	20	9	98	23	12	78	26	15	84
PARAMARIBO, *Suriname*	29	22	209	29	22	149	29	22	168	30	23	219	30	23	307	30	23	302	31	23	227	32	23	163	33	23	80	33	23	82	32	23	117	30	22	204
PUNTA ARENAS, *Chile*	14	7	35	14	7	28	12	5	39	10	4	41	7	2	42	5	1	32	4	-1	34	6	1	33	8	2	28	11	3	24	12	4	29	14	6	32
QUITO, *Ecuador*	22	8	113	22	8	128	22	8	154	21	8	176	21	8	124	22	7	48	22	7	20	23	7	24	23	7	78	22	8	127	22	7	109	22	8	103
RECIFE, *Brazil*	30	25	62	30	25	102	30	24	197	29	24	252	28	23	301	28	23	302	27	22	254	27	22	156	28	23	78	29	24	36	29	24	29	29	25	40
RIO DE JANEIRO, *Brazil*	29	23	135	29	23	124	28	22	134	27	21	109	25	19	78	24	18	52	24	17	45	24	18	46	24	18	62	25	19	82	26	20	100	28	22	137
SANTIAGO, *Chile*	29	12	3	29	11	3	27	9	5	23	7	13	18	5	64	14	3	84	15	3	76	17	4	56	19	6	30	22	7	15	26	9	8	28	11	5
SÃO PAULO, *Brazil*	27	17	225	28	18	208	27	17	160	26	14	71	23	12	67	22	11	54	22	9	35	23	11	48	23	12	77	24	14	117	26	15	139	27	16	185
VALPARAÍSO, *Chile*	22	13	0	22	13	0	21	12	0	19	11	22	17	10	38	16	9	100	16	8	111	16	8	42	17	9	27	18	10	15	21	11	15	22	12	1
EUROPE																																				
AJACCIO, *Corsica*	13	3	76	14	4	58	16	5	66	18	7	56	21	10	41	25	14	23	27	16	71	28	16	18	26	15	43	22	11	97	18	7	112	15	4	79
AMSTERDAM, *Neth.*	4	1	79	5	1	44	8	3	89	11	6	39	16	10	50	18	13	60	21	15	73	20	15	60	18	13	80	13	9	104	8	5	76	5	2	72
ATHENS, *Greece*	13	6	48	14	7	41	16	8	41	20	11	23	25	16	18	30	20	7	33	23	5	33	23	8	29	19	10	24	15	53	19	12	55	15	8	62
BARCELONA, *Spain*	13	6	38	14	7	38	16	9	47	18	11	47	21	14	44	25	18	38	28	21	28	28	21	44	25	19	76	21	15	96	16	11	51	13	8	44
BELFAST, *N. Ireland*	6	2	83	7	2	55	9	3	59	12	4	51	15	6	56	18	9	65	18	11	79	18	11	78	16	9	82	13	7	85	9	4	75	7	3	84
BELGRADE, *Serb. & Mont.*	3	-3	42	5	-2	39	11	2	43	18	7	57	23	12	73	26	15	84	28	17	63	28	17	53	24	13	47	18	8	50	11	4	55	5	0	52
BERLIN, *Germany*	2	-3	43	3	-3	38	8	0	38	13	4	41	19	8	49	22	12	64	24	14	71	23	13	62	20	10	44	13	6	44	7	2	46	3	-1	48
BIARRITZ, *France*	11	4	106	12	4	93	15	6	92	16	8	95	18	11	97	22	14	93	23	16	64	24	16	74	22	15	102	19	11	129	15	7	135	12	5	134
BORDEAUX, *France*	9	2	76	11	2	65	15	4	66	17	6	65	20	9	71	24	12	65	25	14	52	26	14	59	23	12	70	18	8	87	13	5	88	9	3	86
BRINDISI, *Italy*	12	6	57	13	7	61	15	8	67	18	11	35	22	14	26	26	18	20	29	21	9	29	21	25	26	18	47	22	15	71	18	11	72	14	8	65
BRUSSELS, *Belgium*	4	-1	82	7	0	51	10	2	81	14	5	53	18	8	74	22	11	74	23	12	58	22	12	42	21	11	69	15	7	85	9	3	61	6	0	68
BUCHAREST, *Romania*	1	-7	44	4	-5	37	10	-1	35	18	5	46	23	10	65	27	14	86	30	16	56	30	15	56	25	11	35	18	6	28	10	2	45	4	-3	42
BUDAPEST, *Hungary*	1	-4	41	4	-2	36	10	2	41	17	7	49	22	11	69	26	15	71	28	16	53	27	16	53	23	12	45	16	7	52	8	3	58	4	-1	49
CAGLIARI, *Sardinia*	14	7	53	15	7	52	17	9	45	19	11	35	23	14	27	27	18	10	30	21	3	30	21	10	27	19	29	23	15	57	19	11	55	16	9	55
CANDIA, *Crete*	16	9	94	16	9	76	17	10	41	20	12	23	23	15	18	27	19	3	29	21	1	29	22	3	27	19	18	24	17	43	21	14	69	18	11	102
COPENHAGEN, *Denmark*	2	-2	42	2	-3	25	5	-1	35	10	3	40	16	8	42	19	11	52	22	14	67	21	14	75	18	11	51	12	7	53	7	3	52	4	1	51
DUBLIN, *Ireland*	7	2	64	8	2	51	10	3	52	12	5	49	14	7	56	18	9	55	19	11	65	19	11	77	17	10	62	14	7	73	10	4	69	8	3	69
DURAZZO, *Albania*	11	6	76	12	6	84	13	8	99	17	13	56	22	17	41	25	21	48	28	23	13	28	22	48	24	18	43	20	14	180	14	11	216	12	8	185
EDINBURGH, *Scotland*	6	1	55	6	1	41	8	2	47	11	4	39	14	6	50	17	9	50	18	11	64	18	11	69	16	9	63	12	7	62	9	4	63	7	2	61
FLORENCE, *Italy*	9	2	64	11	3	62	14	5	69	19	8	71	23	12	73	27	15	56	30	18	34	30	17	47	26	15	83	20	11	99	14	7	103	11	4	79
GENEVA, *Switzerland*	4	-2	55	6	-1	53	10	2	60	15	5	63	19	9	76	23	13	81	25	15	72	24	14	90	21	12	90	14	7	91	8	3	81	4	0	66
HAMBURG, *Germany*	2	-2	61	3	-2	40	7	-1	52	13	3	47	18	7	55	21	11	74	22	13	81	22	12	79	19	10	68	13	6	62	7	3	65	4	0	71
HELSINKI, *Finland*	-3	-9	46	-4	-9	37	0	-7	35	6	-1	37	14	4	42	19	9	46	22	13	62	20	12	75	15	8	67	8	3	69	3	-1	66	-1	-5	55
LISBON, *Portugal*	14	8	95	15	8	87	17	10	85	20	12	60	21	13	44	25	15	18	27	17	4	28	17	5	26	17	33	22	14	75	17	11	100	15	9	97
LIVERPOOL, *England*	7	2	69	7	2	48	9	3	38	11	5	41	14	8	56	17	11	51	19	13	71	18	13	79	16	11	66	13	8	76	9	5	76	7	3	64
LONDON, *England*	7	2	62	7	2	36	11	8	50	13	4	43	17	7	45	21	11	46	23	13	46	22	12	44	19	11	43	14	7	73	9	4	45	7	2	59
LUXEMBOURG, *Lux.*	3	-1	66	4	-1	54	10	1	55	14	4	53	18	8	66	21	11	65	23	13	70	22	12	69	19	10	62	13	6	70	7	3	71	4	0	74
MADRID, *Spain*	9	2	45	11	2	43	15	5	37	18	7	45	21	10	40	27	15	25	31	17	9	30	17	10	25	14	29	19	10	46	13	5	64	9	2	47
MARSEILLE, *France*	10	2	49	12	2	40	15	5	45	18	8	46	22	11	46	26	15	26	29	17	15	28	17	24	25	15	63	20	10	94	15	6	76	11	3	59

AVERAGE RAINFALL AND TEMPERATURE

Average daily high and low temperatures and monthly rainfall for selected world locations:

	JAN.			FEB.			MARCH			APRIL			MAY			JUNE			JULY			AUG.			SEPT.			OCT.			NOV.			DEC.		
EUROPE																																				
MILAN, Italy	5	0	**61**	8	2	**58**	13	6	**72**	18	10	**85**	23	14	**98**	27	17	**81**	29	20	**68**	28	19	**81**	24	16	**82**	17	11	**116**	10	6	**106**	6	2	**75**
MUNICH, Germany	1	-5	**49**	3	-5	**43**	9	-1	**52**	14	3	**70**	18	7	**101**	21	11	**123**	23	13	**127**	23	12	**112**	20	9	**83**	13	4	**62**	7	0	**54**	2	-4	**51**
NANTES, France	8	2	**79**	9	2	**62**	13	4	**62**	15	6	**54**	19	9	**61**	22	12	**55**	24	14	**50**	24	13	**54**	21	12	**70**	16	8	**89**	11	5	**91**	8	3	**86**
NAPLES, Italy	12	4	**94**	13	5	**81**	15	6	**76**	18	9	**66**	22	12	**46**	26	16	**46**	29	18	**15**	29	18	**18**	26	16	**71**	22	12	**130**	17	9	**114**	14	6	**137**
NICE, France	13	4	**77**	13	5	**73**	15	7	**73**	17	9	**64**	20	13	**49**	24	16	**37**	27	18	**19**	27	18	**32**	25	16	**65**	21	12	**111**	17	8	**117**	13	5	**88**
OSLO, Norway	-2	-7	**41**	-1	-7	**31**	4	-4	**34**	10	1	**36**	16	6	**45**	20	10	**59**	22	13	**75**	21	12	**86**	16	8	**72**	9	3	**71**	3	-1	**57**	0	-4	**49**
PALERMO, Sicily	16	8	**44**	16	8	**35**	17	9	**30**	20	11	**29**	24	14	**14**	27	18	**9**	30	21	**2**	30	21	**8**	28	19	**28**	25	16	**59**	21	12	**66**	18	10	**68**
PALMA, Majorca	14	6	**39**	15	6	**35**	17	8	**37**	19	10	**35**	22	13	**34**	26	17	**20**	29	20	**8**	29	20	**18**	27	18	**52**	23	14	**77**	18	10	**54**	15	8	**54**
PARIS, France	6	1	**46**	7	1	**39**	12	4	**41**	16	6	**44**	20	10	**56**	23	13	**57**	25	15	**57**	24	14	**55**	21	12	**53**	16	8	**57**	10	5	**54**	7	2	**49**
PRAGUE, Czech. Rep.	1	-4	**21**	3	-2	**19**	7	1	**26**	13	4	**36**	18	9	**59**	22	13	**68**	23	14	**67**	23	14	**62**	18	11	**41**	12	7	**30**	5	2	**27**	1	-2	**23**
RIGA, Latvia	-4	10	**32**	-3	-10	**24**	2	-7	**26**	10	1	**35**	16	6	**42**	21	9	**58**	22	11	**72**	21	11	**68**	17	8	**66**	11	4	**54**	4	-1	**52**	-2	-7	**39**
ROME, Italy	11	5	**80**	13	5	**71**	15	7	**69**	19	10	**67**	23	13	**52**	28	17	**34**	30	20	**16**	30	19	**24**	26	17	**69**	22	13	**113**	16	9	**111**	13	6	**97**
SEVILLE, Spain	15	6	**56**	17	7	**74**	20	9	**84**	24	11	**58**	27	13	**33**	32	17	**23**	36	20	**3**	36	20	**3**	32	18	**28**	26	14	**66**	20	10	**94**	16	7	**71**
SOFIA, Bulgaria	2	-4	**34**	4	-3	**34**	10	1	**38**	16	5	**54**	21	10	**69**	24	14	**78**	27	16	**56**	26	15	**43**	22	11	**40**	17	8	**35**	9	3	**52**	4	-2	**44**
SPLIT, Croatia	10	5	**80**	11	5	**65**	14	7	**65**	18	11	**62**	23	16	**62**	27	19	**48**	30	22	**28**	30	22	**43**	26	19	**66**	20	14	**87**	15	10	**111**	12	7	**113**
STOCKHOLM, Sweden	-1	-5	**31**	-1	-5	**25**	3	-4	**26**	8	1	**29**	14	6	**34**	19	11	**44**	22	14	**64**	20	13	**66**	15	9	**49**	9	5	**51**	5	1	**44**	2	-2	**39**
VALENCIA, Spain	15	6	**23**	16	6	**38**	18	8	**23**	20	10	**30**	23	13	**28**	26	17	**33**	29	20	**10**	29	20	**13**	27	18	**56**	23	13	**41**	19	10	**64**	16	7	**33**
VALETTA, Malta	14	10	**84**	15	10	**58**	16	11	**38**	18	13	**20**	22	16	**10**	26	19	**3**	29	22	**1**	29	23	**5**	27	22	**33**	24	19	**69**	20	16	**91**	16	12	**99**
VENICE, Italy	6	1	**51**	8	2	**53**	12	5	**61**	17	10	**71**	21	14	**81**	25	17	**84**	27	19	**66**	27	18	**66**	24	16	**66**	19	11	**94**	12	7	**89**	8	3	**66**
VIENNA, Austria	1	-4	**38**	3	-3	**36**	8	1	**46**	15	6	**51**	19	10	**71**	23	14	**69**	25	15	**76**	24	15	**69**	20	11	**51**	14	7	**25**	7	3	**48**	3	-1	**46**
WARSAW, Poland	0	-6	**28**	0	-6	**26**	6	-2	**31**	12	3	**37**	20	9	**50**	23	12	**66**	24	15	**77**	23	14	**72**	19	10	**47**	13	5	**41**	6	1	**38**	2	-3	**35**
ZÜRICH, Switzerland	2	-3	**61**	5	-2	**61**	10	1	**68**	15	4	**85**	19	8	**101**	23	12	**127**	25	14	**128**	24	13	**124**	20	11	**98**	14	6	**83**	7	2	**71**	3	-2	**72**
ASIA																																				
ADEN, Yemen	27	23	**8**	27	23	**7**	29	24	**8**	31	26	**4**	34	28	**3**	35	29	**1**	34	28	**2**	33	27	**3**	34	28	**4**	32	26	**2**	29	24	**2**	27	23	**4**
ALMATY, Kazakhstan	-5	-14	**33**	-3	13	**23**	4	-6	**56**	13	3	**102**	20	10	**94**	24	14	**66**	27	16	**36**	27	14	**30**	22	8	**25**	13	2	**51**	4	-5	**48**	-2	-9	**33**
ANKARA, Turkey	4	-4	**49**	6	-3	**52**	11	-1	**45**	17	4	**44**	23	9	**56**	26	12	**37**	30	15	**13**	31	15	**8**	26	11	**28**	21	7	**21**	14	3	**28**	6	-2	**63**
ARKHANGEL'SK, Russia	-12	-20	**30**	-10	-18	**28**	-4	-13	**28**	5	-4	**18**	12	2	**33**	17	6	**48**	20	10	**66**	19	10	**69**	12	5	**56**	4	-1	**48**	-2	-7	**41**	-8	-15	**33**
BAGHDAD, Iraq	16	4	**27**	18	6	**28**	22	9	**27**	29	14	**19**	36	19	**7**	41	23	**0**	43	24	**0**	43	24	**0**	40	21	**0**	33	16	**3**	25	11	**20**	18	6	**26**
BALIKPAPAN, Indonesia	29	23	**243**	30	23	**221**	30	23	**249**	29	23	**226**	29	23	**258**	29	23	**252**	28	23	**259**	29	23	**257**	29	23	**201**	29	23	**186**	29	23	**176**	29	23	**245**
BANGKOK, Thailand	32	20	**11**	33	22	**28**	34	24	**31**	35	25	**72**	34	25	**189**	33	24	**152**	32	24	**158**	32	24	**187**	32	24	**320**	31	24	**231**	31	22	**57**	31	20	**9**
BEIJING, China	2	-9	**4**	5	-7	**5**	12	-1	**8**	20	7	**18**	27	13	**33**	31	18	**78**	32	22	**224**	31	21	**170**	27	14	**58**	21	7	**18**	10	-1	**9**	3	-7	**3**
BEIRUT, Lebanon	17	11	**187**	17	11	**151**	19	12	**96**	22	14	**51**	26	18	**19**	28	21	**2**	31	23	**0**	32	23	**0**	30	23	**6**	27	21	**48**	23	16	**119**	18	13	**176**
BOMBAY, India	28	19	**3**	28	19	**1**	30	22	**1**	32	24	**2**	33	27	**14**	32	26	**518**	29	25	**647**	29	24	**384**	29	24	**276**	32	24	**55**	32	23	**15**	31	21	**2**
BRUNEI	30	24	**371**	30	24	**193**	31	24	**198**	32	24	**249**	32	24	**277**	31	24	**241**	31	25	**229**	31	24	**185**	31	24	**300**	31	24	**368**	31	24	**386**	30	24	**330**
CALCUTTA, India	27	13	**12**	29	15	**25**	34	21	**32**	36	24	**53**	36	25	**129**	33	26	**291**	32	26	**329**	32	26	**338**	32	26	**266**	32	23	**131**	29	18	**21**	26	13	**7**
CHONGQING, China	9	5	**18**	13	7	**21**	18	11	**38**	23	16	**94**	27	19	**148**	29	22	**174**	34	24	**151**	35	25	**128**	28	22	**144**	22	16	**103**	16	12	**49**	13	8	**23**
COLOMBO, Sri Lanka	30	22	**84**	31	22	**64**	31	23	**114**	31	24	**255**	31	26	**335**	29	25	**190**	29	25	**129**	29	25	**96**	29	25	**158**	29	24	**353**	29	23	**308**	29	22	**152**
DAMASCUS, Syria	12	2	**39**	14	4	**32**	18	6	**23**	24	9	**13**	29	13	**5**	33	16	**1**	36	18	**0**	37	18	**0**	33	16	**0**	27	12	**9**	19	8	**26**	13	4	**42**
DAVAO, Philippines	31	22	**117**	32	22	**110**	32	22	**109**	33	22	**149**	32	23	**223**	31	23	**205**	31	22	**171**	31	22	**161**	32	22	**177**	32	22	**184**	32	22	**139**	31	22	**139**
DHAKA, Bangladesh	26	13	**8**	28	15	**21**	32	20	**58**	33	23	**116**	33	24	**267**	32	26	**358**	31	26	**399**	31	26	**317**	32	26	**256**	31	24	**164**	29	19	**30**	26	14	**6**
HANOI, Vietnam	20	13	**20**	21	14	**30**	23	17	**64**	28	21	**91**	32	23	**104**	33	26	**284**	33	26	**302**	32	26	**386**	31	24	**254**	29	22	**89**	26	18	**66**	22	15	**71**
HO CHI MINH CITY, Viet.	32	21	**14**	33	22	**4**	34	23	**9**	35	24	**51**	33	24	**213**	32	24	**309**	31	24	**295**	31	24	**271**	31	23	**342**	31	23	**261**	31	23	**119**	31	22	**47**
HONG KONG, China	18	13	**27**	17	13	**44**	19	16	**75**	24	19	**140**	28	23	**298**	29	26	**399**	31	26	**371**	31	26	**377**	29	25	**297**	27	23	**119**	23	18	**38**	20	15	**25**
IRKUTSK, Russia	-16	-26	**13**	-12	-25	**10**	-4	-17	**8**	6	-7	**15**	13	1	**33**	20	7	**56**	21	10	**79**	20	9	**71**	14	2	**43**	5	-6	**18**	-7	-17	**15**	-16	-24	**15**
ISTANBUL, Turkey	8	3	**91**	9	2	**69**	11	3	**62**	16	7	**42**	21	12	**30**	25	16	**28**	28	18	**24**	28	19	**31**	24	16	**48**	20	13	**66**	15	9	**92**	11	5	**114**
JAKARTA, Indonesia	29	23	**342**	29	23	**302**	30	23	**210**	31	24	**135**	31	24	**108**	31	23	**90**	31	23	**59**	31	23	**48**	31	23	**69**	31	23	**106**	30	23	**139**	29	23	**208**
JEDDAH, Saudi Arabia	29	19	**5**	29	18	**1**	29	19	**1**	33	21	**1**	35	23	**1**	36	24	**0**	37	23	**1**	37	27	**1**	36	25	**1**	35	23	**1**	33	22	**25**	30	19	**30**
JERUSALEM, Israel	13	5	**140**	13	6	**111**	18	8	**116**	23	10	**17**	27	14	**6**	29	16	**0**	31	17	**0**	31	18	**0**	29	17	**0**	27	15	**11**	21	12	**68**	15	7	**129**
KABUL, Afghanistan	2	-8	**33**	4	-6	**54**	12	1	**70**	19	6	**66**	26	11	**21**	31	13	**1**	33	16	**5**	33	15	**1**	29	11	**2**	23	6	**4**	17	1	**11**	8	-3	**21**
KARACHI, Pakistan	25	13	**7**	26	14	**10**	29	19	**10**	32	23	**3**	34	26	**0**	34	28	**10**	33	27	**90**	31	26	**58**	31	25	**27**	33	22	**3**	31	18	**3**	27	14	**5**
KATHMANDU, Nepal	18	2	**17**	19	4	**15**	25	7	**30**	28	12	**37**	30	16	**102**	29	19	**201**	29	20	**375**	28	20	**325**	28	19	**189**	27	13	**56**	23	7	**2**	19	3	**10**
KUNMING, China	16	3	**11**	18	4	**14**	21	7	**17**	24	11	**20**	26	14	**90**	25	17	**175**	25	17	**205**	25	17	**203**	24	15	**126**	21	12	**78**	18	7	**40**	17	3	**13**
LAHORE, Pakistan	21	4	**25**	22	7	**24**	28	12	**27**	35	17	**15**	40	22	**17**	41	26	**39**	38	27	**155**	36	26	**135**	36	23	**63**	35	15	**10**	28	8	**3**	23	4	**14**
LHASA, China	7	-10	**0**	9	-7	**3**	12	-2	**4**	16	1	**6**	19	5	**24**	24	9	**72**	23	9	**132**	22	9	**128**	21	7	**58**	17	1	**9**	13	-5	**1**	9	-9	**1**
MADRAS, India	29	19	**29**	31	20	**9**	33	22	**9**	35	26	**17**	38	28	**44**	38	27	**52**	36	26	**99**	35	26	**124**	34	25	**125**	32	24	**285**	29	22	**345**	29	21	**138**
MANAMA, Bahrain	30	14	**14**	21	15	**16**	24	17	**11**	29	21	**8**	33	26	**1**	36	28	**0**	37	29	**0**	38	29	**0**	36	27	**0**	32	24	**0**	28	21	**7**	22	16	**17**
MANDALAY, Myanmar	28	13	**2**	31	15	**13**	36	19	**7**	38	25	**35**	37	26	**142**	34	26	**124**	34	26	**83**	33	25	**113**	33	24	**155**	32	23	**125**	29	19	**45**	27	14	**10**
MANILA, Philippines	30	21	**21**	31	21	**10**	33	22	**15**	34	23	**30**	34	24	**123**	33	24	**262**	31	24	**423**	31	24	**421**	31	24	**353**	31	23	**197**	31	22	**135**	30	21	**65**
MOSCOW, Russia	-9	16	**38**	-6	-14	**36**	0	-8	**28**	10	1	**46**	19	8	**56**	21	11	**74**	23	13	**76**	22	12	**74**	16	7	**48**	9	3	**69**	2	-3	**43**	-5	-10	**41**
MUSCAT, Oman	25	19	**28**	25	19	**18**	28	22	**10**	32	26	**10**	37	30	**1**	38	31	**3**	36	31	**1**	33	29	**1**	34	28	**0**	34	27	**3**	30	23	**10**	26	20	**18**
NAGASAKI, Japan	9	2	**75**	10	2	**87**	14	5	**124**	19	10	**190**	23	14	**191**	26	18	**326**	29	23	**284**	31	23	**187**	27	20	**236**	22	14	**108**	17	9	**89**	12	4	**80**
NEW DELHI, India	21	7	**23**	24	9	**20**	31	14	**15**	36	20	**10**	41	26	**15**	39	28	**68**	36	27	**200**	34	26	**200**	34	24	**123**	34	18	**19**	29	11	**3**	23	8	**10**
NICOSIA, Cyprus	15	5	**70**	16	5	**50**	19	7	**35**	24	10	**21**	29	14	**26**	34	18	**9**	37	21	**1**	37	21	**2**	33	18	**6**	28	14	**23**	22	10	**41**	17	7	**74**
ODESA, Ukraine	0	-6	**25**	2	-4	**18**	5	-1	**18**	12	6	**28**	19	12	**28**	23	16	**48**	26	18	**41**	26	18	**36**	21	14	**28**	16	9	**36**	10	4	**28**	4	-2	**28**
PHNOM PENH, Cambodia	31	21	**7**	32	22	**9**	34	23	**32**	34	24	**73**	33	24	**149**	33	24	**149**	32	24	**151**	32	24	**157**	31	24	**231**	31	24	**259**	30	23	**129**	30	22	**38**
PONTIANAK, Indonesia	31	23	**275**	32	23	**213**	32	23	**242**	33	23	**280**	33	23	**279**	32	23	**228**	32	23	**178**	32	23	**206**	32	23	**245**	32	23	**356**	31	23	**385**	31	23	**321**
RIYADH, Saudi Arabia	21	8	**14**	23	9	**10**	28	13	**30**	32	18	**30**	38	22	**13**	42	25	**0**	42	26	**0**	42	24	**0**	39	22	**0**	34	16	**1**	29	13	**5**	21	9	**11**
ST. PETERSBURG, Russia	-7	-13	**25**	-5	-12	**23**	0	-8	**23**	8	4	**25**	15	6	**41**	20	11	**51**	21	13	**64**	20	13	**71**	15	9	**53**	9	4	**46**	2	-2	**36**	-3	-8	**30**
SANDAKAN, Malaysia	29	23	**454**	29	23	**271**	30	23	**200**	31	23	**118**	32	23	**153**	32	23	**196**	32	23	**185**	32	23	**205**	32	23	**240**	31	23	**263**	31	23	**356**	30	23	**470**
SAPPORO, Japan	-2	-12	**100**	-1	-11	**79**	2	-7	**70**	11	0	**61**	16	4	**59**	21	10	**65**	24	14	**86**	26	16	**117**	22	11	**136**	16	4	**114**	8	-2	**106**	1	-8	**102**
SEOUL, South Korea	0	-9	**21**	3	-7	**28**	8	-2	**49**	17	5	**105**	22	11	**88**	27	16	**151**	29	21	**384**	31	22	**263**	26	15	**160**	19	7	**49**	11	0	**43**	3	-7	**24**
SHANGHAI, China	8	1	**47**	8	1	**61**	13	4	**85**	19	10	**95**	25	15	**104**	28	19	**174**	32	23	**145**	32	23	**137**	28	19	**138**	23	14	**69**	17	7	**52**	12	2	**37**
SINGAPORE, Singapore	30	23	**239**	31	23	**165**	31	24	**174**	31	24	**166**	32	24	**171**	31	24	**163**	31	24	**150**	31	24	**171**	31	24	**164**	31	23	**191**	31	23	**250**	31	23	**269**
TAIPEI, China	19	12	**95**	18	12	**141**	21	14	**162**	25	17	**167**	28	21	**209**	32	23	**280**	33	24	**248**	33	24	**277**	31	23	**201**	27	19	**112**	24	17	**76**	21	14	**76**
T'BILISI, Georgia	6	-2	**16**	7	-1	**21**	12	2	**30**	18	7	**52**	23	12	**83**	27	16	**73**	31	19	**49**	31	19	**40**	26	15	**44**	20	9	**39**	13	4	**32**	8	0	**21**
TEHRAN, Iran	7	-3	**42**	10	0	**37**	15	4	**39**	22	9	**33**	28	14	**15**	34	19	**3**	37	22	**2**	36	22	**2**	32	18	**2**	24	12	**9**	17	6	**24**	11	1	**32**
TEL AVIV-YAFO, Israel	17	9	**165**	18	9	**64**	19	10	**58**	23	12	**13**	27	16	**3**	29	18	**0**	31	21	**0**	31	21	**0**	30	20	**1**	29	18	**14**	25	15	**85**	19	11	**144**
TOKYO, Japan	8	-2	**50**	9	-1	**72**	12	2	**106**	17	8	**129**	22	12	**144**	24	17	**176**	28	21	**136**	30	22	**149**	26	19	**216**	21	13	**194**	16	6	**96**	11	1	**54**
ULAANBAATAR, Mongolia	-19	-32	**1**	-13	-29	**1**	-4	-22	**3**	7	-8	**5**	13	-2	**8**	21	7	**25**	22	11	**74**	21	8	**48**	14	2	**20**	6	-8	**5**	-6	20	**5**	-16	-28	**3**
VIENTIANE, Laos	28	14	**7**	30	17	**18**	33	19	**41**	34	23	**88**	32	23	**212**	32	24	**216**	31	24	**209**	31	24	**254**	31	24	**244**	31	21	**81**	29	18	**16**	28	16	**5**
VLADIVOSTOK, Russia	-11	-18	**8**	-6	-14	**10**	1	-7	**18**	8	1	**30**	13	6	**53**	17	11	**74**	22	16	**84**	24	18	**119**	20	13	**109**	13	5	**48**	2	-4	**30**	-7	-13	**15**

RED FIGURES: Average daily high temperature (°C) **BLUE FIGURES:** Average daily low temperature (°C) **BLACK FIGURES:** Average monthly rainfall (mm)

ASIA	JAN.			FEB.			MARCH			APRIL			MAY			JUNE			JULY			AUG.			SEPT.			OCT.			NOV.			DEC.		
WUHAN, *China*	8	1	**41**	9	2	**57**	14	6	**92**	21	13	**136**	26	18	**165**	31	23	**212**	34	26	**165**	34	26	**114**	29	21	**73**	23	16	**74**	17	9	**49**	11	3	**30**
YAKUTSK, *Russia*	-43	-47	**8**	-33	-40	**5**	-18	-29	**3**	-3	-14	**8**	9	-1	**10**	19	9	**28**	23	12	**41**	19	9	**33**	10	1	**28**	-5	12	**13**	-26	31	**10**	-39	-43	**8**
YANGON, *Myanmar*	32	18	**4**	33	19	**4**	36	22	**17**	36	24	**47**	33	25	**307**	30	24	**478**	29	24	**535**	29	24	**511**	30	24	**368**	31	24	**183**	31	23	**62**	31	19	**11**
YEKATERINBURG, *Russia*	-14	-21	**8**	-10	-17	**10**	-4	-12	**5**	6	-3	**8**	14	4	**15**	18	9	**48**	21	12	**38**	18	10	**53**	12	5	**46**	3	-2	**23**	-7	12	**10**	-12	-18	**8**
AFRICA																																				
ABIDJAN, *Côte d'Ivoire*	31	23	**22**	32	24	**47**	32	24	**110**	32	24	**142**	31	24	**309**	29	23	**543**	28	23	**238**	28	22	**36**	28	23	**74**	29	23	**172**	31	23	**168**	31	23	**85**
ACCRA, *Ghana*	31	23	**15**	31	24	**29**	31	24	**57**	31	24	**90**	31	24	**136**	29	23	**199**	27	23	**50**	27	22	**19**	27	23	**43**	29	23	**64**	31	24	**34**	31	24	**20**
ADDIS ABABA, *Ethiopia*	24	6	**17**	24	8	**38**	25	9	**68**	25	10	**86**	25	10	**86**	23	9	**132**	21	10	**268**	21	10	**281**	22	9	**186**	24	7	**28**	23	6	**11**	23	5	**10**
ALEXANDRIA, *Egypt*	18	11	**52**	19	11	**28**	21	13	**13**	23	15	**4**	26	18	**1**	28	21	**0**	29	23	**0**	31	23	**0**	30	23	**1**	28	20	**8**	25	17	**35**	21	13	**55**
ALGIERS, *Algeria*	15	9	**93**	16	9	**73**	17	11	**67**	20	13	**52**	23	15	**34**	26	18	**14**	28	21	**2**	29	22	**5**	27	21	**33**	23	17	**77**	19	13	**96**	16	11	**114**
ANTANANARIVO, *Madag.*	26	16	**287**	26	16	**262**	26	16	**194**	24	14	**57**	23	12	**18**	21	10	**9**	20	9	**8**	21	9	**10**	23	11	**16**	27	12	**61**	27	14	**153**	27	16	**290**
ASMARA, *Eritrea*	23	7	**0**	24	8	**0**	25	9	**1**	26	11	**7**	26	12	**23**	26	12	**48**	22	12	**114**	22	12	**123**	23	13	**49**	22	12	**4**	22	10	**3**	22	9	**0**
BAMAKO, *Mali*	33	16	**0**	36	19	**0**	39	22	**3**	39	24	**19**	39	24	**59**	34	23	**131**	32	22	**229**	31	22	**307**	32	22	**198**	34	22	**63**	34	18	**7**	33	17	**0**
BANGUI, *Cen. Af. Rep.*	32	20	**20**	34	21	**39**	33	22	**107**	33	22	**133**	32	21	**163**	31	21	**143**	29	21	**181**	29	21	**225**	31	21	**190**	31	21	**202**	31	20	**93**	32	19	**29**
BEIRA, *Mozambique*	32	24	**267**	32	24	**259**	31	23	**263**	30	22	**117**	28	18	**67**	26	16	**40**	25	16	**34**	26	17	**33**	28	18	**25**	31	22	**34**	31	22	**121**	31	23	**243**
BENGHAZI, *Libya*	17	10	**66**	18	11	**41**	21	12	**20**	23	14	**5**	26	17	**3**	28	20	**1**	29	22	**1**	29	22	**1**	28	21	**3**	27	19	**18**	23	16	**46**	19	12	**66**
BUJUMBURA, *Burundi*	29	20	**97**	29	20	**97**	29	20	**126**	29	20	**129**	29	20	**64**	29	19	**11**	30	19	**3**	30	19	**17**	31	20	**43**	31	20	**62**	29	20	**98**	29	20	**100**
CAIRO, *Egypt*	18	8	**5**	21	9	**4**	24	11	**4**	28	14	**2**	33	17	**1**	35	20	**0**	36	21	**0**	35	22	**0**	32	20	**0**	30	18	**1**	26	14	**3**	20	10	**6**
CAPE TOWN, *S. Africa*	26	16	**16**	26	16	**15**	25	14	**22**	22	12	**50**	19	9	**92**	18	8	**105**	17	7	**91**	18	8	**83**	18	9	**54**	21	11	**40**	23	13	**24**	24	14	**19**
CASABLANCA, *Morocco*	17	7	**57**	18	8	**53**	19	9	**51**	21	11	**38**	22	13	**21**	24	16	**6**	26	18	**0**	27	19	**1**	26	17	**6**	24	14	**34**	21	11	**65**	18	8	**73**
CONAKRY, *Guinea*	31	22	**1**	31	23	**1**	32	23	**6**	32	23	**21**	32	24	**141**	30	23	**503**	28	22	**1210**	28	22	**1016**	29	23	**664**	31	23	**318**	31	24	**106**	31	23	**14**
DAKAR, *Senegal*	26	18	**1**	27	17	**1**	27	18	**0**	27	18	**0**	29	20	**1**	31	23	**15**	31	24	**75**	31	24	**215**	32	24	**146**	32	24	**42**	30	23	**3**	27	19	**4**
DAR ES SALAAM, *Tanzania*	31	25	**66**	31	25	**66**	31	24	**130**	30	23	**290**	29	22	**188**	29	20	**33**	28	19	**31**	28	19	**30**	28	19	**30**	29	21	**41**	30	22	**74**	31	24	**91**
DURBAN, *S. Africa*	27	21	**119**	27	21	**126**	27	20	**132**	26	18	**84**	24	14	**56**	23	12	**34**	22	11	**35**	22	13	**49**	23	15	**73**	24	17	**110**	25	18	**118**	26	19	**120**
HARARE, *Zimbabwe*	26	16	**190**	26	16	**177**	26	14	**107**	26	13	**33**	23	9	**10**	21	7	**3**	21	7	**1**	23	8	**2**	26	12	**7**	28	14	**32**	27	16	**93**	26	16	**173**
JOHANNESBURG, *S. Africa*	26	14	**150**	25	14	**129**	24	13	**110**	22	10	**48**	19	6	**24**	17	4	**6**	17	4	**10**	20	6	**10**	23	9	**25**	25	12	**65**	25	13	**126**	26	14	**141**
KAMPALA, *Uganda*	28	18	**58**	28	18	**68**	27	18	**128**	26	18	**185**	26	17	**134**	25	17	**71**	25	17	**55**	26	16	**87**	27	17	**100**	27	17	**119**	27	17	**142**	27	17	**95**
KHARTOUM, *Sudan*	32	15	**0**	34	16	**0**	38	19	**0**	41	22	**0**	42	25	**4**	41	26	**7**	38	25	**49**	37	24	**69**	39	25	**21**	40	24	**5**	36	20	**0**	33	17	**0**
KINSHASA, *D.R.C.*	31	21	**138**	31	22	**148**	32	22	**184**	32	22	**220**	31	22	**145**	29	19	**5**	27	18	**3**	29	18	**4**	31	20	**40**	31	21	**133**	31	22	**235**	30	21	**156**
KISANGANI, *D.R.C.*	31	21	**97**	31	21	**107**	31	21	**172**	31	21	**190**	31	21	**162**	30	21	**128**	29	19	**114**	28	20	**178**	29	20	**164**	30	20	**233**	29	20	**207**	30	20	**105**
LAGOS, *Nigeria*	31	23	**27**	32	25	**44**	32	26	**98**	32	25	**146**	31	24	**252**	29	23	**414**	28	23	**253**	28	23	**69**	28	23	**153**	29	23	**197**	31	24	**66**	31	24	**25**
LIBREVILLE, *Gabon*	31	23	**164**	31	22	**137**	32	23	**248**	32	23	**232**	31	22	**181**	29	21	**24**	28	20	**3**	29	21	**6**	29	22	**69**	30	22	**332**	30	22	**378**	31	22	**197**
LIVINGSTONE, *Zambia*	29	19	**175**	29	19	**160**	29	18	**95**	30	15	**25**	28	11	**5**	25	7	**1**	25	7	**0**	28	10	**0**	32	15	**2**	34	19	**26**	33	19	**78**	31	19	**176**
LUANDA, *Angola*	28	23	**34**	29	24	**35**	30	24	**90**	29	24	**127**	28	23	**18**	25	20	**0**	23	18	**0**	23	18	**1**	24	19	**2**	26	22	**6**	28	23	**32**	28	23	**23**
LUBUMBASHI, *D.R.C.*	28	16	**253**	28	17	**256**	28	16	**210**	28	14	**51**	27	10	**4**	26	7	**1**	26	6	**0**	28	8	**0**	32	11	**6**	33	14	**31**	31	16	**150**	28	17	**272**
LUSAKA, *Zambia*	26	17	**213**	26	17	**172**	26	17	**104**	26	15	**22**	25	12	**3**	23	10	**0**	23	9	**0**	25	12	**0**	29	15	**1**	31	18	**14**	29	18	**86**	27	17	**200**
LUXOR, *Egypt*	23	6	**0**	26	7	**0**	30	10	**0**	35	15	**0**	40	21	**0**	41	21	**0**	42	23	**0**	41	23	**0**	39	22	**0**	37	18	**1**	31	12	**0**	26	7	**0**
MAPUTO, *Mozambique*	30	22	**153**	31	22	**134**	29	21	**99**	28	19	**52**	27	16	**29**	25	13	**18**	24	13	**15**	26	14	**13**	27	16	**32**	28	18	**51**	28	19	**78**	29	21	**94**
MARRAKECH, *Morocco*	18	4	**27**	20	6	**31**	23	9	**36**	26	11	**32**	29	14	**17**	33	17	**7**	38	19	**2**	38	20	**3**	33	17	**7**	28	14	**20**	23	9	**37**	19	6	**28**
MOGADISHU, *Somalia*	30	23	**0**	30	23	**0**	31	24	**8**	32	26	**58**	32	25	**59**	29	23	**78**	28	23	**67**	28	23	**42**	29	23	**21**	30	24	**30**	31	24	**40**	30	24	**9**
MONROVIA, *Liberia*	30	23	**5**	29	23	**3**	31	23	**112**	31	23	**297**	30	22	**340**	27	23	**917**	27	22	**615**	27	23	**472**	27	22	**759**	28	22	**640**	29	23	**208**	30	23	**74**
NAIROBI, *Kenya*	25	12	**45**	26	13	**43**	25	14	**73**	24	14	**160**	22	13	**119**	21	12	**30**	21	11	**13**	21	11	**13**	24	11	**26**	24	13	**42**	23	13	**121**	23	13	**77**
N'DJAMENA, *Chad*	34	14	**0**	37	16	**0**	40	21	**0**	42	23	**8**	40	25	**31**	38	24	**62**	33	22	**150**	31	22	**215**	33	22	**91**	36	21	**22**	36	17	**0**	33	14	**0**
NIAMEY, *Niger*	34	14	**0**	37	18	**0**	41	22	**3**	42	25	**6**	41	27	**35**	38	25	**75**	34	23	**143**	32	23	**187**	34	23	**90**	38	23	**16**	38	18	**1**	34	15	**0**
NOUAKCHOTT, *Maurit.*	29	14	**1**	31	15	**3**	32	17	**1**	32	18	**1**	34	21	**1**	33	23	**3**	32	23	**13**	32	24	**104**	34	24	**23**	33	22	**10**	32	18	**3**	28	13	**1**
TIMBUKTU, *Mali*	31	13	**0**	34	14	**0**	38	19	**0**	42	22	**1**	43	26	**4**	43	27	**19**	39	25	**62**	36	24	**79**	39	24	**33**	40	23	**3**	37	18	**0**	32	13	**0**
TRIPOLI, *Libya*	16	8	**69**	17	9	**40**	19	11	**27**	22	14	**13**	24	16	**5**	27	19	**1**	29	22	**0**	30	22	**1**	29	22	**11**	27	18	**38**	23	14	**60**	18	9	**81**
TUNIS, *Tunisia*	14	6	**62**	16	7	**52**	18	8	**46**	21	11	**38**	24	13	**22**	29	17	**10**	32	20	**3**	33	21	**7**	31	19	**32**	25	15	**55**	20	11	**54**	16	7	**63**
WADI HALFA, *Sudan*	24	9	**0**	27	10	**0**	31	14	**0**	36	18	**0**	40	22	**1**	41	24	**0**	41	25	**1**	41	25	**0**	40	24	**0**	37	21	**0**	30	15	**0**	25	11	**0**
YAOUNDÉ, *Cameroon*	29	19	**26**	29	19	**55**	29	19	**140**	29	19	**193**	28	19	**216**	27	19	**163**	27	19	**62**	27	18	**80**	27	19	**216**	27	18	**292**	28	19	**120**	28	19	**28**
ZANZIBAR, *Tanzania*	32	24	**75**	33	24	**61**	33	25	**150**	30	25	**350**	29	24	**251**	28	23	**54**	28	22	**44**	28	22	**39**	29	22	**48**	30	23	**86**	32	24	**201**	32	24	**145**
ZOMBA, *Malawi*	27	18	**299**	27	18	**269**	26	18	**230**	26	17	**85**	24	14	**23**	22	12	**13**	22	12	**8**	24	13	**8**	27	15	**8**	29	18	**29**	29	19	**124**	27	18	**281**
ATLANTIC LANDS																																				
ASCENSION ISLAND	29	23	**4**	31	23	**8**	31	24	**23**	31	24	**27**	31	23	**10**	29	23	**14**	29	22	**12**	28	22	**10**	28	22	**8**	28	22	**7**	28	22	**4**	29	22	**3**
FALKLAND ISLANDS	13	6	**71**	13	5	**58**	12	4	**64**	9	3	**66**	7	1	**66**	5	-1	**53**	4	-1	**51**	5	-1	**51**	7	1	**38**	9	2	**41**	11	3	**51**	12	4	**71**
FUNCHAL, *Madeira Is.*	19	13	**87**	18	13	**88**	19	13	**79**	19	14	**43**	21	16	**22**	22	17	**9**	24	19	**2**	24	19	**3**	24	19	**27**	23	18	**85**	22	16	**106**	19	14	**87**
HAMILTON, *Bermuda Is.*	20	14	**112**	20	14	**119**	20	14	**122**	22	15	**104**	24	18	**117**	27	21	**112**	29	23	**114**	30	23	**137**	29	22	**132**	26	21	**147**	23	17	**127**	21	16	**119**
LAS PALMAS, *Canary Is.*	21	14	**28**	22	14	**21**	22	15	**15**	22	16	**10**	23	17	**3**	24	18	**1**	25	19	**1**	26	21	**0**	26	21	**6**	26	19	**18**	24	18	**37**	22	16	**32**
																													-3							
NUUK, *Greenland*	-7	-12	**36**	-7	-13	**43**	-4	-11	**41**	-1	-7	**30**	4	-2	**43**	8	1	**36**	11	3	**56**	11	3	**79**	6	1	**84**	2	16	**64**	-2	-7	**48**	-5	-10	**38**
PONTA DELGADA, *Azores*	17	12	**105**	17	11	**91**	17	12	**87**	18	12	**62**	20	13	**57**	22	15	**36**	25	17	**25**	26	18	**34**	25	17	**75**	22	24	**97**	20	14	**108**	18	12	**98**
PRAIA, *Cape Verde*	25	20	**1**	25	19	**2**	26	20	**0**	26	21	**0**	27	21	**0**	28	22	**0**	28	24	**7**	29	24	**63**	29	25	**88**	29	3	**44**	28	23	**15**	26	22	**5**
REYKJAVÍK, *Iceland*	2	-2	**86**	3	-2	**75**	4	-1	**76**	6	1	**56**	10	4	**42**	12	7	**45**	14	9	**51**	14	8	**62**	11	6	**71**	7	-13	**88**	4	0	**83**	2	-2	**84**
THULE, *Greenland*	-17	-27	**7**	-20	-29	**8**	-19	-28	**4**	-13	-23	**4**	-2	-9	**5**	5	-1	**6**	8	2	**14**	6	1	**17**	1	-6	**13**	-5		**11**	-11	-19	**11**	-18	-27	**5**
TRISTAN DA CUNHA	19	15	**103**	20	16	**110**	19	14	**133**	18	14	**137**	16	12	**153**	14	11	**153**	14	10	**54**	13	9	**162**	13	9	**157**	15	11	**148**	16	12	**124**	18	14	**131**
PACIFIC LANDS																																				
APIA, *Samoa*	30	24	**437**	29	24	**360**	30	23	**356**	30	24	**236**	29	23	**174**	29	23	**135**	29	23	**100**	29	24	**111**	29	23	**144**	29	24	**206**	30	23	**259**	29	23	**374**
AUCKLAND, *New Zealand*	23	16	**70**	23	16	**86**	22	15	**77**	19	13	**96**	17	11	**115**	14	9	**126**	13	8	**131**	14	8	**112**	16	9	**94**	17	11	**93**	19	12	**82**	21	14	**78**
DARWIN, *Australia*	32	25	**396**	32	25	**331**	33	25	**282**	33	24	**97**	33	23	**18**	31	21	**3**	31	19	**1**	32	21	**4**	33	23	**15**	34	25	**60**	34	26	**130**	33	26	**239**
DUNEDIN, *New Zealand*	19	10	**81**	19	10	**70**	17	9	**78**	15	7	**75**	12	5	**78**	9	4	**78**	9	3	**70**	11	3	**61**	13	5	**61**	15	6	**70**	17	7	**79**	18	9	**81**
GALÁPAGOS IS., *Ecuador*	30	22	**20**	30	24	**36**	31	24	**28**	31	24	**18**	30	23	**1**	28	22	**1**	27	21	**1**	27	19	**1**	27	19	**1**	27	19	**1**	27	20	**1**	28	21	**1**
GUAM, *Mariana Is.*	29	24	**138**	29	23	**116**	29	24	**121**	31	24	**108**	31	25	**164**	31	25	**150**	30	24	**274**	30	24	**368**	30	24	**374**	30	24	**334**	30	25	**231**	29	24	**160**
HOBART, *Tasmania*	22	12	**51**	22	12	**38**	20	11	**46**	17	9	**51**	14	7	**46**	12	5	**51**	11	4	**51**	13	5	**49**	15	6	**47**	17	8	**60**	19	9	**52**	21	11	**57**
MELBOURNE, *Australia*	26	14	**48**	26	14	**47**	24	13	**52**	20	11	**57**	17	8	**58**	14	7	**49**	13	6	**49**	15	6	**50**	17	8	**59**	19	9	**67**	22	11	**60**	24	12	**59**
NAHA, *Okinawa*	19	13	**125**	19	13	**126**	21	15	**159**	24	18	**165**	27	20	**252**	29	24	**280**	32	25	**178**	31	25	**270**	31	24	**175**	27	21	**165**	24	18	**133**	21	14	**111**
NOUMÉA, *N. Caledonia*	30	22	**111**	29	23	**130**	29	22	**155**	28	21	**121**	26	19	**106**	25	18	**107**	24	17	**91**	24	16	**73**	26	17	**56**	27	18	**53**	28	20	**55**	30	21	**77**
PAPEETE, *Tahiti*	32	22	**335**	32	22	**292**	32	22	**165**	32	22	**173**	31	21	**124**	30	21	**81**	30	20	**66**	30	20	**48**	30	21	**58**	31	21	**86**	31	22	**165**	31	22	**302**
PERTH, *Australia*	29	17	**9**	29	17	**13**	27	16	**19**	24	14	**45**	21	12	**122**	18	10	**182**	17	9	**174**	18	9	**136**	19	10	**80**	21	12	**53**	24	14	**21**	27	16	**13**
PORT MORESBY, *P.N.G.*	32	24	**179**	31	24	**196**	31	24	**190**	31	24	**120**	30	24	**65**	29	23	**39**	28	23	**27**	28	23	**26**	29	23	**33**	30	24	**35**	31	24	**56**	32	24	**121**
SUVA, *Fiji Islands*	30	23	**305**	30	23	**293**	30	23	**367**	29	23	**342**	28	22	**261**	27	21	**166**	26	20	**142**	26	20	**184**	27	21	**200**	27	21	**217**	28	22	**266**	29	23	**296**
SYDNEY, *Australia*	26	18	**103**	26	18	**111**	24	17	**131**	22	14	**130**	19	11	**123**	16	9	**129**	16	8	**103**	17	9	**80**	19	11	**69**	22	13	**83**	23	16	**81**	25	17	**78**
WELLINGTON, *N.Z.*	21	13	**79**	21	13	**80**	19	12	**85**	17	11	**98**	14	8	**121**	13	7	**124**	12	6	**139**	12	6	**121**	14	8	**99**	16	9	**105**	17	10	**88**	19	12	**90**

INDEX

PLACE-NAME INDEX

The following system is used to locate a place on a map in the *National Geographic Concise Atlas of the World.* The boldface type after an entry refers to the plate on which the map is found. The letter-number combination refers to the grid on which the particular place-name is located. The edge of each map is marked horizontally with numbers and vertically with letters. In between, at equally spaced intervals, are index squares (▪). If these ticks were connected with lines, each page would be divided into a grid. Take Amarillo, Texas, for example. The index entry reads "Amarillo, *Tex., U.S.* **40 G8**" On page 40, Abilene is located within the grid square where row G and column 8 intersect.

A place-name may appear on several maps, but the index lists only the best presentation. Usually, this means that a feature is indexed to the largest-scale map on which it appears in its entirety. (Note: Rivers are often labeled multiple times even on a single map. In such cases, the rivers are indexed to labels that are closest to their mouths.) The name of the country or continent in which a feature lies is shown in italic type and is usually abbreviated. (A full list of abbreviations appears on page 104.)

The index lists more than proper names. Some entries include a description, as in "Elba, *island, It.* **58 J6**" and "Amazon, *river, Braz.-Peru* **52 D8**." In languages other than English, the description of a physical feature may be part of the name; e.g., the "Berg" in "Swart Berg, *S. Af.* **81 Q7**," means "mountain." The Glossary of Foreign Terms on pages 106-107 translates such terms into English.

When a feature or place can be referred to by more than one name, both may appear in the index with cross-references. For example, the entry for Cairo, Egypt reads "Cairo *see* El Qâhira, *Egypt* **78 D9**. That entry is "El Qâhira (Cairo), *Egypt* **78 D9**."

Aansluit, *S. Af.* **79 P8**
Aba, *D.R.C.* **78 J9**
Aba, *Nig.* **78 J5**
Ābādān, *Iran* **68 G4**
Abaetetuba, *Braz.* **50 D9**
Abaiang, *island, Kiribati* **96 E6**
Abakan, *Russ.* **68 E9**
Abancay, *Peru* **50 G3**
Ābaya, Lake, *Eth.* **80 H10**
Abbot Ice Shelf, *Antarctica* **102 G3**
Abéché, *Chad* **78 G7**
Abemama, *island, Kiribati* **96 E6**
Abeokuta, *Nig.* **78 H4**
Aberdeen, *S. Dak., U.S.* **40 C9**
Aberdeen, *U.K.* **58 D4**
Aberdeen, *Wash., U.S.* **40 B3**
Abidjan, *Côte d'Ivoire* **78 J3**
Abilene, *Tex., U.S.* **40 H8**
Abingden Downs, *homestead, Qnsld., Austral.* **89 D12**
Abitibi, *river, Can.* **38 H8**
Abitibi, Lake, *Can.* **38 H8**
Abomey, *Benin* **78 H4**
Abou Deïa, *Chad* **78 H7**
Absalom, Mount, *Antarctica* **102 D7**
Absaroka Range, *Mont.-Wyo., U.S.* **42 D6**
Absheron Peninsula, *Azerb.* **61 H14**
Abu Ballâs, *peak, Egypt* **80 E8**
Abu Dhabi *see* Abū Ẕaby, *U.A.E.* **68 H4**
Abuja, *Nig.* **78 H5**
Abu Matariq, *Sudan* **78 H8**
Abunã, *Braz.* **50 F5**
Abū Ẕaby (Abu Dhabi), *U.A.E.* **68 H4**
Academy Glacier, *Antarctica* **102 F7**
Acapulco, *Mex.* **37 P5**
Acarigua, *Venez.* **50 A4**
Accra, *Ghana* **78 J4**
Achacachi, *Bol.* **50 G4**
Achinsk, *Russ.* **68 E9**
Aconcagua, Cerro, *Arg.-Chile* **53 L4**
A Coruña, *Sp.* **58 H2**
Acraman, Lake, *S. Austral., Austral.* **90 J9**
Açu, *Braz.* **50 E11**
Ada, *Okla., U.S.* **40 G9**
Adams, Mount, *Wash., U.S.* **42 B3**
'Adan, *Yemen* **68 J3**
Adana, *Turk.* **59 K11**
Adare, Cape, *Antarctica* **102 M9**
Adavale, *Qnsld., Austral.* **89 G12**
'Ad Dahnā', *region, Saudi Arabia* **70 G4**
Ad Dakhla, *W. Sahara* **78 E1**
Ad Dammām, *Saudi Arabia* **68 H4**
Ad Dawḩah (Doha), *Qatar* **68 H4**
Addis Ababa *see* Ādīs Ābeba, *Eth.* **78 H10**
Adelaide, *S. Austral., Austral.* **89 K10**
Adelaide Island, *Antarctica* **102 D2**
Adelaide River, *N. Terr., Austral.* **88 B7**
Adélie Coast, *Antarctica* **103 M12**
Aden, Gulf of, *Af.-Asia* **70 J3**
Adieu, Cape, *S. Austral., Austral.* **90 J8**
Ādīgrat, *Eth.* **78 G10**
Adirondack Mountains, *N.Y., U.S.* **43 C15**
Ādīs Ābeba (Addis Ababa), *Eth.* **78 H10**
Adıyaman, *Turk.* **59 K12**
Admiralty Island, *Alas., U.S.* **42 L5**
Admiralty Islands, *P.N.G.* **92 B6**
Admiralty Mountains, *Antarctica* **102 M9**
Adrar, *Alg.* **78 E4**
Adrar des Iforas, *mountains, Alg.-Mali* **80 F4**
Adriatic Sea, *Europe* **60 J7**
Ādwa, *Eth.* **78 G10**
Aegean Sea, *Gr.-Turk.* **60 K9**
Afghanistan, *Asia* **68 G6**
Afognak Island, *Alas., U.S.* **42 M3**
Afyon, *Turk.* **59 K10**
Agadez, *Niger* **78 G5**
Agadir, *Mor.* **78 D3**
Agats, *Indonesia* **92 C3**
Agattu, *island, U.S.* **39 R2**
Agen, *Fr.* **58 H4**
Agnes Creek, *homestead, S. Austral., Austral.* **88 G8**
Agnew, *W. Austral., Austral.* **88 H4**
Agra, *India* **68 H7**
Agrihan, *island, N. Mariana Is.* **96 C3**
Aguán, *river, Hond.* **39 P8**
Aguas Blancas, *Chile* **50 J4**
Aguascalientes, *Mex.* **37 N5**
Aguelhok, *Mali* **78 F4**
Aguja Point, *Peru* **52 E1**
Agulhas, Cape, *S. Af.* **81 R7**
Ahaggar Mountains, *Alg.* **80 F5**
Ahmadabad, *India* **68 J7**
Ahvāz, *Iran* **68 G4**
Aiken, *S.C., U.S.* **41 G14**
Aileron, *N. Terr., Austral.* **88 F8**
Ailinglapalap Atoll, *Marshall Is.* **96 E5**
Ailuk Atoll, *Marshall Is.* **96 D6**
Ainsworth, *Nebr., U.S.* **40 E8**
Aiquile, *Bol.* **50 H5**
Aïr (Azbine), *mountains, Niger* **80 F5**
Aitape, *P.N.G.* **92 B4**
Aitutaki Atoll, *Cook Is.* **96 G9**
Aix-en-Provence, *Fr.* **58 H5**
Aiyura, *P.N.G.* **92 C5**
Ajaccio, *Fr.* **58 J5**
Ajajú, *river, Braz.-Col.* **52 C3**
Ajdābiyā, *Lib.* **78 D7**
Ajo, *Ariz., U.S.* **40 H4**
Akbulak, *Russ.* **59 E14**
Akchâr, *region, Maurit.* **80 F1**
Akhḑar, Jabal al, *Lib.* **80 D7**
Akhtuba, *river, Russ.* **61 G13**
Akhtubinsk, *Russ.* **59 F13**
Akimiski Island, *Can.* **38 G8**
Akita, *Jap.* **69 E13**
Akjoujt, *Maurit.* **78 F2**
Akobo, *Sudan* **78 H9**
Akron, *Ohio, U.S.* **41 E13**
Aksu, *China* **68 G8**
Akureyri, *Ice.* **58 A3**
Al Farciya, *W. Sahara* **78 E2**
Alabama, *river, Ala., U.S.* **43 H12**
Alabama, *U.S.* **41 H12**
Alagoinhas, *Braz.* **50 F11**
Alajuela, *C.R.* **37 Q8**
Alakanuk, *Alas., U.S.* **40 K1**
Alamagan, *island, N. Mariana Is.* **96 D3**
Alamogordo, *N. Mex., U.S.* **40 H7**
Alamosa, *Colo., U.S.* **40 F7**
Åland Islands, *Fin.* **60 D8**
Alaska, *U.S.* **40 K3**
Alaska, Gulf of, *Alas., U.S.* **42 M4**
Alaska Peninsula, *Alas., U.S.* **42 M2**
Alaska Range, *Alas., U.S.* **42 L3**
Alatyr', *Russ.* **59 E12**
Albacete, *Sp.* **58 J3**
Albania, *Europe* **58 J8**
Albany, *Ga., U.S.* **41 H13**
Albany, *N.Y., U.S.* **41 D15**
Albany, *Oreg., U.S.* **40 C3**
Albany, *W. Austral., Austral.* **88 L3**
Al Başrah, *Iraq* **68 G4**
Albatross Bay, *Qnsld., Austral.* **91 B11**
Al Bayḑā' (Beida), *Lib.* **78 D7**
Albemarle Sound, *N.C., U.S.* **43 F15**
Albert, Lake, *D.R.C.-Uganda* **80 J9**
Albert, Lake, *S. Austral., Austral.* **91 L10**
Alberta, *Can.* **36 F4**
Albert Lea, *Minn., U.S.* **41 D10**
Albert Nile, *river, Uganda* **80 J9**
Albina Point, *Angola* **81 M6**
Alborán, *island, Sp.* **58 K2**
Alboran Sea, *Mor.-Sp.* **60 K2**
Ålborg, *Den.* **58 E6**
Albuquerque, *N. Mex., U.S.* **40 G6**
Albury, *N.S.W., AUSTRAL.* **89 L13**
Alcoota, *homestead, N. Terr., Austral.* **88 F9**
Aldabra Islands, *Seychelles* **81 L12**
Aldan, *river, Russ.* **71 D11**
Aldan, *Russ.* **69 D11**
Aleg, *Maurit.* **78 F2**
Alegrete, *Braz.* **51 K7**
Aleksandrovsk Sakhalinskiy, *Russ.* **69 D13**
Alençon, *Fr.* **58 G4**
Alenquer, *Braz.* **50 D7**
'Alenuihāhā Channel, *Hawaii, U.S.* **43 L12**
Aleppo *see* Ḩalab, *Syr.* **68 F3**
Alert, *Nunavut* **36 B7**
Ålesund, *Nor.* **58 C6**
Aleutian Islands, *U.S.* **39 R3**
Aleutian Range, *Alas., U.S.* **42 M2**
Alexander Archipelago, *Alas., U.S.* **42 M5**
Alexander Bay, *S. Af.* **79 Q7**
Alexander Island, *Antarctica* **102 E3**
Alexandra, *N.Z.* **92 N3**
Alexandria *see* El Iskandarîya, *Egypt* **78 D9**
Alexandria, *La., U.S.* **41 J11**
Alexandria, *Va., U.S.* **41 E15**
Alexandrina, Lake, *S. Austral., Austral.* **91 L10**
Algeciras, *Sp.* **58 K2**
Algena, *Eritrea* **78 F10**
Alger (Algiers), *Alg.* **78 C5**
Algeria, *Af.* **78 E4**
Algha, *Kaz.* **59 E14**
Algiers *see* Alger, *Alg.* **78 C5**
Algoa Bay, *S. Af.* **81 Q8**
Al Harūjal Aswad, *region, Lib.* **80 E7**
Al Ḩijāz, *region, Saudi Arabia* **68 G3**
Al Ḩudaydah, *Yemen* **68 H3**
Al Hufūf, *Saudi Arabia* **68 H4**
Āli Bayramlı, *Azerb.* **59 H14**
Alicante, *Sp.* **58 K3**
Alice, *Qnsld., Austral.* **89 F13**
Alice, *Tex., U.S.* **40 K9**
Alice Downs, *homestead, W. Austral., Austral.* **88 D6**
Alice Springs, *N. Terr., Austral.* **88 F8**
Alijos Rocks, *Mex.* **39 M3**
Al Jaghbūb, *Lib.* **78 D8**
Al Jawf, *Lib.* **78 E8**
Al Junaynah *see* Geneina, *Sudan* **78 G8**
Al Khums, *Lib.* **78 D6**
Al Kuwayt, *Kuwait* **68 G4**
Allahabad, *India* **68 J8**
Allakaket, *Alas., U.S.* **40 K3**
Allan Hills, *Antarctica* **102 K10**
Allanton, *N.Z.* **92 N4**
Allegheny, *river, N.Y.-Pa., U.S.* **43 D14**
Allegheny Mountains, *U.S.* **43 F14**
Alliance, *Nebr., U.S.* **40 E8**
Allison Peninsula, *Antarctica* **102 F3**
Almaden, *Qnsld., Austral.* **89 D13**
Al Madīnah (Medina), *Saudi Arabia* **68 G3**
Al Manāmah (Manama), *Bahrain* **68 H4**
Al Marj, *Lib.* **78 D7**
Almaty, *Kaz.* **68 F7**
Al Mawşil, *Iraq* **68 F4**
Almenara, *Braz.* **50 G10**
Almería, *Sp.* **58 K3**
Al'met'yevsk, *Russ.* **59 D13**
Al Mukallā, *Yemen* **68 J3**
Alor, *island, Indonesia* **96 F1**
Alor Setar, *Malaysia* **69 L10**
Aloysius, Mount, *W. Austral., Austral.* **90 G7**
Alpena, *Mich., U.S.* **41 C13**
Alpine, *Tex., U.S.* **40 J7**
Alps, *mountains, Europe* **60 H6**
Alroy Downs, *homestead, N. Terr., Austral.* **88 D9**
Alta, *Nor.* **58 A8**
Alta Floresta, *Braz.* **50 F7**
Altamaha, *river, Ga., U.S.* **43 H14**
Altamira, *Braz.* **50 D8**
Altar Desert, *Mex.-U.S.* **39 L3**
Altay, *China* **68 F9**
Altay, *Mongolia* **68 F9**
Altay Mountains, *Asia* **70 F9**
Altiplano, *plateau, Bol.-Peru* **52 G4**
Alto Araguaia, *Braz.* **50 G7**
Alto Garças, *Braz.* **50 G7**
Alto Molócuè, *Mozambique* **79 M10**
Alton, *Ill., U.S.* **41 F11**
Altoona, *Pa., U.S.* **41 E14**
Alto Parnaíba, *Braz.* **50 F9**
Altun Shan, *China* **70 G9**
Al Ubayyiḑ *see* El Obeid, *Sudan* **78 G9**
Al Uwaynāt, *Lib.* **78 E6**
Alvorada, *Braz.* **50 F8**
Amadeus, Lake, *N. Terr., Austral.* **90 F7**
Amadeus Depression, *N. Terr., Austral.* **90 G7**
Amadi, *Sudan* **78 J9**
Amamapare, *Indonesia* **92 C2**
Amami Ō Shima, *Jap.* **96 B1**
Amapá, *Braz.* **50 C8**
Amarillo, *Tex., U.S.* **40 G8**
Amata, *S. Austral., Austral.* **88 G8**
Amazon, *river, Braz.-Peru* **52 D8**
Amazon, Mouths of the, *Braz.* **52 C8**
Amazon, Source of the, *Peru* **52 G3**
Amazonas (Amazon), *river, Braz.-Peru* **50 D8**
Amazon Basin, *S. America* **52 D3**
Ambanja, *Madag.* **79 M12**
Ambarchik, *Russ.* **69 B11**
Ambargasta, Salinas de, *Arg.* **53 K5**
Ambon, *Indonesia* **69 L14**
Ambovombe, *Madag.* **79 P11**
Ambre, Cap d', *Madag.* **81 M12**
Ambriz, *Angola* **79 L6**
Ambunti, *P.N.G.* **92 B4**
American Falls Reservoir, *Idaho, U.S.* **42 D5**
American Highland, *Antarctica* **103 E13**
American Samoa, *Pac. Oc.* **96 G8**
Americus, *Ga., U.S.* **41 H13**
Amery Ice Shelf, *Antarctica* **103 E13**
Ames, *Iowa, U.S.* **41 E10**
Amguid, *Alg.* **78 E5**
Amiens, *Fr.* **58 F5**
Aminuis, *Namibia* **79 P7**
Amistad Reservoir, *Mex.-U.S.* **42 J8**
'Ammān, *Jordan* **68 F3**
Ammaroo, *homestead, N. Terr., Austral.* **88 E9**
Amolar, *Braz.* **50 H7**
Amos, *Que., Can.* **36 H8**
Amravati, *India* **68 J7**
Amritsar, *India* **68 H7**
Amsterdam, *Neth.* **58 F5**
Am Timan, *Chad* **78 H7**
Amu Darya, *river, Turkm.-Uzb.* **70 F6**
Amundsen Bay, *Antarctica* **103 B13**
Amundsen Gulf, *Can.* **38 D4**
Amundsen-Scott South Pole, *station, Antarctica* **102 F8**
Amundsen Sea, *Antarctica* **102 H3**
Amur, *river, China-Russ.* **71 D12**
Amur-Onon, Source of the, *Mongolia* **71 F10**
Anaa, *island, Fr. Polynesia* **97 G10**
Anadyr', *river, Russ.* **71 B12**
Anadyr', *Russ.* **69 A12**
Anadyr, Gulf of, *Russ.* **71 A12**
Anadyrskiy Zaliv (Gulf of Anadyr), *Russ.* **69 A12**
Analalava, *Madag.* **79 M12**
Anápolis, *Braz.* **50 G8**
Anatahan, *island, N. Mariana Is.* **96 D3**
Anatolia (Asia Minor), *region, Turk.* **70 E3**
Anatom, *island, Vanuatu* **96 H6**
Anchorage, *Alas., U.S.* **40 L3**
Ancona, *It.* **58 J6**
Ancud, *Chile* **51 N4**
Andaman Islands, *India* **70 K9**
Andaman Sea, *Asia* **70 K10**
Andamooka, *S. Austral., Austral.* **88 J10**
Anderson, *S.C., U.S.* **41 G13**
Andes, *mountains, S. America* **52 G3**
Andoany (Hell-Ville), *Madag.* **79 M12**
Andoas, *Peru* **50 D2**
Andorra, *Europe* **58 J4**
Andorra, *Andorra* **58 J4**
Andradina, *Braz.* **50 H8**
Andreanof Islands, *U.S.* **39 R3**
Androka, *Madag.* **79 P11**
Andros Island, *Bahamas* **39 M9**
Anefis I-n-Darane, *Mali* **78 F4**
Aneto, Pico de, *Sp.* **60 H4**
Aney, *Niger* **78 F6**
Angamos Point, *Chile* **52 J4**
Angara, *river, Russ.* **70 E9**
Angarsk, *Russ.* **68 E10**
Angel Falls, *Venez.* **52 B5**
Angermanälven, *river, Sweden* **60 C7**
Angers, *Fr.* **58 G4**
Anglem, Mount, *N.Z.* **92 P3**
Ango, *D.R.C.* **78 J8**
Angoche, *Mozambique* **79 M11**
Angola, *Af.* **79 M7**
Angora *see* Ankara, *Turk.* **59 J11**
Angoram, *P.N.G.* **92 B5**
Aniak, *Alas., U.S.* **40 L2**
Anil, *Braz.* **50 D10**
Anixab, *Namibia* **79 N6**
Ankara (Angora), *Turk.* **59 J11**
Ann, Cape, *Antarctica* **103 B14**
Ann, Cape, *Mass., U.S.* **43 D16**
Annaba, *Alg.* **78 C5**
An Nafūd, *region, Saudi Arabia* **70 G3**
An Najaf, *Iraq* **68 G4**
Annam Cordillera, *Laos-Viet.* **71 J11**
Anna Plains, *homestead, W. Austral., Austral.* **88 E4**
Annapolis, *Md., U.S.* **41 E15**
Ann Arbor, *Mich., U.S.* **41 D13**
An Nāşirīyah, *Iraq* **68 G4**
Annean, Lake, *W. Austral., Austral.* **90 H3**
Anningie, *homestead, N. Terr., Austral.* **88 E8**
Annitowa, *homestead, N. Terr., Austral.* **88 E9**
Annobón, *island, Eq. Guinea* **81 K5**
Anqing, *China* **69 G12**
Anshan, *China* **69 F12**
Anshun, *China* **69 H11**
Anson Bay, *N. Terr., Austral.* **90 B7**
Ansudu, *Indonesia* **92 B3**
Antalya, *Turk.* **59 K10**
Antananarivo, *Madag.* **79 N12**
Antarctic Peninsula, *Antarctica* **102 C2**
Anthony Lagoon, *homestead, N. Terr., Austral.* **88 D9**
Anticosti Island, *Can.* **38 G10**
Antigua and Barbuda, *N. America* **37 N12**
Antipodes Islands, *N.Z.* **96 L6**
Antofagasta, *Chile* **50 J4**
Antsirabe, *Madag.* **79 N12**
Antsirañana, *Madag.* **79 M12**
Antwerpen, *Belg.* **58 F5**
Anuta (Cherry Island), *Solomon Is.* **96 G6**
Anvers Island, *Antarctica* **102 C2**
Anvik, *Alas., U.S.* **40 K2**
Anxi, *China* **68 G9**
Aomori, *Jap.* **69 E13**
Aoulef, *Alg.* **78 E4**
Aozou, *Chad* **78 F7**
Aozou Strip, *Chad* **78 F7**
Apalachee Bay, *Fla., U.S.* **43 J13**
Apalachicola, *Fla., U.S.* **41 J13**
Apatity, *Russ.* **58 B9**
Apatzingán, *Mex.* **37 N5**
Apennines, *mountians, It.* **60 H6**
Apennini *see* Apennines, *mountains, It.* **58 H6**
Apia, *Samoa* **96 G7**
Apollo Bay, *Vic., Austral.* **89 M12**
Appalachian Mountains, *U.S.* **43 G13**
Appalachian Plateau, *U.S.* **43 F13**
Appleton, *Wis., U.S.* **41 D11**
Apucarana, *Braz.* **50 J8**
Apure, *river, Venez.* **52 B4**
Apurímac, *river, Peru* **52 G3**
Aqaba, Gulf of, *Egypt-Saudi Arabia* **80 E9**
Aqtaū, *Kaz.* **59 G14**
Aqtöbe, *Kaz.* **59 E14**
Aquidauana, *Braz.* **50 H7**
Aquitaine Basin, *Fr.* **60 H4**
Arabian Peninsula, *Asia* **70 G3**
Arabian Sea, *Asia* **70 K5**
Arabs Gulf, *Egypt* **80 D8**
Aracaju, *Braz.* **50 F11**
Arad, *Rom.* **58 H8**
Arafura Sea, *Asia-Austal.* **71 L16**
Aragarças, *Braz.* **50 G8**
Araguaia, *river, Braz.* **52 E8**
Araguari, *Braz.* **50 H9**
Araguatins, *Braz.* **50 E9**
Arak, *Alg.* **78 E5**
Arāk, *Iran* **68 G4**
Aral, *Kaz.* **59 E16**
Aral Sea, *Kaz.-Uzb.* **70 F6**
Aralsor, Lake, *Kaz.* **61 F13**
Aramac, *Qnsld., Austral.* **89 F13**
Aransas Pass, *Tex., U.S.* **40 K9**
Araouane, *Mali* **78 F3**
Arapiraca, *Braz.* **50 F11**
Araracuara, *Col.* **50 D3**
Araraquara, *Braz.* **50 H9**
Ararat, Mount, *Turk.* **70 F4**
Arauca, *Col.* **50 B4**
Arauco Gulf, *Chile* **53 M4**
Ārba Minch', *Eth.* **78 H10**
Arckaringa Creek, *S. Austral., Austral.* **90 H9**
Arco Pass, *Arg.-Chile* **53 M4**
Arcoverde, *Braz.* **50 F11**
Arctic Bay, *Nunavut* **36 D7**
Arctowski, *station, Antarctica* **102 B1**
Ardabīl, *Iran* **68 F5**
Ardennes, *mountains, Belg.* **60 G5**
Ardmore, *Okla., U.S.* **40 H9**
Areia Branca, *Braz.* **50 E11**
Arena, Point, *Calif., U.S.* **42 E2**
Arenápolis, *Braz.* **50 G7**
Arendal, *Nor.* **58 D6**
Arequipa, *Peru* **50 G4**
Argadargada, *homestead, N. Terr., Austral.* **88 E10**
Argentina, *S. America* **51 Q5**
Argentina Range, *Antarctica* **102 E7**
Argentino, Lake, *Arg.* **53 Q4**
Argun, *river, China-Russ.* **71 E11**
Argus, Dome, *Antarctica* **103 F11**
Argyle, Lake, *W. Austral., Austral.* **90 C7**
Århus, *Den.* **58 E6**
Arica, *Chile* **50 H4**
Arid, Cape, *W. Austral., Austral.* **90 K5**
Aripuanã, *Braz.* **50 F6**
Ariquemes, *Braz.* **50 F5**
Arizona, *U.S.* **40 G5**
Arkadelphia, *Ark., U.S.* **41 H10**
Arkansas, *river, U.S.* **43 G11**
Arkansas, *U.S.* **41 G11**
Arkansas City, *Kans., U.S.* **40 G9**
Arkhangel'sk, *Russ.* **59 B10**
Armavir, *Russ.* **59 H12**
Armenia, *Asia* **59 J13**
Armenia, *Col.* **50 C2**
Armidale, *N.S.W., AUSTRAL.* **89 J15**
Armorican Massif, *Fr.* **60 G4**
Arnhem, Cape, *N. Terr., Austral.* **90 B9**
Arno Atoll, *Marshall Is.* **96 E6**
Arno Bay, *S. Austral., Austral.* **88 K9**
Arorae, *island, Kiribati* **96 F6**
Arowhana, *peak, N.Z.* **92 H7**
Arqalyq, *Kaz.* **59 D16**
Arrabury, *homestead, Qnsld., Austral.* **89 G11**
Arraias, *Braz.* **50 F9**
Ar Riyāḑ (Riyadh), *Saudi Arabia* **68 H4**
Arsuk, *Greenland* **36 E10**
Artemisa, *Cuba* **37 N8**
Artesia, *N. Mex., U.S.* **40 H7**
Arthur's Pass, *N.Z.* **92 L4**
Artigas, *station, Antarctica* **102 B1**
Artigas, *Uru.* **51 K7**
Aru, Kepulauan (Aru Islands), *Indonesia* **69 L15**
Aruanã, *Braz.* **50 G8**
Aruba, *island, Neth. Antilles* **39 P11**
Aru Islands, *Indonesia* **71 L15**
Arusha, *Tanzania* **79 K10**
Aruwimi, *river, D.R.C.* **80 J8**
Arviat, *Nunavut* **36 F6**
Arvidsjaur, *Sweden* **58 B8**
Arvon, Mount, *Mich., U.S.* **43 C11**
Arzamas, *Russ.* **59 E12**
Asahikawa, *Jap.* **69 E13**
Asbest, *Russ.* **59 C14**
Ascención, *Bol.* **50 G5**
Ascension, *island, Atl. Oc.* **81 L1**
Āsela, *Eth.* **78 H10**
Ashburton, *river, W. Austral., Austral.* **90 F2**
Ashburton, *N.Z.* **92 M4**
Ashburton Downs, *homestead, W. Austral., Austral.* **88 F2**
Asheville, *N.C., U.S.* **41 G13**
Ashgabat, *Turkm.* **68 G5**
Ashland, *Ky., U.S.* **41 F13**
Ashland, *Oreg., U.S.* **40 D3**
Ashley, *N. Dak., U.S.* **40 C9**
Ashmore Islands, *W. Austral., Austral.* **90 B4**
Ash Shihr, *Yemen* **68 J3**
Ashtabula, Lake, *N. Dak., U.S.* **42 C9**
Asia, Kepulauan, *Indonesia* **96 E2**
Asia Minor *see* Anatolia, *region, Turk.* **70 E3**
Asīr, *region, Saudi Arabia* **68 H3**
Asmara, *Eritrea* **78 G10**
Āsosa, *Eth.* **78 H10**
Aspiring, Mount, *N.Z.* **92 M3**
Assab, *Eritrea* **78 G11**
Assal, Lake, *Djibouti* **80 G11**
As Sidr, *Lib.* **78 D7**
Astana, *Kaz.* **68 E7**
Astoria, *Oreg., U.S.* **40 B3**
Astra, *Arg.* **51 P5**
Astrakhan', *Russ.* **59 G13**
Asunción, *Para.* **50 J7**
Asuncion, *island, N. Mariana Is.* **96 C3**
Aswân, *Egypt* **78 E9**
Asyûţ, *Egypt* **78 E9**
Ata, *island, Tonga* **96 H7**
Atacama, Puna de, *Arg.* **52 J5**
Atacama Desert, *Chile* **52 H4**
Atafu, *island, Tokelau* **96 F7**
Atakpamé, *Togo* **78 H4**
Atalaya, *Peru* **50 F3**
Atar, *Maurit.* **78 F2**
Atbara, *river, Sudan* **80 G10**
Atbara, *Sudan* **78 F9**
Atbasar, *Kaz.* **59 C16**
Atchafalaya Bay, *La., U.S.* **43 J11**
Athabasca, *river, Can.* **38 G4**
Athabasca, Lake, *Can.* **38 F5**
Athens, *Ga., U.S.* **41 G13**
Athens *see* Athína, *Gr.* **58 K9**
Atherton Tableland, *Qnsld., Austral.* **91 D13**
Athína (Athens), *Gr.* **58 K9**
Atico, *Peru* **50 G3**
Atiu, *island, Cook Is.* **96 H9**
Atka, *island, Alas., U.S.* **37 R3**
Atlanta, *Ga., U.S.* **41 H13**
Atlantic City, *N.J., U.S.* **41 E15**
Atlas Mountains, *Alg.-Mor.* **80 D3**
Atol das Rocas, *island, Braz.* **52 E12**
Atqasuk, *Alas., U.S.* **40 J2**
Aţ Ţā'if, *Saudi Arabia* **68 H3**
Attawapiskat, *river, Can.* **38 G7**
Attawapiskat, *Ont., Can.* **36 G7**
Attu, *island, U.S.* **39 R2**
Attu, *Greenland* **36 D9**
Atyraū, *Kaz.* **59 F14**
Auas Mountains, *Namibia* **81 P7**
Auburn, *homestead, Qnsld., Austral.* **89 G15**
Auckland, *N.Z.* **92 H5**
Auckland Islands, *N.Z.* **96 L5**
Augathella, *Qnsld., Austral.* **89 G13**
Augsburg, *Ger.* **58 G6**
Augusta, *Ga., U.S.* **41 H14**
Augusta, *Me., U.S.* **41 C16**
Augustus, Mount, *W. Austral., Austral.* **90 G2**
Augustus Downs, *homestead, Qnsld., Austral.* **89 D11**
Auld, Lake, *W. Austral., Austral.* **90 F5**
Aurora, *Colo., U.S.* **40 F7**
Aurora, *Ill., U.S.* **41 E12**
Aurukun, *Qnsld., Austral.* **89 B12**
Austin, *Minn., U.S.* **41 D10**
Austin, *Tex., U.S.* **40 J9**
Austin, Lake, *W. Austral., Austral.* **90 H3**
Australian Alps, *mountains, Vic., Austral.* **91 M13**
Australian Capital Territory, *Austral.* **89 L14**
Austral Islands (Tubuai Islands), *Fr. Polynesia* **96 H9**
Austria, *Europe* **58 H6**
Avalon Peninsula, *Can.* **38 G11**
Aveiro, *Braz.* **50 D7**
Aviator Glacier, *Antarctica* **102 L9**
Avon Downs, *homestead, N. Terr., Austral.* **89 E10**
Awarua Bay, *N.Z.* **92 M3**
Awbārī, Şaʻrā', *Lib.* **80 E6**
Awjilah, *Lib.* **78 E7**
Awsard, *W. Sahara* **78 E2**
Axel Heiberg Island, *Can.* **38 B6**
Ayacucho, *Peru* **50 G3**
Ayaköz, *Kaz.* **68 F8**
Ayan, *Russ.* **69 D12**
Aydın, *Turk.* **58 K10**
Ayers Rock, *N. Terr., Austral.* **90 G7**
'Ayoûnel el'Atroûs, *Maurit.* **78 G2**
Ayr, *Qnsld., Austral.* **89 E14**
Azbine *see* Aïr, *mountains, Niger* **80 F5**
Azerbaijan, *Asia-Europe* **59 H14**
Azov, Sea of, *Russ.-Ukr.* **61 H11**
Azov Upland, *Ukr.* **61 G11**
Azuero Peninsula, *Pan.* **39 Q9**
Azul, *Arg.* **51 M6**
Azzel Matti, Sebkha, *Alg.* **80 E4**

Baardheere, *Somalia* **78 J11**
Babahoyo, *Ecua.* **50 D2**
Bab al Mandab, *strait, Af.-Asia* **80 G11**
Babanūsah, *Sudan* **78 H8**
Babar, *island, Indonesia* **96 F1**
Babati, *Tanzania* **79 K10**
Babayevo, *Russ.* **59 D10**
Babelthuap, *island, Palau* **71 J15**
Bābol, *Iran* **68 F5**
Babruysk, *Belarus* **58 F9**
Babuyan Islands, *Philippines* **69 J13**
Bacabal, *Braz.* **50 D9**
Bacău, *Rom.* **58 H9**
Back, *river, Can.* **38 E5**
Backbone Mountain, *Md., U.S.* **43 E14**
Bacolod, *Philippines* **69 K13**

Badajoz, Sp. 58 J2
Badlands, region, N. Dak., U.S. 42 C8
Badogo, Mali 78 H2
Baetic Mountains, Sp. 60 K2
Baffin Bay, Can.-Greenland 38 C8
Baffin Bay, Tex., U.S. 42 K9
Baffin Island, Can. 38 D7
Bafing, river, Guinea-Mali 80 G2
Bagé, Braz. 51 L7
Baghdād, Iraq 68 F4
Baguio, Philippines 69 J13
Bagzane, Mount, Niger 80 F5
Bahama Islands, Atl. Oc. 39 M9
Bahamas, N. America 37 M9
Bahawalpur, Pak. 68 H7
Bahia see Salvador, Braz. 50 G11
Bahía Blanca, Arg. 51 M6
Bahía Laura, Arg. 51 Q5
Bahir Dar, Eth. 78 G10
Bahrain, Asia 68 H4
Bahr el 'Arab, river, Sudan 80 H8
Baía dos Tigres, Angola 79 M6
Baia Mare, Rom. 58 G9
Baïbokoum, Chad 78 H6
Baicheng, China 69 F12
Baidoa see Baydhabo, Somalia 78 J11
Baie-Comeau, Que., Can. 36 G9
Baikal, Lake, Russ. 71 E10
Baile Átha Cliath (Dublin), Ire. 58 E3
Baird Mountains, Alas., U.S. 42 J2
Bairiki see Tarawa, Kiribati 96 E6
Bairnsdale, Vic., Austral. 89 M13
Baja California, region, Mex. 39 L3
Baker, river, Chile 53 Q4
Baker, Mont., U.S. 40 C7
Baker, Mount, Wash., U.S. 42 B3
Baker City, Oreg., U.S. 40 C4
Baker Island, Pac. Oc. 96 E7
Baker Lake, W. Austral., Austral. 90 G6
Baker Lake, Nunavut 36 E6
Bakersfield, Calif., U.S. 40 F3
Bakı (Baku), Azerb. 59 H14
Bakony, mountains, Hung. 60 H7
Baku see Bakı, Azerb. 59 H14
Bakutis Coast, Antarctica 102 J4
Balaklava, S. Austral., Austral. 89 K10
Balakovo, Russ. 59 E13
Balashov, Russ. 59 F12
Balaton, lake, Hung. 60 H7
Balbina, Represa da (Balbina Reservoir), Braz. 50 D6
Balbina Reservoir, Braz. 52 D6
Balcarce, Arg. 51 M6
Balclutha, N.Z. 92 N3
Bald Mountain, Nev., U.S. 42 F4
Baldy Peak, Ariz., U.S. 42 G6
Balearic Islands, Sp. 60 K4
Balearic Sea, Sp. 60 K4
Baleia Point, Braz. 52 H10
Balfes Creek, Qnsld., Austral. 89 E13
Balfour Downs, homestead, W. Austral., Austral. 88 F4
Balgo, W. Austral., Austral. 88 E6
Bali, island, Indonesia 71 M13
Balıkesir, Turk. 58 K10
Balikpapan, Indonesia 69 L13
Balimo, P.N.G. 92 D4
Balkan Mountains, Bulg. 60 J9
Balkan Peninsula, Europe 60 J9
Balkhash, Lake, Kaz. 70 F7
Balladonia, homestead, W. Austral., Austral. 88 K5
Ballarat, Vic., Austral. 89 M12
Ballard, Lake, W. Austral., Austral. 90 J4
Ballina, N.S.W., AUSTRAL. 89 J15
Ball's Pyramid, island, Austral. 96 J4
Balmaceda, Chile 51 P4
Balqash, Kaz. 68 F7
Balqash Köli see Balkhash, Lake, Kaz. 68 F7
Balranald, N.S.W., AUSTRAL. 89 K12
Balsas, river, Mex. 39 P5
Bălţi, Moldova 58 G9
Baltic Plains, Europe 60 E8
Baltic Sea, Europe 60 E8
Baltimore, Md., U.S. 41 E15
Baluchistan, region, Iran-Pak. 68 H5
Bamaga, Qnsld., Austral. 89 A12
Bamako, Mali 78 G3
Bambari, Cen. Af. Rep. 78 J7
Bambaroo, Qnsld., Austral. 89 D13
Bamboo, W. Austral., Austral. 88 E3
Bamenda, Cameroon 78 J5
Bamyili-Beswick, N. Terr., Austral. 88 C8
Banaba (Ocean Island), Kiribati 96 F6
Banana, Qnsld., Austral. 89 G14
Banas, Râs, Egypt 80 E10
Banda Aceh, Indonesia 68 L9
Bandar-e 'Abbās, Iran 68 H5
Bandar-e Būshehr, Iran 68 G4
Bandar Lampung, Indonesia 69 M11
Bandar Seri Begawan, Brunei 69 L12
Banda Sea, Indonesia 71 L14
Bandeira, Pico de la, Braz. 52 H10
Banderas Bay, Mex. 39 N4
Bandundu, D.R.C. 79 K7
Bandung, Indonesia 69 M11
Banff, Alta., Can. 36 G4
Bangalore, India 68 K7
Bangassou, Cen. Af. Rep. 78 J8
Banghāzī (Benghazi), Lib. 78 D7
Bangka, island, Indonesia 71 M11
Bangkok see Krung Thep, Thai. 69 K10
Bangladesh, Asia 68 J9
Bangor, Me., U.S. 41 C16
Bangui, Cen. Af. Rep. 78 J7
Bangweulu, Lake, Zambia 81 L9
Bani, river, Mali 80 G3
Banī Walīd, Lib. 78 D6
Banja Luka, Bosn. Herzg. 58 H7
Banjarmasin, Indonesia 69 M12
Banjul, Gambia 78 G1
Banka Banka, homestead, N. Terr., Austral. 88 D9
Banks Island, Can. 38 C5
Banks Islands, Vanuatu 96 G5
Banks Peninsula, N.Z. 92 M5
Banzare Coast, Antarctica 103 K13
Baoding, China 69 G11
Baoji, China 69 G11
Baoro, Cen. Af. Rep. 78 J6
Baotou, China 69 G11
Baraawe, Somalia 78 J11
Barahona, Dom. Rep. 37 N10
Baranavichy, Belarus 58 F9
Baranof Island, Alas., U.S. 42 M5
Barataria Bay, La., U.S. 43 J11
Barbacena, Braz. 50 H9
Barbados, N. America 37 N12
Barcaldine, Qnsld., Austral. 89 F13
Barcelona, Sp. 58 J4
Barcelona, Venez. 50 A5
Barcelos, Braz. 50 D5
Barcoo, river, Qnsld., Austral. 91 G12
Bardas Blancas, Arg. 51 M4
Bardoc, W. Austral., Austral. 88 J4
Barents Sea, Russ. 61 A10
Bari, It. 58 J7
Barinas, Venez. 50 B4
Barisan Mountains, Indonesia 71 M11
Barkley, Lake, Ky.-Tenn., U.S. 43 F12
Barkly Tableland, N. Terr.-Qnsld., Austral. 90 D10
Barlee, Lake, W. Austral., Austral. 90 J3
Barnaul, Russ. 68 E8
Barquisimeto, Venez. 50 A4
Barra do Bugres, Braz. 50 G7
Barra do São Manuel, Braz. 50 E6
Barrancabermeja, Col. 50 B3
Barranquilla, Col. 50 A3
Barra Point, Mozambique 81 P10
Barras, Col. 50 D3
Barreiras, Braz. 50 F9
Barren Islands, Madag. 81 N11
Barringun, N.S.W., AUSTRAL. 89 H13
Barrow, Alas., U.S. 40 H3
Barrow, Point, Alas., U.S. 42 H3
Barrow Creek, N. Terr., Austral. 88 E9
Barrow Island, W. Austral., Austral. 90 E1
Barrytown, N.Z. 92 L4
Bartle Frere, peak, Qnsld., Austral. 91 D13
Bartlesville, Okla., U.S. 40 G9
Barton Siding, S. Austral., Austral. 88 J8
Barwon, river, N.S.W., AUSTRAL. 91 J13
Basaseachic Falls, Mex. 39 M4
Bascuñán, Cape, Chile 53 K4
Basel, Switz. 58 G5
Bass, Îlots de see Marotiri, Fr. Polynesia 97 H10
Bassas da India, islands, Mozambique Chan. 81 N10
Basseterre, St. Kitts and Nevis 37 N12
Bassikounou, Maurit. 78 G3
Bass Strait, Tas., Austral. 91 L15
Bastia, Fr. 58 J6
Bata, Eq. Guinea 78 J5
Batagay, Russ. 69 C11
Batan Islands, Philippines 69 H13
Bathurst, N.S.W., AUSTRAL. 89 K14
Bathurst Island, Can. 38 C6
Bathurst Island, N. Terr., Austral. 90 A7
Batna, Alg. 78 C5
Baton Rouge, La., U.S. 41 J11
Battambang, Cambodia 69 K10
Batu, peak, Eth. 80 H10
Bat'umi, Ga. 59 H13
Bauchi, Nig. 78 H5
Bauchi Plateau, Nig. 80 H5
Baudó, Serranía de, Col. 52 B2
Bauru, Braz. 50 J8
Baús, Braz. 50 H8
Bawku, Ghana 78 H4
Bayan Har Shan, China 70 G9
Bay City, Mich., U.S. 41 D13
Bay City, Tex., U.S. 41 K10
Baydhabo (Baidoa), Somalia 78 J11
Bay Islands, Hond. 39 P8
Baykal, Ozero (Lake Baikal), Russ. 69 E10
Bay of Whales, station, Antarctica 102 K7
Bayonne, Fr. 58 H3
Baytown, Tex., U.S. 41 J10
Beagle Bay, W. Austral., Austral. 88 D4
Beardmore Glacier, Antarctica 102 H8
Bear Paw Mountains, Mont., U.S. 42 B6
Bear River Range, Idaho-Utah, U.S. 42 D5
Beatrice, Nebr., U.S. 40 E9
Beatty, Nev., U.S. 40 F4
Beaufort, S.C., U.S. 41 H14
Beaufort Sea, Arctic Oc. 42 H3
Beaufort West, S. Af. 79 Q8
Beaumont, Tex., U.S. 41 J10
Beaver, Alas., U.S. 40 K3
Beaver Glacier, Antarctica 103 C13
Bebiram, Indonesia 92 B1
Béchar, Alg. 78 D4
Beckley, W. Va., U.S. 41 F14
Beddouza, Cape, Mor. 80 D3
Bedford, Cape, Qnsld., Austral. 91 C13
Bedourie, Qnsld., Austral. 89 F11
Beenleigh, Qnsld., Austral. 89 H15
Beetaloo, homestead, N. Terr., Austral. 88 D8
Beethoven Peninsula, Antarctica 102 E3
Beeville, Tex., U.S. 40 K9
Bega, N.S.W., AUSTRAL. 89 M14
Behagle see Laï, Chad 78 H7
Beida see Al Bayḍā', Lib. 78 D7
Beijing, China 69 F11
Beira, Mozambique 79 N10
Beirut see Beyrouth, Leb. 68 F3
Bei Shan, China 70 G9
Beitbridge, Zimb. 79 N9
Beja, Tun. 78 C6
Belarus, Europe 58 F9
Bela Vista, Para. 50 H7
Belaya, river, Russ. 61 D13
Belaya Gora, Russ. 69 B11
Belcher Islands, Can. 38 G8
Beledweyne, Somalia 78 J11
Belele, homestead, W. Austral., Austral. 88 G3
Belém, Braz. 50 D9
Belen, N. Mex., U.S. 40 G6
Bélep, Îles, New Caledonia 96 G5
Belfast, U.K. 58 E4
Belgica Mountains, Antarctica 103 B11
Belgium, Europe 58 F5
Belgorod, Russ. 59 F11
Belgrade see Beograd, Serbia and Montenegro 58 H8
Belgrano II, station, Antarctica 102 D6
Belize, N. America 37 P7
Belize City, Belize 37 P7
Bella Bella, B.C., Can. 36 G3
Bella Coola, B.C., Can. 36 G3
Belle Fourche, river, S. Dak.-Wyo., U.S. 42 D7
Belle Fourche, S. Dak., U.S. 40 D8
Belle Isle, Strait of, Can. 38 G10
Belleville, Ill., U.S. 41 F11
Bellingham, Wash., U.S. 40 B3
Bellingshausen, station, Antarctica 102 C1
Bellingshausen Sea, Antarctica 102 F2
Bello, Col. 50 B2
Belmonte, Braz. 50 G11
Belmopan, Belize 37 P7
Belo Horizonte, Braz. 50 H9
Belomorsk, Russ. 58 B10
Beloretsk, Russ. 59 D14
Belo-Tsiribihina, Madag. 79 N11
Beloye, Lake, Russ. 61 D10
Beloye More (White Sea), Russ. 59 B10
Beloye Ozero (Lake Beloye), Russ. 59 D10
Belozersk, Russ. 59 D10
Belukha, peak, Kaz.-Russ. 70 F8
Belyando, river, Qnsld., Austral. 91 F13
Bemaraha Plateau, Madag. 81 N11
Bembe, Angola 79 L6
Bemidji, Minn., U.S. 41 C10
Benadir, region, Somalia 80 J11
Bendena, homestead, Qnsld., Austral. 89 H13
Bender Cassim see Boosaaso, Somalia 78 G12
Bendigo, Vic., Austral. 89 L12
Benevento, It. 58 J7
Bengal, Bay of, Asia 70 K8
Benghazi see Banghāzī, Lib. 78 D7
Bengkulu, Indonesia 69 M11
Bengo Bay, Angola 81 L6
Benguela, Angola 79 M6
Beni, river, Bol. 52 F5
Beni Abbes, Alg. 78 D4
Beni Mazâr, Egypt 78 E9
Benin, Af. 78 H4
Benin, Bight of, Af. 80 J4
Benin City, Nig. 78 H5
Beni Suef, Egypt 78 D9
Benlidi, Qnsld., Austral. 89 G12
Ben Nevis, peak, U.K. 60 D4
Benneydale, N.Z. 92 J6
Bensbach, P.N.G. 92 D4
Benson, Ariz., U.S. 40 H5
Bentiu, Sudan 78 H9
Benue, river, Nig. 80 H5
Beograd (Belgrade), Serbia and Montenegro 58 H8
Berau, Teluk, Indonesia 92 B1
Berber, Sudan 78 F9
Berbera, Somalia 78 H11
Berbérati, Cen. Af. Rep. 78 J6
Berdyans'k, Ukr. 59 G11
Berdychiv, Ukr. 58 G9
Bereina, P.N.G. 92 D5
Berens River, Manitoba, Can. 36 G6
Bereznik, Russ. 59 C11
Berezniki, Russ. 59 C13
Bergamo, It. 58 H6
Bergen, Nor. 58 D6
Beringovskiy, Russ. 69 A12
Bering Sea, Asia-N. America 39 Q3
Bering Strait, Asia-N. America 38 B2
Berkner Island, Antarctica 102 D6
Berlevåg, Nor. 58 A9
Berlin, Ger. 58 F7
Berlin, Mount, Antarctica 102 J5
Bermuda Islands, Atl. Oc. 39 K11
Bern, Switz. 58 G5
Bertholet, Cape, W. Austral., Austral. 90 D4
Bertoua, Cameroon 78 J6
Beru, island, Kiribati 96 F6
Besalampy, Madag. 79 M11
Besançon, Fr. 58 G5
Bessemer, Ala., U.S. 41 H12
Bethanie, Namibia 79 P7
Bethel, Alas., U.S. 40 L2
Betoota, Qnsld., Austral. 89 G11
Betpaqdala, region, Kaz. 70 F7
Betsiboka, river, Madag. 81 M12
Beyla, Guinea 78 H2
Beyneu, Kaz. 59 F15
Beyrouth (Beirut), Leb. 68 F3
Bhopal, India 68 J7
Bhutan, Asia 68 H9
Biak, island, Indonesia 69 K15
Biak, Indonesia 92 A2
Białystok, Pol. 58 F8
Bielefeld, Ger. 58 F6
Bié Plateau, Angola 81 M6
Big Bell, W. Austral., Austral. 88 H3
Big Delta, Alas., U.S. 40 K4
Big Falls, Minn., U.S. 41 C10
Bighorn, river, Mont.-Wyo., U.S. 42 D6
Bighorn Mountains, Mont.-Wyo., U.S. 42 D7
Big Spring, Tex., U.S. 40 H8
Big Trout Lake, Ont., Can. 36 G7
Bikini Atoll, Marshall Is. 96 D5
Bikoro, D.R.C. 78 K7
Bilbao, Sp. 58 H3
Bilibino, Russ. 69 B12
Billiluna, homestead, W. Austral., Austral. 88 E6
Billings, Mont., U.S. 40 C6
Billiton, island, Indonesia 71 M11
Bilma, Niger 78 F6
Biloela, Qnsld., Austral. 89 G15
Biloxi, Miss., U.S. 41 J12
Biltine, Chad 78 G7
Bindle, Qnsld., Austral. 89 H14
Bindura, Zimb. 79 N9
Bingara, homestead, Qnsld., Austral. 89 H12
Bingara, N.S.W., AUSTRAL. 89 J14
Bing Bong, homestead, N. Terr., Austral. 88 C9
Bingham, Me., U.S. 41 C16
Binghamton, N.Y., U.S. 41 D15
Bioko, island, Eq. Guinea 80 J5
Birao, Cen. Af. Rep. 78 H8
Birchip, Vic., Austral. 89 L11
Birch Mountains, Can. 38 F4
Birdsville, Qnsld., Austral. 89 G10
Bīrjand, Iran 68 G5
Birmingham, Ala., U.S. 41 H12
Birmingham, U.K. 58 F4
Bir Mogreïn, Maurit. 78 E2
Birnie Island, Kiribati 96 F8
Birnin Kebbi, Nig. 78 G5
Birni Nkonni, Niger 78 G5
Birrindudu, homestead, N. Terr., Austral. 88 D7
Bisbee, Ariz., U.S. 40 H5
Biscay, Bay of, Fr.-Sp. 60 H3
Biscayne Bay, Fla., U.S. 43 K15
Biscoe Islands, Antarctica 102 D2
Bishkek, Kyrg. 68 F7
Bishop, Calif., U.S. 40 F3
Biskra, Alg. 78 D5
Bismarck, N. Dak., U.S. 40 C8
Bismarck Archipelago, P.N.G. 92 B6
Bismarck Range, P.N.G. 92 C5
Bismarck Sea, P.N.G. 92 B6
Bissagos Islands, Guinea-Bissau 80 G1
Bissau, Guinea-Bissau 78 G1
Bitola, Maced. 58 J8
Bitterfontein, S. Af. 79 Q7
Bitterroot Range, Idaho-MOnt., Can. 42 C5
Biu, Nig. 78 H6
Biysk, Russ. 68 E8
Bizerte, Tun. 78 C6
Black, river, Ark.-Mo., U.S. 43 G11
Blackall, Qnsld., Austral. 89 G13
Blackball, N.Z. 92 L4
Black Belt, region, Ala.-Miss., U.S. 43 H12
Blackburn, Mount, Alas., U.S. 42 L4
Black Coast, Antarctica 102 D3
Blackfoot, Idaho, U.S. 40 D5
Black Forest, Ger. 60 G6
Black Hills, S. Dak.-Wyo., U.S. 42 D7
Black Irtysh, river, China-Kaz. 70 F8
Black Mesa, Okla., U.S. 42 G8
Black Mountain, Ky., U.S. 43 F13
Black Mountains, Ariz., U.S. 42 G4
Black Range, N. Mex., U.S. 42 H6
Black Rock, S. Georgia 53 R9
Black Rock Desert, Nev., U.S. 42 D3
Black Sea, Asia-Europe 61 H11
Black Sea Lowland, Ukr. 61 H10
Black Volta, river, Af. 80 H3
Blackwater, Qnsld., Austral. 89 F14
Blagodarnyy, Russ. 59 G13
Blagoveshchensk, Russ. 69 E12
Blagoyevo, Russ. 59 B11
Blair Athol, Qnsld., Austral. 89 F13
Blanc, Cape, Maurit. 80 F1
Blanc, Cape, Tun. 80 C5
Blanc, Mont, Fr. 60 H5
Blanca Bay, Arg. 53 N6
Blanca Peak, Colo., U.S. 42 F7
Blanche, Lake, S. Austral., Austral. 91 H11
Blanco, Cape, Oreg., U.S. 42 C2
Blantyre, Malawi 79 M10
Blaze, Point, N. Terr., Austral. 90 B7
Blenheim, N.Z. 92 K5
Blinman, S. Austral., Austral. 89 J10
Bloemfontein, S. Af. 79 Q8
Bloomington, Ill., U.S. 41 E11
Blouberg, peak, S. Af. 81 P9
Bluefield, W. Va., U.S. 41 F14
Bluefields, Nicar. 37 Q8
Blue Mountains, Oreg.-Wash., U.S. 42 C4
Blue Nile, river, Eth.-Sudan 80 G9
Blue Ridge, N.C.-Va., U.S. 43 F14
Bluff, N.Z. 92 P3
Bluff Knoll, W. Austral., Austral. 90 K3
Bluff Point, W. Austral., Austral. 90 H1
Blumenau, Braz. 50 K8
Bo, Sierra Leone 78 H2
Boatman, homestead, Qnsld., Austral. 89 H13
Boa Vista, Braz. 50 C6
Bobo Dioulasso, Burkina Faso 78 H3
Boby Peak, Madag. 81 N12
Bôca do Acre, Braz. 50 E4
Bocas del Toro, Pan. 37 Q8
Bodaybo, Russ. 69 D10
Bodele Depression, Chad 80 G7
Boden, Sweden 58 B8
Bodø, Nor. 58 B7
Boende, D.R.C. 78 K7
Bogalusa, La., U.S. 41 J11
Bogan, river, N.S.W., AUSTRAL. 91 K13
Bogantungan, Qnsld., Austral. 89 F13
Bogda Shan, China 70 F9
Boggabilla, N.S.W., AUSTRAL. 89 H14
Bogia, P.N.G. 92 B5
Bogotá, Col. 50 B3
Bo Hai, bay, China 71 F12
Bohemian Forest, Ger. 60 G6
Bohol, island, Philippines 69 K13
Boiaçu, Braz. 50 D6
Boise, Idaho, U.S. 40 D4
Bojnūrd, Iran 68 G5
Boké, Guinea 78 G1
Bolivia, S. America 50 G5
Bollnäs, Sweden 58 D7
Bollon, Qnsld., Austral. 89 H13
Bolobo, D.R.C. 79 K7
Bologna, It. 58 H6
Bol'shevik, Ostrov (Bol'shevik Island), Russ. 68 B9
Bol'shevik Island, Russ. 70 B9
Bol'shezemel'skaya Tundra, Russ. 61 A12
Bolzano, It. 58 H6
Boma, D.R.C. 79 L6
Bomba, Gulf of, Lib. 80 D8
Bombala, N.S.W., AUSTRAL. 89 M13
Bombay see Mumbai, India 68 J6
Bom Jesus da Lapa, Braz. 50 G10
Bomu, river, Cen. Af. Rep.-D.R.C. 80 J8
Bonaire, island, Neth. Antilles 39 P11
Bonang, Vic., Austral. 89 M13
Bonaparte Archipelago, W. Austral., Austral. 90 C5
Bonavista Bay, Can. 38 G11
Bon Bon, homestead, S. Austral., Austral. 88 J9
Bondo, D.R.C. 78 J8
Bonete, Cerro, Arg. 53 K4
Bongandanga, D.R.C. 78 J8
Bongaree, Qnsld., Austral. 89 H15
Bongo Lava, Madag. 81 N11
Bongor, Chad 78 H6
Bonin Islands (Ogasawara Guntō), Jap. 96 C3
Bonn, Ger. 58 F5
Bonners Ferry, Idaho, U.S. 40 B5
Bonney Downs, homestead, W. Austral., Austral. 88 F3
Bonnie Rock, W. Austral., Austral. 88 J3
Bonvouloir Islands, P.N.G. 92 D7
Bookabie, S. Austral., Austral. 88 J8
Booligal, N.S.W., AUSTRAL. 89 K12
Boonah, Qnsld., Austral. 89 H15
Boonderoo, homestead, Qnsld., Austral. 89 E12
Boorama, Somalia 78 H11
Boorara, homestead, Qnsld., Austral. 89 H12
Booroorban, N.S.W., AUSTRAL. 89 L12
Boosaaso (Bender Cassim), Somalia 78 G12
Boothia, Gulf of, Can. 38 D6
Boothia Peninsula, Can. 38 D6
Bora-Bora, island, Fr. Polynesia 96 G10
Borah Peak, Idaho, U.S. 42 D5
Borås, Sweden 58 E7
Borba, Braz. 50 D6
Borborema Plateau, Braz. 52 E11
Borchgrevink Coast, Antarctica 102 L9
Bordeaux, Fr. 58 H4
Borden, W. Austral., Austral. 88 L3
Borden Peninsula, Can. 38 D7
Bordertown, S. Austral., Austral. 89 L11
Bordj Flye Sainte Marie, Alg. 78 E4
Bordj Messouda, Alg. 78 D5
Borger, Tex., U.S. 40 G8
Borg Massif, Antarctica 102 B8
Borisoglebsk, Russ. 59 F12
Borlänge, Sweden 58 D7
Borneo, island, Brunei-Indonesia-Malaysia 71 L12
Borovichi, Russ. 59 D10
Borovskoy, Kaz. 59 C15
Borroloola, N. Terr., Austral. 88 C9
Bosnia and Herzegovina, Europe 58 H7
Bosporus, strait, Turk. 61 J10
Bossangoa, Cen. Af. Rep. 78 H7
Bossut, Cape, W. Austral., Austral. 90 D4
Boston, Mass., U.S. 41 D16
Boston Mountains, Ark., U.S. 43 G10
Botany Bay, N.S.W., AUSTRAL. 91 L14
Bothnia, Gulf of, Fin.-Sweden 60 C8
Botswana, Af. 79 N8
Bouaké, Côte d'Ivoire 78 H3
Bouar, Cen. Af. Rep. 78 J6
Boû Djébéha, Mali 78 F3
Bougainville, island, P.N.G. 92 C8
Bougainville, Cape, W. Austral., Austral. 90 B6
Bouira, Alg. 78 C5
Boujdour, Cape, W. Sahara 80 E2
Boulder, Colo., U.S. 40 E7
Boulder City, Nev., U.S. 40 F4
Boulia, Qnsld., Austral. 89 F11
Boundary Peak, Calif.-Nev. 42 F3
Bounty Islands, N.Z. 96 L7
Bourem, Mali 78 G4
Bourke, N.S.W., AUSTRAL. 89 J13
Bousso, Chad 78 H7
Bouvard, Cape, W. Austral., Austral. 90 K2
Bowen, Qnsld., Austral. 89 E14
Bowling Green, Ky., U.S. 41 F12
Bowman Glacier, Antarctica 102 H8
Bowman Island, Antarctica 103 H15
Boyoma Falls, D.R.C. 80 K8
Bozeman, Mont., U.S. 40 C6
Bozoum, Cen. Af. Rep. 78 H7
Brabant Island, Antarctica 102 C2
Bradenton, Fla., U.S. 41 K14
Bradford, Pa., U.S. 41 D14
Braga, Port. 58 H2
Bragança, Braz. 50 D9
Brahmaputra, river, Bangladesh-India 70 J9
Brainerd, Minn., U.S. 41 C10
Branco, river, Braz. 52 C6
Brandberg, peak, Namibia 81 N6
Brandon, Manitoba, Can. 36 H5
Bransby, homestead, Qnsld., Austral. 89 H11
Bransfield Strait, Antarctica 102 C1
Brasília, Braz. 50 G9
Braşov, Rom. 58 H9
Brasstown Bald, peak, Ga., U.S. 43 G13
Bratislava, Slovakia 58 G7
Bratsk, Russ. 68 E9
Bratsk Reservoir, Russ. 70 E9
Braunschweig, Ger. 58 F6
Brazil, S. America 50 F6
Brazilian Highlands, Braz. 52 F8
Brazos, river, Tex., U.S. 42 H9
Brazzaville, Congo 79 K6
Breadalbane, homestead, Qnsld., Austral. 89 F11
Bredasdorp, S. Af. 79 R7
Breiðafjörður, fjord, Ice. 60 A3
Breid Bay, Antarctica 103 A11
Bremen, Ger. 58 F6
Bremerhaven, Ger. 58 F6
Bremerton, Wash., U.S. 40 B3
Brescia, It. 58 H6
Brest, Belarus 58 F8
Brest, Fr. 58 G3
Breton Sound, La., U.S. 43 J12
Brett, Cape, N.Z. 92 F5
Breves, Braz. 50 D8
Brewarrina, N.S.W., AUSTRAL. 89 J13
Bridgeport, Conn., U.S. 41 D16
Bridgetown, Barbados 37 N12
Bridgetown, W. Austral., Austral. 88 L3
Brindisi, It. 58 J7
Brinkworth, S. Austral., Austral. 88 K10
Brisbane, Qnsld., Austral. 89 H15
Bristol, Tenn., U.S. 41 F13
Bristol, U.K. 58 F4
Bristol Bay, Alas., U.S. 42 M2
British Columbia, Can. 36 F3
British Isles, Ire.-U.K. 60 D3
British Mountains, Can.-U.S. 42 J4
Brno, Czech Rep. 58 G7
Broad, river, N.C.-S.C., U.S. 43 G14
Brochet, Manitoba, Can. 36 F5
Brodeur Peninsula, Can. 38 D7
Broken Hill, N.S.W., AUSTRAL. 89 J11
Brokopondo, Suriname 50 B7
Brookings, S. Dak., U.S. 40 D9
Brooks Range, Alas., U.S. 42 J3
Broome, W. Austral., Austral. 88 D4
Broughton Islands, N.S.W., AUSTRAL. 91 K15
Brown, Point, S. Austral., Austral. 90 K8
Brownfield, Tex., U.S. 40 H8
Brownsville, Tex., U.S. 40 L9
Brownwood, Tex., U.S. 40 J9
Browse Island, W. Austral., Austral. 90 C4
Bruce Rock, W. Austral., Austral. 88 K3
Brumado, Braz. 50 G10
Brunei, Asia 69 L12
Brunette Downs, homestead, N. Terr., Austral. 88 D9
Brunner, Lake, N.Z. 92 L4
Brunswick, Ga., U.S. 41 H14
Brunswick Bay, W. Austral., Austral. 90 C5
Brusque, Braz. 50 K8
Brussels see Bruxelles, Belg. 58 F5
Bruxelles (Brussels), Belg. 58 F5
Bryan, Tex., U.S. 40 J9
Bryan Coast, Antarctica 102 F3
Bryansk, Russ. 59 F10
Buba, Guinea-Bissau 78 G1
Bucaramanga, Col. 50 B3
Buccaneer Archipelago, W. Austral., Austral. 90 C4
Buchanan, Liberia 78 H2
Bucharest see Bucureşti, Rom. 58 H9
Buchon, Point, Calif., U.S. 42 F2
Buckland Tableland, Qnsld., Austral. 91 G13
Bucureşti (Bucharest), Rom. 58 H9
Budapest, Hung. 58 H8
Budd Coast, Antarctica 103 J15
Budgewoi, N.S.W., AUSTRAL. 89 K14
Buenaventura, Col. 50 C2
Buenaventura Bay, Col. 52 C2
Buenos Aires, Arg. 51 L6
Buenos Aires, Lake, Arg.-Chile 53 P4
Buffalo, N.Y., U.S. 41 D14
Buffalo, Wyo., U.S. 40 D7
Buffalo Hump, peak, Idaho, U.S. 42 C5
Bug, river, Belarus-Pol. 60 F8
Buguruslan, Russ. 59 D13
Buin, P.N.G. 92 C8
Bujumbura, Burundi 79 K9
Buka, island, P.N.G. 92 C8
Bukhara see Buxoro, Uzb. 68 G6
Bukittinggi, Indonesia 69 M10
Bulawayo, Zimb. 79 N9
Bulgaria, Europe 58 J9
Bullara, homestead, W. Austral., Austral. 88 F1
Bullfinch, W. Austral., Austral. 88 J3
Bulloo Downs, homestead, Qnsld., Austral. 89 H12
Bulloo Downs, homestead, W. Austral., Austral. 88 G3
Bullo River, N. Terr., Austral. 88 C7
Bull Shoals Lake, Ark.-Mo., U.S. 43 G10
Bumba, D.R.C. 78 J8
Buna, Kenya 78 J10
Bunbury, W. Austral., Austral. 88 K2
Bundaberg, Qnsld., Austral. 89 G15
Bundaleer, homestead, Qnsld., Austral. 89 H13
Bundooma, N. Terr., Austral. 88 G9
Bunia, D.R.C. 78 J9
Burakin, W. Austral., Austral. 88 J3
Buraydah, Saudi Arabia 68 G3
Burco, Somalia 78 H11
Burdekin, river, Qnsld., Austral. 91 E13
Burgas, Bulg. 58 J9

Burgos, *Sp.* **58** H3
Burica Point, *C.R.-Pan.* **39** Q8
Burke Island, *Antarctica* **102** H3
Burketown, *Qnsld., Austral.* **89** D11
Burkina Faso, *Af.* **78** G4
Burley, *Idaho, U.S.* **40** D5
Burlington, *Iowa, U.S.* **41** E11
Burlington, *Vt., U.S.* **41** C15
Burma *see* Myanmar, *Asia* **68** J9
Burnie, *Tas., Austral.* **89** L15
Burns, *Oreg., U.S.* **40** D4
Burnside, Lake, *W. Austral., Austral.* **90** G5
Burrendong Reservoir, *N.S.W., AUSTRAL.* **91** K13
Burren Junction, *N.S.W., AUSTRAL.* **89** J14
Burrundie, *N. Terr., Austral.* **88** B8
Bursa, *Turk.* **59** J10
Būr Sa'īd (Port Said), *Egypt* **78** D9
Būr Sūdān (Port Sudan), *Sudan* **78** F10
Buru, *island, Indonesia* **71** L14
Burundi, *Af.* **79** K9
Bururi, *Burundi* **79** K9
Busan, *S. Korea* **69** F13
Busanga Swamp, *Zambia* **81** M8
Bushy Park, *homestead, N. Terr., Austral.* **88** F9
Busselton, *W. Austral., Austral.* **88** K2
Buta, *D.R.C.* **78** J8
Butaritari, *island, Kiribati* **96** E6
Butchers Hill, *homestead, Qnsld., Austral.* **89** C13
Butembo, *D.R.C.* **78** K9
Buton, *island, Indonesia* **96** F1
Butte, *Mont., U.S.* **40** C5
Buxoro (Bukhara), *Uzb.* **68** G6
Buxton, *Guyana* **50** B6
Buy, *Russ.* **59** D11
Buynaksk, *Russ.* **59** H13
Buyr Nuur, *China-Mongolia* **69** F11
Buzău, *Rom.* **58** H9
Buzaymah, *Lib.* **78** E7
Buzuluk, *Russ.* **59** E13
Bydgoszcz, *Pol.* **58** F7
Byfield, *Qnsld., Austral.* **89** F15
Bylot Island, *Can.* **38** C7
Byrdbreen, *glacier, Antarctica* **103** B11
Byrd Glacier, *Antarctica* **102** J9
Byrock, *N.S.W., AUSTRAL.* **89** J13
Byron, Cape, *N.S.W., AUSTRAL.* **91** J15

Caazapá, *Para.* **50** J7
Caballo Reservoir, *N. Mex., U.S.* **42** H6
Cabanatuan, *Philippines* **69** J13
Cabinda, *Angola* **79** L6
Cabinda, *Angola* **79** L6
Cabo, *Braz.* **50** F12
Caboolture, *Qnsld., Austral.* **89** H15
Cabo San Lucas, *Mex.* **37** M3
Cabot Strait, *Can.* **38** G10
Cáceres, *Braz.* **50** G7
Cáceres, *Sp.* **58** J2
Cachimbo, *Braz.* **50** F7
Cachoeiro do Itapemirim, *Braz.* **50** H10
Cacine, *Guinea-Bissau* **78** G1
Cacolo, *Angola* **79** L7
Cacuri, *Venez.* **50** B5
Cadillac, *Mich., U.S.* **41** D12
Cádiz, *Sp.* **58** K2
Caen, *Fr.* **58** G4
Cagayan de Oro, *Philippines* **69** K14
Cagliari, *It.* **58** K5
Cahora Bassa, Lago de, *Mozambique* **81** M9
Caicó, *Braz.* **50** E11
Caicos Islands, *Atl. Oc.* **39** N10
Caird Coast, *Antarctica* **102** C6
Cairns, *Qnsld., Austral.* **89** D13
Cairo *see* El Qâhira, *Egypt* **78** D9
Cairo, *Ill., U.S.* **41** F11
Cajamarca, *Peru* **50** E2
Cajatambo, *Peru* **50** F2
Calabar, *Nig.* **78** J5
Calabozo, *Venez.* **50** A4
Calabria, *region, It.* **60** K7
Calais, *Me., U.S.* **41** C17
Calama, *Chile* **50** J4
Calamar, *Col.* **50** C3
Calanscio, Sand Sea of, *Lib.* **80** E8
Calanscio, Sarīr, *Lib.* **80** E7
Calçoene, *Braz.* **50** C8
Calcutta *see* Kolkata, *India* **68** J8
Caldwell, *Idaho, U.S.* **40** D4
Calgary, *Alta., Can.* **36** G4
Cali, *Col.* **50** C2
Caliente, *Nev., U.S.* **40** F4
California, *U.S.* **40** E3
California, Gulf of, *Mex.* **39** L3
Callabonna, Lake, *S. Austral., Austral.* **91** J10
Callao, *Peru* **50** F2
Calliope, *Qnsld., Austral.* **89** G15
Calliope Range, *Qnsld., Austral.* **91** G15
Caloundra, *Qnsld., Austral.* **89** H15
Caluula, *Somalia* **78** G12
Calvinia, *S. Af.* **79** Q7
Camagüey, *Cuba* **37** N9
Camapuã, *Braz.* **50** H7
Camargo, *Bol.* **50** H5
Camarón, Cape, *Hond.* **39** P8
Camarones, *Arg.* **51** P5
Camballin, *W. Austral., Austral.* **88** D5
Cambodia, *Asia* **69** K11
Cambrian Mountains, *U.K.* **60** E4
Cambridge Bay, *Nunavut* **36** D5
Cambridge Downs, *homestead, Qnsld., Austral.* **89** E12
Cambundi-Catembo, *Angola* **79** L7
Camden, *Ark., U.S.* **41** H10
Camden Bay, *Alas., U.S.* **42** J4
Cameroon, *Af.* **78** J6
Cameroon Mountain, *Cameroon* **80** J5
Camocim, *Braz.* **50** D10
Camooweal, *Qnsld., Austral.* **89** E10
Campbell, Cape, *N.Z.* **92** L5
Campbell Hill, *Ohio, U.S.* **43** E13
Campbell Island, *N.Z.* **96** M6
Campbell River, *B.C., Can.* **36** G3
Campeche, *Mex.* **37** N7
Campina Grande, *Braz.* **50** E11
Campinas, *Braz.* **50** J9
Campo Grande, *Braz.* **50** H7
Campo Mourão, *Braz.* **50** J8
Campos, *region, Braz.* **52** G9
Campos, *region, Braz.* **52** J8
Cam Ranh, *Viet.* **69** K11
Canada, *N. America* **36** E4
Canadian, *river, U.S.* **42** G8
Canadian Shield, *region, Can.* **38** E5
Canarias, Islas *see* Canary Islands, *Atl. Oc.* **78** D2
Canary Islands, *Atl. Oc.* **80** D2
Canaveral, Cape (Cape Kennedy), *U.S.* **39** M8
Canavieiras, *Braz.* **50** G11
Canberra, *Australian Capital Territory* **89** L13
Cancún, *Mex.* **37** N7
Canea *see* Haniá, *Gr.* **58** L9
Cangamba, *Angola* **79** M7
Canguaretama, *Braz.* **50** E12
Caniapiscau, *river, Can.* **38** F9
Caniapiscau, Réservoir, *Can.* **38** G9
Canindé, *Braz.* **50** E11
Çankırı, *Turk.* **59** J11
Canning Hill, *W. Austral., Austral.* **90** H3
Cann River, *Vic., Austral.* **89** M13
Canoas, *Braz.* **51** K8
Canobie, *homestead, Qnsld., Austral.* **89** E11
Canon City, *Colo., U.S.* **40** F7
Cantabrian Mountains, *Sp.* **60** H2
Canterbury Bight, *N.Z.* **92** M4
Can Tho, *Viet.* **69** K11
Canto do Buriti, *Braz.* **50** E10
Canton, *Ohio, U.S.* **41** E13
Cantwell, *Alas., U.S.* **40** K3
Canutama, *Braz.* **50** E5
Capanema, *Braz.* **50** D9
Cap Barbas, *W. Sahara* **78** E1
Cape Barren Island, *Tas., Austral.* **91** L16
Cape Breton Island, *Can.* **38** H10
Cape Coast, *Ghana* **78** J4
Cape Dorset, *Nunavut* **36** E8
Cape Fear, *river,* N.C., U.S. **43** G15
Cape Girardeau, *Mo., U.S.* **41** F11
Capel, *W. Austral., Austral.* **88** K2
Cape Rodney, *P.N.G.* **92** D6
Cape Town, *S. Af.* **79** Q7
Cape Yakataga, *Alas., U.S.* **40** L4
Cape York Peninsula, *Qnsld., Austral.* **91** B12
Cap-Haïtien, *Haiti* **37** N10
Capitán Arturo Prat, *station, Antarctica* **102** C1
Capitán Pablo Lagerenza, *Para.* **50** H6
Capricorn Channel, *Qnsld., Austral.* **91** F15
Capricorn Group, *Qnsld., Austral.* **91** G15
Caprivi Strip, *Namibia* **79** N8
Cap Rock Escarpment, *Tex., U.S.* **42** H8
Caracaraí, *Braz.* **50** C6
Caracas, *Venez.* **50** A4
Caratasca Lagoon, *Hond.* **39** P8
Carauari, *Braz.* **50** E4
Caravelas, *Braz.* **50** H10
Carbondale, *Ill., U.S.* **41** F11
Carbonia, *It.* **58** K5
Cardabia, *homestead, W. Austral., Austral.* **88** F1
Cardiff, *U.K.* **58** F4
Cardwell, *Qnsld., Austral.* **89** D13
Carey, Lake, *W. Austral., Austral.* **90** H4
Carey Downs, *homestead, W. Austral., Austral.* **88** G2
Caribbean Sea, *N. America* **39** P8
Caribou Mountains, *Can.* **38** F4
Carinda, *N.S.W., AUSTRAL.* **89** J13
Carinhanha, *Braz.* **50** G10
Carlin, *Nev., U.S.* **40** E4
Carlsbad, *N. Mex., U.S.* **40** H7
Carmen de Patagones, *Arg.* **51** N6
Carnamah, *W. Austral., Austral.* **88** J2
Carnarvon, *W. Austral., Austral.* **88** G1
Carnegie, *homestead, W. Austral., Austral.* **88** G5
Carnegie, Lake, *W. Austral., Austral.* **90** G4
Carney Island, *Antarctica* **102** J4
Carnot, Cape, *S. Austral., Austral.* **90** L9
Carolina, *Braz.* **50** E9
Caroline Island, *Fr. Polynesia* **97** F10
Caroline Islands, *F.S.M.* **96** E2
Carpathian Mountains, *Europe* **60** G8
Carpentaria, Gulf of, *Austral.* **91** B10
Carrantuohill, *peak, Ire.* **60** E3
Carrarang, *homestead, W. Austral., Austral.* **88** H1
Carrizal Bajo, *Chile* **51** K4
Carson City, *Nev., U.S.* **40** E3
Carson Sink, *Nev., U.S.* **42** E3
Cartagena, *Col.* **50** A2
Cartagena, *Sp.* **58** K3
Cartier Island, *W. Austral., Austral.* **90** B5
Cartwright, *Nfld. and Lab., Can.* **36** F10
Caruaru, *Braz.* **50** F11
Carúpano, *Venez.* **50** A5
Carutapera, *Braz.* **50** D9
Carvoeiro, *Braz.* **50** D6
Caryapundy Swamp, *N.S.W.-Qnsld., Austral.* **91** H12
Casablanca, *Mor.* **78** D3
Casa Grande, *Ariz., U.S.* **40** H5
Cascade Range, *Can.-U.S.* **42** C3
Cascavel, *Braz.* **50** J7
Casey, *station, Antarctica* **103** J15
Casey Bay, *Antarctica* **103** B13
Casper, *Wyo., U.S.* **40** D7
Caspian Depression, *Kaz.-Russ.* **70** E5
Caspian Sea, *Asia-Europe* **61** G14
Cassiar Mountains, *Can.* **38** E3
Castelló de la Plana, *Sp.* **58** J3
Casterton, *Vic., Austral.* **89** M11
Castlemaine, *Vic., Austral.* **89** L12
Castlereagh, *river, N.S.W., AUSTRAL.* **91** J13
Castlevale, *homestead, Qnsld., Austral.* **89** G13
Castries, *St. Lucia* **37** N12
Castrovillari, *It.* **58** K7
Catalão, *Braz.* **50** H9
Catamarca, *Arg.* **50** K5
Catania, *It.* **58** K7
Catanzaro, *It.* **58** K7
Catawba, *river, N.C.-S.C., U.S.* **43** G14
Catingas, *region, Braz.* **52** E7
Cat Lake, *Ont., Can.* **36** G6
Catoche, Cape, *Mex.* **39** N7
Cato Island, *C.S.I. Terr., Austral.* **91** G16
Catrimani, *Braz.* **50** C6
Catskill Mountains, *N.Y., U.S.* **43** D15
Cauca, *river, Col.* **52** B2
Caucasus Mountains, *Asia-Europe* **61** H12
Caungula, *Angola* **79** L7
Cavalla, *river, Cote d'Ivoire-Liberia* **80** J2
Caxias, *Braz.* **50** E10
Caxias, *Braz.* **50** E3
Caxias do Sul, *Braz.* **51** K8
Caxito, *Angola* **79** L6
Cayenne, *Fr. Guiana* **50** B8
Cayman Islands, *N. America* **37** N8
Cebu, *Philippines* **69** K13
Cedar, *river, Iowa-Minn., U.S.* **43** E10
Cedar City, *Utah, U.S.* **40** F5
Cedar Rapids, *Iowa, U.S.* **41** E11
Celebes, *island, Indonesia* **71** L13
Celebes Sea, *Asia* **71** K13
Celtic Sea, *Ire.-U.K.* **60** F3
Cenderawasih, Teluk, *Indonesia* **96** F2
Central, Cordillera, *S. America* **52** E2
Central African Republic, *Af.* **78** H7
Central America, *region, N. America* **39** P7
Centralia, *Wash., U.S.* **40** B3
Central Lowland, *U.S.* **43** E11
Central Lowlands, *region, Austral.* **91** E10
Central Range, *P.N.G.* **92** C4
Central Range, *Russ.* **71** C13
Central Russian Upland, *Russ.-Ukr.* **61** E11
Central Siberian Plateau, *Russ.* **70** C9
Ceram, *island, Indonesia* **71** L14
Ceram Sea, *Indonesia* **92** B1
Ceres, *Braz.* **50** G8
Cerro de Pasco, *Peru* **50** F2
České Budějovice, *Czech Rep.* **58** G7
Cessnock, *N.S.W., AUSTRAL.* **89** K14
Ceuta, *Sp.* **58** K2
Cévennes, *mountains, Fr.* **60** H4
Chachapoyas, *Peru* **50** E2
Chaco Austral, *plain, Arg.* **53** K6
Chaco Boreal, *plain, Para.* **52** H6
Chad, *Af.* **78** G7
Chad, Lake, *Af.* **80** G6
Chadron, *Nebr., U.S.* **40** D8
Chagda, *Russ.* **69** D11
Chagos Archipelago, *British Ind. Oc. Terr.* **70** M6
Chake Chake, *Tanzania* **79** K11
Chalbi Desert, *Kenya* **80** J10
Chalhuanca, *Peru* **50** G3
Chambeshi, *river, Zambia* **81** M9
Champlain, Lake, *Can.-U.S.* **43** C15
Changchun, *China* **69** F12
Chang Jiang (Yangtze), *river, China* **69** H11
Changsha, *China* **69** H11
Changzhou, *China* **69** G12
Channel Country, *Austral.* **91** G11
Channel Islands, *Calif., U.S.* **42** G3
Channel Islands, *U.K.* **60** F4
Channel-Port aux Basques, *Nfld. and Lab., Can.* **36** G10
Chany, Ozero, *Russ.* **59** B16
Chapadinha, *Braz.* **50** D10
Chapaev, *Kaz.* **59** F13
Chapala, Lake, *Mex.* **39** N5
Chapleau, *Ont., Can.* **36** H7
Charagua, *Bol.* **50** H5
Charcot Island, *Antarctica* **102** E2
Chari, *river, Chad* **80** H7
Charity, *Guyana* **50** B6
Chärjew, *Turkm.* **68** G6
Charleroi, *Belg.* **58** F5
Charles, Cape, *Va., U.S.* **43** F15
Charles Mound, *Ill., U.S.* **43** D11
Charles Point, *N. Terr., Austral.* **90** B7
Charleston, *N.Z.* **92** L4
Charleston, *S.C., U.S.* **41** H14
Charleston, *W. Va., U.S.* **41** F14
Charleville, *Qnsld., Austral.* **89** G13
Charlotte, *N.C., U.S.* **41** G14
Charlotte Harbor, *Fla., U.S.* **43** K14
Charlottesville, *Va., U.S.* **41** F14
Charlottetown, *P.E.I., CAN.* **36** H10
Chatham, *N.B., Can.* **36** H10
Chatham Island, *N.Z.* **96** K7
Chatham Islands, *N.Z.* **96** K7
Chatsworth, *homestead, Qnsld., Austral.* **89** E11
Chattahoochee, *river, Ala.-Fla.-Ga., U.S.* **43** H13
Chattanooga, *Tenn., U.S.* **41** G13
Cheaha Mountain, *Ala., U.S.* **43** H13
Cheboksary, *Russ.* **59** D12
Chech, Erg, *Alg.-Mali* **80** E4
Cheektowaga, *N.Y., U.S.* **41** D14
Cheepie, *Qnsld., Austral.* **89** G12
Cheju Do, *island, S. Korea* **96** B1
Chelyabinsk, *Russ.* **59** C14
Chemnitz, *Ger.* **58** G7
Chengdu, *China* **69** H10
Chennai (Madras), *India* **68** K7
Chepes, *Arg.* **51** L5
Cherbourg, *Fr.* **58** F4
Cherdyn', *Russ.* **59** C13
Cherepovets, *Russ.* **59** D10
Cherevkovo, *Russ.* **59** C11
Cherkasy, *Ukr.* **59** G10
Cherlak, *Russ.* **59** B16
Chernihiv, *Ukr.* **59** F10
Chernivtsi, *Ukr.* **58** G9
Cherokees, Lake of the, *Okla., U.S.* **43** G10
Cherrabun, *homestead, W. Austral., Austral.* **88** D5
Cherry Island *see* Anuta, *Solomon Is.* **96** G6
Cherskiy Range, *Russ.* **71** C11
Cherskogo, Khrebet (Cherskiy Range), *Russ.* **69** C11
Chesapeake Bay, *Md.-Va., U.S.* **43** E15
Chesha Bay, *Russ.* **61** A11
Cheshskaya Guba (Chesha Bay), *Russ.* **59** A11
Chesterfield, Îles, *New Caledonia* **96** G4
Chesterfield Inlet, *Nunavut* **36** E6
Chetumal, *Mex.* **37** P7
Chetumal Bay, *Belize-Mex.* **39** P7
Chew Bahir, Lake, *Eth.* **80** J10
Cheyenne, *river, S. Dak.-Wyo., U.S.* **42** D8
Cheyenne, *Wyo., U.S.* **40** E7
Chibemba, *Angola* **79** M6
Chibougamau, *Que., Can.* **36** H8
Chicago, *Ill., U.S.* **41** E12
Chicapa, *river, Angola-D.R.C.* **81** L7
Chichagof Island, *Alas., U.S.* **42** M5
Chichester Range, *W. Austral., Austral.* **90** F3
Chichi Jima Rettō, *Jap.* **96** C3
Chickasha, *Okla., U.S.* **40** G9
Chiclayo, *Peru* **50** E2
Chicoutimi, *Que., Can.* **36** H9
Chignik, *Alas., U.S.* **40** M2
Chigubo, *Mozambique* **79** P9
Chihuahua, *Mex.* **37** M4
Childers, *Qnsld., Austral.* **89** G15
Childress, *Tex., U.S.* **40** H8
Chile, *S. America* **51** P4
Chillán, *Chile* **51** M4
Chilpancingo, *Mex.* **37** P5
Chilung, *Taiwan* **69** H13
Chilwa, Lake, *Malawi-Mozambique* **81** M10
Chimborazo, *peak, Ecua.* **52** D2
Chimbote, *Peru* **50** F2
China, *Asia* **68** G9
Chinandega, *Nicar.* **37** Q7
Chincha Alta, *Peru* **50** G2
Chincha Islands, *Peru* **52** G2
Chinchilla, *Qnsld., Austral.* **89** H14
Chinde, *Mozambique* **79** N10
Chingola, *Zambia* **79** M8
Chinhoyi, *Zimb.* **79** N9
Chinta, *S. Austral., Austral.* **88** J8
Chiredzi, *Zimb.* **79** N9
Chirinda, *Russ.* **68** D9
Chisasibi, *Que., Can.* **36** G8
Chisimayu *see* Kismaayo, *Somalia* **78** K11
Chişinău, *Moldova* **58** H10
Chita, *Russ.* **69** E11
Chitato, *Angola* **79** L7
Chitembo, *Angola* **79** M7
Chitré, *Pan.* **37** Q9
Chittagong, *Bangladesh* **68** J9
Chitungwiza, *Zimb.* **79** N9
Chobe, *river, Af.* **81** N8
Choele Choel, *Arg.* **51** M5
Choiseul, *island, Solomon Is.* **96** F4
Chokurdakh, *Russ.* **69** B11
Choluteca, *Hond.* **37** P7
Ch'ŏngjin, *N. Korea* **69** F12
Chongqing, *China* **69** H11
Chonos, Archipiélago de los (Chonos Archipelago), *Chile* **51** P4
Chonos Archipelago, *Chile* **53** P4
Chorregon, *Qnsld., Austral.* **89** F12
Chorrillos, *Peru* **50** F2
Chos Malal, *Arg.* **51** M4
Chota Nagpur Plateau, *India* **70** J8
Christchurch, *N.Z.* **92** M4
Christmas Creek, *homestead, W. Austral., Austral.* **88** D6
Christmas Island *see* Kiritimati, *Kiribati* **96** E9
Chubut, *river, Arg.* **53** N4
Chudleigh Park, *homestead, Qnsld., Austral.* **89** E12
Chugach Mountains, *Alas., U.S.* **42** L3
Chukchi Peninsula, *Russ.* **71** A12
Chukchi Range, *Russ.* **71** A12
Chukchi Sea, *Arctic Oc.* **42** J1
Chumikan, *Russ.* **69** D12
Chuquibamba, *Peru* **50** G3
Chuquicamata, *Chile* **50** J4
Churchill, *river, Can.* **38** F6
Churchill, *Manitoba, Can.* **36** F6
Churchill, Cape, *Can.* **38** F6
Churchill Falls, *Nfld. and Lab., Can.* **36** G9
Churchill Mountains, *Antarctica* **102** J9
Chuska Mountains, *Ariz.-N. Mex., U.S.* **42** G6
Chusovoy, *Russ.* **59** C13
Chuuk (Truk Islands), *F.S.M.* **96** E4
Ciego de Ávila, *Cuba* **37** N9
Cienfuegos, *Cuba* **37** N8
Cimarron, *river, U.S.* **42** G9
Cincinnati, *Ohio, U.S.* **41** F13
Circle, *Alas., U.S.* **40** K4
Ciscaucasia, *region, Russ.* **61** H12
Ciudad Bolívar, *Venez.* **50** B5
Ciudad Cortés, *C.R.* **37** Q8
Ciudad del Carmen, *Mex.* **37** P7
Ciudad del Este, *Para.* **50** J7
Ciudad Guayana, *Venez.* **50** B5
Ciudad Juárez, *Mex.* **37** L4
Ciudad Mante, *Mex.* **37** N5
Ciudad Obregón, *Mex.* **37** M4
Ciudad Real, *Sp.* **58** J2
Ciudad Valles, *Mex.* **37** N5
Ciudad Victoria, *Mex.* **37** N5
Civitavecchia, *It.* **58** J6
Clairview, *Qnsld., Austral.* **89** F14
Clarence, *river, N.Z.* **92** L5
Clarence Island, *Antarctica* **102** B1
Clarence Strait, *N. Terr., Austral.* **90** B7
Clarie Coast, *Antarctica* **103** L13
Clarión Island, *Mex.* **39** N2
Clarke Range, *Qnsld., Austral.* **91** E14
Clarksburg, *W. Va., U.S.* **41** E14
Clarksdale, *Miss., U.S.* **41** H11
Clarks Hill Lake, *Ga.-S.C., U.S.* **43** G14
Clarksville, *Tenn., U.S.* **41** G12
Clayton, *N. Mex., U.S.* **40** G7
Clearwater, *Fla., U.S.* **41** K14
Clearwater Mountains, *Idaho, U.S.* **42** C5
Cleburne, *Tex., U.S.* **40** H9
Clermont, *Qnsld., Austral.* **89** F14
Clermont- Ferrand, *Fr.* **58** H4
Cleveland, *Ohio, U.S.* **41** E13
Clifton Hills, *homestead, S. Austral., Austral.* **89** G10
Clingmans Dome, *N.C.-Tenn., U.S.* **43** G13
Clipperton, *island, Pac. Oc.* **97** D14
Cloates, Point, *W. Austral., Austral.* **90** F1
Cloncurry, *river, Qnsld., Austral.* **91** D11
Cloncurry, *Qnsld., Austral.* **89** E11
Cloncurry Plateau, *N. Terr.-Qnsld., Austral.* **91** E11
Cloud Peak, *Wyo., U.S.* **42** D7
Clovis, *N. Mex., U.S.* **40** H7
Cluj-Napoca, *Rom.* **58** H9
Cluny, *homestead, Qnsld., Austral.* **89** F11
Clutha, *river, N.Z.* **92** N3
Clyde River, *Nunavut* **36** D8
Coal Creek, *N.Z.* **92** N3
Coalinga, *Calif., U.S.* **40** F3
Coari, *Braz.* **50** D5
Coastal Plain, *U.S.* **42** K9
Coast Mountains, *Can.* **38** E3
Coast Range, *Venez.* **52** A4
Coast Ranges, *Calif.-Oreg., U.S.* **42** C2
Coats Island, *Can.* **38** F7
Coats Land, *Antarctica* **102** D6
Coatzacoalcos, *Mex.* **37** P6
Cobán, *Guatemala* **37** P7
Cobar, *N.S.W., AUSTRAL.* **89** J13
Cobija, *Bol.* **50** F4
Cobourg Peninsula, *N. Terr., Austral.* **90** A8
Cochabamba, *Bol.* **50** G5
Cochin, *India* **68** K7
Cockburn, *S. Austral., Austral.* **89** J11
Cocklebiddy Motel, *W. Austral., Austral.* **88** J6
Coco, *river, Hond.-Nicar.* **39** P8
Cocoa, *Fla., U.S.* **41** J14
Cocos Island, *C.R.* **39** R7
Cod, Cape, *Mass., U.S.* **43** D16
Codrington, Mount, *Antarctica* **103** C14
Cody, *Wyo., U.S.* **40** D6
Coen, *Qnsld., Austral.* **89** B12
Coeur d'Alene, *Idaho, U.S.* **40** B4
Coffeyville, *Kans., U.S.* **41** G10
Coffs Harbour, *N.S.W., AUSTRAL.* **89** J15
Coiba Island, *Pan.* **39** Q8
Coihaique, *Chile* **51** P4
Coimbatore, *India* **68** K7
Coimbra, *Port.* **58** J2
Colac, *Vic., Austral.* **89** M12
Colby, *Kans., U.S.* **40** F8
Cold Bay, *Alas., U.S.* **40** M1
Colidor, *Braz.* **50** F7
Colima, *Mex.* **37** N4
Colinas, *Braz.* **50** E10
Collerina, *N.S.W., AUSTRAL.* **89** J13
Collie, *W. Austral., Austral.* **88** K3
Collier Bay, *W. Austral., Austral.* **90** C5
Collier Range, *W. Austral., Austral.* **90** G3
Collingwood, *N.Z.* **92** K4
Collinson Peninsula, *Can.* **38** D5
Collinsville, *Qnsld., Austral.* **89** E14
Colombia, *S. America* **50** C3
Colombo, *Sri Lanka* **68** L7
Colón, *Cuba* **37** N8
Colón, *Pan.* **37** Q9
Colón, Archipiélago de *see* Galápagos Islands, *Ecua.* **97** E16
Colorado, *river, Arg.* **53** M5
Colorado, *river, Mex.-U.S.* **42** G4
Colorado, *river, Tex., U.S.* **42** J9
Colorado, *U.S.* **40** F7
Colorado Plateau, *Ariz.-N. Mex., U.S.* **42** F5
Colorado Springs, *Colo., U.S.* **40** F7
Columbia, *river, Can.-U.S.* **42** C3
Columbia, *S.C., U.S.* **41** G14
Columbia, *Tenn., U.S.* **41** G12
Columbia, District of, *U.S.* **41** E15
Columbia Mountains, *Can.* **38** G3
Columbia Plateau, *Idaho-Oreg.-Wash., U.S.* **42** C4
Columbine, Cape, *S. Af.* **81** Q7
Columbus, *Ga., U.S.* **41** H13
Columbus, *Miss., U.S.* **41** H12
Columbus, *Nebr., U.S.* **40** E9
Columbus, *Ohio, U.S.* **41** E13
Colville, *river, Alas., U.S.* **42** J3
Colville, *N.Z.* **92** G6
Colville, *Wash., U.S.* **40** B4
Colville Channel, *N.Z.* **92** G6
Comandante Ferraz, *station, Antarctica* **102** B1
Comandante Luis Piedrabuena, *Arg.* **51** Q5
Comboyne, *N.S.W., AUSTRAL.* **89** K15
Comet, *Qnsld., Austral.* **89** F14
Commandant Charcot Glacier, *Antarctica* **103** L13
Commander Islands, *Russ.* **71** B13
Commonwealth Bay, *Antarctica* **103** M12
Como, Lake, *It.* **60** H6
Comodoro Rivadavia, *Arg.* **51** P5
Comorin, Cape, *India* **70** L7
Comoro Islands, *Comoros* **81** M11
Comoros, *Ind. Oc.* **79** M11
Conakry, *Guinea* **78** H1
Conara Junction, *Tas., Austral.* **89** M16
Conceição do Araguaia, *Braz.* **50** E8
Conceição do Maú, *Braz.* **50** C6
Concepción, *Chile* **51** M4
Concepción del Uruguay, *Arg.* **51** L6
Conception, Point, *Calif., U.S.* **42** G2
Conchos, *river, Mex.* **39** M4
Concord, *N.H., U.S.* **41** C16
Concordia, *station, Antarctica* **103** J12
Condamine, *Qnsld., Austral.* **89** H14
Condobolin, *N.S.W., AUSTRAL.* **89** K13
Conflict Group, *P.N.G.* **92** E7
Congo, *Af.* **79** K6
Congo, *river, Af.* **81** K6
Congo, Source of the, *D.R.C.* **81** M8
Congo Basin, *Congo-D.R.C.* **80** J7
Connecticut, *river, Can.-U.S.* **43** D16
Connecticut, *U.S.* **41** D16
Connmara, *homestead, Qnsld., Austral.* **89** F12
Connors Range, *Qnsld., Austral.* **91** F14
Conselheiro Lafaiete, *Braz.* **50** H9
Constance, Lake, *Ger.-Switz.* **60** G6
Constância dos Baetas, *Braz.* **50** E6
Constanța, *Rom.* **58** H10
Constantine, *Alg.* **78** C5
Constellation Inlet, *Antarctica* **102** F5
Contamana, *Peru* **50** E3
Coober Pedy, *S. Austral., Austral.* **88** H9
Cook, *S. Austral., Austral.* **88** J7
Cook, Mount, *N.Z.* **92** M4
Cook Ice Shelf, *Antarctica* **103** M11
Cook Inlet, *Alas., U.S.* **42** L3
Cook Islands, *Pac. Oc.* **96** G9
Cook Strait, *N.Z.* **92** K5
Cooktown, *Qnsld., Austral.* **89** C13
Coolabah, *N.S.W., AUSTRAL.* **89** J13
Coolabri, *homestead, Qnsld., Austral.* **89** G13
Cooladdi, *Qnsld., Austral.* **89** G13
Coolah, *N.S.W., AUSTRAL.* **89** K14
Coolatai, *N.S.W., AUSTRAL.* **89** J14
Coolgardie, *W. Austral., Austral.* **88** J4
Coonabarabran, *N.S.W., AUSTRAL.* **89** J14
Coonamble, *N.S.W., AUSTRAL.* **89** J13
Coonana, *W. Austral., Austral.* **88** J5
Coonbah, *homestead, N.S.W., AUSTRAL.* **89** K11
Coondambo, *S. Austral., Austral.* **88** J9
Coongoola, *Qnsld., Austral.* **89** H13
Cooper Creek, *S. Austral., Austral.* **91** H10
Coorow, *W. Austral., Austral.* **88** J2
Coos Bay, *Oreg., U.S.* **36** H2
Coos Bay, *Oreg., U.S.* **40** C2
Cootamundra, *N.S.W., AUSTRAL.* **89** L13
Copenhagen *see* København, *Den.* **58** E7
Copper, *river, Alas., U.S.* **42** L4
Copulhue Pass, *Arg.-Chile* **53** M4
Coquimbo, *Chile* **51** K4
Coracora, *Peru* **50** G3
Coral Gables, *Fla., U.S.* **41** K15
Coral Harbour, *Nunavut* **36** E7
Coral Sea, *Pac. Oc.* **96** G4
Coral Sea Islands Territory, *Austral.* **89** D14
Corangamite, Lake, *Vic., Austral.* **91** M11
Cordillo Downs, *homestead, S. Austral., Austral.* **89** G11
Córdoba, *Arg.* **51** L5
Córdoba, *Mex.* **37** P6
Córdoba, *Sp.* **58** J2
Córdoba, Sierras de, *Arg.* **53** L5
Cordova, *Alas., U.S.* **40** L4
Corfu *see* Kérkira, *island, Gr.* **58** K8
Coringa Islets, *C.S.I. Terr., Austral.* **89** D15
Corinna, *Tas., Austral.* **89** M15
Cork, *Ire.* **58** E3
Corner Brook, *Nfld. and Lab., Can.* **36** G10
Corno Grande, *peak, It.* **60** J6
Cornwall, *Ont., Can.* **36** H9
Cornwallis Island, *Can.* **38** C6
Coro, *Venez.* **50** A4
Coroatá, *Braz.* **50** D10
Coromandel Coast, *India* **70** K7
Coromandel Peninsula, *N.Z.* **92** H6
Coronado Bay, *C.R.* **39** Q8
Coronation Island, *Antarctica* **102** A2
Coronel, *Chile* **51** M4
Coronel Oviedo, *Para.* **50** J7
Corpus Christi, *Tex., U.S.* **40** K9
Corpus Christi Bay, *Tex., U.S.* **42** K9
Corrientes, Cape, *Mex.* **39** N4
Corrigin, *W. Austral., Austral.* **88** K3
Corryong, *Vic., Austral.* **89** L13
Corse (Corsica), *Fr.* **58** J5
Corsica, *island, Fr.* **60** J5
Corsicana, *Tex., U.S.* **40** H9
Cortez, *Colo., U.S.* **40** F6
Çorum, *Turk.* **59** J11
Corumbá, *Braz.* **50** H7
Corvallis, *Oreg., U.S.* **40** C3
Cosenza, *It.* **58** K7
Cosmoledo Group, *Seychelles* **81** L12
Cosmo Newberry, *W. Austral., Austral.* **88** H5
Costa Rica, *N. America* **37** Q8
Cotabato, *Philippines* **69** K13
Côte d'Ivoire, *Af.* **78** H3
Cotonou, *Benin* **78** H4
Council Bluffs, *Iowa, U.S.* **41** E10
Covington, *Ky., U.S.* **41** F13
Cowal, Lake, *N.S.W., AUSTRAL.* **91** K13
Cowan, Lake, *W. Austral., Austral.* **90** J5
Cowaramup, *W. Austral., Austral.* **88** L2
Cowarie, *homestead, S. Austral., Austral.* **89** H10
Cowell, *S. Austral., Austral.* **88** K10

Coxim, Braz. 50 H7
Cozumel, Mex. 37 N7
Cozumel Island, Mex. 39 N7
Crafers, S. Austral., Austral. 89 L10
Craig, Colo., U.S. 40 E6
Craiova, Rom. 58 H9
Cranbourne, Vic., Austral. 89 M12
Cranbrook, B.C., Can. 36 H4
Crane, Oreg., U.S. 40 D4
Crary Mountains, Antarctica 102 H5
Crateús, Braz. 50 E10
Crato, Braz. 50 E11
Crescent City, Calif., U.S. 40 D2
Crete, island, Gr. 60 L9
Crete, Sea of, Gr. 60 L9
Crevasse Valley Glacier, Antarctica 102 K6
Criciúma, Braz. 51 K8
Crimea, region, Ukr. 61 H11
Crimean Mountains, Ukr. 61 H11
Cristalina, Braz. 50 G9
Croatia, Europe 58 H7
Croker Island, N. Terr., Austral. 90 A8
Crookston, Minn., U.S. 40 C9
Cross Sound, Alas., U.S. 42 M5
Crown Prince Christian Land, Greenland 38 A8
Croydon, Qnsld., Austral. 89 D12
Cruz Alta, Braz. 51 K7
Cruz del Eje, Arg. 50 K5
Cruzeiro do Sul, Braz. 50 E3
Crystal Mountains, Af. 81 K6
Cuando, river, Af. 81 M7
Cuauhtémoc, Mex. 37 M4
Cuba, N. America 37 N9
Cubango, river, Angola 81 M7
Cuchilla Grande, mountains, Uru. 53 L7
Cucui, Braz. 50 C4
Cúcuta, Col. 50 B3
Cuenca, Ecua. 50 D2
Cuero, Tex., U.S. 40 J9
Cuevo, Bol. 50 H5
Cuiabá, Braz. 50 G7
Cuito Cuanavale, Angola 79 M7
Culiacán, Mex. 37 M4
Culpataro, homestead, N.S.W., AUSTRAL. 89 K12
Culver, Point, W. Austral., Austral. 90 K5
Culverden, N.Z. 92 L5
Cumaná, Venez. 50 A5
Cumberland, river, Ky.-Tenn., U.S. 43 G12
Cumberland, Md., U.S. 41 E14
Cumberland, Lake, Ky., U.S. 43 F13
Cumberland Islands, Qnsld., Austral. 91 E14
Cumberland Peninsula, Can. 38 D8
Cumberland Plateau, Ala.-Ky.-Tenn., U.S. 43 G13
Cumberland Sound, Can. 38 E8
Cumborah, N.S.W., AUSTRAL. 89 J13
Cunaviche, Venez. 50 B4
Cunene, river, Angola-Namibia 81 N6
Cunnamulla, Qnsld., Austral. 89 H13
Cunyu, homestead, W. Austral., Austral. 88 G4
Curaçao, island, Neth. Antilles 39 P11
Curbur, homestead, W. Austral., Austral. 88 H2
Curicó, Chile 51 M4
Curitiba, Braz. 50 J8
Currie, Tas., Austral. 89 L15
Curtin Springs, homestead, N. Terr., Austral. 88 G8
Curtis Island, N.Z. 96 J7
Curuguaty, Para. 50 J7
Curuzú Cuatiá, Arg. 51 K6
Curvelo, Braz. 50 H9
Cusco, Peru 50 G3
Cut, island, Indonesia 92 C11
Cut Bank, Mont., U.S. 40 B6
Cuvier,Cape, W. Austral., Austral. 90 G1
Cuya, Chile 50 H4
Cyclades, islands, Gr. 60 K9
Cyprus, Asia 68 F3
Cyrenaica, region, Lib. 78 E7
Czech Republic, Europe 58 G7
Częstochowa, Pol. 58 G8

Dabakala, Côte d'Ivoire 78 H3
Daegu, S. Korea 69 F13
Daejeon, S. Korea 69 F13
Dahlak Archipelago, Eritrea 80 G10
Dair, Jebel ed, Sudan 80 G9
Dairy Creek, homestead, W. Austral., Austral. 88 G2
Daitō Islands, Jap. 96 C2
Dajarra, Qnsld., Austral. 89 E11
Dakar, Senegal 78 G1
Dalandzadgad, Mongolia 69 F10
Dalbeg, Qnsld., Austral. 89 E14
Dalby, Qnsld., Austral. 89 H15
Dalgonally, homestead, Qnsld., Austral. 89 E11
Dalhart, Tex., U.S. 40 G8
Dali, China 69 H10
Dalian, China 69 F12
Dallas, Tex., U.S. 40 H9
Dall Island, Alas., U.S. 42 M5
Dalmatia, region, Europe 60 J7
Daly, river, N. Terr., Austral. 90 B7
Daly Waters, N. Terr., Austral. 88 C8
Damascus see Dimashq, Syr. 68 F3
Dampier, Selat, Indonesia 92 A1
Dampier Archipelago, W. Austral., Austral. 90 E2
Dampier Downs, homestead, W. Austral., Austral. 88 D4
Dampier Land, W. Austral., Austral. 90 D4
Da Nang, Viet. 69 J11
Danco Coast, Antarctica 102 C2
Daneborg, Greenland 36 A9
Danforth, Me., U.S. 41 B16
Danger Islands see Pukapuka Atoll, Cook Is. 96 G8
Danmark Havn, Greenland 36 A9
Danube, river, Europe 60 J9
Danube, Source of the, Ger. 60 G6
Danube River Delta, Rom.-Ukr. 61 H10
Da Qaidam, China 68 G9
Dardanelles, strait, Turk. 60 K9
Dar es Salaam, Tanzania 79 L10
Dargaville, N.Z. 92 G5
Darhan, Mongolia 69 F10
Darling, river, N.S.W., AUSTRAL. 91 K11
Darling, Source of the, N.S.W., AUSTRAL. 91 H15
Darling Downs, Qnsld., Austral. 91 H14
Darling Range, W. Austral., Austral. 90 K3
Darlot, Lake, W. Austral., Austral. 90 H4
Darmstadt, Ger. 58 G6
Darnah, Lib. 78 D7
Darnley, Cape, Antarctica 103 D14
Dar Rounga, region, Cen. Af. Rep. 80 H7
Dartmouth, N.S., CAN. 36 H10
Daru, P.N.G. 92 D4
Darwin, N. Terr., Austral. 88 B7
Darwin, Isla, Ecua. 97 E16
Darwin Glacier, Antarctica 102 J9
Dashen Terara, Ras, Eth. 80 G10
Daşhowuz, Turkm. 68 F6
Dasht-e Lūt, region, Iran 70 G5
Datong, China 69 G11
Daugavpils, Latv. 58 E9
Dauphin, Manitoba, Can. 36 H5
Davao, Philippines 69 K14
Davenport, Iowa, U.S. 41 E11
Davenport Range, N. Terr., Austral. 90 E9
David, Pan. 37 Q8
Davidson Mountains, Can.-U.S. 42 J4
Davis, station, Antarctica 103 E14
Davis, Mount, Pa., U.S. 43 E14
Davis Inlet, Nfld. and Lab., Can. 36 F9
Davis Sea, Antarctica 103 G15
Davis Strait, Can.-Greenland 38 D9
Davyhurst, W. Austral., Austral. 88 J4
Dawa, river, Eth.-Kenya-Somalia 80 J11
Dawmat al Jandal, Saudi Arabia 68 G3
Dawson, river, Qnsld., Austral. 91 G14
Dawson, Yukon Terr. 36 D3
Dawson Creek, B.C., Can. 36 F4
Daxue Mountains, China 71 H10
Daydawn, W. Austral., Austral. 88 H3
Dayton, Ohio, U.S. 41 E13
Daytona Beach, Fla., U.S. 41 J14
De Aar, S. Af. 79 Q8
Dead Sea, Israel-Jordan-W. Bank 70 F3
Deakin, W. Austral., Austral. 88 J7
Deán Funes, Arg. 50 K5
Dease Inlet, Alas., U.S. 42 H3
Dease Lake, B.C., Can. 36 E3
Death Valley, Calif., U.S. 42 F4
Débo, Lake, Mali 80 G3
Debrecen, Hung. 58 G8
Debre Mark'os, Eth. 78 H10
Decatur, Ala., U.S. 41 G12
Decatur, Ill., U.S. 41 E11
Deccan Plateau, India 70 J7
Deception Island, Antarctica 102 C1
Deep Well, N. Terr., Austral. 88 F9
Deering, Alas., U.S. 40 K2
Deer Lodge, Mont., U.S. 40 C5
DeGrey, homestead, W. Austral., Austral. 88 E3
DeGrey, river, W. Austral., Austral. 90 E3
Deim Zubeir, Sudan 78 H8
De Jongs, Tanjung, Indonesia 92 C3
Delamere, homestead, N. Terr., Austral. 88 C8
De Land, Fla., U.S. 41 J14
Delano, Calif., U.S. 40 F3
Delaware, river, U.S. 43 E15
Delaware, U.S. 41 E15
Delaware Bay, Del.-N.J. 43 E15
Delgado, Cape, Mozambique 81 L11
Delhi, India 68 H7
Delicias, Mex. 37 M4
Délı̨ne, N.W.T., CAN. 36 E4
Delissaville, N. Terr., Austral. 88 B7
De Long Mountains, Alas., U.S. 42 J2
Deloraine, Tas., Austral. 89 L16
Del Rio, Tex., U.S. 40 J8
Delta, Colo., U.S. 40 F6
Delta Downs, homestead, Qnsld., Austral. 89 D11
Demarcation Point, Can.-U.S. 42 J4
Deming, N. Mex., U.S. 40 H6
Democratic Republic of the Congo, Af. 79 K8
Demta, Indonesia 92 B4
Denali see McKinley, Mount, Alas., U.S. 42 K3
Denham, W. Austral., Austral. 88 H1
Deniliquin, N.S.W., AUSTRAL. 89 L12
Denio, Nev., U.S. 40 D4
Denison, Tex., U.S. 40 H9
Denizli, Turk. 59 K10
Denmark, Europe 58 E6
Denmark, W. Austral., Austral. 88 L3
Denmark Strait, Greenland-Ice. 38 B10
Denpasar, Indonesia 69 M12
D'Entrecasteaux, Point, W. Austral., Austral. 90 L3
D'Entrecasteaux Islands, P.N.G. 92 D7
Denver, Colo., U.S. 40 E7
Depósito, Braz. 50 B6
Derbent, Russ. 59 H14
Derby, W. Austral., Austral. 88 D5
Derzhavīnsk, Kaz. 59 D16
Desē, Eth. 78 H10
Deseado, river, Arg. 53 P5
Des Moines, river, Iowa-Minn.-Mo., U.S. 43 E10
Des Moines, Iowa, U.S. 41 E10
Desna, river, Ukr. 61 F10
Detroit, Mich., U.S. 41 D13
Detroit Lakes, Minn., U.S. 41 C10
Devil's Island, Fr. Guiana 52 B8
Devils Lake, N. Dak., U.S. 40 C9
Devon Island, Can. 38 C7
Devonport, Tas., Austral. 89 L16
Dey Dey, Lake, S. Austral., Austral. 90 H8
Dhaka, Bangladesh 68 J9
Dhuusamarreeb, Somalia 78 H12
Diablo Range, Calif., U.S. 42 F2
Diamantina, river, Qnsld., Austral. 91 G11
Diamantina, Braz. 50 H10
Diamantina Lakes, homestead, Qnsld., Austral. 89 F11
Diamantino, Braz. 50 G7
Dibrugarh, India 68 H9
Dickinson, N. Dak., U.S. 40 C8
Dickson, Russ. 68 C8
Diego de Almagro, Chile 50 K4
Diego Garcia, island, British Ind. Oc. Terr. 68 M6
Diemal Find, W. Austral., Austral. 88 J3
Dif, Kenya 78 J11
Diffa, Niger 78 G6
Dijon, Fr. 58 G5
Dili, Timor-Leste 69 M14
Dilling, Sudan 78 G9
Dillingham, Alas., U.S. 40 L2
Dillon, Mont., U.S. 40 C5
Dilolo, D.R.C. 79 L8
Dimashq (Damascus), Syr. 68 F3
Dimitrovgrad, Russ. 59 E13
Dinaric Alps, mountains, Europe 60 H7
Dingo, Qnsld., Austral. 89 F14
Diomede Islands, Russ.-U.S. 42 J1
Diourbel, Senegal 78 G1
Dirē Dawa, Eth. 78 H11
Dirk Hartog Island, W. Austral., Austral. 90 H1
Dirranbandi, Qnsld., Austral. 89 H14
Disappointment, Cape, Wash., U.S. 42 B3
Disappointment, Lake, W. Austral., Austral. 90 F4
Discovery Bay, S. Austral.-Vic., Austral. 91 M11
Divinhe, Mozambique 79 N10
Divinópolis, Braz. 50 H9
Diyarbakır, Turk. 59 K12
Djado, Niger 78 F6
Djanet, Alg. 78 E5
Djelfa, Alg. 78 D5
Djibouti, Af. 78 G11
Djibouti, Djibouti 78 G11
Dnieper, river, Russ.-Ukr. 61 G10
Dnieper, Source of the, Russ. 61 E10
Dnieper Lowland, Belarus-Ukr. 61 F10
Dnieper Upland, Ukr. 61 G10
Dniester, river, Moldova-Ukr. 60 G9
Dnipro (Dnieper), river, Ukr. 59 G11
Dnipropetrovs'k, Ukr. 59 G11
Dnister (Dniester), river, Ukr. 58 G9
Doba, Chad 78 H7
Dobane, Cen. Af. Rep. 78 H8
Dobbs, Cape, Can. 38 E7
Dobson, N.Z. 92 L4
Docker River, N. Terr., Austral. 88 G7
Dodecanese, islands, Gr. 60 K10
Dodge City, Kans., U.S. 40 F8
Dodoma, Tanzania 79 L10
Doha see Ad Dawḩah, Qatar 68 H4
Dolak, island, Indonesia 71 L16
Dolak (Yos Sudarso), island, Indonesia 92 D3
Dolbeau, Que., Can. 36 H9
Dolo Bay, Eth. 78 J11
Dom, peak, Indonesia 92 B3
Dome C, Antarctica 103 J12
Domett, N.Z. 92 L5
Dominica, N. America 37 N12
Dominican Republic, N. America 37 N10
Don, river, Russ. 61 G12
Dondo, Angola 79 L6
Donegal Bay, Ire. 60 E3
Donets, river, Russ.-Ukr. 61 G11
Donets'k, Ukr. 59 G11
Donets Ridge, Russ.-Ukr. 61 G11
Dongara, W. Austral., Austral. 88 J2
Dongola, Sudan 78 F9
Dongting Hu, China 71 H11
Donnellys Crossing, N.Z. 92 G5
Donner Pass, Calif., U.S. 42 E3
Donors Hill, homestead, Qnsld., Austral. 89 D11
Donostia-San Sebastián, Sp. 58 H3
Doomadgee, Qnsld., Austral. 89 D10
Dora, Lake, W. Austral., Austral. 90 F4
Dori, Burkina Faso 78 G4
Dortmund, Ger. 58 F6
Dothan, Ala., U.S. 41 H13
Douala, Cameroon 78 J5
Double Island Point, Qnsld., Austral. 91 H15
Double Point, Qnsld., Austral. 91 D13
Doubtless Bay, N.Z. 92 F5
Douglas, Ariz., U.S. 40 H5
Douglas, Ga., U.S. 41 H14
Douglas, Wyo., U.S. 40 D7
Dourada, Serra, Braz. 52 G8
Dourados, Braz. 50 H7
Douro, river, Port.-Sp. 60 H2
Dover, Del., U.S. 41 E15
Drâa, Hamada du, Alg.-Mor. 80 D3
Drâa, Oued, Alg.-Mor. 80 D3
Drakensberg, mountains, Lesotho-S. Af. 81 Q9
Drammen, Nor. 58 D6
Drava, river, Europe 60 H7
Dresden, Ger. 58 F7
Driskill Mountain, La., U.S. 43 H10
Drummond Island, Mich., U.S. 41 C13
Drummond Range, Qnsld., Austral. 91 F13
Drygalski Ice Tongue, Antarctica 102 L9
Drygalski Island, Antarctica 103 G15
Drygalski Mountains, Antarctica 102 A9
Drysdale, river, W. Austral., Austral. 90 C6
Dry Tortugas, islands, Fla., U.S. 43 L14
Duaringa, Qnsld., Austral. 89 F14
Dubawnt Lake, Can. 38 E6
Dubayy, U.A.E. 68 H5
Dubbo, N.S.W., AUSTRAL. 89 K14
Dublin, Ga., U.S. 41 H13
Dublin see Baile Átha Cliath, Ire. 58 E3
Dubrovnik, Croatia 58 J7
Dubuque, Iowa, U.S. 41 E11
Duc de Gloucester, Îles, Fr. Polynesia 97 H10
Duchess, Qnsld., Austral. 89 E11
Ducie Island, Pitcairn Is. 97 H12
Dudinka, Russ. 68 C8
Duero (Douro), river, Sp. 58 H2
Dufek Coast, Antarctica 102 H8
Duffield, N. Terr., Austral. 88 G9
Duff Islands, Solomon Is. 96 F5
Duifken Point, Qnsld., Austral. 91 B11
Duitama, Col. 50 B3
Dulan, China 68 G10
Duluth, Minn., U.S. 41 C10
Dumas, Tex., U.S. 40 G8
Dumont d'Urville, station, Antarctica 103 M13
Dumyât, Egypt 78 D9
Dunav (Danube), river, Serbia and Montenegro 58 H8
Dundalk, Ire. 58 E3
Dundas, Lake, W. Austral., Austral. 90 K5
Dundee, U.K. 58 D4
Dundee Island, Antarctica 102 B2
Dund-Us, Mongolia 68 F9
Dunedin, N.Z. 92 N4
Dunedoo, N.S.W., AUSTRAL. 89 K14
Dunolly, Vic., Austral. 89 L12
Dunsborough, W. Austral., Austral. 88 K2
Duntroon, N.Z. 92 N4
Duque de Caxias, Braz. 50 J10
Durango, Colo., U.S. 40 F6
Durango, Mex. 37 M4
Durant, Okla., U.S. 40 H9
Durazno, Uru. 51 L7
Durban, S. Af. 79 Q9
Durham, N.C., U.S. 41 F14
Durham Downs, homestead, Qnsld., Austral. 89 H11
Durmitor, peak, Serbia and Montenegro 60 J8
Durong, Qnsld., Austral. 89 H15
D'Urville, Tanjung, Indonesia 92 A3
D'Urville Island, N.Z. 92 K5
Dûsh, Egypt 78 E9
Dushanbe, Taj. 68 G7
Dvina Bay, Russ. 61 B10
Dvinskaya Guba (Dvina Bay), Russ. 59 B10
Dvinskoy, Russ. 59 C11
Dyersburg, Tenn., U.S. 41 G11
Dysart, Qnsld., Austral. 89 F14
Dzhagdy Range, Russ. 71 D12
Dzhugdzhur Range, Russ. 71 D12
Dzungarian Basin, China 70 F8

Eagle, Alas., U.S. 40 K4
Eagle Mountain, Minn., U.S. 43 C11
Eagle Pass, Tex., U.S. 40 K8
Eagle Peak, Calif., U.S. 42 D3
East Antarctica, region, Antarctica 103 F12
East Cape, N.Z. 92 H7
East Cape, Russ. 71 A12
East China Sea, Asia 71 G13
East Coast Bays, N.Z. 92 G5
Easter Island see Pascua, Isla de, Chile 97 H14
Eastern Desert, Egypt 80 E9
Eastern Ghats, India 70 K7
Eastern Sayan Mountains, Russ. 70 E9
East Falkland, island, Falkland Is. 53 Q6
East Fork White, river, Ind., U.S. 43 F12
East London, S. Af. 79 Q8
Eastmain, river, Can. 38 G8
Eastmain, Que., Can. 36 G8
East Prussia, Pol.-Russ. 58 F8
East Saint Louis, Ill., U.S. 41 F11
East Sea see Japan, Sea of, Asia 71 F13
East Siberian Sea, Russ. 71 B11
East Timor see Timor-Leste, Asia 69 M14
Eau Claire, Wis., U.S. 41 D11
Eauripik Atoll, F.S.M. 96 E3
Ebagoola, homestead, Qnsld., Austral. 89 C12
Ebolowa, Cameroon 78 J6
Ebon Atoll, Marshall Is. 96 E5
Ebro, river, Sp. 60 J4
Echo Bay, N.W.T., CAN. 36 E4
Echuca, Vic., Austral. 89 L12
Ecuador, S. America 50 D2
Edah, W. Austral., Austral. 88 H3
Ed Debba, Sudan 78 F9
Edgeøya, island, Nor. 68 B7
Edinburg, Tex., U.S. 40 K9
Edinburgh, U.K. 58 E4
Edirne, Turk. 58 J9
Edmonton, Alta., Can. 36 G4
Edmundston, N.B., Can. 36 H9
Edward, river, N.S.W., AUSTRAL. 91 L12
Edward, Lake, D.R.C.-Uganda 80 K9
Edward River, Qnsld., Austral. 89 C11
Edwards Plateau, Tex., U.S. 42 J8
Edward VIII Bay, Antarctica 103 C14
Edward VII Peninsula, Antarctica 102 K7
Éfaté, island, Vanuatu 96 G5
Egegik, Alas., U.S. 40 M2
Egersund, Nor. 58 D6
Egg Lagoon, Tas., Austral. 89 L15
Egmont, Mount see Taranaki, Mount, N.Z. 92 J5
Egypt, Af. 78 E9
Eiao, island, Marquesas Is. 97 F11
Eidsvold, Qnsld., Austral. 89 G15
Eights Coast, Antarctica 102 G3
Eighty Mile Beach, W. Austral., Austral. 90 E3
Eildon, Lake, Vic., Austral. 91 M12
Einasleigh, Qnsld., Austral. 89 D12
Eirunepé, Braz. 50 E4
Ejin Qi, China 69 G10
Ekibastuz, Kaz. 68 E7
Ekström Ice Shelf, Antarctica 102 A7
El 'Alamein, Egypt 78 D8
Elâzığ, Turk. 59 J12
Elba, island, It. 58 J6
Elba, Cape (Ras Hadarba), Egypt 80 F10
Elbasan, Alban. 58 J8
El Bayadh, Alg. 78 D4
Elbe, river, Ger. 60 F6
Elbert, Mount, Colo., U.S. 42 F7
El'brus, peak, Russ. 61 H13
Elburz Mountains, Iran 70 F5
El Calafate (Lago Argentino), Arg. 51 Q4
El Centro, Calif., U.S. 40 H4
El Djouf, region, Maurit. 80 F3
El Dorado, Ark., U.S. 41 H11
El Dorado, Venez. 50 B6
Eldorado, Arg. 50 J7
Elephant Butte Reservoir, N. Mex., U.S. 42 H6
Elephant Island, Antarctica 102 B1
El Faiyûm, Egypt 78 D9
El Fasher, Sudan 78 G8
El Galpón, Arg. 50 J5
El Gezira, region, Sudan 80 G9
El Gîza, Egypt 78 D9
El Golea, Alg. 78 D5
Elgon, Mount, Kenya-Uganda 80 J10
Eliase, Indonesia 92 D1
El Iskandarîya (Alexandria), Egypt 78 D9
Elista, Russ. 59 G13
El Jadida (Mazagan), Mor. 78 D3
Elkedra, homestead, N. Terr., Austral. 88 E9
El Kef, Tun. 78 C5
El Khandaq, Sudan 78 F9
El Khârga, Egypt 78 E9
Elkhart, Ind., U.S. 41 E12
Elkhorn, river, Nebr., U.S. 42 E9
Elko, Nev., U.S. 40 E4
Ellesmere, Lake, N.Z. 92 M4
Ellesmere Island, Can. 38 B7
Elliott, N. Terr., Austral. 88 D8
Elliston, S. Austral., Austral. 88 K9
Ellsworth Land, Antarctica 102 G4
Ellsworth Mountains, Antarctica 102 F5
El Minya, Egypt 78 E9
Elmira, N.Y., U.S. 41 D15
El Mreyyé, region, Mali-Maurit. 80 F3
El Obeid (Al Ubayyiḑ), Sudan 78 G9
El Oued, Alg. 78 D5
Eloy, Ariz., U.S. 40 H5
El Paso, Tex., U.S. 40 H6
El Qâhira (Cairo), Egypt 78 D9
El Qasr, Egypt 78 E8
El Rosario, Mex. 37 L3
El Salvador, N. America 37 P7
El Sharana, N. Terr., Austral. 88 B8
El Suweis (Suez), Egypt 78 D9
Eltanin Bay, Antarctica 102 F3
Eltham, N.Z. 92 J5
El Tigre, Venez. 50 A5
El Wak, Kenya 78 J11
Ely, Minn., U.S. 41 C10
Ely, Nev., U.S. 40 E4
Emba, Kaz. 59 E15
Embarcación, Arg. 50 J5
Emerald, Qnsld., Austral. 89 F14
Emi Koussi, peak, Chad 80 F7
Emirau, island, P.N.G. 92 B7
Emita, Tas., Austral. 89 L16
Emporia, Kans., U.S. 40 F9
Empress Augusta Bay, P.N.G. 92 C8
Empty Quarter see Ar Rub' al Khālī, desert, Saudi Arabia 68 H4
Emu Park, Qnsld., Austral. 89 F15
Encounter Bay, S. Austral., Austral. 91 L10
Endeavour Hill, N. Terr., Austral. 90 C7
Endeavour Strait, Qnsld., Austral. 91 A11
Enderbury Island, Kiribati 96 F8
Enderby Land, Antarctica 103 C13
Endicott Mountains, Alas., U.S. 42 J3
Enewetak Atoll, Marshall Is. 96 D5
Engels, Russ. 59 F12
England, U.K. 58 F4
English Channel, Fr.-U.K. 60 F4
English Coast, Antarctica 102 E4
Enid, Okla., U.S. 40 G9
En Nahud, Sudan 78 G9
Ennedi, mountains, Chad 80 G7
Enngonia, N.S.W., AUSTRAL. 89 H13
Ensenada, Mex. 37 L3
Entebbe, Uganda 78 K9
Enterprise, Ala., U.S. 41 H13
Entre Ríos, region, Arg. 53 L6
Enugu, Nig. 78 H5
Epéna, Congo 78 J7
Epsilon, homestead, Qnsld., Austral. 89 H11
Epukiro, Namibia 79 N7
Equatorial Guinea, Af. 78 J5
Erebus, Mount, Antarctica 102 K9
Ereğli, Turk. 59 K11
Erfoud, Mor. 78 D4
Erfurt, Ger. 58 F6
Erie, Pa., U.S. 41 D14
Erie, Lake, Can.-U.S. 43 D13
Eritrea, Af. 78 G10
Erldunda, homestead, N. Terr., Austral. 88 G8
Ernabella, S. Austral., Austral. 88 G8
Eromanga, Qnsld., Austral. 89 G12
Er Rachidia, Mor. 78 D4
Er Rif, mountains, Mor. 80 C3
Erromango, island, Vanuatu 96 G6
Erzincan, Turk. 59 J12
Erzurum, Turk. 59 J13
Esbjerg, Den. 58 E6
Escanaba, Mich., U.S. 41 C12
Eşfahān, Iran 68 G5
Esil, Kaz. 59 D16
Esker, Nfld. and Lab., Can. 36 G9
Eskişehir, Turk. 59 K10
Esmeralda, homestead, Qnsld., Austral. 89 D12
Esmeraldas, Ecua. 50 C1
Esperance, W. Austral., Austral. 88 K5
Esperanza, station, Antarctica 102 B2
Esperanza, Peru 50 F4
Espigão Mestre, mountains, Braz. 52 G9
Espinhaço, Serra do, Braz. 52 H9
Espiritu Santo, island, Vanuatu 96 G5
Esquel, Arg. 51 N4
Essen, Ger. 58 F5
Essendon, Mount, W. Austral., Austral. 90 G4
Essequibo, river, Guyana 52 B6
Essington, Port, N. Terr., Austral. 90 A8
Estacado, Llano, N. Mex.-Tex., U.S. 42 H7
Estacado, Llano (Staked Plain), U.S. 39 L5
Estados, Isla de los (Staten Island), Arg. 51 R6
Estância, Braz. 50 F11
Este, Punta del, Uru. 53 M7
Estonia, Europe 58 D9
Etadunna, homestead, S. Austral., Austral. 89 H10
Ethiopia, Af. 78 H10
Ethiopian Highlands, Eth. 80 H10
Etna, peak, It. 60 K7
Etosha Pan, Namibia 81 N7
Ettrick, N.Z. 92 N3
'Eua, island, Tonga 96 H7
Euboea, island, Gr. 60 K9
Eucla Basin, W. Austral., Austral. 90 J6
Eucla Motel, W. Austral., Austral. 88 J7
Eucumbene, Lake, N.S.W., AUSTRAL. 91 L13
Eufaula Lake, Okla., U.S. 43 G10
Eugene, Oreg., U.S. 40 C3
Eugenia Point, Mex. 39 L3
Euphrates, river, Asia 70 F4
Eurardy, homestead, W. Austral., Austral. 88 H2
Eureka, Calif., U.S. 40 D2
Eureka, Nunavut 36 B6
Europa, Île (Europa Island), Ind. Oc. 79 N11
Europa Island, Mozambique Chan. 81 P10
Eva Downs, homestead, N. Terr., Austral. 88 D9
Evanston, Ill., U.S. 41 E12
Evanston, Wyo., U.S. 40 E6
Evansville, Ind., U.S. 41 F12
Everard, Lake, S. Austral., Austral. 90 J9
Everard Park, homestead, S. Austral., Austral. 88 G8
Everest, Mount, China-Nepal 70 H8
Everett, Wash., U.S. 40 B3
Ewaninga, N. Terr., Austral. 88 F9
Executive Committee Range, Antarctica 102 J5
Exmouth, W. Austral., Austral. 88 F1
Exmouth Gulf, W. Austral., Austral. 90 F1
Eyre, Lake, S. Austral., Austral. 91 H10
Eyre North, Lake, S. Austral., Austral. 90 H10
Eyre Peninsula, S. Austral., Austral. 90 K9
Eyre South, Lake, S. Austral., Austral. 90 H10
Ezequiela Ramos Mexia, Embalse, Arg. 53 N5

Fachi, Niger 78 F6
Fada, Chad 78 G7
Faguibine, Lake, Mali 80 G3
Fairbanks, Alas., U.S. 40 K3
Fairview, homestead, Qnsld., Austral. 89 C12
Fairweather, Mount, Can.-U.S. 42 L5
Fais, island, F.S.M. 96 D3
Faisalabad, Pak. 68 H7
Faith, S. Dak., U.S. 40 D8
Fakaofu, island, Tokelau 96 F8
Falcon Lake, Mex.-U.S. 42 K9
Falémé, river, Mali-Senegal 80 G2
Falfurrias, Tex., U.S. 40 K9
Falkland Islands, Atl. Oc. 53 Q6
Fallières Coast, Antarctica 102 D2
False Bay, S. Af. 81 R7
False Cape, Mex. 39 M3
Falun, Sweden 58 D7
Fanning Island see Tabuaeran, Kiribati 96 E9
Farafangana, Madag. 79 P12
Farah, Afghan. 68 G6
Farallon de Pajaros, island, N. Mariana Is. 96 C3
Farallon Islands, Calif., U.S. 42 E2
Farewell, Alas., U.S. 40 L3
Farewell, Cape, Greenland 38 D10
Farewell, Cape, N.Z. 92 K4
Fargo, N. Dak., U.S. 40 C9
Farg'ona, Uzb. 68 G7
Faribault, Minn., U.S. 41 D10
Farmington, N. Mex., U.S. 40 F6
Faro, Port. 58 J1
Faroe Islands, Den. 60 C4
Fataka (Mitre Island), Solomon Is. 96 G6
Fatu Hiva, island, Marquesas Is. 97 F11
Faxaflói, bay, Ice. 60 A3
Faya-Largeau, Chad 78 F7
Fayetteville, Ark., U.S. 41 G10
Fayetteville, N.C., U.S. 41 G14
Fdérik, Maurit. 78 E2
Fear, Cape, N.C., U.S. 43 G15
Federated States of Micronesia, Pac. Oc. 96 E2
Feijó, Braz. 50 E4
Feilding, N.Z. 92 K6
Feira de Santana, Braz. 50 F11
Felipe Carrillo Puerto, Mex. 37 N7
Feni Islands, P.N.G. 92 B8
Fergusson Island, P.N.G. 92 D7
Ferkéssédougou, Côte d'Ivoire 78 H3
Fernandina, Isla, Ecua. 97 E16
Fernando de Noronha, Braz. 52 E12
Fernando de Noronha, Arquipélago de (Fernando de Noronha), Braz. 50 E12
Fernan Vaz see Omboué, Gabon 79 K5
Fernlee, homestead, Qnsld., Austral. 89 H13

Ferrara, *It.* **58** H6
Ferro, *island, Canary Is.* **80** D1
Fès (Fez), *Mor.* **78** D3
Feuet, *Alg.* **78** E6
Fez *see* Fès, *Mor.* **78** D3
Fezzan, *region, Lib.* **78** E6
Fianarantsoa, *Madag.* **79** N12
Fields Find, *W. Austral., Austral.* **88** J3
Fiji Islands, *Pac. Oc.* **96** G6
Filchner Ice Sheet, *Antarctica* **102** D6
Fillmore, *Utah, U.S.* **40** E5
Fimbul Ice Shelf, *Antarctica* **102** A8
Finger Lakes, *N.Y., U.S.* **43** D14
Finisterre, Cape, *Sp.* **60** H2
Finke, *river, N. Terr., Austral.* **90** G8
Finke, *N. Terr., Austral.* **88** G9
Finland, *Europe* **58** C9
Finland, Gulf of, *Est.-Fin.-Russ.* **60** D9
Finnmark Plateau, *Nor.* **60** A8
Finschhafen, *P.N.G.* **92** C6
Firenze, *It.* **58** J6
Fisher, *S. Austral., Austral.* **88** J8
Fisher Glacier, *Antarctica* **103** D12
Fitzgerald, *Ga., U.S.* **41** H13
Fitzroy, *river, Qnsld., Austral.* **91** F14
Fitzroy, *river, W. Austral., Austral.* **90** D5
Fitzroy Crossing, *W. Austral., Austral.* **88** D5
Flagstaff, *Ariz., U.S.* **40** G5
Flaming Gorge Reservoir, *Utah-Wyo., U.S.* **42** E6
Flamingo, Teluk, *Indonesia* **92** C3
Flat, *Alas., U.S.* **40** L2
Flathead Lake, *Mont., U.S.* **42** B5
Flattery, Cape, *Qnsld., Austral.* **91** C13
Flattery, Cape, *Wash., U.S.* **42** A3
Fleming Glacier, *Antarctica* **102** D3
Fletcher Peninsula, *Antarctica* **102** F3
Flinders, *river, Qnsld., Austral.* **91** D11
Flinders Bay, *W. Austral., Austral.* **88** L2
Flinders Island, *Tas., Austral.* **91** L16
Flinders Ranges, *S. Austral., Austral.* **91** J10
Flin Flon, *Manitoba, Can.* **36** G5
Flint, *river, Ga., U.S.* **43** H13
Flint, *Mich., U.S.* **41** D13
Flint Hills, *Kans., U.S.* **42** F9
Flint Island, *Fr. Polynesia* **96** G10
Flood Range, *Antarctica* **102** J5
Florence, *Ala., U.S.* **41** G12
Florence, *S.C., U.S.* **41** G14
Florencia, *Col.* **50** C2
Flores, *island, Indonesia* **71** M13
Flores, *Guatemala* **37** P7
Floriano, *Braz.* **50** E10
Florianópolis, *Braz.* **51** K8
Florida, *U.S.* **41** J13
Florida, Straits of, *Cuba-U.S.* **43** L14
Florida Bay, *Fla., U.S.* **43** K14
Florida Keys, *Fla., U.S.* **43** L14
Florø, *Nor.* **58** C6
Fly, *river, P.N.G.* **92** D4
Foggia, *It.* **58** J7
Fonseca, Gulf of, *Hond.* **39** Q7
Fonte Boa, *Braz.* **50** D5
Ford, Cape, *N. Terr., Austral.* **90** B7
Fordate, *island, Indonesia* **92** C1
Ford Ranges, *Antarctica* **102** J6
Fords Bridge, *N.S.W., AUSTRAL.* **89** J12
Forel, Mont, *Greenland* **38** C10
Forest Home, *homestead, Qnsld., Austral.* **89** D12
Formiga, *Braz.* **50** H9
Formosa, *Arg.* **50** J6
Formosa, *Braz.* **50** G9
Formosa, Serra, *Braz.* **52** F7
Formosa do Rio Prêto, *Braz.* **50** F9
Føroyar *see* Faroe Islands, *Den.* **58** C4
Forrest, *W. Austral., Austral.* **88** J7
Forrestal Range, *Antarctica* **102** E6
Forrest River, *W. Austral., Austral.* **88** C6
Forsayth, *Qnsld., Austral.* **89** D12
Forster-Tuncurry, *N.S.W., AUSTRAL.* **89** K15
Forsyth, *Mont., U.S.* **40** C7
Fortaleza, *Braz.* **50** D11
Fort Benton, *Mont., U.S.* **40** B6
Fort Bragg, *Calif., U.S.* **40** E2
Fort Chipewyan, *Alta., Can.* **36** F5
Fort Collins, *Colo., U.S.* **40** E7
Fort Dodge, *Iowa, U.S.* **41** E10
Fortescue, *river, W. Austral., Austral.* **90** F2
Fort Fraser, *B.C., Can.* **36** F3
Fort Good Hope, *N.W.T., CAN.* **36** D4
Forth, Firth of, *U.K.* **60** E4
Fortín Madrejón, *Para.* **50** H6
Fortín May Alberto Gardel, *Para.* **50** J6
Fortín Presidente Ayala, *Para.* **50** J6
Fortín Suárez Arana, *Bol.* **50** H6
Fort Lauderdale, *Fla., U.S.* **41** K15
Fort Liard, *N.W.T., CAN.* **36** E4
Fort McMurray, *Alta., Can.* **36** F4
Fort McPherson, *N.W.T., CAN.* **36** D4
Fort Miribel, *Alg.* **78** D5
Fort Morgan, *Colo., U.S.* **40** E7
Fort Myers, *Fla., U.S.* **41** K14
Fort Nelson, *B.C., Can.* **36** F4
Fort Peck Lake, *Mont., U.S.* **42** C7
Fort Pierce, *Fla., U.S.* **41** K15
Fort Resolution, *N.W.T., CAN.* **36** F5
Fort Saint John, *B.C., Can.* **36** F4
Fort Severn, *Ont., Can.* **36** G7
Fort Shevchenko, *Kaz.* **59** G14
Fort Simpson, *N.W.T., CAN.* **36** E4
Fort Smith, *Ark., U.S.* **41** G10
Fort Smith, *N.W.T., CAN.* **36** F5
Fort Stockton, *Tex., U.S.* **40** J7
Fort Sumner, *N. Mex., U.S.* **40** G7
Fort Vermilion, *Alta., Can.* **36** F4
Fort Wayne, *Ind., U.S.* **41** E12
Fort Worth, *Tex., U.S.* **40** H9
Fort Yates, *N. Dak., U.S.* **40** C8
Fort Yukon, *Alas., U.S.* **40** K4
Foulwind, Cape, *N.Z.* **92** L4
Foundation Ice Stream, *Antarctica* **102** F6
Fourcroy, Cape, *N. Terr., Austral.* **90** B7
Fouta Djallon, *region, Guinea* **80** G2
Foveaux Strait, *N.Z.* **92** P3
Fowlers Bay, *S. Austral., Austral.* **88** J8
Fox, *river, Ill.-Wisc.* **43** E12
Fox, *river, Wis., U.S.* **43** D12
Foxe Basin, *Can.* **38** E7
Foxe Peninsula, *Can.* **38** E8
Fox Glacier, *N.Z.* **92** M3
Fox Islands, *U.S.* **39** R4
Foyn Coast, *Antarctica* **102** D2
Foz do Cunene, *Angola* **79** N6
Foz do Iguaçu, *Braz.* **50** J7
Framnes Mountains, *Antarctica* **103** D14
Fram Peak, *Antarctica* **103** C14
Franca, *Braz.* **50** H9
France, *Europe* **58** G4
Franceville, *Gabon* **79** K6
Francis Case, Lake, *S. Dak., U.S.* **42** D9
Francistown, *Botswana* **79** N8
Frankfort, *Ky., U.S.* **41** F13
Frankfurt, *Ger.* **58** G6
Franklin Bay, *Can.* **38** D4
Franklin Mountains, *Can.* **38** E4
Frantsa Iosifa, Zemlya *see* Franz Josef Land, *Russ.* **68** B8
Franz Josef Glacier, *N.Z.* **92** M4
Franz Josef Land, *Russ.* **70** B8
Fraser, *river, Can.* **38** G3
Fraser Island (Great Sandy Island), *Qnsld., Austral.* **91** G15
Fraser Range, *homestead, W. Austral., Austral.* **88** K5
Frasertown, *N.Z.* **92** J6
Frederick, Mount, *N. Terr., Austral.* **90** D7
Fredericton, *N.B., Can.* **36** H9
Frederikshavn, *Den.* **58** E6
Fredrikstad, *Nor.* **58** D6
Freeport, *Bahamas* **37** M9
Freeport, *Tex., U.S.* **41** K10
Freetown, *Sierra Leone* **78** H2
Freiburg, *Ger.* **58** G5
Fremantle, *borough, W. Austral., Austral.* **88** K2
Fremont, *Nebr., U.S.* **40** E9
French Guiana, *S. America* **50** B8
French Polynesia, *Pac. Oc.* **97** G10
Fresnillo, *Mex.* **37** N5
Fresno, *Calif., U.S.* **40** F3
Frewena, *homestead, N. Terr., Austral.* **88** D9
Fria, *Guinea* **78** H1
Fridtjof Nansem, Mount, *Antarctica* **102** H8
Frio, Cape, *Braz.* **52** J10
Frisian Islands, *Ger.-Neth.* **60** F5
Frissell, Mount, *Conn., U.S.* **43** D15
Frome, Lake, *S. Austral., Austral.* **91** J11
Frome Downs, *homestead, S. Austral., Austral.* **89** J11
Front Range, *Colo.-Wyo., U.S.* **42** E7
Fuerteventura, *island, Canary Is.* **80** D2
Fuji, *peak, Jap.* **71** F14
Fukuoka, *Jap.* **69** G13
Fukushima, Mount, *Antarctica* **103** B11
Funafuti, *Tuvalu* **96** F7
Fundy, Bay of, *Can.* **43** B17
Furmanovo, *Kaz.* **59** F13
Furneaux Group, *Tas., Austral.* **91** L16
Fushun, *China* **69** F12
Futuna, *island, Vanuatu* **96** G6
Fuzhou, *China* **69** H12
Fyn, *island, Den.* **60** E6

Güeppí, *Peru* **50** D2
Gaalkacyo, *Somalia* **78** H12
Gabes, *Tun.* **78** D6
Gabes, Gulf of, *Tun.* **80** D6
Gabon, *Af.* **79** K6
Gaborone, *Botswana* **79** P8
Gabriel Vera, *Bol.* **50** H5
Gabrovo, *Bulg.* **58** J9
Gäddede, *Sweden* **58** C7
Gadsden, *Ala., U.S.* **41** H12
Gaferut, *island, F.S.M.* **96** D3
Gafsa, *Tun.* **78** D5
Gagnoa, *Côte d'Ivoire* **78** H3
Gainesville, *Fla., U.S.* **41** J14
Gairdner, Lake, *S. Austral., Austral.* **90** J9
Galan, Cerro, *Arg.* **52** J5
Galápagos Islands (Archipiélago de Colón), *Ecua.* **97** E16
Galaţi, *Rom.* **58** H9
Galbraith, *homestead, Qnsld., Austral.* **89** C11
Galdhøpiggen, *peak, Nor.* **60** C6
Galegu, *Sudan* **78** G10
Galena, *Alas., U.S.* **40** K2
Galera Point, *Ecua.* **52** D1
Galilee, Lake, *Qnsld., Austral.* **91** F13
Galina Mine, *W. Austral., Austral.* **88** H2
Galipoli, *homestead, N. Terr., Austral.* **89** D10
Galiwinku, *N. Terr., Austral.* **88** B9
Galle, *Sri Lanka* **68** L7
Gällivare, *Sweden* **58** B8
Gallup, *N. Mex., U.S.* **40** G6
Galveston, *Tex., U.S.* **41** J10
Galveston Bay, *Tex., U.S.* **43** J10
Galway, *Ire.* **58** E3
Gambēla, *Eth.* **78** H10
Gambell, *Alas., U.S.* **40** K1
Gambia, *Af.* **78** G1
Gambia, *river, Gambia-Senegal* **80** G1
Gambier, Îles, *Fr. Polynesia* **97** H11
Gana, *river, Nig.* **80** H6
Gäncä, *Azerb.* **59** H14
Gandajika, *D.R.C.* **79** L8
Gander, *Nfld. and Lab., Can.* **36** G11
Ganga (Ganges), *river, India* **68** H8
Gan Gan, *Arg.* **51** N5
Gangdise Range, *China* **70** H8
Ganges, *river, India* **70** J8
Ganges Plain, *India* **70** H8
Gannett Peak, *Wyo., U.S.* **42** D6
Ganyushkino, *Kaz.* **59** G14
Ganzhou, *China* **69** H12
Gao, *Mali* **78** G4
Gaoua, *Burkina Faso* **78** H3
Gaoual, *Guinea* **78** G2
Garabogaz Bay, *Turkm.* **70** F5
Garacad, *Somalia* **78** H12
Garagum, *region, Turkm.* **70** G6
Garaina, *P.N.G.* **92** D6
Garanhuns, *Braz.* **50** F11
Garda, Lake, *It.* **60** H6
Garden City, *Kans., U.S.* **40** F8
Garden Point, *N. Terr., Austral.* **88** A7
Gardner Pinnacles, *Hawaii, U.S.* **96** C8
Garies, *S. Af.* **79** Q7
Garissa, *Kenya* **79** K11
Garonne, *river, Fr.* **60** H4
Garoowe, *Somalia* **78** H12
Garoua, *Cameroon* **78** H6
Garsen, *Kenya* **79** K11
Gary, *Ind., U.S.* **41** E12
Gascoyne, *river, W. Austral., Austral.* **90** G2
Gascoyne Junction, *W. Austral., Austral.* **88** G2
Gaspé, *Que., Can.* **36** G10
Gaspé Peninsula, *Can.* **38** H9
Gastonia, *N.C., U.S.* **41** G14
Gävle, *Sweden* **58** D7
Gawler, *S. Austral., Austral.* **89** K10
Gawler Ranges, *S. Austral., Austral.* **90** K9
Gaya, *Niger* **78** G4
Gayny, *Russ.* **59** C13
Gaza Strip, *region, Asia* **68** F3
Gaziantep, *Turk.* **59** K12
Gdańsk, *Pol.* **58** F8
Gdańsk, Gulf of, *Pol.-Russ.* **60** E8
Gedaref, *Sudan* **78** G10
Geelong, *Vic., Austral.* **89** M12
Geelvink Channel, *W. Austral., Austral.* **90** J2
Geeveston, *Tas., Austral.* **89** M16
Gefara, *region, Lib.-Tun.* **80** D6
Geidam, *Nig.* **78** G6
Gejiu, *China* **69** J10
Gemena, *D.R.C.* **78** J7
Geneina (Al Junaynah), *Sudan* **78** G8
General Acha, *Arg.* **51** M5
General Alvear, *Arg.* **51** L5
General Bernardo O'Higgins, *station, Antarctica* **102** C2
General Juan Madariaga, *Arg.* **51** M7
General Roca, *Arg.* **51** M5
General San Martín, *Arg.* **51** P4
General Santos, *Philippines* **69** K14
Geneva, Lake of, *Fr.-Switz.* **60** H5
Genève, *Switz.* **58** H5
Genoa *see* Genova, *It.* **58** H6
Genova (Genoa), *It.* **58** H6
Geographe Bay, *W. Austral., Austral.* **90** K2
Geographe Channel, *W. Austral., Austral.* **90** G1
George, *S. Af.* **79** Q8
George, Lake, *N.S.W., AUSTRAL.* **91** L14
George Town, *Tas., Austral.* **89** L16
Georgetown, *Guyana* **50** B6
Georgetown, *Qnsld., Austral.* **89** D12
Georgetown, *S.C., U.S.* **41** G14
George V Coast, *Antarctica* **103** M11
George VI Sound, *Antarctica* **102** E3
Georgia, *Asia-Europe* **59** H13
Georgia, *U.S.* **41** H13
Georgia, Strait of, *Can.* **38** G3
Georgian Bay, *Can.* **38** J8
Georgina, *river, N. Terr.-Qnsld., Austral.* **91** F10
Geral, Serra, *Braz.* **53** K8
Geraldine, *N.Z.* **92** M4
Geraldton, *W. Austral., Austral.* **88** J2
Gerdine, Mount, *Alas., U.S.* **42** L3
Gerlach, *peak, Slovakia* **60** G8
Germany, *Europe* **58** F6
Gesoa, *P.N.G.* **92** D5
Getz Ice Shelf, *Antarctica* **102** J4
Ghadāmis, *Lib.* **78** D6
Ghana, *Af.* **78** H4
Ghanzi, *Botswana* **79** N7
Ghardaïa, *Alg.* **78** D5
Gharyān, *Lib.* **78** D6
Ghāt, *Lib.* **78** E6
Gibb River, *homestead, W. Austral., Austral.* **88** C6
Gibraltar, *Europe* **58** K2
Gibraltar, Strait of, *Af.-Europe* **60** K2
Gibson, *W. Austral., Austral.* **88** K5
Gibson Desert, *W. Austral., Austral.* **90** F5
Gijón, *Sp.* **58** H2
Gila, *river, Ariz.-N. Mex., U.S.* **42** H4
Gila Bend, *Ariz., U.S.* **40** H5
Gilbert, *river, Qnsld., Austral.* **91** D12
Gilbert Islands, *islands, Kiribati* **96** E6
Gilbert River, *Qnsld., Austral.* **89** D12
Gilbués, *Braz.* **50** F9
Gilf Kebîr Plateau, *Egypt* **80** F8
Gilgandra, *N.S.W., AUSTRAL.* **89** K14
Gilgit, *Pak.* **68** G7
Gillen, Lake, *W. Austral., Austral.* **90** G5
Gilles, Lake, *S. Austral., Austral.* **90** K9
Gillette, *Wyo., U.S.* **40** D7
Gilmore Hut, *homestead, Qnsld., Austral.* **89** G12
Gilpeppee, *homestead, Qnsld., Austral.* **89** G11
Gippsland, *region, Vic., Austral.* **91** M13
Girga, *Egypt* **78** E9
Gisborne, *N.Z.* **92** J7
Gitega, *Burundi* **79** K9
Gjoa Haven, *Nunavut* **36** D6
Gjøvik, *Nor.* **58** D6
Gladstone, *Qnsld., Austral.* **89** G15
Gladstone, *S. Austral., Austral.* **89** K10
Glåma, *river, Nor.* **60** D7
Glasgow, *Mont., U.S.* **40** B7
Glasgow, *U.K.* **58** E4
Glazov, *Russ.* **59** C13
Glenavy, *N.Z.* **92** N4
Glenayle, *homestead, W. Austral., Austral.* **88** G4
Glendale, *Calif., U.S.* **40** G3
Glendive, *Mont., U.S.* **40** C7
Glengyle, *homestead, Qnsld., Austral.* **89** G11
Glen Innes, *N.S.W., AUSTRAL.* **89** J15
Glenormiston, *homestead, Qnsld., Austral.* **89** F10
Glenreagh, *N.S.W., AUSTRAL.* **89** J15
Glenroy, *homestead, W. Austral., Austral.* **88** D6
Glenwood Springs, *Colo., U.S.* **40** E6
Globe, *Ariz., U.S.* **40** H5
Glorieuses, Îles, *Ind. Oc.* **79** M12
Gloucester, *N.S.W., AUSTRAL.* **89** K15
Gloucester, *P.N.G.* **92** C6
Gnaraloo, *homestead, W. Austral., Austral.* **88** G1
Goba, *Eth.* **78** H11
Gobi, *desert, China-Mongolia* **71** F11
Godhavn *see* Qeqertarsuaq, *Greenland* **36** D9
Gods Lake, *Manitoba, Can.* **36** G6
Godthåb *see* Nuuk, *Greenland* **36** D9
Godwin Austin *see* K2, *peak, China-Pak.* **70** G7
Gogebic Range, *Mich.-Wisc.* **43** C11
Gogrial, *Sudan* **78** H8
Goianésia, *Braz.* **50** G8
Goiânia, *Braz.* **50** G8
Goiás, *Braz.* **50** G8
Gold Coast, *Ghana* **80** J3
Gold Coast, *Qnsld., Austral.* **89** H15
Golden Bay, *N.Z.* **92** K5
Golden Ridge, *W. Austral., Austral.* **88** J4
Goldfield, *Nev., U.S.* **40** F4
Goldsboro, *N.C., U.S.* **41** G15
Goldsworthy, *W. Austral., Austral.* **88** E3
Golmud, *China* **68** G9
Golovin, *Alas., U.S.* **40** K2
Golyshmanovo, *Russ.* **59** B15
Gombe, *Nig.* **78** H6
Gomera, *island, Canary Is.* **80** D1
Gómez Palacio, *Mex.* **37** M5
Gonâve, Gulf of, *Haiti* **39** N10
Gonder, *Eth.* **78** G10
Gongga Shan, *China* **71** H10
Gongolgon, *N.S.W., AUSTRAL.* **89** J13
Goodenough Island, *P.N.G.* **92** D7
Good Hope, Cape of, *S. Af.* **81** Q7
Goodland, *Kans., U.S.* **40** F8
Goodnews Bay, *Alas., U.S.* **40** L2
Goodooga, *N.S.W., AUSTRAL.* **89** H13
Goodparla, *homestead, N. Terr., Austral.* **88** B8
Goolgowi, *N.S.W., AUSTRAL.* **89** K12
Goomalling, *W. Austral., Austral.* **88** J3
Goondiwindi, *Qnsld., Austral.* **89** H14
Goongarrie, Lake, *W. Austral., Austral.* **90** J4
Goonyella, *Qnsld., Austral.* **89** F14
Goose Lake, *Calif.-Oreg., U.S.* **42** D3
Gordon, Lake, *Tas., Austral.* **91** M15
Gordon Downs, *homestead, W. Austral., Austral.* **88** D7
Goré, *Chad* **78** H7
Gore, *N.Z.* **92** N3
Goreda, *Indonesia* **92** B2
Gor'kiy Reservoir, *Russ.* **61** D11
Goroka, *P.N.G.* **92** C5
Gorongosa, Serra da, *Mozambique* **81** N9
Gorontalo, *Indonesia* **69** L13
Goschen Strait, *P.N.G.* **92** D7
Gosford, *N.S.W., AUSTRAL.* **89** K14
Göteborg, *Sweden* **58** E7
Gotland, *island, Sweden* **60** E8
Gouin, Réservoir, *Can.* **38** H9
Gould Bay, *Antarctica* **102** D6
Gould Coast, *Antarctica* **102** H7
Gouré, *Niger* **78** G6
Gouro, *Chad* **78** F7
Gove Peninsula, *N. Terr., Austral.* **90** B9
Governador Valadares, *Braz.* **50** H10
Goya, *Arg.* **51** K6
Graaff-Reinet, *S. Af.* **79** Q8
Gracias a Dios, Cape, *Nicar.* **39** P8
Gradaús, *Braz.* **50** E8
Grafton, *N. Dak., U.S.* **40** B9
Grafton, *N.S.W., AUSTRAL.* **89** J15
Graham Land, *Antarctica* **102** C2
Grahamstown, *S. Af.* **79** Q8
Grain Coast, *Liberia* **80** J2
Grajaú, *Braz.* **50** E9
Grampian Mountains, *U.K.* **60** D4
Granada, *Nicar.* **37** Q8
Granada, *Sp.* **58** K2
Gran Canaria, *island, Canary Is.* **80** D2
Gran Chaco, *plain, Arg.-Para.* **52** J6
Grand, *river, Mich., U.S.* **43** D12
Grand, *river, S. Dak., U.S.* **42** C8
Grand-Bassam, *Côte d'Ivoire* **78** J3
Grand Canyon, *Ariz., U.S.* **42** G5
Grand Canyon, *Ariz., U.S.* **40** G5
Grand Cayman, *island, Cayman Is.* **39** N8
Grand Cess, *Liberia* **78** J2
Grande, *river, Bol.* **52** G5
Grande, *river, Braz.* **52** H9
Grande, Bahía (Grande Bay), *Arg.* **51** Q5
Grande Bay, *Arg.* **53** Q5
Grande de Chiloé, Isla, *Chile* **53** N4
Grande de Tierra del Fuego, Isla (Tierra del Fuego), *Arg.-Chile* **51** R5
Grande Prairie, *Alta., Can.* **36** F4
Grandes, Salinas, *Arg.* **53** K5
Grand Falls-Windsor, *Nfld. and Lab., Can.* **36** G10
Grand Forks, *N. Dak., U.S.* **40** C9
Grand Island, *Nebr., U.S.* **40** E9
Grand Isle, *La., U.S.* **41** J11
Grand Junction, *Colo., U.S.* **40** F6
Grand Marais, *Minn., U.S.* **41** C11
Grand Rapids, *Manitoba, Can.* **36** G6
Grand Rapids, *Mich., U.S.* **41** D12
Grand Teton, *peak, Wyo., U.S.* **42** D6
Granite Peak, *Mont., U.S.* **42** C6
Granite Peak, *Nev., U.S.* **42** D4
Grant Island, *Antarctica* **102** K5
Grants, *N. Mex., U.S.* **40** G6
Grants Pass, *Oreg., U.S.* **40** D2
Grassmere, *homestead, Qnsld., Austral.* **89** H13
Grass Patch, *W. Austral., Austral.* **88** K4
Graz, *Aust.* **58** H7
Great Artesian Basin, *Austral.* **91** F11
Great Australian Bight, *Austral.* **90** K7
Great Barrier Island, *N.Z.* **92** G6
Great Barrier Reef, *Austral.* **91** E15
Great Basin, *Nev.-Utah, U.S.* **42** E4
Great Bear Lake, *Can.* **38** E4
Great Bend, *Kans., U.S.* **40** F9
Great Britain, *island, U.K.* **60** E4
Great Dismal Swamp, *N.C.-Va., U.S.* **43** F15
Great Divide Basin, *Wyo., U.S.* **42** E6
Great Dividing Range, *Austral.* **91** C12
Great Eastern Erg, *Alg.* **80** D5
Greater Antilles, *islands, N. America* **39** N10
Greater Khingan Range, *China* **71** F11
Greater Sunda Islands, *Asia* **71** L12
Great Falls, *Mont., U.S.* **40** B6
Great Hungarian Plain, *Hung.* **60** H8
Great Inagua Island, *Bahamas* **39** N10
Great Indian Desert, *India-Pak.* **70** H7
Great Karroo, *S. Af.* **81** Q7
Great Miami, *river, Ohio, U.S.* **43** E13
Great Namaland, *region, Namibia* **79** P7
Great Pee Dee, *river, N.C.-S.C., U.S.* **43** G14
Great Plains, *Can.-U.S.* **38** G4
Great Rift Valley, *Af.* **80** J10
Great Ruaha, *river, Tanzania* **81** L10
Great Salt Lake, *Utah, U.S.* **42** E5
Great Salt Lake Desert, *Utah, U.S.* **42** E5
Great Sandy Desert, *Oreg., U.S.* **42** D3
Great Sandy Desert, *W. Austral., Austral.* **90** E5
Great Sandy Island *see* Fraser Island, *Qnsld., Austral.* **91** G15
Great Slave Lake, *Can.* **38** E4
Great Smoky Mountains, *N.C.-Tenn., U.S.* **43** G13
Great Victoria Desert, *S. Austral.-W. Austral., Austral.* **90** H6
Great Wall, *station, Antarctica* **102** C1
Great Western Erg, *Alg.* **80** D4
Great Western Tiers, *mountains, Tas., Austral.* **91** L15
Greece, *Europe* **58** K8
Greeley, *Colo., U.S.* **40** E7
Green, *river, Ky., U.S.* **43** F12
Green, *river, Utah-Wyo., U.S.* **42** F6
Green Bay, *Mich.-Wisc.* **43** C12
Green Bay, *Wis., U.S.* **41** D12
Green Head, *W. Austral., Austral.* **90** J2
Green Islands, *P.N.G.* **92** B8
Greenland (Kalaallit Nunaat), *N. America* **36** C9
Greenland Sea, *Atl. Oc.* **38** A9
Green Mountains, *Vt., U.S.* **43** C15
Greenock, *U.K.* **58** D4
Green River, *Wyo., U.S.* **40** E6
Greensboro, *N.C., U.S.* **41** F14
Greenville, *Liberia* **78** J2
Greenville, *Miss., U.S.* **41** H11
Greenville, *S.C., U.S.* **41** G13
Gregory, *river, Qnsld., Austral.* **91** D10
Gregory, Lake, *S. Austral., Austral.* **91** H10
Gregory Downs, *homestead, Qnsld., Austral.* **89** D10
Gregory Range, *Qnsld., Austral.* **91** D12
Grenada, *N. America* **37** P12
Grenoble, *Fr.* **58** H5
Grenville, Cape, *Qnsld., Austral.* **91** B12
Grey, Mount, *W. Austral., Austral.* **90** J3
Greylock, Mount, *Mass., U.S.* **43** D15
Grey Range, *Qnsld., Austral.* **91** H12
Griffith, *N.S.W., AUSTRAL.* **89** K13
Groningen, *Neth.* **58** F5
Groote Eylandt, *island, N. Terr., Austral.* **90** B9
Grootfontein, *Namibia* **79** N7
Grossglockner, *peak, Aust.* **60** H6
Grosvenor Downs, *homestead, Qnsld., Austral.* **89** F14
Grosvenor Mountains, *Antarctica* **102** H8
Grove Mountains, *Antarctica* **103** E13
Groznyy, *Russ.* **59** H13
Guadalajara, *Mex.* **37** N5
Guadalcanal, *island, Solomon Is.* **96** F5
Guadalquivir, *river, Sp.* **60** K2
Guadalupe, *river, Tex., U.S.* **42** J9
Guadalupe Island, *Mex.* **39** L2
Guadalupe Mountains, *N. Mex.-Tex., U.S.* **42** H7
Guadalupe Peak, *Tex., U.S.* **42** H7
Guadeloupe, *island, N. America* **39** N12
Guadiana, *river, Port.-Sp.* **60** J2
Guaíra, *Braz.* **50** J7
Guajará-Mirim, *Braz.* **50** F5
Guajira Peninsula, *Col.* **52** A3
Guam, *island, Pac. Oc.* **96** D3
Guanajuato, *Mex.* **37** N5
Guanambi, *Braz.* **50** G10
Guanare, *Venez.* **50** A4
Guangzhou, *China* **69** H12
Guantánamo, *Cuba* **37** N9
Guapi, *Col.* **50** C2
Guaporé, *river, Bol.-Braz.* **52** G6
Guaratinguetá, *Braz.* **50** J9
Guasave, *Mex.* **37** M4
Guasdualito, *Venez.* **50** B4
Guatemala, *N. America* **37** P7
Guatemala, *Guatemala* **37** P7
Guaviare, *river, Col.* **52** C4
Guayaquil, *Ecua.* **50** D1
Guayaquil, Golfo de (Gulf of Guayaquil), *Ecua.* **50** D1
Guayaquil, Gulf of, *Ecua.* **52** D1
Guaymas, *Mex.* **37** M3
Gubakha, *Russ.* **59** C13
Gubkin, *Russ.* **59** F11
Guéra Massif, *Chad* **80** G7
Gui, *river, China* **71** H11
Guiana Highlands, *S. America* **52** B5
Guijá, *Mozambique* **79** P9
Guilin, *China* **69** H11
Guimarães, *Braz.* **50** D10
Guinea, *Af.* **78** H2
Guinea-Bissau, *Af.* **78** G1
Guiyang, *China* **69** H11
Gulfport, *Miss., U.S.* **41** J12
Gulgong, *N.S.W., AUSTRAL.* **89** K14
Gulkana, *Alas., U.S.* **40** L4
Gulu, *Uganda* **78** J9
Gumzai, *Indonesia* **92** C2
Guna Terara, *peak, Eth.* **80** G10
Gundagai, *N.S.W., AUSTRAL.* **89** L13
Gunnbjørn, *peak, Greenland* **38** B10
Gunnedah, *N.S.W., AUSTRAL.* **89** J14
Gunnewin, *Qnsld., Austral.* **89** G14
Gunnison, *Colo., U.S.* **40** F7
Guntur, *India* **68** K7
Gurage, *Eth.* **80** H10
Gurimatu, *P.N.G.* **92** C5
Gurney, *P.N.G.* **92** E7
Gurupá Island, *Braz.* **52** D8
Gurupi, *Braz.* **50** F8
Gurupi, Cape, *Braz.* **52** D9
Gusau, *Nig.* **78** G5
Gustavus, *Alas., U.S.* **40** L5
Guwahati, *India* **68** H9
Guyana, *S. America* **50** B6
Guymon, *Okla., U.S.* **40** G8
Guyra, *N.S.W., AUSTRAL.* **89** J15
Gwalior, *India* **68** H7
Gwangju, *S. Korea* **69** G13
Gwardafuy, Cape, *Somalia* **80** G12
Gweru, *Zimb.* **79** N9
Gwydir, *river, N.S.W., AUSTRAL.* **91** J14
Gyangzê, *China* **68** H9
Gyda Peninsula, *Russ.* **70** C8
Gympie, *Qnsld., Austral.* **89** H15
Gy or, *Hung.* **58** G7
Gyumri, *Arm.* **59** J13

Ha'apai Group, *Tonga* **96** G7
Haast, *N.Z.* **92** M3
Haast Bluff, *N. Terr., Austral.* **88** F8
Hachijō Jima, *Jap.* **96** B2
Hadarba, Ras *see* Elba, Cape, *Egypt* **80** F10
Ḥadd, Ra's al, *Oman* **70** H5
Hadejia, *river, Nig.* **80** G5
Hadhramaut, *region, Yemen* **70** J3
Hagemeister Island, *U.S.* **39** Q4
Hagerstown, *Md., U.S.* **41** E14
Haha Jima Rettō, *Jap.* **96** C3
Haig, *W. Austral., Austral.* **88** J6
Haikou, *China* **69** J11
Ḥā'il, *Saudi Arabia* **68** G3
Hailar, *China* **69** E11
Hainan, *island, China* **71** J11
Haines, *Alas., U.S.* **40** L5
Haines Junction, *Yukon Terr.* **36** E3
Haiphong, *Viet.* **69** J11
Haiti, *N. America* **37** N10
Hakataramea, *N.Z.* **92** M4
Ḥalab (Aleppo), *Syr.* **68** F3
Hale'iwa, *Hawaii, U.S.* **41** L11
Halifax, *N.S., CAN.* **36** H10
Halifax, *Qnsld., Austral.* **89** D13
Hall Beach, *Nunavut* **36** D7
Halley, *station, Antarctica* **102** C6
Hall Islands, *F.S.M.* **96** E4
Halls Creek, *W. Austral., Austral.* **88** D6
Halmahera, *island, Indonesia* **71** K14
Halmstad, *Sweden* **58** E7
Hamadān, *Iran* **68** G4
Hamaguir, *Alg.* **78** D4
Hamamatsu, *Jap.* **69** F14
Hamamet, Gulf of, *Tun.* **80** C6
Hamar, *Nor.* **58** D7
Hamburg, *Ger.* **58** F6
Hämeenlinna, *Fin.* **58** D8
Hamelin, *homestead, W. Austral., Austral.* **88** H2
Hamersley Range, *W. Austral., Austral.* **90** F2
Hamhung, *N. Korea* **69** F12
Hami, *China* **68** G9
Hamilton, *N.Z.* **92** H6
Hamilton, *Ont., Can.* **36** J8
Hamilton, *Tas., Austral.* **89** M16
Hamilton, *Vic., Austral.* **89** M11
Ḥammār, Hawr al, *Iraq* **70** G4
Hammerfest, *Nor.* **58** A8
Hampden, *N.Z.* **92** N4
Hampton Tableland, *W. Austral., Austral.* **90** J6
Hāna, *Hawaii, U.S.* **41** L12
Hancock, *Mich., U.S.* **41** C11
Hangzhou, *China* **69** G12
Haniá (Canea), *Gr.* **58** L9
Hannover, *Ger.* **58** F6
Hanoi, *Viet.* **69** J11
Hansen Mountains, *Antarctica* **103** C13
Hao, *island, Fr. Polynesia* **97** G11
Happy Valley-Goose Bay, *Nfld. and Lab., Can.* **36** F10
Harare, *Zimb.* **79** N9
Harbin, *China* **69** E12

Hardangerfjorden, fjord, Nor. 60 D6
Hardin, Mont., U.S. 40 C7
Hārer, Eth. 78 H11
Hargeysa, Somalia 78 H11
Harihari, N.Z. 92 L4
Harlingen, Tex., U.S. 40 L9
Harney Basin, Oreg., U.S. 42 D4
Harney Peak, S. Dak., U.S. 42 D7
Harper, Liberia 78 J2
Harrington Harbour, Que., Can. 36 G10
Harris, Lake, S. Austral., Austral. 90 J9
Harrisburg, Pa., U.S. 41 E15
Harrison, Cape, Can. 38 F10
Harrison Bay, Alas., U.S. 42 J3
Harry S. Truman Reservoir, Mo., U.S. 43 F10
Harstad, Nor. 58 A7
Hartford, Conn., U.S. 41 D16
Harvest Home, homestead, Qnsld., Austral. 89 E13
Harvey, N. Dak., U.S. 40 C9
Harz, mountains, Ger. 60 F6
Hasa Plain, Saudi Arabia 70 H4
Hassi Messaoud, Alg. 78 D5
Hastings, N.Z. 92 J6
Hastings, Nebr., U.S. 40 E9
Hatches Creek, N. Terr., Austral. 88 E9
Hatteras, Cape, N.C., U.S. 43 F15
Hattiesburg, Miss., U.S. 41 J12
Hatutu, island, Marquesas Is. 97 F11
Hat Yai, Thai. 69 L10
Haud, region, Eth.-Somalia 80 H11
Haugesund, Nor. 58 D6
Hauraki Gulf, N.Z. 92 G6
Havana see La Habana, Cuba 37 N8
Havre, Mont., U.S. 40 B6
Hawai'i, island, Hawaii, U.S. 43 M12
Hawaii, U.S. 96 C9
Hawea, Lake, N.Z. 92 M3
Hawi, Hawaii, U.S. 41 L12
Hawke Bay, N.Z. 92 J6
Hawker, S. Austral., Austral. 89 J10
Hawthorne, Nev., U.S. 40 E3
Hay, river, Can. 38 F4
Hay, river, N. Terr., Austral. 90 F10
Hayes Peninsula, Greenland 38 C7
Hay River, N.W.T., CAN. 36 F4
Hays, Kans., U.S. 40 F9
Hazard, Ky., U.S. 41 F13
Healy, Alas., U.S. 36 D2
Hearst, Ont., Can. 36 H7
Hearst Island, Antarctica 102 D3
Heart, river, N. Dak., U.S. 42 C8
Hecate Strait, Can. 38 F2
Hegang, China 69 E12
Heilong (Amur), river, China 69 E11
Hejaz, region, Saudi Arabia 70 G3
Hekla, peak, Ice. 60 A3
Helena, Mont., U.S. 36 H4
Helena, Mont., U.S. 40 C6
Helen Island, Palau 96 E2
Helen Springs, homestead, N. Terr., Austral. 88 D8
Hell-Ville see Andoany, Madag. 79 M12
Helmand, river, Afghan. 70 H6
Helsingborg, Sweden 58 E7
Helsinki, Fin. 58 D8
Henbury, homestead, N. Terr., Austral. 88 F8
Henderson Island, Pitcairn Is. 97 H12
Hengyang, China 69 H11
Herald Cays, C.S.I. Terr., Austral. 91 D14
Herat, Afghan. 68 G6
Herbert, river, Qnsld., Austral. 91 D13
Hercules Dome, Antarctica 102 G8
Hereford, Tex., U.S. 40 G8
Hereheretue, island, Fr. Polynesia 97 G10
Heritage Range, Antarctica 102 F5
Herlacher, Cape, Antarctica 102 H4
Hermannsburg, N. Terr., Austral. 88 F8
Hermidale, N.S.W., AUSTRAL. 89 J13
Hermit Islands, P.N.G. 92 A5
Hermosillo, Mex. 37 L3
Hervey Bay, Qnsld., Austral. 91 G15
Hervey Bay, Qnsld., Austral. 89 G15
Hervey Islands, Cook Is. 96 G9
Hibbing, Minn., U.S. 41 C10
Hicks Bay, N.Z. 92 H7
Hidalgo del Parral, Mex. 37 M4
High Atlas, mountains, Mor. 80 D3
Highlands, U.K. 60 D4
High Plains, U.S. 42 G8
High Point, peak, N.J., U.S. 43 D15
Hiiumaa, island, Est. 60 D8
Hikueru, island, Fr. Polynesia 97 G11
Hikurangi, peak, N.Z. 92 H7
Hilāl, Ras al, Lib. 80 D7
Hillary Coast, Antarctica 102 K9
Hillside, homestead, W. Austral., Austral. 88 F3
Hillston, N.S.W., AUSTRAL. 89 K12
Hilo, Hawaii, U.S. 41 M13
Hilo Bay, Hawaii, U.S. 43 M13
Himalaya, mountains, Asia 70 H8
Hinchinbrook Island, Qnsld., Austral. 91 D13
Hindmarsh, Lake, Vic., Austral. 91 L11
Hindu Kush, mountains, Afghan.-Pak. 70 G7
Hinthada, Myanmar 68 J9
Hios, island, Gr. 58 K9
Hios, Gr. 58 K9
Hiroshima, Jap. 69 F13
Hispaniola, island, N. America 39 N10
Hiva Oa, island, Marquesas Is. 97 F11
Hobart, Tas., Austral. 89 M16
Hobbs, N. Mex., U.S. 40 H7
Hobbs, Mount, Tas., Austral. 91 M16
Hobyo, Somalia 78 H12
Ho Chi Minh City (Saigon), Viet. 69 K11
Hodgson, river, N. Terr., Austral. 90 C9
Hoedspruit, S. Af. 79 P9
Höfn, Ice. 58 B4
Hohhot, China 69 F11
Hokitika, N.Z. 92 L4
Hokkaidō, island, Jap. 71 E13
Holbrook, Ariz., U.S. 40 G5
Holguín, Cuba 37 N9
Hollick-Kenyon Plateau, Antarctica 102 G5
Hollywood, Fla., U.S. 41 K15
Holman, N.W.T., CAN. 36 D5
Holme Bay, Antarctica 103 D14
Holy Cross, Alas., U.S. 40 L2
Hombori, Mali 78 G4
Homer, Alas., U.S. 40 L3
Homestead, Fla., U.S. 41 K15
Homyel', Belarus 58 F10
Honduras, N. America 37 P7
Honduras, Gulf of, Belize-Hond. 39 P7
Hønefoss, Nor. 58 D6
Hong Kong, China 69 J12
Hongshui, river, China 71 H11
Honiara, Solomon Is. 96 F5
Honoka'a, Hawaii, U.S. 41 M12
Honolulu, Hawaii, U.S. 41 L11
Honshu, island, Jap. 71 F13
Hood, Mount, Oreg., U.S. 42 C3
Hoonah, Alas., U.S. 40 M5
Hooper Bay, Alas., U.S. 40 L1
Hope, Ark., U.S. 41 H10
Hope, Lake, W. Austral., Austral. 90 K4
Hope, Point, Alas., U.S. 42 J2
Hopetoun, W. Austral., Austral. 88 K4
Horlick Mountains, Antarctica 102 G7
Horn, Cape, Chile 53 R5
Horne, Îles de, Pac. Oc. 96 G7
Hornos, Cabo de (Cape Horn), Chile 51 R5
Horsham, Vic., Austral. 89 L11
Hotan, China 68 G8
Hot Springs, Ark., U.S. 41 G10
Hot Springs, S. Dak., U.S. 40 D8
Houlton, Me., U.S. 41 B16
Houma, La., U.S. 41 J11
Houston, Tex., U.S. 41 J10
Houtman Abrolhos, islands, W. Austral., Austral. 90 J1
Howe, Cape, N.S.W.-Vic., Austral. 91 M14
Howland Island, Pac. Oc. 96 E7
Hrodna, Belarus 58 F8
Huacho, Peru 50 F2
Huahine, island, Fr. Polynesia 96 G10
Hualien, Taiwan 69 H13
Huambo, Angola 79 M6
Huancavelica, Peru 50 G3
Huancayo, Peru 50 F3
Huanchaca, Bol. 50 H5
Huang (Yellow), river, China 69 G10
Huánuco, Peru 50 F2
Huaral, Peru 50 F2
Huaraz, Peru 50 F2
Hubli, India 68 K7
Hudson, river, N.Y., U.S. 43 D15
Hudson Bay, Can. 38 F7
Hudson Strait, Can. 38 E8
Hue, Viet. 69 J11
Huelva, Sp. 58 J2
Hughenden, Qnsld., Austral. 89 E12
Hughes, Alas., U.S. 40 K3
Hughes, S. Austral., Austral. 88 J7
Hughes Bay, Antarctica 102 C1
Huila Plateau, Angola 81 M6
Hulun Nur, China 69 E11
Humaitá, Braz. 50 E5
Humbe, Angola 79 M6
Humberto de Campos, Braz. 50 D10
Humboldt, river, Nev., U.S. 42 E4
Humpty Doo, homestead, N. Terr., Austral. 88 B7
Hūn, Lib. 78 E6
Húnaflói, bay, Ice. 60 A3
Hungary, Europe 58 H8
Hungerford, N.S.W., AUSTRAL. 89 H12
Huns Mountains, Namibia 81 P7
Hunter, island, Vanuatu 96 H6
Hunter Islands, Tas., Austral. 91 L15
Huntington, W. Va., U.S. 41 F13
Huntly, N.Z. 92 H6
Huntsville, Ala., U.S. 41 G12
Huntsville, Tex., U.S. 41 J10
Huon, Île, New Caledonia 96 G5
Huon Gulf, P.N.G. 92 C6
Huon Peninsula, P.N.G. 92 C6
Huron, S. Dak., U.S. 40 D9
Huron, Lake, Can.-U.S. 43 C13
Hutchinson, Kans., U.S. 40 F9
Hvannadalshnúkur, peak, Ice. 60 B3
Hydaburg, Alas., U.S. 40 M6
Hyden, W. Austral., Austral. 88 K4
Hyderabad, India 68 J7
Hyderabad, Pak. 68 H6

Iamara, P.N.G. 92 D4
Iauaretê, Braz. 50 C4
Ibadan, Nig. 78 H4
Iberia, Peru 50 F4
Iberian Mountains, Sp. 60 J3
Iberian Peninsula, Port.-Sp. 60 J2
Ibiapaba, Serra da, Braz. 52 E10
Ibipetuba, Braz. 50 F9
Ibiza (Iviza), island, Sp. 58 K4
Iboperenda, Bol. 50 H6
Ibotirama, Braz. 50 F10
Ica, Peru 50 G3
İçel, Turk. 59 K11
Iceland, Europe 58 A3
Icoraci, Braz. 50 D9
Icy Cape, Alas., U.S. 42 J2
Idaho, U.S. 40 C5
Idaho, U.S. Falls, Idaho, U.S. 40 D5
Ideriyn, river, Mongolia 70 F9
Ifalik Atoll, F.S.M. 96 E3
Iferouâne, Niger 78 F5
Igarka, Russ. 68 D8
Iglesias, It. 58 K5
Igloolik, Nunavut 36 D7
Igrim, Russ. 59 A13
Iguatu, Braz. 50 E11
Iguazú Falls, Arg.-Braz. 52 J7
Iguidi, Erg, Alg.-Maurit. 80 E3
Ihosy, Madag. 79 N11
Ihu, P.N.G. 92 D5
Iittuarmiit, Greenland 36 D10
IJsselmeer, lake, Neth. 60 F5
Ijuí, Braz. 51 K7
Ilave, Peru 50 G4
Ilbilbie, Qnsld., Austral. 89 F14
Ilbunga, S. Austral., Austral. 88 G9
Île-à-la-Crosse, Sask., Can. 36 G5
Ilebo, D.R.C. 79 K7
Ilfracombe, Qnsld., Austral. 89 F12
Ilhéus, Braz. 50 G11
Ili, river, China-Kaz. 70 F7
Iliamna Lake, Alas., U.S. 42 L2
Illampu, peak, Bol. 52 G4
Illimani, peak, Bol. 52 G4
Illinois, river, Ill., U.S. 43 F11
Illinois, U.S. 41 E11
Illinois Peak, Idaho-MOnt., Can. 42 B5
Illizi, Alg. 78 E5
Il'men', Lake, Russ. 60 D10
Iloilo, Philippines 69 K13
Il'pyrskiy, Russ. 69 B13
Ilulissat, Greenland 36 C9
Imandra, Lake, Russ. 60 B9
Imatra, Fin. 58 D9
Īmī, Eth. 78 H11
Immarna, S. Austral., Austral. 88 J8
Imperatriz, Braz. 50 E9
Imperial Valley, Calif., U.S. 42 G4
Impfondo, Congo 78 J7
Imphal, India 68 J9
Inaccessible Island, Tristan da Cunha Group 81 R2
I-n-Amenas, Alg. 78 E5
Inari, lake, Fin. 60 A9
Incheon, S. Korea 69 F12
Indalsälven, river, Sweden 60 C7
India, Asia 68 J7
Indiana, U.S. 41 E12
Indianapolis, Ind., U.S. 41 E12
Indigirka, river, Russ. 71 C11
Indochina Peninsula, Asia 71 J10
Indonesia, Asia 69 L11
Indore, India 68 J7
Indus, river, Asia 70 H6
I-n-Eker, Alg. 78 E5
Ingal, Niger 78 G5
Ingomar, homestead, S. Austral., Austral. 88 H9
Ingrid Christensen Coast, Antarctica 103 E14
Inhambane, Mozambique 79 P10
Inharrime, Mozambique 79 P10
Inkerman, homestead, Qnsld., Austral. 89 C11
Innamincka, homestead, S. Austral., Austral. 89 H11
Inner Hebrides, islands, U.K. 60 D4
Inner Mongolia, region, China 69 F11
Innesowen, homestead, N.S.W., AUSTRAL. 89 J12
Innisfail, Qnsld., Austral. 89 D13
Innsbruck, Aust. 58 G6
Inongo, D.R.C. 79 K7
I-n-Salah, Alg. 78 E4
Inscription, Cape, W. Austral., Austral. 90 G1
Inta, Russ. 59 A12
International Falls, Minn., U.S. 41 B10
Inukjuak, Que., Can. 36 F8
Inuvik, N.W.T., CAN. 36 D4
Invercargill, N.Z. 92 P3
Inverness, U.K. 58 D4
Inverway, homestead, N. Terr., Austral. 88 D7
Investigator Strait, S. Austral., Austral. 90 L9
Ioánina, Gr. 58 K8
Ioma, P.N.G. 92 D6
Ionian Islands, Gr. 60 K8
Ionian Sea, Gr.-It. 60 K7
Iowa, river, Iowa, U.S. 43 E10
Iowa, U.S. 41 E10
Ipiales, Col. 50 C2
Ipswich, Qnsld., Austral. 89 H15
Iqaluit, Nunavut 36 E8
Iquique, Chile 50 H4
Iquitos, Peru 50 D3
Iracoubo, Fr. Guiana 50 B8
Iráklio, Gr. 58 L9
Iran, Asia 68 G5
Iraq, Asia 68 F4
Ireland, Europe 58 E3
Irian Jaya, region, Indonesia 69 K16
Irimi, Indonesia 92 B1
Irish Sea, Ire.-U.K. 60 E4
Irkutsk, Russ. 69 E10
Iron Gate, pass, Rom.-Serbia and Montenegro 60 H8
Iron Knob, S. Austral., Austral. 88 K10
Iron Mountain, Mich., U.S. 41 C11
Ironwood, Mich., U.S. 41 C11
Irrawaddy, river, Myanmar 70 J9
Irtysh, river, Kaz.-Russ. 70 D7
Isabela, Philippines 69 K13
Isabela, Isla, Ecua. 97 F16
Isachsen Mountain, Antarctica 103 B10
Ísafjör?ur, Ice. 58 A3
Ishim, river, Russ. 59 B15
Ishim, Russ. 59 B15
Ishim Steppe, Kaz.-Russ. 70 E7
Ishinomaki, Jap. 69 E14
Ishpeming, Mich., U.S. 41 C12
Isil'kul', Russ. 59 B16
Isiro, D.R.C. 78 J8
Isisford, Qnsld., Austral. 89 F12
İskenderun, Turk. 68 F3
Iskushuban, Somalia 78 H12
Islamabad, Pak. 68 G7
Island Lagoon, S. Austral., Austral. 90 J10
Island Lake, Manitoba, Can. 36 G6
Islands, Bay of, N.Z. 92 F5
Isna, Egypt 78 E9
Isparta, Turk. 59 K10
Israel, Asia 68 F3
İstanbul, Turk. 59 J10
Isto, Mount, Alas., U.S. 42 J4
Itaberaba, Braz. 50 F10
Itabuna, Braz. 50 G11
Itacoatiara, Braz. 50 D6
Itaituba, Braz. 50 D7
Italy, It. 58 J7
Itapetinga, Braz. 50 G10
Itapipoca, Braz. 50 D11
Itasca, Lake see Mississippi, Source of the, Minn., U.S. 43 C10
Ithaca, N.Y., U.S. 41 D15
Itimbiri, river, D.R.C. 80 J8
Ittoqqortoormiit, Greenland 36 B10
Iturup, island, Russ. 69 D14
Ivalo, Fin. 58 A9
Ivanhoe, homestead, W. Austral., Austral. 88 C6
Ivanhoe, N.S.W., AUSTRAL. 89 K12
Ivano- Frankivs'k, Ukr. 58 G9
Ivanovo, Russ. 59 D11
Ivdel', Russ. 59 B13
Iviza, island, Sp. 60 K4
Ivory Coast, Côte d'Ivoire 80 J3
Ivujivik, Que., Can. 36 E7
Iwembere Steppe, Tanzania 81 K9
Iwo Jima, Jap. 96 C3
Izhevsk, Russ. 59 D13
Izhma, river, Russ. 61 B12
Izmayil, Ukr. 58 H10
İzmir, Turk. 58 K10
Izozog, Bañados del, Bol. 52 H6
Izu Islands, Jap. 71 F14

Jabalpur, India 68 J7
Jabel Abyad Plateau, Sudan 80 F8
Jabiru, N. Terr., Austral. 88 B8
Jaboatão, Braz. 50 F12
Jacareacanga, Braz. 50 E7
Jaciparaná, Braz. 50 F5
Jackson, Miss., U.S. 41 H11
Jackson, Tenn., U.S. 41 G12
Jackson Bay, N.Z. 92 M3
Jackson Lake, Wyo., U.S. 42 D6
Jacksonville, Fla., U.S. 37 L8
Jacksonville, Fla., U.S. 41 J14
Jacquinot Bay, P.N.G. 92 C7
J.A.D. Jensen Nunatakker, peak, Greenland 38 D19
Jaén, Sp. 58 K2
Jaffa, Cape, S. Austral., Austral. 91 L10
Jaffna, Sri Lanka 68 K7
Jahrom, Iran 68 G5
Jaipur, India 68 H7
Jakarta, Indonesia 69 M11
Jakobstad, Fin. 58 C8
Jalingo, Nig. 78 H6
Jaluit Atoll, Marshall Is. 96 E6
Jamaame, Somalia 78 J11
Jamaica, N. America 37 N9
Jambi, Indonesia 69 M11
James, river, N. Dak.-S. Dak., U.S. 42 D9
James, river, Va., U.S. 43 F15
James Bay, Can. 38 G8
James Range, N. Terr., Austral. 90 F8
James Ross Island, Antarctica 102 C2
Jamestown, N. Dak., U.S. 40 C9
Jamestown, N.Y., U.S. 41 D14
Jamshedpur, India 68 J8
Japan, Asia 69 F14
Japan, Sea of (East Sea), Asia 71 F13
Jaramillo, Arg. 51 P5
Jardim, Braz. 50 H7
Jarvis Island, Pac. Oc. 96 E9
Jason Peninsula, Antarctica 102 C2
Jasper, Alta., Can. 36 G4
Jataí, Braz. 50 H8
Jatobal, Braz. 50 D8
Java, island, Indonesia 71 M12
Java Sea, Indonesia 71 M12
Jawhar, Somalia 78 J11
Jaya, Puncak, Indonesia 92 B3
Jaya Peak, Indonesia 71 L16
Jayapura, Indonesia 69 K16
Jayapura, Indonesia 92 B4
Jayawijaya, Pegunungan, Indonesia 92 C3
Jeddah, Saudi Arabia 68 G3
Jefferson, Mount, Nev., U.S. 40 E4
Jefferson City, Mo., U.S. 37 K6
Jefferson City, Mo., U.S. 41 F11
Jelbart Ice Shelf, Antarctica 102 A8
Jelgava, Latv. 58 E8
Jequié, Braz. 50 G10
Jerba Island, Tun. 80 D6
Jeremoabo, Braz. 50 F11
Jerez, Sp. 58 K2
Jericoacoara, Point, Braz. 52 D11
Jerid, Shott el, Tun. 80 D5
Jerilderie, N.S.W., AUSTRAL. 89 L12
Jerimoth Hill, R.I., U.S. 43 D16
Jerome, Idaho, U.S. 40 D5
Jerramungup, W. Austral., Austral. 88 K4
Jersey City, N.J., U.S. 41 D15
Jerseyside, Nfld. and Lab., Can. 36 G11
Jerusalem, Israel 68 F3
Jervis Bay, Australian Capital Territory 91 L14
Jiamusi, China 69 E12
Jiangmen, China 69 J12
Jiayuguan, China 68 G10
Jiggalong, W. Austral., Austral. 88 F4
Jilin, China 69 F12
Jīma, Eth. 78 H10
Jinan, China 69 G12
Jinja, Uganda 78 J9
Jinzhou, China 69 F12
Jiparaná, river, Braz. 52 F6
Ji-Paraná (Rondônia), Braz. 50 F6
Jixi, China 69 E12
Jīzān, Saudi Arabia 68 H3
João Pessoa, Braz. 50 E12
Jodhpur, India 68 H7
Joensuu, Fin. 58 C9
Johannesburg, S. Af. 79 P8
John Day, river, Oreg., U.S. 42 C3
John Day, Oreg., U.S. 40 C4
John Eyre Motel, W. Austral., Austral. 88 K6
Johnston, Lake, W. Austral., Austral. 90 K4
Johnston, Mount, Antarctica 103 E13
Johnston Atoll, Pac. Oc. 96 D8
Johnstown, Pa., U.S. 41 E14
Johor Baharu, Malaysia 69 L11
Joinville, Braz. 50 J8
Joinville Island, Antarctica 102 B2
Joliet, Ill., U.S. 41 E12
Jonesboro, Ark., U.S. 41 G11
Jones Sound, Can. 38 C7
Jönköping, Sweden 58 E7
Joplin, Mo., U.S. 41 G10
Jordan, Asia 68 F3
Joseph Bonaparte Gulf, N. Terr.-W. Austral., Austral. 90 B6
Juan de Fuca, Strait of, Can.-U.S. 42 A3
Juan Fernández, Islas, Chile 53 M2
Juàzeiro, Braz. 50 F10
Juàzeiro do Norte, Braz. 50 E11
Juba, Sudan 78 J9
Jubany, station, Antarctica 102 B1
Jubba, river, Somalia 80 J11
Juchitán, Mex. 37 P6
Juiz de Fora, Braz. 50 J10
Julia Creek, Qnsld., Austral. 89 E11
Jullundur, India 68 H7
Jundah, Qnsld., Austral. 89 G12
Juneau, Alas., U.S. 40 L5
Junín, Arg. 51 L6
Juradó, Col. 50 B2
Jura Mountains, Fr.-Switz. 60 H5
Jurien, W. Austral., Austral. 88 J2
Juruá, river, Braz. 52 E4
Juruena, river, Braz. 52 F6
Jutaí, Braz. 50 E4
Juticalpa, Hond. 37 P8
Jutland, peninsula, Den. 60 E6
Jyväskylä, Fin. 58 C9

K2 (Godwin Austin), peak, China-Pak. 70 G7
Kaabong, Uganda 78 J9
Kaambooni, Somalia 79 K11
Kaambooni, Raas, Somalia 81 K11
Kaap Plateau, S. Af. 81 P8
Kabinda, D.R.C. 79 L8
Kabol (Kabul), Afghan. 68 G6
Kabul see Kabol, Afghan. 68 G6
Kabuli, P.N.G. 92 B5
Kabwe, Zambia 79 M9
Kadavu, island, Fiji 96 G6
Kadé, Guinea 78 G1
Kadugli, Sudan 78 H9
Kaduna, Nig. 78 H5
Kaédi, Maurit. 78 G2
Kaélé, Cameroon 78 H6
Ka'ena Point, Hawaii, U.S. 43 L11
Kaeo, N.Z. 92 F5
Kafia Kingi, Sudan 78 H8
Kafue, river, Zambia 81 M8
Kafue, Zambia 79 M9
Kagoshima, Jap. 69 G13
Kahama, Tanzania 79 K9
Kahemba, D.R.C. 79 L7
Kaho'olawe, island, Hawaii, U.S. 43 L12
Kahramanmaraş, Turk. 59 K12
Kahuku Point, Hawaii, U.S. 43 L11
Kahului, Hawaii, U.S. 41 L12
Kai, Kepulauan, Indonesia 96 F2
Kaibab Plateau, Ariz., U.S. 42 F5
Kaifeng, China 69 G11
Kai Kecil, island, Indonesia 92 C1
Kaikoura, N.Z. 92 L5
Kailua, Hawaii, U.S. 41 M12
Kaimana, Indonesia 92 B2
Kainji Reservoir, Nig. 80 H5
Kaipara Harbour, N.Z. 92 G5
Kaitaia, N.Z. 92 F5
Kaiwi Channel, Hawaii, U.S. 43 L11
Kaiyuh Mountains, Alas., U.S. 42 K2
Kajaani, Fin. 58 C9
Kajabbi, Qnsld., Austral. 89 E11
Kakamas, S. Af. 79 Q7
Kakaramea, N.Z. 92 J5
Kakhovka Reservoir, Ukr. 61 G11
Kaktovik, Alas., U.S. 40 J4
Kalaallit Nunaat see Greenland, N. America 36 C9
Kalabo, Zambia 79 M8
Kalae (South Cape), Hawaii, U.S. 43 M12
Kalahari Desert, Bostwana-Namibia 81 P8
Kalamáta, Gr. 58 K8
Kalamazoo, Mich., U.S. 41 D12
Kalannie, W. Austral., Austral. 88 J3
Kalbarri, W. Austral., Austral. 88 H2
Kalemie, D.R.C. 79 L9
Kalgoorlie, W. Austral., Austral. 88 J4
Kalima, D.R.C. 79 K8
Kalimantan, region, Indonesia 69 L12
Kaliningrad, Russ. 58 E8
Kalispell, Mont., U.S. 40 B5
Kalmar, Sweden 58 E7
Kalohi Channel, Hawaii, U.S. 43 L12
Kaltag, Alas., U.S. 40 K2
Kaluga, Russ. 59 E11
Kalumburu, W. Austral., Austral. 88 C6
Kalyan, India 68 J7
Kama, river, Russ. 61 D13
Kamakou, peak, Hawaii, U.S. 43 L12
Kama Reservoir, Russ. 61 C13
Kamchatka, Poluostrov (Kamchatka Peninsula), Russ. 69 B13
Kamchatka Peninsula, Russ. 71 C13
Kamenka, Kaz. 59 E13
Kamenka, Russ. 59 B11
Kamensk Ural'skiy, Russ. 59 C14
Kamileroi, homestead, Qnsld., Austral. 89 D11
Kamina, D.R.C. 79 L8
Kamloops, B.C., Can. 36 G3
Kampala, Uganda 78 J9
Kamrau, Teluk, Indonesia 92 B2
Kamuela see Waimea, Hawaii, U.S. 41 M12
Kamyshin, Russ. 59 F12
Kanab, Utah, U.S. 40 F5
Kananga, D.R.C. 79 L8
Kanash, Russ. 59 D12
Kandahar, Afghan. 68 H6
Kandalaksha, Russ. 58 B9
Kandalakshskiy Zaliv, Russ. 59 B10
Kandi, Benin 78 H4
Kandrian, P.N.G. 92 C6
Kāne'ohe, Hawaii, U.S. 41 L11
Kangaamiut, Greenland 36 D9
Kangaroo Island, S. Austral., Austral. 90 L9
Kangerlussuaq, Greenland 36 D9
Kangertittivaq, bay, Greenland 38 B10
Kangirsuk, Que., Can. 36 F8
Kaniere, N.Z. 92 L4
Kanin, Poluostrov (Kanin Peninsula), Russ. 59 A10
Kanin Peninsula, Russ. 61 A11
Kankan, Guinea 78 H2
Kano, Nig. 78 G5
Kanpur, India 68 H7
Kansas, river, Kans., U.S. 43 F10
Kansas, U.S. 40 F9
Kansas City, Kans., U.S. 41 F10
Kansas City, Mo., U.S. 41 F10
Kansk, Russ. 68 E9
Kanton, island, Kiribati 96 F7
Kanuku Mountains, Guyana 52 C6
Kaohsiung, Taiwan 69 H12
Kaokoveld, region, Namibia 81 N6
Kaolack, Senegal 78 G1
Kaoma, Zambia 79 M8
Kapaa, Hawaii, U.S. 41 L11
Kapan, Arm. 59 J14
Kapingamarangi Atoll, F.S.M. 96 E4
Kapisillit, Greenland 36 D9
Kapoeta, Sudan 78 J9
Kapuskasing, Ont., Can. 36 H8
Karabük, Turk. 59 J11
Karachi, Pak. 68 H6
Karakoram Range, Asia 70 G7
Karakuwisa, Namibia 79 N7
Karaman, Turk. 59 K11
Karamea, N.Z. 92 K4
Karamea Bight, N.Z. 92 K4
Karasburg, Namibia 79 P7
Kara Sea, Russ. 70 C8
Karas Mountains, Namibia 81 P7
Karbalā', Iraq 68 G4
Kargopol', Russ. 59 C10
Kariba, Zimb. 79 M9
Kariba, Lake, Zambia-Zimb. 81 M8
Karikari, Cape, N.Z. 92 F5
Karitane, N.Z. 92 N4
Karkar, island, P.N.G. 92 C5
Karkük, Iraq 68 F4
Karlskrona, Sweden 58 E7
Karlsruhe, Ger. 58 G6
Karlstad, Sweden 58 D7
Karluk, Alas., U.S. 40 M3
Karonga, Malawi 79 L10
Karonie, W. Austral., Austral. 88 J5
Karpinsk, Russ. 59 B13
Karratha, W. Austral., Austral. 88 E2
Karre Mountains, Cen. Af. Rep. 80 H6
Karridale, W. Austral., Austral. 88 L2
Kartaly, Russ. 59 D15
Karumba, Qnsld., Austral. 89 D11
Karunjie, homestead, W. Austral., Austral. 88 C6
Kasai, river, Angola-D.R.C. 81 K7
Kasama, Zambia 79 L9
Kasane, Botswana 79 N8
Kasar, Ras, Eritrea 80 F10
Kasempa, Zambia 79 M8
Kasese, D.R.C. 79 K8
Kashegelok, Alas., U.S. 40 L2
Kashi, China 68 G7
Kashmir, region, China-India-Pak. 68 G7
Kaskaskia, river, Ill., U.S. 43 F11
Kasongo, D.R.C. 79 K8
Kasongo-Lunda, D.R.C. 79 L7
Kaspiyskiy, Russ. 59 G13
Kassala, Sudan 78 G10
Katahdin, Mount, Me., U.S. 43 B16
Katanga, D.R.C. 79 L8
Katanga Plateau, D.R.C.-Zambia 81 L8
Katanning, W. Austral., Austral. 88 K3

Katherine, river, N. Terr., Austral. 90 B8
Katherine, N. Terr., Austral. 88 C8
Kathmandu, Nepal 68 H8
Katmai, Mount, Alas., U.S. 42 M2
Katoomba, N.S.W., AUSTRAL. 89 K14
Katowice, Pol. 58 G8
Katsina, Nig. 78 G5
Kattegat, strait, Den.-Sweden 60 E6
Kaua'i, island, Hawaii, U.S. 43 K11
Kaua'i Channel, Hawaii, U.S. 43 L11
Kaukau Veld, Bostwana-Namibia 81 N7
Ka'ula, island, Hawaii, U.S. 43 L10
Kaulakahi Channel, Hawaii, U.S. 43 K10
Kaunakakai, Hawaii, U.S. 41 L12
Kaunas, Lith. 58 E8
Kavála, Gr. 58 J9
Kavieng, P.N.G. 92 B7
Kawaihae Bay, Hawaii, U.S. 43 M12
Kawaikini, peak, Hawaii, U.S. 43 L10
Kawakawa, N.Z. 92 G5
Kawambwa, Zambia 79 L9
Kawhia, N.Z. 92 H5
Kayes, Congo 79 K6
Kayes, Mali 78 G2
Kayseri, Turk. 59 K11
Kazach'ye, Russ. 69 C11
Kazakhstan, Asia 68 F7
Kazakh Uplands, Kaz. 70 F7
Kazan', Russ. 59 D12
Kazan Rettō see Volcano Islands, Jap. 69 G15
Kea'au (Olaa), Hawaii, U.S. 41 M13
Kealaikahiki Channel, Hawaii, U.S. 43 L12
Kearney, Nebr., U.S. 40 E9
Kebnekaise, peak, Sweden 60 B8
Keer-weer, Cape, Qnsld., Austral. 91 B11
Keetmanshoop, Namibia 79 P7
Kefallinia, island, Gr. 58 K8
Keflavík, Ice. 58 A3
Keg River, Alta., Can. 36 F4
Keith, S. Austral., Austral. 89 L11
K'elafo, Eth. 78 H11
Kelowna, B.C., Can. 36 G3
Kelso, Wash., U.S. 40 B3
Kem', Russ. 58 B10
Kemerovo, Russ. 68 E8
Kemi, river, Fin. 60 B8
Kemi, Fin. 58 B8
Kemijärvi, Fin. 58 B9
Kemmerer, Wyo., U.S. 40 E6
Kemp Coast, Antarctica 103 C14
Kemp Peninsula, Antarctica 102 D4
Kempsey, N.S.W., AUSTRAL. 89 K15
Kenai, Alas., U.S. 40 L3
Kenai Peninsula, Alas., U.S. 42 L3
Kendall, N.S.W., AUSTRAL. 89 K15
Kenhardt, S. Af. 79 Q7
Kennebec, river, Me., U.S. 43 C16
Kennedy, Cape see Canaveral, Cape, U.S. 39 M8
Kennedy Entrance, strait, Alas., U.S. 42 L3
Kenora, Ont., Can. 36 H6
Kenosha, Wis., U.S. 41 D12
Kentucky, river, Ky., U.S. 43 F13
Kentucky, U.S. 41 F13
Kentucky Lake, Tenn., U.S. 43 G12
Kenya, Af. 78 J10
Kenya, Mount, Kenya 80 K10
Kenya Highlands, Kenya 80 J10
Kepi, Indonesia 92 C3
Kerch, Ukr. 59 H11
Keren, Eritrea 78 G10
Kerikeri, N.Z. 92 F5
Kerinci, peak, Indonesia 71 M10
Kérkira (Corfu), island, Gr. 58 K8
Kermadec Islands, N.Z. 96 J7
Kermān, Iran 68 G5
Kermānshāh, Iran 68 G4
Kerrobert, Sask., Can. 36 G5
Ketchikan, Alas., U.S. 40 M6
Keweenaw Peninsula, Mich., U.S. 43 C11
Keystone Lake, Okla., U.S. 42 G9
Key West, Fla., U.S. 41 L14
Khabarovsk, Russ. 69 E12
Khambhat, Gulf of, India 70 J6
Khamīs Mushayṭ, Saudi Arabia 68 H3
Khandyga, Russ. 69 C11
Khanka, Lake, China-Russ. 71 E12
Khanpur, Pak. 68 H6
Khanty Mansiysk, Russ. 59 A14
Kharkiv, Ukr. 59 F11
Kharlovka, Russ. 58 A10
Kharovsk, Russ. 59 D11
Khartoum, Sudan 78 G9
Khartoum North, Sudan 78 G9
Khaskovo, Bulg. 58 J9
Khatanga, Russ. 68 C9
Kherson, Ukr. 59 H10
Khmel'nyts'kyy, Ukr. 58 G9
Khoper, river, Russ. 61 F12
Khorāsān, region, Iran 68 G5
Khulna, Bangladesh 68 J9
Kiama, N.S.W., AUSTRAL. 89 L14
Kiana, Alas., U.S. 40 J2
Kidal, Mali 78 F4
Kidnappers, Cape, N.Z. 92 J6
Kiel, Ger. 58 E6
Kielce, Pol. 58 G8
Kiev see Kyyiv, Ukr. 59 G10
Kiffa, Maurit. 78 F2
Kigali, Rwanda 79 K9
Kikládes, islands, Gr. 58 K9
Kikori, river, P.N.G. 92 C5
Kikori, P.N.G. 92 D5
Kikwit, D.R.C. 79 K7
Kilauea, Hawaii, U.S. 41 K11
Kīlauea, peak, Hawaii, U.S. 43 M12
Kilbuck Mountains, Alas., U.S. 42 L2
Kilcowera, homestead, Qnsld., Austral. 89 H12
Kili Island, Marshall Is. 96 E6
Kilimanjaro, peak, Tanzania 81 K10
Killiniq Island, Can. 38 E9
Kilombero, river, Tanzania 81 L10
Kilwa Kivinje, Tanzania 79 L10
Kimaam, Indonesia 92 D3
Kimbe Bay, P.N.G. 92 C7
Kimberley, region, W. Austral., Austral. 88 D5
Kimberley, S. Af. 79 Q8
Kimberley, Cape, Qnsld., Austral. 91 C13
Kimberley Plateau, W. Austral., Austral. 90 C6
Kinabalu, peak, Malaysia 71 K12
Kindia, Guinea 78 H2
Kindu, D.R.C. 79 K8
Kineshma, Russ. 59 D11
King Christian IX Land, Greenland 38 C10
King Christian X Land, Greenland 38 B9
King Frederik VI Coast, Greenland 38 D10
King Frederik VIII Land, Greenland 38 A8
King George Island, Antarctica 102 B1
King George Sound, W. Austral., Austral. 90 L3
King Island, Tas., Austral. 91 L15
King Leopold Ranges, W. Austral., Austral. 90 D5
Kingman, Ariz., U.S. 40 G4
Kingoonya, S. Austral., Austral. 88 J9
King Peak, Antarctica 102 G7
King Salmon, Alas., U.S. 40 M2
Kingscote, S. Austral., Austral. 88 L10
King Sejong, station, Antarctica 102 B1
King Sound, W. Austral., Austral. 90 D4
Kings Peak, Utah, U.S. 42 E6
Kingsport, Tenn., U.S. 41 F13
Kingston, Jamaica 37 N9
Kingston, Ont., Can. 36 J8
Kingston, Tas., Austral. 89 M16
Kingston South East, S. Austral., Austral. 89 L10
Kingstown, St. Vincent and the Grenadines 37 P12
Kingsville, Tex., U.S. 40 K9
King Wilhelm Land, Greenland 38 B9
Kinshasa, D.R.C. 79 K6
Kipili, Tanzania 79 L9
Kiri, D.R.C. 79 K7
Kiribati, Pac. Oc. 96 F7
Kırıkkale, Turk. 59 J11
Kiritimati (Christmas Island), Kiribati 96 E9
Kiriwina, island, P.N.G. 92 D7
Kirkenes, Nor. 58 A9
Kirksville, Mo., U.S. 41 E10
Kirkwall, U.K. 58 D4
Kirov, Russ. 59 C12
Kirovo Chepetsk, Russ. 59 C12
Kirovohrad, Ukr. 59 G10
Kirs, Russ. 59 C12
Kiruna, Sweden 58 B8
Kirwan Escarpment, Antarctica 102 B8
Kisangani, D.R.C. 78 J8
Kisigo, river, Tanzania 81 L10
Kiska, island, Alas., U.S. 37 R2
Kismaayo (Chisimayu), Somalia 78 K11
Kisumu, Kenya 78 K10
Kita, Mali 78 G2
Kita Daitō Jima, Jap. 96 C2
Kita Iwo Jima, Jap. 96 C3
Kitakyūshū, Jap. 69 G13
Kitale, Kenya 78 J10
Kitchener, W. Austral., Austral. 88 J5
Kitimat, B.C., Can. 36 F3
Kitty Hawk, N.C., U.S. 41 F15
Kitwe, Zambia 79 M9
Kiunga, P.N.G. 92 C4
Kivalina, Alas., U.S. 40 J2
Kivu, Lake, D.R.C.-Rwanda 81 K9
Kizema, Russ. 59 C11
Klaipėda, Lith. 58 E8
Klamath Falls, Oreg., U.S. 40 D3
Klamath Mountains, Calif., U.S. 42 D2
Klarälven, river, Sweden 60 D7
Klintsy, Russ. 59 F10
Klyaz'ma, river, Russ. 61 E11
Klyuchevskaya Sopka, peak, Russ. 71 C13
Knob, Cape, W. Austral., Austral. 90 L4
Knox Coast, Antarctica 103 H15
Knoxville, Tenn., U.S. 41 G13
Knud Rasmussen Land, Greenland 38 B8
Kōbe, Jap. 69 F13
København (Copenhagen), Den. 58 E7
Kobuk, river, Alas., U.S. 42 J2
Kobuk, Alas., U.S. 40 J2
Kocaeli, Turk. 59 J10
Kodiak, Alas., U.S. 40 M3
Kodiak Island, Alas., U.S. 42 M3
Kohler Glacier, Antarctica 102 H4
Kokas, Indonesia 92 B1
Kokkola, Fin. 58 C8
Kokomo, Ind., U.S. 41 E12
Kökshetaū, Kaz. 59 C16
Kola, island, Indonesia 92 C2
Kola Peninsula, Russ. 60 B10
Kolguyev, Ostrov (Kolguyev Island), Russ. 59 A11
Kolguyev Island, Russ. 61 A11
Kolhapur, India 68 J7
Kolkata (Calcutta), India 68 J8
Köln, Ger. 58 F5
Kolomna, Russ. 59 E11
Kolpashevo, Russ. 68 E8
Kol'skiy Poluostrov (Kola Peninsula), Russ. 58 B10
Kolwezi, D.R.C. 79 L8
Kolyma, river, Russ. 71 B11
Kolyma Lowland, Russ. 71 B11
Kolyma Range, Russ. 71 B12
Komoé, river, Burkina Faso-Cote d'Ivoire 80 H3
Kôm Ombo, Egypt 78 E9
Komoran, island, Indonesia 92 D3
Komsomolets, Ostrov (Komsomolets Island), Russ. 68 B9
Komsomolets Island, Russ. 70 B9
Komsomol'sk na Amure, Russ. 69 D12
Konda, Indonesia 92 B1
Kondinin, W. Austral., Austral. 88 K3
Kondopoga, Russ. 59 C10
Konduz, Afghan. 68 G6
Kongolo, D.R.C. 79 K8
Konnongorring, W. Austral., Austral. 88 J3
Konosha, Russ. 59 C11
Konotop, Ukr. 59 F10
Konya, Turk. 59 K11
Kookynie, W. Austral., Austral. 88 J4
Koolburra, homestead, Qnsld., Austral. 89 C12
Koonalda, homestead, S. Austral., Austral. 88 J7
Koonibba, S. Austral., Austral. 88 J8
Kopet Mountains, Iran-Turkm. 70 G5
K'orahē, Eth. 78 H11
Korçë, Alban. 58 J8
Korea, region, Asia 71 F12
Korhogo, Côte d'Ivoire 78 H3
Korla, China 68 G8
Koror, Palau 96 E2
Korosten', Ukr. 58 F9
Koro Toro, Chad 78 G7
Koryak Range, Russ. 71 B12
Kosciuszko, Mount, N.S.W., AUSTRAL. 91 L13
Košice, Slovakia 58 G8
Koslan, Russ. 59 B11
Kosrae (Kusaie), island, F.S.M. 96 E5
Kosti, Sudan 78 G9
Kostroma, Russ. 59 D11
Koszalin, Pol. 58 F7
Kota, India 68 J7
Kota Baharu, Malaysia 69 L10
Kota Kinabalu, Malaysia 69 K12
Kotel'nich, Russ. 59 D12
Kotel'nyy Island, Russ. 71 B10
Kotka, Fin. 58 D9
Kotlas, Russ. 59 C11
Kotlik, Alas., U.S. 40 K2
Kotto, river, Cen. Af. Rep. 80 J7
Kotzebue, Alas., U.S. 40 J2
Kotzebue Sound, Alas., U.S. 42 J2
Koudougou, Burkina Faso 78 G3
Koulikoro, Mali 78 G3
Koumra, Chad 78 H7
Kourou, Fr. Guiana 50 B8
Kovel', Ukr. 58 F9
Kovrov, Russ. 59 D11
Kowanyama, Qnsld., Austral. 89 C12
Koyda, Russ. 59 B10
Koyuk, Alas., U.S. 40 K2
Koyukuk, river, Alas., U.S. 42 K3
Kozhikode, India 68 K7
Kpalimé, Togo 78 H4
Kraków, Pol. 58 G8
Kramators'k, Ukr. 59 G11
Kramfors, Sweden 58 C7
Krasavino, Russ. 59 C11
Krasnoarmeysk, Russ. 59 F12
Krasnodar, Russ. 59 H12
Krasnokamensk, Russ. 69 E11
Krasnoleninskiy, Russ. 59 A14
Krasnotur'insk, Russ. 59 B13
Krasnoural'sk, Russ. 59 C14
Krasnovishersk, Russ. 59 B13
Krasnoyarsk, Russ. 68 E9
Kraul Mountains, Antarctica 102 B7
Kremenchuk, Ukr. 59 G10
Krishna, river, India 70 K7
Kristiansand, Nor. 58 D6
Kristiansund, Nor. 58 C6
Kríti (Crete), island, Gr. 58 L9
Kroonstad, S. Af. 79 P8
Kropotkin, Russ. 59 G12
Krung Thep (Bangkok), Thai. 69 K10
Kruzof Island, Alas., U.S. 42 M5
Krychaw, Belarus 59 F10
Kryvyy Rih, Ukr. 59 G10
Kuala Lumpur, Malaysia 69 L10
Kuala Terengganu, Malaysia 69 L11
Kuban', river, Russ. 61 H11
Kuban Lowland, Russ. 61 G12
Kubeno, Lake, Russ. 61 D11
Kuching, Malaysia 69 L12
Kudgee, homestead, N.S.W., AUSTRAL. 89 K11
Kudymkar, Russ. 59 C13
Kufra Oasis, Lib. 80 E8
Kugluktuk, Nunavut 36 D5
Kuikuina, Nicar. 37 P8
Kuito, Angola 79 M7
Kuiu Island, Alas., U.S. 42 M5
Kule, Botswana 79 P7
Kulgera, homestead, N. Terr., Austral. 88 G8
Kulin, W. Austral., Austral. 88 K3
Kullorsuaq, Greenland 36 C8
Kuloy, river, Russ. 61 B11
Kulumadau, P.N.G. 92 D7
Kuma, river, Russ. 61 G13
Kumara Junction, N.Z. 92 L4
Kumasi, Ghana 78 H3
Kumawa, Pegunungan, Indonesia 92 B1
Kumba, Cameroon 78 J5
Kunashir, island, Russ. 69 E13
Kungur, Russ. 59 C13
Kunié see Pins, Île des, New Caledonia 96 H5
Kunlun Mountains, China 70 G8
Kunlun Shan (Kunlun Mountains), China 68 G8
Kunming, China 69 H10
Kununurra, W. Austral., Austral. 88 C6
Kuopio, Fin. 58 C9
Kupang, Indonesia 69 M14
Kupreanof Island, Alas., U.S. 42 M5
Kuqa, China 68 G8
Kura, river, Asia 70 F5
Kure Atoll, Hawaii, U.S. 96 B7
Kurgan, Russ. 59 C15
Kuri Bay, W. Austral., Austral. 88 C5
Kuril Islands, Russ. 71 D14
Kursk, Russ. 59 F11
Kuruman, S. Af. 79 P8
Kusaie see Kosrae, island, F.S.M. 96 E5
Kuskokwim, river, Alas., U.S. 42 L2
Kuskokwim Bay, Alas., U.S. 42 L2
Kuskokwim Mountains, Alas., U.S. 42 L2
Kütahya, Turk. 59 K10
K'ut'aisi, Ga. 59 H13
Kutch, Gulf of, India 70 J6
Kutu, D.R.C. 79 K7
Kuujjuaq, Que., Can. 36 F9
Kuujjuarapik, Que., Can. 36 G8
Kuvango, Angola 79 M7
Kuwait, Asia 68 G4
Kuybyshev Reservoir, Russ. 61 D13
Kuybyshevskaye Vodokhranilishche (Kuybyshev Reservoir), Russ. 59 D13
Kwajalein Atoll, Marshall Is. 96 D5
Kwango, river, Angola-D.R.C. 81 L7
Kwanza, river, Angola 81 L6
Kwinana, W. Austral., Austral. 88 K2
Kwoka, peak, Indonesia 92 A1
Kynuna, Qnsld., Austral. 89 E11
Kyōto, Jap. 69 F13
Kyrgyzstan, Asia 68 G7
Kyshtym, Russ. 59 C14
Kyushu, island, Jap. 71 G13
Kyyiv (Kiev), Ukr. 59 G10
Kyzyl, Russ. 68 E9
Kzyltu, Kaz. 59 C16

Laascaanood, Somalia 78 H12
Laayoune, W. Sahara 78 E2
Labé, Guinea 78 G2
Labrador, region, Nfld. and Lab., Can. 36 F9
Labrador City, Nfld. and Lab., Can. 36 G9
Labrador Sea, Atl. Oc. 38 E10
Lábrea, Braz. 50 E5
Laccadive Sea, India 70 K7
La Ceiba, Hond. 37 P7
Lachlan, river, N.S.W., AUSTRAL. 91 K12
Lac La Biche, Alta., Can. 36 G4
La Crosse, Wis., U.S. 41 D11
Ladoga, Lake, Russ. 60 D9
La Dorada, Col. 50 B3
Ladozhskoye Ozero (Lake Ladoga), Russ. 58 D9
Ladysmith, S. Af. 79 Q9
Lae, P.N.G. 92 C6
La Esmeralda, Venez. 50 C5
Lafayette, La., U.S. 41 J11
Laghouat, Alg. 78 D5
Lago Argentino see El Calafate, Arg. 51 Q4
Lagos, Nig. 78 H4
La Grande, Oreg., U.S. 40 C4
La Grange, Ga., U.S. 41 H13
Lagrange, W. Austral., Austral. 88 D4
Laguna, Braz. 51 K8
Laguna Grande, Arg. 51 Q5
La Habana (Havana), Cuba 37 N8
Lahaina, Hawaii, U.S. 41 L12
Lahore, Pak. 68 H7
Lahti, Fin. 58 D9
Laï (Behagle), Chad 78 H7
Laird, river, Can. 38 E4
Laisamis, Kenya 78 J10
Lajamanu, N. Terr., Austral. 88 D7
Lajes, Braz. 51 K8
La Junta, Colo., U.S. 40 F7
Lake Cargelligo, N.S.W., AUSTRAL. 89 K13
Lake Charles, La., U.S. 41 J10
Lake City, Fla., U.S. 41 J14
Lake Coleridge, N.Z. 92 M4
Lake Eyre Basin, S. Austral., Austral. 90 H10
Lake Grace, W. Austral., Austral. 88 K3
Lake King, W. Austral., Austral. 88 K4
Lakeland, Fla., U.S. 41 J14
Lake Louise, Alta., Can. 36 G4
Lake Minchumina, Alas., U.S. 40 K3
Lake Murray, P.N.G. 92 C4
Lake Nash, homestead, N. Terr., Austral. 89 E10
Lake Region, U.K. 60 C9
Lake Stewart, homestead, N.S.W., AUSTRAL. 89 H11
Lake Violet, homestead, W. Austral., Austral. 88 G4
Lakselv, Nor. 58 A8
Lakshadweep, islands, India 70 K6
Lamar, Colo., U.S. 40 F8
Lambaréné, Gabon 78 K6
Lambert Glacier, Antarctica 103 E13
Lambert's Bay, S. Af. 79 Q7
Lamesa, Tex., U.S. 40 H8
La Montaña, region, Braz.-Peru 52 F3
Lamu, Kenya 79 K11
Lana'i, island, Hawaii, U.S. 43 L12
Lāna'i City, Hawaii, U.S. 41 L12
Lancaster Sound, Can. 38 C7
Lander, river, N. Terr., Austral. 90 E8
Lander, Wyo., U.S. 40 D6
Landor, homestead, W. Austral., Austral. 88 G2
Landsborough Creek, Qnsld., Austral. 91 F12
Land's End, point, U.K. 60 F3
Länkäran, Azerb. 59 J14
Lansdowne, homestead, W. Austral., Austral. 88 D6
Lansdowne House, Ont., Can. 36 G7
L'Anse aux Meadows, Nfld. and Lab., Can. 36 F10
Lansing, Mich., U.S. 41 D12
Lanzarote, island, Canary Is. 80 D2
Lanzhou, China 69 G10
Laoag, Philippines 69 J13
La Oroya, Peru 50 F2
Laos, Asia 69 J10
La Palma, island, Canary Is. 80 D1
La Paragua, Venez. 50 B5
La Paz, Bol. 50 G4
La Paz, Mex. 37 M3
La Pedrera, Col. 50 D4
La Perouse Pinnacle, Hawaii, U.S. 96 C8
Lapland, Fin.-Russ.-Sweden 58 B8
La Plata, Arg. 51 L6
Lappeenranta, Fin. 58 D9
Laptev Sea, Russ. 70 B10
La Quiaca, Arg. 50 J5
Laramie, Wyo., U.S. 40 E7
Laramie Mountains, Wyo., U.S. 42 E7
Laramie Peak, Wyo., U.S. 42 E7
Larat, island, Indonesia 92 C1
Laredo, Tex., U.S. 40 K8
La Rioja, Arg. 50 K5
Lárissa, Gr. 58 K8
La Rochelle, Fr. 58 G4
La Ronge, Sask., Can. 36 G5
Larrimah, N. Terr., Austral. 88 C8
Lars Christensen Coast, Antarctica 103 D14
Larsen Ice Shelf, Antarctica 102 D2
La Rubia, Arg. 51 K6
Lascelles, Vic., Austral. 89 L11
Las Cruces, N. Mex., U.S. 40 H6
La Serena, Chile 51 K4
Las Heras, Arg. 51 L4
Las Heras, Arg. 51 P5
Las Lomitas, Arg. 50 J6
Las Palmas, Canary Is. 78 D2
La Spezia, It. 58 H6
Lassen Peak, Calif., U.S. 42 D3
Lassiter Coast, Antarctica 102 D4
Las Tunas, Cuba 37 N9
Las Vegas, N. Mex., U.S. 40 G7
Las Vegas, Nev., U.S. 40 F4
Latady Island, Antarctica 102 E3
Latady Mountains, Antarctica 102 E4
Latouche Treville, Cape, W. Austral., Austral. 90 D4
Latvia, Europe 58 E8
Laughlan Islands, P.N.G. 92 D8
Lau Group, Fiji 96 G7
Launceston, Tas., Austral. 89 L16
Laura, Qnsld., Austral. 89 C13
Laurel, Miss., U.S. 41 H12
Laurel, Mont., U.S. 40 C6
Laurentian Scarp, Can. 38 H8
Laurentide Scarp, Can. 38 G9
Laurie Island, Antarctica 102 A2
Lausanne, Switz. 58 H5
Laverton, W. Austral., Austral. 88 H5
Lawrence, Kans., U.S. 41 F10
Lawton, Okla., U.S. 40 G9
Laysan Island, Hawaii, U.S. 96 C8
Lead, S. Dak., U.S. 40 D8
Leaf, river, Can. 38 F8
Learmonth, W. Austral., Austral. 88 F1
Lebanon, Asia 68 F3
Lebanon, Mo., U.S. 41 F10
Lebombo Mountains, Mozambique-S. Af.-Swaziland 81 P9
Lecce, It. 58 K7
Leech Lake, Minn., U.S. 43 C10
Leeds, U.K. 58 E4
Leesburg, Fla., U.S. 41 J14
Leeuwin, Cape, W. Austral., Austral. 90 L2
Leeward Islands, N. America 39 N12
Lefkáda, island, Gr. 58 K8
Lefkosia (Nicosia), Cyprus 68 F3
Lefroy, Lake, W. Austral., Austral. 90 J4
Legune, homestead, N. Terr., Austral. 88 C7
Le Havre, Fr. 58 F4
Leigh, N.Z. 92 G5
Leigh Creek, S. Austral., Austral. 89 J10
Leipzig, Ger. 58 F6
Le Mans, Fr. 58 G4
Lemmon, S. Dak., U.S. 40 C8
Lena, river, Russ. 71 C10
Lenghu, China 68 G9
Lengua de Vaca Point, Chile 53 L4
Lennox-King Glacier, Antarctica 102 H9
Lensk, Russ. 69 D10
Léo, Burkina Faso 78 H3
León, Mex. 37 N5
León, Nicar. 37 Q7
León, Sp. 58 H2
Leongatha, Vic., Austral. 89 M12
Leonora, W. Austral., Austral. 88 H4
Leopold and Astrid Coast, Antarctica 103 F15
Ler, Sudan 78 H9
Lerida, homestead, Qnsld., Austral. 89 F12
Lerma, river, Mex. 39 N5
Lerwick, U.K. 58 C5
Les Cayes, Haiti 37 N10
Leshukonskoye, Russ. 59 B11
Lesotho, Af. 79 Q8
Lesozavodsk, Russ. 69 E12
L'Esperance Rock, N.Z. 96 J7
Lesser Antilles, islands, N. America 39 P12
Lesser Khingan Range, China 71 E12
Lesser Sunda Islands, Indonesia 71 M13
Lésvos, island, Gr. 58 K9
Lethbridge, Alta., Can. 36 H4
Lethem, Guyana 50 C6
Levant Coast, Asia 70 F3
Leveque, Cape, W. Austral., Austral. 90 C4
Levin, N.Z. 92 K6
Lewis, Isle of, U.K. 58 D4
Lewis Pass, N.Z. 92 L4
Lewis Range, N. Terr.-W. Austral., Austral. 90 E6
Lewis Smith Lake, Ala., U.S. 43 G12
Lewiston, Idaho, U.S. 40 C4
Lewiston, Me., U.S. 41 C16
Lewistown, Mont., U.S. 40 C6
Lexington, Ky., U.S. 41 F13
Leyte, island, Philippines 96 D1
Lhasa, China 68 H9
Lianyungang, China 69 G12
Liao, river, China 71 F12
Libenge, D.R.C. 78 J7
Liberal, Okla., U.S. 40 G8
Liberia, Af. 78 H2
Liberia, C.R. 37 Q8
Libreville, Gabon 79 K5
Libya, Af. 78 E7
Libyan Desert, Egypt-Lib.-Sudan 80 E8
Libyan Plateau, Egypt-Lib. 80 D8
Lichinga, Mozambique 79 M10
Lida, Belarus 58 F9
Liechtenstein, Europe 58 G6
Liepāja, Latv. 58 E8
Lifou, island, New Caledonia 96 H5
Ligurian Sea, Fr.-It. 60 J6
Lihir, island, P.N.G. 92 B7
Lihir Group, P.N.G. 92 B7
Līhu'e, Hawaii, U.S. 41 L11
Likasi, D.R.C. 79 M8
Lilian, Point, W. Austral., Austral. 90 H6
Lille, Fr. 58 F5
Lillehammer, Nor. 58 D6
Lillie Glacier, Antarctica 102 M10
Lillooet, B.C., Can. 36 G3
Lilongwe, Malawi 79 M9
Lima, Ohio, U.S. 41 E13
Lima, Peru 50 F2
Limay, river, Arg. 53 N4
Limerick, Ire. 58 E3
Limmen Bight, N. Terr., Austral. 90 C9
Limoges, Fr. 58 H4
Limoquije, Bol. 50 G5
Limpopo, river, Af. 81 P9
Linares, Chile 51 M4
Linares, Mex. 37 M5
Linares, Sp. 58 J2
Lincoln, Nebr., U.S. 40 E9
Lincoln Sea, Arctic Ocean 38 A7
Linda Downs, homestead, Qnsld., Austral. 89 F10
Lindi, Tanzania 79 L10
Line Islands, Kiribati 96 E9
Linhares, Braz. 50 H10
Linköping, Sweden 58 D7
Linz, Aust. 58 G7
Lions, Gulf of, Fr. 60 J4
Lipetsk, Russ. 59 F11
Lisala, D.R.C. 78 J7
Lisboa (Lisbon), Port. 58 J1
Lisbon see Lisboa, Port. 58 J1
Lisburne, Cape, Alas., U.S. 42 J2
Lisianski Island, Hawaii, U.S. 96 C7
Lismore, N.S.W., AUSTRAL. 89 J15
Lister, Mount, Antarctica 102 K9
Listowel Downs, homestead, Qnsld., Austral. 89 G13
Lithgow, N.S.W., AUSTRAL. 89 K14
Lithuania, Europe 58 E8
Little Barrier Island, N.Z. 92 G6
Little Missouri, river, Mont.-N. Dak.-S. Dak., U.S. 42 C8
Little Rock, Ark., U.S. 41 G11
Liuzhou, China 69 H11
Liverpool, U.K. 58 E4
Liverpool Range, N.S.W., AUSTRAL. 91 K14
Livingston, Mont., U.S. 40 C6
Livingstone, Zambia 79 N8
Livingston Island, Antarctica 102 C1
Livny, Russ. 59 F11
Ljubljana, Slov. 58 H7
Llaima Volcano, Chile 53 M4
Llanos, plains, Col.-Venez. 52 B4
Lleida, Sp. 58 J4
Lobaya, river, Cen. Af. Rep. 80 J6
Lobería, Arg. 51 N5
Lobito, Angola 79 M6
Lobos Islands, Peru 52 E1
Lockhart River, Qnsld., Austral. 89 B12
Lodja, D.R.C. 79 K8
Lodwar, Kenya 78 J10
Łódź, Pol. 58 F8
Lofoten, island, Nor. 60 B7
Lofty Range, W. Austral., Austral. 90 G3
Logan, Utah, U.S. 40 E5
Logan, Mount, Can. 38 E2
Logone, river, Cameroon-Chad 80 H6
Loire, river, Fr. 60 G4
Loja, Ecua. 50 E2
Lokitaung, Kenya 78 J10
Lomami, river, D.R.C. 81 K8
Loma Mountains, Guinea-Sierra Leone 80 H2
Lombadina, W. Austral., Austral. 88 C4
Lomblen, island, Indonesia 96 F1
Lombok, island, Indonesia 71 M13
Lomé, Togo 78 H4
Lomela, D.R.C. 79 K8
Lomié, Cameroon 78 J6
Lompoc, Calif., U.S. 40 G2
London, U.K. 58 F4
Londonderry, U.K. 58 E3
Londonderry, Cape, W. Austral., Austral. 90 B6
Londrina, Braz. 50 J8
Long Beach, Calif., U.S. 40 G3
Long Island, N.Y., U.S. 43 D16
Long Island, P.N.G. 92 C6
Long Island Sound, Conn.-N.Y., U.S. 43 D16
Longmont, Colo., U.S. 40 E7
Long Range Mountains, Can. 38 G10
Longreach, Qnsld., Austral. 89 F12
Longs Peak, Colo., U.S. 42 E7
Longton, homestead, Qnsld., Austral. 89 E13
Longview, Tex., U.S. 41 H10

Longview, Wash., U.S. 40 B3
Long Xuyen, Viet. 69 K11
Lookout, Cape, N.C., U.S. 43 G15
Lookout, Point, Qnsld., Austral. 91 H15
Loongana, W. Austral., Austral. 88 J6
Lopatka, Cape, Russ. 71 C13
Lopez, Cape, Gabon 81 K5
Lop Nur, China 70 G9
Lord Howe Island, Austral. 96 J4
Lordsburg, N. Mex., U.S. 40 H6
Lorian Swamp, Kenya 80 J10
Lorient, Fr. 58 G3
Lorne, homestead, Qnsld., Austral. 89 G13
Los Alamos, N. Mex., U.S. 40 G7
Los Ángeles, Chile 51 M4
Los Angeles, Calif., U.S. 40 G3
Los Mochis, Mex. 37 M4
Los Plumas, Arg. 51 N5
Los Teques, Venez. 50 A4
Losuia, P.N.G. 92 D7
Los Vilos, Chile 51 L4
Lota, Chile 51 M4
Lot's Wife see Sōfu Gan, island, Jap. 96 B2
Lou, island, P.N.G. 92 B6
Louangphrabang, Laos 69 J10
Loubomo, Congo 79 K6
Louisiade Archipelago, P.N.G. 92 E8
Louisiana, U.S. 41 J11
Louisville, Ky., U.S. 41 F12
Loup, river, Nebr., U.S. 42 E9
Lourdes-de-Blanc-Sablon, Que., Can. 36 G10
Louth, N.S.W., AUSTRAL. 89 J12
Lovelock, Nev., U.S. 40 E3
Lowell, Mass., U.S. 41 D16
Lower Guinea, region, Af. 81 K6
Lower Hutt, N.Z. 92 K5
Lower Peninsula, Mich., U.S. 43 D12
Lower Red Lake, Minn., U.S. 43 C10
Loyalty Islands, New Caledonia 96 H5
Luanda, Angola 79 L6
Luangwa, river, Zambia 81 M9
Luanshya, Zambia 79 M9
Luapula, river, D.R.C.-Zambia 81 L9
Lubango, Angola 79 M6
Lubbock, Tex., U.S. 40 H8
Lübeck, Ger. 58 F6
Lubefu, D.R.C. 79 K8
Lublin, Pol. 58 F8
Lubumbashi, D.R.C. 79 M8
Lubutu, D.R.C. 78 K8
Lucena, Sp. 58 K2
Lucira, Angola 79 M6
Lucknow, homestead, Qnsld., Austral. 89 F11
Lucknow, India 68 H8
Lucy Creek, homestead, N. Terr., Austral. 88 F9
Lüderitz, Namibia 79 P6
Ludhiana, India 68 H7
Ludogorie, region, Bulg. 60 J9
Luena, Angola 79 M7
Lufkin, Tex., U.S. 41 J10
Luga, Russ. 58 D9
Lugenda, river, Mozambique 81 M10
Lugo, Sp. 58 H2
Luhans'k, Ukr. 59 G12
Luitpold Coast, Antarctica 102 D6
Luiza, D.R.C. 79 L8
Lukenie, river, D.R.C. 81 K7
Luleå, Sweden 58 B8
Luleälven, river, Sweden 60 B8
Lüliang Shan, China 71 G11
Lulonga, river, D.R.C. 80 J7
Lulua, river, D.R.C. 81 L7
Lumberton, N.C., U.S. 41 G14
Lumi, P.N.G. 92 B4
Lungwebungu, river, Angola-Zambia 81 M7
Luoyang, China 69 G11
Lupin, Nunavut 36 E5
Lúrio, river, Mozambique 81 M10
Lúrio, Mozambique 79 M11
Lusaka, Zambia 79 M9
Lusancay Islands, P.N.G. 92 D7
Lusk, Wyo., U.S. 40 D7
Łutselk'e, N.W.T., CAN. 36 E5
Luts'k, Ukr. 58 G9
Lützow-Holm Bay, Antarctica 103 B12
Luxembourg, Europe 58 G5
Luxembourg, Lux. 58 G5
Luxor, Egypt 78 E9
Luza, Russ. 59 C12
Luzhou, China 69 H10
Luzon, island, Philippines 71 J13
Luzon Strait, Philippines-Taiwan 71 J13
L'viv, Ukr. 58 G9
Lyddan Island, Antarctica 102 B6
Lynchburg, Va., U.S. 41 F14
Lyndhurst, S. Austral., Austral. 89 J10
Lyndon, homestead, W. Austral., Austral. 88 G2
Lynn Lake, Manitoba, Can. 36 G5
Lynton, W. Austral., Austral. 88 H2
Lyon, Fr. 58 H5
Lyons, river, W. Austral., Austral. 90 G2
Lys'va, Russ. 59 C13
Lytton, B.C., Can. 36 G3
Lyudinovo, Russ. 59 E10

Maan Ridge, Fin.-Russ. 60 B9
Macapá, Braz. 50 C8
Macaroni, homestead, Qnsld., Austral. 89 C11
Macau, Braz. 50 E11
Macau, China 69 J12
Macauley Island, N.Z. 96 J7
Macdonnell Ranges, N. Terr., Austral. 90 F8
Macedonia, Europe 58 J8
Maceió, Braz. 50 F11
Machala, Ecua. 50 D1
Mackay, Qnsld., Austral. 89 E14
Mackay, Lake, N. Terr.-W. Austral., Austral. 90 F6
Mackenzie, river, Can. 38 E4
Mackenzie, river, Qnsld., Austral. 91 F14
Mackenzie, B.C., Can. 36 F3
Mackenzie Bay, Can. 38 C4
Mackenzie Mountains, Can. 38 E4
Mackenzie-Peace, Source of the, Can. 38 F3
Mackinac, Straits of, Mich., U.S. 43 C12
Macknade, Qnsld., Austral. 89 D13
Macleod, Lake, W. Austral., Austral. 90 G1
Macon, Ga., U.S. 41 H13
Macondo, Angola 79 M8
Macquarie, river, N.S.W., AUSTRAL. 91 J13
Macquarie, Port, N.S.W., AUSTRAL. 91 K15
Macquarie Island, Austral. 96 M4
Mac. Robertson Land, Antarctica 103 D13
Madagascar, Af. 79 N11
Madang, P.N.G. 92 C5
Madeira, island, Atl. Oc. 80 C2
Madeira, river, Braz. 52 E6
Madeira Islands, Atl. Oc. 80 D2
Madison, Wis., U.S. 41 D11
Madisonville, Ky., U.S. 41 F12
Madley, Mount, W. Austral., Austral. 90 F5
Mado Gashi, Kenya 78 J10
Madras see Chennai, India 68 K7
Madre, Sierra, Guatemala-Mex. 39 P6
Madre del Sur, Sierra, Mex. 39 P5
Madre Lagoon, Mex. 39 M6
Madre Occidental, Sierra, Mex. 39 M4
Madre Oriental, Sierra, Mex. 39 M5
Madrid, Sp. 58 J3
Madrid Point, Chile 52 H4
Madura, homestead, W. Austral., Austral. 88 J6
Madurai, India 68 K7
Maevatanana, Madag. 79 M12
Maéwo, island, Vanuatu 96 G5
Mafia Island, Tanzania 81 L10
Magadan, Russ. 69 C12
Magadi, Kenya 79 K10
Magallanes, Estrecho de (Strait of Magellan), Chile 51 R5
Magangué, Col. 50 A3
Magazine Mountain, Ark., U.S. 43 G10
Magdagachi, Russ. 69 E11
Magdalena, river, Col. 52 A2
Magdalena, river, Mex. 39 L3
Magdalena, Bol. 50 F5
Magdalena, Mex. 37 L4
Magdalena, N. Mex., U.S. 40 G6
Magdalena Bay, Mex. 39 M3
Magdeburg, Ger. 58 F6
Magdelaine Cays, C.S.I. Terr., Austral. 91 D15
Magellan, Strait of, Chile 53 R5
Magnitogorsk, Russ. 59 D14
Mahajamba Bay, Madag. 81 M12
Mahajanga, Madag. 79 M12
Mahalapye, Botswana 79 P8
Mahenge, Tanzania 79 L10
Maheno, N.Z. 92 N4
Mahia Peninsula, N.Z. 92 J7
Mahilyow, Belarus 58 F10
Maiduguri, Nig. 78 H6
Maikoor, island, Indonesia 92 C2
Main, river, Ger. 60 G6
Maine, U.S. 41 C16
Maine, Gulf of, U.S. 38 J9
Mainland, island, Orkney Is. 58 D4
Mainland, island, Shetland Is. 58 C5
Mainoru, homestead, N. Terr., Austral. 88 B9
Maintirano, Madag. 79 N11
Maipo Volcano, Arg.-Chile 53 L4
Maitland, N.S.W., AUSTRAL. 89 K14
Maitri, station, Antarctica 102 A9
Majī, Eth. 78 H10
Majorca, island, Sp. 60 J4
Majuro, Marshall Is. 96 E6
Makassar Strait, Indonesia 71 L13
Makatea, island, Fr. Polynesia 97 G10
Makemo, island, Fr. Polynesia 97 G10
Makgadikgadi Pans, Botswana 81 N8
Makhachkala, Russ. 59 H14
Makkah (Mecca), Saudi Arabia 68 H3
Makkovik, Nfld. and Lab., Can. 36 F10
Makokou, Gabon 78 J6
Makurdi, Nig. 78 H5
Malabar Coast, India 70 K7
Malabo, Eq. Guinea 78 J5
Malacca, Strait of, Asia 71 L10
Málaga, Sp. 58 K2
Malaita, island, Solomon Is. 96 F5
Malakal, Sudan 78 H9
Malakula, island, Vanuatu 96 G5
Malang, Indonesia 69 M12
Malanje, Angola 79 L7
Mälaren, lake, Sweden 60 D7
Malatya, Turk. 59 K12
Malawi, Af. 79 M10
Malawi, Lake, Malawi-Mozambique-Tanzania 81 M10
Malay Peninsula, Malaysia-Thai. 71 L10
Malaysia, Asia 69 L10
Malcolm, W. Austral., Austral. 88 H4
Malden Island, Kiribati 96 F9
Maldive Islands, Ind. Oc. 70 L6
Maldives, Ind. Oc. 68 L6
Male, Maldives 68 L6
Mali, Af. 78 G3
Malindi, Kenya 79 K11
Mallacoota, Vic., Austral. 89 M14
Mallawi, Egypt 78 E9
Mallorca (Majorca), island, Sp. 58 J4
Malmö, Sweden 58 E7
Maloelap Atoll, Marshall Is. 96 E6
Malozemel'skaya Tundra, Russ. 61 A11
Malpelo, Isla de (Malpelo Island), Col. 50 C1
Malpelo Island, Col. 52 C1
Malta, Europe 58 L7
Malta, Mont., U.S. 40 B7
Maltahöhe, Namibia 79 P7
Maltese Islands, Malta 60 L7
Malvinas, Islas (Falkland Islands), Atl. Oc. 51 Q6
Mamberamo, Indonesia 92 A3
Mamoré, river, Bol. 52 F5
Man, Côte d'Ivoire 78 H2
Man, Isle of, U.K. 60 E4
Mana, Fr. Guiana 50 B7
Manado, Indonesia 69 L14
Managua, Nicar. 37 Q8
Managua, Lake, Nicar. 39 Q8
Manaia, N.Z. 92 J5
Manakara, Madag. 79 N12
Manakau, peak, N.Z. 92 L5
Manam, island, P.N.G. 92 B5
Manama see Al Manāmah, Bahrain 68 H4
Mananjary, Madag. 79 N12
Manapouri, Lake, N.Z. 92 N3
Manaus, Braz. 50 D6
Manchester, N.H., U.S. 41 D16
Manchester, U.K. 58 E4
Manchuria, region, China 69 E12
Manchurian Plain, China 71 F12
Mandal, Nor. 58 D6
Mandala, Puncak, Indonesia 92 C4
Mandalay, Myanmar 68 J9
Mandalgovĭ, Mongolia 69 F10
Mandan, N. Dak., U.S. 40 C8
Mandera, Kenya 78 J11
Mandimba, Mozambique 79 M10
Mandritsara, Madag. 79 M12
Mandurah, W. Austral., Austral. 88 K2
Manga, region, Chad-Niger 80 G6
Manga, Braz. 50 G10
Mangaia, island, Cook Is. 96 H9
Mangareva, island, Fr. Polynesia 97 H11
Mangeigne, Chad 78 H7
Mango, Togo 78 H4
Mangueni Plateau, Niger 80 F6
Manguinho Point, Braz. 52 F11
Manhattan, Kans., U.S. 40 F9
Manicoré, Braz. 50 E6
Manicouagan, Réservoir, Can. 38 G9
Manifold, Cape, Qnsld., Austral. 91 F15
Manihi, island, Fr. Polynesia 97 G10
Manihiki Atoll, Cook Is. 96 F9
Manila, Philippines 69 J13
Maningrida, N. Terr., Austral. 88 B9
Manitoba, Can. 36 G6
Manitoba, Lake, Can. 38 H6
Manizales, Col. 50 B2
Manja, Madag. 79 N11
Mankato, Minn., U.S. 41 D10
Mannheim, Ger. 58 G6
Manokwari, Indonesia 92 A2
Manono, D.R.C. 79 L8
Manra, island, Kiribati 96 F8
Mansa, Zambia 79 L9
Mansel Island, Can. 38 F7
Manseriche, Pongo de, Peru 52 E2
Mansfield, Vic., Austral. 89 M12
Mansfield, Mount, Vt., U.S. 43 C15
Manta, Ecua. 50 D1
Manti, Utah, U.S. 40 E5
Mantiqueira, Serra da, Braz. 52 J9
Manturovo, Russ. 59 D12
Manū, Peru 50 F4
Manuae, island, Fr. Polynesia 96 G9
Manua Islands, American Samoa 96 G8
Manukau, N.Z. 92 H5
Manus, island, P.N.G. 92 B6
Manych Guidilo, Lake, Russ. 61 G12
Manzanillo, Cuba 37 N9
Manzanillo Bay, Mex. 39 N4
Maoke, Pegunungan, Indonesia 92 B3
Maoke Mountains, Indonesia 71 L16
Mapi, Indonesia 92 C3
Mapia, Kepulauan, Indonesia 96 E2
Mapimí, Bolsón de, Mex. 39 M5
Maprik, P.N.G. 92 B4
Maputo, Mozambique 79 P9
Maputo, Baia de, Mozambique 81 P9
Maqat, Kaz. 59 F14
Mar, Serra do, Braz. 53 K8
Maraã, Braz. 50 D5
Marabá, Braz. 50 E8
Maracaibo, Venez. 50 A3
Maracaibo, Lake, Venez. 52 A3
Maracaibo Basin, Venez. 52 A3
Maracá Island, Braz. 52 C8
Maracaju, Serra de, Braz. 52 H7
Maracay, Venez. 50 A4
Maradi, Niger 78 G5
Marajó, Ilha de (Marajó Island), Braz. 50 D8
Marajó Bay, Braz. 52 D9
Marajó Island, Braz. 52 D8
Marakei, island, Kiribati 96 E6
Maralinga, S. Austral., Austral. 88 J8
Marambio, station, Antarctica 102 C2
Maranboy, N. Terr., Austral. 88 C8
Marañón, river, Peru 52 E2
Mara Rosa, Braz. 50 G8
Marawi, Philippines 69 K13
Marble Bar, W. Austral., Austral. 88 E3
Mar Chiquita, Laguna, Arg. 53 K6
Marcus see Minami Tori Shima, island, Jap. 96 C4
Marcy, Mount, N.Y., U.S. 43 C15
Mar del Plata, Arg. 51 M7
Maré, island, New Caledonia 96 H5
Marechal Taumaturgo, Braz. 50 F3
Marfa, Tex., U.S. 40 J7
Margaret River, homestead, W. Austral., Austral. 88 D6
Margarita Island, Venez. 52 A5
Marguerite Bay, Antarctica 102 D2
Maria, Îles, Fr. Polynesia 96 H9
Mariana Islands, Pac. Oc. 71 G16
Marías Islands, Mex. 39 N4
Maria van Diemen, Cape, N.Z. 92 F4
Maribor, Slov. 58 H7
Maridi, Sudan 78 J9
Marie Byrd Land, Antarctica 102 H5
Mariental, Namibia 79 P7
Marietta, Ga., U.S. 41 G13
Marília, Braz. 50 J8
Marillana, homestead, W. Austral., Austral. 88 F3
Maringá, Braz. 50 J8
Marion, Ohio, U.S. 41 E13
Marion Downs, homestead, Qnsld., Austral. 89 F11
Maritsa, river, Bulg.-Gr.-Turk. 60 J9
Mariupol', Ukr. 59 G11
Marka (Merca), Somalia 78 J11
Markovo, Russ. 69 B12
Marlborough, Qnsld., Austral. 89 F14
Marmara, Sea of, Turk. 60 J10
Marmara Denizi (Sea of Marmara), Turk. 58 J10
Maroantsetra, Madag. 79 M12
Marobee Range, N.S.W., AUSTRAL. 91 K13
Maromokotro, peak, Madag. 81 M12
Maroni, river, Fr. Guiana-Suriname 52 B7
Maroochydore, Qnsld., Austral. 89 H15
Marotiri (Îlots de Bass), Fr. Polynesia 97 H10
Maroua, Cameroon 78 H6
Marovoay, Madag. 79 M12
Marquesas Islands, Fr. Polynesia 97 F11
Marquesas Keys, Fla., U.S. 43 L14
Marquette, Mich., U.S. 41 C12
Marrakech, Mor. 78 D3
Marra Mountains, Sudan 80 G8
Marrawah, Tas., Austral. 89 L15
Marree, S. Austral., Austral. 89 H10
Marrupa, Mozambique 79 M10
Marsabit, Kenya 78 J10
Marsala, It. 58 K6
Marseille, Fr. 58 H5
Marshall, river, N. Terr., Austral. 90 F9
Marshall Islands, Pac. Oc. 96 D6
Marsh Island, La., U.S. 43 J11
Martha's Vineyard, island, Mass., U.S. 43 D16
Martin, S. Dak., U.S. 40 D8
Martinique, island, N. America 39 N12
Martinsville, Va., U.S. 41 F14
Maru, island, Indonesia 92 C1
Marutea, island, Fr. Polynesia 97 H11
Marvel Loch, W. Austral., Austral. 88 J4
Mary, Turkm. 68 G6
Maryborough, Qnsld., Austral. 89 G15
Maryland, U.S. 41 E15
Marzūq, Şahrā', Lib. 80 E6
Masai Steppe, Tanzania 81 K10
Masasi, Tanzania 79 L10
Mascara, Alg. 78 C4
Maseru, Lesotho 79 Q8
Mashhad, Iran 68 G6
Masira, Gulf of, Oman 70 J5
Maşīrah, Jazīrat, Oman 68 J5
Mason, Iowa, U.S. 41 D10
Mason Bay, N.Z. 92 P3
Masqaţ (Muscat), Oman 68 H5
Massachusetts, U.S. 41 D16
Massakory, Chad 78 G6
Massangena, Mozambique 79 N9
Massawa, Eritrea 78 G10
Massenya, Chad 78 H6
Massif Central, Fr. 60 H4
Masson Island, Antarctica 103 G15
Masterton, N.Z. 92 K6
Masvingo, Zimb. 79 N9
Matadi, D.R.C. 79 L6
Matagami, Que., Can. 36 H8
Matagorda Bay, Tex., U.S. 42 K9
Mataiva, island, Fr. Polynesia 97 G10
Matam, Senegal 78 G2
Matamoros, Mex. 37 M6
Matane, Que., Can. 36 H9
Matanzas, Cuba 37 N8
Mataranka, N. Terr., Austral. 88 C8
Matatiele, S. Af. 79 Q9
Mateguá, Bol. 50 F5
Matehuala, Mex. 37 N5
Matiere, N.Z. 92 J5
Mato Grosso, Braz. 50 G6
Mato Grosso Plateau, Braz. 52 G6
Matopo Hills, Zimb. 81 N9
Matterhorn, peak, It.-Switz. 60 H5
Matthew, island, Vanuatu 96 H6
Matthews Peak, Ariz., U.S. 42 G6
Maturín, Venez. 50 A5
Maudheim, station, Antarctica 102 A7
Maui, island, Hawaii, U.S. 43 L12
Mauke, island, Cook Is. 96 H9
Maumee, river, Ohio, U.S. 43 E13
Maun, Botswana 79 N8
Mauna Kea, peak, Hawaii, U.S. 43 M12
Mauna Loa, peak, Hawaii, U.S. 43 M12
Maunaloa, Hawaii, U.S. 41 L12
Maupihaa, island, Fr. Polynesia 96 G9
Maurice, Lake, S. Austral., Austral. 90 H8
Mauritania, Af. 78 F2
Maury Bay, Antarctica 103 K14
Mavinga, Angola 79 M7
Mawlamyine, Myanmar 68 K10
Mawson, station, Antarctica 103 D14
Mawson Coast, Antarctica 103 D14
Mawson Escarpment, Antarctica 103 E13
Mawson Peninsula, Antarctica 103 M11
Maxixe, Mozambique 79 P10
Maykop, Russ. 59 H12
Mayo, Yukon Terr. 36 D3
Mayotte, island, Ind. Oc. 79 M11
May Pen, Jamaica 37 N9
Mayumba, Gabon 79 K6
Mazagan see El Jadida, Mor. 78 D3
Mazar-e Sharif, Afghan. 68 G6
Mazatán, Mex. 37 L4
Mazatlán, Mex. 37 N4
Mazyr, Belarus 58 F9
Mbabane, Swaziland 79 P9
Mbala, Zambia 79 L9
Mbale, Uganda 78 J10
Mbamba Bay, Tanzania 79 L10
Mbandaka, D.R.C. 78 K7
Mbang Mountains, Cameroon-Chad 80 H6
M'banza Congo, Angola 79 L6
Mbanza-Ngungu, D.R.C. 79 K6
Mbarara, Uganda 78 K9
Mbeya, Tanzania 79 L9
M'Binda, Congo 79 K6
Mbuji-Mayi, D.R.C. 79 L8
McAlester, Okla., U.S. 41 G10
McAllen, Tex., U.S. 40 K9
McArthur River, homestead, N. Terr., Austral. 88 C9
McCook, Nebr., U.S. 40 E8
McDermitt, Nev., U.S. 40 D4
McDouall Peak, homestead, S. Austral., Austral. 88 J9
McGill, Nev., U.S. 40 E4
McGrath, Alas., U.S. 40 K3
McKean Island, Kiribati 96 F7
McKinlay, Qnsld., Austral. 89 E11
McKinley, Mount (Denali), Alas., U.S. 42 K3
M'Clintock Channel, Can. 38 D6
M'Clure Strait, Can. 38 C5
McMurdo, station, Antarctica 102 K9
McMurdo Sound, Antarctica 102 K9
Mead, Lake, Ariz.-Nev. 42 F4
Meadow, homestead, W. Austral., Austral. 88 H2
Meadow Lake, Sask., Can. 36 G5
Meandarra, Qnsld., Austral. 89 H14
Meander River, Alta., Can. 36 F4
Mecca see Makkah, Saudi Arabia 68 H3
Mecula, Mozambique 79 M10
Medan, Indonesia 69 L10
Médea, Alg. 78 C5
Medellín, Col. 50 B2
Medford, Oreg., U.S. 40 D3
Medicine Bow Mountains, Colo.-Wyo., U.S. 42 E7
Medicine Hat, Alta., Can. 36 H4
Medina see Al Madīnah, Saudi Arabia 68 G3
Mednogorsk, Russ. 59 E14
Medvezh'yegorsk, Russ. 58 C10
Meekatharra, W. Austral., Austral. 88 H3
Meerut, India 68 H7
Mēga, Eth. 78 J10
Meharry, Mount, W. Austral., Austral. 90 F3
Mékambo, Gabon 78 J6
Mek'elē, Eth. 78 G10
Mekerrhane, Sebkha, Alg. 80 E4
Meknès, Mor. 78 C3
Mekong, river, Asia 71 K11
Mekoryuk, Alas., U.S. 40 L1
Melanesia, islands, Pac. Oc. 96 E3
Melbourne, Fla., U.S. 41 J14
Melbourne, Vic., Austral. 89 M12
Melbourne, Mount, Antarctica 102 L9
Melfort, Sask., Can. 36 G5
Melilla, Sp. 58 K2
Melinka, Chile 51 P4
Melitopol', Ukr. 59 G11
Melo, Uru. 51 L7
Melrhir, Chott, Alg. 80 D5
Melrose, homestead, W. Austral., Austral. 88 H4
Melton, Vic., Austral. 89 M12
Melville Bay, Greenland 38 C8
Melville Hills, Can. 38 D4
Melville Island, Can. 38 C5
Melville Island, N. Terr., Austral. 90 A7
Melville Peninsula, Can. 38 E7
Memphis, Tenn., U.S. 41 G11
Ménaka, Mali 78 G4
Mendebo Mountains, Eth. 80 H10
Mendi, P.N.G. 92 C5
Mendocino, Cape, Calif., U.S. 42 D2
Meningie, S. Austral., Austral. 89 L10
Menominee, river, Mich.-Wisc. 43 C11
Menongue, Angola 79 M7
Menorca (Minorca), island, Sp. 58 J4
Mentawai Islands, Indonesia 71 M10
Menyamya, P.N.G. 92 C5
Menzies, W. Austral., Austral. 88 J4
Menzies, Mount, Antarctica 103 D12
Meramangye, Lake, S. Austral., Austral. 90 H8
Merauke, Indonesia 69 L16
Merauke, Indonesia 92 D4
Merca see Marka, Somalia 78 J11
Mercedario, Cerro, Arg.-Chile 53 L4
Mercedes, Arg. 51 L5
Mercedes, Uru. 51 L6
Meredith, Lake, Tex., U.S. 42 G8
Mereeg, Somalia 78 J12
Mergenevo, Kaz. 59 F14
Mérida, Mex. 37 N7
Mérida, Sp. 58 J2
Mérida, Venez. 50 B3
Mérida, Cordillera de, Venez. 52 B3
Meridian, Miss., U.S. 41 H12
Merimbula, N.S.W., AUSTRAL. 89 M14
Merir, island, Palau 96 E2
Merowe, Sudan 78 F9
Merredin, W. Austral., Austral. 88 J3
Merrick Mountains, Antarctica 102 E4
Merrimack, river, Mass.-N.H. 43 D16
Merritt Island, Fla., U.S. 41 J14
Mertz Glacier, Antarctica 103 M12
Mertz Glacier Tongue, Antarctica 103 M12
Meru, Kenya 78 K10
Mesa, Ariz., U.S. 40 H5
Mesabi Range, Minn., U.S. 43 C10
Meseta, plateau, Sp. 60 J2
Mesopotamia, region, Iraq-Syr. 70 F4
Messina, It. 58 K7
Messina, S. Af. 79 N9
Meta Incognita Peninsula, Can. 38 E8
Meuse, river, Belg.-Fr.-Neth. 60 F5
Mexicali, Mex. 37 L3
México, Mex. 37 N5
Mexico, N. America 37 M4
Mexico, Gulf of, N. America 39 M7
Meyanodas, Indonesia 92 D1
Mezen', river, Russ. 61 B11
Mezen', Russ. 59 B11
Mezen' Bay, Russ. 61 B11
Miahuatlán, Mex. 37 P6
Miami, river, U.S. 38 K8
Miami, Fla., U.S. 41 K15
Miami Beach, Fla., U.S. 41 K15
Miangas, island, Indonesia 96 E1
Mianyang, China 69 H10
Miass, Russ. 59 D14
Michigan, U.S. 41 C12
Michigan, Lake, U.S. 43 D12
Michurinsk, Russ. 59 E11
Micronesia, islands, Pac. Oc. 96 D3
Middelburg, S. Af. 79 Q8
Middlemarch, N.Z. 92 N4
Middle Park, homestead, Qnsld., Austral. 89 E12
Midland, Tex., U.S. 40 H8
Midway Islands, Hawaii, U.S. 96 B7
Mikhaylovka, Russ. 59 F12
Mikkeli, Fin. 58 C9
Mikun', Russ. 59 B12
Milagro, Ecua. 50 D2
Milan see Milano, It. 58 H6
Milano (Milan), It. 58 H6
Milbank, S. Dak., U.S. 40 D9
Mildura, Vic., Austral. 89 K11
Miles, Qnsld., Austral. 89 H14
Miles City, Mont., U.S. 40 C7
Mileura, homestead, W. Austral., Austral. 88 H3
Milford Sound, N.Z. 92 M3
Milgarra, homestead, Qnsld., Austral. 89 D11
Milgun, homestead, W. Austral., Austral. 88 G3
Mili Atoll, Marshall Is. 96 E6
Milikapiti, N. Terr., Austral. 88 A7
Milingimbi, N. Terr., Austral. 88 B9
Milk, river, Can.-U.S. 42 B6
Mille Lacs Lake, Minn., U.S. 43 C10
Mill Island, Antarctica 103 H15
Millmerran, Qnsld., Austral. 89 H15
Millungera, homestead, Qnsld., Austral. 89 E11
Milly Milly, homestead, W. Austral., Austral. 88 G2
Milpa, homestead, N.S.W., AUSTRAL. 89 J11
Milparinka, N.S.W., AUSTRAL. 89 J11
Milwaukee, Wis., U.S. 41 D12
Minami Iwo Jima, Jap. 96 C3
Minami Tori Shima (Marcus), Jap. 96 C4
Minas, Uru. 51 L7
Mindanao, island, Philippines 71 K14
Mindoro, island, Philippines 71 J13
Mingäçevir, Azerb. 59 H14
Mingenew, W. Austral., Austral. 88 J2
Mingiwal, Lake, W. Austral., Austral. 90 J5
Minilya, homestead, W. Austral., Austral. 88 G1
Minjilang, N. Terr., Austral. 88 A8
Minneapolis, Minn., U.S. 41 D10
Minnedosa, Manitoba, Can. 36 H5
Minnesota, river, Minn.-S. Dak., U.S. 43 D10
Minnesota, U.S. 41 C10
Minorca, island, Sp. 60 J4
Minot, N. Dak., U.S. 40 B8
Minsk, Belarus 58 F9
Minto, Mount, Antarctica 102 M9
Miraflores, Col. 50 C3
Miriam Vale, Qnsld., Austral. 89 G15
Mirnyy, station, Antarctica 103 G15
Mirnyy, Russ. 69 D10
Misima, island, P.N.G. 92 E7
Misión San José Estero, Para. 50 J6
Miskitos, Cayos, Nicar. 37 P8
Miskolc, Hung. 58 G8
Mişrātah, Lib. 78 D6
Mississippi, river, U.S. 43 H11
Mississippi, U.S. 41 H11
Mississippi, Source of the (Lake Itasca), Minn., U.S. 43 C10
Mississippi River Delta, La., U.S. 43 J12
Mississippi Sound, Miss., U.S. 43 J12
Missoula, Mont., U.S. 40 C5
Missouri, river, U.S. 43 F11
Missouri, U.S. 41 F10
Missouri-Red Rock, Source of the, U.S. 38 H4
Misurata, Cape, Lib. 80 D6
Mitchell, river, Qnsld., Austral. 91 C12
Mitchell, Qnsld., Austral. 89 G14
Mitchell, S. Dak., U.S. 40 D9
Mitchell, Mount, N.C., U.S. 43 G13
Mitiaro, island, Cook Is. 96 G9
Mitre, peak, N.Z. 92 K6
Mitre Island see Fataka, Solomon Is. 96 G6
Mittelland Canal, Ger. 60 F6
Mitú, Col. 50 C4
Mitumba Mountains, D.R.C. 81 L8
Mjøsa, lake, Nor. 60 D7
Moa, island, Indonesia 96 F1
Moab, Utah, U.S. 40 F6
Mobayi-Mbongo, D.R.C. 78 J7

Mobile, *Ala., U.S.* **41** J12
Mobile Bay, *Ala., U.S.* **43** J12
Mobridge, *S. Dak., U.S.* **40** C8
Mocoa, *Col.* **50** C2
Moctezuma, *Mex.* **37** L4
Modena, *It.* **58** H6
Modesto, *Calif., U.S.* **40** F3
Moe, *Vic., Austral.* **89** M12
Mogadishu *see* Muqdisho, *Somalia* **78** J11
Mogollon Rim, *Ariz., U.S.* **42** G5
Mogotes Point, *Arg.* **53** M7
Mohotani (Motane), *island, Marquesas Is.* **97** F11
Mo i Rana, *Nor.* **58** B7
Mojave, *Calif., U.S.* **40** G3
Mojave Desert, *Calif.-Nev.* **42** F4
Molde, *Nor.* **58** C6
Moldova, *Europe* **58** G9
Molepolole, *Botswana* **79** P8
Molesworth, *N.Z.* **92** L5
Mollendo, *Peru* **50** G3
Molodezhnaya, *station, Antarctica* **103** B13
Moloka'i, *Hawaii, U.S.* **43** L12
Molopo, *river, Botswana-S. Af.* **81** P7
Moloundou, *Cameroon* **78** J6
Molu, *island, Indonesia* **92** C1
Moluccas, *islands, Indonesia* **71** L14
Molucca Sea, *Indonesia* **96** E1
Mombasa, *Kenya* **79** K11
Momote, *P.N.G.* **92** B6
Monaco, *Europe* **58** H5
Mona Passage, *Dom. Rep.-P.R.* **39** N11
Mona Point (Monkey Point), *Nicar.* **39** Q8
Monchegorsk, *Russ.* **58** B9
Monclova, *Mex.* **37** M5
Moncton, *N.B., Can.* **36** H10
Mongers Lake, *W. Austral., Austral.* **90** J2
Mongo, *Chad* **78** G7
Mongolia, *Asia* **68** F10
Mongolian Plateau, *China-Mongolia* **71** F10
Mongororo, *Chad* **78** G8
Mongos, Chaîne des, *Cen. Af. Rep.-Chad* **80** H7
Mongu, *Zambia* **79** M8
Monitor Range, *Nev., U.S.* **42** E4
Monkey Point *see* Monkey Point, *Nicar.* **39** Q8
Monkira, *Qnsld., Austral.* **89** G11
Mono Lake, *Calif., U.S.* **42** E3
Monroe, *La., U.S.* **41** H11
Monrovia, *Liberia* **78** H2
Montague Island, *Alas., U.S.* **42** L3
Montana, *U.S.* **40** C6
Montauban, *Fr.* **58** H4
Monteagle, Mount, *Antarctica* **102** L9
Monte Azul, *Braz.* **50** G10
Monte Dinero, *Arg.* **51** Q5
Montego Bay, *Jamaica* **37** N9
Montemayor, Meseta de, *Arg.* **53** P5
Monte Quemado, *Arg.* **50** J5
Monterey, *Calif., U.S.* **40** F2
Monterey Bay, *Calif., U.S.* **42** F2
Montería, *Col.* **50** B2
Monterrey, *Mex.* **37** M5
Montes Claros, *Braz.* **50** G10
Montevideo, *Uru.* **51** L7
Montgomery, *Ala., U.S.* **41** H12
Monticello, *Utah, U.S.* **40** F6
Monto, *Qnsld., Austral.* **89** G15
Montpelier, *Idaho, U.S.* **40** D6
Montpelier, *Vt., U.S.* **41** C15
Montpellier, *Fr.* **58** H4
Montréal, *Que., Can.* **36** H9
Montrose, *Colo., U.S.* **40** F6
Montserrat, *island, N. America* **39** N12
Monywa, *Myanmar* **68** J9
Moolawatana, *homestead, S. Austral., Austral.* **89** J11
Mooloogool, *homestead, W. Austral., Austral.* **88** G3
Moora, *W. Austral., Austral.* **88** J2
Mooraberree, *homestead, Qnsld., Austral.* **89** G11
Moore, Lake, *W. Austral., Austral.* **90** J3
Moorhead, *Minn., U.S.* **40** C9
Moosehead Lake, *Me., U.S.* **43** B16
Moose Jaw, *Sask., Can.* **36** H5
Moose Lake, *Minn., U.S.* **41** C10
Moosonee, *Ont., Can.* **36** G8
Mootwingee, *homestead, N.S.W., AUSTRAL.* **89** J11
Mopti, *Mali* **78** G3
Moquegua, *Peru* **50** G4
Morane, *island, Fr. Polynesia* **97** H11
Morava, *river, Serbia and Montenegro* **60** H8
Morawhanna, *Guyana* **50** B6
Moray Firth, *U.K.* **60** D4
Moreau, *river, S. Dak., U.S.* **42** D8
Morelia, *Mex.* **37** N5
Morella, *Qnsld., Austral.* **89** F12
Morena, Sierra, *Sp.* **60** J2
Morenci, *Ariz., U.S.* **40** H6
Morere, *N.Z.* **92** J7
Moreton, *Qnsld., Austral.* **89** B12
Moreton Island, *Qnsld., Austral.* **91** H15
Morgan, *S. Austral., Austral.* **89** K10
Morganito, *Venez.* **50** B4
Moriah, Mount, *Nev., U.S.* **42** E5
Mornington, *Qnsld., Austral.* **89** C11
Mornington Island, *Qnsld., Austral.* **91** C11
Morocco, *Af.* **78** D3
Morogoro, *Tanzania* **79** L10
Morondava, *Madag.* **79** N11
Moroni, *Comoros* **79** M11
Morotai, *island, Indonesia* **96** E1
Morris Jesup, Cape, *Greenland* **38** A7
Morrosquillo, Gulf of, *Col.* **52** A2
Morshansk, *Russ.* **59** E12
Mortlake, *Vic., Austral.* **89** M11
Mortlock Islands, *F.S.M.* **96** E4
Moruroa, *island, Fr. Polynesia* **97** H11
Morven, *Qnsld., Austral.* **89** G13
Moscow, *river, Russ.* **61** E11
Moscow *see* Moskva, *Russ.* **59** E11
Moscow University Ice Shelf, *Antarctica* **103** K14
Mose, Cape, *Antarctica* **103** L13
Moselle, *river, Fr.-Ger.-Lux.* **60** G5
Moshi, *Tanzania* **79** K10
Mosjøen, *Nor.* **58** B7
Moskva (Moscow), *Russ.* **59** E11
Mosquito Coast, *Nicar.* **39** Q8
Mosquitos, Gulf of, *Pan.* **39** Q9
Mossburn, *N.Z.* **92** N3
Mossel Bay, *S. Af.* **81** Q7
Mossgiel, *N.S.W., AUSTRAL.* **89** K12
Mossoró, *Braz.* **50** E11
Mostaganem, *Alg.* **78** C4
Mostar, *Bosn. Herzg.* **58** J7
Motane *see* Mohotani, *island, Marquesas Is.* **97** F11
Mott, *N. Dak., U.S.* **40** C8
Motu, *river, N.Z.* **92** H7
Motueka, *N.Z.* **92** K5
Motul, *Mex.* **37** N7
Motu One, *island, Fr. Polynesia* **96** G9
Moulamein, *N.S.W., AUSTRAL.* **89** L12
Mould Bay, *N.W.T., CAN.* **36** C5
Moultrie, Lake, *S.C., U.S.* **43** G14
Moundou, *Chad* **78** H6
Mountain Home, *Idaho, U.S.* **40** D4
Mountain Nile, *river, Sudan* **80** H9
Mountain Village, *Alas., U.S.* **40** L2
Mount Arrowsmith, *homestead, N.S.W., AUSTRAL.* **89** J11
Mount Barker, *W. Austral., Austral.* **88** L3
Mount Barnett, *homestead, W. Austral., Austral.* **88** C5
Mount Cavenagh, *homestead, N. Terr., Austral.* **88** G8
Mount Cook, *N.Z.* **92** M4
Mount Coolon, *Qnsld., Austral.* **89** E14
Mount Desert Island, *Me., U.S.* **43** C16
Mount Douglas, *homestead, Qnsld., Austral.* **89** E13
Mount Ebenezer, *homestead, N. Terr., Austral.* **88** G8
Mount Elsie, *homestead, Qnsld., Austral.* **89** E13
Mount Gambier, *S. Austral., Austral.* **89** M11
Mount Hagen, *P.N.G.* **92** C5
Mount Hope, *N.S.W., AUSTRAL.* **89** K13
Mount House, *homestead, W. Austral., Austral.* **88** D5
Mount Ida, *W. Austral., Austral.* **88** H4
Mount Isa, *Qnsld., Austral.* **89** E11
Mount Keith, *homestead, W. Austral., Austral.* **88** H4
Mount Lofty Ranges, *S. Austral., Austral.* **91** K10
Mount Magnet, *W. Austral., Austral.* **88** H3
Mount Maunganui, *N.Z.* **92** H6
Mount Molloy, *Qnsld., Austral.* **89** D13
Mount Mulgrave, *homestead, Qnsld., Austral.* **89** C12
Mount Murchison, *homestead, N.S.W., AUSTRAL.* **89** J12
Mount Riddock, *homestead, N. Terr., Austral.* **88** F9
Mount Sanford, *homestead, N. Terr., Austral.* **88** D7
Mount Sarah, *S. Austral., Austral.* **88** G9
Mount Stuart, *homestead, W. Austral., Austral.* **88** F2
Mount Vernon, *homestead, W. Austral., Austral.* **88** G3
Mount Wedge, *homestead, N. Terr., Austral.* **88** F8
Mount Willoughby, *homestead, S. Austral., Austral.* **88** H9
Mouroubra, *homestead, W. Austral., Austral.* **88** J3
Moussoro, *Chad* **78** G7
Moyale, *Kenya* **78** J10
Moyo, *Uganda* **78** J9
Moyobamba, *Peru* **50** E2
Mozambique, *Af.* **79** N10
Mozambique Channel, *Af.* **81** N10
Mozdok, *Russ.* **59** H13
Mpandamatenga, *Botswana* **79** N8
Mpika, *Zambia* **79** M9
Mtsensk, *Russ.* **59** F11
Mtwara, *Tanzania* **79** L11
Mubi, *Nig.* **78** H6
Muchea, *W. Austral., Austral.* **88** K2
Muchinga Mountains, *Zambia* **81** M9
Muckety, *homestead, N. Terr., Austral.* **88** D8
Muconda, *Angola* **79** L7
Mucusso, *Angola* **79** N7
Mudamuckla, *S. Austral., Austral.* **88** J9
Mudanjiang, *China* **69** E12
Mudgee, *N.S.W., AUSTRAL.* **89** K14
Mufulira, *Zambia* **79** M9
Muğla, *Turk.* **59** K10
Muḩammad, Râs, *Egypt* **80** E9
Muhembo, *Botswana* **79** N7
Mühlig-Hofmann Mountains, *Antarctica* **102** A8
Mukinbudin, *W. Austral., Austral.* **88** J3
Muko Jima Rettō, *Jap.* **96** B3
Mulchén, *peak, Sp.* **60** K2
Mulgildie, *Qnsld., Austral.* **89** G15
Mulhouse, *Fr.* **58** G5
Mulka, *homestead, S. Austral., Austral.* **89** H10
Mullewa, *W. Austral., Austral.* **88** H2
Mullumbimby, *N.S.W., AUSTRAL.* **89** J15
Multan, *Pak.* **68** H7
Mumbai (Bombay), *India* **68** J6
Munburra, *homestead, Qnsld., Austral.* **89** C13
München (Munich), *Ger.* **58** G6
Muncie, *Ind., U.S.* **41** E12
Mundabullangana, *W. Austral., Austral.* **88** E3
Mundiwindi, *W. Austral., Austral.* **88** F4
Mundrabilla, *homestead, W. Austral., Austral.* **88** J6
Mundubbera, *Qnsld., Austral.* **89** G15
Mungana, *Qnsld., Austral.* **89** D12
Mungindi, *N.S.W., AUSTRAL.* **89** H14
Munich *see* München, *Ger.* **58** G6
Muqdisho (Mogadishu), *Somalia* **78** J11
Murashi, *Russ.* **59** C12
Murchison, *river, W. Austral., Austral.* **90** H2
Murcia, *Sp.* **58** K3
Mures, *river, Hung.-Rom.* **60** H8
Murfreesboro, *Tenn., U.S.* **41** G12
Murgoo, *homestead, W. Austral., Austral.* **88** H2
Murman Coast, *Russ.* **60** A10
Murmansk, *Russ.* **58** A9
Murom, *Russ.* **59** E11
Murray, *river, Austral.* **91** K11
Murray, *river, W. Austral., Austral.* **90** K3
Murray, Lake, *P.N.G.* **92** C4
Murray, Source of the, *Vic., Austral.* **91** L13
Murray Bridge, *S. Austral., Austral.* **89** L10
Murray River Basin, *Austral.* **91** K11
Murrayville, *Vic., Austral.* **89** L11
Murrenja Hill, *N. Terr., Austral.* **90** B7
Murrin Murrin, *W. Austral., Austral.* **88** H4
Murrumbidgee, *river, N.S.W., AUSTRAL.* **91** K12
Muscat *see* Masqaţ, *Oman* **68** H5
Musgrave, Port, *Qnsld., Austral.* **91** B11
Musgrave Ranges, *S. Austral., Austral.* **90** G8
Mushie, *D.R.C.* **79** K7
Muskegon, *river, Mich., U.S.* **43** D12
Muskegon, *Mich., U.S.* **41** D12
Muskingum, *river, Ohio, U.S.* **43** E13
Muskogee, *Okla., U.S.* **41** G10
Mussau, *island, P.N.G.* **92** A6
Mussau Islands, *P.N.G.* **92** A6
Musselshell, *river, Mont., U.S.* **42** C6
Mussuma, *Angola* **79** M8
Muswellbrook, *N.S.W., AUSTRAL.* **89** K14
Mutare, *Mozambique* **79** N9
Muting, *Indonesia* **92** D4
Muttaburra, *Qnsld., Austral.* **89** F12
Muturi, *Indonesia* **92** B2
Muztag, *peak, China* **70** G8
Mwanza, *Tanzania* **79** K9
Mweka, *D.R.C.* **79** K7
Mwene-Ditu, *D.R.C.* **79** L8
Mweru, Lake, *D.R.C.-Zambia* **81** L9
Myanmar (Burma), *Asia* **68** J9
Mykolayiv, *Ukr.* **59** G10
Myrtle Beach, *S.C., U.S.* **41** G15
Mysore, *India* **68** K7
Mzuzu, *Malawi* **79** M9
Nā'ālehu, *Hawaii, U.S.* **41** M12
Naberezhnyye Chelny, *Russ.* **59** D13
Nabire, *Indonesia* **92** B2
Nacala, *Mozambique* **79** M11
Nacogdoches, *Tex., U.S.* **41** J10
Nadym, *Russ.* **68** D8
Nafūsah, Jabal, *Lib.* **80** D6
Naga, *Philippines* **69** J13
Nagasaki, *Jap.* **69** G13
Nagēlē, *Eth.* **78** J10
Nagoya, *Jap.* **69** F13
Nagpur, *India* **68** J7
Naha, *Jap.* **69** H13
Nain, *Nfld. and Lab., Can.* **36** F9
Nairobi, *Kenya* **79** K10
Najd, *region, Saudi Arabia* **68** G3
Nakfa, *Eritrea* **78** G10
Nakhodka, *Russ.* **69** E13
Naknek, *Alas., U.S.* **40** L2
Nakuru, *Kenya* **78** K10
Nal'chik, *Russ.* **59** H13
Nālūt, *Lib.* **78** D6
Namanga, *Kenya* **79** K10
Namangan, *Uzb.* **68** G7
Namapa, *Mozambique* **79** M10
Namatanai, *P.N.G.* **92** B7
Nambour, *Qnsld., Austral.* **89** H15
Nam Dinh, *Viet.* **69** J11
Namib Desert, *Namibia* **81** P6
Namibe, *Angola* **79** M6
Namibia, *Af.* **79** N6
Namoi, *river, N.S.W., AUSTRAL.* **91** J14
Namonuito Atoll, *F.S.M.* **96** E4
Namorik Atoll, *Marshall Is.* **96** E5
Nampa, *Idaho, U.S.* **40** D4
Nampala, *Mali* **78** G3
Nampō Shotō, *Jap.* **69** F14
Nampula, *Mozambique* **79** M10
Namsos, *Nor.* **58** C7
Namuli, *peak, Mozambique* **81** M10
Nanaimo, *B.C., Can.* **36** G3
Nanchang, *China* **69** H12
Nancy, *Fr.* **58** G5
Nanjing, *China* **69** G12
Nanning, *China* **69** J11
Nannup, *W. Austral., Austral.* **88** L3
Nanortalik, *Greenland* **36** D10
Nanping, *China* **69** H12
Nansei Shotō *see* Ryukyu Islands, *Jap.* **69** H13
Nantes, *Fr.* **58** G4
Nantong, *China* **69** G12
Nantucket Island, *Mass., U.S.* **43** D16
Nānu'alele Point, *Hawaii, U.S.* **43** L12
Nanumanga, *island, Tuvalu* **96** F6
Nanumea, *island, Tuvalu* **96** F6
Nanuque, *Braz.* **50** H10
Nanutarra, *homestead, W. Austral., Austral.* **88** F2
Napier, *N.Z.* **92** J6
Napier Mountains, *Antarctica* **103** C14
Naples *see* Napoli, *It.* **58** J7
Napo, *river, Ecua.-Peru* **52** D3
Napoli (Naples), *It.* **58** J7
Napuka, *island, Fr. Polynesia* **97** G11
Naracoorte, *S. Austral., Austral.* **89** L11
Nardoo, *homestead, Qnsld., Austral.* **89** D11
Narembeem, *W. Austral., Austral.* **88** K3
Naretha, *W. Austral., Austral.* **88** J5
Narib, *Namibia* **79** P7
Narmada, *river, India* **70** J7
Narndee, *homestead, W. Austral., Austral.* **88** H3
Narngulu, *W. Austral., Austral.* **88** J2
Narodnaya, *peak, Russ.* **61** A13
Narooma, *N.S.W., AUSTRAL.* **89** L14
Narrabri, *N.S.W., AUSTRAL.* **89** J14
Narran Lake, *N.S.W., AUSTRAL.* **91** J13
Narrandera, *N.S.W., AUSTRAL.* **89** L13
Narrogin, *W. Austral., Austral.* **88** K3
Narsarsuaq, *Greenland* **36** D10
Narva, *Est.* **58** D9
Narvik, *Nor.* **58** B8
Nar'yan Mar, *Russ.* **59** A11
Naryilco, *homestead, Qnsld., Austral.* **89** H11
Nasca, *Peru* **50** G3
Nashua, *N.H., U.S.* **41** D16
Nashville, *Tenn., U.S.* **41** G12
Nasik, *India* **68** J7
Nassau, *island, Cook Is.* **96** G8
Nassau, *Bahamas* **37** M9
Nasser, Lake, *Egypt* **80** F9
Natal, *Braz.* **50** E12
Natal Downs, *homestead, Qnsld., Austral.* **89** E13
Natashquan, *Que., Can.* **36** G10
Natchez, *Miss., U.S.* **41** J11
Natchitoches, *La., U.S.* **41** H10
National City, *Calif., U.S.* **40** H3
Natividade, *Braz.* **50** F9
Natuna Besar, *island, Indonesia* **69** L11
Natuna Islands, *Indonesia* **71** L11
Naturaliste, Cape, *W. Austral., Austral.* **90** K2
Nauru, *Pac. Oc.* **96** F5
Nauta, *Peru* **50** E3
Navapolatsk, *Belarus* **58** E9
Navarin, Cape, *Russ.* **71** A13
Navojoa, *Mex.* **37** M4
Naxçıvan, *Azerb.* **59** J14
Nazyvayevsk, *Russ.* **59** B16
N'dalatando, *Angola* **79** L6
Ndélé, *Cen. Af. Rep.* **78** H7
Ndeni *see* Nendo, *island, Solomon Is.* **96** G5
N'Djamena, *Chad* **78** G6
Ndola, *Zambia* **79** M9
Neagh, Lake, *U.K.* **60** E3
Neale, Lake, *S. Austral., Austral.* **90** F7
Near Islands, *U.S.* **39** R2
Nebine Creek, *N.S.W.-Qnsld., Austral.* **91** H13
Neblina, Pico da, *Braz.-Venez.* **52** C5
Nebraska, *U.S.* **40** E8
Neches, *river, Tex., U.S.* **43** J10
Neckarboo Range, *N.S.W., AUSTRAL.* **91** K12
Necker Island, *Hawaii, U.S.* **96** C8
Necochea, *Arg.* **51** M6
Needles, *Calif., U.S.* **40** G4
Neftekamsk, *Russ.* **59** D13
Nefteyugansk, *Russ.* **59** A15
Negomane, *Mozambique* **79** M10
Negro, *river, Arg.* **53** N5
Negro, *river, Braz.* **52** D6
Negro, *river, Uru.* **53** L7
Negros, *island, Philippines* **71** K13
Neiva, *Col.* **50** C2
Nellore, *India* **68** K7
Nelson, *river, Can.* **38** G6
Nelson, *N.Z.* **92** K5
Nelson, Cape, *Vic., Austral.* **91** M11
Nelson House, *Manitoba, Can.* **36** G6
Néma, *Maurit.* **78** G3
Neman, *river, Lith.-Russ.* **60** E8
Nemiscau, *Que., Can.* **36** G8
Nenana, *Alas., U.S.* **40** K3
Nendo (Ndeni), *island, Solomon Is.* **96** G5
Neosho, *river, Kans.-Okla., U.S.* **43** F10
Nepal, *Asia* **68** H8
Nephi, *Utah, U.S.* **40** E5
Neptune Range, *Antarctica* **102** E7
Neriquinha, *Angola* **79** M7
Nerrima, *homestead, W. Austral., Austral.* **88** D5
Neryungri, *Russ.* **69** D11
Neskaupsta?ur, *Ice.* **58** B4
Netherdale, *Qnsld., Austral.* **89** E14
Netherlands, *Europe* **58** F5
Netzahualcóyotl, *Mex.* **37** N5
Neumayer, *station, Antarctica* **102** A7
Neuquén, *Arg.* **51** M5
Neuse, *river, N.C., U.S.* **43** G15
Neusiedler Lake, *Aust.-Hung.* **60** G7
Nevada, *U.S.* **40** E4
Nevada, Sierra, *U.S.* **38** J3
Nevada de Santa Marta, Serra, *Col.* **52** A3
Nevado Huascarán, *peak, Peru* **52** F2
Nevinnomyssk, *Russ.* **59** H12
New Albany, *Ind., U.S.* **41** F12
New Amsterdam, *Guyana* **50** B7
Newark, *N.J., U.S.* **41** D15
New Bedford, *Mass., U.S.* **41** D16
New Bern, *N.C., U.S.* **41** G15
New Braunfels, *Tex., U.S.* **40** J9
New Britain, *island, P.N.G.* **92** C7
New Brunswick, *Can.* **36** H9
Newburgh, *N.Y., U.S.* **41** D15
New Caledonia, *Pac. Oc.* **96** H5
Newcastle, *N.S.W., AUSTRAL.* **89** K14
Newcastle, *U.K.* **58** E4
Newcastle, *Wyo., U.S.* **40** D7
Newcastle Waters, *N. Terr., Austral.* **88** D8
Newdegate, *W. Austral., Austral.* **88** K4
New Delhi, *India* **68** H7
New England Range, *N.S.W., AUSTRAL.* **91** J15
Newenham, Cape, *Alas., U.S.* **42** L2
Newfoundland, Island of, *Can.* **38** G10
Newfoundland and Labrador, *Can.* **36** F10
New Georgia, *island, Solomon Is.* **96** F4
New Glasgow, *N.S., CAN.* **36** H10
New Guinea, *island, Indonesia-P.N.G.* **92** B4
Newhalen, *Alas., U.S.* **40** L3
New Hampshire, *U.S.* **41** C16
New Hanover, *island, P.N.G.* **92** B7
New Haven, *Conn., U.S.* **41** D16
New Iberia, *La., U.S.* **41** J11
New Ireland, *island, P.N.G.* **92** B7
New Jersey, *U.S.* **41** E15
Newman, *W. Austral., Austral.* **88** F3
New Mexico, *U.S.* **40** G6
New Orleans, *La., U.S.* **41** J11
New Plymouth, *N.Z.* **92** J5
Newport, *Oreg., U.S.* **40** C2
Newport News, *Va., U.S.* **41** F15
Newry, *homestead, N. Terr., Austral.* **88** C7
New Schwabenland, *region, Antarctica* **102** B8
New Siberian Islands, *Russ.* **71** B10
New South Wales, *Austral.* **89** J13
New Springs, *homestead, W. Austral., Austral.* **88** G4
Newton, *Kans., U.S.* **40** F9
New York, *U.S.* **41** D15
New York, *N.Y., U.S.* **41** D15
Neya, *Russ.* **59** D11
Ngabordamlu, Tanjung, *Indonesia* **92** C2
Nganglong Range, *China* **70** H8
Ngaoundéré, *Cameroon* **78** H6
Ngara, *Tanzania* **79** K9
Ngaruawahia, *N.Z.* **92** H6
Ngatik Atoll, *F.S.M.* **96** E4
Ngauruhoe, Mount, *N.Z.* **92** J6
Ngoko, *river, Cameroon-D.R.C.* **80** J6
Ngourti, *Niger* **78** G6
Nguigmi, *Niger* **78** G6
Nguiu, *N. Terr., Austral.* **88** A7
Ngukurr, *N. Terr., Austral.* **88** C9
Ngulu Atoll, *F.S.M.* **96** E2
Nguru, *Nig.* **78** G6
Nhamundá, *Braz.* **50** D7
Nha Trang, *Viet.* **69** K11
Nhulunbuy, *N. Terr., Austral.* **88** B10
Niagara Falls, *N.Y., U.S.* **41** D14
Niagara Falls, *Can.-U.S.* **43** D14
Niamey, *Niger* **78** G4
Nias, *island, Indonesia* **71** L10
Nicaragua, *N. America* **37** Q8
Nicaragua, Lake, *Nicar.* **39** Q8
Nice, *Fr.* **58** H5
Nicholson, *homestead, W. Austral., Austral.* **88** D7
Nicholson Range, *W. Austral., Austral.* **90** H2
Nickavilla, *homestead, Qnsld., Austral.* **89** G12
Nicobar Islands, *India* **70** L9
Nicosia *see* Lefkosia, *Cyprus* **68** F3
Nicoya Peninsula, *C.R.* **39** Q8
Nieuw Amsterdam, *Suriname* **50** B7
Nieuw Nickerie, *Suriname* **50** B7
Niger, *Af.* **78** G5
Niger, *river, Af.* **80** H5
Niger, Source of the, *Guinea* **80** H2
Nigeria, *Af.* **78** H5
Niger River Delta, *Nig.* **80** J5
Nightingale Island, *Tristan da Cunha Group* **81** R2
Nihoa, *island, Hawaii, U.S.* **96** C9
Niigata, *Jap.* **69** F13
Ni'ihau, *island, Hawaii, U.S.* **43** L10
Nikel', *Russ.* **58** A9
Nikolayevsk, *Russ.* **59** F13
Nikolayevsk na Amure, *Russ.* **69** D12
Nikolski, *Alas., U.S.* **37** R4
Nikumaroro, *island, Kiribati* **96** F7
Nile, *river, Egypt-Sudan* **80** E9
Nile, Sources of the, *Burundi-Rwanda* **81** K9
Nile River Delta, *Egypt* **80** D9
Nimba Mountains, *Côte d'Ivoire-Guinea-Liberia* **80** H2
Nimbin, *N.S.W., AUSTRAL.* **89** H15
Nîmes, *Fr.* **58** H5
Nimrod Glacier, *Antarctica* **102** H9
Ninety Mile Beach, *N.Z.* **92** F5
Ninety Mile Beach, *Vic., Austral.* **91** M13
Ningbo, *China* **69** G12
Ninigo Group, *P.N.G.* **92** A5
Ninnis Glacier, *Antarctica* **103** M12
Niobrara, *river, Nebr.-Wyo., U.S.* **42** D8
Nioro du Sahel, *Mali* **78** G2
Nipigon, *Ont., Can.* **36** H7
Nipigon, Lake, *Can.* **38** H7
Niquelândia, *Braz.* **50** G9
Niš, *Serbia and Montenegro* **58** J8
Niterói, *Braz.* **50** J10
Niuafo'ou, *island, Tonga* **96** G7
Niuatoputapu, *island, Tonga* **96** G7
Niue, *island, N.Z.* **96** G8
Niulakita, *island, Tuvalu* **96** G7
Niutao, *island, Tuvalu* **96** F6
Nizhnekamsk, *Russ.* **59** D13
Nizhnevartovsk, *Russ.* **68** D8
Nizhniy Novgorod, *Russ.* **59** D12
Nizhniy Tagil, *Russ.* **59** C14
Nizhnyaya Tunguska, *river, Russ.* **68** D9
Nizhyn, *Ukr.* **59** F10
Nizwá, *Oman* **68** H5
Njombe, *Tanzania* **79** L10
Nkongsamba, *Cameroon* **78** J5
Noatak, *river, Alas., U.S.* **42** J2
Noatak, *Alas., U.S.* **40** J2
Nogales, *Ariz., U.S.* **40** H5
Nogales, *Mex.* **37** L4
Nome, *Alas., U.S.* **40** K1
Nonouti, *island, Kiribati* **96** E6
Nord, *Greenland* **36** A8
Nordaustlandet, *island, Nor.* **68** A7
Norfolk, *Nebr., U.S.* **40** E9
Norfolk, *Va., U.S.* **41** F15
Norfolk Island, *Austral.* **96** H5
Noril'sk, *Russ.* **68** C9
Norman, *river, Qnsld., Austral.* **91** D11
Normanby Island, *P.N.G.* **92** D7
Normanton, *Qnsld., Austral.* **89** D11
Norman Wells, *N.W.T., CAN.* **36** D4
Nornalup, *W. Austral., Austral.* **88** L3
Ñorquincó, *Arg.* **51** N4
Norrköping, *Sweden* **58** D7
Norseman, *W. Austral., Austral.* **88** K4
Northampton, *W. Austral., Austral.* **88** H2
North Battleford, *Sask., Can.* **36** G5
North Bay, *Ont., Can.* **36** H8
North Bend, *Oreg., U.S.* **40** C2
North Canadian, *river, N. Mex.-Okla.-Tex., U.S.* **42** G9
North Cape, *N.Z.* **92** F5
North Cape, *Nor.* **60** A9
North Carolina, *U.S.* **41** G14
North China Plain, *China* **71** G11
Northcliffe, *W. Austral., Austral.* **88** L3
North Dakota, *U.S.* **40** C8
Northern Dvina, *river, Russ.* **61** C11
Northern Ireland, *U.K.* **58** E3
Northern Karroo, *region, S. Af.* **81** Q8
Northern Mariana Islands, *Pac. Oc.* **96** C3
Northern Sporades, *islands, Gr.* **60** K9
Northern Territory, *Austral.* **88** D8
Northern Uvals, *hills, Russ.* **61** C12
North Head, *N.Z.* **92** G5
North Island, *N.Z.* **92** H5
North Korea, *Asia* **69** F12
North Land, *Russ.* **70** B9
North Magnetic Pole, *N. America* **38** B6
North Platte, *river, Nebr.-Wyo., U.S.* **42** E8
North Platte, *Nebr., U.S.* **40** E8
North Saskatchewan, *river, Can.* **38** G4
North Sea, *Europe* **60** E5
North Siberian Lowland, *Russ.* **70** C9
North Slope, *Alas., U.S.* **42** J3
North Stradbroke Island, *Qnsld., Austral.* **91** H15
North Taranaki Bight, *N.Z.* **92** J5
Northumberland, Cape, *S. Austral., Austral.* **91** M10
Northumberland Islands, *Qnsld., Austral.* **91** F14
Northway, *Alas., U.S.* **40** K4
North West Basin, *W. Austral., Austral.* **90** F1
North West Cape, *W. Austral., Austral.* **90** F1
Northwest Territories, *Can.* **36** E4
Norton, *Kans., U.S.* **40** F8
Norton Bay, *Alas., U.S.* **42** K2
Norton Sound, *Alas., U.S.* **42** K2
Norvegia, Cape, *Antarctica* **102** A7
Norway, *Europe* **58** C6
Norway House, *Manitoba, Can.* **36** G6
Norwegian Sea, *Europe* **60** B5
Nossob, *river, Botswana-Namibia-South Africa* **81** P7
Nouadhibou, *Maurit.* **78** F1
Nouakchott, *Maurit.* **78** F1
Nouamrhar, *Maurit.* **78** F1
Nouméa, *New Caledonia* **96** H5
Nova Friburgo, *Braz.* **50** J10
Nova Iguaçu, *Braz.* **50** J9
Nova Mambone, *Mozambique* **79** N10
Nova Olinda do Norte, *Braz.* **50** D6
Nova Scotia, *Can.* **36** H10
Nova Xavantina, *Braz.* **50** G8
Novaya Zemlya, *Russ.* **70** C7
Novi Pazar, *Serbia and Montenegro* **58** J8
Novi Sad, *Serbia and Montenegro* **58** H8
Novodvinsk, *Russ.* **59** B10
Novo Hamburgo, *Braz.* **51** K8
Novokuznetsk, *Russ.* **68** E8
Novolazarevskaya, *station, Antarctica* **102** A9
Novomoskovsk, *Russ.* **59** E11
Novorossiysk, *Russ.* **59** H11
Novorybnoye, *Russ.* **68** C9
Novosibirsk, *Russ.* **68** E8
Novosibirskiye Ostrova (New Siberian Islands), *Russ.* **69** B10
Novotroitsk, *Russ.* **59** E14
Novouzensk, *Russ.* **59** F13
Novyy Urengoy, *Russ.* **68** D8
Nowa Nowa, *Vic., Austral.* **89** M13
Nowra, *N.S.W., AUSTRAL.* **89** L14
Ntem, *river, Cameroon-Eq. Guinea-Gabon* **80** J6
Nu (Salween), *river, China* **68** H9
Nuba Mountains, *Sudan* **80** H9
Nubia, Lake, *Sudan* **80** F9
Nubian Desert, *Sudan* **80** F9
Nueces, *river, Tex., U.S.* **42** K9
Nueva Imperial, *Chile* **51** M4
Nueva Rosita, *Mex.* **37** M5
Nuevo Casas Grandes, *Mex.* **37** L4
Nuevo Laredo, *Mex.* **37** M5
Nuevo Rocafuerte, *Ecua.* **50** D2
Nuguria Islands, *P.N.G.* **92** B8
Nui, *island, Tuvalu* **96** F6
Nuku'alofa, *Tonga* **96** H7
Nukufetau, *island, Tuvalu* **96** F6
Nuku Hiva, *island, Marquesas Is.* **97** F11
Nukulaelae, *island, Tuvalu* **96** F7
Nukumanu Islands, *Solomon Is.* **96** F4
Nukunonu, *island, Tokelau* **96** F7
Nukuoro Atoll, *F.S.M.* **96** E4
Nukus, *Uzb.* **68** F6
Nulato, *Alas., U.S.* **40** K2
Nullagine, *W. Austral., Austral.* **88** F3
Nullarbor Plain, *S. Austral.-W. Austral., Austral.* **90** J6
Numbulwar, *N. Terr., Austral.* **88** B9
Numfoor, *island, Indonesia* **92** A2
Nunap Isua (Cape Farewell), *Greenland* **36** D10
Nunavut, *Can.* **36** E6
Nunivak Island, *Alas., U.S.* **42** L1
Nuoro, *It.* **58** J6
Nupani, *island, Solomon Is.* **96** F5
Nurina, *W. Austral., Austral.* **88** J6
Nurmes, *Fin.* **58** C9
Nürnberg, *Ger.* **58** G6
Nutwood Downs, *homestead, N. Terr., Austral.* **88** C9
Nuuk (Godthåb), *Greenland* **36** D9
Nyac, *Alas., U.S.* **40** L2
Nyagan', *Russ.* **59** A14
Nyainqêntanglha Shan, *China* **70** H9
Nyala, *Sudan* **78** G8
Nyamlell, *Sudan* **78** H8
Nyeri, *Kenya* **78** K10
Nyíregyháza, *Hung.* **58** G8

Nymagee, N.S.W., AUSTRAL. 89 K13
Nyngan, N.S.W., AUSTRAL. 89 J13
Nyunzu, D.R.C. 79 L9
Nzérékoré, Guinea 78 H2
N'zeto, Angola 79 L6

Oahe, Lake, S. Dak., U.S. 42 C8
O'ahu, island, Hawaii, U.S. 43 L11
Oakes, N. Dak., U.S. 40 C9
Oakland, Calif., U.S. 40 E2
Oak Ridge, Tenn., U.S. 41 G13
Oakvale, homestead, S. Austral., Austral. 89 K11
Oakwood, homestead, Qnsld., Austral. 89 G13
Oamaru, N.Z. 92 N4
Oaro, N.Z. 92 L5
Oates Coast, Antarctica 103 M10
Oaxaca, Mex. 37 P6
Ob, river, Russ. 70 D7
Ob, Gulf of, Russ. 70 C8
Oba, Ont., Can. 36 H7
Oban, homestead, Qnsld., Austral. 89 E10
Oban, N.Z. 92 P3
Obando, Col. 50 C4
Ob' Bay, Antarctica 102 M10
Ob-Irtysh, Source of the, China 70 F9
Obo, Cen. Af. Rep. 78 J8
Obshchiy Syrt, hills, Russ. 61 E13
Obskaya Guba (Gulf of Ob), Russ. 68 C8
Ocala, Fla., U.S. 41 J14
Ocaña, Col. 50 B3
Occidental, Cordillera, S. America 52 B2
Ocean Island see Banaba, Kiribati 96 F6
Ocheyedan Mound, Iowa, U.S. 43 D10
Ocmulgee, river, Ga., U.S. 43 H13
Oconee, river, Ga., U.S. 43 H13
October Revolution Island, Russ. 70 B9
Odense, Den. 58 E6
Oder, river, Ger.-Pol. 60 F7
Odesa, Ukr. 59 H10
Odessa, Tex., U.S. 40 H8
Odienné, Côte d'Ivoire 78 H3
Oeiras, Braz. 50 E10
Oeno Island, Pitcairn Is. 97 H12
Oenpelli, N. Terr., Austral. 88 B8
Oficina Dominador, Chile 50 J4
Ogadēn, region, Eth. 80 H11
Ogasawara Guntō see Bonin Islands, Jap. 96 C3
Ogbomosho, Nig. 78 H4
Ogden, Utah, U.S. 40 E5
Ogilvie Mountains, Can. 38 D3
Ogmore, Qnsld., Austral. 89 F14
Ogoki, Ont., Can. 36 G7
Ohau, Lake, N.Z. 92 M3
Ohio, river, U.S. 43 F11
Ohio, U.S. 41 E13
Ohrid, Lake, Alban.-Maced. 60 J8
Oiapoque, Braz. 50 C8
Oil Islands see Chagos Archipelago, British Ind. Oc. Terr. 68 M6
Oka, river, Russ. 61 E11
Okaba, Indonesia 92 D3
Oka-Don Plain, Russ. 61 E11
Okanogan, river, Can.-U.S. 42 B4
Okaukuejo, Namibia 79 N7
Okavango, river, Angola-Botswana-Namibia 81 N7
Okavango Delta, Botswana 81 N8
Okeechobee, Lake, Fla., U.S. 43 K14
Okefenokee Swamp, U.S. 39 L8
Okha, Russ. 69 D12
Okhotsk, Sea of, Russ. 71 D13
Okiep, S. Af. 79 Q7
Okinawa, island, Jap. 71 H13
Okino Daitō Jima, Jap. 96 C2
Oklahoma, U.S. 40 G9
Oklahoma City, Okla., U.S. 40 G9
Okmulgee, Okla., U.S. 41 G10
Oktyabr'sk, Kaz. 59 E15
Oktyabr'skiy, Russ. 59 D13
Oktyabr'skoy Revolyutsii, Ostrov (October Revolution Island), Russ. 68 B9
Olaa see Kea'au, Hawaii, U.S. 41 M13
Öland, island, Sweden 60 E7
Olary, S. Austral., Austral. 89 J11
Olavarría, Arg. 51 M6
Olbia, It. 58 J6
Old Cork, homestead, Qnsld., Austral. 89 F11
Old Crow, Yukon Terr. 36 D3
Oldenburg, Ger. 58 F6
Olduvai Gorge, Tanzania 81 K10
Olekminsk, Russ. 69 D11
Olenek, river, Russ. 71 C10
Olga, Mount, N. Terr., Austral. 90 G7
Olinda, Braz. 50 F12
Olio, Qnsld., Austral. 89 F12
Ollagüe (Oyahue), Chile 50 H4
Olomouc, Czech Rep. 58 G7
Olsztyn, Pol. 58 F8
Olt, river, Rom. 60 H9
Olympia, Wash., U.S. 40 B3
Olympus, peak, Gr. 60 K8
Olympus, Mount, Wash., U.S. 42 B3
Olyutorskiy, Cape, Russ. 71 B13
Omaha, Nebr., U.S. 41 E10
Oman, Asia 68 H5
Oman, Gulf of, Iran-Oman 70 H5
Omboué (Fernan Vaz), Gabon 79 K5
Omdurman (Umm Durmān), Sudan 78 G9
Omihi, N.Z. 92 L5
Omsk, Russ. 59 B16
Ondangwa, Namibia 79 N7
Ondjiva, Angola 79 N6
Onega, river, Russ. 61 C10
Onega, Russ. 59 C10
Onega, Lake, Russ. 61 C10
Onega Bay, Russ. 61 B10
Oneida Lake, N.Y., U.S. 43 D15
Onezhskaya Guba (Onega Bay), Russ. 59 B10
Onezhskoye Ozero (Lake Onega), Russ. 59 C10
Ongarue, N.Z. 92 J6
Onitsha, Nig. 78 J5
Ono-i-Lau, island, Fiji 96 H7
Onon, river, Mongolia-Russ. 71 E11
Onslow, W. Austral., Austral. 88 F2
Ontario, Can. 36 H7
Ontario, Oreg., U.S. 40 C4
Ontario, Lake, Can.-U.S. 43 D14
Oodnadatta, S. Austral., Austral. 88 H9
Opelousas, La., U.S. 41 J11
Open Bay, P.N.G. 92 C7
Ophthalmia Range, W. Austral., Austral. 90 F3
Opotiki, N.Z. 92 H6
Opunake, N.Z. 92 J5
Opuwo, Namibia 79 N6
Oradea, Rom. 58 H8
Oral, Kaz. 59 E13
Oran, Alg. 78 C4
Orange, river, Namibia-S. Af. 81 Q7
Orange, N.S.W., AUSTRAL. 89 K14
Orange, Tex., U.S. 41 J10
Orange, Cape, Braz. 52 B8
Orangeburg, S.C., U.S. 41 G14
Oranjemund, Namibia 79 Q7
Orbost, Vic., Austral. 89 M13
Orcadas, station, Antarctica 102 A2
Ord, river, W. Austral., Austral. 90 C6
Ord, Mount, W. Austral., Austral. 90 D5
Ord River, homestead, W. Austral., Austral. 88 D7
Ordu, Turk. 59 J12
Örebro, Sweden 58 D7
Oregon, U.S. 40 C3
Orel, Russ. 59 F11
Ore Mountains, Ger. 60 G7
Orenburg, Russ. 59 E14
Orepuki, N.Z. 92 N3
Oreti, river, N.Z. 92 N3
Orhon, river, Mongolia 71 F10
Oriental, Cordillera, S. America 52 E2
Orinduik, Guyana 50 B6
Orinoco, river, Col.-Venez. 52 B5
Orinoco, Source of the, Venez. 52 C5
Orinoco River Delta, Venez. 52 A6
Oristano, It. 58 K5
Oriximiná, Braz. 50 D7
Orizaba, peak, Mex. 39 N6
Orkney Islands, U.K. 60 D4
Orlando, Fla., U.S. 41 J14
Orléans, Fr. 58 G4
Örnsköldsvik, Sweden 58 C8
Orocué, Col. 50 B3
Oroluk Atoll, F.S.M. 96 E4
Orona, island, Kiribati 96 F7
Orsha, Belarus 58 E10
Orsk, Russ. 59 E15
Oruro, Bol. 50 H5
Osage, river, Kans.-Mo., U.S. 43 F10
Ōsaka, Jap. 69 F13
Oscar II Coast, Antarctica 102 C2
Oscoda, Mich., U.S. 41 D13
Oshawa, Ont., Can. 36 J8
Oshkosh, Wis., U.S. 41 D11
Oshogbo, Nig. 78 H5
Osijek, Croatia 58 H8
Öskemen, Kaz. 68 F8
Oslo, Nor. 58 D6
Osorno, Chile 51 N4
Ossa, Mount, Tas., Austral. 91 M15
Östersund, Sweden 58 C7
Ostrava, Czech Rep. 58 G8
Otaki, N.Z. 92 K5
O.T. Downs, homestead, N. Terr., Austral. 88 C9
Otish, Mts., Can. 38 G9
Otjiwarongo, Namibia 79 N7
Otranto, Strait of, Alban.-It. 60 K8
Ottawa, river, Can. 38 H8
Ottawa, Ont., Can. 36 H8
Ottumwa, Iowa, U.S. 41 E10
Otuzco, Peru 50 E2
Otway, Cape, Vic., Austral. 91 M11
Ouachita, river, Ark., U.S. 43 H10
Ouachita Mountains, Ark.-Okla., U.S. 43 G10
Ouadane, Maurit. 78 F2
Ouadda, Cen. Af. Rep. 78 H8
Ouagadougou, Burkina Faso 78 G4
Ouahigouya, Burkina Faso 78 G3
Oualâta, Maurit. 78 F3
Ouanda Djallé, Cen. Af. Rep. 78 H8
Ouargla, Alg. 78 D5
Oudtshoorn, S. Af. 79 Q8
Ouesso, Congo 78 J6
Oujda, Mor. 78 C4
Oulu, river, Fin. 60 C9
Oulu, Fin. 58 B8
Oulujärvi, lake, Fin. 60 C9
Ounianga, Chad 78 F7
Ourense, Sp. 58 H2
Ouse, Tas., Austral. 89 M16
Outer Hebrides, islands, U.K. 60 D4
Outjo, Namibia 79 N7
Ouvéa, island, New Caledonia 96 H5
Ouyen, Vic., Austral. 89 L11
Ovalle, Chile 51 L4
Ovamboland, region, Namibia 79 N6
Oviedo, Sp. 58 H2
Owaka, N.Z. 92 P3
Owen, Mount, N.Z. 92 K4
Owensboro, Ky., U.S. 41 F12
Owen Stanley Range, P.N.G. 92 D6
Oxford, N.Z. 92 M4
Oyahue see Ollagüe, Chile 50 H4
Oyem, Gabon 78 J6
Oyo, Congo 79 K6
Ozark Plateau, Ark.-Mo., U.S. 43 G10
Ozarks, Lake of the, Mo., U.S. 43 F10
Ozona, Tex., U.S. 40 J8

Paamiut, Greenland 36 E10
Paarl, S. Af. 79 Q7
Pa'auilo, Hawaii, U.S. 41 M12
Pacaraima, Sierra, Braz.-Venez. 52 C5
Padang, Indonesia 69 M10
Padova, It. 58 H6
Padre Island, Tex., U.S. 42 K9
Paducah, Ky., U.S. 41 F12
Paeroa, N.Z. 92 H6
Pafúri, Mozambique 79 N9
Pagan, island, N. Mariana Is. 96 D3
Pago Pago, American Samoa 96 G8
Pāhala, Hawaii, U.S. 41 M12
Pāhoa, Hawaii, U.S. 41 M13
Päijänne, lake, Fin. 60 D8
Paili, P.N.G. 92 D6
Pailolo Channel, Hawaii, U.S. 43 L12
Painted Desert, Ariz., U.S. 42 G5
Paita, Peru 50 E1
Pakaraima Mountains, Guyana-Venez. 52 B6
Pakistan, Asia 68 H6
Palana, Russ. 69 C13
Palatka, Fla., U.S. 41 J14
Palau, Pac. Oc. 96 E2
Palawan, island, Philippines 71 K13
Palembang, Indonesia 69 M11
Palermo, It. 58 K6
Palikir, F.S.M. 96 E4
Palliser, Cape, N.Z. 92 K6
Palma de Mallorca, Sp. 58 J4
Palmares, Braz. 50 F12
Palmas, Cape, Liberia 80 J2
Palmeira dos Índios, Braz. 50 F11
Palmeirinhas Point, Angola 81 L6
Palmer, station, Antarctica 102 C2
Palmer, Alas., U.S. 40 L3
Palmer Archipelago, Antarctica 102 C1
Palmer Land, Antarctica 102 D3
Palmerston Atoll, Cook Is. 96 G8
Palmerston North, N.Z. 92 K6
Palmerville, Qnsld., Austral. 89 C12
Palmira, Col. 50 C2
Palm Springs, Calif., U.S. 40 G4
Palmyra Atoll, Pac. Oc. 96 E9
Palo Alto, Calif., U.S. 40 E2
Palomar Mountain, Calif., U.S. 42 G3
Palopo, Indonesia 69 L13
Palparara, homestead, Qnsld., Austral. 89 G11
Palu, Indonesia 69 L13
Pamlico Sound, N.C., U.S. 43 F15
Pampa, Tex., U.S. 40 G8
Pampas, Arg. 53 M5
Pamplona, Col. 50 B3
Pamplona, Sp. 58 H3
Panamá, Pan. 37 Q9
Panama, N. America 37 Q9
Panama, Gulf of, Pan. 39 Q9
Panama, Isthmus of, Pan. 39 Q9
Panama Canal, Pan. 39 Q9
Panama City, Fla., U.S. 41 J13
Panay, island, Philippines 71 K13
Pandie Pandie, homestead, S. Austral., Austral. 89 G10
Panevėžys, Lith. 58 E9
Pangalanes, Canal des, Madag. 81 N12
Pangkalpinang, Indonesia 69 M11
Pangnirtung, Nunavut 36 D8
Panguitch, Utah, U.S. 40 F5
Pāni'au, Hawaii, U.S. 43 L10
Pannawonica, W. Austral., Austral. 88 F2
Pantanal, wetland, Braz. 52 H7
Pantelleria, island, It. 58 L6
Panzhihua, China 69 H10
Papakura, N.Z. 92 H5
Papeete, Fr. Polynesia 97 G10
Papua, Gulf of, P.N.G. 92 D5
Papua New Guinea, New Guinea 92 C4
Papunya, N. Terr., Austral. 88 F8
Paracatu, Braz. 50 G9
Parachilna, S. Austral., Austral. 89 J10
Paragould, Ark., U.S. 41 G11
Paraguaná Peninsula, Venez. 52 A4
Paraguay, S. America 50 H6
Paraguay, river, S. America 52 H6
Paraíso do Tocantins, Braz. 50 F8
Parakou, Benin 78 H4
Paramaribo, Suriname 50 B7
Paramushir, island, Russ. 69 C13
Paranã, Braz. 50 F9
Paraná, river, Arg.-Braz. 53 L6
Paraná, Arg. 51 L6
Paraná, Source of the, Braz. 52 J9
Paranaguá, Braz. 50 J8
Paranaguá Bay, Braz. 52 J9
Paranaíba, river, Braz. 52 H8
Pardoo, homestead, W. Austral., Austral. 88 E3
Parece Vela, island, Jap. 96 C2
Parecis, Serra dos, Braz. 52 F6
Paren', Russ. 69 B12
Parepare, Indonesia 69 L13
Paria Peninsula, Venez. 52 A5
Parintins, Braz. 50 D7
Paris, Fr. 58 G5
Paris Basin, Fr. 60 G4
Parkersburg, W. Va., U.S. 41 E13
Parkes, N.S.W., AUSTRAL. 89 K13
Parnaíba, river, Braz. 52 E10
Parnaíba, Braz. 50 D10
Parnassus, peak, Gr. 60 K8
Parnassus, N.Z. 92 L5
Pärnu, Est. 58 D8
Paroo, homestead, W. Austral., Austral. 88 G3
Parowan, Utah, U.S. 40 F5
Parraburdoo, W. Austral., Austral. 88 F3
Parry Islands, Can. 38 C6
Parsons, Kans., U.S. 41 F10
Parsons Range, N. Terr., Austral. 90 B9
Paru, river, Braz. 52 C7
Pasadena, Calif., U.S. 40 G3
Pasadena, Tex., U.S. 41 J10
Pascagoula, Miss., U.S. 41 J12
Pascua, Isla de (Easter Island), Chile 97 H14
Pasley, Cape, W. Austral., Austral. 90 K5
Paso Robles, Calif., U.S. 40 F2
Passo Fundo, Braz. 51 K8
Pasto, Col. 50 C2
Patagonia, region, Arg. 53 Q5
Patna, India 68 J8
Patos, Braz. 50 E11
Patos de Minas, Braz. 50 H9
Patos Lagoon, Braz. 53 L8
Patquía, Arg. 50 K5
Pátra, Gr. 58 K8
Patuxent Range, Antarctica 102 F7
Pau, Fr. 58 H4
Pauini, Braz. 50 E4
Paulatuk, N.W.T., CAN. 36 D4
Paulistana, Braz. 50 E10
Paulo Afonso, Braz. 50 F11
Pavlodar, Kaz. 68 E8
Pavlovo, Russ. 59 D12
Pawarenga, N.Z. 92 G5
Payer Mountains, Antarctica 102 B9
Payette, Idaho, U.S. 40 C4
Paynes Find, W. Austral., Austral. 88 J3
Paysandú, Uru. 51 L6
Peace, river, Can. 38 F4
Peace River, Alta., Can. 36 F4
Peak Hill, W. Austral., Austral. 88 G3
Pearl, river, La.-Miss., U.S. 43 J11
Pearl and Hermes Atoll, Hawaii, U.S. 96 C7
Pearl Harbor, Hawaii, U.S. 43 L11
Peary Land, Greenland 38 A7
Peawanuk, Ont., Can. 36 G7
Pebas, Peru 50 D3
Pechora, river, Russ. 61 A11
Pechora, Russ. 59 A12
Pechora Basin, Russ. 61 A12
Pecos, river, N. Mex.-Tex., U.S. 42 J8
Pecos, Tex., U.S. 40 J7
Pedder, Lake, Tas., Austral. 91 M16
Pedra Azul, Braz. 50 G10
Pedras Negras, Braz. 50 F5
Pedro Cays, Jamaica 39 P9
Pedro Juan Caballero, Para. 50 J7
Peedamulla, homestead, W. Austral., Austral. 88 F2
Pegasus Bay, N.Z. 92 L5
Pehuajó, Arg. 51 M6
Peipus, Lake, Est.-Russ. 60 D9
Pekanbaru, Indonesia 69 L10
Pelagie, Isole, It. 58 L6
Peleng, island, Indonesia 96 F1
Pelican Point, Namibia 81 P6
Pelly Crossing, Yukon Terr. 36 D3
Peloponnesus, peninsula, Gr. 60 K8
Pelotas, Braz. 51 L8
Pemba, Mozambique 79 M11
Pemba Bay, Mozambique 81 M11
Pemba Island, Tanzania 81 K10
Pemberton, W. Austral., Austral. 88 L3
Pembroke, Ont., Can. 36 H8
Pendleton, Oreg., U.S. 40 C4
Pend Oreille Lake, Idaho, U.S. 42 B5
Penha do Tapauá, Braz. 50 E5
Pennell Coast, Antarctica 102 M9
Pennsylvania, U.S. 41 E14
Penobscot, river, Me., U.S. 43 B16
Penola, S. Austral., Austral. 89 L11
Penrhyn Atoll (Tongareva), Cook Is. 96 F9
Pensacola, Fla., U.S. 41 J12
Pensacola Bay, Fla., U.S. 43 J12
Pensacola Mountains, Antarctica 102 E7
Penza, Russ. 59 E12
Peoria, Ill., U.S. 41 E11
Percival Lakes, W. Austral., Austral. 90 E5
Pereira, Col. 50 B2
Perenjori, W. Austral., Austral. 88 J2
Peri Lake, N.S.W., AUSTRAL. 91 J12
Perito Moreno, Arg. 51 P4
Perm', Russ. 59 C13
Peron, Cape, W. Austral., Austral. 90 K2
Perpignan, Fr. 58 J4
Perry, Fla., U.S. 41 J13
Perry Island, Nunavut 36 E6
Perryville, Alas., U.S. 37 R5
Persian Gulf, Asia 70 H4
Perth, U.K. 58 D4
Perth, W. Austral., Austral. 88 K2
Peru, S. America 50 E3
Perugia, It. 58 J6
Pervoural'sk, Russ. 59 C14
Pescara, It. 58 J7
Peshawar, Pak. 68 G7
Petacalco Bay, Mex. 39 P5
Peterborough, Ont., Can. 36 J8
Peter I Island, Antarctica 102 G2
Petermann Ranges, N. Terr.-W. Austral., Austral. 90 G7
Petersburg, Alas., U.S. 40 M5
Petersburg, Va., U.S. 41 F15
Petoskey, Mich., U.S. 41 C12
Petrolândia, Braz. 50 F11
Petrolina, Braz. 50 F10
Petropavl, Kaz. 59 C15
Petropavlovsk Kamchatskiy, Russ. 69 C13
Petrozavodsk, Russ. 59 C10
Pevek, Russ. 69 A11
Phenix City, Ala., U.S. 41 H13
Philadelphia, Pa., U.S. 41 E15
Philippi Glacier, Antarctica 103 F15
Philippine Islands, Philippines 71 J13
Philippines, Asia 69 J13
Philippine Sea, Asia 71 H14
Philip Smith Mountains, Alas., U.S. 42 J3
Phillip Island, Austral. 96 J5
Phnom Penh, Cambodia 69 K11
Phoenix, Ariz., U.S. 40 H5
Phoenix Islands, Kiribati 96 F7
Pibor Post, Sudan 78 H9
Pickle Lake, Ont., Can. 36 H7
Picos, Braz. 50 E10
Piedmont, region, It. 60 H5
Piedmont, region, U.S. 43 G14
Piedras Negras, Mex. 37 M5
Pielinen, lake, Fin. 60 C9
Pierre, S. Dak., U.S. 40 D8
Pietermaritzburg, S. Af. 79 Q9
Pietersburg (Polokwane), S. Af. 79 P9
Pikes Peak, Colo., U.S. 42 F7
Pilar, Para. 50 K6
Pilcomayo, river, Arg.-Bol. 52 J6
Pilliga, N.S.W., AUSTRAL. 89 J14
Pilot Point, Alas., U.S. 40 M2
Pilottown, La., U.S. 41 J12
Pimba, S. Austral., Austral. 88 J10
Pinar del Río, Cuba 37 N8
Pindus Mountains, Alban.-Gr. 60 K8
Pine Barrens, region, N.J., U.S. 43 E15
Pine Bluff, Ark., U.S. 41 H11
Pine Creek, N. Terr., Austral. 88 B8
Pinega, river, Russ. 61 B11
Pinegrove, homestead, W. Austral., Austral. 88 H2
Pine Hill, homestead, N. Terr., Austral. 88 F8
Pinehill, Qnsld., Austral. 89 F13
Pine Island Bay, Antarctica 102 H4
Pine Island Glacier, Antarctica 102 G4
Pingelly, W. Austral., Austral. 88 K3
Pingliang, China 69 G11
Pinheiro, Braz. 50 D9
Pinjarra, W. Austral., Austral. 88 K2
Pins, Île des (Kunié), New Caledonia 96 H5
Pinsk, Belarus 58 F9
Pinsk Marshes, Belarus 60 F9
Pintharuka, W. Austral., Austral. 88 J2
Pioche, Nev., U.S. 40 F4
Piracicaba, Braz. 50 J9
Piranhas, Braz. 50 F11
Pireás, Gr. 58 K9
Pires do Rio, Braz. 50 H8
Pirimapun, Indonesia 92 C3
Piripiri, Braz. 50 E10
Pisa, It. 58 H6
Pisco, Peru 50 G2
Piso Firme, Bol. 50 G6
Pitcairn Island, Pitcairn Is. 97 H12
Piteå, Sweden 58 B8
Pithara, W. Austral., Austral. 88 J3
Pitt Island, N.Z. 96 K7
Pittsburgh, Pa., U.S. 41 E14
Piura, Peru 50 E1
Plainwell, Tex., U.S. 40 H8
Plata, Río de la (River Plate), Arg.-Uru. 51 L7
Plate, River, Arg.-Uru. 53 M7
Plateau Station, station, Antarctica 103 D10
Platte, river, Nebr., U.S. 42 E9
Plenty, river, N. Terr., Austral. 90 F9
Plenty, Bay of, N.Z. 92 H6
Pleven, Bulg. 58 J9
Ploieşti, Rom. 58 H9
Plovdiv, Bulg. 58 J9
Plymouth, U.K. 58 F3
Plzeň, Czech Rep. 58 G7
Po, river, It. 60 H6
Pocatello, Idaho, U.S. 40 D5
Poconé, Braz. 50 G7
Podgorica, Serbia and Montenegro 58 J8
Podporozh'ye, Russ. 59 D10
Pohnpei (Ponape), island, F.S.M. 96 E4
Poinsett, Cape, Antarctica 103 J15
Pointe-Noire, Congo 79 K6
Point Hope, Alas., U.S. 40 J2
Point Lay, Alas., U.S. 40 J2
Point Samson, W. Austral., Austral. 88 E2
Poitiers, Fr. 58 G4
Pokataroo, N.S.W., AUSTRAL. 89 J14
Poland, Europe 58 F8
Polar Plateau, Antarctica 102 F8
Polatsk, Belarus 58 E9
Polevskoy, Russ. 59 C14
Polokwane see Pietersburg, S. Af. 79 P9
Polson, Mont., U.S. 40 B5
Poltava, Ukr. 59 G11
Polyarnyy, Russ. 58 A9
Polynesia, islands, Pac. Oc. 96 D8
Pom, Indonesia 92 B2
Pomene, Mozambique 79 P10
Ponape see Pohnpei, island, F.S.M. 96 E4
Ponca City, Okla., U.S. 40 G9
Pondicherry, India 68 K7
Pond Inlet, Nunavut 36 D7
Pongaroa, N.Z. 92 K6
Ponoy, Russ. 59 B10
Ponta Grossa, Braz. 50 J8
Ponta Porã, Braz. 50 J7
Pontchartrain, Lake, La., U.S. 43 J11
Pontiac, Mich., U.S. 41 D13
Pontianak, Indonesia 69 L12
Poochera, S. Austral., Austral. 88 K9
Pooncarie, N.S.W., AUSTRAL. 89 K11
Popayán, Col. 50 C2
Poplar Bluff, Mo., U.S. 41 G11
Popocatépetl, Mex. 39 N5
Popondetta, P.N.G. 92 D6
Porangahau, N.Z. 92 K6
Porcupine, river, Can.-U.S. 42 J4
Pori, Fin. 58 D8
Porirua, N.Z. 92 K5
Porlamar, Venez. 50 A5
Porongurup, W. Austral., Austral. 88 L3
Porpoise Bay, Antarctica 103 L13
Portal, N. Dak., U.S. 40 B8
Port Albert, Vic., Austral. 89 M13
Port Arthur, Tex., U.S. 41 J10
Port Augusta, S. Austral., Austral. 89 K10
Port-au-Prince, Haiti 37 N10
Port Broughton, S. Austral., Austral. 89 K10
Port Burwell, Nfld. and Lab., Can. 36 E9
Port Douglas, Qnsld., Austral. 89 C13
Porteira, Braz. 50 D7
Port Elizabeth, S. Af. 79 Q8
Port Fairy, Vic., Austral. 89 M11
Port-Gentil, Gabon 78 K5
Port Harcourt, Nig. 78 J5
Port Hardy, B.C., Can. 36 G2
Port Hedland, W. Austral., Austral. 88 E3
Portland, Me., U.S. 41 C16
Portland, Oreg., U.S. 40 C3
Portland, Vic., Austral. 89 M11
Port Lincoln, S. Austral., Austral. 88 K9
Port Macquarie, N.S.W., AUSTRAL. 89 K15
Port-Menier, Que., Can. 36 G10
Port Moresby, P.N.G. 92 D6
Porto, Port. 58 H2
Porto Alegre, Braz. 51 K8
Porto Amboim, Angola 79 L6
Pôrto Artur, Braz. 50 F7
Pôrto dos Gauchos, Braz. 50 F7
Pôrto Esperidião, Braz. 50 G6
Port-of-Spain, Trinidad and Tobago 37 P12
Porto-Novo, Benin 78 H4
Pôrto Seguro, Braz. 50 G11
Pôrto Velho, Braz. 50 E5
Portoviejo, Ecua. 50 D1
Port Phillip Bay, Vic., Austral. 91 M12
Port Pirie, S. Austral., Austral. 89 K10
Port Royal Sound, Ga.-S.C., U.S. 41 H14
Port Said see Būr Sa'īd, Egypt 78 D9
Portsmouth, Ohio, U.S. 41 F13
Port Sudan see Būr Sūdān, Sudan 78 F10
Portugal, Europe 58 J2
Port-Vila, Vanuatu 96 G5
Port Warrender, W. Austral., Austral. 88 C5
Porvenir, Chile 51 R5
Posadas, Arg. 50 K7
Potenza, It. 58 J7
Potomac, river, Md.-Va.-W. Va., U.S. 43 E14
Potosí, Bol. 50 H5
Powder, river, Mont.-Wyo., U.S. 42 C7
Powell, Wyo., U.S. 40 D6
Powell, Lake, Ariz.-Utah, U.S. 42 F5
Powell River, B.C., Can. 36 G3
Poxoréo, Braz. 50 G7
Poyang Hu, China 71 H12
Poza Rica, Mex. 37 N6
Pozheg, Russ. 59 B12
Poznań, Pol. 58 F7
Prague see Praha, Czech Rep. 58 G7
Praha (Prague), Czech Rep. 58 G7
Prainha, Braz. 50 E6
Prairie du Chien, Wis., U.S. 41 D11
Prescott, Ariz., U.S. 40 G5
Presidente Dutra, Braz. 50 E10
Presidente Eduardo Frei, station, Antarctica 102 B1
Presidente Prudente, Braz. 50 J8
Presidente Roque Sáenz Peña, Arg. 50 K6
Presque Isle, Me., U.S. 41 B16
Preston, Idaho, U.S. 40 D5
Pretoria, S. Af. 79 P8
Pribilof Islands, U.S. 39 Q4
Price, Utah, U.S. 40 E6
Prichard, Ala., U.S. 41 J12
Prince Albert, Sask., Can. 36 G5
Prince Albert Mountains, Antarctica 102 K9
Prince Alfred, Cape, Can. 38 C5
Prince Charles Island, Can. 38 D7
Prince Charles Mountains, Antarctica 103 D13
Prince Edward Island, Can. 36 H10
Prince George, B.C., Can. 36 G3
Prince Harald Coast, Antarctica 103 B12
Prince of Wales, Cape, Alas., U.S. 42 K1
Prince of Wales Island, Alas., U.S. 42 M5
Prince of Wales Island, Can. 38 D6
Prince of Wales Island, Qnsld., Austral. 91 A12
Prince Olav Coast, Antarctica 103 B12
Prince Patrick Island, Can. 38 C5
Prince Rupert, B.C., Can. 36 F2
Princess Astrid Coast, Antarctica 102 A9
Princess Charlotte Bay, Qnsld., Austral. 91 C12
Princess Martha Coast, Antarctica 102 B7
Princess Ragnhild Coast, Antarctica 103 B11
Prince William Sound, Alas., U.S. 42 L4
Príncipe, island, São Tomé and Príncipe 80 J5
Príncipe da Beira, Braz. 50 F5
Priština, Serbia and Montenegro 58 J8
Prizren, Serbia and Montenegro 58 J8
Progress, station, Antarctica 103 E14
Prokop'yevsk, Russ. 68 E8
Propriá, Braz. 50 F11
Proserpine, Qnsld., Austral. 89 E14
Providence, R.I., U.S. 41 D16
Provo, Utah, U.S. 40 E5
Prudhoe Bay, Alas., U.S. 42 J3
Prudhoe Bay, Alas., U.S. 40 J3
Prut, river, Moldova-Rom.-Ukr. 60 G9
Prydz Bay, Antarctica 103 E14

Pryluky, *Ukr.* **59** F10
Prypyats', *river, Belarus-Ukr.* **60** F9
Przemyśl, *Pol.* **58** G8
Pskov, *Russ.* **58** D9
Pskov, Lake, *Est.-Russ.* **60** D9
Pucallpa, *Peru* **50** F3
Puca Urco, *Peru* **50** D3
Puebla, *Mex.* **37** N5
Pueblo, *Colo., U.S.* **40** F7
Puerto Acosta, *Bol.* **50** G4
Puerto América, *Peru* **50** E2
Puerto Ángel, *Mex.* **37** P6
Puerto Armuelles, *Pan.* **37** Q8
Puerto Ayacucho, *Venez.* **50** B4
Puerto Berrío, *Col.* **50** B3
Puerto Cabezas, *Nicar.* **37** P8
Puerto Carreño, *Col.* **50** B4
Puerto Deseado, *Arg.* **51** P5
Puerto Heath, *Bol.* **50** F4
Puerto Leguízamo, *Col.* **50** D3
Puerto Limón, *C.R.* **37** Q8
Puerto Maldonado, *Peru* **50** F4
Puerto Montt, *Chile* **51** N4
Puerto Natales, *Chile* **51** Q4
Puerto Páez, *Venez.* **50** B4
Puerto Plata, *Dom. Rep.* **37** N10
Puerto Portillo, *Peru* **50** F3
Puerto Rico, *U.S.* **37** N11
Puerto San Carlos, *Chile* **51** P4
Puerto San Julián, *Arg.* **51** Q5
Puerto Suárez, *Bol.* **50** H7
Puerto Tres Palmas, *Para.* **50** H6
Puerto Vallarta, *Mex.* **37** N4
Puerto Williams, *Chile* **51** R5
Pugachev, *Russ.* **59** E13
Puget Sound, *Wash., U.S.* **42** B3
Pukaki, Lake, *N.Z.* **92** M4
Pukapuka, *island, Fr. Polynesia* **97** G11
Pukapuka Atoll (Danger Islands), *Cook Is.* **96** G8
Pulacayo, *Bol.* **50** H5
Pulap Atoll, *F.S.M.* **96** E3
Pullman, *Wash., U.S.* **40** B4
Pulo Anna, *island, Palau* **96** E2
Pulusuk, *island, F.S.M.* **96** E3
Puluwat Atoll, *F.S.M.* **96** E3
Pune, *India* **68** J7
Puno, *Peru* **50** G4
Punta Alta, *Arg.* **51** M6
Punta Arenas, *Chile* **51** R5
Punta Delgada, *Arg.* **51** N6
Puntarenas, *C.R.* **37** Q8
Puntland, *region, Somalia* **78** H12
Punto Fijo, *Venez.* **50** A4
Puntudo, Cerro, *Arg.* **53** Q5
Puquio, *Peru* **50** G3
Purari, *river, P.N.G.* **92** C5
Purdy Islands, *P.N.G.* **92** B5
Purus, *river, Braz.-Peru* **52** E5
Pu'uwai, *Hawaii, U.S.* **41** L10
Puy de Sancy, *peak, Fr.* **60** H4
Puysegur Point, *N.Z.* **92** N2
Pweto, *D.R.C.* **79** L9
Pya, Lake, *Russ.* **60** B9
Pyatigorsk, *Russ.* **59** H13
Pyay, *Myanmar* **68** J9
P'yŏngyang, *N. Korea* **69** F12
Pyramid Lake, *Nev., U.S.* **42** E3
Pyrenees, *mountains, Fr.-Sp.* **60** H4

Qaidam Basin, *China* **70** G9
Qairouan, *Tun.* **78** C6
Qal at Bīshah, *Saudi Arabia* **68** H3
Qamdo, *China* **68** H9
Qaraghandy, *Kaz.* **68** F7
Qardho, *Somalia* **78** H12
Qaṣr Farâfra, *Egypt* **78** E8
Qatar, *Asia* **68** H4
Qattara Depression, *Egypt* **80** D8
Qazaly, *Kaz.* **68** F6
Qazvīn, *Iran* **68** F5
Qeissan, *Sudan* **78** H10
Qena, *Egypt* **78** E9
Qeqertarsuaq (Godhavn), *Greenland* **36** D9
Qeqertarsuatsiaat, *Greenland* **36** D9
Qerqertarsuaq, *island, Greenland* **38** D9
Qiemo, *China* **68** G8
Qikiqtarjuaq, *Nunavut* **36** D8
Qilian Shan, *China* **70** G9
Qingdao, *China* **69** G12
Qinghai Hu, *China* **71** G10
Qin Lin, *mountains, China* **71** G11
Qiqihar, *China* **69** E12
Qizilqum, *region, Uzb.* **70** F6
Qom, *Iran* **68** G5
Qostanay, *Kaz.* **59** D15
Quairading, *W. Austral., Austral.* **88** K3
Quamby, *Qnsld., Austral.* **89** E11
Queanbeyan, *N.S.W., AUSTRAL.* **89** L14
Québec, *Que., Can.* **36** H9
Quebec, *Can.* **36** G9
Queen Adelaida Archipelago, *Chile* **53** R4
Queen Alexandra Range, *Antarctica* **102** H9
Queen Charlotte Islands, *Can.* **38** F2
Queen Elizabeth Islands, *Can.* **38** B6
Queen Elizabeth Range, *Antarctica* **102** H9
Queen Fabiola Mountains (Yamato Mountains), *Antarctica* **103** B12
Queen Mary Coast, *Antarctica* **103** G15
Queen Maud Gulf, *Can.* **38** D6
Queen Maud Land, *Antarctica* **102** B8
Queen Maud Mountains, *Antarctica* **102** H8
Queensland, *Austral.* **89** F12
Queenstown, *N.Z.* **92** N3
Queenstown, *S. Af.* **79** Q8
Queenstown, *Tas., Austral.* **89** M15
Quelimane, *Mozambique* **79** N10
Quellón, *Chile* **51** N4
Querétaro, *Mex.* **37** N5
Quṣeir, *Egypt* **78** E9
Quetta, *Pak.* **68** H6
Quetzaltenango, *Guatemala* **37** P7
Quezon City, *Philippines* **69** J13
Quibala, *Angola* **79** L6
Quibdó, *Col.* **50** B2
Quillota, *Chile* **51** L4
Quilpie, *Qnsld., Austral.* **89** G12
Quincy, *Ill., U.S.* **41** E11
Quinhagak, *Alas., U.S.* **40** L2
Qui Nhon, *Viet.* **69** K11
Quipungo, *Angola* **79** M6
Quirindi, *N.S.W., AUSTRAL.* **89** K14
Quito, *Ecua.* **50** D2
Quixadá, *Braz.* **50** E11
Qulsary, *Kaz.* **59** F14
Quobba, *homestead, W. Austral., Austral.* **88** G1
Qusmuryn, *Kaz.* **59** D15
Quzhou, *China* **69** H12
Qyzylorda, *Kaz.* **68** F6

Raahe, *Fin.* **58** C8
Raba, *Indonesia* **69** M13
Rabat, *Mor.* **78** D3
Rabaul, *P.N.G.* **92** B7
Racine, *Wis., U.S.* **41** D12
Radisson, *Que., Can.* **36** G8
Radom, *Pol.* **58** F8
Rae Lakes, *N.W.T., CAN.* **36** E4
Raeside, Lake, *W. Austral., Austral.* **90** H4
Raetihi, *N.Z.* **92** J6
Rafaela, *Arg.* **51** L6
Ragged, Mount, *W. Austral., Austral.* **90** K5
Ragusa, *It.* **58** L7
Raiatea, *island, Fr. Polynesia* **96** G10
Rainier, Mount, *Wash., U.S.* **42** B3
Rainy Lake, *Can.-U.S.* **43** B10
Raivavae (Vavitu), *island, Fr. Polynesia* **97** H10
Rajkot, *India* **68** J6
Rajshahi, *Bangladesh* **68** J9
Rakahanga Atoll, *Cook Is.* **96** F9
Rakaia, *N.Z.* **92** M4
Rakops, *Botswana* **79** N8
Raleigh, *N.C., U.S.* **37** K8
Raleigh, *N.C., U.S.* **41** G14
Ralik Chain, *Marshall Is.* **96** D5
Rambutyo, *island, P.N.G.* **92** B6
Rampart, *Alas., U.S.* **40** K3
Ramu, *river, P.N.G.* **92** B5
Rancagua, *Chile* **51** L4
Ranchi, *India* **68** J8
Randers, *Den.* **58** E6
Rangiroa, *island, Fr. Polynesia* **97** G10
Rangitaiki, *river, N.Z.* **92** J6
Rangoon *see* Yangon, *Myanmar* **68** K10
Rankin Inlet, *Nunavut* **36** E6
Ransiki, *Indonesia* **92** A2
Raoul Island (Sunday), *N.Z.* **96** J7
Rapa, *island, Fr. Polynesia* **97** H10
Rapid City, *S. Dak., U.S.* **40** D8
Rarotonga, *island, Cook Is.* **96** H9
Rasa Point, *Arg.* **53** N6
Rasht, *Iran* **68** F5
Rason Lake, *W. Austral., Austral.* **90** H5
Rasskazovo, *Russ.* **59** E12
Ratak Chain, *Marshall Is.* **96** D6
Rat Islands, *U.S.* **39** R2
Raton, *N. Mex., U.S.* **40** G7
Rauma, *Fin.* **58** D8
Ravenshoe, *Qnsld., Austral.* **89** D13
Ravensthorpe, *W. Austral., Austral.* **88** K4
Ravenswood, *Qnsld., Austral.* **89** E13
Rawaki, *island, Kiribati* **96** F8
Rawalpindi, *Pak.* **68** G7
Rawlinna, *W. Austral., Austral.* **88** J6
Rawlins, *Wyo., U.S.* **40** E7
Rawson, *Arg.* **51** N5
Raymond Terrace, *N.S.W., AUSTRAL.* **89** K15
Raymondville, *Tex., U.S.* **40** K9
Ray Mountains, *Alas., U.S.* **42** K3
Rayner Glacier, *Antarctica* **103** B13
Reading, *Pa., U.S.* **41** E15
Realicó, *Arg.* **51** L5
Rebecca, Lake, *W. Austral., Austral.* **90** J5
Rebiana Sand Sea, *Lib.* **80** E7
Recherche, Archipelago of the, *W. Austral., Austral.* **90** L5
Recife, *Braz.* **50** F12
Recife, Cape, *S. Af.* **81** Q8
Reconquista, *Arg.* **51** K6
Red, *river, China-Viet.* **71** J10
Red, *river, U.S.* **43** H10
Red Bluff, *Calif., U.S.* **40** D2
Red Bluff Lake, *Tex., U.S.* **42** H7
Redcliffe, Mount, *W. Austral., Austral.* **90** H4
Red Deer, *Alta., Can.* **36** G4
Red Devil, *Alas., U.S.* **40** L2
Redding, *Calif., U.S.* **36** J2
Redding, *Calif., U.S.* **40** D2
Red Hills, *Kans., U.S.* **42** F9
Red Lake, *Ont., Can.* **36** H6
Red Lake, *W. Austral., Austral.* **88** K4
Red River of the North, *Can.-U.S.* **42** C9
Red Rocks Point, *W. Austral., Austral.* **90** K6
Red Sea, *Af.-Asia* **70** G2
Reedy Glacier, *Antarctica* **102** G7
Reefton, *N.Z.* **92** L4
Reggane, *Alg.* **78** E4
Reggio di Calabria, *It.* **58** K7
Regina, *Sask., Can.* **36** H5
Rehoboth, *Namibia* **79** P7
Reid, *W. Austral., Austral.* **88** J7
Reid River, *Qnsld., Austral.* **89** E13
Reims, *Fr.* **58** G5
Reina Adelaida, Archipiélago (Queen Adelaida Archipelago), *Chile* **51** R4
Reindeer Lake, *Can.* **38** F5
Reinga, Cape, *N.Z.* **92** F5
Remada, *Tun.* **78** D6
Remanso, *Braz.* **50** F10
Renmark, *S. Austral., Austral.* **89** K11
Rennell, *island, Solomon Is.* **96** G5
Rennes, *Fr.* **58** G4
Rennick Glacier, *Antarctica* **103** M10
Reno, *Nev., U.S.* **40** E3
Republican, *river, Colo.-Kans.-Nebr.* **42** E9
Repulse Bay, *Qnsld., Austral.* **91** E14
Repulse Bay, *Nunavut* **36** E7
Resistencia, *Arg.* **50** K6
Resolute, *Nunavut* **36** C6
Resolution Island, *N.Z.* **92** N2
Resolution Island, *Nunavut* **36** E9
Revelstoke, *B.C., Can.* **36** G3
Revillagigedo, Islas *see* Revillagigedo Islands, *Mex.* **37** N3
Revillagigedo Island, *Alas., U.S.* **42** M6
Revillagigedo Islands, *Mex.* **39** N3
Reyes, *Bol.* **50** G4
Reyes, Point, *Calif., U.S.* **42** E2
Reykjanes, *point, Ice.* **60** A3
Reykjavík, *Ice.* **58** A3
Reynosa, *Mex.* **37** M5
Rēzekne, *Latv.* **58** E9
Rhine, *river, Europe* **60** F5
Rhine, Sources of the, *Switz.* **60** H6
Rhinelander, *Wis., U.S.* **41** C11
Rhir, Cape, *Mor.* **80** D3
Rhode Island, *U.S.* **41** D16
Rhodes, *island, Gr.* **61** L10
Rhodope Mountains, *Bulg.* **60** J9
Rhône, *river, Fr.* **60** H5
Riachão, *Braz.* **50** E9
Ribeirão Prêto, *Braz.* **50** H9
Riberalta, *Bol.* **50** F5
Richardson Mountains, *Can.* **38** D3
Richfield, *Utah, U.S.* **40** F5
Richland, *Wash., U.S.* **40** C4
Richmond, *N.S.W., AUSTRAL.* **89** K14
Richmond, *Qnsld., Austral.* **89** E12
Richmond, *S. Af.* **79** Q8
Richmond, *Va., U.S.* **41** F15
Ridgecrest, *Calif., U.S.* **40** F3
Rifstangi, *point, Ice.* **60** A4
Rīga, *Latv.* **58** E8
Riga, Gulf of, *Est.-Latv.* **60** E8
Rigo, *P.N.G.* **92** D6
Riiser-Larsen Ice Shelf, *Antarctica* **102** B7
Riiser-Larsen Peninsula, *Antarctica* **103** B12
Rimatara, *island, Fr. Polynesia* **96** H9
Rimini, *It.* **58** H6
Rimouski, *Que., Can.* **36** H9
Rincón del Bonete, Lake, *Uru.* **53** L7
Ringwood, *homestead, N. Terr., Austral.* **88** F9
Riobamba, *Ecua.* **50** D2
Rio Branco, *Braz.* **50** F4
Río Cuarto, *Arg.* **51** L5
Rio de Janeiro, *Braz.* **50** J9
Río Gallegos, *Arg.* **51** Q5
Rio Grande, *river, Mex.-U.S.* **42** K8
Rio Grande, *Braz.* **51** L8
Rio Grande, Source of the, *U.S.* **39** K4
Riohacha, *Col.* **50** A3
Río Muni, *region, Eq. Guinea* **78** J6
Rio Verde, *Braz.* **50** H8
Rio Verde de Mato Grosso, *Braz.* **50** H7
Ritscher Upland, *Antarctica* **102** B7
Rivera, *Uru.* **51** L7
River Cess, *Liberia* **78** J2
Riverina, *homestead, W. Austral., Austral.* **88** J4
Riverina, *region, N.S.W., AUSTRAL.* **91** L12
Riverside, *Calif., U.S.* **40** G3
Riversleigh, *homestead, Qnsld., Austral.* **89** D10
Riverton, *Wyo., U.S.* **40** D6
Riviera, *coast, Fr.-It.* **60** H5
Rivne, *Ukr.* **58** G9
Riyadh *see* Ar Riyāḑ, *Saudi Arabia* **68** H4
Rize, *Turk.* **59** J12
Roan Cliffs, *Utah, U.S.* **42** E6
Roanoke, *river, N.C.-Va., U.S.* **43** F15
Roanoke, *Va., U.S.* **41** F14
Robe, *S. Austral., Austral.* **89** L10
Robert Glacier, *Antarctica* **103** C14
Roberts Butte, *Antarctica* **103** L10
Roberts Mountain, *Alas., U.S.* **42** L1
Robertsport, *Liberia* **78** H2
Robinson Range, *W. Austral., Austral.* **90** G3
Robinson River, *homestead, N. Terr., Austral.* **88** C10
Robinvale, *Vic., Austral.* **89** K11
Roboré, *Bol.* **50** H6
Roca Partida Island, *Mex.* **39** N3
Rocha, *Uru.* **51** L7
Rochester, *Minn., U.S.* **41** D10
Rochester, *N.Y., U.S.* **41** D14
Rock, *river, Ill.-Wisc.* **43** E11
Rockall, *island, U.K.* **58** C3
Rockefeller Plateau, *Antarctica* **102** J6
Rockford, *Ill., U.S.* **41** E11
Rockhampton, *Qnsld., Austral.* **89** F15
Rockhampton Downs, *homestead, N. Terr., Austral.* **88** D9
Rockingham, *W. Austral., Austral.* **88** K2
Rockingham Bay, *Qnsld., Austral.* **91** D13
Rock Island, *Ill., U.S.* **41** E11
Rocklea, *homestead, W. Austral., Austral.* **88** F2
Rock Springs, *Wyo., U.S.* **40** E6
Rocky Mountains, *N. America* **38** F3
Roddickton, *Nfld. and Lab., Can.* **36** G10
Rodeo, *Arg.* **51** K4
Rodinga, *N. Terr., Austral.* **88** F9
Ródos, *Gr.* **59** L10
Ródos (Rhodes), *island, Gr.* **59** L10
Roebourne, *W. Austral., Austral.* **88** E2
Roebuck Bay, *W. Austral., Austral.* **90** D4
Roebuck Plains, *homestead, W. Austral., Austral.* **88** D4
Rogers, Mount, *Va., U.S.* **43** F14
Rojo, Cape, *Mex.* **39** N6
Rolla, *Mo., U.S.* **41** F11
Rolleston, *N.Z.* **92** M4
Rolleston, *Qnsld., Austral.* **89** G14
Roma, *Qnsld., Austral.* **89** H14
Roma (Rome), *It.* **58** J6
Romania, *Europe* **58** H9
Romano, Cape, *Fla., U.S.* **43** K14
Romanzof, Cape, *Alas., U.S.* **42** L1
Rome, *Ga., U.S.* **41** G13
Rome *see* Roma, *It.* **58** J6
Roncador, Serra do, *Braz.* **52** G8
Roncador Cay, *Col.* **39** P9
Rondônia *see* Ji-Paraná, *Braz.* **50** F6
Rondonópolis, *Braz.* **50** G7
Ronge, Lac la, *Can.* **38** G5
Rongelap Atoll, *Marshall Is.* **96** D5
Ronne Entrance, *Antarctica* **102** E3
Ronne Ice Shelf, *Antarctica* **102** E5
Roosevelt Island, *Antarctica* **102** J7
Roper Valley, *homestead, N. Terr., Austral.* **88** C9
Roraima, Mount, *Braz.-Guyana-Venez.* **52** B6
Røros, *Nor.* **58** C7
Rosario, *Arg.* **51** L6
Rosario, *Mex.* **37** N4
Rose Atoll, *American Samoa* **96** G8
Roseau, *Dominica* **37** N12
Rosebery, *Tas., Austral.* **89** M15
Roseburg, *Oreg., U.S.* **40** C2
Rosedale, *Qnsld., Austral.* **89** G15
Ross, *N.Z.* **92** L4
Ross, Mount, *N.Z.* **92** K6
Rossel Island, *P.N.G.* **92** E8
Ross Ice Shelf, *Antarctica* **102** J8
Ross Island, *Antarctica* **102** K9
Rossosh', *Russ.* **59** F11
Ross River, *N. Terr., Austral.* **88** F9
Ross River, *Yukon Terr.* **36** E3
Ross Sea, *Antarctica* **102** K8
Rossville, *Qnsld., Austral.* **89** C13
Rostock, *Ger.* **58** F6
Rostov na Donu, *Russ.* **59** G12
Roswell, *N. Mex., U.S.* **40** H7
Rota, *island, N. Mariana Is.* **96** D3
Rothera, *station, Antarctica* **102** D2
Rothschild Island, *Antarctica* **102** E2
Roti, *island, Indonesia* **90** A4
Roto, *N.S.W., AUSTRAL.* **89** K12
Rotorua, *N.Z.* **92** H6
Rotterdam, *Neth.* **58** F5
Rotuma, *island, Fiji* **96** G6
Rouen, *Fr.* **58** G4
Roundup, *Mont., U.S.* **40** C6
Rouyn-Noranda, *Que., Can.* **36** H8
Rovaniemi, *Fin.* **58** B8
Rowena, *N.S.W., AUSTRAL.* **89** J14
Royale, Isle, *Mich., U.S.* **43** B11
Royal Society Range, *Antarctica* **102** K9
Roy Hill, *W. Austral., Austral.* **88** F3
Ruapehu, Mount, *N.Z.* **92** J6
Ruapuke Island, *N.Z.* **92** P3
Ruatoria, *N.Z.* **92** H7
Ruawai, *N.Z.* **92** G5
Rub al Khali, *Saudi Arabia* **70** H4
Rubtsovsk, *Russ.* **68** E8
Ruby, *Alas., U.S.* **40** K3
Ruby Dome, *Nev., U.S.* **42** E4
Ruby Mountains, *Nev., U.S.* **42** E4
Rūdnyy, *Kaz.* **59** D15
Rudolf, Lake *see* Turkana, Lake, *Eth.-Kenya* **80** J10
Rufiji, *river, Tanzania* **81** L10
Rufino, *Arg.* **51** L6
Rugby, *N. Dak., U.S.* **40** B9
Rui Barbosa, *Braz.* **50** F10
Rukwa, Lake, *Tanzania* **81** L9
Rumbalara, *N. Terr., Austral.* **88** G9
Rum Cay, *Bahamas* **39** M9
Runanga, *N.Z.* **92** L4
Runaway, Cape, *N.Z.* **92** H7
Rundu, *Namibia* **79** N7
Rupert, *Idaho, U.S.* **40** D5
Ruppert Coast, *Antarctica* **102** K6
Rurrenabaque, *Bol.* **50** G4
Rurutu, *island, Fr. Polynesia* **96** H10
Ruse, *Bulg.* **58** J9
Russell, *Kans., U.S.* **40** F9
Russia, *Asia-Europe* **68** D7
Rust'avi, *Ga.* **59** H13
Ruvuma, *river, Mozambique-Tanzania* **81** L10
Ruwenzori, *peak, D.R.C.-Uganda* **80** J9
Rwanda, *Af.* **79** K9
Ryazan', *Russ.* **59** E11
Rybinsk, *Russ.* **59** D11
Rybinskoye Vodokhranilishche (Rybinsk Reservoir), *Russ.* **59** D11
Rybinsk Reservoir, *Russ.* **61** D11
Ryn Peski, *Kaz.* **61** F13
Ryukyu Islands, *Jap.* **71** H13
Rzeszów, *Pol.* **58** G8
Rzhev, *Russ.* **59** E10

Saaremaa, *island, Est.* **60** D8
Sabah, *region, Malaysia* **69** K13
Sabhā, *Lib.* **78** E6
Sabidana, Jebel, *Sudan* **80** F10
Sabine, *river, La.-Tex., U.S.* **43** J10
Sable, Cape, *Can.* **38** H10
Sable, Cape, *Fla., U.S.* **43** K14
Sable Island, *Can.* **38** H10
Sabrina Coast, *Antarctica* **103** K14
Sabzevār, *Iran* **68** G5
Sachs Harbour, *N.W.T., CAN.* **36** C4
Sacramento, *river, Calif., U.S.* **42** E2
Sacramento, *Calif., U.S.* **40** E3
Sacramento Mountains, *N. Mex., U.S.* **42** H7
Sacramento Valley, *Calif., U.S.* **42** E2
Şa'dah, *Yemen* **68** H3
Sae Islands, *P.N.G.* **92** A5
Safford, *Ariz., U.S.* **40** H5
Safi, *Mor.* **78** D3
Safonovo, *Russ.* **59** E10
Saginaw, *Mich., U.S.* **41** D13
Saginaw Bay, *Mich., U.S.* **43** D13
Sahara, *desert, Af.* **80** F2
Saharan Atlas, *mountains, Alg.-Mor.* **80** D4
Sahel, *region, Af.* **80** G3
Saïda, *Alg.* **78** C4
Saidor, *P.N.G.* **92** C6
Saigon *see* Ho Chi Minh City, *Viet.* **69** K11
Saimaa, *lake, Fin.* **60** C9
Saint André, Cap, *Madag.* **81** M11
Saint Andrews, *N.Z.* **92** M4
Saint Anthony, *Nfld. and Lab., Can.* **36** G10
Saint Arnaud, *Vic., Austral.* **89** L12
Saint Augustin Bay, *Madag.* **81** P11
Saint Augustine, *Fla., U.S.* **41** J14
Saint Clair, Lake, *Can.-U.S.* **43** D13
Saint Cloud, *Minn., U.S.* **41** C10
Saint Croix, *island, Virgin Is.* **39** N11
Saint Croix, *river, Minn.-Wisc.* **43** C10
Saint Elias, Mount, *Can.-U.S.* **42** L4
Saint Elias Mountains, *Can.-U.S.* **42** L4
Sainte Marie, Cape, *Madag.* **81** P11
Sainte Marie, Nosy, *Madag.* **81** N12
Saint-Étienne, *Fr.* **58** H5
Saint Francis, *river, Ark.-Mo., U.S.* **43** G11
Saint Francis Bay, *S. Af.* **81** Q8
Saint George, *Qnsld., Austral.* **89** H14
Saint George, *Utah, U.S.* **40** F5
Saint George, Cape, *P.N.G.* **92** C7
Saint George's, *Grenada* **37** P12
Saint George's Channel, *P.N.G.* **92** C7
Saint Helena, *Atl. Oc.* **81** M3
Saint Helena Bay, *S. Af.* **81** Q7
Saint Helens, Mount, *Wash., U.S.* **42** B3
Saint John, *river, Can.-U.S.* **43** B16
Saint John, *N. Dak., U.S.* **40** B9
Saint John, *N.B., Can.* **36** H10
Saint John's, *Antigua and Barbuda* **37** N12
Saint John's, *Nfld. and Lab., Can.* **36** G11
Saint Joseph, *Mo., U.S.* **41** F10
Saint Joseph, Lake, *Can.* **38** H7
Saint Kitts, *island, St. Kitts and Nevis* **39** N12
Saint Kitts and Nevis, *N. America* **37** N12
Saint-Laurent du Maroni, *Fr. Guiana* **50** B7
Saint Lawrence, *river, Can.-U.S.* **38** G9
Saint Lawrence, Gulf of, *Can.* **38** G10
Saint Lawrence Island, *Alas., U.S.* **42** K1
Saint Louis, *Mo., U.S.* **41** F11
Saint-Louis, *Senegal* **78** F1
Saint Lucia, *N. America* **37** N12
Saint Marys, *Tas., Austral.* **89** M16
Saint-Mathieu, Point, *Fr.* **60** G3
Saint Matthew Island, *U.S.* **39** Q3
Saint Michael, *Alas., U.S.* **36** C2
Saint Paul, *Minn., U.S.* **41** D10
Saint Petersburg, *Fla., U.S.* **41** K14
Saint Petersburg, *Russ.* **58** D9
Saint-Pierre and Miquelon, *N. America* **36** G11
Saint Thomas, *U.S.* **37** N11
Saint Vincent, Gulf, *S. Austral., Austral.* **91** L10
Saint Vincent, *island, St. Vincent and the Grenadines* **39** P12
Saint Vincent, Cape, *Madag.* **81** N11
Saint Vincent, Cape, *Port.* **60** J1
Saint Vincent and the Grenadines, *N. America* **37** P12
Saipan, *island, N. Mariana Is.* **96** D3
Sakakawea, Lake, *N. Dak., U.S.* **42** C8
Sakarya, *Turk.* **59** J10
Sakhalin, *island, Russ.* **71** D13
Sakhalin, Ostrov (Sakhalin), *Russ.* **69** D13
Şäki, *Azerb.* **59** H14
Sakishima Shotō, *Jap.* **96** C1
Salado, *river, Arg.* **53** K5
Salado, *river, Arg.* **53** M5
Salālah, *Oman* **68** J4
Salamanca, *Mex.* **37** N5
Salamanca, *Sp.* **58** J2
Salapaly Bay, *Madag.* **81** P11
Salavat, *Russ.* **59** D14
Sala-y-Gómez, *island, Chile* **97** H14
Sale, *Vic., Austral.* **89** M13
Salekhard, *Russ.* **68** D7
Salem, *India* **68** K7
Salem, *Oreg., U.S.* **40** C3
Salerno, *It.* **58** J7
Salgueiro, *Braz.* **50** E11
Salida, *Colo., U.S.* **40** F7
Salihorsk, *Belarus* **58** F9
Salina, *Kans., U.S.* **40** F9
Salinas, *Calif., U.S.* **40** F2
Saline, *river, Ark.-La., U.S.* **43** H11
Salinópolis, *Braz.* **50** D9
Salluit, *Que., Can.* **36** E8
Salmon, *river, Idaho, U.S.* **42** C4
Salmon, *Idaho, U.S.* **40** C5
Salmon Gums, *W. Austral., Austral.* **88** K4
Salmon River Mountains, *Idaho, U.S.* **42** C5
Salpaus Ridge, *Fin.* **60** D9
Sal'sk, *Russ.* **59** G12
Salt, *river, Ariz., U.S.* **42** G5
Salta, *Arg.* **50** J5
Saltillo, *Mex.* **37** M5
Salt Lake City, *Utah, U.S.* **40** E5
Salto, *Uru.* **51** L6
Salton Sea, *Calif., U.S.* **42** G4
Saluda, *river, S.C., U.S.* **43** G14
Salûm, *Egypt* **78** D8
Salûm, Gulf of, *Egypt-Lib.* **80** D8
Salvador (Bahia), *Braz.* **50** G11
Salvage Islands, *Canary Is.* **80** D2
Salween, *river, China-Myanmar* **70** J10
Salyan, *Azerb.* **59** J14
Salzburg, *Aust.* **58** G6
Samar, *island, Philippines* **71** J13
Samara, *river, Russ.* **61** E13
Samara, *Russ.* **59** E13
Samarai, *P.N.G.* **92** E7
Samarinda, *Indonesia* **69** L13
Samarqand, *Uzb.* **68** G6
Sambava, *Madag.* **79** M12
Samborombón Bay, *Arg.* **53** M7
Samo, *P.N.G.* **92** B7
Samoa, *Pac. Oc.* **96** G7
Samoa Islands, *Samoa* **96** G8
Sampwe, *D.R.C.* **79** L8
Sam Rayburn Reservoir, *Tex., U.S.* **43** J10
Samsun, *Turk.* **59** J11
Şanā', *Yemen* **68** H3
Sanae IV, *station, Antarctica* **102** A8
Sanaga, *river, Cameroon* **80** J6
San Ambrosio, Isla, *Chile* **53** K2
Sanandaj, *Iran* **68** F4
San Andrés, Isla de, *Col.* **50** A1
San Andres Mountains, *N. Mex., U.S.* **42** H6
San Angelo, *Tex., U.S.* **40** J8
San Antonio, *river, Tex., U.S.* **42** K9
San Antonio, *Chile* **51** L4
San Antonio, *Tex., U.S.* **40** J9
San Antonio, Cape, *Arg.* **53** M7
San Antonio, Cape, *Cuba* **39** N8
San Antonio, Mount, *Calif., U.S.* **42** G3
San Benedicto Island, *Mex.* **39** N3
San Bernardino, *Calif., U.S.* **40** G3
San Bernardo, *Chile* **51** L4
San Blas, Cape, *Fla., U.S.* **43** J13
San Borja, *Bol.* **50** G5
San Carlos, *Venez.* **50** A3
San Carlos de Bariloche, *Arg.* **51** N4
San Carlos de Río Negro, *Venez.* **50** C4
San Clemente, *island, Calif., U.S.* **42** G3
San Cristóbal, *Venez.* **50** B3
San Cristóbal, Isla, *Ecua.* **97** F16
San Cristobal, *island, Solomon Is.* **96** G5
Sancti Spíritus, *Cuba* **37** N9
Sandakan, *Malaysia* **69** K13
Sanderson, *Tex., U.S.* **40** J8
Sand Hills, *Nebr., U.S.* **42** E8
San Diego, *Calif., U.S.* **40** G3
Sandoa, *D.R.C.* **79** L8
Sand Point, *Alas., U.S.* **40** M2
Sandpoint, *Idaho, U.S.* **40** B5
Sandstone, *W. Austral., Austral.* **88** H3
Sandusky, *Ohio, U.S.* **41** E13
Sandy Cape, *Qnsld., Austral.* **91** G15
Sandy Lake, *Ont., Can.* **36** G6
San Felipe, *Chile* **51** L4
San Felipe, *Col.* **50** C4
San Felipe, *Mex.* **37** L3
San Felipe, *Venez.* **50** A4
San Félix, Isla, *Chile* **53** K2
San Fernando, *Chile* **51** L4
San Fernando de Apure, *Venez.* **50** B4
San Fernando de Atabapo, *Venez.* **50** C4
Sanford, *Fla., U.S.* **41** J14
San Francisco, *Calif., U.S.* **40** E2
San Francisco Bay, *Calif., U.S.* **42** E2
San Francisco Mountain, *Ariz., U.S.* **42** G5
Sangamon, *river, Ill., U.S.* **43** E11
Sangar, *Russ.* **69** C11
Sangre de Cristo Mountains, *Colo.-N. Mex., U.S.* **42** F7
San Ignacio, *Bol.* **50** G6
San Joaquin, *river, Calif., U.S.* **42** F3
San Joaquín, *Bol.* **50** F5
San Joaquin Valley, *Calif., U.S.* **42** F3
San Jorge, Golfo (Gulf of San Jorge), *Arg.* **51** P5
San Jorge, Gulf of, *Arg.* **53** P5
San José, *C.R.* **37** Q8
San Jose, *Calif., U.S.* **40** F2
San José de Amacuro, *Venez.* **50** A6
San José del Guaviare, *Col.* **50** C3
San José de Mayo, *Uru.* **51** L7
San José de Ocuné, *Col.* **50** C4
San Juan, *Arg.* **51** L4
San Juan, *P.R.* **37** N11
San Juan, *Peru* **50** G3
San Juan Bautista, *Para.* **50** K7
San Juan Mountains, *Colo.-N. Mex., U.S.* **42** F6
San Julián Bay, *Arg.* **53** Q5
San Justo, *Arg.* **51** L6
Sankuru, *river, D.R.C.* **81** K7
Şanlıurfa, *Turk.* **59** K12
San Luis, *Arg.* **51** L5
San Luis Obispo, *Calif., U.S.* **40** F2
San Luis Potosí, *Mex.* **37** N5
San Luis Río Colorado, *Mex.* **37** L3
San Marcos, *Tex., U.S.* **40** J9
San Marino, *Europe* **58** H6
San Martín, *station, Antarctica* **102** D2
San Martín de los Andes, *Arg.* **51** N4
San Mateo, *Calif., U.S.* **40** E2
San Matías, Golfo (San Matías Gulf), *Arg.* **51** N5
San Matías Gulf, *Arg.* **53** N5
San Miguel, *island, Calif., U.S.* **42** G2
San Miguel, *El Salv.* **37** P7

San Miguel de Tucumán, *Arg.* **51** K5
San Nicolás, *Arg.* **51** L6
San Nicolas, *island,* Calif., U.S. **42** G3
San Pablo, *Philippines* **69** J13
San Pedro, *river, Mex.* **39** N4
San Pedro, *Arg.* **50** J5
San Pedro Sula, *Hond.* **37** P7
San Rafael, *Arg.* **51** L5
San Rafael, *Bol.* **50** G6
San Salvador, *island, Bahamas* **39** M9
San Salvador, *El Salv.* **37** P7
San Salvador de Jujuy, *Arg.* **50** J5
Santa Ana, *Bol.* **50** G5
Santa Ana, *Calif., U.S.* **40** G3
Santa Ana, *El Salv.* **37** P7
Santa Barbara, *Calif., U.S.* **40** G3
Santa Barbara Channel, *Calif., U.S.* **42** G3
Santa Catalina, *island,* Calif., U.S. **42** G3
Santa Catalina, Gulf of, *Calif., U.S.* **42** G3
Santa Clara, *Cuba* **37** N9
Santa Clotilde, *Peru* **50** D3
Santa Cruz, *island,* Calif., U.S. **42** G3
Santa Cruz, *Bol.* **50** H5
Santa Cruz, *Calif., U.S.* **40** F2
Santa Cruz, *Canary Is.* **78** D2
Santa Cruz, Isla, *Ecua.* **97** E16
Santa Cruz Islands, *Solomon Is.* **96** G5
Santa Elena, *Venez.* **50** B6
Santa Elena Peninsula, *Ecua.* **52** D1
Santa Fe, *Arg.* **51** L6
Santa Fe, *N. Mex., U.S.* **40** G7
Santa Helena, *Braz.* **50** E7
Santa Inês, *Braz.* **50** D9
Santa Isabel, *island, Solomon Is.* **96** F4
Santa Isabel, *Arg.* **51** M5
Santa Lucía, *Arg.* **51** L4
Santa Lucia Range, *Calif., U.S.* **42** F2
Santa Maria, *Braz.* **50** D6
Santa Maria, *Braz.* **51** K7
Santa Maria, *Calif., U.S.* **40** F2
Santa María, Isla, *Ecua.* **97** F16
Santa Maria da Vitória, *Braz.* **50** G9
Santa María de Nanay, *Peru* **50** D3
Santa Marta, *Col.* **50** A3
Santa Marta Grande, Cape, *Braz.* **53** K8
Santana, *Braz.* **50** F10
Santana do Araguaia, *Braz.* **50** E8
Santana do Livramento, *Braz.* **51** K7
Santander, *Sp.* **58** H3
Santarém, *Braz.* **50** D7
Santarém, *Port.* **58** J1
Santa Rita do Weil, *Braz.* **50** D4
Santa Rosa, *island,* Calif., U.S. **42** G2
Santa Rosa, *Arg.* **51** M5
Santa Rosa, *Bol.* **50** F4
Santa Rosa, *Calif., U.S.* **40** E2
Santa Rosa, *Peru* **50** F4
Santa Rosalía, *Mex.* **37** M3
Santa Teresa, *N. Terr., Austral.* **88** F9
Santa Teresinha, *Braz.* **50** F8
Santa Vitória do Palmar, *Braz.* **51** L7
Santee, *river, S.C., U.S.* **43** G14
San Telmo Point, *Mex.* **39** P4
Santiago, *Chile* **51** L4
Santiago, *Dom. Rep.* **37** N10
Santiago, *Pan.* **37** Q9
Santiago, Isla, *Ecua.* **97** E16
Santiago de Compostela, *Sp.* **58** H2
Santiago de Cuba, *Cuba* **37** N9
Santiago del Estero, *Arg.* **50** K5
Santo André, *Braz.* **50** J9
Santo Ângelo, *Braz.* **51** K7
Santo Antônio do Içá, *Braz.* **50** D4
Santo Corazón, *Bol.* **50** G6
Santo Domingo, *Dom. Rep.* **37** N10
Santos, *Braz.* **50** J9
Santos Dumont, *Braz.* **50** E4
Santo Tomé, *Arg.* **51** K7
San Vincente del Caguán, *Col.* **50** C3
São Borja, *Braz.* **51** K7
São Carlos, *Braz.* **50** J9
São Félix, *Braz.* **50** F8
São Félix do Xingu, *Braz.* **50** E8
São Francisco, *river, Braz.* **52** F11
São Gabriel, *Braz.* **51** K7
São Gabriel da Cachoeira, *Braz.* **50** C4
São João da Aliança, *Braz.* **50** G9
São João del Rei, *Braz.* **50** H9
São José de Anauá, *Braz.* **50** C6
São José do Rio Prêto, *Braz.* **50** H8
São José dos Campos, *Braz.* **50** J9
São Leopoldo, *Braz.* **51** K8
São Luís, *Braz.* **50** D10
Sao Manuel *see* Teles Pires, *river, Braz.* **50** E7
São Marcos Bay, *Braz.* **52** D10
São Mateus, *Braz.* **50** H10
São Miguel do Araguaia, *Braz.* **50** F8
Saône, *river, Fr.* **60** G5
São Paulo, *Braz.* **50** J9
São Paulo de Olivença, *Braz.* **50** D4
São Raimundo Nonato, *Braz.* **50** F10
São Romão, *Braz.* **50** E4
São Roque, Cape, *Braz.* **52** E12
São Sebastião, Cape, *Mozambique* **81** N10
São Tomé, *island, São Tomé and Príncipe* **80** K5
São Tomé, *São Tomé and Príncipe* **78** K5
São Tomé, Cape, *Braz.* **52** J10
São Tomé and Príncipe, *Af.* **78** J5
Sapporo, *Jap.* **69** E13
Sarajevo, *Bosn. Herzg.* **58** J7
Saranac Lake, *N.Y., U.S.* **41** C15
Saransk, *Russ.* **59** E12
Sarapul, *Russ.* **59** D13
Sarasota, *Fla., U.S.* **41** K14
Saratov, *Russ.* **59** E12
Sarawak, *region, Malaysia* **69** L12
Sardegna (Sardinia), *island, It.* **58** J5
Sardinia, *island, It.* **60** J5
Sarh, *Chad* **78** H7
Sarigan, *island, N. Mariana Is.* **96** D3
Sarina, *Qnsld., Austral.* **89** F14
Sarmi, *Indonesia* **92** B3
Saryözek, *Kaz.* **68** F8
Saskatchewan, *Can.* **36** G5
Saskatchewan, *river, Can.* **38** G5
Saskatoon, *Sask., Can.* **36** G5
Sasolburg, *S. Af.* **79** P8
Sasovo, *Russ.* **59** E11
Sassafras Mountain, *S.C., U.S.* **43** G13
Sassandra, *Côte d'Ivoire* **78** J3
Sassari, *It.* **58** J5
Satadougou Tintiba, *Mali* **78** G2
Satawal, *island, F.S.M.* **96** E3
Saudi Arabia, *Asia* **68** G3
Saukorem, *Indonesia* **92** A1
Sault Sainte Marie, *Mich., U.S.* **41** C12
Sault Sainte Marie, *Ont., Can.* **36** H7
Saunders Coast, *Antarctica* **102** K6
Saurimo, *Angola* **79** L7
Sava, *river, Europe* **60** H8
Savai'i, *island, Samoa* **96** G7
Savannah, *river, Ga.-S.C., U.S.* **43** H14
Savannah, *Ga., U.S.* **41** H14
Savannakhet, *Laos* **69** J11
Save, *river, Mozambique* **81** N9
Savissivik, *Greenland* **36** C7
Savonlinna, *Fin.* **58** C9
Savoonga, *Alas., U.S.* **40** K1
Savu Sea, *Indonesia* **90** A3
Sawdā', Jabal as, *Lib.* **80** E6
Sawkanah, *Lib.* **78** E6
Sawu, *island, Indonesia* **90** A4
Saxby Downs, *homestead, Qnsld., Austral.* **89** E12
Saylac, *Somalia* **78** G11
Saywūn, *Yemen* **68** J3
Scandinavia, *region, Europe* **60** D7
Schefferville, *Nfld. and Lab., Can.* **36** F9
Schell Creek Range, *Nev., U.S.* **42** E4
Schenectady, *N.Y., U.S.* **41** D15
Schouten Islands, *P.N.G.* **92** B5
Scilly, Isles of, *U.K.* **58** F3
Scioto, *river, Ohio, U.S.* **43** E13
Scotland, *U.K.* **58** D4
Scott Base, *station, Antarctica* **102** K9
Scott Coast, *Antarctica* **102** K9
Scott Glacier, *Antarctica* **103** H15
Scottsbluff, *Nebr., U.S.* **40** E7
Scottsdale, *Ariz., U.S.* **40** G5
Scranton, *Pa., U.S.* **41** D15
Scrubby Creek, *Qnsld., Austral.* **89** B12
Sea Islands, *Ga., U.S.* **43** H14
Sea Lake, *Vic., Austral.* **89** L11
Seaton Glacier, *Antarctica* **103** C14
Seattle, *Wash., U.S.* **40** B3
Sebakor, Teluk, *Indonesia* **92** B1
Sebastián Vizcaíno Bay, *Mex.* **39** L3
Sebring, *Fla., U.S.* **41** K14
Sechura Desert, *Peru* **52** E1
Secretary Island, *N.Z.* **92** N2
Securé, *river, Bol.* **52** G5
Seddon, *N.Z.* **92** L5
Seg, Lake, *Russ.* **60** C10
Segezha, *Russ.* **58** C10
Ségou, *Mali* **78** G3
Segovia, *Sp.* **58** J3
Seinäjoki, *Fin.* **58** C8
Seine, *river, Fr.* **60** G4
Sekondi-Takoradi, *Ghana* **78** J3
Selawik, *Alas., U.S.* **40** K2
Selawik Lake, *Alas., U.S.* **42** J2
Seldovia, *Alas., U.S.* **40** L3
Selenga, *river, Mongolia-Russ.* **71** E10
Selkirk Mountains, *Can.* **38** G4
Sellheim, *Qnsld., Austral.* **89** E13
Selma, *Ala., U.S.* **41** H12
Selvas, *region, Braz.* **52** E3
Selwyn, *Qnsld., Austral.* **89** E11
Selwyn Mountains, *Can.* **38** E3
Semarang, *Indonesia* **69** M12
Semenov, *Russ.* **59** D12
Semey, *Kaz.* **68** F8
Seminole, Lake, *Fla.-Ga., U.S.* **43** J13
Sena Madureira, *Braz.* **50** F4
Sendai, *Jap.* **69** E14
Sénégal, *river, Mali-Maurit.-Senegal* **80** G2
Senegal, *Af.* **78** G1
Sennar, *Sudan* **78** G9
Sentinel Range, *Antarctica* **102** F5
Senyavin Islands, *F.S.M.* **96** E4
Seoul, *S. Korea* **69** F12
Sepik, *river, P.N.G.* **92** B4
Sept-Îles, *Que., Can.* **36** G9
Serbia and Montenegro, *Europe* **58** H8
Serdobsk, *Russ.* **59** E12
Serengeti Plain, *Tanzania* **81** K10
Sergino, *Russ.* **59** A13
Serov, *Russ.* **59** B13
Serowe, *Botswana* **79** N8
Serpentine Lakes, *S. Austral.-W. Austral., Austral.* **90** H7
Serpukhov, *Russ.* **59** E11
Serrinha, *Braz.* **50** F11
Sertão, *region, Braz.* **52** F10
Sesfontein, *Namibia* **79** N6
Sete Lagoas, *Braz.* **50** H9
Sete Quedas Falls, *Braz.-Para.* **52** J7
Sétif, *Alg.* **78** C5
Settat, *Mor.* **78** D3
Setúbal, *Port.* **58** J1
Sevastopol', *Ukr.* **59** H11
Severn, *river, Can.* **38** G7
Severn, *S. Af.* **79** P8
Severnaya Dvina (Northern Dvina), *river, Russ.* **59** C11
Severnaya Zemlya (North Land), *Russ.* **68** B9
Severobaykal'sk, *Russ.* **69** E10
Severodvinsk, *Russ.* **59** B10
Severoural'sk, *Russ.* **59** B13
Severo Yeniseyskiy, *Russ.* **68** D9
Sevier Lake, *Utah, U.S.* **42** E5
Sevilla, *Sp.* **58** K2
Seward, *Alas., U.S.* **40** L3
Seward Peninsula, *Alas., U.S.* **42** K2
Seychelles, *Ind. Oc.* **68** M3
Seychelles, *islands,* Ind. Oc. **70** M4
Seylla Glacier, *Antarctica* **103** D13
Seymchan, *Russ.* **69** C12
Seymour, *Vic., Austral.* **89** L12
Sfax, *Tun.* **78** D6
Shache, *China* **68** G7
Shackleton Coast, *Antarctica* **102** J9
Shackleton Ice Shelf, *Antarctica* **103** H15
Shackleton Range, *Antarctica* **102** D7
Shag Rocks, *S. Georgia* **53** R9
Shakhty, *Russ.* **59** G12
Shalqar, *Kaz.* **59** E15
Shamattawa, *Manitoba, Can.* **36** G6
Shambe, *Sudan* **78** H9
Shanghai, *China* **69** G12
Shannon, *river, Ire.* **60** E3
Shantar Islands, *Russ.* **71** D12
Shantou, *China* **69** H12
Shaoguan, *China* **69** H12
Shark Bay, *W. Austral., Austral.* **90** G1
Sharpe, Lake, *S. Dak., U.S.* **42** D9
Shar'ya, *Russ.* **59** D12
Shashe, *river, Botswana-Zimb.* **81** N9
Shasta, Mount, *Calif., U.S.* **42** D3
Shawnee, *Okla., U.S.* **40** G9
Shay Gap, *W. Austral., Austral.* **88** E3
Shchüchїnsk, *Kaz.* **59** C16
Shebele, *river, Somalia* **80** J11
Sheboygan, *Wis., U.S.* **41** D12
Sheffield, *U.K.* **58** E4
Shelburne, *N.S., CAN.* **36** H10
Shelby, *Mont., U.S.* **40** B6
Shelikhova, Zaliv *see* Shelikhov Gulf, *Russ.* **69** C12
Shelikhov Gulf, *Russ.* **71** C12
Shelikof Strait, *Alas., U.S.* **42** M2
Shell Beach, *Guyana* **52** B6
Shenyang, *China* **69** F12
Shepparton, *Vic., Austral.* **89** L12
Sheridan, *Wyo., U.S.* **40** D7
Sherkaly, *Russ.* **59** A13
Sherman, *Tex., U.S.* **40** H9
Sherman Peak, *Idaho, U.S.* **42** D5
Shetland Islands, *U.K.* **60** C5
Sheyenne, *river,* N. Dak., U.S. **42** C9
Shihezi, *China* **68** F8
Shijiazhuang, *China* **69** G11
Shikoku, *island, Jap.* **71** F13
Shiliguri, *India* **68** H9
Shimanovsk, *Russ.* **69** E12
Shirase Coast, *Antarctica* **102** J7
Shirase Glacier, *Antarctica* **103** B12
Shīrāz, *Iran* **68** G4
Shire, *river, Malawi-Mozambique* **81** N10
Shishmaref, *Alas., U.S.* **40** J2
Shizuishan, *China* **69** G10
Shkodër, *Alban.* **58** J8
Sholapur, *India* **68** J7
Shoshone Falls, *Idaho, U.S.* **42** D5
Shoshone Mountains, *Nev., U.S.* **42** E4
Shoyna, *Russ.* **59** A10
Shreveport, *La., U.S.* **41** H10
Shubarkuduk, *Kaz.* **59** E14
Shumagin Islands, *U.S.* **39** R5
Shungnak, *Alas., U.S.* **40** J2
Shuya, *Russ.* **59** D11
Shymkent, *Kaz.* **68** F7
Sia, *Indonesia* **92** C2
Šiauliai, *Lith.* **58** E8
Sibay, *Russ.* **59** D14
Siberia, *region, Russ.* **70** D8
Sibidiro, *P.N.G.* **92** D4
Sibiti, *Congo* **79** K6
Sibiu, *Rom.* **58** H9
Sibu, *Malaysia* **69** L12
Sibut, *Cen. Af. Rep.* **78** J7
Sichuan Basin, *China* **71** H10
Sicily, *island, It.* **60** K6
Sidi Bel Abbès, *Alg.* **78** C4
Sidi Ifni, *Mor.* **78** D3
Sidmouth, Cape, *Qnsld., Austral.* **91** B12
Sidney, *Mont., U.S.* **40** C8
Sidney, *Nebr., U.S.* **40** E8
Sidra, Gulf of, *Lib.* **80** D7
Sierra Blanca Peak, *N. Mex., U.S.* **42** H7
Sierra Leone, *Af.* **78** H2
Sierra Nevada, *Calif., U.S.* **42** E3
Siguiri, *Guinea* **78** G2
Siirt, *Turk.* **59** J13
Sikasso, *Mali* **78** G3
Sikhote Alin' Range, *Russ.* **71** E13
Silet, *Alg.* **78** F5
Silver City, *N. Mex., U.S.* **40** H6
Silver Plains, *homestead, Qnsld., Austral.* **89** B12
Silverton, *Colo., U.S.* **40** F6
Silves, *Braz.* **50** D6
Simeulue, *island, Indonesia* **68** L10
Simferopol', *Ukr.* **59** H11
Simpson Desert, *N. Terr., Austral.* **90** G9
Sinai, *region, Egypt* **80** D9
Sinai, Mount, *Egypt* **80** E9
Sincelejo, *Col.* **50** A2
Singapore, *Asia* **69** L11
Singida, *Tanzania* **79** K10
Singkawang, *Indonesia* **69** L11
Singkiang, *region, China* **68** G8
Singleton, *N.S.W., AUSTRAL.* **89** K14
Sinop, *Braz.* **50** F7
Sinop, *Turk.* **59** J11
Siorapaluk, *Greenland* **36** C7
Sioux City, *Iowa, U.S.* **40** E9
Sioux Falls, *S. Dak., U.S.* **40** D9
Sioux Lookout, *Ont., Can.* **36** H6
Siping, *China* **69** F12
Siple, Mount, *Antarctica* **102** J4
Siple Coast, *Antarctica* **102** J7
Siple Island, *Antarctica* **102** J4
Siracusa, *It.* **58** K7
Siret, *river, Rom.* **60** H9
Siri, Jabal, *Egypt* **80** F9
Sir Thomas, Mount, *S. Austral., Austral.* **90** H7
Sitka, *Alas., U.S.* **40** M5
Sittwe, *Myanmar* **68** J9
Sivas, *Turk.* **59** J12
Sīwa, *Egypt* **78** D8
Skagerrak, *strait, Den.-Nor.* **60** D6
Skagway, *Alas., U.S.* **40** L5
Skeleton Coast, *Namibia* **81** N6
Skellefteå, *Sweden* **58** C8
Skien, *Nor.* **58** D6
Skikda, *Alg.* **78** C5
Skopje, *Maced.* **58** J8
Skovorodino, *Russ.* **69** E11
Skwentna, *Alas., U.S.* **40** L3
Skye, Island of, *U.K.* **58** D4
Slantsy, *Russ.* **58** D9
Slatina, *Rom.* **58** H9
Slave Coast, *Benin-Nig.-Togo* **80** J4
Slessor Glacier, *Antarctica* **102** D7
Slide Mountain, *N.Y., U.S.* **43** D15
Sligo, *Ire.* **58** E3
Slovakia, *Europe* **58** G8
Slovenia, *Europe* **58** H7
Słupsk, *Pol.* **58** F7
Smallwood Reservoir, *Can.* **38** G9
Smeïda *see* Taoudenni, *Mali* **78** F3
Smith *see* Sumisu, *island, Jap.* **96** B2
Smith Bay, *Alas., U.S.* **42** H3
Smith Bay, *Can.-Greenland* **38** C7
Smithers, *B.C., Can.* **36** F3
Smith Glacier, *Antarctica* **102** H4
Smokey Hill, *river, Colo.-Kans., U.S.* **42** F8
Smoky Bay, *S. Austral., Austral.* **88** J9
Smoky Hills, *Kans., U.S.* **42** F9
Smolensk, *Russ.* **59** E10
Smolensk-Moscow Upland, *Russ.* **61** E10
Smyley Island, *Antarctica* **102** F3
Snake, *river, U.S.* **38** H3
Snake, *river, U.S.* **42** B4
Snake River Plain, *Idaho, U.S.* **42** D5
Sneeu Berg, *S. Af.* **81** Q8
Snowdon, *peak, U.K.* **60** E4
Snow Hill Island, *Antarctica* **102** C2
Snowy, *river, N.S.W.-Vic., Austral.* **91** M13
Snyder, *Tex., U.S.* **40** H8
Soala *see* Sokolo, *Mali* **78** G3
Sobradinho, Represa de (Sobradinho Reservoir), *Braz.* **50** F10
Sobradinho Reservoir, *Braz.* **52** F10
Sobral, *Braz.* **50** D11
Sochi, *Russ.* **59** H12
Society Islands, *Fr. Polynesia* **96** G10
Socorro, *N. Mex., U.S.* **40** H6
Socorro Island, *Mex.* **39** N3
Socotra, *island, Yemen* **70** J4
Sodo, *Eth.* **78** H10
Sofia *see* Sofiya, *Bulg.* **58** J9
Sofiya (Sofia), *Bulg.* **58** J9
Sōfu Gan (Lot's Wife), *island, Jap.* **96** B2
Sogamoso, *Col.* **50** B3
Sognefjorden, *fjord, Nor.* **60** C6
Sokhumi, *Ga., U.S.* **59** H12
Sokodé, *Togo* **78** H4
Sokol, *Russ.* **59** D11
Sokolo (Soala), *Mali* **78** G3
Sokoto, *Nig.* **78** G5
Solander Island, *N.Z.* **92** P2
Solikamsk, *Russ.* **59** C13
Solimões *see* Amazon, *river, Braz.* **52** D5
Solitary Islands, *N.S.W., AUSTRAL.* **91** J15
Sol'Iletsk, *Russ.* **59** E14
Solomon, *river,* Kans., U.S. **42** F9
Solomon Islands, *Pac. Oc.* **96** F5
Solomon Sea, *P.N.G.* **92** D7
Somalia, *Af.* **78** J12
Somaliland, *region, Somalia* **78** H11
Somali Peninsula, *Eth.-Somalia* **80** H12
Somerset Island, *Can.* **38** D6
Sommariva, *Qnsld., Austral.* **89** G13
Somuncurá, Meseta de, *Arg.* **53** N5
Songea, *Tanzania* **79** L10
Songhua, *river, China* **71** E12
Songhua Hu, *China* **71** F12
Sonora, *Tex., U.S.* **40** J8
Sonoran Desert, *Mex.-U.S.* **39** L3
Sonsonate, *El Salv.* **37** P7
Sonsorol Islands, *Palau* **96** E2
Sorocaba, *Braz.* **50** J9
Sorong, *Indonesia* **69** L15
Sorong, *Indonesia* **92** A1
Soroti, *Uganda* **78** J9
Sørøya, *island, Nor.* **58** A8
Sør Rondane Mountains, *Antarctica* **103** B10
Sortavala, *Russ.* **58** C9
Sosnogorsk, *Russ.* **59** B12
Sos'va, *Russ.* **59** A13
Sos'va, *Russ.* **59** B14
Soudan, *homestead, N. Terr., Austral.* **88** E10
Soure, *Braz.* **50** D9
Souris, *river, Can.-U.S.* **42** B8
Sousa, *Braz.* **50** E11
Sousse, *Tun.* **78** C6
South Africa, *Af.* **79** P8
South Alligator, *river, N. Terr., Austral.* **90** B8
Southampton, *U.K.* **58** F4
Southampton Island, *Can.* **38** E7
South Australia, *Austral.* **88** H9
South Bend, *Ind., U.S.* **41** E12
South Cape *see* Kalae, *Hawaii, U.S.* **43** M12
South Carolina, *U.S.* **41** G14
South China Sea, *Asia* **71** K12
South Dakota, *U.S.* **40** D8
Southern Alps, *N.Z.* **92** M3
Southern Bug, *river, Ukr.* **61** G10
Southern Cross, *W. Austral., Austral.* **88** J4
Southern Uplands, *U.K.* **60** E4
Southesk Tablelands, *W. Austral., Austral.* **90** E6
South Geomagnetic Pole, *Antarctica* **103** H11
South Georgia, *island, Atl. Oc.* **53** R9
South Island, *N.Z.* **92** M4
South Korea, *Asia* **69** F13
South Magnetic Pole, *Antarctica* **103** M13
South Orkney Islands, *Antarctica* **102** A2
South Platte, *river, Colo.-Nebr.* **42** E8
South Saskatchewan, *river, Can.* **38** H5
South Shetland Islands, *Antarctica* **102** C1
South Taranaki Bight, *N.Z.* **92** J5
South West Cape, *Tas., Austral.* **91** M15
Sovetsk, *Russ.* **59** D12
Sovetskiy, *Russ.* **59** B13
Soweto, *S. Af.* **79** P8
Soyo, *Angola* **79** L6
Spaatz Island, *Antarctica* **102** E3
Spain, *Europe* **58** J3
Spartanburg, *S.C., U.S.* **41** G14
Spencer, *Iowa, U.S.* **41** D10
Spencer, Cape, *S. Austral., Austral.* **90** L9
Spencer Gulf, *S. Austral., Austral.* **90** K10
Spitsbergen, *islands, Nor.* **68** A7
Split, *Croatia* **58** J7
Split Lake, *Manitoba, Can.* **36** G6
Spokane, *Wash., U.S.* **40** B4
Spooner, *Wis., U.S.* **41** C11
Sporades, *islands, Gr.* **60** K9
Spring Creek, *homestead, W. Austral., Austral.* **88** C7
Springer, *N. Mex., U.S.* **40** G7
Springfield, *Ill., U.S.* **41** E11
Springfield, *Mass., U.S.* **41** D16
Springfield, *Mo., U.S.* **41** F10
Springfield, *Ohio, U.S.* **41** E13
Springfield, *Oreg., U.S.* **40** C3
Spring Mountains, *Nev., U.S.* **42** F4
Springsure, *Qnsld., Austral.* **89** G14
Spruce Knob, *W. Va., U.S.* **43** E14
Srednekolymsk, *Russ.* **69** B11
Sri Lanka, *Asia* **68** L8
Srinagar, *India* **68** G7
St. Michael, *Alas., U.S.* **40** K2
Staked Plain *see* Estacado, Llano, *U.S.* **39** L5
Stancomb-Wills Glacier, *Antarctica* **102** C7
Stanley, *Falkland Is.* **51** Q6
Stanley, *N. Dak., U.S.* **40** B8
Stanley, *Tas., Austral.* **89** L15
Stanovoy Range, *Russ.* **71** D11
Stara Zagora, *Bulg.* **58** J9
Starbuck Island, *Kiribati* **96** F9
Staryy Oskol, *Russ.* **59** F11
Staten Island, *Arg.* **53** R6
Staunton, *Va., U.S.* **41** F14
Stavanger, *Nor.* **58** D6
Stavropol', *Russ.* **59** H12
Stavropol' Plateau, *Russ.* **61** G13
Stawell, *Vic., Austral.* **89** L11
Steens Mountain, *Oreg., U.S.* **42** D4
Steinkjer, *Nor.* **58** C7
Stepanakert, *Azerb.* **59** J14
Stephenson, Mount, *Antarctica* **102** E3
Stepnyak, *Kaz.* **59** C16
Sterlitamak, *Russ.* **59** D14
Stewart, *B.C., Can.* **36** F3
Stewart Island, *N.Z.* **92** P3
Stillwater, *Okla., U.S.* **40** G9
Stockholm, *Sweden* **58** D8
Stockton, *Calif., U.S.* **40** E3
Stokes, Mount, *N.Z.* **92** K5
Stonehenge, *Qnsld., Austral.* **89** G12
Storavan, *lake, Sweden* **60** B8
Stornoway, *U.K.* **58** D4
Storuman, *Sweden* **58** C7
Strahan, *Tas., Austral.* **89** M15
Strangways, *S. Austral., Austral.* **88** H9
Strasbourg, *Fr.* **58** G5
Strathalbyn, *S. Austral., Austral.* **89** L10
Strathcona, Mount, *Antarctica* **103** H15
Streaky Bay, *S. Austral., Austral.* **88** K9
Strickland, *river, P.N.G.* **92** C4
Stuart Island, *Alas., U.S.* **42** K2
Stuart Range, *S. Austral., Austral.* **90** H9
Stuart Stony Desert, *S. Austral., Austral.* **91** G11
Stuttgart, *Ger.* **58** G6
Suakin Archipelago, *Sudan* **80** F10
Subotica, *Serbia and Montenegro* **58** H8
Sucre, *Bol.* **50** H5
Sudan, *Af.* **78** G9
Sudan, *region, Af.* **80** H3
Sudbury, *Ont., Can.* **36** H8
Sudd, *wetland, Sudan* **80** H9
Sudeten, *region, Czech Rep.* **60** G7
Suez *see* El Suweis, *Egypt* **78** D9
Suez, Gulf of, *Egypt* **80** E9
Suez Canal, *Egypt* **80** D9
Sukhona, *river, Russ.* **61** C11
Sukkur, *Pak.* **68** H6
Sula, Kepulauan, *Indonesia* **96** F1
Sulawesi *see* Celebes, *island, Indonesia* **69** L13
Sullana, *Peru* **50** E1
Sulphur, *river, Ark.-Tex., U.S.* **43** H10
Sulu Sea, *Malaysia-Philippines* **71** K13
Sumatra, *island, Indonesia* **71** L10
Sumba, *island, Indonesia* **71** M13
Sumbawa, *island, Indonesia* **71** M13
Sumbawanga, *Tanzania* **79** L9
Sumbe, *Angola* **79** M6
Sumisu (Smith), *island, Jap.* **96** B2
Sumqayıt, *Azerb.* **59** H14
Sumy, *Ukr.* **59** F11
Sunbury, *Vic., Austral.* **89** M12
Sunday *see* Raoul Island, *N.Z.* **96** J7
Sunderland, *U.K.* **58** E4
Sundsvall, *Sweden* **58** C7
Sunflower, Mount, *Kans., U.S.* **42** F8
Sun Valley, *Idaho, U.S.* **40** D5
Suomen Ridge, *Fin.* **60** C9
Superior, *Wis., U.S.* **41** C10
Superior, Lake, *Can.-U.S.* **43** C11
Supiori, *island, Indonesia* **92** A2
Support Force Glacier, *Antarctica* **102** E7
Suquṭrá *see* Socotra, *island, Yemen* **68** J4
Şūr, *Oman* **68** H5
Sur, Point, *Calif., U.S.* **42** F2
Sura, *river, Russ.* **61** E12
Surabaya, *Indonesia* **69** M12
Surat, *India* **68** J7
Surat, *Qnsld., Austral.* **89** H14
Surat Thani, *Thai.* **69** K10
Surgut, *Russ.* **59** A15
Suriname, *S. America* **50** B7
Surt, *Lib.* **78** D7
Surtsey, *island, Ice.* **60** B3
Susanville, *Calif., U.S.* **40** D3
Susitna, *river,* Alas., U.S. **42** L3
Susquehanna, *river, Md.-Pa., U.S.* **43** E15
Susuman, *Russ.* **69** C12
Susunu, *Indonesia* **92** B2
Sutlej, *river, India-Pak.* **70** H7
Suva, *Fiji* **96** G6
Suwannee, *river, Fla.-Ga., U.S.* **43** J14
Suwarrow Atoll, *Cook Is.* **96** G8
Svobodnyy, *Russ.* **69** E12
Svolvær, *Nor.* **58** B7
Swain Reefs, *Austral.* **91** F15
Swains Island, *American Samoa* **96** G8
Swakopmund, *Namibia* **79** N6
Swan, *river, W. Austral., Austral.* **90** K2
Swansea, *U.K.* **58** F4
Swart Berg, *S. Af.* **81** Q7
Swaziland, *Af.* **79** P9
Sweden, *Europe* **58** D7
Sweeney Mountains, *Antarctica* **102** E4
Sweetwater, *Tex., U.S.* **40** H8
Swift Current, *Sask., Can.* **36** H5
Switzerland, *Europe* **58** H5
Sydney, *N.S., CAN.* **36** H10
Sydney, *N.S.W., AUSTRAL.* **89** L14
Syktyvkar, *Russ.* **59** C12
Sylvester, Lake, *N. Terr., Austral.* **90** D9
Synya, *Russ.* **59** A12
Syowa, *station, Antarctica* **103** B12
Syracuse, *N.Y., U.S.* **41** D15
Syr Darya, *river, Kaz.* **70** F7
Syria, *Asia* **68** F3
Syrian Desert, *Asia* **70** F3
Syzran', *Russ.* **59** E13
Szczecin, *Pol.* **58** F7
Szeged, *Hung.* **58** H8

Términos Lagoon, *Mex.* **39** P7
Tabalo, *P.N.G.* **92** A6
Tabar Islands, *P.N.G.* **92** B7
Tabelbala, *Alg.* **78** D4
Tabiteuea, *island, Kiribati* **96** F6
Table Rock Lake, *Mo., U.S.* **43** G10
Tabora, *Tanzania* **79** K9
Tabrīz, *Iran* **68** F4
Tabuaeran (Fanning Island), *Kiribati* **96** E9
Tabūk, *Saudi Arabia* **68** G3
Tacheng, *China* **68** F8
Tacloban, *Philippines* **69** J13
Tacna, *Peru* **50** H4
Tacoma, *Wash., U.S.* **40** B3
Tacuarembó, *Uru.* **51** L7
Tacutu, *river, Braz.-Guyana* **52** C6
Tademaït Plateau, *Alg.* **80** E4
Tadjoura, Gulf of, *Djibouti* **80** G11
Tafahi, *island, Tonga* **96** G7
Taganrog, *Russ.* **59** G12
Tagant, *region, Maurit.* **80** F2
Tagounit, *Mor.* **78** D3
Taguatinga, *Braz.* **50** F9
Tagula, *island, P.N.G.* **92** E8
Tagus, *river, Port.-Sp.* **60** J1
Tahat, Mount, *Alg.* **80** F5
Tahiti, *island, Fr. Polynesia* **97** G10
Tahoe, Lake, *Calif.-Nev.* **42** E3
Tahoua, *Niger* **78** G5
Tahuata, *island, Marquesas Is.* **97** F11
Taihape, *N.Z.* **92** J6
Tailem Bend, *S. Austral., Austral.* **89** L10
T'ainan, *Taiwan* **69** H12
T'aipei, *Taiwan* **69** H12
Taiwan, *Asia* **69** H13
Taiwan Strait, *China* **71** H12
Taiyuan, *China* **69** G11
Ta'izz, *Yemen* **68** J3
Tajarḥī, *Lib.* **78** E6
Tajikistan, *Asia* **68** G7
Tajo (Tagus), *river, Sp.* **58** J2
Tak, *Thai.* **69** J10

Takahe, Mount, Antarctica 102 H4
Takaka, N.Z. 92 K5
Takapau, N.Z. 92 K6
Takaroa, island, Fr. Polynesia 97 G10
Taklimakan Desert, China 70 G8
Taklimakan Shamo (Taklimakan Desert), China 68 G8
Talamanca, Cordillera de, C.R.-Pan. 39 Q8
Talara, Peru 50 E1
Talaud, Kepulauan, Indonesia 96 E1
Talbot, Cape, W. Austral., Austral. 90 B6
Talca, Chile 51 M4
Taldora, homestead, Qnsld., Austral. 89 E11
Taldyqorghan, Kaz. 68 F8
Talia, S. Austral., Austral. 88 K9
Talkeetna Mountains, Alas., U.S. 42 L3
Tallahassee, Fla., U.S. 41 J13
Tallinn, Est. 58 D8
Tallulah, La., U.S. 41 H11
Talos Dome, Antarctica 103 L10
Taloyoak, Nunavut 36 D6
Taltal, Chile 50 J4
Tamale, Ghana 78 H4
Tamana, island, Kiribati 96 F6
Tamanrasset, Alg. 78 F5
Tambacounda, Senegal 78 G2
Tambo, Qnsld., Austral. 89 G13
Tambov, Russ. 59 E12
Tambura, Sudan 78 J8
Tamchaket, Maurit. 78 F2
Tamel Aike, Arg. 51 Q4
Tampa, Fla., U.S. 41 J14
Tampa Bay, Fla., U.S. 43 K14
Tampere, Fin. 58 D8
Tampico, Mex. 37 N5
Tamworth, N.S.W., AUSTRAL. 89 J14
Tana, Lake, Eth. 80 G10
Tanacross, Alas., U.S. 40 K4
Tanahmerah, Indonesia 92 C4
Tanami, N. Terr., Austral. 88 E7
Tanami, Mount, N. Terr., Austral. 90 E7
Tanami Desert, N. Terr., Austral. 90 D8
Tanana, river, Alas., U.S. 42 K4
Tanana, Alas., U.S. 40 K3
Tandil, Arg. 51 M6
Tandil, Sierra del, Arg. 53 M6
Tanega Shima, island, Jap. 96 B2
Tanezrouft, region, Alg. 80 E4
Tanga, Tanzania 79 K10
Tanga Islands, P.N.G. 92 B8
Tanganyika, Lake, Af. 81 L9
Tange Promontory, Antarctica 103 B13
Tanggula Range, China 70 H9
Tangier, Mor. 78 C3
Tangorin, Qnsld., Austral. 89 E12
Tangshan, China 69 F11
Tanimbar, Kepulauan (Tanimbar Islands), Indonesia 69 L15
Tanimbar Islands, Indonesia 71 L15
Tanna, island, Vanuatu 96 G6
Tânout, Niger 78 G5
Ţanţa, Egypt 78 D9
Tan-Tan, Mor. 78 D2
Tanumbirini, homestead, N. Terr., Austral. 88 C9
Tanzania, Af. 79 L10
Taongi Atoll, Marshall Is. 96 D5
Taoudenni (Smeïda), Mali 78 F3
Tapachula, Mex. 37 P6
Tapajós, river, Braz. 52 D7
Tapawera, N.Z. 92 K5
Tapeta, Liberia 78 H2
Tapini, P.N.G. 92 D6
Tapuaenuku, peak, N.Z. 92 L5
Tapurucuará, Braz. 50 D5
Tar, river, N.C., U.S. 43 F15
Tara, Qnsld., Austral. 89 H14
Tara, Russ. 59 B16
Ţarābulus (Tripoli), Lib. 78 D6
Taranaki, Mount (Mount Egmont), N.Z. 92 J5
Taranto, It. 58 K7
Tarapoto, Peru 50 E2
Tarawa (Bairiki), town, Kiribati 96 E6
Tarawera, Mount, N.Z. 92 H6
Taraz, Kaz. 68 F7
Tarazit Massif, Niger 80 F5
Tarbrax, homestead, Qnsld., Austral. 89 E12
Tarcoola, S. Austral., Austral. 88 J9
Tardun, W. Austral., Austral. 88 J2
Taree, N.S.W., AUSTRAL. 89 K15
Tari, P.N.G. 92 C4
Tarija, Bol. 50 H5
Tariku-Taritatu Plain, Indonesia 92 B3
Tarim, river, China 70 G8
Tarim Basin, China 70 G8
Taritatu, river, Indonesia 92 B3
Taroom, Qnsld., Austral. 89 G14
Tarrabool Lake, N. Terr., Austral. 90 D9
Tarragona, Sp. 58 J4
Tarraleah, Tas., Austral. 89 M16
Tarras, N.Z. 92 N3
Tartu, Est. 58 D9
Tasāwah, Lib. 78 E6
Tashkent see Toshkent, Uzb. 68 F7
Tasiilaq, Greenland 36 C10
Tasiusaq, Greenland 36 C8
Tasman, N.Z. 92 K5
Tasman Bay, N.Z. 92 K5
Tasmania, Austral. 89 M15
Tasman Peninsula, Tas., Austral. 91 M16
Tasman Sea, Pac. Oc. 96 K5
Tassili-n-Ajjer, Alg. 80 E5
Tassili Oua-n-Ahaggar, region, Alg. 80 F5
Tatakoto, island, Fr. Polynesia 97 G11
Tatarsk, Russ. 59 B16
Tatarskiy Proliv (Tatar Strait), Russ. 69 D13
Tatar Strait, Russ. 71 D13
Tatnam, Cape, Can. 38 F6
Tauá, Braz. 50 E10
Taumarunui, N.Z. 92 J6
Taumatawhakatangihangakoauauotamateapokai-whenuakitanatahu, peak, N.Z. 92 K6
Taum Sauk Mountain, Mo., U.S. 43 F11
Taupo, N.Z. 92 J6
Taupo, Lake, N.Z. 92 J6
Tauranga, N.Z. 92 H6
Taurus Mountains, Turk. 70 E3
Tavda, Russ. 59 B14
Taveuni, island, Fiji 96 G7
Taylor Glacier, Antarctica 102 K9
Taymyr, Lake, Russ. 70 C9
Taymyr, Poluostrov (Taymyr Peninsula), Russ. 68 C9
Taymyr Peninsula, Russ. 70 C9
Taz, river, Russ. 70 D8
Taza, Mor. 78 C4
Tāzirbū, Lib. 78 E7
T'bilisi, Ga. 59 H13
Tchibanga, Gabon 79 K6
Tchin-Tabaradene, Niger 78 G5
Te Anau, N.Z. 92 N3
Te Anau, Lake, N.Z. 92 N3
Tea Tree, N. Terr., Austral. 88 E8
Techla, W. Sahara 78 F2
Tecka, Arg. 51 N4
Tecomán, Mex. 37 N4
Tecuala, Mex. 37 N4
Tefé, Braz. 50 D5
Tegucigalpa, Hond. 37 P7
Te Hapua, N.Z. 92 F5
Tehrān, Iran 68 G5
Tehuacán, Mex. 37 P6
Tehuantepec, Mex. 37 P6
Tehuantepec, Gulf of, Mex. 39 P6
Tehuantepec, Isthmus of, Mex. 39 P6
Tekapo, Lake, N.Z. 92 M4
Te Karaka, N.Z. 92 J7
Tekirdağ, Turk. 59 J10
Telefomin, P.N.G. 92 C4
Teles Pires, river, Braz. 52 E7
Teljo, Jebel, Sudan 80 G8
Tell Atlas, mountains, Alg. 80 C4
Teller, Alas., U.S. 40 K1
Tema, Ghana 78 J4
Tematagi, island, Fr. Polynesia 97 H11
Teminabuan, Indonesia 92 A1
Temoe, island, Fr. Polynesia 97 H11
Temora, N.S.W., AUSTRAL. 89 L13
Temple, Tex., U.S. 40 J9
Temple Bay, Qnsld., Austral. 91 B12
Temuco, Chile 51 M4
Temuka, N.Z. 92 M4
Ténéré, region, Niger 80 F6
Tenerife, island, Canary Is. 80 D2
Tengiz, Lake, Kaz. 70 E7
Tenkeli, Russ. 69 B11
Tenkodogo, Burkina Faso 78 G4
Tennant Creek, N. Terr., Austral. 88 E9
Tennessee, river, U.S. 43 G12
Tennessee, U.S. 41 G12
Teófilo Otoni, Braz. 50 H10
Tepic, Mex. 37 N4
Teraina (Washington Island), Kiribati 96 E9
Teramo, It. 58 J7
Terek, river, Russ. 61 H13
Teresina, Braz. 50 E10
Termiz, Uzb. 68 G6
Ternate, Indonesia 69 L14
Terni, It. 58 J6
Ternopil', Ukr. 58 G9
Terrace, B.C., Can. 36 F3
Terrebonne Bay, La., U.S. 43 J11
Terre Haute, Ind., U.S. 41 F12
Teshekpuk Lake, Alas., U.S. 42 J3
Tesouro, Braz. 50 G7
Tessalit, Mali 78 F4
Tete, Mozambique 79 M9
Te Teko, N.Z. 92 H6
Tétouan, Mor. 78 C3
Tewantin, Qnsld., Austral. 89 H15
Texarkana, Ark., U.S. 41 H10
Texas, U.S. 40 J8
Texas City, Tex., U.S. 41 J10
Texoma, Lake, Okla.-Tex., U.S. 42 H9
Thabana Ntlenyana, peak, Lesotho 81 Q9
Thailand, Asia 69 K10
Thailand, Gulf of, Asia 71 K10
Thames, river, U.K. 60 F4
Thangool, Qnsld., Austral. 89 G15
Thargomindah, Qnsld., Austral. 89 H12
The Caves, Qnsld., Austral. 89 F15
The Dalles, Oreg., U.S. 40 C3
Theebine, Qnsld., Austral. 89 G15
The Everglades, wetland, Fla., U.S. 43 K14
The Father, peak, P.N.G. 92 C7
Thelon, river, Can. 38 E5
The Lynd, homestead, Qnsld., Austral. 89 D13
Theodore, Qnsld., Austral. 89 G14
The Pas, Manitoba, Can. 36 G5
The Pennines, mountains, U.K. 60 E4
The Remarkables, peak, N.Z. 92 N3
Thermopolis, Wyo., U.S. 40 D6
The Snares, islands, N.Z. 96 L5
Thessaloníki, Gr. 58 J9
Thessaly, region, Gr. 60 K8
The Steppes, Kaz. 70 E6
The Twins, homestead, S. Austral., Austral. 88 J9
Thief River Falls, Minn., U.S. 40 C9
Thimphu, Bhutan 68 H9
Thíra, island, Gr. 58 L9
Thohoyandou, S. Af. 79 P9
Thomasville, Ga., U.S. 41 J13
Thompson, Manitoba, Can. 36 G6
Thomson, river, Qnsld., Austral. 91 G12
Thorntonia, homestead, Qnsld., Austral. 89 E10
Three Kings Islands, N.Z. 92 F4
Throssell, Lake, W. Austral., Austral. 90 H5
Thunder Bay, Ont., Can. 36 H7
Thurso, U.K. 58 D4
Thurston Island, Antarctica 102 G3
Thylungra, homestead, Qnsld., Austral. 89 G12
Tianjin, China 69 G11
Tian Shan, Asia 70 G7
Tianshui, China 69 G10
Tiaro, Qnsld., Austral. 89 G15
Tiber, river, It. 60 J6
Tibesti, mountains, Chad 80 F7
Tibet, region, China 68 H8
Tibet, Plateau of, China 70 H8
Tibooburra, N.S.W., AUSTRAL. 89 H11
Tîchît, Maurit. 78 F2
Tidjikdja, Maurit. 78 F2
Tiel, Senegal 78 G1
Tierra del Fuego, island, Arg.-Chile 53 R5
Tieyon, homestead, S. Austral., Austral. 88 G9
Tiger Bay, Angola 81 N6
Tigris, river, Iraq-Turk. 70 F4
Tihamah, region, Saudi Arabia-Yemen 70 H3
Tijuana, Mex. 37 L3
Tikei, island, Fr. Polynesia 97 G10
Tikhoretsk, Russ. 59 G12
Tikhvin, Russ. 59 D10
Tikopia, island, Solomon Is. 96 G5
Tiksi, Russ. 69 C10
Tilbooroo, homestead, Qnsld., Austral. 89 H12
Tillabéri, Niger 78 G4
Tilpa, N.S.W., AUSTRAL. 89 J12
Timan Ridge, Russ. 61 B11
Timaru, N.Z. 92 M4
Timbalier Bay, La., U.S. 43 J11
Timbaúba, Braz. 50 E12
Timber Creek, N. Terr., Austral. 88 C7
Timbuktu see Tombouctou, Mali 78 G3
Timimoun, Alg. 78 D4
Timiris, Cape, Maurit. 80 F1
Timişoara, Rom. 58 H8
Timmiarmiut, Greenland 36 D10
Timmins, Ont., Can. 36 H8
Timms Hill, Wis., U.S. 43 C11
Timor, island, Indonesia-Timor-Leste 71 M14
Timor-Leste (East Timor), Asia 69 M14
Timor Sea, Austral.-Indonesia 90 A6
Tindouf, Alg. 78 E3
Tingmerkpuk Mountain, Alas., U.S. 42 J2
Tinian, island, N. Mariana Is. 69 H16
Tinian, island, N. Mariana Is. 96 D3
Tinnenburra, homestead, Qnsld., Austral. 89 H13
Tinogasta, Arg. 50 K5
Tinrhert, Hamada de, Alg.-Lib. 80 E5
Tintina, Arg. 50 K6
Tintinara, S. Austral., Austral. 89 L11
Ti-n-Zaouâtene, Alg. 78 F4
Tipperary, homestead, N. Terr., Austral. 88 B7
Tipuani, Bol. 50 G4
Tiracambu, Serra do, Braz. 52 D9
Tirana see Tiranë, Alban. 58 J8
Tiranë (Tirana), Alban. 58 J8
Tiraspol, Moldova 59 H10
Tîrgu Mureş, Rom. 58 H9
Tiruchchirappalli, India 68 K7
Tisza, river, Hung.-Serbia and Montenegro 60 H8
Titan Dome, Antarctica 102 G8
Titicaca, Lago (Lake Titicaca), Bol.-Peru 50 G4
Titicaca, Lake, Bol.-Peru 52 G4
Titusville, Fla., U.S. 41 J14
Tiz Ouzou, Alg. 78 C5
Tlaxiaco, Mex. 37 P5
Tmassah, Lib. 78 E6
Toamasina, Madag. 79 N12
Tobago, island, Trinidad and Tobago 39 P12
Tobermorey, homestead, N. Terr., Austral. 89 F10
Tobermory, homestead, Qnsld., Austral. 89 H12
Tobi, island, Palau 96 E2
Tobol, river, Kaz.-Russ. 70 E7
Tobol'sk, Russ. 59 B15
Tobruk see Ţubruq, Lib. 78 D8
Tobyl, river, Kaz. 59 D15
Tobyl, Kaz. 59 D15
Tocal, Qnsld., Austral. 89 F12
Tocantinópolis, Braz. 50 E9
Tocantins, river, Braz. 52 D8
Toconao, Chile 50 J4
Tocopilla, Chile 50 J4
Todmorden, homestead, S. Austral., Austral. 88 G9
Todo Santos, Peru 50 D3
Todos os Santos Bay, Braz. 52 G11
Togiak, Alas., U.S. 40 L2
Togliatti, Russ. 59 E13
Togo, Af. 78 H4
Toiyabe Range, Nev., U.S. 42 E4
Tok, Alas., U.S. 36 D2
Tokar, Sudan 78 F10
Tokat, Turk. 59 J12
Tokelau, islands, Pac. Oc. 96 F8
Tokomaru Bay, N.Z. 92 H7
Tokoroa, N.Z. 92 H6
Tōkyō, Jap. 69 F14
Tôlañaro, Madag. 79 P12
Tolarno, homestead, N.S.W., AUSTRAL. 89 K11
Tolchin, Mount, Antarctica 102 F7
Toledo, Ohio, U.S. 41 E13
Toledo, Sp. 58 J3
Toledo Bend Reservoir, La.-Tex., U.S. 43 H10
Toliara, Madag. 79 P11
Tomahawk, Wis., U.S. 41 C11
Tombador, Serra do, Braz. 52 F6
Tombigbee, river, Ala.-Miss., U.S. 43 H12
Tombouctou (Timbuktu), Mali 78 G3
Tombstone, Ariz., U.S. 40 H5
Tomé, Chile 51 M4
Tomo, river, Col. 52 B4
Tom Price, W. Austral., Austral. 88 F3
Tomsk, Russ. 68 E8
Tondou Massif, Cen. Af. Rep. 80 H8
Tonga, Pac. Oc. 96 H7
Tonga Islands, Tonga 96 G7
Tongareva see Penrhyn Atoll, Cook Is. 96 F9
Tongatapu Group, Tonga 96 H7
Tongliao, China 69 F12
Tongo, homestead, N.S.W., AUSTRAL. 89 J12
Tongtian (Yangtze), river, China 68 H9
Tongue, river, Mont.-Wyo., U.S. 42 C7
Tonkin, Gulf of, China-Viet. 71 J11
Tonle Sap, lake, Cambodia 71 K11
Tonopah, Nev., U.S. 40 F4
Toodyay, W. Austral., Austral. 88 K3
Tooele, Utah, U.S. 40 E5
Toompine, homestead, Qnsld., Austral. 89 H12
Toowoomba, Qnsld., Austral. 89 H15
Top, Lake, Russ. 60 B9
Topeka, Kans., U.S. 41 F10
Top Ozero (Lake Top), Russ. 58 B9
Top Springs, homestead, N. Terr., Austral. 88 C8
Torbay, W. Austral., Austral. 88 L3
Torino, It. 58 H5
Torneälven, river, Sweden 60 B8
Torngat Mountains, Can. 38 F9
Torokina, P.N.G. 92 C8
Toronto, Ont., Can. 36 J8
Torrens, Lake, S. Austral., Austral. 90 J10
Torreón, Mex. 37 M5
Torres Islands, Vanuatu 96 G5
Torres Strait, Qnsld., Austral. 91 A12
Tórshavn, Faroe Is. 58 C4
Tortuga Island, Venez. 52 A5
Toruń, Pol. 58 F8
Torzhok, Russ. 59 E10
Toshkent (Tashkent), Uzb. 68 F7
Totness, Suriname 50 B7
Tottan Hills, Antarctica 102 C7
Toubkal, Jebel, Mor. 80 D3
Touggourt, Alg. 78 D5
Toulon, Fr. 58 J5
Toulouse, Fr. 58 H4
Toummo, Niger 78 F6
Toungo, Nig. 78 H6
Tours, Fr. 58 G4
Touside, Pic, Chad 80 F6
Townsville, Qnsld., Austral. 89 E13
Towot, Sudan 78 H10
Toyama, Jap. 69 F13
Trabzon, Turk. 59 J12
Tralee, Ire. 58 E3
Trangan, island, Indonesia 92 C2
Trangie, N.S.W., AUSTRAL. 89 K13
Transantarctic Mountains, Antarctica 102 E7
Transylvania, region, Rom. 60 H9
Transylvanian Alps, mountains, Rom. 60 H9
Traralgon, Vic., Austral. 89 M13
Trarza, region, Maurit. 80 F1
Trayning, W. Austral., Austral. 88 J3
Tregrosse Islets, C.S.I. Terr., Austral. 91 D15
Treinta-y-Tres, Uru. 51 L7
Trelew, Arg. 51 N5
Tremblant, Mount, Can. 38 H9
Trenque Lauquen, Arg. 51 M6
Trento, It. 58 H6
Trenton, N.J., U.S. 41 E15
Trepassey, Nfld. and Lab., Can. 36 G11
Tres Arroyos, Arg. 51 M6
Tres Esquinas, Col. 50 C3
Três Lagoas, Braz. 50 H8
Tres Montes Peninsula, Chile 53 P4
Tres Puntas, Cape, Arg. 53 P5
Triabunna, Tas., Austral. 89 M16
Tribulation, Cape, Qnsld., Austral. 91 C13
Trieste, It. 58 H7
Trikora, Puncak, Indonesia 92 B3
Trindade, Braz. 50 G8
Trinidad, Trinidad and Tobago 39 P12
Trinidad, Bol. 50 G5
Trinidad, Colo., U.S. 40 F7
Trinidad and Tobago, N. America 37 P12
Trinity, river, Tex., U.S. 43 J10
Trinity Beach, Qnsld., Austral. 89 D13
Trinity Islands, Alas., U.S. 42 M3
Trinity Peninsula, Antarctica 102 C2
Tripoli see Ţarābulus, Lib. 78 D6
Tripolitania, region, Lib. 78 D6
Tristan da Cunha Group, Atl. Oc. 81 R2
Tristan da Cunha Island, Atl. Oc. 81 R2
Trivandrum, India 68 K7
Trobriand Islands, P.N.G. 92 D7
Trois-Rivières, Que., Can. 36 H9
Troitsk, Russ. 59 D15
Troitsko Pechorsk, Russ. 59 B12
Trollhättan, Sweden 58 D7
Tromsø, Nor. 58 A8
Trondheim, Nor. 58 C7
Trondheimsfjorden, fjord, Nor. 60 C6
Trout Lake, Can. 38 H6
Troyes, Fr. 58 G5
Troy Peak, Nev., U.S. 42 F4
Trujillo, Peru 50 F2
Truk Islands, F.S.M. 96 E4
Trumbull, Mount, Ariz., U.S. 42 F5
Truth or Consequences, N. Mex., U.S. 40 H6
Tsao see Tsau, Botswana 79 N8
Tsau (Tsao), Botswana 79 N8
Tshabong, Botswana 79 P8
Tshane, Botswana 79 P7
Tshikapa, D.R.C. 79 L7
Tsiigehtchic, N.W.T., CAN. 36 D4
Tsil'ma, river, Russ. 61 B11
Tsimlyansk Reservoir, Russ. 61 G12
Tuakau, N.Z. 92 H5
Tual, Indonesia 69 L15
Tuamotu Archipelago, Fr. Polynesia 97 G11
Tuapse, Russ. 59 H12
Tuatapere, N.Z. 92 N3
Tubarão, Braz. 51 K8
Tubmanburg, Liberia 78 H2
Ţubruq (Tobruk), Lib. 78 D8
Tubuai, island, Fr. Polynesia 97 H10
Tubuai Islands see Austral Islands, Fr. Polynesia 96 H9
Tucano, Braz. 50 F11
Tucson, Ariz., U.S. 40 H5
Tucumcari, N. Mex., U.S. 40 G7
Tucupita, Venez. 50 A6
Tucuruí, Braz. 50 D8
Tuen, Qnsld., Austral. 89 H13
Tufi, P.N.G. 92 D6
Tugela Falls, S. Af. 81 Q9
Tūkrah, Lib. 78 D7
Tuktoyaktuk, N.W.T., CAN. 36 D4
Tula, Russ. 59 E11
Tullah, Tas., Austral. 89 M15
Tullamore, N.S.W., AUSTRAL. 89 K13
Tully, Qnsld., Austral. 89 D13
Tulsa, Okla., U.S. 41 G10
Tuluá, Col. 50 C2
Tulun, Russ. 68 E9
Tumaco, Col. 50 C2
Tumbes, Peru 50 E1
Tumby Bay, S. Austral., Austral. 88 K9
Tumucumaque, Serra de, Braz. 52 C7
Tunis, Tun. 78 C6
Tunis, Gulf of, Tun. 80 C6
Tunisia, Af. 78 D6
Tunja, Col. 50 B3
Tununak, Alas., U.S. 40 L1
Tupelo, Miss., U.S. 41 H12
Tupungato, Cerro, Arg.-Chile 53 L4
Tura, Russ. 68 D9
Turan Lowland, Kaz.-Turkm.-Uzb. 70 F6
Turbat, Pak. 68 H6
Turbo, Col. 50 B2
Tureia, island, Fr. Polynesia 97 H11
Turkana, Lake (Lake Rudolf), Eth.-Kenya 80 J10
Turkey, Asia-Europe 59 K11
Turkey Creek, W. Austral., Austral. 88 D6
Türkmenbashy, Turkm. 68 F5
Turkmenistan, Asia 68 F6
Turks and Caicos Islands, N. America 37 M10
Turks Islands, Turks and Caicos Is. 39 N10
Turku, Fin. 58 D8
Turnagain, Cape, N.Z. 92 K6
Turner, Mont., U.S. 40 B6
Turpan, China 68 F9
Turpan Depression, China 70 G9
Tuscaloosa, Ala., U.S. 41 H12
Tutira, N.Z. 92 J6
Tutoko, Mount, N.Z. 92 M3
Tutuila, island, American Samoa 96 G8
Tuvalu, Pac. Oc. 96 F6
Tuwayq Mountains, Saudi Arabia 70 H3
Tuxpan, Mex. 37 N6
Tuxtla Gutiérrez, Mex. 37 P6
Tuz Gölü, Turk. 59 K11
Tuzla, Bosn. Herzg. 58 H8
Tver', Russ. 59 E10
Tweed Heads, N.S.W., AUSTRAL. 89 H15
Twin Falls, Idaho, U.S. 40 D5
Twin Peaks, Idaho, U.S. 42 C5
Twizel, N.Z. 92 M4
Tyler, Tex., U.S. 37 L6
Tyler, Tex., U.S. 41 H10
Tynda, Russ. 69 D11
Tyrrell, Lake, Vic., Austral. 91 L11
Tyrrhenian Sea, It. 60 K6
Tyukalinsk, Russ. 59 B16
Tyumen', Russ. 59 C14

Ua Huka, island, Marquesas Is. 97 F11
Ua Pu, island, Marquesas Is. 97 F11
Uaroo, homestead, W. Austral., Austral. 88 F2
Ubangi, river, Congo-D.R.C. 80 J7
Uberaba, Braz. 50 H9
Uberlândia, Braz. 50 H9
Ucayali, river, Peru 52 E3
Uchiza, Peru 50 F2
Udaipur, India 68 J7
Udon Thani, Thai. 69 J10
Uele, river, D.R.C. 80 J8
Uelen, Russ. 69 A12
Ufa, river, Russ. 61 C14
Ufa, Russ. 59 D14
Uganda, Af. 78 J9
Uige, Angola 79 L6
Uinta Mountains, Utah, U.S. 42 E6
Uitenhage, S. Af. 79 Q8
Ujelang Atoll, Marshall Is. 96 D5
Ujiji, Tanzania 79 K9
Ujungpandang, Indonesia 69 M13
Ukhta, Russ. 59 B12
Ukiah, Calif., U.S. 40 E2
Ukraine, Europe 59 G10
Ulaanbaatar, Mongolia 69 F10
Ulaangom, Mongolia 68 F9
Ulaga, Russ. 69 C11
Ulan Ude, Russ. 69 E10
Uliastay, Mongolia 68 F9
Ulingan, P.N.G. 92 B5
Ulithi Atoll, F.S.M. 96 D2
Ulmarra, N.S.W., AUSTRAL. 89 J15
Ul'yanovsk, Russ. 59 E12
Umari, Indonesia 92 B2
Umba, Russ. 58 B9
Umboi, island, P.N.G. 92 C6
Umbukul, P.N.G. 92 B6
Umeå, Sweden 58 C8
Umeälven, river, Sweden 60 C8
Umiat, Alas., U.S. 40 J3
Umm al Arānib, Lib. 78 E6
Umm Durmān see Omdurman, Sudan 78 G9
Unalakleet, Alas., U.S. 40 K2
Unalaska, Alas., U.S. 37 R4
Uncompahgre Peak, Colo., U.S. 42 F6
Uncompahgre Plateau, Colo., U.S. 42 F6
Ungama Bay, Kenya 81 K11
Ungava Bay, Can. 38 F9
Ungava Peninsula, Can. 38 F8
União da Vitória, Braz. 50 J8
Unimak Pass, Alas., U.S. 37 R4
United Arab Emirates, Asia 68 H4
United Kingdom, Europe 58 E4
United States, U.S. 36 J3
Upemba, Lake, D.R.C. 81 L8
Upernavik Kujalleq, Greenland 36 C8
Upington, S. Af. 79 P7
Upolu, island, Samoa 96 G8
'Upolu Point, Hawaii, U.S. 43 L12
Upper Guinea, region, Af. 80 H3
Upper Hutt, N.Z. 92 K5
Upper Kama Upland, Russ. 61 C13
Upper Peninsula, Mich., U.S. 43 C12
Upper Red Lake, Minn., U.S. 43 C10
Uppsala, Sweden 58 D7
Urabá, Gulf of, Col. 52 A2
Ural, river, Kaz.-Russ. 70 E6
Uralla, N.S.W., AUSTRAL. 89 J15
Ural Mountains, Russ. 61 B13
Urana, N.S.W., AUSTRAL. 89 L13
Urandangi, Qnsld., Austral. 89 E10
Uranium City, Sask., Can. 36 F5
Urbano Santos, Braz. 50 D10
Uriah, Mount, N.Z. 92 L4
Urmia, Lake, Iran 70 F4
Uruapan, Mex. 37 N5
Uruçuí, Serra do, Braz. 52 F9
Uruguaiana, Braz. 51 K7
Uruguay, S. America 51 L7
Uruguay, river, Arg.-Braz. 53 K7
Ürümqi, China 68 F8
Urup, island, Russ. 69 D14
Usa, river, Russ. 61 A12
Uşak, Turk. 59 K10
Usakos, Namibia 79 N6
Usarp Mountains, Antarctica 103 L10
Ushuaia, Arg. 51 R5
Usinsk, Russ. 59 A12
Ussuri, river, China-Russ. 71 E12
Ussuriysk, Russ. 69 E12
Ust' Ilimsk, Russ. 68 E9
Ust' Kamchatsk, Russ. 69 C13
Ust' Kut, Russ. 69 E10
Ust' Maya, Russ. 69 D11
Ust' Nera, Russ. 69 C11
Ust' Tsil'ma, Russ. 59 A12
Ust' Usa, Russ. 59 A12
Ustyurt Plateau, Kaz.-Uzb. 70 F6
Usumacinta, river, Mex. 39 P6
Utah, U.S. 40 E5
Utah, U.S. Lake, Utah, U.S. 42 E5
Utiariti, Braz. 50 F6
Utica, N.Y., U.S. 41 D15
Utirik Atoll, Marshall Is. 96 D6
Utopia, homestead, N. Terr., Austral. 88 F9
Utupua, island, Solomon Is. 96 G5
Uummannaq, Greenland 36 C9
Uvalde, Tex., U.S. 40 J8
Uvea, Pac. Oc. 96 G7
Uvol, P.N.G. 92 C7
'Uweinat, Jebel, Sudan 80 F8
Uyuni, Salar de, Bol. 52 H4
Uzbekistan, Asia 68 F6

Vaal, river, S. Af. 81 P8
Vaasa, Fin. 58 C8
Vadodara, India 68 J7
Vadsø, Nor. 58 A9
Vaga, river, Russ. 61 C11
Vaitupu, island, Tuvalu 96 F7
Valcheta, Arg. 51 N5
Valdés, Península (Valdés Peninsula), Arg. 51 N5
Valdés Peninsula, Arg. 53 N5
Valdez, Alas., U.S. 40 L4
Valdivia, Chile 51 N4
Val-d'Or, Que., Can. 36 H8
Valdosta, Ga., U.S. 41 J13
Valence, Fr. 58 H5
Valencia, Sp. 58 J3
Valencia, Venez. 50 A4
Valencia, Lake, Venez. 52 A4
Valentine, Nebr., U.S. 40 D8
Valera, Venez. 50 A4
Valkyrie Dome, Antarctica 103 D10
Valladolid, Mex. 37 N7
Valladolid, Sp. 58 H3
Valledupar, Col. 50 A3
Vallejo, Calif., U.S. 40 E2
Vallenar, Chile 51 K4
Valletta, Malta 58 L7
Valley City, N. Dak., U.S. 40 C9
Valmiera, Latv. 58 E9
Valparaíso, Chile 51 L4
Vals, Tanjung, Indonesia 92 D3
Van, Turk. 59 J13
Van, Lake, Turk. 70 F4
Vanadzor, Arm. 59 J13
Vancouver, B.C., Can. 36 G3

Vancouver, Wash., U.S. 40 C3
Vancouver Island, Can. 38 G2
Vanderford Glacier, Antarctica 103 J14
Van Diemen, Cape, N. Terr., Austral. 90 A7
Van Diemen Gulf, N. Terr., Austral. 90 B8
Vänern, lake, Sweden 60 D7
Van Gölü, Turk. 59 J13
Van Horn, Tex., U.S. 40 J7
Vanikolo Islands, Solomon Is. 96 G5
Vanimo, P.N.G. 92 B4
Vanino, Russ. 69 D13
Vanrook, homestead, Qnsld., Austral. 89 D12
Vanua Levu, island, Fiji 96 G7
Vanuatu, Pac. Oc. 96 G6
Varanasi, India 68 J8
Varangerfjorden, fjord, Nor. 60 A9
Varna, Bulg. 58 J10
Västerås, Sweden 58 D7
Vasyugan'ye, wetland, Russ. 70 E8
Vatican City, Europe 58 J6
Vatnajökull, Ice. 60 B3
Vatoa, island, Fiji 96 G7
Vättern, lake, Sweden 60 D7
Vaughn, N. Mex., U.S. 40 G7
Vava'u Group, Tonga 96 G7
Vavitu, island, Fr. Polynesia 97 H10
Växjö, Sweden 58 E7
Velikaya, river, Russ. 60 E9
Velikiye Luki, Russ. 58 E9
Velikiy Novgorod, Russ. 58 D10
Velikiy Ustyug, Russ. 59 C11
Vélingara, Senegal 78 G1
Vel'sk, Russ. 59 C11
Venable Ice Shelf, Antarctica 102 F3
Venezia (Venice), It. 58 H6
Venezuela, S. America 50 B4
Venezuela, Golfo de (Gulf of Venezuela), Venez. 50 A3
Venezuela, Gulf of, Venez. 52 A3
Veniaminof, Mount, Alas., U.S. 42 M2
Venice see Venezia, It. 58 H6
Venice, Gulf of, Croatia-It.-Slov. 60 H6
Ventspils, Latv. 58 E8
Veracruz, Mex. 37 N6
Verde, Cape, Senegal 80 G1
Verdigris, river, Kans.-Okla., U.S. 43 G10
Verkhnyaya Salda, Russ. 59 C14
Verkhoyansk, Russ. 69 C11
Verkhoyanskiy Khrebet (Verkhoyansk Range), Russ. 69 C11
Verkhoyansk Range, Russ. 71 C11
Vermont, U.S. 41 C15
Vernadsky, station, Antarctica 102 C2
Vernal, Utah, U.S. 40 E6
Vernon, Tex., U.S. 40 H9
Vero Beach, Fla., U.S. 41 K14
Verona, It. 58 H6
Vesterålen, island, Nor. 60 A7
Vestfjorden, Nor. 60 B7
Vestfold Hills, Antarctica 103 E14
Vestmannaeyjar, island, Ice. 60 B3
Veststraumen Glacier, Antarctica 102 B7
Vesuvius, peak, It. 60 J7
Vetluga, river, Russ. 61 D12
Viacha, Bol. 50 G4
Viangchan (Vientiane), Laos 69 J10
Vicksburg, Miss., U.S. 41 H11
Victor, Mount, Antarctica 103 B11
Victor Harbor, S. Austral., Austral. 89 L10
Victoria, Austral. 89 M12
Victoria, river, N. Terr., Austral. 90 C7
Victoria, B.C., Can. 36 G3
Victoria, Chile 50 H4
Victoria, Seychelles 68 L4
Victoria, Tex., U.S. 40 K9
Victoria, Lake, Kenya-Tanzania-Uganda 81 K9
Victoria, Mount, Myanmar 70 J9
Victoria, Mount, P.N.G. 92 D6
Victoria Falls, Zimb. 79 N8
Victoria Falls, Zambia-Zimb. 81 N8
Victoria Island, Can. 38 D5
Victoria Land, Antarctica 102 L10
Victoria River Downs, homestead, N. Terr., Austral. 88 C7
Victorica, Arg. 51 M5
Victory Peak, peak, China-Kyrg. 70 G8
Viedma, Arg. 51 N6
Viedma, Lake, Arg. 53 Q4
Vienna see Wien, Aust. 58 G7
Vientiane see Viangchan, Laos 69 J10
Vietnam, Asia 69 K11
Vigan, Philippines 69 J13
Vigo, Sp. 58 H2
Vijayawada, India 68 K7
Vila Bittencourt, Braz. 50 D4
Vilanculos, Mozambique 79 N10
Vila Velha, Braz. 50 C8
Vilhena, Braz. 50 F6
Villahermosa, Mex. 37 P6
Villamontes, Bol. 50 H5
Villarrica, Para. 50 J7
Villa Unión, Arg. 51 K4
Villavicencio, Col. 50 C3
Villazón, Bol. 50 H5
Vilnius, Lith. 58 E9
Vilyuy, river, Russ. 71 D10
Vincennes Bay, Antarctica 103 J15
Vindhya Range, India 70 J7
Vinh, Viet. 69 J11
Vinnytsya, Ukr. 58 G9
Vinson Massif, Antarctica 102 F5
Viranşehir, Turk. 59 K12
Virgenes, Cape, Arg. 53 R5
Virginia, U.S. 41 F14
Virginia Beach, Va., U.S. 41 F15
Virginia Falls, Can. 38 E4
Virgin Islands, N. America 39 N11
Visalia, Calif., U.S. 40 F3
Visby, Sweden 58 E8
Viscount Melville Sound, Can. 38 C5
Vishakhapatnam, India 68 J8
Vistula, river, Pol. 60 F8
Viti Levu, island, Fiji 96 G6
Vitim, river, Russ. 71 E10
Vitim, Russ. 69 D10
Vitória, Braz. 50 H10
Vitória da Conquista, Braz. 50 G10
Vitoria-Gasteiz, Sp. 58 H3
Vitsyebsk, Belarus 58 E9
Vladikavkaz, Russ. 59 H13
Vladimir, Russ. 59 E11
Vladivostok, Russ. 69 E13
Vlorë, Alban. 58 K8
Volcano Islands (Kazan Rettō), Jap. 96 C3
Volga, river, Russ. 61 G13
Volga, Source of the, Russ. 61 E10
Volga-Don Canal, Russ. 61 F12
Volga River Delta, Russ. 61 G13
Volga Upland, Russ. 61 F12
Volgograd, Russ. 59 F12
Volgograd Reservoir, Russ. 61 F12
Volgogradskoye Vodokhranilishche (Volgograd Reservoir), Russ. 59 F12
Volkhov, river, Russ. 60 D10
Vologda, Russ. 59 D11
Volonga, Russ. 59 A11
Vólos, Gr. 58 K9
Volta, Lake, Ghana 80 H4
Voltaire, Cape, W. Austral., Austral. 90 C5
Volyn-Podolian Upland, Ukr. 60 G9
Volzhskiy, Russ. 59 F12
Vorkuta, Russ. 68 C7
Voronezh, Russ. 59 F11
Vosges, mountains, Fr. 60 G5
Vostok, station, Antarctica 103 G11
Vostok Island, Fr. Polynesia 96 F10
Votkinsk, Russ. 59 D13
Voyvozh, Russ. 59 B12
Vrangelya, Ostrov (Wrangel Island), Russ. 69 A11
Vratsa, Bulg. 58 J9
Vryheid, S. Af. 79 P9
Vuktyl, Russ. 59 B12
Vyatka, river, Russ. 61 D12
Vyazemskiy, Russ. 69 E12
Vychegda, river, Russ. 61 B12
Vychegda Lowland, Russ. 61 B11
Vyg, Lake, Russ. 61 C10
Vym', river, Russ. 61 B12
Vyshniy Volochek, Russ. 59 D10
Vytegra, Russ. 59 C10

Wabash, river, Ill.-Ind., U.S. 43 F12
Waco, Tex., U.S. 40 J9
Wadeye, N. Terr., Austral. 88 B7
Wadi Halfa, Sudan 78 F9
Waeshe, Mount, Antarctica 102 J5
Wagga Wagga, N.S.W., AUSTRAL. 89 L13
Wagin, W. Austral., Austral. 88 K3
Wahiawā, Hawaii, U.S. 41 L11
Waiau, river, N.Z. 92 N3
Waigeo, island, Indonesia 96 E2
Waiheke Island, N.Z. 92 G6
Waikato, river, N.Z. 92 H6
Waikawa, N.Z. 92 P3
Waikouaiti, N.Z. 92 N4
Wailuku, Hawaii, U.S. 41 L12
Waimarama, N.Z. 92 J6
Waimate, N.Z. 92 M4
Waimea, Hawaii, U.S. 41 L10
Waimea (Kamuela), Hawaii, U.S. 41 M12
Wainwright, Alas., U.S. 40 H2
Waipa, river, N.Z. 92 H6
Waipahi, N.Z. 92 N3
Waipahu, Hawaii, U.S. 41 L11
Waipu, N.Z. 92 G5
Waipukurau, N.Z. 92 K6
Wakatipu, Lake, N.Z. 92 N3
Wake Island, Pac. Oc. 96 C5
Wakunai, P.N.G. 92 C8
Wałbrzych, Pol. 58 G7
Wales, U.K. 58 F4
Wales, Alas., U.S. 40 K1
Walgreen Coast, Antarctica 102 H4
Walkaway, W. Austral., Austral. 88 J2
Wallabadah, homestead, Qnsld., Austral. 89 D12
Wallace, Idaho, U.S. 40 B5
Wallal Downs, homestead, W. Austral., Austral. 88 E4
Wallam Creek, Qnsld., Austral. 91 H13
Wallara, N. Terr., Austral. 88 F8
Walla Walla, Wash., U.S. 40 C4
Wallis, Îles, Pac. Oc. 96 G7
Wallowa Mountains, Oreg., U.S. 42 C4
Walsenburg, Colo., U.S. 40 F7
Walterboro, S.C., U.S. 41 H14
Walvis Bay, Namibia 79 P6
Walyahmoning Rock, W. Austral., Austral. 90 J3
Wamba, D.R.C. 78 J8
Wanaaring, N.S.W., AUSTRAL. 89 J12
Wanaka, N.Z. 92 M3
Wanaka, Lake, N.Z. 92 M3
Wandoan, Qnsld., Austral. 89 G14
Wangal, Indonesia 92 C2
Wanganui, river, N.Z. 92 J5
Wanganui, N.Z. 92 J5
Wangaratta, Vic., Austral. 89 L13
Wangary, S. Austral., Austral. 88 K9
Wanigela, P.N.G. 92 D6
Waranga Basin, Vic., Austral. 91 L12
Waratah, Tas., Austral. 89 L15
Warbreccan, homestead, Qnsld., Austral. 89 F12
Warburton, W. Austral., Austral. 88 G6
Warialda, N.S.W., AUSTRAL. 89 J14
Warner Mountains, Calif.-Oreg., U.S. 42 D3
Waroona, W. Austral., Austral. 88 K2
Warrabri, N. Terr., Austral. 88 E9
Warracknabeal, Vic., Austral. 89 L11
Warrawagine, homestead, W. Austral., Austral. 88 E4
Warrego, river, N.S.W.-Qnsld., Austral. 91 J13
Warrina, S. Austral., Austral. 88 H9
Warrnambool, Vic., Austral. 89 M11
Warsaw see Warszawa, Pol. 58 F8
Warszawa (Warsaw), Pol. 58 F8
Warwick, Qnsld., Austral. 89 H15
Wasado, peak, Indonesia 92 B2
Wasatch Range, Utah, U.S. 42 E5
Washington, U.S. 40 B3
Washington, D.C., U.S. 41 E15
Washington, Cape, Antarctica 102 L9
Washington, Mount, N.H., U.S. 43 C16
Washington Island see Teraina, Kiribati 96 E9
Washita, river, Okla.-Tex., U.S. 42 G9
Waskaganish, Que., Can. 36 G8
Waterford, Ire. 58 E3
Waterloo, homestead, N. Terr., Austral. 88 C7
Waterloo, Iowa, U.S. 41 E10
Watertown, N.Y., U.S. 41 C15
Watertown, S. Dak., U.S. 40 D9
Watsa, D.R.C. 78 J9
Watson, S. Austral., Austral. 88 J8
Watson Lake, Yukon Terr. 36 E3
Watubela, Kepulauan, Indonesia 92 B1
Wau, P.N.G. 92 C6
Wau, Sudan 78 H8
Wauchope, N. Terr., Austral. 88 E9
Waukarlycarly, Lake, W. Austral., Austral. 90 E4
Waukegan, Ill., U.S. 41 D12
Wausau, Wis., U.S. 41 D11
Wave Hill, homestead, N. Terr., Austral. 88 D7
Wāw al Kabīr, Lib. 78 E7
Waycross, Ga., U.S. 41 H14
Weddell Sea, Antarctica 102 C5
Weilmoringle, N.S.W., AUSTRAL. 89 J13
Weipa, Qnsld., Austral. 89 B12
Weir, river, Qnsld., Austral. 91 H14
Welbourn Hill, homestead, S. Austral., Austral. 88 H9
Weldiya, Eth. 78 G10
Welford, homestead, Qnsld., Austral. 89 G12
Wellesley Islands, Qnsld., Austral. 91 D11
Wellington, N.Z. 92 K5
Wellington, Lake, Vic., Austral. 91 M13
Wellington Island, Chile 53 Q4
Wells, Nev., U.S. 40 E4
Wells, Lake, W. Austral., Austral. 90 H5
Welshpool, Vic., Austral. 89 M12
Wenatchee, Wash., U.S. 40 B4
Wenshan, China 69 J10
Wentworth, N.S.W., AUSTRAL. 89 K11
Wenzhou, China 69 H12
Werdër, Eth. 78 H11
Weri, Indonesia 92 B1
Werris Creek, N.S.W., AUSTRAL. 89 J14
Weser, river, Ger. 60 F6
Wessel Islands, N. Terr., Austral. 90 A9
West Antarctica, region, Antarctica 102 G5
West Bank, region, Asia 68 F3
West Cape Howe, W. Austral., Austral. 90 L3
Western Australia, Austral. 88 F3
Western Desert, Egypt 80 E8
Western Dvina, river, Belarus-Latv. 60 E9
Western Ghats, India 70 K7
Western Plateau, Austral. 90 F4
Western Sahara, Mor. 78 E2
Western Sayan Mountains, Russ. 70 E9
West Falkland, island, Falkland Is. 53 Q6
West Ice Shelf, Antarctica 103 F15
West Indies, islands, N. America 39 N10
West Islet, C.S.I. Terr., Austral. 89 F16
West Lafayette, Ind., U.S. 41 E12
West Memphis, Ark., U.S. 41 G11
Westmoreland, homestead, Qnsld., Austral. 89 D10
West Palm Beach, Fla., U.S. 41 K15
West Point, S. Austral., Austral. 90 L9
Westport, N.Z. 92 L4
West Siberian Plain, Russ. 70 E8
West Virginia, U.S. 41 E14
Westwood Downs, homestead, N.S.W., AUSTRAL. 89 J11
West Wyalong, N.S.W., AUSTRAL. 89 K13
Wetar, island, Indonesia 69 M14
Wetaskiwin, Alta., Can. 36 G4
Wewak, P.N.G. 92 B5
Weymouth, Cape, Qnsld., Austral. 91 B12
Whakapunake, peak, N.Z. 92 J7
Whakatane, N.Z. 92 H6
Whangamata, N.Z. 92 H6
Whangarei, N.Z. 92 G5
Wheeler Peak, N. Mex., U.S. 42 G7
Wheeler Peak, Nev., U.S. 42 E4
Wheeling, W. Va., U.S. 41 E14
Whidbey, Point, S. Austral., Austral. 90 K9
Whim Creek, W. Austral., Austral. 88 E3
White, river, Ark., U.S. 43 G11
White, river, Ind., U.S. 43 F12
White, river, Nebr.-S. Dak., U.S. 42 D8
White, Lake, N. Terr.-W. Austral., Austral. 90 E7
White Butte, N. Dak., U.S. 42 C8
White Cliffs, N.S.W., AUSTRAL. 89 J12
Whitehorse, Yukon Terr. 36 E3
White Island, Antarctica 103 B13
White Mountains, Alas., U.S. 42 K3
White Mountains, N.H., U.S. 43 C16
White Nile, river, Sudan 80 H9
White Sea, Russ. 61 B10
White Sea-Baltic Canal, Russ. 58 C10
White Volta, river, Burkina Faso-Ghana 80 H4
Whitewood, Qnsld., Austral. 89 E12
Whitmore Mountains, Antarctica 102 G6
Whitney, Mount, Calif., U.S. 42 F3
Whittier, Alas., U.S. 40 L3
Whyalla, S. Austral., Austral. 88 K10
Wialki, W. Austral., Austral. 88 J3
Wichita, Kans., U.S. 40 F9
Wichita Falls, Tex., U.S. 40 H9
Wichita Mountains, Okla., U.S. 42 G9
Wickenburg, Ariz., U.S. 40 G5
Wickepin, W. Austral., Austral. 88 K3
Wide Bay, P.N.G. 92 C7
Wien (Vienna), Aust. 58 G7
Wiesbaden, Ger. 58 G6
Wilberforce, Cape, N. Terr., Austral. 90 B9
Wilcannia, N.S.W., AUSTRAL. 89 J12
Wilhelm, Mount, P.N.G. 92 C5
Wilhelm II Coast, Antarctica 103 G15
Wilhelmina Mountains, Suriname 52 C7
Wilkes-Barre, Pa., U.S. 41 D15
Wilkes Land, Antarctica 103 L12
Wilkins Coast, Antarctica 102 D3
Willamette, river, Oreg., U.S. 42 C3
Willcox, Ariz., U.S. 40 H5
Willeroo, homestead, N. Terr., Austral. 88 C8
William, Mount, Vic., Austral. 91 L11
William Creek, S. Austral., Austral. 88 H9
Williams, Ariz., U.S. 40 G5
Williams, W. Austral., Austral. 88 K3
Williams Lake, B.C., Can. 36 G3
Williamson Glacier, Antarctica 103 J14
Williamsport, Pa., U.S. 41 D15
Willis Islets, C.S.I. Terr., Austral. 89 D15
Williston, N. Dak., U.S. 40 B8
Williston Lake, Can. 38 F3
Willmar, Minn., U.S. 41 D10
Willowra, homestead, N. Terr., Austral. 88 E8
Wilmington, Del., U.S. 41 E15
Wilmington, N.C., U.S. 41 G15
Wilmington, S. Austral., Austral. 89 K10
Wilson Hills, Antarctica 103 M10
Wilsons Promontory, Vic., Austral. 91 M13
Wiluna, W. Austral., Austral. 88 H4
Windhoek, Namibia 79 N7
Windorah, Qnsld., Austral. 89 G12
Wind River Range, Wyo., U.S. 42 D6
Windward Islands, N. America 39 P12
Windward Passage, Cuba-Haiti 39 N10
Winneba, Ghana 78 J4
Winnebago, Lake, Wis., U.S. 43 D11
Winnemucca, Nev., U.S. 40 E4
Winnipeg, Manitoba, Can. 36 H6
Winnipeg, Lake, Can. 38 G6
Winnipegosis, Lake, Can. 38 G5
Winnipesaukee, Lake, N.H., U.S. 43 C16
Winona, Minn., U.S. 41 D11
Winslow, Ariz., U.S. 40 G5
Winston-Salem, N.C., U.S. 41 F14
Wirrulla, S. Austral., Austral. 88 K9
Wisconsin, river, Wis., U.S. 43 D11
Wisconsin, U.S. 41 D11
Wiseman, Alas., U.S. 40 J3
Witchcliffe, W. Austral., Austral. 88 L2
Wittenoom, W. Austral., Austral. 88 F3
Witu Islands, P.N.G. 92 B6
Wodonga, Vic., Austral. 89 L13
Wohlthat Mountains, Antarctica 102 A9
Wokam, island, Indonesia 92 C2
Woleai Atoll, F.S.M. 96 E3
Wolf, river, Wis., U.S. 43 C11
Wolf Point, Mont., U.S. 40 B7
Wollaston Lake, Can. 38 F5
Wollaston Peninsula, Can. 38 D5
Wollogorang, homestead, N. Terr., Austral. 89 D10
Wollongong, N.S.W., AUSTRAL. 89 L14
Wondai, Qnsld., Austral. 89 H15
Wongan Hills, W. Austral., Austral. 88 J3
Wongawal, homestead, W. Austral., Austral. 88 G4
Wonthaggi, Vic., Austral. 89 M12
Wonti, Indonesia 92 B2
Woodall Mountain, Miss., U.S. 43 G12
Woodburn, N.S.W., AUSTRAL. 89 J15
Woodlark, island, P.N.G. 92 D7
Woods, Lake, N. Terr., Austral. 90 D8
Woods, Lake of the, Can.-U.S. 43 B10
Woodstock, homestead, Qnsld., Austral. 89 D12
Woodville, N.Z. 92 K6
Woodward, Okla., U.S. 40 G9
Woody Head, N.S.W., AUSTRAL. 91 J15
Woomera, S. Austral., Austral. 88 J10
Woorabinda, Qnsld., Austral. 89 G14
Wooramel, homestead, W. Austral., Austral. 88 G2
Worcester, Mass., U.S. 41 D16
Worcester, S. Af. 79 Q7
Worland, Wyo., U.S. 40 D6
Wotje Atoll, Marshall Is. 96 D6
Wrangel Island, Russ. 71 A11
Wrangell, Alas., U.S. 40 M6
Wrangell Mountains, Alas., U.S. 42 L4
Wreck Point, S. Af. 81 Q6
Wrigley Gulf, Antarctica 102 J5
Wrocław, Pol. 58 F7
Wubin, W. Austral., Austral. 88 J3
Wudinna, S. Austral., Austral. 88 K9
Wuhan, China 69 H11
Wuliaru, island, Indonesia 92 D1
Wundowie, W. Austral., Austral. 88 K3
Wurarga, W. Austral., Austral. 88 H2
Wurung, homestead, Qnsld., Austral. 89 D11
Würzburg, Ger. 58 G6
Wuvulu Island, P.N.G. 92 B4
Wuwei, China 69 G10
Wuxi, China 69 G12
Wuyi Shan, China 71 H12
Wyandra, Qnsld., Austral. 89 H13
Wyloo, homestead, W. Austral., Austral. 88 F2
Wynbring, S. Austral., Austral. 88 J8
Wyndham, W. Austral., Austral. 88 C6
Wyoming, U.S. 40 D6

Xaçmaz, Azerb. 59 H14
Xai-Xai, Mozambique 79 P9
Xangongo, Angola 79 M6
Xánthi, Gr. 58 J9
Xapecó, Braz. 50 K8
Xapuri, Braz. 50 F4
Xi, river, China 71 J11
Xiamen, China 69 H12
Xi'an, China 69 G11
Xiangfan, China 69 G11
Xiangtan, China 69 H11
Xichang, China 69 H10
Xigazê, China 68 H9
Xingu, river, Braz. 52 D8
Xinguara, Braz. 50 E8
Xining, China 69 G10
Xinyang, China 69 G11
Xique Xique, Braz. 50 F10
Xuddur, Somalia 78 J11
Xuzhou, China 69 G12

Yablonovyy Range, Russ. 71 E11
Yacuiba, Bol. 50 H5
Yafi, Indonesia 92 B4
Yakima, Wash., U.S. 40 B4
Yakossi, Cen. Af. Rep. 78 J8
Yaksha, Russ. 59 B13
Yaku Shima, Jap. 96 B1
Yakutat, Alas., U.S. 40 L4
Yakutat Bay, Alas., U.S. 42 L4
Yakutsk, Russ. 69 D11
Yalgoo, W. Austral., Austral. 88 H3
Yalleroi, Qnsld., Austral. 89 F13
Yallock, N.S.W., AUSTRAL. 89 K12
Yalta, Ukr. 59 H11
Yamal Peninsula, Russ. 70 C8
Yamato Glacier, Antarctica 103 B11
Yamato Mountains see Queen Fabiola Mountains, Antarctica 103 B12
Yamba, N.S.W., AUSTRAL. 89 J15
Yambio, Sudan 78 J9
Yamdena, island, Indonesia 92 D1
Yamma Yamma, Lake, Qnsld., Austral. 91 G11
Yamoussoukro, Côte d'Ivoire 78 H3
Yana, river, Russ. 71 C11
Yanbu' al Baḩr, Saudi Arabia 68 G3
Yancannia, homestead, N.S.W., AUSTRAL. 89 J12
Yangambi, D.R.C. 78 J8
Yangon (Rangoon), Myanmar 68 K10
Yangtze, river, China 71 G12
Yangtze, Source of the, China 70 H9
Yangtze Gorges, China 71 H11
Yankton, S. Dak., U.S. 40 D9
Yantabulla, N.S.W., AUSTRAL. 89 H12
Yantai, China 69 G12
Yaoundé, Cameroon 78 J6
Yapen, island, Indonesia 92 B2
Yapen, Selat, Indonesia 92 A2
Yapero, Indonesia 92 C3
Yap Islands, F.S.M. 96 D2
Yaqui, river, Mex. 39 M4
Yaraka, Qnsld., Austral. 89 G12
Yarle Lakes, S. Austral., Austral. 90 J8
Yarmouth, N.S., CAN. 36 H10
Yaroslavl', Russ. 59 D11
Yarraden, homestead, Qnsld., Austral. 89 C12
Yazd, Iran 68 G5
Yazoo, river, Miss., U.S. 43 H11
Yeeda, homestead, W. Austral., Austral. 88 D5
Yefremov, Russ. 59 E11
Yekaterinburg, Russ. 59 C14
Yelets, Russ. 59 F11
Yellow, river, China 71 G12
Yellow, Source of the, China 70 G9
Yellowknife, N.W.T., CAN. 36 E4
Yellow Sea, Asia 71 G12
Yellowstone, river, Mont.-N. Dak.-Wyo., U.S. 42 C7
Yellowstone Lake, Wyo., U.S. 42 D6
Yemanzhelinsk, Russ. 59 C14
Yemen, Asia 68 J3
Yenisey, river, Russ. 70 C8
Yenisey-Angara, Source of the, Mongolia 70 F9
Yenisey Gulf, Russ. 70 C8
Yeniseysk, Russ. 68 E9
Yeniseyskiy Zaliv (Yenisey Gulf), Russ. 68 C8
Yeppoon, Qnsld., Austral. 89 F15
Yerevan, Arm. 59 J13
Yergeni Hills, Russ. 61 G13
Yerilla, homestead, W. Austral., Austral. 88 J4
Yermitsa, Russ. 59 A11
Yessey, Russ. 68 C9
Yetman, N.S.W., AUSTRAL. 89 J14
Yevpatoriya, Ukr. 59 H11
Yichun, China 69 E12
Yinchuan, China 69 G10
Yindarlgooda, Lake, W. Austral., Austral. 90 J5
Yindi, homestead, W. Austral., Austral. 88 J5
Yining, China 68 F8
Yin Shan, China 71 F11
Yirga Alem, Eth. 78 H10
Yirrkala, N. Terr., Austral. 88 B10
Yobe, river, Niger-Nig. 80 G6
Yokohama, Jap. 69 F14
Yola, Nig. 78 H6
York, Cape, Greenland 38 C7
York, Cape, Qnsld., Austral. 91 A12
Yorke Peninsula, S. Austral., Austral. 90 L10
Yorkton, Sask., Can. 36 H5
Yoshkar Ola, Russ. 59 D12
Yos Sudarso see Dolak, island, Indonesia 92 D3
Young, N.S.W., AUSTRAL. 89 L13
Young, Mount, N. Terr., Austral. 90 C9
Youngstown, Ohio, U.S. 41 E14
Youth, Isle of, Cuba 39 N8
Ypé Jhú, Para. 50 J7
Yreka, Calif., U.S. 40 D3
Ysabel Channel, P.N.G. 92 B7
Yuba City, Calif., U.S. 40 E3
Yucatan Channel, Cuba-Mex. 39 N8
Yucatan Peninsula, Mex. 39 N7
Yuendumu, N. Terr., Austral. 88 F8
Yugorenok, Russ. 69 D12
Yukon, river, Can.-U.S. 38 C1
Yukon, Source of the, Can. 38 E3
Yukon Delta, Alas., U.S. 42 K1
Yukon Flats, Alas., U.S. 42 K4
Yukon Plateau, Can. 38 D3
Yukon Territory, Can. 36 D3
Yulara, N. Terr., Austral. 88 G7
Yuleba, Qnsld., Austral. 89 H14
Yuma, Ariz., U.S. 40 H4
Yumen, China 68 G9
Yungas, region, Bol. 52 G5
Yunta, S. Austral., Austral. 89 K10
Yurimaguas, Peru 50 E2
Yuxi, China 69 J10
Yuzhno Sakhalinsk, Russ. 69 E13
Yuzhnoural'sk, Russ. 59 D14

Zābol, Iran 68 G5
Zacatecas, Mex. 37 N5
Zadar, Croatia 58 H7
Zagora, Mor. 78 D3
Zagreb, Croatia 58 H7
Zagros Mountains, Iran 70 G4
Zāhedān, Iran 68 H5
Zaječar, Serbia and Montenegro 58 J8
Zákinthos, island, Gr. 58 K8
Zambeze (Zambezi), river, Angola 79 M8
Zambezi, river, Af. 81 N10
Zambezi, Zambia 79 M8
Zambezi, Source of the, Zambia 81 L8
Zambezi River Delta, Mozambique 81 N10
Zambia, Af. 79 M8
Zamboanga, Philippines 69 K13
Zanthus, W. Austral., Austral. 88 J5
Zanzibar, Tanzania 79 L10
Zanzibar Island, Tanzania 81 L10
Zapala, Arg. 51 M4
Zaporizhzhya, Ukr. 59 G11
Zaragoza, Sp. 58 J3
Zaria, Nig. 78 H5
Zarzis, Tun. 78 D6
Zāwiyat Masūs, Lib. 78 D7
Zaysan Köli, Kaz. 68 F8
Zealand, island, Den. 60 E6
Zednes, peak, Maurit. 80 E2
Zeil, Mount, N. Terr., Austral. 90 F8
Zelenokumsk, Russ. 59 H13
Zemio, Cen. Af. Rep. 78 J8
Zemongo, Cen. Af. Rep. 78 H8
Zhangaözen, Kaz. 59 G15
Zhangaqazaly, Kaz. 59 F16
Zhanjiang, China 69 J11
Zhanyi, China 69 H10
Zhaotong, China 69 H10
Zhayyq (Ural), river, Kaz. 59 F14
Zheleznodorozhnyy, Russ. 59 B12
Zheleznogorsk, Russ. 59 F11
Zhengzhou, China 69 G11
Zhetiqara, Kaz. 59 D15
Zhigansk, Russ. 69 C10
Zhilinda, Russ. 68 C10
Zhongshan, station, Antarctica 103 E14
Zhytomyr, Ukr. 58 G9
Zibo, China 69 G12
Zigey, Chad 78 G6
Zigong, China 69 H10
Ziguinchor, Senegal 78 G1
Zillah, Lib. 78 E7
Zima, Russ. 68 E10
Zimbabwe, Af. 79 N9
Zinder, Niger 78 G5
Zlatoust, Russ. 59 D14
Zomba, Malawi 79 M10
Zongo, D.R.C. 78 J7
Zonguldak, Turk. 59 J10
Zouar, Chad 78 F7
Zugdidi, Ga. 59 H12
Zumberge Coast, Antarctica 102 F5
Zumbo, Mozambique 79 M9
Zürich, Switz. 58 G6
Zvishavane, Zimb. 79 N9
Zwickau, Ger. 58 G6
Zyryanka, Russ. 69 C12

ACKNOWLEDGMENTS

CONSULTANTS

PHYSICAL AND POLITICAL MAPS

Bureau of the Census, U.S. Department of Commerce
Bureau of Land Management, U.S. Department of the Interior
Central Intelligence Agency (CIA)
National Geographic Maps
National Imagery and Mapping Agency (NIMA)
National Park Service, U.S. Department of the Interior
Office of the Geographer, U.S. Department of State
U.S. Board on Geographic Names (BGN)
U.S. Geological Survey, U.S. Department of the Interior

WORLD SECTION

Geographical Comparisons
George Sharman
NOAA/NESDIS/NGDC

Peter H. Gleick
Pacific Institute for Studies in Development, Environment, and Security

R.L. Fisher
Scripps Institution of Oceanography

Philip Micklin
Western Michigan University

National Imagery and Mapping Agency (NIMA)

NOAA/National Climatic Data Center (NCDC)

World Economy
Daniel Cannistra
Ernst and Young LLP

Susan Martin
Institute for the Study of International Migration, Georgetown University

Richard Fix
World Bank

World Population
Gregory Yetman
Center for International Earth Science Information Network (CIESIN), Columbia University

Carl Haub
Population Reference Bureau

World Religions
Arthur Green, Reuven Kimelman
Brandeis University

Bob Thurman, Neguin Yavari
Columbia University

Richard Jaffe
Duke University

Stephen Fields, Ariel Glucklich
Georgetown University

Harry Yeide, Jr.
George Washington University

Todd Johnson
Center for the Study of Global Christianity

International Population Center, San Diego State University

World Time Zones
National Geographic Maps

FLAGS AND FACTS

Whitney Smith
Flag Research Center

Carl Haub
Population Reference Bureau

COUNTRY DATES OF INDEPENDENCE

Leo Dillon
Department of State, Office of the Geographer

Harm J. de Blij
Michigan State University

Carl Haub
Population Reference Bureau

ART AND ILLUSTRATIONS

Cover: Globe, Tibor G. Tóth (The Living Earth, Inc. data)
Pages 2–3, Tibor G. Tóth (The Living Earth, Inc. data)
Pages 20-21, *continents adrift in time:* Christopher R. Scotese/PALEOMAP Project; *cutaway of the earth:* Tibor G. Tóth; *tectonic block diagrams:* Susan Sanford
Page 128, Tibor G. Tóth (The Living Earth, Inc. data)

SATELLITE IMAGES

World and Continental Land cover Satellite Images: *Global land cover classification at 1km spatial resolution using a classification tree approach:* Hansen, M.C., DeFries, R.S., Townshend, J.R.G., and Sohlberg, R., 2000, *International Journal of Remote Sensing,* volume 21, numbers 6 and 7, pp. 1331–1364. (Note: Data derived from NOAA/AVHRR and NASA.) Image processing assistance from Global Land Cover Facility, University of Maryland Institute for Advanced Computer Studies.

Cover Globe, Title-Spread Globe (pp. 2-3), and Credit-Page Globe (p. 128): The Living Earth, Inc. and Tibor G. Tóth, composite imagery of spring and summer months, 1997 to 2003 (Note: Data derived from NOAA/AVHRR) 1 kilometer spatial resolution

PHOTOGRAPHY

Page 48, (left) Jodi Cobb, National Geographic Photographer
Page 48, (right) James L. Stanfield
Page 48–49, Tony Heiderer
Page 49, (left) Thomas J. Abercrombie
Page 49, (right) Annie Griffiths Belt

PRINCIPAL REFERENCE SOURCES

Columbia Gazetteer of the World, Cohen, Saul B., ed. New York: Columbia University Press, 1998

International Migration 2002, New York: United Nations Population Division, 2003

International Trade Statistics, 2001, Geneva, Switzerland: World Trade Organization

Matras, Judah, *Populations and Societies.* Englewood Cliffs, New Jersey: Prentice Hall, 1973

Merriam Webster's Geographical Dictionary, 3rd ed. Springfield, Ma.: Merriam-Webster, Incorporated, 1997

National Geographic Atlas of the World, 7th ed. Washington, D.C.: The National Geographic Society, 1999

The Statesman's Yearbook, 139th ed., Turner, Barry, ed. Exeter, United Kingdom: MacMillan Press Ltd., 2002.

Statistical Yearbook, 1999, United Nations Educational, Scientific and Cultural Organization. Paris and Lanham: UNESCO Publishing and Bernan Press, 1999

World Christian Encyclopedia: A Comparative Survey of Churches and Religions in the Modern World, 2nd ed. Barrett, David B., et al., eds., New York: Oxford University Press, 2001

World Development Indicators, 2003, Washington, D.C.: World Bank

The World Factbook 2002, Washington, D.C.: Central Intelligence Agency, 2002

World Investment Report, 2001, New York and Geneva: United Nations Conference on Trade and Development, 2001

World Urbanization Prospects: The 2001 Revision. Population Division of the Department of Economic and Social Affairs of the United Nations Secretariat, New York: United Nations, 2002

PRINCIPAL ONLINE SOURCES

British Antarctic Survey
www.nerc-bas.ac.uk

Central Intelligence Agency
www.cia.gov

GEOnet Names Server (GNS)
www.nima.mil/gns/html/

Population Reference Bureau
www.prb.org

United Nations
www.un.org

UN Population Division
www.unpopulation.org

World Bank
www.worldbank.org

World Trade Organization
www.wto.org

KEY TO FLAGS AND FACTS

The National Geographic Society, whose cartographic policy is to recognize de facto countries, counted 192 independent nations in mid-2003. At the end of each chapter of the ***Concise Atlas of the World*** there is a fact box for every independent nation and for most dependencies located on the continent or region covered in that chapter. Each box includes the flag of a political entity, as well as important statistical data. Boxes for some dependencies show two flags—a local one and the sovereign flag of the administering country. Dependencies are nonindependent political entities associated in some way with a particular independent nation.

The statistical data provide highlights of geography, demography, and economy. These details offer a brief overview of each political entity; they present general characteristics and are not intended to be comprehensive studies. The structured nature of the text results in some generic collective or umbrella terms. The industry category, for instance, includes services in addition to traditional manufacturing sectors. Space limitations dictate the amount of information included. For example, the only languages listed for the U.S. are English and Spanish, although many others are spoken. The North America chapter also includes concise fact boxes for U.S. states, showing the state flag, population, and capital.

Fact boxes are arranged alphabetically by the conventional short forms of the country or dependency names. Country and dependency boxes are grouped separately. The conventional long forms of names appear in colored type below the conventional short form; if there are no long forms, the short forms are repeated.

AREA accounts for the total area of a country, or dependency, including all land and inland water delimited by international boundaries, intranational boundaries, or coastlines.

POPULATION figures for independent nations and dependencies are mid-2003 figures from the Population Reference Bureau in Washington, D.C. Next to CAPITAL is the name of the seat of government, followed by the city's population. Capital city populations for both independent nations and dependencies are from 2001 United Nations estimates and represent the populations of metropolitan areas. In the POPULATION category, the figures for U.S. state populations are from the U.S. Census Bureau's 2001 midyear estimates.

POPULATION figures for countries, dependencies, and U.S. states are rounded to the nearest thousand.

Under RELIGION, the most widely practiced faith appears first. "Traditional" or "indigenous" connotes beliefs of important local sects, such as the Maya in Middle America. Under LANGUAGE, if a country has an official language, it is listed first. Often, a country may list more than one official language. Otherwise both RELIGION and LANGUAGE are in rank ordering.

LITERACY generally indicates the percentage of the population above the age of 15 who can read and write. There are no universal standards of literacy, so these estimates (from the CIA's *World Factbook*) are based on the most common definition available for a nation. LIFE EXPECTANCY represents the average number of years a group of infants born in the same year can be expected to live if the mortality rate at each age remains constant in the future.

GDP PER CAPITA is Gross Domestic Product divided by midyear population estimates. GDP estimates for independent nations and dependencies use the purchasing power parity (PPP) conversion factor designed to equalize the purchasing powers of different currencies.

Individual income estimates such as GDP PER CAPITA are among the many indicators used to assess a nation's well-being. As statistical averages, they hide extremes of poverty and wealth. Furthermore, they take no account of factors that affect quality of life, such as environmental degradation, educational opportunities, and health care.

ECONOMY information for the independent nations and dependencies is divided into three general categories: Industry, Agriculture, and Exports. Because of structural limitations, only the primary industries (IND), agricultural commodities (AGR), and exports (EXP) are reported. Agriculture serves as an umbrella term for not only crops but also livestock, products, and fish. In the interest of conciseness, agriculture for the independent nations presents, when applicable (but is not limited to), two major crops, followed respectively by leading entries for livestock, products, and fish.

NA indicates that data are not available.

One of the world's largest nonprofit scientific and educational organizations, the National Geographic Society was founded in 1888 "for the increase and diffusion of geographic knowledge." Fulfilling this mission, the Society educates and inspires millions every day through its magazines, books, television programs, videos, maps and atlases, research grants, the National Geographic Bee, teacher workshops, and innovative classroom materials. The Society is supported through membership dues, charitable gifts, and income from the sale of its educational products. This support is vital to National Geographic's mission to increase global understanding and promote conservation of our planet through exploration, research, and education.

For more information, please call 1-800-NGS LINE (647-5463)
or write to the following address:

National Geographic Society
1145 17th Street N.W
Washington, D.C. 20036-4688
U.S.A.

Visit the Society's Web site at www.nationalgeographic.com.

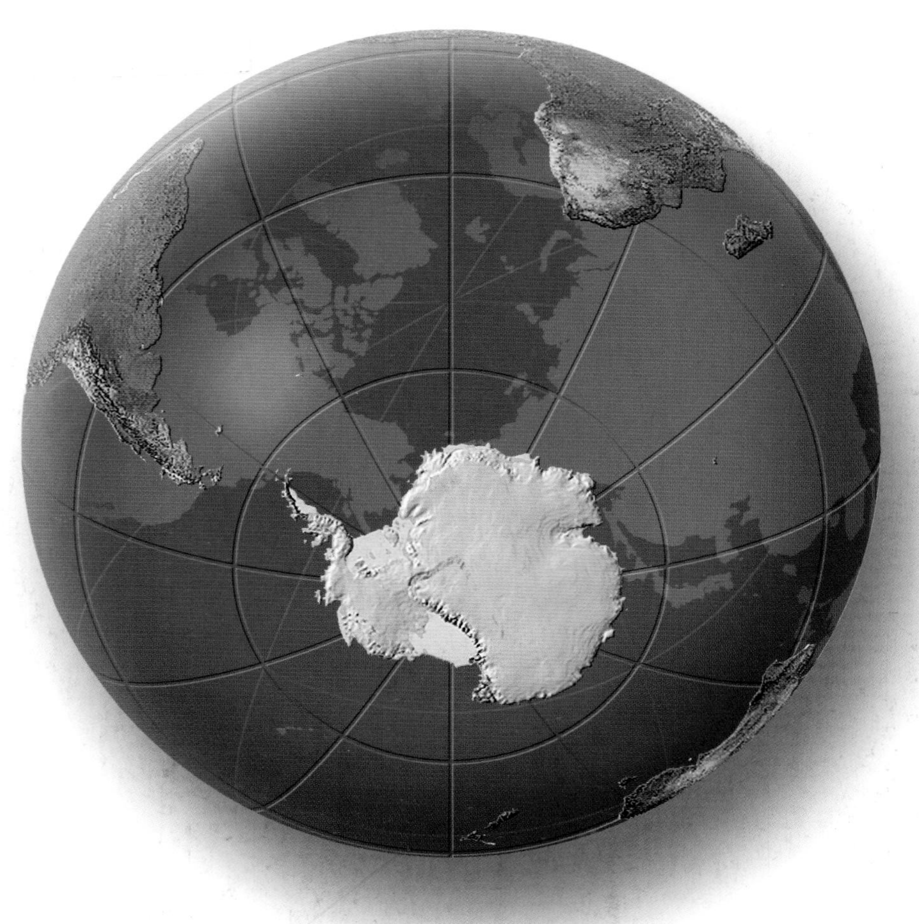

NATIONAL GEOGRAPHIC

CONCISE ATLAS of the WORLD

PUBLISHED BY THE NATIONAL GEOGRAPHIC SOCIETY

PREPARED BY THE BOOK DIVISION

Kevin Mulroy	Vice President and Editor-in-Chief
Marianne R. Koszorus	Design Director

STAFF FOR THIS ATLAS

Carl Mehler	Project Editor and Director of Maps
Laura Exner, Thomas L. Gray, Joseph F. Ochlak, Nicholas P. Rosenbach	Map Editors
Nathan Eidem and XNR Productions	Map Research and Compilation
Gregory Ugiansky	Map Production Manager
Matt Chwastyk, James Huckenpahler, and XNR Productions	Map Production
National Geographic Maps: Kevin Allen, Director of Map Services; Jan D. Morris, Project Manager; Mary Kate Cannistra, Windy A Robertson	Geographic Information System (GIS) Support
National Geographic Maps: Michael J. Horner, David B. Miller, Scott A. Zillmer	Contributing Geographers
Melissa Farris, Lyle Rosbotham	Book Design
Rebecca Lescaze, Melanie Patt-Corner	Text Editors
Elisabeth B. Booz, Patrick Booz, Noel Grove, Antony Shugaar,	Contributing Writers
Elisabeth B. Booz, Nathan Eidem, Joseph F. Ochlak	Text Researchers
Tibor G. Tóth	Art and Illustrations
R. Gary Colbert	Production Director

MANUFACTURING AND QUALITY CONTROL

Christopher A. Liedel	Chief Financial Officer
Phillip L. Schlosser	Managing Director
John T. Dunn	Technical Director
Vincent P. Ryan	Manager

Reproduction by Quad/Graphics, Alexandria, Virginia
Printed and Bound by Mondadori S.p.A., Verona, Italy